Avizandum Statutes on

Scots Property, Trusts and Succession Law
2023–2024

20th edition

AVIZANDUM STATUTES

Avizandum Statutes are designed specifically to provide undergraduates at Scottish universities with legislation and, where appropriate, other core materials in a readily accessible format. All materials have been selected on the basis of their relevance to university courses and appear in updated form. The lack of annotation and commentary means that the volumes are ideal for use in examinations.

Volumes in the series:

Alisdair D J MacPherson (ed), *Avizandum Statutes on Scots Commercial and Consumer Law 2023–2024, 21st edition* (2023)

Jane Mair (ed), *Avizandum Statutes on Scots Family Law 2023–2024, 21st edition* (2023)

Andrew J M Steven and Scott Wortley (eds), *Avizandum Statutes on Scots Property, Trusts and Succession Law 2023–2024, 20th edition* (2023)

Laura J Macgregor (ed), *Avizandum Legislation on the Scots Law of Obligations, 9th edition* (2021)

Elizabeth B Crawford and Janeen M Carruthers (eds), *Avizandum Legislation on International Private Law, 5th edition* (2020)

Navraj Singh Ghaleigh (ed), *Avizandum Statutes on Scots Public Law, 5th edition* (2020)

https://edinburghuniversitypress.com/series-avizandum-statutes

Avizandum Statutes on

Scots Property, Trusts and Succession Law

2023–2024

20th edition

Editors

Andrew J M Steven LLB, PhD, WS
Professor of Property Law, University of Edinburgh
and former Scottish Law Commissioner

and

Scott Wortley LLB, Solicitor
Lecturer in Private Law, University of Edinburgh

EDINBURGH
University Press

Edinburgh University Press is one of the leading university presses in the UK. We publish academic books and journals in our selected subject areas across the humanities and social sciences, combining cutting-edge scholarship with high editorial and production values to produce academic works of lasting importance. For more information visit our website: edinburghuniversitypress.com

First published   2004
20th edition published   2023

© Edinburgh University Press, 2023

Edinburgh University Press Ltd
The Tun – Holyrood Road
12(2f) Jackson's Entry
Edinburgh EH8 8PJ

Typeset in 9/10 pt, Palatino
by Deanta Global Publishing Services, Chennai, India, and
printed and bound in Great Britain by Clays

A CIP record for this book is available from the British Library

ISBN 978 1 3995 2882 5 (paperback)
ISBN 978 1 3995 2883 2 (webready PDF)
ISBN 978 1 3995 2884 9 (epub)

Public sector information is licensed under the Open Government Licence 3.0
(http://www.nationalarchives.gov.uk/doc/open-government-licence/version/3)

EDITORS' PREFACE

This collection, first published in 2004, aims to bring together the key statutory provisions necessary for a study of property, trusts and succession law at LLB level in Scotland.

Part I covers property law. Whilst this can be regarded as a unitary subject, there is of course a classic division between heritable and moveable property. The law of heritable property has undergone revolutionary change in recent times, culminating in the abolition of the feudal system on 28 November 2004. This volume seeks to include all the statutory material governing the post-feudal era. In relation to moveable property, we have included a number of important provisions, notably from the Sale of Goods Act 1979. As ever, we have to be selective in our coverage.

In this, the twentieth edition of the collection, we are delighted to include the Moveable Transactions (Scotland) Act 2023. It is a major new piece of legislation with which we have both been heavily involved since its genesis in the work of the Scottish Law Commission. The 2023 Act is expected to come into force next year. We have also taken account of amendments made by the Coronavirus (Recovery and Reform) (Scotland) Act 2022 and the Economic Crime (Transparency and Enforcement) Act 2022 to some of the statutes already in the collection, notably the Land Registration etc (Scotland) Act 2012.

In Part II, we have collected the main trusts and succession statutes. Some of the statutes included in Part I have effect in this area too, in particular the Requirements of Writing (Scotland) Act 1995.

We welcome feedback as to any material omissions, which we can then address in future editions. We are grateful to our fellow teachers at Edinburgh and the other Scottish universities for their assistance in deciding what material should be included.

We thank Malcolm Combe, Chris Cooper and Diana MacDonald for their help in originally bringing together the materials and checking for amendments and repeals. We are grateful to Chathuni Jayatilaka for her checking of the materials in 2015.

The materials are intended to be up to date to June 2023. All amendments to the legislation appear in square brackets. Where part of a statutory provision has been repealed this is indicated by [. . .]. Where it is not in force, it is normally indicated by *italics*.

Andrew J M Steven
Scott Wortley
University of Edinburgh
June 2023

CONTENTS

PART II: TRUSTS AND SUCCESSION

PART I
PROPERTY

STATUTES

ROYAL MINES ACT 1424
(1424, c 12)

Of mynis of golde and silver

Item Gif ony myne of golde or siluer be fundyn in ony lordis landis of the realme and it may be prowyt that thre halfpennys of siluer may be fynit owt of the punde of leide The lordis of parliament consentis that sik myne be the kingis as is vsuale in vthir realmys.

LEASES ACT 1449
(1449, c 18)

Of takis of landis for termes

Item It is ordanit for the sauftie and fauour of the pure pepil that labouris the grunde that thai and al vthiris that has takyn or sal tak landis in tym to cum fra lordis and has termes and yeris thereof that suppose the lordis sel or analy thai landis that the takaris sall remayn with thare takis on to the ische of thare termes quhais handis at euir thai landis cum to for sic lik male as thai tuk thaim of befoir [. . .].

MINES AND METALS ACT 1592
(1592, c 31)

For furthering of the kingis commoditie be the Mynes and metallis

OURE Souerane Lord vnderstanding that this lang tyme bygane Nather his Maiestie nor the cuntrie hes Importit ony commoditie of the mynis and metallis quhilk in great abundance micht be easelie found in this realme to the interteynement and sustentatioun of ane greit nowmer of the liegis thairof And that the said inconvenient hes ensewit be resone Oure said souerane lord and his maist noble progenitouris wes in vse commonlie to sett the saidis haill mynis within thair dominionis to ane or tua strangearis for ane small dewtie quha nather haid substance to caus labour and wirk the hundreth pairt of ony ane of the saidis mynis nor yit instructed vtheris leigis of this realme in the knawlege thairof quhilk is mair nor notour be the doingis of the present takisman of the mynes quha nether wirkis presentlie nor hes wrocht thir mony yeiris bypast nor euir hes serchit socht nor discoverit ony new mettall sen his entrie nor hes instructit ony of the leigis of the cuntrie in that knawlege And quhilk is maist inconvenient of all hes maid na sufficient payment of the dewtie of his tak to oure souerane lordis thesaurair sua that na pairt of the said yeirlie dewtie is euir cum in the said thesauraris compt to his hienes vse and commoditie Quhairby Oure souerane lord and the haill cuntrie will sustene greit loss gif ane strangear sall bruik in this maner the haill mettallis within his maiesties dominionis but payment of ony dewtie ffor the space of xxj yeris altogidder Lyk as also in respect the richt of all mynis pertenit to his maiestie and his hienes predicessouris Thairfoir quhensoeuir ony myne or seme of mettaill wes found be ony of the leigis of this realme the same wes ather neglectit or be all moyanis possible obscurit be ressone that na pairt of the commoditie thairof micht redound to thame selffis quhairby ane greit proffite quhilk micht haue bene gottin baith to oure souerane lord and als to the cuntrie wes allutirlie owir sene And now our said souerane lord vnderstanding the inconvenientis foirsaidis To haue procedit cheiflie becaus ther wes nocht ane speciall man of witt and knawlege appointit to quhais office propirlie the owirsicht of the haill mater of the mettallis suld pertene And of quhome his Maiestie and estaitis micht seik ane compt and ressone of the administratioun of his said office that his mynis be nocht neglectit (as thay ar) dyuerse vtheris princes makand sa greit commoditie of the lyk . . . . And als oure souerane willing that all his Maiesties liegis quha will tak on hand to discouer and work the saidis mynis may haue reasonable proffite and recompence of thair panis [and] a sufficient securitie maid to thame of thair awin mynis within thair awin landis And als vnderstanding that the dewtie of the said mynis quhilk baith of the commoun law and consuetude obseruit be vther foreign princes properlie pertenis to the prince Extendis onlie to the tent part fre Thairfore our said souerane lord with auise of his estaittis in parliament hes dissoluit the saidis mynis and mettallis in safer as thay war part of his propirtie annext or ony wyis to the effect the same may be sett in few for augmentatioun of oure said souerane lordis rentall And statutis and ordanis that it salbe lesum to his hienes and his successouris . . . forreasonable compositioun to [dispone] to every erle lord barroun and vther [owner] within this realme all and quhatsumeuir mynis of gould siluer copper leid tin and vther quhatsumeuir mettallis or minerallis quhilk is or may be found within thair awin landis and heretageis with pouer to thame to seik and discouer lauboure and work the saidis mettallis and minerallis and to sell dispone or sett the mynis thairof in takkis . . . to vtheris thair subtenentis at thair pleasure as thair proper gudis and heretage And with sic vther ample priuilegeis as oure said souerane lord . . . sall think expedient for the wining and working of the saidis mettallis be cuntrie men or strangearis Payand thairfore yeirlie the saidis Erlis Lordis barounis and vtheris quha sall accept the [disposition of the saidis mynis] as said is to oure said souerane Lord and his thesaurare thair factouris and seruitouris in thair Name the Just tent part of all and haill the said gould siluer copper leid tin and vtheris minerallis quhilk salbe found and gottin yeirlie within thair saidis landis and heretageis vpoun the ground quhair the same salbe found in sic vre and qualitie as the same salbe gottin out of the erth frelie but ony deductioun . . . . Provyding that in cace ony mynis being sufficientlie discouerit to be within ony of the landis pertening to ony subiect of this realme and the lord of the ground sufficientlie aduertesit thairof and lauchfullie requirit to work the same himself befoir ane Notar [ane witness] as efferis gif he refuisses or delayis the space of thre monethis thairefter Than and in that cace It salbe lesum to our said souerane lord to [dispone the same or set the same] or tak or vtherwyis to caus work the same or to mak rycht thairof to ony vther persone at his grace pleasure That be the wilfull refuise or delay of the awnar of the ground his grace and his cuntrie be not defraudit of the commoditie of the said myne And oure said souerane lord with auise foirsaid of the parliament Declaris that this act of dissolutioun salbe perpetuall to last for all tyme cuming . [. . .]

REGISTRATION ACT 1617
(1617, c 16)

Anent the Registratione of reuersiones Seasingis and vtheris writis

OURE Souerane Lord Considdering the gryit hurt sustened by his Maiesties Liegis by the fraudulent dealing of pairties who haveing annaliet thair Landis and ressauit gryit soumes of money thairfore Yit be thair vniust concealing of sum privat Right formarlie made by thame rendereth subsequent alienatioun done for gryit soumes of money altogidder vnproffitable whiche can not be avoyded vnles the saidis privat rightis be maid publict and patent to his hienes liegis FOR remedie whereoff and of the manye Inconvenientis whiche may ensew thairupoun HIS Maiestie with aduyis and consent of the estaittis of Parliament statutes and ordanis That thair salbe ane publick Register In the whiche all Reuersiounes regresses bandis and writtis for making of reuersiounes or regresses assignatiounes thairto dischargis of the same renunciatiounes of wodsettis and grantis off redemptioun and siclyik all instrumentis of seasing salbe registrat. [. . .] It is alwayis declared that it sall not be necessar to registrat anye bandis and wreatis for making of reuersiounes or regresses vnles seasing pas in fauoures off the pairties makeris of the saidis bandis or writtis In the whiche cace It is ordaned that the samen salbe registrat. [. . .] The extract off the whiche Register sall mak faith in all caces except where the writtis so registrated ar offered to be improvin And gif it salhappin any of the saidis writtis whiche ar appoynted to be registrat as said is not to be dewlie registrat. [. . .] Then and in that cace his maiestie with aduyse and consent foirsaid Decernis the same to mak no faithe in Judgment by way off actioun or exceptioun in preiudice of a third pairtie who hathe acquyred ane perfyit and lauchfull right to the saidis landis and heretages but preiudice alwayis to thame to vse the saidis writtis aganis the pairtye maker thairof his heiris and successoures It is alwayes declared that this present Act sall nowayis be extendit to [. . .] reuersiounes incorporate in the bodye of the Infeftmentis maid to the persounes aganis quhome the saidis reuersiounes ar vseit It is also declaired that gif anye renunciaciones or grantis of redemptioun whiche salhappin to be consignit in proces betuix pairties salbe registrat within thriescore dayes efter the daittis of the decreitis whereby the same salbe Ordaned to be gevin up to the pairties haveand right thairto The same salbe sufficient And to the effect the said register may presentlie and in all tyme cuming be the moir faithfullie keipit THAIRFORE Oure said souerane Lord with aduyis and consent foirsaid Statutes and ordanis the same registeris and registratiounes foirsaidis to be insert thairin to appertene and belang to the present Clerk of Register and his deputtis to be appoynted be him to that effect and decernis and ordanis the same Registeris to be annexed and incorporated with the said office And that the Clerk of Register present and to cum haue the said office as ane proper pairt and pertinent of the Clerk of Register his office [. . .] AND OURE SAID SOUERANE LORD with aduyse and Consent of the estaittis Decernis and Declairis this present act to haue the force strenth and effect of ane decreit and statute of parliament whiche sall have force strenth and executioun according to the tennoure thairoff in all tyme to cum. [. . .]

REAL RIGHTS ACT 1693
(1693, c 22)

Act concerning the preference of Real Rights

OUR Soveraigne Lord and Lady The King and Queens Majesties for the better clearing and determining of Competitions and Preferences of Reall Rights and Infeftments Do hereby with advice and consent of the Estates of Parliament Enact Statute and Declare That [Reall Rights in land shall in all competitions be preferable and preferred according to the date and priority of registration in the General Register of Sasines].

REGISTRATION OF LEASES (SCOTLAND) ACT 1857
(20 & 21 Vict, c 26)

AN ACT to provide for the Registration of Long Leases in Scotland, and Assignations thereof

1 Long leases, and assignations thereof [registrable in Land Register of Scotland or in Register of Sasines]

[(1)] It shall be lawful to [register in the Land Register of Scotland or as the case may be] record in the general register of sasines in Scotland [. . .] probative leases, whether executed before or after the passing of this Act, for a period [exceeding twenty years] of lands and heritages in Scotland [. . .], and to [register or record assignations and translations of such leases], all herein-after mentioned.

[(2) In subsection (1) above, the expression 'lands and heritages in Scotland' is, without prejudice to its generality, to be construed as including the seabed of the territorial sea of the United Kingdom adjacent to Scotland.]

2 [Registered and recorded] leases effectual against singular successors in the lands let

Leases registerable under this Act, and valid and binding as in a question with the granters thereof, which shall have been duly [registered or] recorded, as herein provided [. . .] shall, by virtue of such registration, be effectual against any singular successor in the lands and heritages thereby let, whose [title is completed after] the date of such registration: Provided always, that, except for the purposes of [and subject to section 20C of] this Act, it shall not be necessary to record any such lease as aforesaid, but that all such leases which would, under the existing law prior to the passing of this Act, have been valid and effectual against any such singular successor as aforesaid, shall, though not recorded, be valid and effectual against such singular successor, as well as against the granters of the said leases.

3 Assignations of [registered or] recorded leases

[(1)] When any such lease as aforesaid shall have been [registered or] recorded as herein provided, it shall be lawful for the party in right of such lease, and whose right is [registered or] recorded in terms of this Act, but in accordance always with the conditions and stipulations of such lease, and not otherwise, to assign the same, in whole or in part, by assignation in the form as nearly as may be of the schedule [(ZA) or, as the case may be,] (A) to this Act annexed; and the [registering or] recording of such assignation shall fully and effectually vest the assignee with the right of the granter thereof in and to such lease to the extent assigned: Provided always, that such assignation shall be without prejudice to the right of hypothec, or other rights of the landlord.

[(2) Notwithstanding—

(a) any restriction imposed by subsection (1) above on the power under that subsection to assign such a lease; or

(b) any rule of law to the contrary,

it shall be, and shall be deemed always to have been, competent in an assignation under this section

[(i)] to impose conditions and make stipulations, or

[(ii)] to import such conditions and stipulations,]

which, upon [. . .] registration under the Land Registration (Scotland) Act 1979 of the assignee's interest [or the registration of such assignation under the Land Registration etc (Scotland) Act 2012 (asp 5) or the recording of such assignation] shall be as effectual against any singular successor of the assignee in the subjects assigned as if such assignee had been a grantee of the lease [and, as the case may be, the grantee's interest or the lease had been so registered or the lease had been duly recorded].]

[(2A) Any person entitled to grant an assignation under this section may—

(a) execute a deed containing such conditions, or stipulations, as may be specified in an assignation under subsection (2) above; and

(b) register such conditions and stipulations in the Land Register of Scotland or, as the case may be, record the deed in the Register of Sasines,

and, subject to subsection (2C) below, on such registration or, as the case may be, recording such conditions and stipulations shall be effectual.

(2B) 'Import' in subsection (2)(ii) above means to import into itself from a deed of conditions ('deed of conditions' having the meaning given by section 122(1) of the Title Conditions (Scotland) Act 2003 (asp 9)) the terms of the conditions or stipulations; and importation in or as nearly as may be in the form set out in schedule 1 to that Act (but with the modification that for the references in that form to the terms of the title conditions there are substituted references to the terms of the conditions or stipulations) shall suffice in that regard.

(2C) Where [. . .] a deed provides for the postponement of effectiveness of any conditions or, as the case may be, stipulations to—

(a) a date specified in that deed (the specification being of a fixed date and not, for example, of a date determinable by reference to the occurrence of an event); or

(b) the date of—

(i) registration [. . .] or

(ii) recording of,

some other deed so specified,

the conditions, or stipulations, shall take effect in accordance with such provision.]

[(3) Nothing in subsection (2) [or (2A)] above makes effectual against any successor of the assignee any obligation of periodical payment other than a payment—

(a) of rent or of an apportionment of rent;

(b) in defrayal of a contribution towards some continuing cost related to the lands and heritages subject to the lease assigned; or

(c) under a heritable security.

(4) A provision in an assignation [, or as the case may be in a deed such as is mentioned in subsection (2A) above] which purports to make effectual against any successor of the assignee any obligation of periodic payment other than one specified in paragraphs (a) to (c) of subsection (3) above shall not render the deed void or unenforceable, but the assignation [, or as the case may be the deed,] shall have, and shall be deemed always to have had, effect only to the extent (if any) that it would have had effect if it had not imposed such obligation.]

6 Translation of assignations in security. Creditor's entry to possession in default of payment

All such assignations in security as aforesaid shall, when recorded, be transferable, in whole or in part, by translation in the form as nearly as may be of the schedule (D) to this Act annexed; and the recording of such translation shall fully and effectually vest the party in whose favour it was granted with the right of the granter thereof in such assignation in security to the extent assigned; and the creditor or party in right of such assignation in security, without prejudice to the exercise of any power of sale therein contained, shall be entitled, in default of payment of the capital sum for which such assignation in security has been granted, or of a term's interest thereof, or of a term's annuity, for six months after such capital sum or term's interest or annuity shall have fallen due, to apply to the sheriff for a warrant to enter on possession of the lands and heritages leased; and the sheriff, after intimation to the lessee for the time being, and to the landlord, shall, if he see cause, grant such warrant, which shall be a sufficient title for such creditor or party to enter into possession of such lands and heritages, and to uplift the rents from any sub-tenant therein, and to sub-let the same, as freely and to the like effect as the lessee might have done: Provided always, that no such creditor or party, unless and until he enter into possession as aforesaid, shall be personally liable to the landlord in any of the obligations and prestations of the lease.

10   Adjudgers to complete right by recording abbreviate

When an adjudication of any such lease [registered or recorded] or assignation in security recorded as aforesaid shall have been obtained against the party vested in the right thereof respectively, or against the heir of such party, the [registering or] recording of the abbreviate of adjudication in the register in which the lease is [registered or] recorded shall complete the right of the adjudger to such lease or assignation in security.

12   Preferences regulated by date of registering or recording transfer

All such leases executed after the passing of this Act, and all assignations [of any such lease registered or recorded as aforesaid], assignations in security of any such lease recorded as aforesaid, and translations thereof, and all adjudications of such leases [registered or] recorded as aforesaid, or assignations in security, shall in competition be preferable according to their dates of [registering or] recording.

13   Renunciations and discharges to be [registered or] recorded

On the production to the keeper of the register of a renunciation of any such lease as aforesaid [registered or] recorded therein, or of a discharge of any such assignation in security as aforesaid therein recorded, by or on behalf of the party appearing on the register as in right of such lease or assignation in security, which renunciation or discharge may be in the form of the schedules [(ZG) or (G)] and (H) respectively to this Act annexed, and may be endorsed on such lease or assignation in security, he shall forthwith duly [register or] record the same.

14   Entry of decree of reduction

On the production to any such keeper of an extract of a decree of reduction of any such lease, assignation, assignation in security, translation, adjudication, instrument, discharge, or renunciation [registered or as the case may be] recorded in the register of which he is the keeper, he shall forthwith duly [register or] record the same.

15   Mode of registering—extracts to make faith as writs registered

[(1)]   Leases, assignations, assignations in security, translations, adjudications, instruments, discharges, renunciations, and other writs, duly presented for registration in pursuance of this Act, shall be forthwith shortly entered in the minute book of the register in common form, and shall, with all due despatch, be fully registered in the register book, and thereafter re-delivered to the parties, with certificates of due registration thereon, which shall be probative of such registration, such certificates specifying the date of presentation, and the book and folio in which the engrossment has been made [. . .]; and the date of entry in the minute book shall be held to be the date of registration [. . .].

[(2)   References in subsection (1) above to registration are not to be construed as including references to registration in the Land Register of Scotland.]

16   Registration equivalent to possession

[(1)]   The registration of all such leases, assignations, assignations in security, translations, adjudications [and writs of acknowledgement] as aforesaid, in manner herein provided, shall complete the right under the same respectively, to the effect of establishing a preference in virtue thereof, as effectually as if the grantee, or party in his right, had entered into the actual possession of the subjects leased under such writs respectively at the date of registration thereof.

[(2)   The registration of any such lease or other writ as aforesaid, in manner herein provided, on or after 1st September 1974, shall, without prejudice to the foregoing provisions of this section and to the provisions of section 2 of the Prescription and Limitation (Scotland) Act 1973, complete the right under the same to the effect of establishing in virtue thereof such a preference as aforesaid over the right of any party to any such lease or writ, or of any party in his right, granted after that date and not registered in manner herein provided at the time of the registration of the lease or writ first mentioned.]

[(3) References in subsections (1) and (2) above to registration are not to be construed as including references to registration in the Land Register of Scotland.]

17 Leases, with obligation to renew, registerable

Leases containing an obligation upon the granter to renew the same from time to time at fixed periods, or upon the termination of a life or lives, or otherwise, shall be deemed leases within the meaning of this Act, and registerable as such, provided such leases shall by the terms of such obligation be renewable from time to time so as to endure for a period [exceeding twenty years].

20 Clauses in schedules to be held to import and to have effect as declared by 10 & 11 Vict c 50, ss 2, 3, &c

The several clauses in the schedules to this Act annexed shall be held to import such and the like meaning and to have such and the like effect as is declared by the Act of the tenth and eleventh of Queen Victoria, chapter fifty, sections second and third, to belong to the corresponding clauses in the schedule to the said recited Act annexed; and the procedure thereby prescribed for a sale under a bond and disposition in security shall be applicable to a sale of any such lease as aforesaid under any such assignation in security as is herein-before mentioned.

[20A Certain transactions or events registrable in the Land Register of Scotland

(1) A deed mentioned in subsection (2) which affects a lease registered in the Land Register of Scotland is registrable in that register.

(2) The deed is one—
    (a) terminating the lease,
    (b) extending the duration of the lease,
    (c) otherwise altering the terms of the lease.]

[20B Effect of registration in the Land Register of Scotland

(1) Registration in the Land Register of Scotland has the effect of—
    (a) vesting in the person registered as entitled to the lease a real right in and to the lease and in and to any right or pertinent, express or implied, forming part of the lease, subject only to the effect of any matter entered in that register so far as adverse to the entitlement,
    (b) making any registered right or obligation relating to the registered lease a real right or obligation, and
    (c) affecting any registered real right or obligation relating to the registered lease,
in so far as the right or obligation is capable, under any enactment or rule of law, of being vested as a real right, of being made real or (as the case may be) of being affected as a real right.

(2) Registration in the Land Register of Scotland is the only means—
    (a) whereby rights or obligations relating to a registered lease become real rights or obligations, or
    (b) of affecting such real rights or obligations.

(3) Subject to Part 9 of the Land Registration etc. (Scotland) Act 2012 (asp 5) (rights to persons acquiring etc. in good faith), registration of an invalid deed confers no real effect.]

[20C Disapplication of Leases Act 1449

The Leases Act 1449 (c.6) does not apply to a lease registrable under this Act and granted on or after the date on which—
    (a) the land to which the lease relates, or any part of that land, became land within an operational area (that is to say within an area in respect of which the

provisions of the Land Registration (Scotland) Act 1979 (c.33) had come into operation), or

   (b)   section 52 of the Land Registration etc. (Scotland) Act 2012 (asp 5) (amendment of Registration of Leases (Scotland) Act 1857 (c.26)) comes into force.]

[20D   Long fishing leases

This Act applies to a contract within the meaning of section 66 of the Salmon and
Freshwater Fisheries (Consolidation) (Scotland) Act 2003 (asp 15) (application of
Leases Act 1449) as it does to a lease described in section 1 of this Act provided that
the contract in question—

   (a)   is for a period exceeding 20 years, or
   (b)   includes an obligation such as is described in section 17 of this Act.]

[20E   The expression 'the register'

Except where the context otherwise requires, in this Act—

   (a)   the expression 'the register' is to be construed as including a reference to the
Land Register of Scotland, and
   (b)   analogous expressions are to be construed accordingly.]

21   Short title

This Act may be cited for all purposes as 'The Registration of Leases (Scotland) Act,
1857.'

SCHEDULES

[SCHEDULE (ZA)
Form of Assignation of Lease Registered in the Land Register of Scotland

   I, *A.B.*, [*designation*] in consideration of the sum now paid to me, [*or otherwise, as
the case may be,*] assign to *C.D.* [*designation*] a lease registered in the Land Register of
Scotland under title number [*number*] [but (*where the lease is assigned in part only*) in
so far only as regards the following portion of the subjects leased; viz. (*specify particularly the portion,*)] with entry as at (*term of entry*). And [*where sub-lease*] I assign the
rents from [*term*]; and I grant warrandice; and I bind myself to free and relieve the
said *C.D.* of all rents and burdens due to the landlord or others at and prior to the
term of entry in respect of said lease; and I consent to registration for preservation
and execution.

[*Testing clause* †]

† Note—In the case of a traditional document, subscription of it by the granter will be sufficient
for the document to be formally valid, but witnessing of it may be necessary or desirable for
other purposes: see the Requirements of Writing (Scotland) Act 1995 (c 7) (which also makes
provision as regards the authentication of an electronic document).]

SCHEDULE (A)   Sect 3

Form of Assignation of Lease [recorded in the Register of Sasines]

   I, *A.B.*, [*designation*] in consideration of the sum of   now paid to
me, [*or otherwise, as the case may be,*] assign to *C.D.* [*designation*] a lease, dated
                        , and recorded in the   register of sasines at
                  , of date   , granted by *E.F.* [*designation*] in my favour [*or
if not in assigner's favour, name and design grantee*], of [*shortly mention subjects*] in the
parish of   and county of   [. . .], [but (*where the lease
is assigned in part only*) in so far only as regards the following portion of the subjects leased; viz. (*specify particularly the portion,*)] with entry as at (*term of entry*). And
[*where sub-lease*] I assign the rents from [*term*]; and I grant warrandice; and I bind
myself to free and relieve the said *C.D.* of all rents and burdens due to the land-

lord or others at and prior to the term of entry in respect of said lease; and I consent to registration for preservation and execution.

[*Testing clause* †]

[† Note—[In the case of a traditional document, subscription of it by the granter] will be sufficient for the document to be formally valid, but witnessing of it may be necessary or desirable for other purposes (see the Requirements of Writing (Scotland) Act 1995) [, which also makes provision as regards the authentication of an electronic document].]

[SCHEDULE (ZG)
Renunciation of Lease Registered in the Land Register of Scotland

I, *A.B.* [*designation*] renounce as from the term of [*term*] in favour of *C.D.* [*or as the case may be*] a lease granted by the said *C.D.* [*or as the case may be*] and registered in the Land Register of Scotland under title number [*number*].

[*Testing clause* †]

[† Note—In the case of a traditional document, subscription of it by the granter will be sufficient for the document to be formally valid, but witnessing of it may be necessary or desirable for other purposes: see the Requirements of Writing (Scotland) Act 1995 (c 7) which also makes provision as regards the authentication of an electronic document.]

Sect 13   SCHEDULE (G)
Renunciation of Lease [recorded in the Register of Sasines]

I, *A.B.* [*designation,*] renounce as from the term of   in favour of *C.D.* [*designation*] a lease granted by the said *C.D.* [*or as the case may be*] of [*shortly set forth subjects*] in the parish of   , and county of   , which lease is dated   , and recorded [*register, and date of recording,*] [. . .]

[*Testing clause* †]

[† Note—[In the case of a traditional document, subscription of it by the granter] will be sufficient for the document to be formally valid, but witnessing of it may be necessary or desirable for other purposes (see the Requirements of Writing (Scotland) Act 1995) [, which also makes provision as regards the authentication of an electronic document].]

Sect 13   SCHEDULE (H)
Form of Discharge of Bond and Assignation in Security

I, *A.B.,* [*designation*] in consideration of the sum of   , now paid to me by *C.D.,* [*designation,*] discharge a bond and assignation in security for the sum of   , granted by the said *C.D.* in my favour [*or as the case may be*[1]], and which is dated   , and recorded in the [*register, and date of recording*]; and I declare to be disburdened thereof a lease granted by *E.F.* [*designation*] of [*shortly mention subjects leased*] in the parish of   and county of   , which lease is dated   , and recorded [*register, and date of recording*].

[*Testing clause* †]

[† Note—[In the case of a traditional document, subscription of it by the granter] will be sufficient for the document to be formally valid, but witnessing of it may be necessary or desirable for other purposes (see the Requirements of Writing (Scotland) Act 1995) [, which also makes provision as regards the authentication of an electronic document].]

[1] Note—If granter not original creditor, [name and design original creditor].

TRANSMISSION OF MOVEABLE PROPERTY (SCOTLAND) ACT 1862
(1862 c 85)

1   Personal bond or conveyance of moveable estate may be assigned in the form set forth in schedule A

It shall be competent to any party, in right of a personal bond or of a conveyance of moveable estate, to assign such bond or conveyance by assignation in or as nearly as may be in the form set forth in schedule A hereto annexed; and it shall be competent to write the assignation or assignations on the bond or conveyance itself in or as nearly as may be in the form set forth in schedule B. hereto annexed; which assignation shall be registrable in the books of any court, in terms of any clause of registration contained in the bond or conveyance so assigned; and such assignation, upon being duly stamped and duly intimated, shall have the same force and effect as a duly stamped and duly intimated assignation according to the forms at present in use.

2   Certified copy to be delivered to person or persons to whom intimation may in any case be requisite

An assignation shall be validly intimated (1) by a notary public delivering a copy thereof, certified as correct, to the person or persons to whom intimation may in any case be requisite, or (2) by the holder of such assignation, or any person authorized by him, transmitting a copy thereof certified as correct by post to such person; and (in the first case) a certificate by such notary public in or as nearly as may be in the form set forth in schedule C. hereto annexed, and (in the second case) a written acknowledgment by the person to whom such copy may have been transmitted by post as aforesaid of the receipt of the copy, shall be sufficient evidence of such intimation having been duly made: Provided always, that if the deed or instrument containing such assignation shall likewise contain other conveyances or declarations of trust purposes, it shall not be necessary to deliver or transmit a full copy thereof, but only a copy of such part thereof as respects the subject matter of such assignation.

3   As to transmission of personal bond, &c

Nothing in this Act contained shall prevent the transmission of any personal bond or conveyance of moveable estate, or the intimation of any assignation according to the forms at present in use.

4   Interpretation of terms

The following words in this Act, and in the schedules annexed to this Act, shall have the several meanings hereby assigned to them, unless there be something in the subject or context repugnant to such construction; that is to say, the word 'bond' and the word 'conveyance' shall extend to and include personal bonds for payment or performance, bonds of caution, bonds of guarantee, bonds of relief, bonds and assignations in security of every kind, decreets of any court, policies of assurance of any assurance company or association in Scotland, whether held by parties resident in Scotland or elsewhere, protests of bills or of promissory notes, dispositions, assignations, or other conveyances of moveable or personal property or effects, assignations, translations, and retrocessions, and also probative extracts of all such deeds from the books of any competent court; the word 'assignation' shall also include translations and retrocessions, and probative extracts thereof; the words 'moveable estate' shall extend to and include all personal debts and obligations, and moveable or personal property or effects of every kind.

5   Short title

This Act may be cited for all purposes as the 'Transmission of Moveable Property (Scotland) Act, 1862.'

SCHEDULES referred to in the foregoing Act

SCHEDULE A

I, A.B., in consideration of, &c [*or otherwise, as the case may be*], do hereby assign to C.D. and his heirs or assignees [*or otherwise, as the case may be,*] the bond [*or other deed, describing it*], granted by E.F., dated, &c, by which [*here specify the nature of the deed, and specify also any connecting title, and any circumstances requiring to be stated in regard to the nature and extent of the right required*],

[† Note—[In the case of a traditional document, subscription of it by the granter] will be sufficient for the document to be formally valid, but witnessing of it may be necessary or desirable for other purposes (see the Requirements of Writing (Scotland) Act 1995) [, which also makes provision as regards the authentication of an electronic document].]

SCHEDULE B

I, A.B., in consideration of, &c [*or otherwise, as the case may be*], do hereby assign to C.D. and his heirs or assignees [*or otherwise, as the case may be,*] the foregoing [*or within-written*] bond [*or other writ or deed, describing it,*] granted in my favour [*or otherwise, as the case may be, specifying any connecting title, and any circumstances requiring to be stated in regard to the nature and extent of the right assigned*].

[† Note—[In the case of a traditional document, subscription of it by the granter] will be sufficient for the document to be formally valid, but witnessing of it may be necessary or desirable for other purposes (see the Requirements of Writing (Scotland) Act 1995) [, which also makes provision as regards the authentication of an electronic document].]

SCHEDULE C

I (A.), of the city of notary public, do hereby attest and declare, that upon the day of, and between the hours of and, I duly intimated to B. [*here describe the party*] the within-written assignation [*or otherwise, as the case may be*], or an assignation granted by [*here describe it*], and that by delivering to the said A. personally [*or otherwise*] by leaving for the said A. within his dwelling house at E., in the hands of [*here describe the party*], a full copy thereof, [*or if a partial copy here quote the portion of the deed which has been delivered*], to be given to him; all of which was done in presence of C. [. . .]

LAND REGISTERS (SCOTLAND) ACT 1868
(31 & 32 Vict, c 64)

3   In general register of sasines, writs of each county to be kept separate
The general register of sasines for Scotland shall be so kept that the writs applicable to each county shall be entered in a separate series of presentment books, and the writs shall be minuted in a separate series of minute books, and engrossed in a separate series of register volumes, in the order of presentment; and where any writ shall contain land in more than one county, such writ shall be entered by the ingiver in the presentment book of such of these counties as may be specified in the [application for registration] and shall be minuted in the minute book of such of these counties or county as are specified in [that application], and shall be engrossed at length in the division of the register applicable to one only of the said counties; and a memorandum shall be entered in each division of the register applicable to the other counties or county in the presentment book of which it is entered as aforesaid, setting forth the volume of the register and the folio or folios of

such volume in which such engrossment is made; and such memorandum shall be deemed to be equivalent to full engrossment of such writ in the division of the register wherein such memorandum shall be entered as aforesaid: For the purposes of this Act, the barony and regality of Glasgow, and also the stewartry of Kirkcudbright, shall each be treated as a county.

6   Provision for writs transmitted by post to general register of sasines

Where [an application for registration of a writ in the general register of sasines is transmitted by post], the keeper of said register shall, upon the receipt of such [application], cause the same to be acknowledged to the sender, and [cause the writ] to be presented [. . .] by a clerk in his office to be appointed by him for that purpose, and who shall be held as the ingiver of the writ; and such clerk shall [in the presentment book enter] the name of the sender; and such writ shall be recorded in the same manner as any other writ [which is a traditional document] presented for registration; and on the writ being ready for delivery [. . .], the keeper shall transmit the writs to the sender by post; and where two or more [such applications] shall be received by the keeper at the same time, the entries [. . .] in the presentment book and minute book [for the writs in respect of which such applications are made] shall be of the same year, month [and day,] and such writs shall be deemed and taken to be presented and registered contemporaneously.

[6A   Provision for writs transmitted electronically to general register of sasines

(1)   This section applies where an application is transmitted electronically for recording in the general register of sasines of a writ [. . .] which may be recorded in the register.

(2)   The keeper of the register must on receipt of an application cause it to be acknowledged to the sender.

(3)   The keeper must cause the name of the sender to be entered in the presentment book.

(4)   The writ is to be recorded in the same manner as a traditional document, save that the copy or copies are to be entered in and kept on a computer or similar device under the keeper's management and control.

(5)   Following recording, the keeper must confirm recording to the sender.]

[(6)   For the purposes of this section, submission by electronic means of a copy of the writ is sufficient evidence of the original for the purposes of accepting an application.

(7)   But subsection (6) applies only where submission of the copy is by a means (and in a form) which is specified on the Keeper's website as being acceptable.

(8)   In subsection (6), the reference to submission by electronic means is to submission—

(a)   by means of an electronic communications network (for example as an attachment to an email), or

(b)   by other means but in a form which requires the use of electronic apparatus by the recipient to render the thing delivered intelligible.

(9) In this section—

'electronic communications network' has the meaning given by section 32 of the Communications Act 2003,

'the Keeper's website' means the website maintained by, or on behalf of, the Keeper of the Registers of Scotland.]

[6B   Writs received at the same time as writs transmitted electronically

(1)   This section applies where an application transmitted electronically under section 6A is received by the keeper at the same time as—

(a)   another such application, or

(b)   another application by post under section 6.

(2)   The entries in the presentment book and minute book for the writs in respect of which such applications are made are to be of the same year, month and day, and such writs are to be deemed to be presented and registered contemporaneously.]

TITLES TO LAND CONSOLIDATION (SCOTLAND) ACT 1868
(31 & 32 Vict, c 101)

[Preamble]

1 Short title
This Act may be cited for all purposes as 'The Titles to Land Consolidation (Scotland) Act, 1868.'

2 Commencement of Act
This Act shall take effect from and after the thirty-first day of December one thousand eight hundred and sixty-eight, unless in so far as it is herein appointed to take effect at an earlier date.

3 Interpretation of terms
The following words and expressions in this Act, and in the schedules annexed to this Act, shall have the several meanings hereby assigned to them, unless there be something in the subject or context repugnant to such construction; that is to say,

The words [. . .] 'grantor,' 'grantee,' 'disponer,' 'disponee,' 'legatee,' 'adjudger,' and 'purchaser' shall extend to and include the heirs, successors, and representatives of such [. . .] grantor, grantee, disponer, disponee, legatee, adjudger, or purchaser respectively; and the word 'successors' shall extend to and include heirs, disponees, assignees legal as well as voluntary, executors, and representatives:

[. . .]

The words 'sheriff of Chancery' shall extend to and include the sheriff of Chancery and his substitute under this Act, or under the Act of the tenth and eleventh Victoria, chapter forty-seven, and the word 'sheriff' shall extend to and include the sheriff of any county and his substitute, and the sheriff of Chancery and his substitute:

The words 'sheriff clerk of Chancery' shall extend to and include the sheriff clerk of Chancery acting under this Act, or who acted under the Act of the tenth and eleventh Victoria, chapter forty-seven, and the depute of such sheriff clerk; and the words 'sheriff clerk' shall extend to and include the sheriff clerk of Chancery, and the sheriff clerk of any county and their respective deputes:

[. . .] The word 'Prince' shall extend to and include the Prince and Steward of Scotland and his successors:

[. . .]

The word 'deed' and the word 'conveyance' shall each extend to and include all [. . .] writs, dispositions, [. . .] whether inter vivos or mortis causa, and whether absolute or in trust, [. . .] heritable securities, reversions, assignations, instruments, decrees of constitution relating to land to be afterwards adjudged, decrees of adjudication for debt, and of adjudication in implement, and of constitution and adjudication combined, whether for debt or implement, decrees of declarator and adjudication, decrees of sale, and decrees of general and of special service [. . .] and the summonses, petitions, or warrants on which any such decrees proceed, warrants to judicial factors, trustees, or beneficiaries of a lapsed trust, to make up titles to lands, and the petitions on which such warrants proceed, writs of acknowledgment, contracts of excambion, deeds of entail [. . .] and all deeds, decrees, and writings by which lands, or rights in lands, are constituted or completed or conveyed, or discharged, whether dated, granted, or obtained before or after the passing of this Act, and official extracts of all deeds and conveyances; and all codicils, deeds of nomination, and other writings annexed to or endorsed on deeds or conveyances or bearing reference to deeds or conveyances separately granted, and decrees of declarator naming or appointing persons to exercise or enjoy the rights or powers conferred by such deeds or conveyances, shall be deemed and taken for the purposes of this Act to be parts of the deeds or conveyances to which they severally relate, and shall have the same effect in all respects as to the persons so named and appointed as if they had been named and appointed in the deeds or conveyances themselves:

[. . .]

The word 'instrument' shall extend to and include all notarial instruments [. . .] and also all instruments of sasine, instruments of resignation ad remanentiam, instruments of resignation and sasine and instruments of cognition and sasine, and instruments of cognition:

The words 'heritable security' and 'security' shall each extend to and include all heritable bonds, bonds and dispositions in security, bonds of annual rent, bonds of annuity, and all securities authorised to be granted by the seventh section of the Debts Securities (Scotland) Act, 1856, and all deeds and conveyances whatsoever, legal as well as voluntary, which are or may be used for the purpose of constituting or completing or transmitting a security over lands or over the rents and profits thereof, as well as such lands themselves and the rents and profits thereof, and the sums, principal, interest, and penalties, secured by such securities; but shall not include securities by way of ground annual, whether redeemable or irredeemable, or absolute dispositions qualified by back bonds or letters:

The word 'creditor' shall extend to and include the party in whose favour an heritable security is granted, and his successors in right thereof:

The word 'debtor' shall include the debtor and his successors:

The word 'lands' shall extend to and include all heritable subjects, securities, and rights:

The words 'notary public' shall be held to mean a notary public duly admitted to practise in Scotland:

The word 'petitioner' shall extend to and include any person who may have presented or may present a petition within the meaning of this Act, or of any Act hereby repealed:

[. . .]

8   Import of clauses in Schedule (B) nos 1 and 2

[. . .] The clause of assignation of writs and evidents in [Form No 1] of schedule (B) hereto annexed shall, unless specially qualified, be held to import an absolute and unconditional assignation to such writs and evidents [. . .] therein contained, and to all unrecorded conveyances to which the disponer has right; and the clause of assignation of rents [. . .] shall, unless specially qualified, be held to import an assignation to the rents to become due for the possession following the term of entry, according to the legal and not the conventional terms, unless in the case of forehand rents, in which case it shall be held to import an assignation to the rents payable at the conventional terms subsequent to the date of entry; and the clause of warrandice [. . .] shall, unless specially qualified, be held to imply absolute warrandice as regards the lands and writs and evidents, and warrandice from fact and deed as regards the rents; and the clause of obligation to free and relieve from [public burdens] shall, unless specially qualified, be held to import an obligation to relieve of all [public] and local burdens due from or on account of the lands conveyed prior to the date of entry; [. . .]; and the clause of consent to registration [shall, unless specially qualified, have the meaning and effect assigned].

12   Clause directing part of conveyance to be recorded

Immediately before the testing clause of any conveyance of lands, it shall be competent to insert a clause of direction, in or as nearly as may be in the form No 1 of schedule (F) hereto annexed, specifying the part or parts of the conveyance which the grantor thereof desires to be recorded in the register of sasines; and when such clause is so inserted in any conveyance, whether dated before or after the commencement of this Act, and [. . .] is presented to the keeper of the appropriate register of sasines for registration, such keeper shall record such part or parts only, together with the clause of direction, and the testing clause [. . .]: Provided, that notwithstanding such clause of direction it shall be competent for the person entitled to present the conveyance for registration to record the whole conveyance. [. . .]

13 Several lands conveyed by the same deed may be comprehended under one general name

Where several lands are comprehended in one conveyance in favour of the same person or persons, it shall be competent to insert a clause in the conveyance, declaring that the whole lands conveyed and therein particularly described shall be designed and known in future by one general name, to be therein specified; and on the conveyance containing such clause, whether dated before or after the commencement of this Act, or on an instrument following thereon, whether dated before or after the commencement of this Act, and containing such particular description and clause, being duly recorded in the appropriate register of sasines, it shall be competent in all subsequent conveyances and deeds and discharges of or relating to such several lands to use the general name specified in such clause as the name of the several lands declared by such clause to be comprehended under it; and such subsequent conveyances and deeds and discharges of or relating to such several lands under the general name so specified shall be as effectual in all respects as if the same contained a particular description of each of such several lands, exactly as the same is set forth in such recorded conveyance or instrument: Provided always, that reference be made in such subsequent conveyances and deeds and discharges to a prior conveyance or instrument recorded as aforesaid, in which such particular description and clause are contained: Provided also, that it shall not be necessary in such clause to comprehend under one general name the whole lands contained in the conveyance in which such clause is inserted, but that it shall be competent to comprehend certain lands under one general name and certain other lands under another general name, it being clearly specified what lands are comprehended under each general name; and such reference shall be in or as nearly as may be in the terms set forth in schedule (G) hereunto annexed. [. . .]

20 De praesenti words, or words of style unnecessary in mortis causa deeds

From and after the commencement of this Act it shall be competent to any owner of lands to settle the succession to the same in the event of his death, not only by conveyances de præsenti, according to the existing law and practice, but likewise by testamentary or mortis causa deeds or writings; and no testamentary or mortis causa deed or writing purporting to convey or bequeath lands which shall have been granted by any person alive at the commencement of this Act, or which shall be granted by any person after the commencement of this Act, shall be held to be invalid as a settlement of the lands to which such deed or writing applies on the ground that the grantor has not used with reference to such lands the word 'dispone,' or other word or words importing a conveyance de præsenti; and where such deed or writing shall not be expressed in the terms required by the existing law or practice for the conveyance of lands, but shall contain with reference to such lands any word or words which would, if used in a will or testament with reference to moveables, be sufficient to confer upon the executor of the grantor, or upon the grantee or legatee of such moveables, a right to claim and receive the same, such deed or writing, if duly executed in the manner required or permitted in the case of any testamentary writing by the law of Scotland, shall be deemed and taken to be [valid as a settlement on a grantee or legatee of the lands to which it applies; and the executor of the grantor may complete title to such lands by expeding and recording a notarial instrument as aforesaid]: Provided always, that nothing herein contained shall be held to confer any right to such lands on the successors of any such grantee or legatee who shall predecease the grantor, unless the deed or writing shall be so expressed as to give them such right in the event of the predecease of such grantee or legatee.

21   Trustee or executor to apply lands for purposes of trust or will

Where such testamentary or mortis causa deed or writing shall be conceived in favour of a grantee as trustee or executor of the grantor and shall not be expressed to be wholly in favour of such trustee or executor for his own benefit, such trustee or executor shall apply such whole lands for the purposes specified in such deed or writing; and where such purposes cannot, in whole or in part, be carried into effect, or where no purposes with reference to such lands have been or shall be specified in such deed or writing, such trustee or executor shall convey such lands, or so much thereof, or shall apply so much of the proceeds thereof, if such lands shall have been sold and realized by him, as may not be required for the purposes of such deed or writing, to or for behoof of the person or the successors of the person who, but for the passing of this Act and the granting of such deed or writing, would have been entitled to succeed to such lands on the death of such grantor.

24   Mode of completing title by a judicial factor on a trust estate, &c

Where in a petition to the Court of Session for the appointment of a judicial factor authority has been or shall be asked for the completion of a title by such factor to any lands forming the whole or part of the estate to be managed by such judicial factor, or where a judicial factor has applied or shall apply, by petition or note to the said Court, for authority to complete a title to such lands, either in his own person as judicial factor, or in the person of any persons under legal disability by reason of nonage, or mental or other incapacity to whom he may have been appointed judicial factor, and where any petition or note has specified and described or shall specify and describe the lands to which such title is to be completed, or has referred or shall refer to the description of the same, in the form or as nearly as may be in the form [. . .] of schedule (G) hereto annexed, as the case may be, the warrant granted for completing such title shall also so specify and describe the lands to which such title is to be completed, or shall so refer to the description thereof; and such warrant shall be held to be a conveyance in due and common form of the lands therein specified in favour of such judicial factor, granted by the person, whether in life or deceased, whose estate is under judicial management, or where the estate is that of a person under legal disability by reason of nonage, or mental or other incapacity, in whose person a title has not been made up, such warrant shall be held to be such a conveyance in favour of the persons under legal disability by reason of nonage, or mental or other incapacity, or of a judicial factor appointed to such persons under legal disability by reason of nonage, or mental or other incapacity, as the case may be, granted by a predecessor or author having such title, or where such judicial factor has been or shall be appointed on an estate which shall have been vested in a trustee or former judicial factor, such warrant shall be held to be such a conveyance granted by such trustee or former factor, whether in life or deceased, for the purposes of such estate, or trust, or factory, [. . .] to be holden of Her Majesty in free burgage; and such warrant may [. . .] be recorded in the appropriate register of sasines as a conveyance in favour of such judicial factor, or persons under legal disability by reason of nonage, or mental or other incapacity, or of the factor on his estate, and being so recorded shall have the same force and effect as if at the date of such recording such conveyance had been granted to the judicial factor, or persons under legal disability by reason of nonage, or mental or other incapacity, or the judicial factor appointed to such persons under legal disability by reason of nonage, or mental or other incapacity, as the case may be, and recorded in the appropriate register of sasines: Provided always, that for enabling the person in whom such lands were last vested, or his representatives, or other parties interested, to bring forward competent objections against such warrant being granted, or claims upon the estate, the Court shall order such intimation and service of the petition or note as to them shall seem proper: Declaring always, that the whole enactments and provisions herein contained shall extend and apply to all petitions to and warrants by the Court of Session under the Trusts (Scotland) Act, 1867, unless in so far as such provisions and enactments may be inapplicable to the form or objects of such petitions or warrants.]

[25   Deduction of title by liquidator
The liquidator in the winding up of a company shall, for the purposes of sections 3 (disposition etc by person with unrecorded title) and 4 (completion of title) of the Conveyancing (Scotland) Act 1924 (c 27) (including those sections as applied to registered leases by section 24 of that Act), be taken to be a person having right to any land belonging to the company.]

26   Heritable property conveyed for religious or educational purposes to vest in disponees or their successors
Wherever lands have been or may hereafter be acquired by any congregation, society, or body of men associated for religious purposes, or for the promotion of education, including the general assemblies, synods, and presbyteries of the Established Church of Scotland, and of all other Presbyterian churches in Scotland, as a chapel, meeting house, or other place of worship, or as a manse or dwelling house for the minister of such congregation or society or body of men, or offices, garden, or glebe for his use, or as a schoolhouse, or schoolmaster's house, garden, or playground, or as a college, academy, or seminary, or as a hall or rooms for meeting for the transaction of business, or as part of the property belonging to such congregation, society, or body of men, and wherever the conveyance or lease of such lands has been or may be taken in favour of the moderator, minister, kirk session, vestrymen, deacons, managers, or other office bearers or office bearer of such congregation or society or body of men, or any of them, or of trustees appointed or to be from time to time appointed, or of any party or parties named in such conveyance or lease in trust for behoof of the congregation or society or body of men, or of the individuals comprising the same, such conveyance, when recorded [. . .] in terms of this Act, or such lease, shall not only vest the party or parties named therein in the lands thereby [. . .] conveyed, or leased, but shall also, after the death or resignation or removal from office of such party or parties, or any of them, effectually vest their successors in office for the time being chosen and appointed in the manner provided or referred to in such conveyance or lease, or if no mode of appointment be therein set forth or prescribed, then in terms of the rules or regulations of such congregation or society or body of men, in such lands, subject to such and the like trusts, and with and under the same powers and provisions, as are contained or referred to in the conveyance or lease given and granted to the parties disponees or lessees therein, and that without any transmission or renewal of the investiture whatsoever, anything in such conveyance or lease contained to the contrary notwithstanding: And the provisions of this section shall apply also to all trusts for the maintenance, support, or endowment of ministers of religion, missionaries, or schoolmasters, or for the maintenance of the fabric of churches, chapels, meeting houses, or other places of worship, or of manses or dwelling houses or offices for ministers of the gospel, or of schoolhouses or schoolmaster's houses, or other like buildings.

[26A   Application for declarator of succession as heir in general or to specified lands
On an application being made by any person having an interest, the sheriff of Chancery may, if satisfied that—
     (a)   such deceased person as may be specified in the application died before 10th September 1964 and that person either—
          (i)   was domiciled in Scotland at the date of his death; or
          (ii)   was the owner of lands situated in Scotland to which the application relates; and

(b) the applicant, or as the case may be such person as may be specified in the application, has succeeded as heir to that deceased, and is either—

(i)   heir in general; or

(ii) heir to such lands as may be specified in the application,

grant declarator that the applicant, or as the case may be such person as may be specified in the declarator, is the heir in general or heir to the lands so specified.

26B Application for declarator of succession as heir to last surviving trustee under a trust

On an application being made under this section, the sheriff of Chancery may, if satisfied that—

(a) such deceased person as may be specified in the application was the last surviving trustee named in, or assumed under, a trust;

(b) the trust provides for the heir of such last surviving trustee to be a trustee;

(c) either—

(i)   the trust is governed by the law of Scotland; or

(ii) lands subject to the trust and to which the application relates are situated in Scotland; and

(d) the applicant has succeeded as heir to the deceased,

grant declarator that the applicant is the heir of the deceased and accordingly is a trustee under the trust.

26C Construction of reference to service of heir

A reference in any enactment or deed to a decree of service of heir (however expressed) shall include a reference to a declarator granted under section 26A or 26B of this Act.]

51 Power to the Court of Session to pass Acts of Sederunt

It shall be competent to the [. . .] Court of Session, and they are hereby authorized and required, from time to time to pass such acts of sederunt as shall be necessary or proper for regulating in all respects the proceedings under this Act before the sheriff of Chancery [. . .].

62 Effect of a decree of adjudication or of sale

In all cases a decree of adjudication, whether for debt or in implement, or a decree of constitution and adjudication, whether for debt or in implement, if duly obtained in the form prescribed by this Act, or obtained, if prior to the commencement of this Act, in the form then in use, or a decree of declarator and adjudication, or a decree of sale, shall, except in the case where the subjects contained in the decree of adjudication, or of constitution and adjudication, or of declarator and adjudication, are heritable securities, be held equivalent to and shall have the legal operation and effect of a conveyance in ordinary form of the lands therein contained granted in favour of the adjudger or purchaser by the ancestor of such apparent heir, or by the owner or proprietor, in trust or otherwise, and whether in life or deceased, of the lands adjudged, or by the seller of the lands sold, although [under legal disability by reason of non-age] or [mental or other incapacity] [. . .] and it shall be lawful and competent to such adjudger or purchaser to complete [title by recording the decree as a conveyance or by using the decree as a midcouple or link of title].

[117 Heritable security in succession of creditor in the security

In the succession of the creditor in a heritable security, the security shall be moveable estate; except that in relation to the legal rights of the spouse, or of the descendants, of the deceased it shall be heritable estate.]

120 Securities may be registered during lifetime of grantee, or title completed after his death

Heritable securities [. . .] may be registered in the appropriate register of sasines at any time during the lifetime of the grantee, and shall in competition be preferred according to the date of the registration thereof [. . .].

[129   Adjudgers may complete their title to heritable securities by recording abbreviate of adjudication
In all cases of adjudication, whether for debt or in implement, or of constitution and adjudication, whether for debt or in implement, in which the adjudger has obtained a decree of adjudication, or of constitution and adjudication, in the manner and to the effect provided by this Act, or in cases of declarator and adjudication, where the subjects contained in any such decree are heritable securities, it shall be competent for the adjudger to complete his title to such securities by recording either the abbreviate of adjudication or an extract of such decree in the appropriate register of sasines, in either of which cases he shall be in the same position as if an assignation of such heritable securities had been granted in his favour by the ancestor or person or creditor, in trust or otherwise, and whether in life or deceased, whose estate is adjudged, and as if such assignation had been duly recorded in the appropriate register of sasines at the date of so recording such abbreviate or such extract decree.]

138   Short clauses of consent to registration may be used in any deed
The short clauses of consent to registration for preservation, and for preservation and execution contained in [form No 1] of schedule (B) hereto annexed, when occurring in any deed or conveyance under this Act, or in any deed or writing or document of whatsoever nature, and whether relating to lands or not, shall, unless specially qualified, import a consent to registration and a procuratory of registration in the books of council and session, or other judges books competent, therein to remain for preservation; and also, if for execution, that [, upon the issue of an extract containing a warrant for execution, all lawful execution shall pass thereon].

140   Additional sheets may be added to writs
In all cases where writs or deeds of any description are by this or any other Act permitted or directed to be engrossed on any conveyance or deed, it shall be competent, when necessary, to engross such deeds or writs on a sheet or sheets of paper, or of whatever other material the conveyance itself consists, added to such conveyance, provided that the engrossing of the deed or writ shall be commenced on some part of the conveyance or deed itself on which it is permitted or directed to be engrossed; and the first of such additional sheets shall be chargeable with the stamp duty applicable to the writ or deed partly engrossed thereon [. . .]

142   Recording of conveyances in the Register of Sasines authorised
All conveyances and deeds [. . .] authorized to be recorded in the register of sasines, may [. . .] be recorded at any time in the life of the person on whose behalf the [application for registration of such conveyance or deed is made and on such application the conveyance or deed] shall be presented for registration [and] when presented for registration shall be forthwith shortly registered in the minute books of the said register in common form, and shall with all due despatch be fully registered in the register books, and thereafter redelivered to the parties with certificates of due registration thereon, which shall specify the date of presentation, and the book and folios in which the engrossment has been made, [. . .] and shall be probative of such registration, and when so registered shall in competition be preferable according to the date of registration, and the date of entry in the minute book shall be held to be the date of registration: Provided, that where two or more [applications for registration of] deeds or conveyances [. . .] shall be received by the keeper of the register of sasines [on the same day], the entries [. . .] in the presentment book and minute book [for the conveyances or deeds in respect of which

such applications are made] shall be of the same year, month [and day], and such deeds and conveyances shall be deemed and taken to be presented and registered contemporaneously [. . .].

[143   **Recording anew**
Where there is an error or defect in recording a deed or conveyance in the Register of Sasines it shall be competent to record it anew.]

159   **Litigiosity not to begin before date of registration of notice of summons**
   [(1)]   It shall be competent to register in the general register of inhibitions a notice of any signeted summons of reduction of any conveyance or deed of or relating to lands, and in the register of adjudications a notice of any signeted summons of adjudication or of constitution and adjudication combined for debt or in security or in implement, which notice shall [be in (or as nearly as may be in) the form prescribed*]; and no summons of reduction, constitution, adjudication, or constitution and adjudication combined, shall have any effect in rendering litigious the lands to which such summons relates, except from and after the date of the registration of such notice.
   [(2)   A notice registered under subsection (1) on or after the date on which section 67 of the Land Registration etc (Scotland) Act 2012 (asp 5) (warrant to place a caveat) comes into force shall not have any effect in rendering litigious any land a title sheet for which is comprised in the Land Register of Scotland or in placing in bad faith any person acquiring such land.]

---

* The form is prescribed under s 159B.

SCHEDULES

SCHEDULE (B)   Sects 5–8, 46, 138

No 1

Formal clauses of a disposition of land, &c [. . .]

[*After the inductive and dispositive clauses, the deed may proceed thus:*] With entry at the term of [*here specify the date of entry*]; [. . .] and I assign the writs, and have delivered the same according to inventory; and I assign the rents; and I bind myself to free and relieve the said disponee and his foresaids of all [. . .] public burdens; and I grant warrandice; and I consent to registration hereof for preservation [*or* for preservation and execution]. [. . .]

[*Testing clause* †]

[† Note— [In the case of a traditional document, subscription of it by the granter] will be sufficient for the document to be formally valid, but witnessing of it may be necessary or desirable for other purposes (see the Requirements of Writing (Scotland) Act 1995) [, which also makes provision as regards the authentication of an electronic document].]
   [. . .]

SCHEDULE (F)   Sect 12

No 1

Clause of direction specifying part of deed which grantor desires to be recorded

And I direct to be recorded in the register of sasines the part of this deed from its commencement to the words [*insert words*] on the   line of the   page [and also the part from the words [*insert words*] on the   line of the page to the words [*insert words*] on the   line of the   page]. [*Or,* I direct the whole of this deed to be recorded in the register of sasines, with the exception of the part [*or* parts, *as the case may be, specifying the part or parts excepted, as above*].]

   [. . .]

SCHEDULE (G)   Sects 13, 24

Clause of reference to conveyance, containing general designation of lands

[*After giving the general name or names of the lands, and the name of the county or burgh and county, as the case may be, add*] as particularly described in the disposition [*or other deed, as the case may be,*] granted by C.D., and bearing date [*here insert date*], and recorded in the [*specify the register of sasines*] on the   day of   , in the year   , and in which the lands hereby conveyed are declared to be designed and known by the said name of [*here insert name*] [*or,* 'as particularly described in the instrument (*specify instrument*) recorded, *&c*, and in which the lands hereby conveyed are declared,' *&c*] [*If part only of lands is conveyed, then follow form for similar case given in schedule (E)*]

   [. . .]

CONVEYANCING (SCOTLAND) ACT 1874
(37 & 38 Vict, c 94)

[Preamble]

1 Short title
This Act may be cited for all purposes as 'The Conveyancing (Scotland) Act 1874'.

2 Commencement of Act
This Act shall, except where otherwise provided, come into operation on the first day of October one thousand eight hundred and seventy-four, which date is hereinafter referred to as the commencement of this Act.

3 Interpretation
The following words and expressions in this Act shall have the several meanings hereby assigned to them; that is to say,

'Land' or 'lands' shall include all subjects of heritable property which [prior to the day appointed by order made under section 71 of the Abolition of Feudal Tenure etc (Scotland) Act 2000 (asp 5) were, or might be,] held of a superior according to feudal tenure, or which prior to the commencement of this Act have been or might have been held by burgage tenure, or by tenure of booking:

[. . .]

'Conveyance' and 'deed' and 'instrument' shall each have the meaning attached thereto by the Titles to Land Consolidation (Scotland) Act, 1868 and the Titles to Land Consolidation (Scotland) (Amendment) Act, 1869, and shall also, when used in this Act, include all the deeds, instruments, decrees, petitions, and writings specified in this Act; and the words 'heritable securities' and 'securities' shall have the meaning attached thereto by the said recited Acts. [. . .]

27 The word 'dispone' unnecessary
It shall not be competent to object to the validity of any deed or writing as a conveyance of heritage coming into operation after the passing of this Act, on the ground that it does not contain the word 'dispone,' provided it contains any other word or words importing conveyance or transference, or present intention to convey or transfer.

28 Date of entry
Where no term of entry is stated in a conveyance of lands, the entry shall be at the first term of Whitsunday or Martinmas after the date or last date of the conveyance, unless it shall appear from the terms of the conveyance that another term of entry was intended.

29 General dispositions forming links of series of titles not objectionable on certain grounds
No decree, instrument, or conveyance [. . .], whether dated before or after the commencement of this Act, shall be deemed to be invalid because the series of titles connecting the person obtaining such decree, or expeding such instrument, or holding such conveyance, with the person [who last held a recorded title contains] as links of the series two or more general dispositions, or because any general disposition forming a part of the series does not contain a clause of assignation of writs.

35 Registration of a decree of division
A decree of division of commonty or of common property or runrig lands, whether pronounced by a court of law, or by arbiters or by an oversman, shall have the effect of a conveyance containing assignations of writs by all the [. . .] proprietors in favour of the several parties participating in the division of the shares severally allotted to them, and the extract decree pronounced by the court

or the decree pronounced by the arbiters or oversman, or an extract thereof from any competent court books, may be recorded in the appropriate register of sasines, in ordinary form on behalf of all or any of the parties, or may be used by all or any of the parties for the purpose of [deducing title] to the shares severally allotted to them, or to any portion thereof [. . .].

36 Effect of decree of sale of glebe
A decree of sale obtained in terms of section seventeen of the Glebe Lands (Scotland) Act 1866, shall have the effect of a conveyance by the minister of the parish at the sight of the heritors of the parish and of the presbytery of the bounds, to the heritor in whose favour it is pronounced, and his heirs and assignees whomsoever, of the glebe or portion of glebe therein contained; and, on an extract of such decree being recorded in the appropriate register of sasines, shall vest in such heritor the glebe or portion of the glebe described therein [. . .].

44 Provisions for the case of a person appointed by the court to administer a trust
When a trust title [to land or to a real right in or over land] has been duly completed and recorded, and any person is subsequently appointed by the Court to administer the trust in whole or in part as a trustee or judicial factor, the interlocutor whereby the appointment is made shall specify the trust deed, and the other title or titles (if any) by which the trust title had been completed as aforesaid, in such manner as to identify the same, and shall refer to the register or registers of sasines where such deed or title or titles is or are recorded, and also set forth the lands by description or reference; and an extract of such interlocutor, being recorded in the appropriate register of sasines, shall operate [to complete] in favour of the trustee or judicial factor thereby appointed [title to the land or real right,] in the same manner as if he had been a trustee named in the completed and recorded title in conformity always with the nature and terms of the appointment, and to the effect of enabling him to perform the duties of the office to which he is appointed.

45 How title shall be completed when the holder of an office or proprietor is ex officio a trustee and his successor in office takes the trust
When by the tenor of the title to any [land, or any real right in or over land] held in trust duly completed in favour of the trustee or trustees therein named, or any of them, and recorded in the appropriate register of sasines, the office of a trustee has been or shall be conferred upon the holder of any place or office, or proprietor of any estate, and his successors therein, any person subsequently becoming a trustee by appointment or succession to the place or office or estate to which the office of trustee has thus been or shall be annexed shall be deemed and taken to have a valid and complete title [to the land or real right] in the same manner and to the same effect as if he had been named in the completed and recorded title, without the necessity of any deed of conveyance or other procedure.

47 Securities upon land, and relative personal obligations, shall transmit against heirs and disponees [. . .]
An heritable security for money, duly constituted [over land, or over a real right in land,] shall, together with any personal obligation to pay principal, interest, and penalty contained in the deed or instrument whereby the security is constituted, transmit against any person taking [such land or real right] by succession, gift, or bequest, or by conveyance, when an agreement to that effect appears in gremio of the conveyance, and shall be a burden upon his title in the same manner as it was upon that of his ancestor or author, without the necessity of a bond of corroboration or other deed or procedure; and the personal obligation may be enforced against such person by summary diligence or otherwise, in the same manner as against the original debtor. A warrant to charge may be applied for and validly granted in the Bill Chamber or in a Sheriff Court, in the form set forth in

Schedule K hereto annexed, or in a similar form, and all diligence may thereafter proceed against the party in common form. A discharge of the personal obligation of the original or any subsequent debtor, whether granted before or after the commencement of this Act, shall not where the debt still exists prejudice the security on [the land or real right] or the obligation as hereby made transmissible against the existing proprietor.

50   Form and effect of assigning right of relief or other right affecting land
An assignation or conveyance of any obligation or right of relief or other right connected with lands, but the title to which does not, according to the present law, pass under the general assignation of writs in the disposition of the lands, may be granted in, or as nearly as may be in, the form of Schedule M hereto annexed, and may either be a separate deed or part of another deed, and shall have the effect of vesting in the person or persons in whose favour it is granted, and his or their successors, a valid and complete right and title to the obligation or right thereby assigned or conveyed, with all the intermediate transmissions thereof, to the same effect in all respects as if an assignation or conveyance in the form at present in use had been granted in his or their favour.

51   Probate equivalent to will or extract for completing title
The [. . .] probate of the will or other testamentary settlement of a person deceased, issued by
    [(a)]   any court of probate in England or in Ireland, or in any British colony or dependency, or
    [(b)   a district court in Palestine before 15th May 1948, or
    (c)   the Supreme Court of Aden before 30th November 1967,]
or of [an exemplification of such probate, shall for the purpose of completing a title to any land, or real right in land,] or to any heritable security, be held to be equivalent to and as effectual as [. . .] the will or settlement itself, or of an extract thereof from the books of council and session [. . .].

54   Recorded deed or instrument unchallengeable on certain grounds
No challenge of any deed, instrument, or writing recorded in any register of sasines shall receive effect on the ground that any part of the record of such deed, instrument, or writing is written on erasure, unless such erasure be proved to have been made for the purpose of fraud, or the record is not conformable to the deed, instrument, or writing as presented for registration.

61   Description of lands contained in recorded deeds may be inserted in subsequent writs by reference merely—reference already made in recorded deed not challengeable if certain particulars correctly given
[. . .] In all cases where any lands have been particularly described in any conveyance, deed, or instrument of or relating thereto, recorded in the appropriate register of sasines, it shall not be necessary in any subsequent conveyance, deed, or instrument, conveying or referring to the whole or any part of such lands, to repeat the particular description of the lands at length; but it shall be sufficient to specify the name of the county, and where the lands were held by burgage or by any similar tenure prior to the commencement of this Act, the name of the burgh and county in which the lands are situated, and to refer to the particular description of such lands as contained in such prior conveyance, deed, or instrument so recorded in or as nearly as may be in the form set forth in Schedule O hereto annexed; and the specification and reference so made in any such subsequent conveyance, deed, or instrument, whether dated prior or subsequent to the commencement of this Act, shall be held to be equivalent to the full insertion of the particular description contained in such prior conveyance, deed, or instrument, and shall have the same effect as if the particular description had been inserted in such subsequent conveyance, deed, or instrument exactly as it is contained in such prior conveyance, deed, or instrument; and it shall not be competent . . . to object

to any specification and reference to any particular description of lands contained in any conveyance, deed, or instrument recorded prior to the commencement of this Act, provided such specification and reference states correctly the name of the county, and where the lands were held by burgage or by any similar tenure prior to the commencement of this Act, the name of the burgh and county in which the lands are situated, and refers correctly to the prior recorded conveyance, deed, or instrument containing the particular description of such lands; and where any conveyance, deed, or instrument recorded prior to the commencement of this Act contains a specification and reference stating these particulars correctly, the specification and reference so made shall be held to have been equivalent to the full insertion of the particular description contained in the prior conveyance, deed, or instrument referred to, as if the particular description had been inserted in such recorded conveyance, deed, or instrument exactly as it is contained in the prior conveyance, deed, or instrument referred to.

[Note the effect here of the Conveyancing (Scotland) Act 1924, s 8.]

66 Schedules to be part of Act
The schedules annexed to this Act, and the directions therein contained, and notes thereto appended, shall have the same effect as if they were contained in the body of this Act.

67 Repeal of Acts, &c
All statutes, laws, and usages at variance with any of the provisions of this Act are hereby repealed.

Sect 47   SCHEDULE K
FORM OF MINUTE TO BE PRESENTED IN BILL CHAMBER OF COURT OF
SESSION, OR IN SHERIFF COURT, FOR WARRANT TO CHARGE AN HEIR OR
DISPONEE UNDER A PERSONAL OBLIGATION BY HIS ANCESTOR
OR AUTHOR

Warrant is craved, in virtue of the Conveyancing (Scotland) Act, 1874, at the instance of A.B. [*name and design applicant*], the creditor [*if he is not the original creditor, or only a partial creditor, add,* in virtue of (*or* to the extent and in virtue of) the assignation (*or* general disposition and notarial instrument *or other writ or writs forming the title in the creditor's person*) in his favour after mentioned] under a bond and disposition in security over the lands of [*specify shortly the lands*], for the principal sum of £   with corresponding interest and penalties, granted by C.D. [*design him*], then proprietor of the said lands, in favour of the said A.B. [*or of G.H. (design him) as the case may be*], and dated [*state date*] [*and if recorded, say,* and recorded in the register of sasines (*state register and date of recording*), *or* and instrument of sasine thereon recorded, &c, *as the case may be*]: To charge E.F. [*design him*], the present proprietor of the said lands, and as such the present debtor in the said bond and disposition in security, to make payment to the said A.B. of the said principal sum of £   contained in and due by the said bond and disposition in security [*if A.B. is only a partial creditor, say,* of the principal sum of £   being the extent to which the said A.B. is in right of the said bond and disposition in security]: And also of the further sum of £   being the amount of the interest due thereon. Produced herewith the said bond and disposition in security [*or an extract thereof from the books of council and session or from the register of sasines; if the applicant is not the original creditor, the title in his own person to the security will also be stated and produced*].

Dated the   day of   .
(Signed)   A.B., W.S., Edinburgh, [*or as the case may be*].
The Clerk of the Bills, or Sheriff Clerk, as the case may be, will subjoin
Fiat ut petitur.
[*To be dated and signed by the Clerk.*]

Sect 50   SCHEDULE M
                        FORM OF ASSIGNATION OF RIGHT OF RELIEF, &c

I [*here insert the name and designation of the granter, and the cause of granting, unless
the assignation forms part of another deed*] hereby assign to C.D. [*here insert the designation of the grantee, unless already given*], and his heirs and assignees [*or and his
foresaids*], a disposition [*or other deed, as the case may be*] granted by [*here insert the
names and designations of the persons by and in whose favour the deed to be assigned
was granted, with its date and also the date of registration, and the register in which it is
recorded, if it has been recorded*], whereby the said [*name of the original granter of the
disposition or obligation*] bound and obliged himself, his heirs and successors [*here
insert the terms of the obligation in the terms so far as possible of the disposition or other
deed. If the right to be assigned was originally granted in favour of some other person
than the granter of the assignation, here specify the series of writs by which he acquired
right.*]

[*Testing clause* †]

[† Note—[In the case of a traditional document, subscription of it by the granter] will be
sufficient for the document to be formally valid, but witnessing of it may be necessary or desirable for other purposes (see the Requirements of Writing (Scotland) Act 1995) [, which also
makes provision as regards the authentication of an electronic document].]

HERITABLE SECURITIES (SCOTLAND) ACT 1894
(57 & 58 Vict, c 44)

1   Short title
This Act may be cited for all purposes as the Heritable Securities (Scotland) Act,
1894.

2   Extent and commencement of Act
This Act shall apply to Scotland only.

3   Tenants need not be parties to actions of maills and duties
The creditor in a heritable security may, without calling the tenants of the lands
disponed in security as defenders, raise an action of maills and duties either in
the sheriff court, in the form as nearly as may be of Schedule (A) annexed to this
Act, or in the Court of Session in common form, with the necessary alterations
consequent upon the provisions of this Act, and may give notice of the raising of
such action to the tenants by registered letter in the form as nearly as may be of
Schedule (B) annexed to this Act, and from and after the date when such notice
is received by the tenants they shall be held as interpelled from making payment
of the rents due by them, in the same manner and to the same effect as if they
were called as defenders in an action of maills and duties according to the present
law and practice, and upon intimation of the decree obtained in said action being
made to the tenants by registered letter in the form as nearly as may be of Schedule
(C) annexed to this Act, the said tenants shall make payment of the rents due by
them respectively in the same manner and under the like legal compulsitors as if
the same had been decerned for and a charge for payment given in an action of
maills and duties according to the existing law and practice, and payment when
so made shall be a complete exoneration and discharge to such tenants respectively: Provided always, that no decree in such action shall affect the right of the
tenants to refuse payment of such rents on any ground not affecting the title of

such creditor or the right of any prior creditor to enter into possession, and nothing herein contained shall prevent an action of maills and duties from being raised in the form heretofore in use, or deprive a creditor of any existing right competent to him of entering into possession without having recourse to an action of maills and duties.

4   Power to interpel security holder
Any person interested may take proceedings to interpel the creditor from entering into possession of the lands disponed in security or collecting the rents thereof.

5   Power to eject proprietor in personal occupation
[(1)]   Where a creditor desires to enter into possession of the lands disponed in security, and the proprietor thereof is in personal occupation of the same, or any part thereof, such proprietor shall be deemed to be an occupant without a title, and the creditor may take proceedings to eject him in all respects in the same way as if he were such occupant: Provided that this section shall not apply in any case unless such proprietor has made default in the punctual payment of the interest due under the security, or in due payment of the principal after formal requisition.

[(2)   Proceedings under subsection (1) by a creditor in a security over land or a real right in land used to any extent for residential purposes are to be brought by summary application (regardless of whether they include a crave for any other remedy).

[(2A)   *Subsection (2) is subject to section 72(3) of the Courts Reform (Scotland) Act 2014 (which provides for certain proceedings for the recovery of heritable property to be subject to simple procedure).]*

(3)   Before making an application under subsection (1) in a case referred to in subsection (2), the creditor must comply with the pre-action requirements imposed by section 5B.]

[5A   Court powers on section 5 proceedings relating to residential property
(1)   This section applies to an application under section 5(1) by a creditor in a security over land or a real right in land used to any extent for residential purposes.

(2)   The creditor must—

(a)   serve on the proprietor a notice in conformity with Form 1 in Part 2 of the schedule to the Mortgage Rights (Scotland) Act 2001,

(b)   serve on the occupier of the security subjects a notice in conformity with Form 2 in that Part of that schedule, and

(c)   give notice of the application to the local authority in whose area the security subjects are situated, unless the creditor is that local authority.

(3)   A notice under subsection (2)(a) or (b) must be sent by recorded delivery letter addressed—

(a)   in the case of a notice under subsection (2)(a), to the proprietor at the proprietor's last known address,

(b)   in the case of a notice under subsection (2)(b), to 'The Occupier' at the security subjects.

(4)   Notice under subsection (2)(c) is to be given in the form and manner prescribed under section 11(3) of the Homelessness etc (Scotland) Act 2003.

(5)   The court may continue the proceedings or make any other order that it thinks fit on the application; but it may not grant the application unless it is satisfied that—

(a)   the creditor has complied with section 5(3); and

(b)   it is reasonable in the circumstances of the case to do so.

(6)   In considering the application in a case where the debtor appears or is represented, the court is to have regard in particular to the matters set out in subsection (7).

(7)   Those matters are—
   (a)   the nature of and reasons for the default,
   (b)   the ability of the debtor to fulfil within a reasonable time the obligations under the security in respect of which the debtor is in default,
   (c)   any action taken by the creditor to assist the debtor to fulfil those obligations,
   (d)   where appropriate, participation by the debtor in a debt payment programme approved under Part 1 of the Debt Arrangement and Attachment (Scotland) Act 2002, and
   (e)   the ability of the debtor and any other person residing at the security subjects to secure reasonable alternative accommodation.
(8)   Subsections (5) and (6) do not affect—
   (a)   any power that the court may have, or
   (b)   any rights that the debtor may have,
by virtue of any other enactment or rule of law.]
[(9)   For the avoidance of doubt, a decree granted on an application to which this section applies is not an order for possession of a house let on an assured tenancy (within the meaning of Part II of the Housing (Scotland) Act 1988 (c 43)).]

[5B   Section 5 proceedings relating to residential property: pre-action requirements
(1)   The pre-action requirements referred to in section 5(3) are set out in subsection s (2) to (6) below.
(2)   The creditor must provide the debtor with clear information about—
   (a)   the terms of the security,
   (b)   the amount due to the creditor under the security, including any arrears and any charges in respect of late payment or redemption, and
   (c)   any other obligation under the security in respect of which the debtor is in default.
(3)   The creditor must make reasonable efforts to agree with the debtor proposals in respect of future payments to the creditor under the security and the fulfilment of any other obligation under the security in respect of which the debtor is in default.
(4)   The creditor must not make an application under section 5(1) to which section 5A applies if the debtor is taking steps which are likely to result in—
   (a)   the payment to the creditor within a reasonable time of any arrears, or the whole amount, due to the creditor under the security, and
   (b)   fulfilment by the debtor within a reasonable time of any other obligation under the security in respect of which the debtor is in default.
(5)   The creditor must provide the debtor with information about sources of advice and assistance in relation to management of debt.
(6)   The creditor must encourage the debtor to contact the local authority in whose area the security subjects are situated.
(7)   In complying with the pre-action requirements the creditor must have regard to any guidance issued by the Scottish Ministers.
(8)   The Scottish Ministers may by order made by statutory instrument make further provision about the pre-action requirements, including provision—
   (a)   specifying particular steps to be taken, or not to be taken, by a creditor in complying with any requirement,
   (b)   modifying or removing any requirement,
   (c)   making different provision for different circumstances.
(9)   A statutory instrument containing an order under subsection (8) above is not to be made unless a draft of the instrument has been laid before, and approved by resolution of, the Scottish Parliament.]

[5C   Application to court by entitled residents
(1)   An entitled resident may, in proceedings on an application to which section

5A applies, apply to the court to continue the proceedings or make any other order that the court thinks fit, despite not being called as a defender in the application.

(2)   In determining an application under subsection (1) of this section the court is to have regard in particular to the matters set out in subsection (7) of section 5A, reading the first reference to the debtor in paragraph (b) as including a reference to the entitled resident.

(3)   Subsection (2) does not affect—

(a)   any power that the court may have, or

(b)   any rights that an entitled resident may have,

under any other enactment or rule of law.]

[5D   Entitled residents: definition

(1)   For the purposes of sections 5C, 5E and 5F, an entitled resident is a person whose sole or main residence is the security subjects (in whole or in part) and who is—

(a)   the proprietor of the security subjects (where the proprietor is not the debtor in the security),

(b)   the non-entitled spouse of the debtor or the proprietor of security subjects which are (in whole or in part) a matrimonial home,

(c)   the non-entitled civil partner of the debtor or the proprietor of security subjects which are (in whole or in part) a family home,

(d)   a person living together with the debtor or the proprietor as husband and wife,

(e)   a person living together with the debtor or the proprietor in a relationship which has the characteristics of the relationship between civil partners,

(f)   a person who lived together with the debtor or the proprietor in a relationship described in paragraph (d) or (e) if—

(i)   the security subjects (in whole or in part) are not the sole or main residence of the debtor or the proprietor,

(ii)   the person lived together with the debtor or the proprietor throughout the period of 6 months ending with the date on which the security subjects ceased to be the sole or main residence of the debtor or the proprietor, and

(iii)   the security subjects (in whole or in part) are the sole or main residence of a child aged under 16 who is a child of both parties in that relationship.

(2)   In this section—

'child' includes a stepchild and any person brought up, or treated, by both parties to the relationship as their child,

'family home' has the meaning given by section 135(1) of the Civil Partnership Act 2004,

'matrimonial home' has the meaning given by section 22 of the Matrimonial Homes (Family Protection) (Scotland) Act 1981,

'non-entitled civil partner' has the same meaning as 'non-entitled partner' in section 101(1) of the Civil Partnership Act 2004,

'non-entitled spouse' has the meaning given by section 1 of the Matrimonial Homes (Family Protection) (Scotland) Act 1981.]

[5E   Recall of decree

(1)   A person mentioned in subsection (2) may apply to the court for recall of a decree granted on an application to which section 5A applies.

(2)   Those persons are—

(a)   the creditor,

(b)   the debtor, but only if the debtor did not appear and was not represented in the proceedings on the application,

(c)   an entitled resident, but only if the entitled resident did not make an application under section 5C(1) in the proceedings.

(3)   An application under subsection (1) may be made at any time before the decree has been fully implemented.

(4)   An application by any person under subsection (1) is not competent if an application under that subsection has already been made by that person in relation to the application to which section 5A applies.

(5)   An applicant under subsection (1) must give notice of the application to—

(a)   the creditor (unless the applicant is the creditor),

(b)   the debtor (unless the applicant is the debtor),

(c)   every entitled resident (or, if the applicant is an entitled resident, every other entitled resident).]

[5F   Lay representation in section 5 proceedings relating to residential property etc

(1)   In proceedings on an application to which section 5A applies and proceedings under section 5E(1), the debtor and any entitled resident may be represented by an approved lay representative except in prescribed circumstances.

(2)   An approved lay representative must throughout the proceedings satisfy the sheriff that the representative is a suitable person to represent the debtor or entitled resident and is authorised by the debtor or entitled resident to do so.

(3)   References in this section to an approved lay representative are to an individual (other than an advocate or solicitor) approved for the purposes of this section by a person or body prescribed, or of a description prescribed, by the Scottish Ministers by order made by statutory instrument.

(4)   An order under subsection (3) may—

(a)   prescribe persons or bodies, or descriptions of persons or bodies, for the purposes of that subsection,

(b)   make provision about the procedure for, and form and manner of—

(i)   approval,

(ii)   withdrawal of approval,

of an individual for the purposes of this section,

(c)   make provision requiring a prescribed person or body, or a person or body of a prescribed description, to provide information to the Scottish Ministers about approvals and withdrawals of approval,

(d)   prescribe circumstances in which an approved lay representative may not represent a debtor or entitled resident.

(5)   Before making an order under subsection (3) the Scottish Ministers must consult the Lord President of the Court of Session.

(6)   A statutory instrument containing an order under subsection (3) is subject to annulment in pursuance of a resolution of the Scottish Parliament.]

6   Power to lease security subjects for seven years or under

Any creditor in possession of lands [by virtue of an adjudication] may let such lands held in security, or part thereof, on lease, for a period not exceeding seven years in duration.

7   Sheriff may grant power to lease security subjects for longer periods, not more than 21 years for heritable property in general, and 31 years for minerals

Any creditor in possession of lands [by virtue of an adjudication] may apply to the sheriff for warrant to let the lands [. . .] or part thereof, for a period exceeding seven years, setting forth the name of the proposed tenant or tenants, the duration and conditions of the proposed lease; and the sheriff may, after service on the proprietor and on the other heritable creditors, if any, and after such intimation and inquiry as he may think proper, and if satisfied that a lease for a longer period than seven years is expedient for the beneficial occupation of the lands, approve of the proposed lease on the terms and conditions proposed, or on such other terms and conditions as may appear to him expedient: Provided always, that such lease shall in no case exceed twenty-one years for heritable property in general and thirty-one years for minerals.

11   Sheriff may grant power to *pari passu* security holder to sell *pari passu* security
Any creditor holding a security ranking *pari passu* with another security who desires to sell the lands conveyed in security by his security, and who is unable to obtain the consent of the creditor holding such other *pari passu* security to a sale, may apply to the sheriff for warrant to sell the said lands, calling such other creditor as defender; and the sheriff, after hearing parties and making such inquiry as he thinks fit, may order a sale of the said lands, if in his opinion it is reasonable and expedient that such sale should take place; and in case of difference of opinion, the sheriff may fix the price, authorise both or either of the parties or some other person to carry through the sale, and upon payment or consignation of the price to grant a conveyance and disencumber the lands of the said securities in the same way and as fully as if the creditors therein were by agreement carrying through said sale, and also to fix the times and conditions of sale in conformity with the law and practice relating to pre-monition and advertisement. And the expenses of and connected with the sale shall be payable preferably out of the price or proceeds of the sale, and the balance of such price or proceeds after providing for such expenses shall be paid to the creditors in the securities charged upon the lands according to their just rights and preferences.

12   Provisions anent procedure
The following provisions shall have effect with regard to applications under sections seven [. . .] and eleven of this Act:—
   (1)   The interlocutor of the sheriff who pronounces any order or decree shall be final, and not subject to review, except (1) as to questions of title and (2) where the principal sum due under the heritable security exceeds one thousand pounds.
   (2)   The sheriff may award expenses, or may direct that the expenses be treated as part of the expenses of the sale.

13   Provisions of Act to have effect not withstanding incapacity of debtor.
Trustees and others to have powers conferred by Act
The rights and powers [under a heritable security] may be exercised by any creditor, although the debtor or any other creditor holding a security over the same lands, or other person to whom intimation may require or be ordered to be given is [subject to any legal disability by reason of nonage or otherwise] and any action or proceeding [by a creditor in exercise of those rights and powers] shall have the same force and effect as it would have had if [the debtor, proprietor, other] creditor, or other person had been of full age and not subject to any legal incapacity when such action or proceeding was taken; [and
   (a)   any person entitled, within the meaning of Part I of the Children (Scotland) Act 1995, to act as the legal representative of a child; and
   (b)   trustees; [and]
   (c)   the person entitled to act as the legal representative of any such person,] executors, [guardians], judicial factors, and other officers of court may exercise all or any of the powers conferred by this Act.

18   Interpretation clause
In this Act the words 'conveyance,' 'heritable security,' 'security,' 'creditor,' 'debtor,' and 'purchaser' shall have the same meanings respectively as in the Titles to Land Consolidation (Scotland) Act, 1868.
   The word 'lands' shall extend to and include all heritable subjects.

19   Saving as to rights of Crown
Nothing in this Act contained shall affect the present law and practice in regard to the preferential character of debts due to the Crown, nor shall anything done

under the new procedure by this Act authorised prejudice the rights of the Crown as these exist according to the present law and practice.

SCHEDULES

SCHEDULE (A)   Section 3

In the sheriff court of   at

A.B., Pursuer,
against
C.D., Defender.

The above-named pursuer submits to the court the condescendence and note of plea-in-law hereto annexed, and prays the court—

To grant a decree against the above-named defender, finding and declaring that the pursuer has right to the rents, maills, and duties of the subjects and others specified in the bond and disposition in security for £   , granted by   in favour of   , dated the
and recorded in the
register
or, at least so much of the said rents, maills, and duties as will satisfy and pay the pursuer the principal sum of £   with interest thereon at the rate of   per centum per annum from the
day of   18   , liquidate penalty and termly failures all as specified and contained in the said bond and disposition in security dated and recorded as aforesaid, and to find the said C.D. liable in expenses, and to decern therefor.

Add condescendence and pleas-in-law.

SCHEDULE (B)   Section 3

In the court of session   [or]
In the sheriff court of   shire, at
Notice.

An action has been raised of this date [*specify place and date*] in the above court, at the instance of A.B. [*design him*], pursuer, against C.D. [*design him*], defender, in which the said pursuer asks that it be declared that as holding a bond and disposition in security over the subjects situated at [*here give such description of the subjects*, e.g., *their name or the number of street in which they are situated, as may identify them*], he has right to the rents due, current, and to become due, from the subjects.

Should you, after receiving this notice, pay your rent to the defender, you will do so at the risk of having to pay again to the pursuer should he obtain decree in the action.

[*To be signed by the pursuer or his law agent, or messenger at arms, or sheriff officer.*]

Section 3   SCHEDULE (C)

In the court of session   [*or*]
In the sheriff court of   shire, at

Notice.

Decree having been obtained of this date [*specify place and date*] in the above court, at the instance of A.B. [*design him*] pursuer, against C.D. [*design him*] defender, finding and declaring that the pursuer has right to the rents, maills, and duties of the subjects and others situated at [*here give such description of the subjects*, e.g., *their name, or the number of street in which they are situated, as may identify them*] specified in a bond and disposition in security for £   granted by   in favour of   dated the   and recorded in the register, you are hereby notified of the same, and desired and required to make payment to the said *A.B.* of the rents, maills, and duties due by you in respect of the occupancy of said subjects or part thereof.

[*To be signed by the pursuer or his law agent, or messenger at arms, or sheriff officer.*]

CONVEYANCING (SCOTLAND) ACT 1924
(1924, 14 & 15 Geo 5, c 27)

1 Short title, extent and commencement of Act
(1)   This Act may be cited as the Conveyancing (Scotland) Act, 1924.

[. . .]

(3)   This Act shall apply to Scotland only.

2 Interpretation clause
The words and expressions after mentioned or referred to shall have the several meanings hereby assigned to them, unless there be something in the subject or context repugnant to such construction (that is to say):—

(1)   The words and expressions used in this Act and in the schedules annexed to this Act which are interpreted in the Titles to Land Consolidation (Scotland) Act, 1868, and the Conveyancing (Scotland) Act, 1874, shall have the meaning assigned thereto respectively by these Acts, subject to the following qualifications:—

(a) 'Land' or 'lands' shall not include 'securities';

(b) 'Heritable securities' and 'securities' shall include [. . .] securities over a lease, but shall not include securities constituted by ex facie absolute disposition; and

(c) 'Conveyance' and 'deed' and 'instrument' shall include all deeds, notices of title, decrees, petitions and writings specified in this Act; and these words and the words 'writing,' 'writ' and 'decree' occurring in the said Acts and in this Act shall each mean and include an extract or office copy of such 'conveyance,' 'deed,' 'instrument,' 'writing,' 'writ' or 'decree':

(2)   'Extract' and 'office copy' shall each mean and include a duly authenticated extract of any act, decree or warrant of the Lords of Council and Session, or any inferior court or a duly authenticated extract or office copy from the Register of the Great Seal, or from the Books of Council and Session, or of any sheriff court, or of any other public authentic register of probative writs, or from the appropriate Register of Sasines, of any conveyance, deed, instrument, writing, writ or decree, and shall also mean and include a probate of the will or testamentary settlement of a person deceased issued by any court of probate in England or Northern Ireland, or in any part of His Majesty's Dominions, or an exemplification of such probate:

(3)   'Deduction of title' shall mean the specification in a deed, decree or instrument of the writ or series of writs (without narration of the contents thereof) by which the person granting such deed or in whose favour such decree is conceived or by whom such instrument is expede, has acquired right from the person from whom such title is deduced, and such specification shall be a compliance with an instruction to 'deduce' a title in terms of this Act:

(4)   'Adjudication' shall include adjudication whether for debt or in implement, and constitution and adjudication whether for debt or in implement, and declarator and adjudication:

(5)   'Lease' shall mean a lease which has been registered or is registrable [in the Land Register of Scotland or] in the Register of Sasines in virtue of the Registration of Leases (Scotland) Act, 1857, and Acts amending the same:

(6) 'Law agent' shall mean and include writers to the signet, solicitors in the supreme courts, procurators in any sheriff court, and every person entitled to practise as an agent in a court of law in Scotland:

(7) 'Agent' in the Schedules hereto shall mean law agent or notary public:

(8) 'Register of Sasines,' shall mean and include the General Register of Sasines, the Particular Registers of Sasines now discontinued, the Register of Sasines kept for any royal or other burgh and the Register of Booking in the burgh of Paisley.

3 Disposition &c by person uninfeft

If a disposition of land, or an assignation, discharge or deed of restriction of a heritable security duly recorded in the appropriate Register of Sasines, or of any part of such security, is granted by a person having a right to such land, or to such heritable security, or such part thereof, but whose title to such land or heritable security or part thereof has not been completed by being so recorded, and who in such disposition or other deed deduces his title from the person [. . .] having the last recorded title, in or as nearly as may be in the terms of Form No 1 of Schedule A to this Act in the case of land, or in or as nearly as may be in [such manner as was (immediately before the repeal of the note)] prescribed in Note 2 to Schedule K to this Act in the case of a heritable security, then on such disposition or other deed being recorded in the appropriate Register of Sasines, the title of the grantee thereof shall be [completed].

4 [Completion of title: General Register of Sasines]

Any person having right either to land or to a heritable security [may, if the last recorded title to the right is recorded in the General Register of Sasines] complete his title in manner following:—

(1) A person having such right to land may complete a title thereto by recording in the appropriate Register of Sasines a notice of title in or as nearly as may be in the terms of Form No 1 of Schedule B to this Act, in which notice of title such person shall deduce his title from the person [having the last recorded title]:

(2) When the writ forming the immediate connection with the person [having the last recorded title] is an unrecorded conveyance, deed or decree, the recording of which in the appropriate Register of Sasines on behalf of the person in whose favour the same is conceived would have completed his title [. . .], the person having such right to the land therein contained or part thereof may complete a title thereto by recording in the appropriate Register of Sasines such conveyance, deed or decree, docqueted in manner prescribed in Note 7 to Schedule B to this Act, along with a notice of title in or as nearly as may be in the terms of Form No 2 of that Schedule, in which notice of title such person shall deduce his title from the person in whose favour such conveyance, deed or decree is conceived:

(3) A person having such right to a heritable security, or part thereof, which appears in the appropriate Register of Sasines as a burden on land, may complete a title thereto by recording in the appropriate Register of Sasines a notice of title in or as nearly as may be in the terms of Form No 3 of Schedule B to this Act [. . .], in which notice of title such person shall deduce his title from the person [having the last recorded title to the heritable security]:

(4) A person having such right to an unrecorded heritable security or part thereof contained in a deed the recording of which in the appropriate Register of Sasines on behalf of the original creditor would have [completed his title thereto and to] the land out of which it is payable, or either of them, but which has not been so recorded, may complete a title thereto by recording in the appropriate Register of Sasines such heritable security, which shall be docqueted in manner prescribed in Note 7 to Schedule B to this Act, along with a notice of title in or as nearly as may be in the terms of Form No 5 of that Schedule [. . .], in which notice of title such person shall deduce his title from the original creditor in such heritable security.

[. . .]

[4A   Completion of title: Land Register

[(1)]   Any person having right either to land or to a heritable security may complete title by registration in the Land Register of a notice of title in or as nearly as may be in the terms of the form in schedule BA to this Act.]

[(2)   Subsection (1) is subject to paragraphs 3 and 4 of schedule 1A to the Land Registration etc. (Scotland) Act 2012.]

[4B   Further provision as regards completion of title

(1)   If it is competent to register a disposition or assignation in the Land Register, it is not competent for the disponee or assignee to complete title in the manner provided for in section 4 of this Act.

(2)   In this section and in section 4A of this Act, 'Land Register' means the Land Register of Scotland.]

5   Deduction of title

(1)   In a deduction of title in terms of this Act it shall be competent to specify as a title or as a midcouple or link of title, any statute, conveyance, deed, instrument, decree or other writing whereby a right to land or to [any real right in] land is vested in or transmitted to any person, or in virtue of which a notarial instrument could [(before the day appointed by order made under section 71 of the Abolition of Feudal Tenure etc (Scotland) Act 2000 (asp 5))] be expede, or which could be used as a midcouple or link of title in expeding such instrument, or any minute of a meeting at which any person is appointed to any place or office, if such appointment involves a right to land or to [a real right in] land; and any copy of or excerpt from such minute of meeting certified as correct by the chairman of such meeting or other person duly authorised to sign such minute or to give extracts therefrom, or by any law agent or notary public shall be primaˆ facie evidence of the terms of such minute of meeting.

(2)(a)   When the holder of a heritable security [. . .] has died, whether [. . .] with or without a recorded title, and whether testate or intestate, any confirmation in favour of an executor of such deceased which includes such security shall of itself be a valid title to the debt thereby secured, and shall also be a warrant for such executor dealing with such debt and also with such security in terms of the third [section] of this Act, and also for completing a title to such security in terms of the fourth section of this Act.

(b)   For the purposes of this subsection, 'confirmation' shall include any probate or letters of administration or other grant of representation to movable or personal estate of a deceased person [issued—

(a)   by any court in England and Wales or Northern Ireland and noting his domicile in England and Wales or in Northern Ireland, as the case may be, or

(b)   by any court outwith the United Kingdom and sealed in Scotland under section 2 of the Colonial Probates Act 1892

and] the confirmation thereby implied shall operate in favour of the person or the persons or the survivors or survivor of them to whom such probate, letters of administration or other grant of representation were granted; and 'executor' shall include such person or persons; and such implied confirmation shall be deemed to include all heritable securities which belonged to the deceased [. . .].

(3)(a)   It shall be competent in any warrant, interlocutor or decree of court conferring a right to land or to a heritable security, or granting authority to complete a title thereto, and also in the application upon which such warrant, interlocutor or decree proceeds, to insert a deduction of title from the person [. . .] holding the last recorded title, and an extract of such warrant, interlocutor or decree shall be equivalent to a disposition of land or an assignation of a heritable security granted in terms of section three of this Act and on being recorded in the appropriate Register of Sasines shall have the same force and effect as such a disposition or assignation duly recorded in such register.

(b)   Section twenty-four of the Titles to Land Consolidation (Scotland) Act, 1868, and section forty-four of the Conveyancing (Scotland) Act, 1874, are hereby amended in accordance with the provisions of this subsection, and the procedure

prescribed in section forty-four of the said Act of 1874, as hereby amended, shall be
competent irrespective of whether the trust title has or has not been duly completed
and recorded, and shall be applicable to all judicial factors within the meaning of
section three of the said Act of 1868, and both of such sections hereby amended shall
apply to heritable securities, and such heritable security may be referred to in any
warrant, interlocutor or decree, or in any application upon which the same proceeds,
in the manner prescribed in the forms relative thereto referred to in section four of
this Act.

8   Description by reference and short reference to deed bearing more than one date

(1)   It shall be no objection to a description by reference to a particular description of land in accordance with section sixty-one of the Conveyancing (Scotland) Act,
1874, that the description referred to contains a description by reference of a larger
piece of land of which the land particularly described forms part, and Schedule O
annexed to the said Act of 1874 is hereby repealed and Schedule D to this Act is substituted therefor: The provisions of this section shall be retrospective.

[. . .]

(3)   In specifying any writ recorded in any Register of Sasines, it shall be competent for the better identification of such writ, to state the number of the volume or
book of the register in which, and of the folio on which, the same has been recorded;
but it shall be no objection to the specification of any writ that such volume or
book and folio or either of them are not stated or are misstated, provided that such
specification is sufficient for the identification of such writ.

(4)   Where any deed, instrument, or writing bearing more than one date is [. . .]
specified or referred to in any other deed, instrument, or writing, it shall be no objection to such specification or reference that only the first date is given with the addition of the words 'and subsequent date' (or 'dates').

[(5)   Note 1 to Schedule D to this Act shall apply to a reference competently made
to any deed for reservations, real burdens, conditions, provisions, limitations, obligations and stipulations affecting lands and to the form of such reference given in
[schedule 1 to the Title Conditions (Scotland) Act 2003 (asp 9)].]

14   Abolition of real warrandice

(1)   From and after the commencement of this Act, it shall not be competent
to dispone lands in real warrandice of a conveyance of other lands, and such real
warrandice shall not arise ex lege from any contract or agreement entered into
after the commencement of this Act.

[. . .]

15   Transmission of personal obligation

(1)   The personal obligation contained in any deed or writing whereby any heritable security is constituted shall not transmit in terms of section forty-seven of the
Conveyancing (Scotland) Act, 1874, against any person taking the estate by conveyance in the sense of that section dated after the commencement of this Act, unless
such conveyance be signed by such person.

(2)   After the commencement of this Act, summary diligence, in terms of the said
section, shall not be competent against any obligant whose obligation is created by
succession, gift or bequest, unless in cases in which there shall be an agreement to the
transmission of such obligation executed by such obligant.

(3)   An agreement for transmission of a personal obligation pursuant to the said
section may be in terms of Form No 2 of Schedule A to this Act, or in any other form
sufficiently expressing such agreement.

19   Applicability of forms prescribed by Act

The forms prescribed by this Act for the completion of the titles to and the conveyance, assignation, discharge or restriction of rights of property [. . .] in land or
heritable securities shall respectively be applicable to all other rights in or over

land or in or over a heritable security the title to which may according to the present law and practice be competently completed by the recording of such title in the appropriate Register of Sasines.

22 Assimilation of law as regards legitim and jus relictæ, &c

(1) In the case of any person dying after the commencement of this Act, the rules of law which determine what estate belonging to a deceased is subject to claims for legitim shall be applicable in determining what estate belonging to the deceased is subject to the claim for jus relictæ or jus relicti: And the estates of all such persons shall be distributed on the footing that there shall no longer be any distinction between the description of estate subject to claims for legitim and the description of estate subject to claims for jus relictæ and jus relicti.

(2) All debts which if due to any person dying after the commencement of this Act would, according to the present law and practice or in terms of this section, be subject to legitim and jus relictæ or jus relicti shall, if due by the deceased or out of his or her estate, form, so far as the estate on which such debts are secured may be insufficient to meet the same, deductions from the deceased's moveable estate before ascertaining legitim and jus relictæ or jus relicti.

24 Registered leases. Assimilation of forms

All enabling powers and rights which, by this Act, are conferred upon or implied in favour of a person in right of land or of a security over land [. . .] shall, so far as applicable, be held as conferred upon a person who has right to a lease, or to a security over a lease respectively; and the forms prescribed by this Act may be used in connection with the constitution, transmission, restriction and discharge of securities over leases, and the completion of titles to leases and to securities over the same, and to sales thereof under such securities, [. . .] and the clauses held as implied in any of the forms prescribed by this Act shall, so far as applicable, be held as implied when such forms are used in connection with leases and securities over the same: Provided that in applying this Act and relative schedules to leases and securities over the same the following modifications and such other verbal modifications as may be necessary shall be given effect to:—

(1) For 'lands,' 'lands and others' or 'subjects' there shall be substituted 'lease,' for 'conveyance' or 'disposition' there shall be substituted 'assignation' [. . .], for 'bond and disposition in security' there shall be substituted 'bond and assignation in security,' for 'assignation of a bond and disposition in security' there shall be substituted 'translation of a bond and assignation in security,' for 'dispone' or 'convey' there shall be substituted 'assign,' for 'proprietor' there shall be substituted 'lessee,' [and] for 'disponee' there shall be substituted 'assignee':

(2) In an assignation of a lease, or in a bond and assignation in security of a lease, or in a notice of title relating to a lease, there may be substituted for a description of the land a reference to such lease in or as nearly as may be in the terms of Schedule J to this Act:

(3) In the event of the lease, to which a title is being completed by notice of title under this Act, not having been recorded in the appropriate Register of Sasines, it shall be recorded therein along with such notice of title in which the lease shall be referred to in manner prescribed in Note 5 to Schedule J to this Act, and such lease, before being so recorded, shall be docqueted in manner prescribed in Note 7 to Schedule B to this Act, and, on the same being so recorded, it shall have the same force and effect as a recorded title under the Registration of Leases (Scotland) Act, 1857, and Acts amending the same:

(4) [. . .]

(5) A renunciation of a lease in terms of Schedule G to the Registration of Leases (Scotland) Act, 1857, may competently be granted by a person not holding a recorded title to such lease, provided that he shall therein deduce his title from the person holding the last recorded title in manner prescribed in Note 4 to Schedule J to this Act, and on such renunciation being recorded in the appropriate Register of

Sasines such lease shall be as effectually renounced as if the title of the granter of such renunciation had been completed as at the date of such recording [. . .], and section thirteen of the said Act of 1857, and Schedule G annexed to that Act, are hereby amended accordingly:

(6)   Section twenty-four of the Titles to Land Consolidation (Scotland) Act, 1868, and section forty-four of the Conveyancing (Scotland) Act, 1874, as amended by section five of this Act, shall apply to a lease and to a security over a lease, and in the warrant, interlocutor or decree of Court conferring a right to such lease or security over the same or granting authority to complete title thereto, and also in the application upon which such warrant, interlocutor or decree proceeds, such lease may be referred to in or as nearly as may be in the terms of Schedule J hereto:

(7)   An adjudger or purchaser of a lease, or an adjudger or assignee of a security over a lease, may complete his title thereto by recording in the appropriate Register of Sasines an extract of the decree of adjudication or of sale (as the case may be) or may use such extract decree as an assignation or one of a series of assignations of an unrecorded lease or of an unrecorded security over a lease, and section ten of the Registration of Leases (Scotland) Act, 1857, is hereby amended accordingly.

27   Restriction of agent's lien
From and after the commencement of this Act it shall be incompetent for any law agent or notary public acting for the proprietor or creditors or others, whose rights in or over land conveyed in security are postponed to those of the creditor in such heritable security, to acquire over the writs and evidents as against such creditor any right of hypothec, lien or retention after the date of recording such heritable security.

40   Exposure in lots and apportionment of feu-duty
[(1)   [Land, or any part thereof, sold in exercise of a power of sale under a bond and disposition in security] may be exposed to, or offered for, sale either in whole or in lots, and in the former case at such upset price or prices as the creditor may think proper, and in the latter case at the best price that can be reasonably obtained] subject to such proportion of any existing [. . .] valued rent or land tax, as the creditor may think proper, and, without prejudice to the rights of any third party, the creditor may, in selling the land in lots, provide that the proprietor for the time being of any lot shall be obliged to relieve the proprietor or proprietors of another lot or lots of the whole or such part of an existing [. . .] land tax, as the creditor may think proper, and for that purpose the creditor may create such obligation a real burden on such lot.

[(2)   Where there is a sale as aforesaid in lots, the creditor shall have power to create such rights and impose such duties and conditions [(whether or not by creating a real burden)] as he considers may be reasonably required for the proper management, maintenance and use of any part of the land to be held in common by the owners for the time being of the lots.]

41   Purchasers protected
(1)   All proceedings [relating to the redemption or calling up of, or a sale under, a bond and disposition in security] shall be valid and effectual notwithstanding that any person to whom premonition or notice requires to be given in terms of this Act may be [subject to any legal disability by reason of nonage or otherwise] and any sale and disposition in implement thereof shall be as valid to the purchaser as if made by the proprietor of the land not being under disability, and any such disposition shall import an assignation to the purchaser of the warrandice contained or implied in the bond and disposition in security under which the land is sold, and also an obligation by the granter of the security to ratify, approve and confirm the sale and disposition.

[(2)   Where a disposition of land is duly recorded in the appropriate Register of Sasines and that disposition bears to be granted in the exercise of a power of sale contained in a deed granting a bond and disposition in security, and the exercise of that power was *ex facie* regular, the title of a *bona fide* purchaser of the land for value shall not be challengeable on the ground that the debt had ceased to exist, unless that fact appeared in the said Register, or was known to the purchaser prior to the payment of the price, or on the ground of any irregularity relating to the sale or in any preliminary procedure thereto; but nothing in the provisions of this subsection shall affect the competency of any claim for damages in respect of the sale of the land against the person exercising the said power.]

44   General register of inhibitions and register of adjudications to be combined; limitation of effect of entries therein

(1)   The General Register of Inhibitions and Interdictions and the Register of Adjudications shall be combined, and the Keeper thereof shall keep only one register for inhibitions, interdictions, adjudications, reductions, and notices of litigiosity, and such register shall be called the Register of Inhibitions and Adjudications; and a reference in any public, general or local Act to the General Register of Inhibitions or the Register of Adjudications shall be deemed to mean and include such Register of Inhibitions and Adjudications.

(2)(a)   No action whether raised before or after the commencement of this Act relating to land or to a lease or to a heritable security, shall be deemed to have had or shall have the effect of making such land, lease or heritable security litigious, unless and until

[(i)]   a notice relative to such action in or as nearly as may be in the form of Schedule RR annexed to the Titles to Land Consolidation (Scotland) Act, 1868, shall have been or shall be registered in the Register of Inhibitions and Adjudications in the manner provided by section one hundred and fifty-nine of that Act [; or

(ii)   a notice of an application under section 8 of the Law Reform (Miscellaneous Provisions) (Scotland) Act 1985 has been registered in the said register.]

(b)   No decree in any action of adjudication of land or of a lease or of a heritable security, whether pronounced before or after the commencement of this Act, and no abbreviate of any such decree shall be deemed have had or to have any effect in making such land, lease or heritable security litigious.

[(2A)   A notice registered under subsection (2)(a)(i) of this section on or after the date on which section 67 of the Land Registration etc (Scotland) Act 2012 (asp 5) (warrant to place a caveat) comes into force shall not have any effect in rendering—

(a)   a land or lease for which there is a title sheet in the Land Register of Scotland, or

(b)   any heritable security the particulars of which are entered in a title sheet in that register,

litigious or in placing in bad faith any person acquiring such land, lease or heritable security.]

(3)(a)   All inhibitions and all notices of litigiosity registered in terms of section one hundred and fifty-nine of the Titles to Land Consolidation (Scotland) Act, 1868, subsisting at the commencement of this Act shall prescribe and be of no effect on the lapse of five years after such commencement or at such earlier date as they would prescribe according to the present law and practice; and all [. . .] [notices of litigiosity and notices of applications under section 8 of the Law Reform (Miscellaneous Provisions) (Scotland) Act 1985] which relate to land or to a lease or to a heritable security and which shall be first registered after the commencement of this Act, shall prescribe and be of no effect on the lapse of five years from the date on which the same shall respectively take effect:

Provided that in no case shall litigiosity be pleadable or be founded on to any effect after the expiry of six months from and after final decree is pronounced in the action creating such litigiosity.

[(aa)   all inhibitions shall cease to have effect on the lapse of five years from the date on which they take effect.]

(b)   From and after the commencement of this Act interdiction, whether judicial or voluntary, shall be incompetent, and any interdiction which is legally operative at such commencement shall remain legally operative for not longer than the period of five years thereafter.

(4)(a), (b)   [. . .]

(c)   No deed, decree, instrument or writing granted or expede by a person whose estates have been sequestrated under the Bankruptcy (Scotland) Act, 1856, or the Bankruptcy (Scotland) Act, 1913 [, or the Bankruptcy (Scotland) Act 1985 [*or the Bankruptcy (Scotland) Act 2016*]], or the heirs, executors, successors or assignees of such person relative to any land or lease or heritable security belonging to such person at the date of such sequestration or subsequently acquired by him shall be challengeable or denied effect on the ground of such sequestration if such deed, decree, instrument or writing shall have been granted or expede, or shall come into operation at a date when the effect of recording (a) the abbreviate provided for under section forty-four of the said Act of 1913, as amended by this Act, shall have expired in terms of the said section as amended as aforesaid [; or (b) under subsection (1)(a) of section 14 of the Bankruptcy (Scotland) Act 1985 [*or (1)(a) of section 26 of the Bankruptcy (Scotland) Act 2016*] the certified copy of an order shall have expired by virtue of subsection (3) of [*the said section 14 or (4) of the said section 26*]], unless the trustee in such sequestration shall before the recording of such deed, decree, instrument or writing in the appropriate Register of Sasines have completed his title to such land, lease or heritable security by recording the same in such register [or have recorded a memorandum in such register in the form provided by Schedule O to this Act]: Provided always, in case of sequestrations awarded under the Bankruptcy (Scotland) Act, 1856, that the provisions of this section shall not apply to any deed, decree, instrument or writing dated within five years after the commencement of this Act.

(5)   The provisions of this section shall not affect the ranking of adjudgers inter se, or any real right obtained in virtue of a decree of adjudication, or in virtue of a decree pronounced in an action creating litigiosity, or by a trustee in bankruptcy, if such right has been completed by the recording in the appropriate Register of Sasines of any deed, decree, abbreviate, or instrument necessary to effect the completion of such right.

(6)   Section one hundred and fifty-nine of the Titles to Land Consolidation (Scotland) Act, 1868, and sections sixteen and seventeen of the Land Registers (Scotland) Act, 1868, [. . .] are hereby amended in accordance with this section, and section forty-two of the Conveyancing (Scotland) Act, 1874, and Schedule J thereto annexed, are hereby repealed.

45   Provision for termination of perpetual trusts of moveables

In any case where the provisions of section nine of the Trusts (Scotland) Act, 1921, would apply to any deed, and to the right of any party thereunder if such deed had been dated after the thirty-first day of July, eighteen hundred and sixty-eight, the provisions of the said section shall, from and after the passing of this Act, apply to such deed and to the right of any party thereunder notwithstanding that the same be dated on or prior to the said thirty-first day of July, eighteen hundred and sixty-eight:

Provided that, in the application of the said provisions to the deeds to which this section refers and to the right of any party thereunder, the date of such deeds shall be deemed to be the date of the passing of this Act.

46 Extract decree of reduction to be recorded

[(1)] In the case of the reduction of a deed, decree or instrument recorded in the Register of Sasines or forming a midcouple or link of title in a title recorded in the said register there shall be recorded in the said register either an extract of the decree of reduction of such deed, decree or instrument, or a title in which such extract decree forms a midcouple or link of title, and such decree of reduction shall not be pleadable against a third party who shall in bona fide onerously acquire right to the land, lease or heritable security contained in the deed, decree, or instrument reduced by such decree of reduction prior to an extract of such decree of reduction, or a title, in which it forms a midcouple or link of title, being recorded in the Register of Sasines.

[(2) [Subsection (1)] shall apply to the rectification of a document by an order under section 8 of the Law Reform (Miscellaneous Provisions) (Scotland) Act 1985 as it applies to the reduction of a deed but with the substitution of any reference to the decree of reduction of the deed with a reference to the order rectifying the document.]

[(3) Where—

(a) an arbitral award orders the reduction of a deed or other document recorded in the Register of Sasines (or forming a midcouple or link of title in a title recorded in that Register), and

(b) the court orders that the award may be enforced in accordance with section 12 of the Arbitration (Scotland) Act 2010 (asp 1),

subsection (1) applies to the arbitral award as it applies to a decree of reduction of a deed recorded in the Register of Sasines.]

[46A Further provision as regards decree of reduction

(1) Where a deed mentioned in subsection (2) is reduced, the decree of reduction—

(a) may be registered in the Land Register of Scotland, and

(b) does not have real effect until so registered.

(2) The deed is one which—

(a) is voidable, and

(b) relates to a plot of land or lease registered in the Land Register of Scotland.

(3) Subsection (1) applies to an arbitral award which—

(a) orders the reduction of a deed mentioned in subsection (2), and

(b) may be enforced in accordance with section 12 of the Arbitration (Scotland) Act 2010 (asp 1),

as it applies to a decree of reduction.]

47 Re-recording of deeds relative to leasehold subjects

Where in terms of the Registration of Leases (Scotland) Act, 1857, or of section twenty-four of this Act, any deed or extract shall have been recorded in the appropriate Register of Sasines, and where in terms of that Act or of the said section any such deed or extract shall fall to be recorded again, or where any extract from a competent register of any deed the principal of which has already been recorded in the appropriate Register of Sasines falls to be so recorded, it shall not be necessary for the keeper of the Register of Sasines in which such deed or extract falls to be recorded, or in which such extract of any recorded deed falls to be recorded, to engross such deed or extract in the register at length, but the keeper of such Register of Sasines may in place of such engrossment enter in the register a short memorandum specifying the deed or extract and the book and folio in which the same is already engrossed, and in the case of an extract of a deed the principal of which has already been recorded in the appropriate Register of Sasines the book and folio in which the principal is already engrossed, and such memorandum shall have the same effect as if the deed or extract were engrossed in the register at length in place of such memorandum.

48 Duplicate plans may be retained with register

Where any writ which refers to a plan signed as relative thereto is presented or transmitted by post for registration in the General Register of Sasines it shall be competent to ingive to the said register along therewith a duplicate of such plan, docqueted with reference to the said writ and authenticated in the same manner as the principal plan, and such duplicate plan shall be retained in the said register. The ingiving of such duplicate plan shall be noted in the register, and acknowledgement of the receipt thereof shall be marked by the keeper of the register on the plan signed as relative to the writ.

Along with each register volume transmitted to the Keeper of the Records for custody there shall be sent the duplicate plans, if any, relative to any of the writs engrossed in such volume.

Such duplicate plans when transmitted to the Keeper of the Records shall remain in his custody, subject to the same rights on the part of the public to have access thereto as apply to the Record Volumes.

49   Saving clause

(1)   [...]

(2)   Nothing in this Act contained shall affect the preparation of the printed minutes and printed indexes of persons and places applicable to each county in Scotland, and the Keeper of the General Register of Sasines shall supply as full information in the printed minute books as hitherto according to the existing law and practice.

[49A   Power of the Scottish Ministers to prescribe forms

(1)   The Scottish Ministers may, by order, modify any schedule to this Act.

(2)   Such an order may, in particular, substitute for any form, notice, clause, warrant or other deed for the time being set out in such a schedule another such form, notice, clause, warrant or other deed.

(3)   An order under this section is subject to the affirmative procedure.]

SCHEDULES

SCHEDULE A

FORM NO 1
CLAUSE OF DEDUCTION OF TITLE IN A DISPOSITION OF
LAND WHERE THE GRANTER [DOES NOT HAVE A RECORDED TITLE]

Section 3

[To be inserted immediately after the clause specifying the date or term of entry or after the dispositive clause where no date or term of entry is specified.]

Which lands and others (*or* subjects) were last vested [*or* are part of the lands and others (*or* subjects) last vested] in *A.B.*, (*designation of person* [*having last recorded title*]), whose title thereto is recorded in (*specify Register of Sasines and date of recording, or if the last* [*recorded title*] *has already been mentioned say* in the said *A.B.* as aforesaid), and from whom I acquired right by (*here specify shortly the writ or series of writs by which right was so acquired*).

NOTE TO FORM NO 1 OF SCHEDULE A

If any conditions, reservations, provisions, obligations, servitudes or other burdens which affect the land or any part thereof or qualify the granter's right thereto be contained in or imposed by the writ or any of the writs by which the granter acquired right and are proper to be inserted, insert the same at length in the dispositive clause, and if they affect only part of the land specify the part or parts of the land affected thereby, and in case of money burdens specify the amounts thereof and the name and designation or designative description of the creditor therein, all as in the writ containing or imposing such money burdens, and in all cases specify the writ or writs containing or imposing such conditions and others.

FORM NO 2
CLAUSE TRANSMITTING PERSONAL OBLIGATION IN A HERITABLE SECURITY IN A
DISPOSITION OF LAND

Section 15

I, *A.B.* (*designation*), in consideration of (*specify any part of price paid in money*) and in consideration also of *C.D.* (*designation*) undertaking as by his signature hereto he undertakes the personal obligation contained in a bond and disposition in security for the sum of (*insert amount*) granted by me [*or by E.F. (original debtor)*] in favour of *G.H.* (*original creditor*), dated (*insert date*), and recorded in (*specify Register of Sasines and date of recording*) do hereby dispone, &c.

[SCHEDULE BA
Form of Notice of Title: Land Register

Be it known that *A.B.* (*designation*) has right as proprietor to all and whole (*description*) conform to the last completed title and subsequent writ (*or writs*), which title and writ (*or writs*), which title and writ (*or writs*) have been examined by me, *Y.Z.* (*designation*), Notary Public (*or Law Agent*).

[*Testing clause*]
Y.Z.

NOTES TO SCHEDULE BA

Note 1: Where the notice is in respect of a subordinate real right, other than a registered lease having its own title sheet, for 'proprietor to' substitute 'holder of liferent (*or other right, as the case may be*) over'.

Note 2: Where the notice is in respect of a registered lease having its own title sheet, for 'proprietor to' substitute 'tenant of'.

Note 3: If any writ by which A.B. acquired right contains a new title condition, whether burdening or benefiting the property, the condition is to be inserted in full after the description of the property.

Note 4: In the case of a traditional document, subscription of it by the notary public (or law agent) on behalf of the granter will suffice for the document to be formally valid, but witnessing of it may be necessary or desirable for other purposes: see Requirements of Writing (Scotland) Act 1995 (c 7) (which also makes provision as regards the authentication of an electronic document).]

SCHEDULE B
[FORMS OF NOTICE OF TITLE IN THE REGISTER OF SASINES]

FORM NO 1
ON BEHALF OF A PERSON WHO HAS RIGHT TO LAND BY A TITLE WHICH HAS NOT BEEN
RECORDED IN THE APPROPRIATE REGISTER OF SASINES AND WHICH IS NOT TO BE
RECORDED ALONG WITH THE NOTICE OF TITLE

Section 4(1)

Be it known that *A.B.* (*designation*) has right as proprietor (*or life-renter or proprietor in trust or otherwise, as the case may be*) to all and whole [*here describe the land or refer to description thereof as in Schedule D to this Act or as in Schedule G to the Titles to Land Consolidation (Scotland) Act, 1868; and if* [. . .] *any conditions, reservations, provisions, obligations, servitudes, or other burdens which affect the land or any part thereof* [. . .] *or qualify A.B.'s right thereto be contained in or imposed by the writ or any of the writs by which A.B. acquired right and are proper to be inserted, here insert the same at length, and if they affect only part of the land specify the part or parts of the land affected thereby, and in case of money burdens specify the amount thereof and the name and designation*

*or designative description of the creditor therein all as in the writ containing or imposing
such money burdens, and in all cases specify the writ or writs containing or imposing such
conditions and others];* Which lands and others (*or* subjects) were last vested [*or* are
part of the lands and others (*or* subjects) last vested] in *C.D.* (*design person [having last
recorded title]*), whose title thereto was recorded in (*specify Register of Sasines and date
of recording, or if the last [recorded title] has already been mentioned say* in the said *C.D.* as
aforesaid), and from whom the said *A.B.* acquired right by (*here specify shortly the writ
or series of writs by which he acquired right*); Which last recorded title and subsequent
writ (*or* writs) have been presented to me, *Y.Z.* (*designation*), Notary Public, (*or* Law
Agent).

[*Testing clause †*]

Y.Z.

FORM NO 2
ON BEHALF OF A PERSON WHO HAS RIGHT TO LAND CONVEYED BY
AN UNRECORDED SPECIAL CONVEYANCE WHICH IS TO BE RECORDED ALONG WITH THE
NOTICE OF TITLE
Section 4(2)

Be it known that *A.B.* (*designation*) has right as proprietor (*or* life-renter *or* proprietor in trust *or otherwise, as the case may be*) to all and whole the lands and
others (*or* subjects) disponed by (*or* contained in) the disposition (*or feu charter or
other special conveyance*) granted by *C.D.* (*designation*) in favour of *E.F.* (*designation*)
dated (*insert date*), and recorded in (*specify Register of Sasines*) of even date herewith [*if any conditions, reservations, provisions, obligations, servitudes or other burdens
affecting the land or any part thereof or qualifying A.B.'s right thereto be contained in
or imposed by the writ or any of the writs by which A.B. acquired right other than such
special conveyance and are proper to be inserted, here insert the same at length, and if
they affect only part of the land specify the part or parts of the land affected thereby, and
in case of money burdens specify the amount thereof and the name and designation or
designative description of the creditor therein, all as in the writ containing or imposing
such money burdens, and in all cases specify the writ or writs containing or imposing
such conditions and others];* To which lands and others (*or* subjects) the said *A.B.*
acquired right by the foresaid disposition (*or as the case may be*) and by (*here specify
shortly the subsequent writ or series of writs by which he acquired right*); Which disposition and subsequent writ (*or* writs) have been presented to me (*as in Form No 1
of this Schedule*).

[*Testing clause †*]

FORM NO 3
ON BEHALF OF A PERSON WHO HAS RIGHT TO A RECORDED HERITABLE SECURITY
BY A TITLE WHICH HAS NOT BEEN RECORDED IN THE APPROPRIATE REGISTER OF
SASINES AND WHICH IS NOT TO BE RECORDED ALONG WITH THE NOTICE OF
TITLE
Section 4(3)

Be it known that *A.B.* (*designation*) has right (*adding if such be the case* to the extent
aftermentioned) to a bond and disposition in security (*or as the case may be*) for
the sum of (*insert amount*) granted by *C.D.* (*design original debtor*) in favour of *E.F.*
(*design original creditor*), dated (*insert date*) and recorded in [*specify Register of Sasines
and date of recording; adding, if necessary,* but only to the extent of (*insert sum*) of prin-
cipal]; Which bond and disposition in security was last vested in the said *E.F.* as
aforesaid [*or if E.F. is not the person [. . .] holding the last recorded title thereto, say*
Which bond and disposition in security (*adding, if necessary,* to the extent foresaid

or as the case may be) was last vested in *G.H.* (*design person holding the last recorded title thereto*), whose title thereto was recorded in said Register of Sasines (*or as the case may be, and give date of recording*)], and from whom the said *A.B.* acquired right (*adding, if necessary*, to the extent foresaid, *or as the case may be*), by (*here specify shortly the writ or series of writs by which he acquired right*); Which last recorded title and subsequent writ (*or writs*) have been presented to me (*as in Form No 1 of this Schedule*).

[*Testing clause* †]

FORM NO 5
ON BEHALF OF A PERSON WHO HAS RIGHT TO AN UNRECORDED HERITABLE SECURITY
WHICH IS TO BE RECORDED ALONG WITH THE NOTICE OF TITLE
Section 4(4)

Be it known that *A.B.* (*designation*) has right (*adding if such be the case* to the extent aftermentioned) to a bond and disposition in security (*or as the case may be*) for the sum of (*insert amount*) granted by *C.D.* (*designation*) in favour of *E.F.* (*designation*) dated (*insert date*), and recorded in (*specify Register of Sasines*) of even date herewith [*adding if necessary* but only to the extent of (*insert sum*) of principal]; To which bond and disposition in security (*adding if necessary* to the extent foresaid *or as the case may be*) the said *A.B.* acquired right by (*here specify shortly the writ or series of writs by which he acquired right*); Which bond and disposition in Security (*or as the case may be*) and subsequent writ (*or writs*) have been presented to me (*as in Form No 1 of this Schedule*).

[*Testing clause* †]

NOTES TO SCHEDULE B
Sections 4(2), (4), 24(3)

Note 1.—Where the description in the last [recorded title] is a particular description, the description in Form No 1 of this Schedule should be by reference thereto, unless there is reason to the contrary.

Note 2.—In adapting Form No 2 of this Schedule to the case of a person who has right to only a part of the land contained in an unrecorded conveyance, deed, or decree there shall be inserted immediately before the words 'all and whole' a description of such part of the land, and the form may then proceed *which lands and others* (or *subjects*) *are part of.*

Note 3.—If the original [title to] a bond and disposition in security or other heritable security [has been completed] otherwise than by recording the same in the appropriate Register of Sasines add immediately after the mention of the date thereof *and instrument of sasine* (or *notarial instrument*, or if such be the case *and along with notice of title*) thereon (adding if such instrument or notice is not in favour of the original creditor the name and designation of the person in whose favour it is conceived) *recorded in* (specify Register of Sasines and date of recording).

Note 4.—In adapting Forms Nos 3 and 5 of this Schedule to real burdens for capital sums, there shall be substituted for the specification of the bond and disposition in security the following: *A real burden for the sum of* (insert amount) *payable to E.F.* (designation) *in terms of* (specify the disposition or other deed under which the real burden was reserved or constituted, giving the names and designations of the granter and grantee, or of the parties thereto), *dated* (insert date) *and recorded in* (specify Register of Sasines and date of recording); and in specifying the writs by which *A.B.* acquired right to such real burden there shall in Form No. 5 be mentioned as the first of such writs *the said disposition* (or other deed as above), and the same shall along with the other writ or writs be presented to the Agent expeding the notice of title.

Note 5.—[*repealed*]

Note 6.—Where in place of the principal titles or writs on which any notice of title bears to proceed there are presented to the agent expeding such notice extracts or office copies thereof, the statement in the notice as to the presentation of such titles or writs may be varied accordingly; but it shall be no objection to any notice of title that it states that the principal titles or writs were so presented although there were presented only extracts or office copies of such titles or writs.

Note 7.—Where a deed, decree or heritable security is to be recorded along with a notice of title it should be docqueted as follows:—*Docqueted with reference to notice of title in favour of* A.B. recorded of even date herewith.

[† Note 8.—[In the case of a traditional document, subscription of it] by the notary public (or law agent) on behalf of granter of it will be sufficient for the document to be formally valid, but witnessing of it may be necessary or desirable for other purposes (see the Requirements of Writing (Scotland) Act 1995) [, which also makes provision as regards the authentication of an electronic document].]

[. . .]

SCHEDULE D
CLAUSE OF REFERENCE TO A DESCRIPTION OF LAND CONTAINED IN A PRIOR CONVEYANCE, DEED, OR INSTRUMENT
Section 8

All and whole the lands and others (*or* subjects) in the county of
(*or* in the burgh of   and county of   *as the case may be*)
described in (*refer to the conveyance, deed, or instrument in such terms as shall be sufficient to identify it, and specify the Register of Sasines in which it is recorded and date of recording, or where the conveyance, deed, or instrument referred to is recorded on the same date as the conveyance, deed, or instrument containing the reference substitute for the date of recording the words* of even date with the recording of these presents):—

NOTES TO SCHEDULE D

Note 1.—In referring to a Deed containing a particular description [or to a Deed containing reservations, real burdens, conditions, provisions, limitations, obligations and stipulations affecting lands] it shall be sufficient to give the names of the granter and grantee or of the parties thereto without adding their designations, and when there are several granters or grantees or several parties acting in the same category it shall be sufficient to give the name of the first mentioned person only with the addition of the words *and others*; and where the granter or granters or grantee or grantees, or the parties or one of the parties thereto acts or act in a fiduciary capacity it shall be sufficient to state such capacity without giving their individual name or names, *e.g.*:

(a) *Feu Charter granted by A.B. in favour of C.D., dated* (insert date) *and recorded in* (specify Register of Sasines and give date of recording).

(b) *Disposition granted by C.D. and others in favour of E.F. and others, dated, &c* (as above).

(c) *Notarial Instrument* (or *Notice of title*) *in favour of the Trustee* (or *Trustees*) *of G.H.* (or *the Judicial Factor of J.K. or the Trustee on the Sequestrated Estates of L.M. or the Liquidator of the N.O. Company, Limited, or* as the case may be) *recorded in* (specify Register of Sasines and date of recording).

Note 2.—Where it is desired to insert a short description of the land or subjects, this may be done as follows:—*All and whole that dwelling-house, number ten, Rosebery Crescent, Edinburgh,* (or *the eastmost half-flat on the second storey of the tenement entering from number fifteen, Lothian Street, Edinburgh,* or otherwise, in the case may be) *in the county of Edinburgh, described in, &c.* (as above).

Note 3.—If part only of the land or subjects described in a former recorded conveyance, deed, instrument, or notice of title is being conveyed or otherwise dealt with for the first time as a separate subject, such part should be described at length, adding *being part of the lands and others* (or *subjects*) *in the county of*   or *in the burgh of*   *and county of*   *described in, &c* (as above); or thus: *All and Whole the lands and others* (or *subjects*) *in the county of*   or *in the burgh of*   *and county of*   *described in, &c* (as above), *with the exception of* (describe, the part excepted).

Note 4.—If several lands or subjects are described in the conveyance, deed, or instrument referred to, and it is intended to specify one or more of them, these may be distinguished from the others thus: *All and Whole the lands and others* (or *subjects*) *first* (or *second and third*) *described in*, &c (as above, or otherwise, as the case may be).

[. . .]

SCHEDULE J
REGISTRABLE LEASES

Section 24

A lease (*or* tack) granted by E.F. (*designation*) in my favour [*or* in favour of *G.H.* (*designation*) *or as the case may be*] of the subjects therein described lying in the county of
(*or* burgh of   and county of   ) dated (*insert date*)
and recorded in (*specify Register of Sasines and date of recording*).

NOTES TO SCHEDULE J

Note 1.—If the recording of a lease in the appropriate Register of Sasines has been effected by a successor of the original lessee, add immediately after the mention of the date thereof *and along with notarial instrument* (or *notice of title*) *thereon in favour of* (giving the name and designation of the person in whose favour it is conceived) *recorded in* (specify Register of Sasines and date of recording).

Note 2.—Where any deed authorised by this Act relates to part only of the subjects contained in a lease add *but in so far only as regards the following portion of the subjects leased, viz.* (here describe the portion or refer to description thereof as in Schedule D hereto).

Note 3.—Where the granter of an assignation of a recorded lease or of a bond and assignation in security of a recorded lease is not the original lessee but has a recorded title [no specification of the granter's title is required].

Note 4.—In an assignation or renunciation of a recorded lease the title of the granter of which assignation or renunciation is not recorded, and in a notice of title to a recorded lease, insert *which lease* (adding if necessary *to the extent foresaid* or as the case may be) *was last vested in the said G.H. as aforesaid* [or if *G.H.* is not the person having such title say *in J.K.* (design person having such title) *whose title thereto is recorded in said Register of Sasines* (or as the case, may be, and give date of recording)], *and from whom I* (in the case of an assignation or renunciation) or *the said A.B.* (in the case of a notice of title) *acquired right by* (here specify shortly the writ or series of writs by which right was so acquired by the person granting the assignation or renunciation, or expeding the notice of title.)

Note 5.—Where a title to an unrecorded lease is being completed by notice of title under this Act the lease shall be referred to in manner above prescribed except that the Register of Sasines shall be specified, and for the date of recording of the lease there shall be substituted the words *of even date herewith*.

[SCHEDULE O
FORM OF MEMORANDUM TO BE RECORDED IN THE REGISTER OF SASINES

Section 44

Memorandum with regard to the subjects after described:

With reference to the subjects (*describe particularly or by reference*) T the trustee in the sequestration of B has obtained a vesting order under section 98 of the Bankruptcy (Scotland) Act 1913 dated (*insert date of order*).

The memorandum should be signed by the trustee or his law agent, dated, and recorded [. . .] in the appropriate division or divisions of the Register of Sasines.

The form may be adapted in the case of a lease thus:—

Memorandum with regard to the lease after-mentioned:

With reference to the lease granted by C in favour of D of the subjects therein described lying in the county of K, dated (*insert date*), and recorded in [*specify Register of Sasines and date of recording*], T the trustee &c.

And in the case of a heritable security thus:—

Memorandum with regard to the bond and disposition in security after-mentioned:

With reference to the bond and disposition in security for the sum of (*insert sum*) granted by E in favour of F dated (*insert date*) and recorded in (*specify Register of Sasines and date of recording*), T the trustee &c.]

CONVEYANCING AND FEUDAL REFORM (SCOTLAND) ACT 1970
(1970, c 35)

PART II
THE STANDARD SECURITY

9 The standard security

(1) The provisions of this Part of this Act shall have effect for the purpose of enabling a new form of heritable security to be created to be known as a standard security.

(2) It shall be competent to [grant and register in the Land Register of Scotland or to] grant and record in the Register of Sasines a standard security over any [land or real right in land] to be expressed in conformity with one of the forms prescribed in Schedule 2 to this Act.

[(2B) It shall not be competent to grant a standard security over a personal preemption burden or personal redemption burden (both within the meaning of Part 4 of the Abolition of Feudal Tenure etc (Scotland) Act 2000 (asp 5) [or, as the case may be, of section 23 of the Long Leases (Scotland) Act 2012 (asp 9)]).]

(3) A grant of any right over [land or a real right] in land for the purpose of securing any debt by way of a heritable security shall only be capable of being affected at law if it is embodied in a standard security.

(4) Where for the purpose last-mentioned any deed which is not in the form of a standard security contains a disposition or assignation [of land or of a real right] in land, it shall to that extent be void and unenforceable, and where that deed has been duly [registered or] recorded the creditor in the purported security may be required, by any person having an interest, to grant any deed which may be appropriate to clear [the Land Register of Scotland or] the Register of Sasines of that security.

(5) A standard security may be used for any other purpose for which a heritable security may be used if any of the said forms is appropriate to that purpose, and for the purpose of any enactment affecting heritable securities a standard security, if so used, or if used as is required by this Act instead of a heritable security as defined therein, shall be a heritable security for the purposes of that enactment.

(6) The Bankruptcy Act 1696, in so far as it renders a heritable security of no effect in relation to a debt contracted after the recording of that security, and any rule of law which requires that a real burden for money may only be created in respect of a sum specified in the deed of creation, shall not apply in relation to a standard security.

[. . .]

(8) For the purposes of this Part of this Act—

(a) 'heritable security' (except in subsection (5) of this section if the context otherwise requires) means any security capable of being constituted over any [land or real right] in land by disposition or assignation of that [land or real right] in security of any debt and of being [registered in the Land Register of Scotland or] recorded in the Register of Sasines;

[(b) 'real right in land' means any such right, other than ownership or a real burden, which is capable of being held separately and to which a title may be [registered in the Land Register of Scotland or] recorded in the Register of Sasines;]

(c) 'debt' means any obligation due, or which will or may become due, to repay or pay money, including any such obligation arising from a transaction or part of a transaction in the course of any trade, business or profession, and any obligation to pay an annuity or *ad factum praestandum*, but does not include an obligation to pay any [. . .], rent or other periodical sum payable in respect of land, and 'creditor' and 'debtor', in relation to a standard security, shall be construed accordingly.

10 Import of forms of, and certain clauses in, standard security

(1) The import of the clause relating to the personal obligation contained in Form A of Schedule 2 to this Act expressed in any standard security shall, unless specially qualified, be as follows—

(a) where the security is for a fixed amount advanced or payable at, or prior to, the delivery of the deed, the clause undertaking to make payment to the creditor shall import an acknowledgment of receipt by the debtor of the principal sum advanced or an acknowledgment by the debtor of liability to pay that sum and a personal obligation undertaken by the debtor to repay or pay to the creditor on demand in writing at any time after the date of delivery of the standard security the said sum, with interest at the rate stated payable on the dates specified, together with all expenses for which the debtor is liable by virtue of the deed or of this Part of this Act;

(b) where the security is for a fluctuating amount, whether subject to a maximum amount or not and whether advanced or due partly before and partly after delivery of the deed or whether to be advanced or to become due wholly after such delivery, the clause undertaking to make payment to the creditor shall import a personal obligation by the debtor to repay or pay to the creditor on demand in writing the amount, not being greater than the maximum amount, if any, specified in the deed, advanced or due and outstanding at the time of demand, with interest on each advance from the date when it was made until repayment thereof, or on each sum payable from the date on which it became due until payment thereof, and at the rate stated payable on the dates specified, together with all expenses for which the debtor is liable by virtue of the deed or of this Part of this Act.

(2) The clause of warrandice in the forms of standard security contained in Schedule 2 to this Act expressed in any standard security shall, unless specially qualified, import absolute warrandice as regards the [land or real right] in land over which the security is granted and the title deeds thereof, and warrandice from fact and deed as regards the rents thereof.

(3) The clause relating to consent to registration for execution contained in Form A of Schedule 2 to this Act expressed in any standard security shall, unless specially qualified, import a consent to registration in the Books of Council and Session, or, as the case may be, in the books of the appropriate sheriff court, for execution.

(4) The forms of standard security contained in Schedule 2 to this Act shall, unless specially qualified, import an assignation to the creditor of the title deeds, including searches, and all conveyances not duly [registered or] recorded, affecting the security subjects or any part thereof, with power to the creditor in the event of a sale under the powers conferred by the security, but subject to the rights of any person holding prior rights to possession of those title deeds, to deliver them, so far as in the creditor's possession, to the purchaser, and to assign to the purchaser any right he may possess to have the title deeds made forthcoming.

11 Effect of [registered or] recorded standard security, and incorporation of standard conditions

(1) Where a standard security is duly [registered or] recorded, it shall operate

to vest [in the grantee a real right in security] for the performance of the contract to which the security relates.

(2)   Subject to the provisions of this Part of this Act, the conditions set out in Schedule 3 to this Act, either as so set out or with such variations as have been agreed by the parties in the exercise of the powers conferred by the said Part (which conditions are hereinafter in this Act referred to as 'the standard conditions'), shall regulate every standard security.

(3)   Subject to the provisions of this Part of this Act, the creditor and debtor in a standard security may vary any of the standard conditions, other than [standard condition 11 (procedure on redemption) and] the provisions of Schedule 3 to this Act relating to the powers of sale [. . .] and foreclosure and to the exercise of those powers, but no condition capable of being varied shall be varied in a manner inconsistent with any condition which may not be varied by virtue of this subsection.

(4)   In this Part of this Act—

(a)   any reference to a variation of the standard conditions shall include a reference to the inclusion of an additional condition and to the exclusion of a standard condition;

(b)   any purported variation of a standard condition which contravenes the provisions of subsection (3) of this section shall be void and unenforceable.

12   Standard security may be granted by person uninfeft

[(1)   Notwithstanding any rule of law, a standard security may be granted over land or a real right in land by a person whose title thereto has not been completed by being duly registered or recorded.]

[(1A)   If the deed expressing the security is to be recorded in the Register of Sasines, the grantor must, in that deed, deduce his title to the land or real right from the person who appears in the Register of Sasines as having the last recorded title thereto.]

(2)   A deduction of title in a deed for the purposes of the foregoing subsection shall be expressed in the form prescribed by Note 2 or 3 of Schedule 2 to this Act, and on [a deed expressing the security being registered or] recorded as aforesaid the title of the grantee shall, for the purposes of the rights and obligations between the grantor and the grantee thereof and those deriving right from them, but for no other purpose, in all respects be of the same effect as if the title of the grantor of the deed to the [land or real right in land] [. . .] had been duly completed; and any references to a proprietor or to a person [having the last [registered or] recorded title] shall in this Part of this Act be construed accordingly.

(3)   There may be specified for the purposes of any deduction of title in pursuance of any provision of this Part of this Act any writing which it is competent to specify as a title, midcouple, or link in title for the purposes of section 5 of the Conveyancing (Scotland) Act 1924 (deduction of title).

13   Ranking of standard securities

(1)   Where the creditor in a standard security duly [registered or] recorded has received notice of the creation of a subsequent security over the same [land or real right in land or over any part thereof, or of the subsequent assignation or conveyance of that land or real right,] in whole or in part, being a security, assignation or conveyance so [registered or] recorded, the preference in ranking of the security of that creditor shall be restricted to security for

[(a)   the present debt incurred (whenever payable); and

(b)   any future debt which, under the contract to which the security relates, he is required to allow the debtor in the security to incur,]

and interest present or future due thereon (including any such interest which has accrued or may accrue) and for any expenses or outlays (including interest thereon) which may be, or may have been, reasonably incurred in the exercise of any power conferred on any creditor by the deed expressing the existing security.

(2)   For the purposes of the foregoing subsection—

(a)   a creditor in an existing standard security duly [registered or] recorded shall not be held to have had any notice referred to in that subsection, by reason only of the subsequent [registration or] recording of the relevant deed in the [the Land Register of Scotland or] the Register of Sasines;

(b)   any assignation, conveyance or vesting in favour of or in any other person of the interest of the debtor in the security subjects or in any part thereof resulting from any judicial decree, or otherwise by operation of law, shall constitute sufficient notice thereof to the creditor.

(3)   Nothing in the foregoing provisions of this section shall affect—

(a)   any preference in ranking enjoyed by the Crown; and

(b)   any powers of the creditor and debtor in any heritable security to regulate the preference to be enjoyed by creditors in such manner as they may think fit.

[(4)   An agreement as to the ranking among themselves of two or more standard securities which are granted over the same land or the same real right in land may be registered in the Land Register of Scotland.]

14   Assignation of standard security

(1)   Any standard security duly [registered or] recorded may be transferred, in whole or in part, by the creditor by an assignation in conformity with Form A or B of Schedule 4 to this Act, and upon such an assignation being duly [registered or] recorded, the security, or, as the case may be, part thereof, shall be vested in the assignee as effectually as if the security or the part had been granted in his favour.

(2)   An assignation of a standard security shall, except so far as otherwise therein stated, be deemed to convey to the grantee all rights competent to the grantor to the writs, and shall have the effect *inter alia* of vesting in the assignee—

(a)   the full benefit of all corroborative or substitutional obligations for the debt, or any part thereof, whether those obligations are contained in any deed or arise by operation of law or otherwise,

(b)   the right to recover payment from the debtor of all expenses properly incurred by the creditor in connection with the security, and

(c)   the entitlement to the benefit of any notices served and of all procedure instituted by the creditor in respect of the security to the effect that the grantee may proceed as if he had originally served or instituted such notices or procedure.

15   Restriction of standard security

(1)   The security constituted by any standard security duly [registered or] recorded may be restricted, as regards any part of the [land or real right] in land burdened by the security, by a deed of restriction in conformity with Form C of Schedule 4 to this Act, and, upon that deed being duly [registered or] recorded, the security shall be restricted [to the land or real right contained in the standard security other than the part of that land or real right disburdened by the deed; and the land or real right] thereby disburdened shall be released from the security wholly or to the extent specified in the deed.

(2)   A partial discharge and deed of restriction of a standard security, which has been duly [registered or] recorded, may be combined in one deed, which shall be in conformity with Form D of the said Schedule 4.

16   Variation of standard security

(1)   Any alteration in the provisions (including any standard condition) of a standard security duly [registered or] recorded, other than an alteration which may appropriately be effected by an assignation, discharge or restriction of that

standard security, or an alteration which involves an addition to, or an extension of, the [land or real right] in land mentioned therein, may be effected by a variation endorsed on the standard security in conformity with Form E of Schedule 4 to this Act, or by a variation contained in a separate deed in a form appropriate for that purpose, duly [registered or] recorded in either case.

(2)　Where a standard security has been duly [registered or] recorded, but the personal obligation or any other provision (including any standard condition) relating to the security has been created or specified in a deed which has not been so [registered or] recorded, nothing contained in this section shall prevent any alteration in that personal obligation or provision, other than an alteration which may be appropriately effected by an assignation, discharge or restriction of the standard security, or an alteration which involves an addition to, or an extension of, the [land or real right] in land mentioned therein, by a variation contained in any form of deed appropriate for that purpose, and such a variation shall not require to be [registered in the Land Register of Scotland or] recorded in the Register of Sasines.

(3)　[. . .]

(4)　Any variation effected in accordance with this section shall not prejudice any other security or right over the same [land or real right in land, or over] any part thereof, effectively constituted before the variation is [registered or] recorded, or, where the variation is effected by an [unregistered or] unrecorded deed, before that deed is executed, as the case may be.

17　Discharge of standard security

A standard security duly [registered or] recorded may be discharged, and the [land or real right] in land burdened by that security may be disburdened thereof, in whole or in part, by a discharge in conformity with Form F of Schedule 4 to this Act, duly [registered or] recorded.

18　Redemption of standard security

(1)　[Subject to the provisions of subsection (1A) of this section,] the debtor in a standard security or, where the debtor is not the proprietor, the proprietor of the security subjects shall be entitled to redeem the security [on giving two months' notice of his intention so to do, and] in conformity with the terms of standard condition 11 and the appropriate Forms of Schedule 5 to this Act.

[(1A)　Without prejudice to section 11 of the Land Tenure Reform (Scotland) Act 1974 the provisions of the foregoing subsection shall be subject to any agreement to the contrary, but any right to redeem the security shall be exercisable in conformity with the terms and Forms referred to in that subsection.]

(2)　Where owing to the death or absence of the creditor, or to any other cause, the debtor in a standard security or, as the case may be, the proprietor of the security subjects [(being in either case a person entitled to redeem the security)] is unable to obtain a discharge under the [foregoing provisions of this section], he may—

(a)　where the security was granted in respect of any obligation to repay or pay money, consign in any bank in Scotland, incorporated by or under Act of Parliament or by Royal Charter, the whole amount due to the creditor on redemption, other than any unascertained expenses of the creditor, for the person appearing to have the best right thereto, and

(b)　in any other case, apply to the court for declarator that the whole obligations under the contract to which the security relates have been performed.

(3)　On consignation, or on the court granting declarator as aforesaid, a certificate to that effect may be expede by a solicitor in the appropriate form prescribed by Form D of Schedule 5 to this Act, which on being duly [registered or] recorded shall disburden the [land or real right] in land, to which the standard security relates, of that security.

(4)　For the purposes of this section, 'whole amount due' means the debt to which the security relates, so far as outstanding, and any other sums due thereunder by way of interest or otherwise.

19   Calling-up of standard security

(1)   Where a creditor in a standard security intends to require discharge of the debt thereby secured and, failing that discharge, to exercise any power conferred by the security to sell any subjects of the security or any other power which he may appropriately exercise on the default of the debtor within the meaning of standard condition 9(1)(a), he shall serve a notice calling-up the security in conformity with Form A of Schedule 6 to this Act (hereinafter in this Act referred to as a 'calling-up notice'), in accordance with the following provisions of this section.

(2)   Subject to the following provisions of this section, a calling-up notice shall be served on the person [having the last [registered or] recorded title to] the security subjects and appearing [in the Land Register of Scotland or] on the record [of the Register of Sasines] as the proprietor, and should the proprietor of those subjects, or any part thereof, be dead then on his representative or the person entitled to the subjects in terms of the last [registered or] recorded title thereto, notwithstanding any alteration of the succession not appearing in the [Land Register of Scotland or] Register of Sasines.

(3)   Where the person [having the last [registered or] recorded title to] the security subjects was an incorporated company which has been removed from the Register of Companies, or a person deceased who has left no representatives, a calling-up notice shall be served on the Lord Advocate and, where the estates of the person [having the last [registered or] recorded title have] been sequestrated under the Bankruptcy (Scotland) Act [2016], the notice shall be served on the trustee in the sequestration (unless such trustee has been discharged) as well as on the bankrupt.

(4)   If the proprietor be a body of trustees, it shall be sufficient if the notice is served on a majority of the trustees [having title to] the security subjects.

(5)   It shall be an obligation on the creditor to serve a copy of the calling-up notice on any other person against whom he wishes to preserve any right of recourse in respect of the debt.

(6)   For the purposes of the foregoing provisions of this section, the service of a calling-up notice may be made by delivery to the person on whom it is desired to be served or the notice may be sent by registered post or by the recorded delivery service to him at his last known address, or, in the case of the Lord Advocate, at the Crown Office, Edinburgh, and an acknowledgment, signed by the person on whom service has been made, in conformity with Form C of Schedule 6 to this Act, or, as the case may be, a certificate in conformity with Form D of that Schedule, accompanied by the postal receipt shall be sufficient evidence of the service of that notice; and if the address of the person on whom the notice is desired to be served is not known, or if it is not known whether that person is still alive, or if the packet containing a calling-up notice is returned to the creditor with an intimation that it could not be delivered, that notice shall be sent to the Extractor of the Court of Session, and shall be equivalent to the service of a calling-up notice on the person on whom it is desired to be served.

(7)   For the purposes of the last foregoing subsection, an acknowledgment of receipt by the said Extractor on a copy of a calling-up notice shall be sufficient evidence of the receipt by him of that notice.

(8)   A calling-up notice served by post shall be held to have been served on the next day after the day of posting.

(9)   Where a creditor in a standard security has indicated in a calling-up notice that any sum and any interest thereon due under the contract may be subject to adjustment in amount, he shall, if the person on whom notice has been served so requests, furnish the debtor with a statement of the amount as finally determined

within a period of one month from the date of service of the calling-up notice, and a failure by the creditor to comply with the provisions of this subsection shall cause the calling-up notice to be of no effect.

(10) The period of notice mentioned in the calling-up notice may be effectively dispensed with or shortened by the person on whom it is served, with the consent of the creditors, if any, holding securities *pari passu* with, or postponed to, the security held by the creditor serving the calling-up notice, by a minute written or endorsed upon the said notice, or a copy thereof, in conformity with Form C of Schedule 6 to this Act.

[Provided, that without prejudice to the foregoing generality, if the standard security is over a matrimonial home as defined in section 22 of the Matrimonial Homes (Family Protection) (Scotland) Act 1981, the spouse on whom the callingup notice has been served may not dispense with or shorten the said period without the consent in writing of the other spouse.]

[(10A) Subsection (10B) below applies where the calling-up notice relates to a standard security over land or a real right in land used to any extent for residential purposes.

(10B) The period of notice mentioned in the calling-up notice may be shortened under subsection (10) above only with the consent in writing (in addition to any other consent required by that subsection) of—

(a) any person entitled to make an application under section 24B(1) of this Act as an entitled resident falling within paragraph (d), (e) or (f) of section 24C(1), and

(b) where the debtor in the standard security is not the proprietor—
(i) the debtor, and
(ii) if the standard security is over a matrimonial home or a family home (within the definitions in section 23A(3)), the debtor's spouse or civil partner.]

(11) [Subject to subsection (12) below,] a calling-up notice shall cease to have effect for the purpose of a sale in the exercise of any power conferred by the security on the expiration of a period of five years, which period shall run—

(a) in the case where the subjects of the security, or any part thereof, have not been offered for or exposed to sale, from the date of the notice,

(b) in the case where there has been such an offer or exposure, from the date of the last offer or exposure.

[(12) A calling-up notice calling up a standard security over land or a real right in land used to any extent for residential purposes ceases to have effect on the expiration of a period of 5 years from the date of the notice.]

[19A   Notice to occupier of calling-up

(1) Where a creditor in a standard security over [land or a real right] in land used to any extent for residential purposes serves a calling-up notice, he shall serve a notice in conformity with Form BB (notice to occupier) of Schedule 6 to this Act together with a copy of the calling-up notice.

(2) Notices under subsection (1) above shall be sent by recorded delivery letter addressed to 'The Occupier' at the security subjects.

(3) If a creditor fails to comply with subsections (1) and (2) above, the callingup notice shall be of no effect.]

[19B   Notice to local authority of calling-up

(1) Where a creditor in a standard security over an interest in land used to any extent for residential purposes serves a calling-up notice, the creditor shall give notice of that fact to the local authority in whose area the security subjects are situated, unless the creditor is that local authority.

(2) Notice under subsection (1) shall be given in the form and manner prescribed under section 11(3) of the Homelessness etc (Scotland) Act 2003 (asp 10).]

20   Exercise of rights of creditor on default of debtor in complying with a calling-up notice

(1)   Where the debtor in a standard security is in default within the meaning of standard condition 9(1)(a), the creditor may exercise such of his rights under the security as he may consider appropriate, and any such right shall be in addition to and not in derogation from any other remedy arising from the contract to which the security relates or from any right conferred by any enactment or by any rule of law on the creditor in a heritable security.

(2)   Where the debtor is in default as aforesaid, the creditor shall have the right to sell the security subjects, or any part thereof, in accordance with the provisions of this Part of this Act.

[(2A)   Where the standard security is over land or a real right in land used to any extent for residential purposes, the creditor is entitled to exercise the rights specified in standard condition 10(2) and (3)(and mentioned in subsections (1) and (2) above) only—

   (a)   where the conditions in section 23A of this Act are satisfied, or

   (b)   with the warrant of the court, granted on an application under section 24 of this Act.]

(3)   A creditor in a standard security who is in lawful possession of the security subjects may let the security subjects, or any part thereof, for any period not exceeding seven years, or may make application to the court for warrant to let those subjects, or any part thereof, for a period exceeding seven years, and the application shall state the proposed tenant, and the duration and conditions of the proposed lease, and shall be served on the proprietor of the subjects and on any other heritable creditor having interest as such a creditor in the subjects.

(4)   The court, on such an application as aforesaid and after such inquiry and such further intimation of the application as it may think fit, may grant the application as submitted, or subject to such variation as it may consider reasonable in all the circumstances of the case, or may refuse the application.

(5)   There shall be deemed to be assigned to a creditor who is in lawful possession of the security subjects all rights and obligations of the proprietor relating to—

   (a)   leases, or any permission or right of occupancy, granted in respect of those subjects or any part thereof, and

   (b)   the management and maintenance of the subjects and the effecting of any reconstruction, alteration or improvement reasonably required for the purpose of maintaining the market value of the subjects.

21   Notice of default

(1)   Where the debtor in a standard security is in default within the meaning of standard condition 9(1)(b), and the default is remediable, the creditor may, without prejudice to any other powers he may have by virtue of this Act or otherwise, proceed in accordance with the provisions of this section to call on the debtor and on the proprietor, where he is not the debtor, to purge the default.

(2)   For the aforesaid purpose the creditor may serve on the debtor and, as the case may be, on the proprietor a notice in conformity with Form B of Schedule 6 to this Act (hereinafter in this Act referred to as a 'notice of default') which shall be served in the like manner and with the like requirements as to proof of service as a calling-up notice.

[(2A)   Sections 19A and 19B of this Act apply where the creditor serves a notice of default as they apply where he serves a calling-up notice.]

(3)   For the purpose of dispensing with, or shortening, the period of notice mentioned in a notice of default, [subsections (10) and (10B) of section 19 of this Act shall apply as they apply] in relation to a calling-up notice.

(4)   Notwithstanding the failure to comply with any requirement contained in the notice, a notice of default shall cease to be authority for the exercise of the

rights mentioned in section 23(2) of this Act on the expiration of a period of five years from the date of the notice.

22   Objections to notice of default

(1)   Where a person on whom a notice of default has been served considers himself aggrieved by any requirement of that notice he may, within a period of fourteen days of the service of the notice, object to the notice by way of application to the court; and the applicant shall, not later than the lodging of that application, serve a copy of his application on the creditor, and on any other party on whom the notice has been served by the creditor.

(2)   On any such application the court, after hearing the parties and making such inquiry as it may think fit, may order the notice appealed against to be set aside, in whole or in part, or otherwise to be varied, or to be upheld.

(3)   The respondent in any such application may make a counter-application craving for any of the remedies conferred on him by this Act or by any other enactment relating to heritable securities, and the court may grant any such remedy as aforesaid as it may think proper.

(4)   For the purposes of such a counter-application as aforesaid, a certificate which conforms with the requirements of Schedule 7 to this Act may be lodged in court by the creditor, and that certificate shall be *prima facie* evidence of the facts directed by the said Schedule to be contained therein.

23   Rights and duties of parties after service of notice of default to which objection is not taken, or where the notice is not set aside

(1)   Where a person does not object to a notice of default in accordance with the provisions of the last foregoing section, or where he has so objected and the notice has been upheld or varied under that section, it shall be his duty to comply with any requirement, due to be performed or fulfilled by him, contained in the notice or, as the case may be, in the notice as so varied.

(2)   Subject to the provisions of section 21(4) of this Act [and subsection (4) below], where a person fails to comply as aforesaid, the creditor, subject to the next following subsection, may proceed to exercise such of his rights on default under standard condition 10(2), (6) and (7) as he may consider appropriate.

(3)   At any time after the expiry of the period stated in a notice of default, or in a notice varied as aforesaid, but before the conclusion of any enforceable contract to sell the security subjects, or any part thereof, by virtue of the last foregoing subsection , the debtor or proprietor [(being in either case a person entitled to redeem the security)] may, subject to any agreement to the contrary, redeem the security without the necessity of observance of any requirement as to notice.

[(4)   Where the standard security is over land or a real right in land used to any extent for residential purposes—

(a)   the creditor is entitled to exercise the right specified in standard condition 10(2) only—

(i)   where the conditions in section 23A of this Act are satisfied, or

(ii)   with the warrant of the court, granted on an application under section 24 of this Act, and

(b)   subsection (3) above has effect as if the reference to the last foregoing subsection were a reference to section 24 of this Act.]

[23A   Voluntary surrender of residential property following calling-up notice or notice of default

(1)   The conditions referred to in sections 20(2A)(a) and 23(4)(a)(i) are that—

(a)   the security subjects are unoccupied; and

(b)   each of the persons specified in subsection (2) below has, in writing—

(i)   certified that that person does not occupy the security subjects and is not aware of the security subjects being occupied by any other person;

(ii)   consented to the exercise by the creditor of the creditor's rights on default; and

(iii)   certified that the consent is given freely and without coercion of any kind.

(2)   Those persons are—

(a)   the debtor;

(b)   the proprietor of the security subjects (where the proprietor is not the debtor);

(c)   the non-entitled spouse of the debtor or the proprietor of security subjects which are (in whole or in part) a matrimonial home;

(d)   the non-entitled civil partner of the debtor or the proprietor of security subjects which are (in whole or in part) a family home; and

(e)   a person who has occupancy rights in the security subjects by virtue of an order under section 18(1) (occupancy rights of cohabiting couples) of the Matrimonial Homes (Family Protection) (Scotland) Act 1981.

(3)   In this section—

'family home' has the meaning given by section 135(1) of the Civil Partnership Act 2004;

'matrimonial home' has the meaning given by section 22 of the Matrimonial Homes (Family Protection) (Scotland) Act 1981;

'non-entitled civil partner' has the same meaning as 'non-entitled partner' in section 101(1) of the Civil Partnership Act 2004;

'non-entitled spouse' has the meaning given by section 1 of the Matrimonial Homes (Family Protection) (Scotland) Act 1981.]

24   Application by creditor to court for remedies on default

(1)   Without prejudice to his proceeding by way of notice of default in respect of a default within the meaning of standard condition 9(1)(b), a creditor in a standard security, where the debtor is in default within the meaning of that standard condition or standard condition 9(1)(c), may apply to the court for warrant to exercise any of the remedies which he is entitled to exercise on a default within the meaning of standard condition 9(1)(a).

[(1A)   Subsection (1) above does not apply in relation to a creditor in a standard security over land or a real right in land used to any extent for residential purposes.

(1B)   A creditor in a standard security of that kind may, where the debtor is in default within the meaning of paragraph (a), (b) or (c) of standard condition 9(1), apply to the court for warrant to exercise any of the remedies which the creditor is entitled to exercise on a default within the meaning of standard condition 9(1)(a).

(1C)   Before making an application under subsection (1B) above the creditor must comply with the pre-action requirements imposed by section 24A of this Act. (1D) An application under subsection (1B) above is to be made by summary application (regardless of whether it includes a crave for any other remedy).]

[(1E)   *Subsection (1D) is subject to section 72(3) of the Courts Reform (Scotland) Act 2014 (which provides for certain proceedings for the recovery of heritable property to be subject to simple procedure).]*

(2)   For the purposes of [an application under subsection (1) or (1B)] in respect of a default within the meaning of standard condition 9(1)(b), a certificate which conforms with the requirements of Schedule 7 to this Act may be lodged in court by the creditor, and that certificate shall be *prima facie* evidence of the facts directed by the said Schedule to be contained therein.

[(3)   Where the creditor applies to the court under [subsection (1B)] above, he shall, [. . .]

(a)   serve on the debtor and (where the proprietor is not the debtor) or the proprietor a notice in conformity with Form E of Schedule 6 to this Act,

(b) serve on the occupier of the security subjects a notice in conformity with Form F of that Schedule, [and

(c) give notice of the application to the local authority in whose area the security subjects are situated, unless the creditor is that local authority].

(4) Notices under subsection [(3)(a) or (b)] above shall be sent by recorded delivery letter addressed—

(a) in the case of a notice under subsection (3)(a), to the debtor or, as the case may be, the proprietor at his last known address,

(b) in the case of a notice under subsection (3)(b) to 'The Occupier' at the security subjects.

[(4A) Notice under subsection (3)(c) above shall be given in the form and manner prescribed under section 11(3) of the Homelessness etc (Scotland) Act 2003 (asp 10).]

[(5) The court may, on an application under subsection (1B) above, continue the proceedings or make any other order that it thinks fit; but it may not grant the application unless it is satisfied that—

(a) the creditor has complied with subsection (1C) above; and

(b) it is reasonable in the circumstances of the case to do so.

(6) In considering an application under subsection (1B) above where the debtor appears or is represented, the court is to have regard in particular to the matters set out in subsection (7) below.

(7) Those matters are—

(a) the nature of and reasons for the default;

(b) the ability of the debtor to fulfil within a reasonable time the obligations under the standard security in respect of which the debtor is in default;

(c) any action taken by the creditor to assist the debtor to fulfil those obligations;

(d) where appropriate, participation by the debtor in a debt payment programme approved under Part 1 of the Debt Arrangement and Attachment (Scotland) Act 2002; and

(e) the ability of the debtor and any other person residing at the security subjects to secure reasonable alternative accommodation.

(8) Subsections (5) and (6) above do not affect—

(a) any power that the court may have; or

(b) any rights that the debtor may have, by virtue of any other enactment or rule of law.

(9) Where—

(a) the default in respect of which an application is made under subsection (1B) above is a default within the meaning of paragraph (a) or (b) of standard condition 9(1); and

(b) before a decree is granted on the application, the obligations under the standard security in respect of which the debtor is in default are fulfilled,

the standard security has effect as if the default had not occurred.]

[(10) For the avoidance of doubt, a decree granted on an application under subsection (1B) above is not an order for possession of a house let on an assured tenancy (within the meaning of Part II of the Housing (Scotland) Act 1988 (c 43)).]

[24A   Section 24(1B) proceedings: pre-action requirements

(1) The pre-action requirements referred to in section 24(1C) of this Act are set out in subsections (2) to (6) below.

(2) The creditor must provide the debtor with clear information about—

(a) the terms of the standard security;

(b) the amount due to the creditor under the standard security, including any arrears and any charges in respect of late payment or redemption; and

(c) any other obligation under the standard security in respect of which the debtor is in default.

(3)   The creditor must make reasonable efforts to agree with the debtor proposals in respect of future payments to the creditor under the standard security and the fulfilment of any other obligation under the standard security in respect of which the debtor is in default.

(4)   The creditor must not make an application under section 24(1B) of this Act if the debtor is taking steps which are likely to result in—

(a)   the payment to the creditor within a reasonable time of any arrears, or the whole amount, due to the creditor under the standard security; and

(b)   fulfilment by the debtor within a reasonable time of any other obligation under the standard security in respect of which the debtor is in default.

(5)   The creditor must provide the debtor with information about sources of advice and assistance in relation to management of debt.

(6)   The creditor must encourage the debtor to contact the local authority in whose area the security subjects are situated.

(7)   In complying with the pre-action requirements the creditor must have regard to any guidance issued by the Scottish Ministers.

(8)   The Scottish Ministers may by order made by statutory instrument make further provision about the pre-action requirements, including provision—

(a)   specifying particular steps to be taken, or not to be taken, by a creditor in complying with any requirement;

(b)   modifying or removing any requirement;

(c)   making different provision for different circumstances.

(9)   A statutory instrument containing an order under subsection (8) above is not to be made unless a draft of the instrument has been laid before, and approved by resolution of, the Scottish Parliament.]

[24B   Section 24(1B) applications: application to court by entitled residents

(1)   An entitled resident may, in proceedings on an application under section 24(1B) of this Act, apply to the court to continue the proceedings or make any other order that the court thinks fit, despite not being called as a defender in the application.

(2)   In determining an application under subsection (1) above the court is to have regard in particular to the matters set out in subsection (7) of section 24, reading the first reference to the debtor in paragraph (b) as including a reference to the entitled resident.

(3)   Subsection (2) above does not affect—

(a)   any power that the court may have; or

(b)   any rights that an entitled resident may have, under any other enactment or rule of law.]

[24C   Entitled residents: definition

(1)   For the purposes of sections 24B, 24D and 24E, an entitled resident is a person whose sole or main residence is the security subjects (in whole or in part) and who is—

(a)   the proprietor of the security subjects (where the proprietor is not the debtor in the standard security);

(b)   the non-entitled spouse of the debtor or the proprietor of security subjects which are (in whole or in part) a matrimonial home;

(c)   the non-entitled civil partner of the debtor or the proprietor of security subjects which are (in whole or in part) a family home;

(d)   a person living together with the debtor or the proprietor as husband and wife;

(e)   a person living together with the debtor or the proprietor in a relationship which has the characteristics of the relationship between civil partners;

(f)   a person who lived together with the debtor or the proprietor in a relationship described in paragraph (d) or (e) if—

    (i)   the security subjects (in whole or in part) are not the sole or main residence of the debtor or the proprietor;

    (ii)   the person lived together with the debtor or the proprietor throughout the period of 6 months ending with the date on which the security subjects ceased to be the sole or main residence of the debtor or the proprietor; and

    (iii)   the security subjects (in whole or in part) are the sole or main residence of a child aged under 16 who is a child of both parties in that relationship.

(2)   In this section—

'child' includes a stepchild and any person brought up, or treated, by both parties to the relationship as their child;

'family home' has the meaning given by section 135(1) of the Civil Partnership Act 2004;

'matrimonial home' has the meaning given by section 22 of the Matrimonial Homes (Family Protection) (Scotland) Act 1981;

'non-entitled civil partner' has the same meaning as 'non-entitled partner' in section 101(1) of the Civil Partnership Act 2004;

'non-entitled spouse' has the meaning given by section 1 of the Matrimonial Homes (Family Protection) (Scotland) Act 1981.]

[24D   Section 24(1B) proceedings: recall of decree

(1)   A person mentioned in subsection (2) below may apply to the court for recall of a decree granted on an application under section 24(1B) of this Act.

(2)   Those persons are—

    (a)   the creditor;

    (b)   the debtor, but only if the debtor did not appear and was not represented in the proceedings on the application under section 24(1B);

    (c)   an entitled resident, but only if the entitled resident did not make an application under section 24B(1) in the proceedings.

(3)   An application under subsection (1) may be made at any time before the decree has been fully implemented.

(4)   An application by any person under subsection (1) above is not competent if an application under that subsection has already been made by that person in relation to the application under section 24(1B).

(5)   An applicant under subsection (1) above must give notice of the application to—

    (a)   the creditor (unless the applicant is the creditor);

    (b)   the debtor (unless the applicant is the debtor);

    (c)   every entitled resident (or, if the applicant is an entitled resident, every other entitled resident).]

[24E   Lay representation in section 24(1B) proceedings etc

(1)   In proceedings under sections 24(1B) and 24D(1) of this Act, the debtor and any entitled resident may be represented by an approved lay representative except in prescribed circumstances.

(2)   An approved lay representative must throughout the proceedings satisfy the sheriff that the representative is a suitable person to represent the debtor or entitled resident and is authorised by the debtor or entitled resident to do so.

(3)   References in this section to an approved lay representative are to an individual (other than an advocate or solicitor) approved for the purposes of this section by a person or body prescribed, or of a description prescribed, by the Scottish Ministers by order made by statutory instrument.

(4)   An order under subsection (3) above may—

    (a)   prescribe persons or bodies, or descriptions of persons or bodies, for the purposes of that subsection;

    (b)   make provision about the procedure for, and form and manner of—

        (i)   approval,

(ii)   withdrawal of approval,
of an individual for the purposes of this section;
   (c)   make provision requiring a prescribed person or body, or a person or body of a prescribed description, to provide information to the Scottish Ministers about approvals and withdrawals of approval;
   (d)   prescribe circumstances in which an approved lay representative may not represent a debtor or entitled resident.
(5)   Before making an order under subsection (3) above the Scottish Ministers must consult the Lord President of the Court of Session.
(6)   A statutory instrument containing an order under subsection (3) above is subject to annulment in pursuance of a resolution of the Scottish Parliament.]

25   Exercise of power of sale
A creditor in a standard security having right to sell the security subjects may [, subject to sections 37(5)(e) or 40(1) of the Land Reform (Scotland) Act 2003 (asp 2) (prohibition of transfer of land registered under that Act except in accordance with its provisions),] exercise that right either by private bargain or by exposure to sale, and in either event it shall be the duty of the creditor to advertise the sale and to take all reasonable steps to ensure that the price at which all or any of the subjects are sold is the best that can be reasonably obtained.

26   Disposition by creditor on sale
(1)   Where a creditor in a standard security has effected a sale of the security subjects, or any part thereof, and grants to the purchaser or his nominee a disposition of the subjects sold thereby, which bears to be in implement of the sale, then, on that disposition being duly [registered or] recorded, those subjects shall be disburdened of the standard security and of all other heritable securities and diligences ranking *pari passu* with, or postponed to, that security.
(2)   Where on a sale as aforesaid the security subjects remain subject to a prior security, the [registration or] recording of a disposition under the foregoing subsection shall not affect the rights of the creditor in that security, but the creditor who has effected the sale shall have the like right as the debtor to redeem the security.

27   Application of proceeds of sale
(1)   The money which is received by the creditor in a standard security, arising from any sale by him of the security subjects, shall be held by him in trust to be applied by him in accordance with the following order of priority—
   (a)   first, in payment of any expenses properly incurred by him in connection with the sale, or any attempted sale;
   (b)   secondly, in payment of the whole amount due under any prior security to which the sale is not made subject;
   (c)   thirdly, in payment of the whole amount due under the standard security, and in payment, in due proportion, of the whole amount due under a security, if any, ranking *pari passu* with his own security, which has been duly [registered or] recorded;
   (d)   fourthly, in payment of any amounts due under any securities with a ranking postponed to that of his own security, according to their ranking,
and any residue of the money so received shall be paid to the person entitled to the security subjects at the time of sale, or to any person authorised to give receipts for the proceeds of the sale thereof.
(2)   Where owing to the death or absence of any other creditor, or to any other cause, a creditor is unable to obtain a receipt or discharge for any payment he is required to make under the provisions of the foregoing subsection, he may, without prejudice to his liability to account therefor, consign the amount due (so far as ascertainable) in the sheriff court for the person appearing to have the best right thereto; and where consignation is so made, the creditor shall lodge in court a statement of the amount consigned.

(3)   A consignation made in pursuance of the last foregoing subsection shall operate as a discharge of the payment of the amount due, and a certificate under the hand of the sheriff clerk shall be sufficient evidence thereof.

28   Foreclosure

(1)   Where the creditor in a standard security has exposed the security subjects to sale at a price not exceeding the amount due under the security and under any security ranking prior to, or *pari passu* with, the security, and has failed to find a purchaser, or where, having so failed, he has succeeded in selling only a part of the subjects at a price which is less than the amount due as aforesaid, he may, on the expiration of a period of two months from the date of the first exposure to sale, apply to the court for a decree of foreclosure.

(2)   In any application under the last foregoing subsection the creditor shall lodge a statement setting out the whole amount due under the security but, without prejudice to the right of the debtor or of the proprietor to challenge that statement, it shall be sufficient for the purposes of the application for the creditor to establish to the satisfaction of the court that the amount so stated is not less than the price at which the security subjects have been exposed to sale or sold, where part of the subjects has been sold as aforesaid.

(3)   Any application under subsection (1) of this section shall be served on the debtor in the standard security, the proprietor of the security subjects (if he is a person other than the debtor) and the creditor in any other heritable security affecting the security subjects as disclosed by a search of the Register of Sasines for a period of twenty years immediately preceding the last date to which the appropriate Minute Book of the said Register has been completed at the time when the application is made [or by an examination of the title sheet of the security subjects in the Land Register of Scotland].

(4)   The court may order such intimation and inquiry as it thinks fit and may in its discretion allow the debtor or the proprietor of the security subjects a period not exceeding three months in which to pay the whole amount due under the security and, subject to any such allowance, may—

(a)   appoint the security subjects or the unsold part thereof to be re-exposed to sale at a price to be fixed by the court, in which event the creditor in the security may bid and purchase at the sale, or

(b)   grant a decree of foreclosure in conformity with the provisions of the next following subsection.

(5)   A decree of foreclosure shall contain a declaration that, on the extract of the decree being duly [registered or] recorded, [any right to redeem the security] has been extinguished and that the creditor has right to the security subjects or the unsold part thereof, described by means of a particular description or by reference to a description thereof as in Schedule D to the Conveyancing (Scotland) Act 1924 or in Schedule G to the Titles to Land Consolidation (Scotland) Act 1868, including a reference to any conditions or clauses affecting the subjects or the unsold part thereof [or in accordance with [the Land Registration etc (Scotland) Act 2012 (asp 5)]], at the price at which the said subjects were last exposed to sale under deduction of the price received for any part thereof sold, and shall also contain a warrant [for registering the extract of the decree in the Land Register of Scotland or] for recording the extract of the decree in the Register of Sasines.

(6)   Upon an extract of the decree of foreclosure being duly [registered or] recorded, the following provisions of this subsection shall have effect in relation to the security subjects to which the decree relates—

(a)   [any right to redeem the security] shall be extinguished, and the creditor shall have right to, and be vested in, the subjects as if he had received an irredeemable disposition thereof duly [registered or] recorded from the proprietor of the subjects at the date [of the registration or] of the recording of the extract of the decree;

(b) the subjects shall be disburdened of the standard security and all securities and diligences postponed thereto;

(c) the creditor who has obtained the decree shall have the like right as the debtor to redeem any security prior to, or *pari passu* with, his own security.

(7) Notwithstanding the due [registration or] recording of an extract of a decree of foreclosure, any personal obligation of the debtor under the standard security shall remain in full force and effect so far as not extinguished by the price at which the security subjects have been acquired and the price for which any part thereof has been sold.

(8) Where the security subjects or any part thereof have been acquired by a creditor in the security by virtue of a decree of foreclosure under the provisions of this section, the title thereto of the creditor shall not be challengeable on the ground of any irregularity in the proceedings for foreclosure or on calling-up or default which preceded it; but nothing in the provisions of this subsection shall affect the competency of any claim for damages in respect of such proceedings against the creditor.

29 Procedure

(1) The court for the purposes of this Part of this Act, and for the operation of section 11 of the Heritable Securities (Scotland) Act 1894 (application by *pari passu* creditor to sell), in relation to a standard security, shall be the sheriff having jurisdiction over any part of the security subjects, and the sheriff shall be deemed to have such jurisdiction whatever the value of the subjects.

[. . .]

30 Interpretation of Part II

(1) In this Part of this Act, unless the context otherwise requires, the following expressions have the meanings hereby respectively assigned to them, that is to say—

'creditor' and 'debtor' shall include any successor in title, assignee or representative of a creditor or debtor;

'debt' and 'creditor' and 'debtor', in relation to a standard security, have the meanings assigned to them by section 9(8) of this Act;

['duly registered or recorded' means registered in the Land Register of Scotland or recorded in the General Register of Sasines;]

'exposure to sale' means exposure to sale by public roup, and exposed or reexposed to sale shall be construed accordingly;

'heritable security' has the meaning assigned to it by the said section 9(8); ['real right in land'] has the meaning assigned to it by the said section 9(8); ['recorded' means recorded in the Register of Sasines,]

'Register of Sasines' means the appropriate division of the General Register of Sasines;

['registered' means registered in the Land Register of Scotland,]

'the standard conditions' are the conditions (whether varied or not) referred to in section 11(2) of this Act;

'whole amount due' has the meaning assigned to it by section 18(4) of this Act.

(2) For the purpose of construing this Part of this Act in relation to the creation of a security over a registered lease and to any subsequent transactions connected with that security, the following expressions shall have the meanings hereby respectively assigned to them, that is to say—

'conveyance' or 'disposition' means assignation;

'convey' or 'dispone' means assign;

[. . .]

'proprietor' means lessee;

'security subjects' means a registered lease subject to a security.

31   Saving

Nothing in the provisions of this Part of this Act shall affect the validity of any heritable security within the meaning of this Part which has been duly recorded before the commencement of this Act, and any such security may be dealt with and shall be as capable of being enforced, as if this Part had not been passed.

32   Application of enactments

The provisions of any enactment relating to a bond and disposition or assignation in security shall apply to a standard security, except in so far as such provisions are inconsistent with the provisions of this Part of this Act, but, without prejudice to the generality of that exception, the enactments specified in Schedule 8 to this Act shall not so apply.

PART III

PROVISIONS AS TO HERITABLE SECURITIES

40   Discharge of heritable security constituted by *ex facie* absolute conveyance

(1)   Where land is held in security by virtue of a heritable security constituted by *ex facie* absolute conveyance, whether qualified by a back letter or not, a discharge by the creditor in security in conformity with Schedule 9 to this Act, either as a separate deed or as a deed endorsed on the conveyance, shall, as from the date on which that discharge is duly recorded, discharge that heritable security, disburden the land to the extent that it is the subject of the security, and vest that land in the person entitled thereto in like manner and to the like effect as if a conveyance containing a clause of warrandice from fact and deed only and all other usual and necessary clauses had been granted by the creditor to that person and duly recorded.

(2)   Nothing in the provisions of the foregoing subsection shall affect any method of granting a discharge in existence at the commencement of this Act.

41   Restriction on effect of reduction of certain discharges of securities

(1)   Where the discharge, in whole or in part, of a security over land is duly recorded, whether before or after the commencement of this Act, and that discharge bears to be granted by a person entitled so to do, the title of a person [who subsequently acquires the land or a real right in or over it] *bona fide* and for value, shall not be challengeable, after the expiration of a period of five years commencing with the date of the recording of the discharge, by reason only of the recording of an extract of a decree of reduction of the discharge, whether or not the date of that decree was before or after the date on which the acquisition [. . .] was duly recorded.

(2)   Section 46 of the Act of 1924 (which requires extract decrees of reduction of certain deeds to be recorded) shall cease to apply in relation to a decree of reduction of a discharge of a security where that discharge has been duly recorded for a period of five years or more, but the provisions of this subsection shall not preclude the recording of such a decree of reduction as provided for in the said section 46.

(3)   Nothing in the provisions of this section shall affect any rights of a creditor in a security as against the debtor therein.

(4)   The provisions of this section shall not be pleadable to any effect in any action begun, whether before or after the date of the commencement of this Act, before the expiry of a period of two years beginning with that date.

[(5)   This section shall apply to an order under section 8 of the Law Reform (Miscellaneous Provisions) (Scotland) Act 1985 rectifying a discharge as it applies to a decree of reduction of a discharge.]

42   Extension of s 13 to certain existing forms of heritable securities

Section 13 of this Act shall apply, in relation to the effect on the preference in ranking of any heritable security, constituted by *ex facie* absolute disposition or assignation, as it applies to the preference in ranking of a standard security.

43 Interpretation of Part III

(1) In this Part of this Act, unless the context otherwise requires, the following expressions have the meanings hereby respectively assigned to them, that is to say—

[. . .]

'the Act of 1924' means the Conveyancing (Scotland) Act 1924;

'land' has the meaning assigned to it by section 2(1) of the Act of 1924.

(2) For the purpose of construing this Part of this Act in relation to the creation of a security over a registered lease and to any subsequent transactions connected with that security, section 30(2) shall apply as it applies to Part II of this Act, and any reference to a security over land, however expressed, shall be construed as a reference to a registered lease subject to a security, and 'land' shall be construed accordingly.

PART IV
OTHER CONVEYANCING REFORMS

45 Status of sasine extracts

An extract, whether issued before or after the commencement of this Act, of a conveyance, deed instrument or other document bearing to have been recorded in the Register of Sasines shall be accepted for all purposes as sufficient evidence of the contents of the original so recorded and of any matter relating thereto appearing on the extract.

PART VI
GENERAL

51 Application to Crown

This Act shall, subject to any exceptions stated therein, apply to land [owned by the Crown or by] the Prince and Steward of Scotland, and to land in which there is any other interest belonging to Her Majesty in right of the Crown or to a Government department, or held on behalf of Her Majesty for the purposes of a Government department, in like manner as it applies to other land.

52 Saving amendment and repeal

(1) Any procedure, notice, advertisement, certificate or warrant instituted, given or granted, or any other thing done under any enactment amended or disapplied by this Act, shall not be invalidated by the coming into force of that amendment or disapplication, but it and any sale or other proceedings dependent thereon shall have effect as if this Act had not come into operation.

(2), (3) [*Amendments and repeals*]

53 Interpretation

(1) It shall be sufficient compliance with any provisions in this Act which require any deed, notice, certificate or procedure to be in conformity with a Form or Note, or other requirement of this Act, that that deed, notice, certificate or procedure so conforms as closely as may be, and nothing in this Act shall preclude the inclusion of any additional matter which the person granting the deed or giving or serving the notice or giving the certificate or adopting the procedure may consider relevant.

(2) In any Form prescribed by Schedules 2, 4, 5, 6 and 9 to this Act, and in any Note to those Schedules, the expression 'Register for' means the Register of Sasines appropriate for.

(3) Any reference in this Act to any other enactment is a reference thereto as

amended, and includes a reference thereto as extended or applied, by or under any other enactment, including this Act.

(4)   In this Act, except Part II, unless the context otherwise requires—

'conveyance', 'deed' and 'instrument' have the meanings assigned to them in section 3 of the Titles to Land Consolidation (Scotland) Act 1868, section 3 of the Conveyancing (Scotland) Act 1874, and section 2 of the Conveyancing (Scotland) Act 1924;

['duly registered or recorded' means registered in the Land Register of Scotland or recorded in the Register of Sasines;]

'Lands Tribunal' means the Lands Tribunal for Scotland;

[. . .]

'Register of Sasines' has the meaning assigned to it in section 2 of the Conveyancing (Scotland) Act 1924.

54   Short title, commencement and extent

(1)   This Act may be cited as the Conveyancing and Feudal Reform (Scotland) Act 1970.

(2)   This Act shall come into operation—

(a)   except as respects sections 1 to 6, section 50, sections 51 to 53 in so far as they relate to those sections, and this section, at the expiration of a period of six months beginning with the date on which it is passed,

(b)   as respects sections 1 to 6 and sections 51 to 53 in so far as they relate to those sections, on such date as the Secretary of State may by order made by statutory instrument appoint, and different days may be appointed for different provisions,

(c)   as respects section 50, sections 51 to 53 in so far as they relate thereto, and this section, on the passing of this Act;

and any reference in any provision of this Act to the commencement of this Act shall, unless otherwise provided by any such order, be construed as a reference to the date on which that provision comes into operation.

(3)   This Act shall extend to Scotland only.

SCHEDULES

[. . .]

Sections 9 and 10   SCHEDULE 2
                              FORMS OF STANDARD SECURITY

FORM A
[To be used where the personal obligation is included in the deed]

I, AB (*designation*), hereby undertake to pay to CD (*designation*), the sum of £   (*or a maximum sum of £   *) (*or all sums due and that may become due by me to the said CD in respect of ....(here specify the matter for which the under-taking is granted*)) with interest from .... (*or from the respective times of advance*) at .... per centum per annum (*or otherwise as the case may be*) (annually, *half-yearly, or otherwise as the case may be*) on ....
.. in each year commencing on ....; For which I grant a standard security in favour of the said CD over ALL and WHOLE (*here describe the security subjects as indicated in Note 1 hereto*): The standard conditions specified in Schedule 3 to the Conveyancing and Feudal Reform (Scotland) Act 1970, and any lawful varia-tion thereof operative for the time being, shall apply: And I grant warrandice: And I consent to registration for execution.

[*Testing clause* †]

FORM B

[To be used where the personal obligation is constituted in a separate instrument or instruments]

I, AB (*designation*) hereby in security of (*here specify the nature of the debt or obligation in respect of which the security is given and the instrument(s) by which it is constituted in such manner as will identify these instruments*) grant a standard security in favour of CD (*designation*) over ALL and WHOLE (*here describe the security subjects as indicated in Note 1 hereto*): The standard conditions specified in Schedule 3 to the Conveyancing and Feudal Reform (Scotland) Act 1970, and any lawful variation thereof operative for the time being, shall apply: And I grant warrandice.

[Testing clause †]

NOTES TO SCHEDULE 2

[*Note 1.*—The security subjects shall be described sufficiently to identify them; but this note is without prejudice to any additional requirement imposed as respects any register.]

Note 2.—Where the grantor has not a recorded title to the security subjects [and the deed is to be recorded in the Register of Sasines], insert after the description thereof a clause of deduction of title as follows:—*Which subjects* ([. . .] *lease* (or *tack*) or, as the case may be) *were last vested* (or *are part of the subjects last vested*) *in EF whose title thereto was recorded in the Register for* .... (or *the said Register of Sasines*) on .... (or, if the last [recorded title] has already been mentioned, say *in the said EF as aforesaid*), *and from whom I acquired right by* (here specify shortly the writ or writs by which that right was so acquired).

Note 3.—Where the grantor of a standard security [to be recorded in the Register of Sasines] has granted a conveyance *ex facie* absolute of the security subjects, or any part thereof, that conveyance shall be referred to in accordance with Note 5 to this Schedule. In any such case:—(a) where the grantor [has a recorded title to] the security subjects, no clause of deduction of title is required in the standard security, (b) where the grantor [does not have a recorded title to] the security subjects but has right thereto by virtue of an unrecorded title insert in the standard security after the description of the security subjects a clause of deduction of title as follows.—*Which subjects* (or [. . .] *lease* (or *tack*) or, as the case may be) *were formerly vested in* (or *are part of the subjects formerly vested in*) (give name of person [who last had a recorded title to] the subjects before the grantor acquired right thereto) *whose title thereto was recorded in the Register for* .... (or *the said Register of Sasines*) on .... (or if such [recorded title] has already been mentioned say *in the said* .... *as aforesaid*) *and from whom I acquired right by* (here specify shortly the writ or writs by which that right was so acquired).

Note 4.—Where it is desired to vary any of the standard conditions contained in Schedule 3 to this Act, such variations shall be effected either by an instrument or instruments other than the standard security, and any such instrument shall not require to be [registered in the Land Register of Scotland or] recorded in the Register of Sasines or by inserting in the standard security after the description of the security subjects (and after the clause of deduction of title, if any) *And I agree that the standard conditions shall be varied to the effect that* (here insert particulars of the variations desired).

(As regards future variations, see section 16 of, and Form E and Notes 5 and 6 in Schedule 4 to, this Act).

Note 5.—Where the security subjects are burdened by any other standard security or heritable security, or by any security by way of *ex facie* absolute conveyance which ranks prior to the standard security which is being granted, insert immediately before the clause of warrandice the following:— *But the security hereby granted is subject to* (here specify any deed by which such preferable rights were created and any deed modifying or altering such rights), and amend the clause of warrandice to read *And, subject as aforesaid, I grant warrandice.* Where the standard security is to rank prior or postponed to, or *pari passu* with, any other existing heritable security or any other standard security, a ranking clause may be inserted in appropriate terms immediately prior to the warrandice clause, and the warrandice clause shall, where necessary, be qualified accordingly.

Note 6.—Where a standard security is granted in Form A for a fluctuating or uncertain amount, provisions for ascertaining the amount due at any time may be inserted immediately prior to the clause of granting of the security, and the registration clause shall, where necessary, be amended accordingly.

Note 7.—In the case of a standard security for a non-monetary obligation, the forms in this Schedule shall be adapted as appropriate.

[† Note 8.—[In the case of a traditional document, subscription of it by the granter] will be sufficient for the document to be formally valid, but witnessing of it may be necessary or desirable for other purposes (see the Requirements of Writing (Scotland) Act 1995) [, which also makes provision as regards the authentication of an electronic document].]

SCHEDULE 3   Section 11

THE STANDARD CONDITIONS

Maintenance and repair

1.   It shall be an obligation on the debtor—

(a)   to maintain the security subjects in good and sufficient repair to the reasonable satisfaction of the creditor;

(b)   to permit, after seven clear days notice in writing, the creditor or his agent to enter upon the security subjects at all reasonable times to examine the condition thereof;

(c)   to make all necessary repairs and make good all defects in pursuance of his obligation under head (a) of this condition within such reasonable period as the creditor may require by notice in writing.

Completion of buildings etc and prohibition of alterations etc

2.   It shall be an obligation on the debtor—

(a)   to complete, as soon as may be practicable, any unfinished buildings and works forming part of the security subjects to the reasonable satisfaction of the creditor;

(b)   not to demolish, alter or add to any buildings or works forming part of the security subjects, except in accordance with the terms of a prior written consent of the creditor and in compliance with any consent, licence or approval required by law;

(c)   to exhibit to the creditor at his request evidence of that consent, licence or approval.

Observance of conditions in title, payment of duties, charges, etc, and general compliance with requirements of law relating to security subjects

3.   It shall be an obligation on the debtor—

(a)   to observe any condition or perform any obligation in respect of the security subjects lawfully binding on him in relation to the security subjects;

(b)   to make due and punctual payment of any ground burden, teind, stipend, or standard charge, and any rates, taxes and other public burdens, and any other payments exigible in respect of the security subjects;

(c)   to comply with any requirement imposed upon him in relation to the security subjects by virtue of any enactment.

Planning notices, etc

4.   It shall be an obligation on the debtor—

(a)   where he has received any notice or order, issued or made by virtue of the Town and Country Planning (Scotland) Acts 1947 to 1969 or any amendment thereof, or any proposal so made for the making or issuing of any such notice or order, or any other notice or document affecting or likely to affect the security subjects, to give to the creditor, within fourteen days of the receipt of that notice, order or proposal, full particulars thereof;

(b)　to take, as soon as practicable, all reasonable or necessary steps to comply with such a notice or order or, as the case may be, duly to object thereto;

(c)　in the event of the creditor so requiring, to object or to join with the creditor in objecting to any such notice or order or in making representations against any proposal therefor.

Insurance

5.　It shall be an obligation on the debtor—

(a)　to insure the security subjects or, at the option of the creditor, to permit the creditor to insure the security subjects in the names of the creditor and the debtor to the extent of the market value thereof against the risk of fire and such other risks as the creditor may reasonably require;

(b)　to deposit any policy of insurance effected by the debtor for the aforesaid purpose with the creditor;

(c)　to pay any premium due in respect of any such policy, and, where the creditor so requests, to exhibit a receipt therefor not later than the fourteenth day after the renewal date of the policy;

(d)　to intimate to the creditor, within fourteen days of the occurrence, any occurrence which may give rise to a claim under the policy, and to authorise the creditor to negotiate the settlement of the claim;

(e)　without prejudice to any obligation to the contrary enforceable against him, to comply with any reasonable requirement of the creditor as to the application of any sum received in respect of such a claim;

(f)　to refrain from any act or omission which would invalidate the policy.

Restriction on letting

6.　It shall be an obligation on the debtor not to let, or agree to let, the security subjects, or any part thereof, without the prior consent in writing of the creditor, and 'to let' in this condition includes to sub-let.

General power of creditor to perform obligations etc on failure of debtor and power to charge debtor

7.—(1)　The creditor shall be entitled to perform any obligation imposed by the standard conditions on the debtor, which the debtor has failed to perform.

(2)　Where it is necessary for the performance of any obligation as aforesaid, the creditor may, after giving seven clear days notice in writing to the debtor, enter upon the security subjects at all reasonable times.

(3)　All expenses and charges (including any interest thereon), reasonably incurred by the creditor in the exercise of a right conferred by this condition, shall be recoverable from the debtor and shall be deemed to be secured by the security subjects under the standard security, and the rate of any such interest shall be the rate in force at the relevant time in respect of advances secured by the security, or, where no such rate is prescribed, shall be the bank rate in force at the relevant time.

Calling-up

8.　The creditor shall be entitled, subject to the terms of the security and to any requirement of law, to call-up a standard security in the manner prescribed by section 19 of this Act.

Default

9.—(1)   The debtor shall be held to be in default in any of the following circumstances, that is to say—

(a)   where a calling-up notice in respect of the security has been served and has
not been complied with;

(b)   where there has been a failure to comply with any other requirement arising
out of the security;

(c)   where the proprietor of the security subjects has become insolvent.

(2)   For the purposes of this condition, the proprietor shall be taken to be in sol-
vent if—

(a)   he has become notour bankrupt, or he has executed a trust deed for
behoof of, or has made a composition contract or arrangement with, his
creditors;

(b)   he has died and a judicial factor has been appointed under section [11A of
the Judicial Factors (Scotland) Act 1889] to divide his insolvent estate among his
creditors, [or his estate falls to be administered in accordance with an order under
section [421 of the Insolvency Act 1986]];

(c)   where the proprietor is a company, a winding-up order has been made with
respect to it, or a resolution for voluntary winding-up (other than a members' voluntary winding-up) has been passed with respect to it, or a receiver or manager of
its undertaking has been duly appointed, or possession has been taken, by or on
behalf of the holders of any debentures secured by a floating charge, of any property of the company comprised in or subject to the charge.

Rights of creditor on default

10.—(1)   Where the debtor is in default, the creditor may, without prejudice to his
exercising any other remedy arising from the contract to which the standard security relates, exercise, in accordance with the provisions of Part II of this Act and of
any other enactment applying to standard securities, such of the remedies specified
in the following sub-paragraphs of this standard condition as he may consider
appropriate.

(2)   He may proceed to sell the security subjects or any part thereof.

(3)   He may enter into possession of the security subjects and may receive or
recover [. . .] the rents of those subjects or any part thereof.

(4)   Where he has entered into possession as aforesaid, he may let the security
subjects or any part thereof.

(5)   Where he has entered into possession as aforesaid there shall be transferred
to him all the rights of the debtor in relation to the granting of leases or rights of
occupancy over the security subjects and to the management and maintenance of
those subjects.

(6)   He may effect all such repairs and may make good such defects as are necessary to maintain the security subjects in good and sufficient repair, and may
effect such reconstruction, alteration and improvement on the subjects as would
be expected of a prudent proprietor to maintain the market value of the subjects, and for the aforesaid purposes may enter on the subjects at all reasonable
times.

(7)   He may apply to the court for a decree of foreclosure.

Exercise of right of redemption

11.—(1)   The debtor shall be entitled to exercise his [right (if any) to redeem the
security on giving notice] of his intention so to do, being a notice in writing (hereinafter referred to as a 'notice of redemption').

(2)   Nothing in the provisions of [this Act] shall preclude a creditor from waiv-

ing the necessity for a notice of redemption, or from agreeing to a period of notice of less than [that to which he is entitled].

(3)(a) A notice of redemption may be delivered to the creditor or sent by registered post or recorded delivery to him at his last known address, and an acknowledgment signed by the creditor or his agent or a certificate of postage by the person giving the notice accompanied by the postal receipt shall be sufficient evidence of such notice having been given.

(b) If the address of the creditor is not known, or if the packet containing the notice of redemption is returned to the sender with intimation that it could not be delivered, a notice of redemption may be sent to the Extractor of the Court of Session and an acknowledgment of receipt by him shall be sufficient evidence of such notice having been given.

(c) A notice of redemption sent by post shall be held to have been given on the day next after the day of posting.

(4) When a notice of redemption states that a specified amount will be repaid, and it is subsequently ascertained that the whole amount due to be repaid is more or less than the amount specified in the notice, the notice shall nevertheless be effective as a notice of repayment of the amount due as subsequently ascertained.

(5) [Where the debtor has exercised a right to redeem, and has made payment] of the whole amount due, or [has performed] the whole obligations of the debtor under the contract to which the security relates, the creditor shall grant a discharge in the terms prescribed in section 17 of this Act.

12. The debtor shall be personally liable to the creditor for the whole expenses of the preparation and execution of the standard security and any variation, restriction and discharge thereof and, where any of those deeds are [registered or] recorded, the [registration or] recording thereof, and all expenses reasonably incurred by the creditor in calling-up the security and realising or attempting to realise the security subjects, or any part thereof, and exercising any other powers conferred upon him by the security.

Interpretation

In this Schedule, where the debtor is not the proprietor of the security subjects, 'debtor' means 'proprietor', except

(a) in standard conditions 9(1), 10(1) and 12, and

(b) in standard condition 11, where 'debtor' includes the proprietor.

SCHEDULE 4   Sections 14, 15, 16 and 17
FORMS OF DEEDS OF ASSIGNATION, RESTRICTION, &c

FORM A
ASSIGNATION OF STANDARD SECURITY

Separate

I, AB (*designation*), in consideration of £   hereby assign to CD (*designation*) a standard security for £   (*or* a maximum sum of £   , to the extent of £   being the amount now due thereunder; *in other cases describe as indicated in Note 2 to this Schedule*) by EF in my favour (*or* in favour of GH) [registered in the Land Register of Scotland on .... over title number .... (*or* recorded in the Register for .... on ....)] (*adding if necessary*, but only to the extent of £   of principal); With interest from ....

[*Testing clause †*]

FORM B
[To be endorsed on the standard security]

As above save that instead of the words 'a standard security for £   ' (or other-wise, as the case may be) insert 'the foregoing standard security'. *Where the security is for a fluctuating amount whether subject to a maximum or not, add* 'to the extent of £   being the amount now due thereunder.'.

FORM C
RESTRICTION OF STANDARD SECURITY
I, AB (*designation*), in consideration of (*specify consideration, if any*) hereby disbur-den of a standard security for £   (*or a maximum sum of £   ; in other cases, describe as indicated in Note 2 to this Schedule*) by CD in my favour (*or in favour of EF*) [registered in the Land Register of Scotland on .... over title number .... (*or recorded in the Register for .... on ....*)] (*adding if necessary,* but only to the extent of £   of principal) ALL and WHOLE (*describe the subjects disburdened in the same way as directed in Note 1 to Schedule 2 to this Act in the case of a description of security subjects*).

[*Testing clause* †]

FORM D
COMBINED PARTIAL DISCHARGE AND DEED OF RESTRICTION
OF STANDARD SECURITY

I, AB (*designation*) in consideration of £   paid by CD (*designation*) (*or, as the case may be*), hereby discharge a standard security for £   (*or a maximum sum of £   ; in other cases, describe as indicated in Note 2 to this Schedule*) by the said CD (*or by EF*) in my favour (*or in favour of GH*) [registered in the Land Register of Scotland on .... over title number .... (*or recorded in the Register for .... on ....*)] but only to the extent of £   of principal; And I disburden of the said standard security (*adding if necessary,* but only to the extent of £   of principal) ALL and WHOLE (*describe the subjects disburdened in the same way as directed in Note 1 to Schedule 2 to this Act in the case of a description of security subjects*).

[*Testing clause* †]

FORM E
VARIATION OF STANDARD SECURITY
[To be endorsed on the standard security]

I, AB (*designation*), agree that the foregoing standard security granted by me (*or by CD*) in favour of EF [registered in the Land Register of Scotland on .... over title number .... (*or recorded in the Register for .... on ....*)] (*if there have been previous variations insert* 'as varied') shall with effect from .... be varied so that (*here insert particulars of the variation agreed*); And I, EF (*designation*) (*or if the creditor is not the per-son in whose favour the standard security was granted say* GH (*designation*) the creditor now in right of the said standard security) consent to the variation hereby effected.

[*Testing clause* †]

FORM F
DISCHARGE OF STANDARD SECURITY

Separate

I, AB *(designation)*, in consideration of £   *(where the security is in respect of a maximum sum or of all sums due or to become due or is in respect of a personal obligation constituted in an instrument or instruments other than the standard security add* being the whole amount secured by the standard security aftermentioned) paid by CD, *(designation) (or, as the case may be)* hereby discharge a standard security for £
(or a maximum sum of £   *in other cases describe as indicated in Note 2 to this Schedule*) by the said CD (or by EF) in my favour *(or in favour of GH)* recorded in the Register for .... on .... *(adding if necessary,* but only to the extent of £   of principal).

[Testing clause †]

[To be endorsed on the standard security]

As above save that instead of the words 'a standard security for £   *(or a* maximum sum of £   *in other cases describe as indicated in Note 2 to this Schedule)' insert* 'the foregoing standard security'.

NOTES TO SCHEDULE 4

General

Note 1.—Where the grantor of an assignation, discharge or deed of restriction of a standard security, or the creditor consenting to a variation of a standard security, is not the original creditor and has not a recorded title [and the deed is to be recorded in the Register of Sasines], insert at the end of the deed a clause of deduction of title as follows: *Which standard security* (adding, if necessary, *to the extent aforesaid* or, as the case may be) *was last vested in the said* (give name of original creditor) *as aforesaid* (or where the last recorded title to the standard security was in favour of a person other than the original creditor say *in JK whose title thereto was recorded in the said Register of Sasines on* ....) *and from whom I acquired right by* (here specify shortly the writ or writs by which right was so acquired).
    Where the grantor of an assignation, discharge or deed of restriction of a standard security, or the creditor consenting to a variation of a standard security, although not the original creditor, has a [registered or] recorded title, no specification of the title of the grantor or creditor is required.
    Note 2.—In an assignation, discharge or deed of restriction, (1) a standard security in respect of an uncertain amount may be described by specifying shortly the nature of the debt or obligation (e.g., all sums due or to become due) for which the security was granted, adding in the case of an assignation, *to the extent of £   being the amount now due thereunder* and (2) a standard security in respect of a personal obligation constituted in an instrument or instruments other than the standard security itself may be described by specifying shortly the nature of the debt or obligation and referring to the other instrument or instruments by which it is constituted in such manner as will be sufficient identification thereof.
    Note 3.—If the original [title to a standard security has been completed] otherwise than by [registration of the security in the Land Register of Scotland or] recording the security in the Register of Sasines, insert immediately after the word ['registered' (or 'recorded')] the words *along with notice of title thereon* (adding, if such notice is not in favour of the original creditor, the name of the person in whose favour it is drawn).
    Note 4.—If part of the security subjects has already been disburdened, there may be inserted in an assignation, after the specification of the standard security assigned, a reference to the previous partial discharge or deed of restriction.
    Note 5.—The variation docket Form E of this Schedule shall be used only when the personal obligation or other matter to which the variation relates was contained in the standard security, or in a variation thereof which has been duly [registered or] recorded. Variations in

a personal obligation or other matter constituted in an instrument or instruments which have not been so [registered or] recorded may be altered by an instrument in appropriate terms which shall not be required to be [registered in the Land Register of Scotland or] recorded in the Register of Sasines.

Note 6.—Where the grantor of a variation docket does not have a recorded title to the security subjects [and the deed is to be recorded in the Register of Sasines], insert at the end of the variation and immediately before the consent by the creditor a clause of deduction of title as follows: *the security subjects to which the said standard security relates being last vested in* (give the name of the person in whom the security subjects were last vested) *whose title thereto was recorded in the said Register of Sasines on ....) and from whom I acquired right by* (here specify the writ or writs by which such right was so acquired).

[† Note 7—[In the case of a traditional document, subscription of it by the granter], or in the case of form E the granter and the consenter to the variation, will be sufficient for the document to be formally valid, but witnessing of it may be necessary or desirable for other purposes (see the Requirements of Writing (Scotland) Act 1995) [, which also makes provision as regards the authentication of an electronic document].]

SCHEDULE 5   Section 18
PROCEDURES AS TO REDEMPTION

FORM A
NOTICE OF REDEMPTION OF STANDARD SECURITY

To AB (*address*)

TAKE NOTICE that on .... (*state date of repayment*) CD (*designation*), will repay the sum of £   (*or the whole amount due*) secured by a standard security by the said CD (*or by EF*) in your favour (*or in favour of GH*) [registered in the Land Register of Scotland on .... over title number .... (*or recorded in the Register for .... on ....)] Dated this .... day of ....

(*To be signed by the debtor, or proprietor, or by his agent, who will add his designation and the words* Agent of the said CD.)

In the case of a standard security for a non-monetary obligation this Form shall be adapted accordingly.

FORM B

I, AB, above named, hereby acknowledge receipt of the Notice of Redemption of which the foregoing is a copy. Dated this .... day of ....

(*To be signed by the creditor, or by his agent, who will add his designation and the words* Agent of the said AB)

FORM C

Notice of Redemption, of which the foregoing is a copy, was posted (*or otherwise, as the case may be*) to AB above named on the .... day of ....

(*To be signed by the debtor, or proprietor, or by his agent, who will add his designation and the words* Agent of the said CD *and if posted the postal receipt to be attached.*)

FORM D

NO. 1
CERTIFICATE OF CONSIGNATION ON REDEMPTION OF STANDARD SECURITY WHERE
DISCHARGE CANNOT BE OBTAINED

I, AB (*designation*) (solicitor) certify that consignation of the whole amount due under the standard security aftermentioned was made as after stated and was necessitated by reason of a discharge being unobtainable after due notice of redemption had been given.

STANDARD SECURITY for £   (*or* a maximum of £   ; *in other cases describe as indicated in Note 2 to Schedule 4 to this Act*) by CD in favour of EF [registered in the Land Register of Scotland on .... over title number .... (*or* recorded in the Register for .... on ....)]

AMOUNT CONSIGNED £   , being £   of principal, £   of interest and £   in respect of ascertained expenses.

BANK IN WHICH CONSIGNED (*specify bank or branch of bank, with address, in which above amount consigned*) conform to deposit receipt dated .... in name of the person appearing to have the best right thereto (*specifying his name and designation if known*) (*or if he is only a partial creditor say* to the extent of £   ).

[Testing clause †]

[† Note—[In the case of a traditional document, subscription of it by the granter] will be sufficient for the document to be formally valid, but witnessing of it may be necessary or desirable for other purposes (see the Requirements of Writing (Scotland) Act 1995) [, which also makes provision as regards the authentication of an electronic document].]

NO. 2
CERTIFICATE OF DECLARATOR OF PERFORMANCE OF DEBTOR'S OBLIGATIONS UNDER
STANDARD SECURITY WHERE DISCHARGE CANNOT BE OBTAINED

I, AB (*designation*) (solicitor) certify that a decree of declarator of performance of the obligations of the debtor under the standard security aftermentioned was pronounced as after stated and was necessitated by reason of a discharge being unobtainable after due notice of redemption had been given.

STANDARD SECURITY by CD in favour of EF [registered in the Land Register of Scotland on .... over title number .... (*or* recorded in the Register for .... on ....)]

DECREE OF DECLARATOR by the Sheriff of .... at .... in the application of the said CD (*or* JK (*designation*), who is now the debtor (*or* the proprietor of the interest in land contained) in the said standard security).

[Testing clause †]

[† Note—[In the case of a traditional document, subscription of it by the granter] will be sufficient for the document to be formally valid, but witnessing of it may be necessary or desirable for other purposes (see the Requirements of Writing (Scotland) Act 1995) [, which also makes provision as regards the authentication of an electronic document].]

SCHEDULE 6   Sections 19 and 21
PROCEDURES AS TO CALLING-UP AND DEFAULT

[FORM A
NOTICE OF CALLING UP OF STANDARD SECURITY

IT IS IMPORTANT THAT YOU READ THIS LETTER—YOUR HOME MAY BE AT RISK OF REPOSSESSION

To AB (*address*)

TAKE NOTICE that CD (*designation*) requires payment of the principal sum of £ .... with interest thereon at the rate of.................. per centum per annum from the .... day of .... (*adding if necessary*, subject to such adjust-ment of the principal sum and the amount of interest as may subsequently be determined) secured by a standard security by you (or by EF) over (*insert address*) ('the property') in favour of CD (or of GH to which CD has now right) [registered in the Land Register of Scotland on .... over title number .... (*or* recorded in the Register for on ....)] And that failing full payment of the said sum and interest thereon (adding if necessary, subject to any adjustment as aforesaid), and expenses within two months after the date of service of this demand—

• IF THE PROPERTY IS A RESIDENTIAL PROPERTY, CD may apply to the sheriff court for warrant to exercise the remedies available to a creditor on default for example to repossess and sell the property.

• IF THE PROPERTY IS A NON-RESIDENTIAL PROPERTY, it may be sold without the need to go to court.

Dated this .... day of ....

(*To be signed by the creditor, or by his agent, who will add his designation and the words Agent of the said CD*)

IT IS STRONGLY RECOMMENDED THAT YOU SEEK ADVICE:
You can get advice about this Notice and what it means for you from a solicitor, Citizens Advice Bureau or other advice agency or, in the case of a residential prop-erty, an approved lay representative. A Citizens Advice Bureau or other advice agency may also be able to give you advice about how to manage debt. Take this Notice with you when seeking advice. You may be eligible for legal aid depending on your circumstances. You can get information about legal aid from a solicitor.

A solicitor or approved lay representative may represent you in any court proceed-ings in relation to an application by CD for possession and sale of your home. You can find out more about approved lay representatives from the housing department of your local authority or from a Citizens Advice Bureau or other advice agency.

YOUR RIGHTS IN RELATION TO RESIDENTIAL PROPERTY ARE PROTECTED BY LAW:
In the case of a residential property, CD must comply with statutory pre-action requirements before being allowed to apply to the court. These requirements include providing you with specified information and contacting you to discuss alternatives to repossession. CD may also be prevented from applying to the court if you have made an application to an insurer under a payment protection policy or to a mortgage support scheme. It is important to discuss with your solicitor or

advisor any doubts you have about whether CD has complied with these requirements.

YOU MAY WISH TO VOLUNTARILY SURRENDER YOUR HOME:
In the case of a residential property it is open to you, in certain circumstances, to voluntarily surrender the property to CD if all entitled residents in it consent. If you wish to consider voluntary surrender you should discuss with your solicitor or advisor whether this option is right for you. You should not proceed with voluntary surrender unless you understand the consequences of doing so, for example that you may still owe money to CD.

(In the case of a standard security for a non-monetary obligation this Form shall be adapted accordingly.)

FORM B
NOTICE OF DEFAULT UNDER STANDARD SECURITY

**IT IS IMPORTANT THAT YOU READ THIS LETTER—YOUR HOME MAY
BE AT RISK OF REPOSSESSION**

To AB (*address*)

TAKE NOTICE that CD (*designation*), the creditor in a standard security by you (or by EF) over (*insert address*) ('the property') in favour of CD (*or* of GH to which CD has now right) [registered in the Land Register of Scotland on .... over title number .... (*or* recorded in the Register for .... on ....
..................)] requires fulfilment of the obligation(s) specified in the Schedule hereto in respect of which there is default; And that failing such fulfilment within one month after the date of service of this notice—
• IF THE PROPERTY IS A RESIDENTIAL PROPERTY, CD may apply to the sheriff court for warrant to exercise the remedies available to a creditor on default for example to repossess and sell the property.
• IF THE PROPERTY IS A NON-RESIDENTIAL PROPERTY, it may be sold without the need to go to court.

Dated this .... day of ....

(*To be signed by the creditor, or by his agent, who will add his designation and the words Agent of the said CD*)

Schedule of Obligation(s) in respect of which there is default.

To (*specify in detail the obligation(s) in respect of which there is default*)

IT IS STRONGLY RECOMMENDED THAT YOU SEEK ADVICE:
You can get advice about this Notice and what it means for you from a solicitor, Citizens Advice Bureau or other advice agency or, in the case of a residential property, an approved lay representative. A Citizens Advice Bureau or other advice agency may also be able to give you advice about how to manage debt. Take this Notice with you when seeking advice. You may be eligible for legal aid depending on your circumstances. You can get information about legal aid from a solicitor.

A solicitor or an approved lay representative may represent you in any court proceedings in relation to an application by CD for possession and sale of your home. You can find out more about approved lay representatives from the housing department of your local authority or from a Citizens Advice Bureau or other advice agency.

YOUR RIGHTS IN RELATION TO RESIDENTIAL PROPERTY ARE PROTECTED BY LAW:
In the case of residential property, CD must comply with statutory pre-action requirements before being allowed to apply to the court. These requirements include providing you with specified information and contacting you to discuss alternatives to repossession. CD may also be prevented from applying to the court if you have made an application to an insurer under a payment protection policy or to a mortgage support scheme. It is important to discuss with your solicitor or advisor any doubts you have about whether CD has complied with these requirements.

YOU MAY WISH TO VOLUNTARILY SURRENDER YOUR HOME:
In the case of a residential property it is open to you, in certain circumstances, to voluntarily surrender the property to CD if all entitled residents in it consent. If you wish to consider voluntary surrender you should discuss with your solicitor or advisor whether this option is right for you. You should not proceed with voluntary surrender unless you understand the consequences of doing so, for example, that you may still owe money to CD.

FORM BB
NOTICE TO THE OCCUPIER

IT IS IMPORTANT THAT YOU READ THIS LETTER—YOUR HOME MAY BE AT RISK OF REPOSSESSION

To the Occupier (including any Tenant) (*address*)

A Notice of Calling-up of a standard security/ Default under a standard security (*delete as appropriate*) has been served by CD on AB in relation to (*address of subjects*) ('the property'). A copy of the Notice is attached. CD may apply to the sheriff court for warrant to exercise the remedies available to a creditor on default including the rights to enter into possession of and sell the property.

Dated this .... day of ....

(*Signature of CD, or signature and designation of CD's agent followed by the words Agent of CD*)

IT IS STRONGLY RECOMMENDED THAT YOU SEEK ADVICE:
You can get advice about this Notice and what it means for you from a solicitor, Citizens Advice Bureau or other advice agency or, in certain cases, an approved lay representative. Take this Notice with you when seeking advice. You may be eligible for legal aid depending on your circumstances. You can get information about legal aid from a solicitor.

YOUR RIGHTS IN RELATION TO RESIDENTIAL PROPERTY ARE PROTECTED BY LAW:
CD must comply with statutory pre-action requirements before being allowed to apply to the court. These requirements include providing AB with specified information and contacting AB to discuss alternatives to repossession. It is important to discuss with your solicitor or advisor any doubts you have about whether CD has complied with these requirements.

IF YOU ARE OR WERE THE SPOUSE, CIVIL PARTNER OR PARTNER OF AB OR ARE THE OWNER OF THE HOUSE:

You may be an ENTITLED RESIDENT and should discuss this with your solicitor or advisor. This means that AB cannot voluntarily surrender the property if you or anyone else is living there or without your written consent. You may be asked to give your consent—it is recommended that you do not do so until you have discussed this with a solicitor or other advisor.

You have a RIGHT TO BE HEARD IN COURT. If CD does make an application to the court, you are entitled to intervene to ask the court to continue the proceedings or to make any other order (for example an order suspending CD's rights or refusing CD's application). You may represent yourself, or be represented by a solicitor or approved lay representative. You can find out more about approved lay representatives from the housing department of your local authority or from a Citizens Advice Bureau or other advice agency.

IF YOU ARE A TENANT OF AB:

You should contact CD to let them know about your tenancy as soon as possible as they may not be aware that you live in the property.

If you have an assured or short assured tenancy you may have rights under the Housing (Scotland) Act 1988—in certain circumstances CD cannot take possession of the property or evict you without making a separate application to the court under that Act. Whatever your type of tenancy, you should obtain legal advice about your rights as a tenant.]

FORM C

I, AB, above named, hereby acknowledge receipt of the foregoing Notice of (Calling-up), (Default) of which the foregoing is a copy of the notice *adding where appropriate* 'and I agree to the period of notice being dispensed with (*or* shortened to ....).'

Dated this .... day of ....

(*To be signed by the person on whom notice is served, or by his agent, who will add his designation and the words* Agent of the said AB.)

FORM D

Notice of (Calling-up) (Default), of which the foregoing is a copy, was posted (*or otherwise, as the case may be*) to AB above named on the .... day of ....

(*To be signed by the creditor, or by his agent, who will add his designation and the words* Agent of the said CD *and if posted the postal receipt to be attached.*)

[FORM E
NOTICE OF PROCEEDINGS

IT IS IMPORTANT THAT YOU READ THIS LETTER—YOUR HOME MAY BE AT RISK OF REPOSSESSION

To AB (*address*)

CD (*designation*), the creditor in a standard security by you (*or* by EF) in favour of CD (*or* of GH to which CD now has right) recorded in the Register for .... (*or, as the case may be,* registered in the Land Register for Scotland) on (*date*) has applied to the court under section 24 of the Conveyancing and Feudal Reform (Scotland) Act 1970 for warrant to exercise in relation to (*address of security subjects*) remedies to which he is entitled on the following default—

(specify in detail the default in respect of which the application is made)

A copy of the application is attached.

Dated this .... day of ....

(*Signature of CD, or signature and designation of CD's agent followed by the words Agent of CD*)

IT IS STRONGLY RECOMMENDED THAT YOU SEEK ADVICE:
You can get advice about this Notice and what it means for you from a solicitor, Citizens Advice Bureau or other advice agency or an approved lay representative. A Citizens Advice Bureau or other advice agency may also be able to give you advice about how to manage debt. Take this Notice with you when seeking advice. You may be eligible for legal aid depending on your circumstances. You can get information about legal aid from a solicitor.

A solicitor or approved lay representative may represent you in any court proceedings in relation to an application by CD for possession and sale of your home. You can find out more about approved lay representatives from the housing department of your local authority or from a Citizens Advice Bureau or other advice agency.

YOUR RIGHTS IN RELATION TO RESIDENTIAL PROPERTY ARE PROTECTED BY LAW:
CD's application is not valid and can be challenged by you (or by EF) if CD has failed to comply with certain pre-action requirements. These requirements include providing specified information and to contacting you (*or the debtor*) to discuss alternatives to repossession. It is important to discuss with your solicitor or advisor if you have doubts about whether CD has complied with these requirements.

YOU HAVE THE RIGHT TO BE HEARD IN COURT:
You are (*or the debtor is*) entitled to intervene in the court proceedings following from CD's application. You (*or the debtor*) can appear personally or be represented by a solicitor or approved lay representative. For example, you (*or the debtor*) might want to argue that the pre-action requirements have not been complied with or that it would not be reasonable for the sheriff to grant the application. Even if they have, you have (*or the debtor has*) the right to ask the sheriff to continue the proceedings or make any other order. The sheriff will take into account matters such as the nature of and reasons for the default, your (*or the debtor's*) ability to fulfil your (*or the*) obligations under the security within a reasonable time, any action taken by CD to assist you (*or the debtor*) to fulfil your (*or the*) obligations, your (*or the debtor's*) participation in a relevant debt payment programme and your (*or the debtor's*) ability, or the ability of any other person residing in the property, to secure reasonable alternative accommodation.

YOU MAY WISH TO VOLUNTARILY SURRENDER YOUR HOME:
It is open to you (*or the debtor*), in certain circumstances, to voluntarily surrender the property to CD if all entitled residents in it consent. If you wish to consider voluntary surrender you should discuss with your solicitor or advisor whether this option is right for you. You should not proceed with voluntary surrender unless you understand the consequences of doing so, for example, that you may still owe money to CD.

WHAT IF AN ORDER FOR REPOSSESSION HAS ALREADY BEEN GRANTED AND I HAVE JUST BECOME AWARE OF THE APPLICATION?
It may not be too late to intervene so you should urgently seek advice. You have the right to apply to the court to ask for the order to be recalled at any time before repossession has taken place. If the court recalls the order it will fix a hearing, giving you (*or* the debtor) the opportunity to appear or be represented.

FORM F
NOTICE OF PROCEEDINGS TO THE OCCUPIER

IT IS IMPORTANT THAT YOU READ THIS LETTER—YOUR HOME MAY BE AT RISK OF REPOSSESSION

To the Occupier (including any Tenant) (*address*)

CD (*designation*) has applied to the court under section 24 of the Conveyancing and Feudal Reform (Scotland) Act 1970 for warrant to exercise in relation to (*address of security subjects*) ('the property') remedies to which he is entitled on the default of AB (designation) in the performance of his obligations under a standard security over the property. A copy of the application is attached.

Dated this .... day of ....

(Signature of CD, or signature and designation of CD's agent followed by the words
Agent of CD)

IT IS STRONGLY RECOMMENDED THAT YOU SEEK ADVICE:
You can get advice about this Notice and what it means for you from a solicitor, Citizens Advice Bureau or other advice agency or, in certain cases, an approved lay representative. Take this Notice with you when seeking advice. You may be eligible for legal aid depending on your circumstances. You can get information about legal aid from a solicitor.

YOUR RIGHTS IN RELATION TO RESIDENTIAL PROPERTY ARE PROTECTED BY LAW:
CD must comply with statutory pre-action requirements before being allowed to apply to the court. These requirements include providing AB with specified information and contacting AB to discuss alternatives to repossession. It is important to discuss with your solicitor or advisor any doubts you have about whether CD has complied with these requirements.

IF YOU ARE OR WERE THE SPOUSE, CIVIL PARTNER OR PARTNER OF AB OR ARE THE OWNER OF THE HOUSE:

You may be an ENTITLED RESIDENT and should discuss this with your solicitor or advisor. This means that AB cannot voluntarily surrender the property if you or anyone else is living there or without your written consent. You may be asked to give your consent—it is recommended that you do not do so until you have discussed this with a solicitor or other advisor.

You have the RIGHT TO BE HEARD IN COURT. You are entitled to intervene to ask the court to continue the proceedings or to make any other order (for example an order suspending CD's rights or refusing CD's application). For example, you might want to argue that the pre-action requirements have not been complied with or that it would not be reasonable for the sheriff to grant the application. Even if they have, you have the right to ask the sheriff to continue the proceedings or make any other order. The sheriff will take into account matters such as the nature of and reasons for the default, your or the debtor's ability to fulfil the obligations under the security within a reasonable time, any action taken by CD to assist the debtor to fulfil the obligations, the debtor's participation in a relevant debt payment programme and your ability, or the ability of any other person residing in the property (including you), to secure reasonable alternative accommodation.

You may represent yourself, or be represented by a solicitor or approved lay representative. You can find out more about approved lay representatives from the housing department of your local authority or from a Citizens Advice Bureau or other advice agency.

IF YOU ARE A TENANT OF AB:

You should contact CD to let them know about your tenancy as soon as possible as they may not be aware that you live in the property.

If you have an assured or short assured tenancy you may have rights under the Housing (Scotland) Act 1988—in certain circumstances CD cannot take possession of the property or evict you without making a separate application to court under that Act. The sheriff may also permit you to intervene in the proceedings for possession as an interested party. Whatever your type of tenancy, you should obtain legal advice about your rights as a tenant.

WHAT IF AN ORDER FOR REPOSSESSION HAS ALREADY BEEN GRANTED AND I HAVE JUST BECOME AWARE OF THE APPLICATION?
If you are an ENTITLED RESIDENT it may not be too late to intervene so you should urgently seek advice. You have the right to apply to court to ask for the order to be recalled at any time before repossession has taken place. If the court recalls the order it will fix a hearing, giving you the opportunity to appear or be represented.

If you are a TENANT, CD may need to obtain a separate order for eviction, depending on your tenancy type. You should urgently obtain legal advice about your rights as a tenant.]

Sections 22 and 24   SCHEDULE 7
CONTENTS OF CERTIFICATE STATING A DEFAULT

1.   A certificate which is lodged in court by the creditor for the purposes of section 22 or 24 of this Act shall contain the information required by the following provisions of this Schedule.

2.   A certificate shall state—

     (i)   the name and address of the creditor and shall specify the standard security in respect of which the default is alleged to have occurred by reference to the original creditor and debtor therein and to the particulars of its registration;

     (ii)   the nature of the default with full details thereof.

3.   The certificate shall be signed by the creditor or his solicitor, and a certificate which does not comply with the foregoing requirements of this Schedule shall not be received in evidence for the purposes of the said section 22 or 24.

Section 32   SCHEDULE 8
                                EXCLUDED ENACTMENTS

The Debts Securities (Scotland) Act 1856

1.   Section 7 (Securities for cash accounts or credits).

Registration of Long Leases (Scotland) Act 1857

[. . .]
4.   Section 6 (Translation of assignations in security and creditor's entry on possession in default of payment), so far as relating to such a translation.
5.   Section 13 (Renunciations and discharges to be recorded) so far as affecting
discharges.
6.   Section 20 (Interpretation of clauses in Schedules).
[. . .]

Section 40   SCHEDULE 9
                DISCHARGE OF HERITABLE SECURITY CONSTITUTED
                      BY *EX FACIE* ABSOLUTE CONVEYANCE

I, AB, *(designation)* hereby acknowledge that [the disposition *(or assignation)* granted
by CD, *(designation)* *(or by EF, (designation) with consent of CD, (designation))* in my
favour *(or in favour of GH, (designation of original creditor))* recorded in the Register
for .... on ....] [*or, where endorsed on the disposition or assignation,* the
foregoing disposition *(or assignation)*] [*describe security discharged by reference to the
parties thereto and to the details of its recording*] although in its terms *ex facie* absolute
was truly in security of an advance of £   (*or a maximum amount of
£   in other cases describe as indicated in Note 2 to Schedule 4 to this Act*), and
that all moneys intended to be secured thereby have been fully paid.

                              [*Testing clause* †]

                          NOTES TO SCHEDULE 9

   Note 1.—The discharge may be separate or endorsed on the *ex facie* absolute disposition or
assignation.
   Note 2.—Where the grantor of the discharge is not the original creditor, the separate form of
discharge shall be used.
   Note 3.—Where the grantor of the discharge is not the original creditor but has a recorded
title, no specification of the grantor's title is required. Where the grantor of the discharge is not
the original creditor and has not a recorded title, insert at the end of the discharge a clause of
deduction of title as follows:

   The subjects conveyed by the said disposition (or otherwise, as the case may be) *were last vested in
the said GH as aforesaid* (or, where the last recorded title to the subjects was in favour of a person other than the original creditor, say *in JK whose title thereto was recorded in the said Register
of Sasines on* ....) *and from whom I acquired right by* (here specify shortly the writ or
writs by which right was so acquired).

   [† Note 4—[In the case of a traditional document, subscription of it by the granter] will be
sufficient for the document to be formally valid, but witnessing of it may be necessary or desirable for other purposes (see the Requirements of Writing (Scotland) Act 1995) [, which also
makes provision as regards the authentication of an electronic document].]

PRESCRIPTION AND LIMITATION (SCOTLAND) ACT 1973
(1973 c 52)

PART I
PRESCRIPTION

Positive prescription

[1   Validity of right
(1)   If land has been possessed by any person, or by any person and his successors, for a continuous period of ten years openly, peaceably and without any judicial
interruption and the possession was founded on, and followed—
(a) the recording of a deed which is sufficient in respect of its terms to constitute in favour of that person a real right in—
(i)   that land; or
(ii) land of a description *habile* to include that land; or
[(b) the registration of a deed which is sufficient in respect of its terms to constitute in favour of that person a real right in—
(i)   that land; or
(ii) land of a description habile to include that land.]
then, as from the expiry of that period, the real right so far as relating to that land
shall be exempt from challenge.
(2)   Subsection (1) above shall not apply where—
(a) possession was founded on the recording of a deed which is invalid *ex facie*
or was forged; or
(b) possession was founded on registration in the Land Register of Scotland
proceeding on a forged deed and the person appearing from the Register to have
the real right in question was aware of the forgery at the time of registration in his
favour.
(3)   In subsection (1) above, the reference to a real right is to a real right which is
registrable in the Land Register of Scotland or a deed relating to which can competently be recorded; but this section does not apply to [real burdens,] servitudes or
public rights of way.
(4)   In the computation of a prescriptive period for the purposes of this section
in a case where the deed in question is a decree of adjudication for debt, any period
before the expiry of the legal shall be disregarded.
(5)   Where, in any question involving any foreshore or any salmon fishings, this
section is pled against the Crown as owner of the regalia, subsection (1) above shall
have effect as if for the words 'ten years' there were substituted 'twenty years'.
(6)   This section is without prejudice to section 2 of this Act.]

[2   Special cases
(1)   If—
(a) land has been possessed by any person, or by any person and his successors, for a continuous period of twenty years openly, peaceably and without any
judicial interruption; and
(b) the possession was founded on, and followed the execution of, a deed
(whether [or not registered or recorded]) which is sufficient in respect of its terms
to constitute in favour of that person a real right in that land, or in land of a description *habile* to include that land, then, as from the expiry of that period, the real right
so far as relating to that land shall be exempt from challenge except on the ground
that the deed is invalid *ex facie* or was forged.
(2)   This section applies—
(a) to the real right of the lessee under a lease; and
(b) to any other real right in land, being a real right of a kind which, under
the law in force immediately before the commencement of this Part of this Act,

was sufficient to form a foundation for positive prescription without the deed constituting the title to the real right having been [registered or] recorded,
but does not apply to servitudes or public rights of way.

(3) This section is without prejudice to section 1 of this Act or to [section 20B or 20C of the Registration of Leases (Scotland) Act 1857 (c 26)].]

3 Positive servitudes and public rights of way

(1) If in the case of a positive servitude over land—

(a) the servitude has been possessed for a continuous period of twenty years openly, peaceably and without any judicial interruption, and

(b) the possession was founded on, and followed the execution of, a deed which is sufficient in respect of its terms (whether expressly or by implication) to constitute the servitude,

then, as from the expiration of the said period, the validity of the servitude as so constituted shall be exempt from challenge except on the ground that the deed is invalid *ex facie* or was forged.

(2) If a positive servitude over land has been possessed for a continuous period of twenty years openly, peaceably and without judicial interruption, then, as from the expiration of that period, the existence of the servitude as so possessed shall be exempt from challenge.

(3) If a public right of way over land has been possessed by the public for a continuous period of twenty years openly, peaceably and without judicial interruption, then, as from the expiration of that period, the existence of the right of way as so possessed shall be exempt from challenge.

(4) References in subsections (1) and (2) of this section to possession of a servitude are references to possession of the servitude by any person in possession of the relative dominant tenement.

(5) This section is without prejudice to the operation of section 7 of this Act.

4 Judicial interruption of periods of possession for purposes of sections 1, 2 and 3

(1) In sections 1, 2 and 3 of this Act references to a judicial interruption, in relation to possession, are references to the making in appropriate proceedings, by any person having a proper interest to do so, of a claim which challenges the possession in question.

(2) In this section 'appropriate proceedings' means—

(a) any proceedings in a court of competent jurisdiction in Scotland or elsewhere, except proceedings in the Court of Session initiated by a summons which is not subsequently called;

(b) any arbitration in Scotland;

(c) any arbitration in a country other than Scotland, being an arbitration an award in which would be enforceable in Scotland.

(3) The date of a judicial interruption shall be taken to be—

(a) where the claim has been made in an arbitration and the nature of the claim has been stated in a preliminary notice relating to that arbitration, the date when the preliminary notice was served;

(b) in any other case, the date when the claim was made.

(4) In the foregoing subsection 'preliminary notice' in relation to an arbitration means a notice served by one party to the arbitration on the other party or parties requiring him or them to appoint an arbiter or to agree to the appointment of an arbiter, or, where the arbitration agreement or any relevant enactment provides that the reference shall be to a person therein named or designated, a notice requiring him or them to submit the dispute to the person so named or designated.

5 Further provisions supplementary to sections 1, 2 and 3

(1) In sections 1, 2 and 3 of this Act 'deed' includes a judicial decree; and for the purposes of the said sections any of the following, namely an instrument of

sasine, a notarial instrument and a notice of title, which narrates or declares that a person has a [right in land shall be treated as a deed sufficient to constitute that right].

[(1A) Any reference in those sections to a real right's being exempt from challenge as from the expiration of some continuous period is to be construed, if the real right of the possessor was void immediately before that expiration, as including reference to acquisition of the real right by the possessor.]

[. . .]

Negative prescription

6   Extinction of obligations by prescriptive periods of five years

(1) If, after the appropriate date, an obligation to which this section applies has subsisted for a continuous period of five years—

(a) without any relevant claim having been made in relation to the obligation, and

(b) without the subsistence of the obligation having been relevantly acknowledged,

then as from the expiration of that period the obligation shall be extinguished:

Provided that in its application to an obligation under a bill of exchange or a promissory note this subsection shall have effect as if paragraph (b) thereof were omitted.

(2) Schedule 1 to this Act shall have effect for defining the obligations to which this section applies.

(3) In subsection (1) above the reference to the appropriate date, in relation to an obligation of any kind specified in Schedule 2 to this Act is a reference to the date specified in that Schedule in relation to obligations of that kind, and in relation to an obligation of any other kind is a reference to the date when the obligation became enforceable.

(4) In the computation of a prescriptive period in relation to any obligation for the purposes of this section—

(a) any period during which by reason of—

(i) fraud on the part of the debtor or any person acting on his behalf, or

(ii) error induced by words or conduct of the debtor or any person acting on his behalf,

the creditor was induced to refrain from making a relevant claim in relation to the obligation, and

(b) any period during which the original creditor (while he is the creditor) was under legal disability,

shall not be reckoned as, or as part of, the prescriptive period:

Provided that any period such as is mentioned in paragraph (a) of this subsection shall not include any time occurring after the creditor could with reasonable diligence have discovered the fraud or error, as the case may be, referred to in that paragraph.

(5) Any period such as is mentioned in paragraph (a) or (b) of subsection (4) of this section shall not be regarded as separating the time immediately before it from the time immediately after it.

7   Extinction of obligations by prescriptive periods of twenty years

(1) If, after the date when any obligation to which this section applies has become enforceable, the obligation has subsisted for a continuous period of twenty years—

(a) without any relevant claim having been made in relation to the obligation, and

(b) without the subsistence of the obligation having been relevantly acknowledged,

then as from the expiration of that period the obligation shall be extinguished:

Provided that in its application to an obligation under a bill of exchange or a promissory note this subsection shall have effect as if paragraph (b) thereof were omitted.

(2)   This section applies to an obligation of any kind (including an obligation to which section 6 of this Act applies), not being an obligation [to which section 22A of this Act applies or an obligation] specified in Schedule 3 to this Act as an impre-scriptible obligation [or an obligation to make reparation in respect of personal inju-ries within the meaning of Part II of this Act or in respect of the death of any person as a result of such injuries.]

8   Extinction of other rights relating to property by prescriptive periods of twenty years

(1)   If, after the date when any right to which this section applies has become exer-cisable or enforceable, the right has subsisted for a continuous period of twenty years unexercised or unenforced, and without any relevant claim in relation to it having been made, then as from the expiration of that period the right shall be extinguished.

(2)   This section applies to any right relating to property, whether heritable or moveable, not being a right specified in Schedule 3 to this Act as an imprescriptible right or falling within section 6 or 7 of this Act as being a right correlative to an obli-gation to which either of those sections applies.

[8A   Extinction of obligations to make contribution between wrongdoers

(1)   If any obligation to make a contribution by virtue of section 3(2) of the Law Reform (Miscellaneous Provisions) (Scotland) Act 1940 in respect of any damages or expenses has subsisted for a continuous period of 2 years after the date on which the right to recover the contribution became enforceable by the creditor in the obligation—

(a)   without any relevant claim having been made in relation to the obligation; and

(b)   without the subsistence of the obligation having been relevantly acknowledged;

then as from the expiration of that period the obligation shall be extinguished.

(2)   Subsections (4) and (5) of section 6 of this Act shall apply for the purposes of this section as they apply for the purposes of that section.]

9   Definition of 'relevant claim' for purposes of sections 6, 7 and 8

(1)   In sections 6 [, 7 and 8A] of this Act the expression 'relevant claim', in relation to an obligation, means a claim made by or on behalf of the creditor for implement or part-implement of the obligation, being a claim made—

(a)   in appropriate proceedings, or

[(b) by the presentation of, or the concurring in, a petition for sequestration or by the submission of a claim under section [46 or 122 of the Bankruptcy (Scotland) Act 2016] [. . .]; or

(c)   by a creditor to the trustee acting under a trust deed as defined in section [228(1) of the Bankruptcy (Scotland) Act 2016]; or

(d)   by the presentation of, or the concurring in, a petition for the winding up of a company or by the submission of a claim in a liquidation in accordance with rules made under section 411 of the Insolvency Act 1986;]

and for the purposes of the said sections 6 [, 7 and 8A] the execution by or on behalf of the creditor in an obligation of any form of diligence directed to the enforcement of the obligation shall be deemed to be a relevant claim in relation to the obligation.

(2)   In section 8 of this Act the expression 'relevant claim', in relation to a right, means a claim made in appropriate proceedings by or on behalf of the creditor to establish the right or to contest any claim to a right inconsistent therewith.

(3)   Where a claim which, in accordance with the foregoing provisions of this section, is a relevant claim for the purposes of section 6, 7 [, 8 or 8A] of this Act is made in an arbitration, and the nature of the claim has been stated in a preliminary notice relating to that arbitration, the date when the notice was served shall be taken for those purposes to be the date of the making of the claim.

(4)   In this section the expression 'appropriate proceedings' and, in relation to an arbitration, the expression 'preliminary notice' have the same meanings as in section 4 of this Act.

10   Relevant acknowledgement for purposes of sections 6 and 7

(1)   The subsistence of an obligation shall be regarded for the purposes of sections 6 [, 7 and 8A] of this Act as having been relevantly acknowledged if, and only if, either of the following conditions is satisfied, namely—

(a)   that there has been such performance by or on behalf of the debtor towards implement of the obligation as clearly indicates that the obligation still subsists;

(b)   that there has been made by or on behalf of the debtor to the creditor or his agent an unequivocal written admission clearly acknowledging that the obligation still subsists.

(2)   Subject to subsection (3) below, where two or more persons are bound jointly by an obligation so that each is liable for the whole, and the subsistence of the obligation has been relevantly acknowledged by or on behalf of one of those persons then—

(a)   if the acknowledgment is made in the manner specified in paragraph (a) of the foregoing subsection it shall have effect for the purposes of the said sections 6 [, 7 and 8A] as respects the liability of each of those persons, and

(b)   if it is made in the manner specified in paragraph (b) of that subsection it shall have effect for those purposes only as respects the liability of the person who makes it.

(3)   Where the subsistence of an obligation affecting a trust has been relevantly acknowledged by or on behalf of one two or more co-trustees in the manner specified in paragraph (a) or (b) of subsection (1) of this section, the acknowledgment shall have effect for the purposes of the said sections 6 [, 7 and 8A] as respects the liability of the trust estate and any liability of each of the trustees.

(4)   In this section references to performance in relation to an obligation include, where the nature of the obligation so requires, references to refraining from doing something and to permitting or suffering something to be done or maintained.

11   Obligations to make reparation

(1)   Subject to subsections (2) and (3) below, any obligation (whether arising from any enactment, or from any rule of law or from, or by reason of any breach of, a contract or promise) to make reparation for loss, injury or damage caused by an [act or omission] shall be regarded for the purposes of section 6 of this Act as having become enforceable on the date when the loss, injury or damage occurred.

(2)   Where as a result of a continuing [act or omission] loss, injury or damage has occurred before the cessation of the [act or omission] the loss, injury or damage shall be deemed for the purposes of subsection (1) above to have occurred on the date when the [act or omission] ceased.

(3)   In relation to a case where on the date referred to in subsection (1) above (or, as the case may be, that subsection as modified by subsection (2) above) the

creditor was not aware, and could not with reasonable diligence have been aware, [of each of the facts mentioned in subsection (3A)], the said subsection (1) shall have effect as if for the reference therein to that date there were substituted a reference to the date when the creditor first became, or could with reasonable diligence have become, so aware.

[(3A)   The facts referred to in subsection (3) are—
  (a)   that loss, injury or damage has occurred,
  (b)   that the loss, injury or damage was caused by a person's act or omission, and
  (c)   the identity of that person.

(3B)   It does not matter for the purposes of subsections (3) and (3A) whether the creditor is aware that the act or omission that caused the loss, injury or damage is actionable in law.]

(4)   Subsections (1) and (2) above (with the omission of any reference therein to subsection (3) above) shall have effect for the purposes of section 7 of this Act as they have effect for the purposes of section 6 of this Act.

12   Savings

(1)   Where by virtue of any enactment passed or made before the passing of this Act a claim to establish a right or enforce implement of an obligation may be made only within a period of limitation specified in or determined under the enactment, and, by the expiration of a prescriptive period determined under section 6, 7 or 8 of this Act the right or obligation would, apart from this subsection, be extinguished before the expiration of the period of limitation, the said section shall have effect as if the relevant prescriptive period were extended so that it expires—
  (a)   on the date when the period of limitation expires, or
  (b)   if on that date any such claim made within that period has not been finally disposed of, on the date when the claim is so disposed of.

(2)   Nothing in section 6, 7 or 8 of this Act shall be construed so as to exempt any deed from challenge at any time on the ground that it is invalid *ex facie* or was forged.

[13   Restrictions on contracting out

(1)   The creditor and debtor in an obligation to which a prescriptive period under section 6 or 8A applies may agree to extend the prescriptive period under section 6 or, as the case may be, 8A in relation to the obligation.

(2)   A prescriptive period may be extended by agreement under subsection (1) only—
  (a)   after the period has commenced (and before it would, but for this section, expire),
  (b)   by a period of no more than one year, and
  (c)   once in relation to the same obligation.

(3)   Where there is an agreement under subsection (1) in relation to an obligation—
  (a)   the prescriptive period which is the subject of the agreement expires, in relation to the parties to the agreement, on the date specified in or determined in accordance with the agreement, but
  (b)   that does not otherwise affect the operation of this Act in relation to the obligation or the prescriptive period.

(4)   Except as provided for in subsections (1) to (3), a provision in an agreement is of no effect so far as the provision would (apart from this subsection) have the effect, in relation to a right or obligation to which section 6, 7, 8 or 8A (the 'section in question') applies, of—

(a) disapplying the section in question in relation to the right or obligation, or

(b) otherwise altering the operation of the section in question in relation to the right or obligation.]

General

14 Computation of prescriptive periods

(1) In the computation of a prescriptive period for the purposes of any provision of this Part of this Act—

(a) time occurring before the commencement of this Part of this Act shall be reckonable towards the prescriptive period in like manner as time occurring thereafter, but subject to the restriction that any time reckoned under this paragraph shall be less than the prescriptive period;

(b) any time during which any person against whom the provision is pled was under legal disability shall (except so far as otherwise provided by [subsection (4) of section 6 of this Act including that subsection as applied by section 8A of this Act] be reckoned as if the person were free from that disability;

(c) if the commencement of the prescriptive period would, apart from this paragraph, fall at a time in any day other than the beginning of the day, the period shall be deemed to have commenced at the beginning of the next following day;

(d) if the last day of the prescriptive period would, apart from this paragraph, be a holiday, the period shall, notwithstanding anything in the said provision, be extended to include any immediately succeeding day which is a holiday, any further immediately succeeding days which are holidays, and the next succeeding day which is not a holiday;

(e) save as otherwise provided in this Part of this Act regard shall be had to the like principles as immediately before the commencement of this Part of this Act were applicable to the computation of periods of prescription for the purposes of the Prescription Act 1617.

[. . .]

(1D) The prescriptive period calculated in relation to a relevant consumer dispute for the purposes of any provision of this Part of this Act is extended where the last day of the period would, apart from this subsection fall—

(a) after the date when the non-binding ADR procedure starts but before the date that such a procedure ends;

(b) on the date that a non-binding ADR procedure in relation to the dispute ends; or

(c) in the 8 weeks after the date that a non-binding ADR procedure in relation to the dispute ends.

(1E) Where subsection (1D) applies, the prescriptive period is extended so that it expires on the date falling 8 weeks after the date on which the non-binding ADR procedure ends.

(1F) For the purposes of subsections (1D)(a) and (1E), a non-binding ADR procedure starts in relation to a relevant dispute on the date when the dispute is first sent or otherwise communicated to the ADR entity in accordance with the entity's rules regarding the submission of complaints.

(1G) For the purposes of subsections (1D) and (1E), a non-binding ADR procedure ends on the date that any of the following occurs—

(a) all of the parties reach an agreement in resolution of the relevant consumer dispute;

(b) a party completes the notification of the other parties that it has withdrawn from the non-binding ADR procedure;

(c)   a party to whom a qualifying request is made fails to give a response reaching the other parties within 14 days of the request;

(d)   the ADR entity notifies the party that submitted the relevant dispute to the ADR entity that, in accordance with its policy, the ADR entity refuses to deal with the relevant consumer dispute;

(e)   after the parties are notified that the ADR entity can no longer act in relation to the relevant dispute (for whatever reason), the parties fail to agree within 14 days to submit the dispute to an alternative ADR entity;

(f)   the non-binding ADR procedure otherwise comes to an end pursuant to the rules of the ADR entity.

(2)   In this section [—

[. . .]

["ADR entity" means a person whose name appears on a list maintained in accordance with regulation 10 of the Alternative Dispute Resolution for Consumer Disputes (Competent Authorities and Information) Regulations 2015 (SI 2015/ 542);]

[. . .]

["ADR procedure" means a procedure for the out-of-court resolution of disputes through the intervention of an ADR entity which proposes or imposes a solution or brings the parties together with the aim of facilitating an amicable solution;]

["consumer" means an individual acting for purposes which are wholly or mainly outside that individual's trade, business, craft or profession;]

[. . .]

"holiday" means a day of any of the following descriptions, namely, a Saturday, a Sunday and a day which, in Scotland, is a bank holiday under the Banking and Financial Dealings Act 1971[;]

[. . .]

["non-binding ADR procedure" means an ADR procedure the outcome of which is not binding on the parties;

"qualifying request" is a request by a party that another (A) confirm to all parties that A is continuing with the non-binding ADR procedure;

["relevant consumer dispute" means a dispute that—

(a)   concerns obligations under a sales contract or a service contract, and

(b)   is between a trader established in the United Kingdom or the European Union and a consumer resident in the United Kingdom,

which the parties attempt to settle by recourse to a non-binding ADR procedure;]]

[. . .]

["sales contract" means a contract under which a trader transfers, or agrees to transfer, the ownership of goods to a consumer and the consumer pays, or agrees to pay, the price, including any contract that has both goods and services as its object;

"service contract" means a contract, other than a sales contract, under which a trader supplies, or agrees to supply, a service to a consumer and the consumer pays, or agrees to pay, the price;

"trader" means a person acting for purposes relating to that person's trade, business, craft or profession, whether acting personally or through another person acting in the trader's name or on the trader's behalf.]]

15   Interpretation of Part I

(1)   In this Part of this Act, unless the context otherwise requires, the following expressions have the meanings hereby assigned to them, namely—

'bill of exchange' has the same meaning as it has for the purposes of the Bills of Exchange Act 1882;

'date of execution', in relation to a deed executed on several dates, means the last of those dates;

'enactment' includes an order, regulation, rule or other instrument having effect by virtue of an Act;

'holiday' has the meaning assigned to it by section 14 of this Act;

'land' includes heritable property of any description;

'lease' includes a sub-lease;

'legal disability' means legal disability by reason of nonage or unsoundness of mind;

'possession' includes civil possession, and 'possessed' shall be construed accordingly;

'prescriptive period' means a period required for the operation of section 1, 2, 3, 6, 7 [, 8 or 8A] of this Act;

'promissory note' has the same meaning as it has for the purposes of the Bills of Exchange Act 1882;

'trustee' includes any person holding property in fiduciary capacity for another and, without prejudice to that generality, includes a trustee within the meaning of the Trusts (Scotland) Act 1921; and 'trust' shall be construed accordingly; and references to the recording of a deed are references to the recording thereof in the General Register of Sasines [and to the registering of a deed are to the registering thereof in the Land Register of Scotland].

(2)   In this Part of this Act, unless the context otherwise requires, any reference to an obligation or to a right includes a reference to the right or, as the case may be, to the obligation (if any), correlative thereto.

(3)   In this Part of this Act any reference to an enactment shall, unless the context otherwise requires, be construed as a reference to that enactment as amended or extended, and as including a reference thereto as applied, by or under any other enactment.

16   Amendments and repeals related to Part I

(1)   The enactment specified in Part I of Schedule 4 to this Act shall have effect subject to the amendment there specified, being an amendment related to this Part of this Act.

(2)   Subject to the next following subsection, the enactments specified in Part I of Schedule 5 to this Act (which includes certain enactments relating to the limitation of proof) are hereby repealed to the extent specified in column 3 of that Schedule.

(3)   Where by virtue of any Act repealed by this section the subsistence of an obligation in force at the date of the commencement of this Part of this Act was immediately before that date, by reason of the passage of time, provable only by the writ or oath of the debtor the subsistence of the obligation shall [(notwithstanding anything in sections 16(1) and 17(2)(a) of the Interpretation Act 1978, which relates to the effect of repeals)] as from that date be provable as if the said repealed Act had not passed.

SCHEDULES

Section 6   SCHEDULE 1
OBLIGATIONS AFFECTED BY PRESCRIPTIVE PERIODS OF FIVE YEARS
UNDER SECTION 6

1.   Subject to paragraph 2 below, section 6 of this Act applies—

(a)   to any obligation to pay a sum of money due in respect of a particular period—

(i)   by way of interest;

(ii)   by way of an instalment of an annuity;
[. . .]
(v)   by way of rent or other periodical payment under a lease;
(vi)   by way of a periodical payment in respect of the occupancy or use of land, not being an obligation falling within any other provision of this subparagraph;
(vii)   by way of a periodical payment under a [title condition], not being an obligation falling within any other provision of this sub-paragraph;
[(aa)   to any obligation to make a compensatory payment ('compensatory payment' being construed in accordance with section 8(1) of the Abolition of Feudal Tenure etc (Scotland) Act 2000 (asp 5), including that section as read with section 56 of that Act);

(aa)   to any obligation to pay compensation by virtue of section 2 of the Leasehold Casualties (Scotland) Act 2001 (asp 5);
(ab)   to any obligation arising by virtue of a right—
(i)   of reversion under the third proviso to section 2 of the School Sites Act 1841 (4 & 5 Vict c 38) (or of reversion under that proviso as applied by virtue of any other enactment);
(ii)   to petition for a declaration of forfeiture under section 7 of the Entail Sites Act 1840 (3 & 4 Vict c 48);]
[(ac)   to any obligation to pay a sum of money by way of costs to which section 12 of the Tenements (Scotland) Act 2004 (asp 11) applies;]
[(aca)   to any obligation to make a payment under section 46, 53(2) or 54(5) of the Long Leases (Scotland) Act 2012 (asp 9);]
[(ad)   to any obligation of the Keeper of the Registers of Scotland to pay compensation by virtue of section 84 of the Land Registration etc (Scotland) Act 2012 (asp 5);
(ae)   to any obligation to pay compensation by virtue of section 111 of that Act;]
[(af)   to any obligation arising by virtue of a right of redress under Part 4A of the Consumer Protection from Unfair Trading Regulations 2008;]
(b)   to any obligation based on redress of unjustified enrichment, including without prejudice to that generality any obligation of restitution, repetition or recompense;
(c)   to any obligation arising from *negotiorum gestio*;
(d)   to any obligation arising from liability (whether arising from any enactment or from any rule of law) to make reparation;
[(dd)   to any obligation arising by virtue of section 74(1) of the Criminal Injuries Compensation Act 1995 (recovery of compensation from offenders: general);]
(e)   to any obligation under a bill of exchange or a promissory note;
(f)   to any obligation of accounting, other than accounting for trust funds;
(g)   to any obligation arising from, or by reason of any breach of, a contract or promise, not being an obligation falling within any other provision of this paragraph.
2.   Notwithstanding anything in the foregoing paragraph, section 6 of this Act does not apply—
(a)   to any obligation to recognise or obtemper a decree of court, an arbitration award or an order of a tribunal or authority exercising jurisdiction under any enactment;
(b)   to any obligation arising from the issue of a bank note;
[. . .]
(d)   to any obligation under a contract of partnership or of agency, not being an obligation remaining, or becoming prestable on or after the termination of the relationship between the parties under the contract;

(e) except as provided in paragraph 1(a) to [(ae)] of this Schedule, to any obligation relating to land (including an obligation to recognise a servitude) [and any obligation of the Keeper of the Registers of Scotland to pay compensation by virtue of section 77 or 94 of the Land Registration etc (Scotland) Act 2012 (asp 5)];

[(ee) so as to extinguish, before the expiry of the continuous period of five years which immediately follows the coming into force of section 88 of the Title Conditions (Scotland) Act 2003 (asp 9) (prescriptive period for obligations arising by virtue of 1841 Act or 1840 Act), an obligation mentioned in sub-paragraph (ab) of paragraph 1 of this Schedule;]

(f) to any obligation to satisfy any claim to [. . .] legitim, jus relicti or jus relictae, or to any prior right of a surviving spouse under section 8 or 9 of the Succession (Scotland) Act 1964;

(g) to any obligation to make reparation in respect of personal injuries within the meaning of Part II of this Act or in respect of the death of any person as a result of such injuries;

[(gg) to any obligation to make reparation or otherwise make good in respect of defamation within the meaning of section 18A of this Act;

(ggg) to any obligation arising from liability under section 2 of the Consumer Protection Act 1987 (to make reparation for damage caused wholly or partly by a defect in a product);]

(h) to any obligation specified in Schedule 3 to this Act as an imprescriptible obligation.

[. . .]

[4. In this Schedule, 'title condition' shall be construed in accordance with section 122(1) of the Title Conditions (Scotland) Act 2003 (asp 9).]

SCHEDULE 2   Section 6

APPROPRIATE DATES FOR CERTAIN OBLIGATIONS FOR PURPOSES OF SECTION 6

1—(1) This paragraph applies to any obligation, not being part of a banking transaction, to pay money in respect of—

(a) goods supplied on sale or hire, or

(b) services rendered,

in a series of transactions between the same parties (whether under a single contract or under several contracts) and charged on continuing account.

(2) In the foregoing sub-paragraph—

(a) any reference to the supply of goods on sale includes a reference to the supply of goods under a hire-purchase agreement, a credit-sale agreement or a conditional sale agreement as defined (in each case) by section 1 of the Hire-Purchase (Scotland) Act 1965; and

(b) any reference to services rendered does not include the work of keeping the account in question.

(3) Where there is a series of transactions between a partnership and another party, the series shall be regarded for the purposes of this paragraph as terminated (without prejudice to any other mode of termination) if the partnership or any partner therein becomes bankrupt; but, subject to that, if the partnership (in the further provisions of this sub-paragraph referred to as 'the old partnership') is dissolved and is replaced by a single new partnership having among its partners any person who was a partner in the old partnership, then, for the purposes of this paragraph, the new partnership shall be regarded as if it were identical with the old partnership.

(4) The appropriate date in relation to an obligation to which this paragraph applies is the date on which payment for the goods last supplied, or, as the case may be, the services last rendered, became due.

2—(1) This paragraph applies to any obligation to repay the whole, or any part of, a sum of money lent to, or deposited with, the debtor under a contract of loan or, as the case may be, deposit.

(2) The appropriate date in relation to an obligation to which this paragraph applies is—

(a) if the contract contains a stipulation which makes provision with respect to the date on or before which repayment of the sum or, as the case may be, the part thereof is to be made, the date on or before which, in terms of that stipulation, the sum or part thereof is to be repaid; and

(b) if the contract contains no such stipulation, but a written demand for repayment of the sum, or, as the case may be, the part thereof, is made by or on behalf of the creditor to the debtor, the date when such demand is made or first made.

3—(1) This paragraph applies to any obligation under a contract of partnership or of agency, being an obligation remaining, or becoming, prestable on or after the termination of the relationship between the parties under the contract.

(2) The appropriate date in relation to an obligation to which this paragraph applies is—

(a) if the contract contains a stipulation which makes provision with respect to the date on or before which performance on the obligation is to be due, the date on or before which, in terms of that stipulation, the obligation is to be performed; and

(b) in any other case the date when the said relationship terminated.

4—(1) This paragraph applies to any obligation—

(a) to pay an instalment of a sum of money payable by instalments,

(b) to execute any instalment of work due to be executed by instalments, not being an obligation to which any of the foregoing paragraphs applies.

(2) The appropriate date in relation to an obligation to which this paragraph applies is the date on which the last of the instalments is due to be paid or, as the case may be, to be executed.

Sections 7 & 8: Schedule 1   SCHEDULE 3
RIGHTS AND OBLIGATIONS WHICH ARE IMPRESCRIPTIBLE FOR THE
PURPOSES OF SECTIONS 7 AND 8 AND SCHEDULE 1

The following are imprescriptible rights and obligations for the purposes of sections 7(2) and 8(2) of, and paragraph 2(h) of Schedule 1 to, this Act, namely—

(a) any real right of ownership in land;

(b) the right in land of the lessee under a recorded lease;

(c) any right exercisable as a *res merae facultatis*;

(d) any right to recover property *extra commercium*;

(e) any obligation of a trustee—

(i) to produce accounts of the trustee's intromissions with any property of the trust;

(ii) to make reparation or restitution in respect of any fraudulent breach of trust to which the trustee was a party or was privy;

(iii) to make furthcoming to any person entitled thereto any trust property, or the proceeds of any such property, in the possession of the trustee, or to make good the value of any such property previously received by the trustee and appropriated to his own use;

(f)   any obligation of a third party to make furthcoming to any person entitled thereto any trust property received by the third party otherwise than in good faith and in his possession;

(g)   any right to recover stolen property from the person by whom it was stolen or from any person privy to the stealing thereof;

(h)   any right to be served as heir to an ancestor or to take any steps necessary for making up or completing title to any [real right] in land;

[(i)   any obligation of the Keeper of the Registers of Scotland to rectify an inaccuracy in the Land Register of Scotland].

LAND TENURE REFORM (SCOTLAND) ACT 1974
(1974, c 38)

2   Prohibition of new ground annuals and other periodical payments from land

(1)   No deed executed after the commencement of this Act shall impose ground annual, skat or any other periodical payment [. . .] in respect of the tenure or use of land or under a [title condition] not being a payment in respect of a lease, liferent or other right of occupancy, [. . .] a payment in defrayal of or contribution towards some continuing cost related to the land, or a payment under a heritable security.

(2)   A provision in a deed executed after such commencement which purports to impose any payment to which subsection (1) above applies shall not render the deed void or unenforceable, but the deed shall have effect only to the extent (if any) that it would have had effect under the law in force before such commencement if it had not imposed any such payment.

[(3)   In subsection (1) above, 'title condition' has the meaning given by section 122(1) of the Title Conditions (Scotland) Act 2003 (asp 9).]

PART II
LIMITATIONS ON RESIDENTIAL USE OF PROPERTY LET UNDER FUTURE LONG LEASES

8   Property let under future long lease, etc not to be used as private dwelling-house

(1)   It shall be a condition of every long lease executed after the commencement of this Act that, subject to the provisions of this Part of this Act, no part of the property which is subject to the lease shall be used as or as part of a private dwelling-house.

(2)   For the purposes of this Part of this Act, any garden, yard, garage, outhouse or pertinent used along with any dwelling-house shall be deemed to form part of a dwelling-house, and use as a dwelling-house shall not include use as the site of a caravan.

(3)   The use as or as part of a private dwelling-house of part of a property which is subject to a long lease shall not constitute a breach of the condition contained in subsection (1) above if such use is ancillary to the use of the remainder of the property otherwise than as or as part of a private dwelling-house and it would be detrimental to the efficient exercise of the use last-mentioned if the said ancillary use did not occur on that property.

[(3ZA)   The condition contained in subsection (1) above does not apply in relation to a private residential tenancy as defined in the Private Housing (Tenancies) (Scotland) Act 2016.]

[(3A)   The condition contained in subsection (1) above does not apply to a long lease executed after the commencement of section 138 of the Housing

(Scotland) Act 2010 (asp 17) where at the time the lease is executed the lessee is—

(a) a social landlord (within the meaning of section 165 of the Housing (Scotland) Act 2010);

(b) a body connected to a social landlord (within the meaning of section 164 of the Housing (Scotland) Act 2010);

(c) a rural housing body (within the meaning of section 122(1) of the Title Conditions (Scotland) Act 2003) [; or

(d) a body prescribed, or of a type prescribed, by the Scottish Ministers by order made by statutory instrument].]

[3B) An order under subsection (3A)(d) may—

(a) prescribe a body or type of body subject to conditions or restrictions,

(b) prescribe conditions which a body or type of body must meet for the purposes of subsection (3A),

(c) restrict the application of subsection (3A) to specified leases, or leases of specified descriptions,

(d) prescribe circumstances in which subsection (3A) is to apply or cease to apply in relation to a body or type of body or any lease,

(e) make provision about the consequences, in relation to any lease, of—

(i) a breach of any condition or restriction prescribed by the order, or

(ii) subsection (3A) otherwise ceasing to apply in relation to a body or type of body or the lease.

(3C) Provision made by virtue of subsection (3B)(e) may, in particular, include provision for the protection of the interests of tenants or occupiers of any dwelling-houses on the property which is subject to the lease.

(3D) An order under subsection (3A)(d)—

(a) may modify any enactment, and

(b) is not to be made unless a draft of the statutory instrument containing the order has been laid before, and approved by resolution of, the Scottish Parliament.]

(4) For the purposes of this Part of this Act—

'lessor' and 'lessee' mean any person holding for the time being the interest of lessor or lessee (as the case may be); and

'long lease' means any grant of—

(a) a lease, or

(b) a liferent or other right of occupancy granted for payment (other than payment in defrayal of or contribution towards some continuing cost related to such liferent use or such occupancy, as the case may be),

which is either—

(i) subject to a duration, whether definite or indefinite, which could (in terms of the grant and without any subsequent agreement, express or implied, between the persons holding the interests of the grantor and the grantee) extend for more than 20 years, or

(ii) subject to any provision whereby any person holding the interest of the grantor or the grantee is under a future obligation, if so requested by the other, to renew the grant so that the total duration could so extend for more than 20 years, or whereby, if he does not so renew it, he will be liable to make some payment or to perform some other obligation.

[but, in relation to a lease granted before 1st September 1974, does not include its renewal (whether before or after the commencement of section 1 of the Law Reform (Miscellaneous Provisions) (Scotland) Act 1985) in implement of an obligation in or under it].

(5) This Part of this Act shall not apply in relation to the use of property for the time being forming part or deemed to form part of—

[(a) the land comprised in a lease constituting a 1991 Act tenancy, within the meaning of the Agricultural Holdings (Scotland) Act 2003 (asp 11);

(aa)   the land comprised in a lease constituting a short limited duration tenancy [, a limited duration tenancy, a modern limited duration tenancy or a repairing tenancy] within the meaning of that Act;]

(b)   a holding, within the meaning of the Small Landholders (Scotland) Acts 1886 to 1931;

(c)   a croft, within the meaning of the Crofters (Scotland) Acts 1955 and 1961.

(6)   Nothing in this Part of this Act shall affect the right of the lessor to terminate the lease and recover possession of the property subject thereto on the ground of breach of a conventional condition of the lease which has the effect of prohibiting such use of the property as constitutes a breach of the condition contained in subsection (1) above.

(7)   Nothing in this Part of this Act shall prevent a tenancy from being or becoming a protected or statutory tenancy within the meaning of the Rent (Scotland) Act [1984 or a Scottish secure tenancy within the meaning of the Housing (Scotland) Act 2001 (asp 10)], but nothing in [either of those Acts] restricting the power of a court to make an order for possession of a dwelling-house shall prevent the granting of a decree of removing under section 9(1) of this Act.

9   Consequences of use as dwelling-house of property subject to long lease

(1)   A breach of the condition of a long lease executed after the commencement of this Act, contained in section 8(1) of this Act, shall not render the lease void or unenforceable, but, subject to the provisions of this section and of section 10 of this Act, where such a breach occurs, the lessor shall be entitled to give to the lessee notice to terminate the use constituting the breach within 28 days from the date of the notice; and, if the lessee shall fail to terminate that use within that period, the lessor shall be entitled to raise an action of removing against the lessee concluding for his removal from such part of the property as is subject to the use at the expiry of 28 days after the decree of removing is extracted, and the court may decern for the termination of the lease in respect of such part and the removal of the lessee therefrom and, failing such removal, for his ejection therefrom on expiry of the 28 days last mentioned.

(2)   A notice under subsection (1) above shall be in or as nearly as may be in the form contained in Schedule 5 to this Act.

(3)   It shall be a defence to an action under subsection (1) above that the breach of condition constituting the ground of action has ceased.

(4)   Subject to section 10(3) of this Act, in an action under subsection (1) above, if it is proved that the use of the property constituting the ground of action has at any time been approved by the person holding at that time the interest of the lessor in the lease, either expressly or by his actings, and the said use has not subsequently been discontinued, the court shall not decern in terms of that subsection, but—

(a)   where the lease is subject to a duration expiring in a year more than 20 years after the year in which the notice under subsection (1) above relative to the breach was given, the court shall decern that the lease shall, in respect of such part of the property as is subject to the use, have effect as if for the year of expiry there were substituted the year 20 years after the year in which the said notice was given;

(b)   where the lease is subject to a duration expiring in a year less than 20 years after that year, the lease shall continue in force according to its terms; and the said part of the property subject to the lease (and, during the remaining period of the lease as determined by reference to this subsection, any over-lease, insofar as it relates to that part) shall cease to be subject to the condition contained in section 8(1) of this Act.

(5)   Where the breach of condition constituting the ground of action under subsection (1) above relates to part only of the property subject to the lease, any

decree granted to the pursuer in the action under subsection (1) or (4)(a) above shall contain a particular description or a description by reference (in accordance with the provisions of the Conveyancing (Scotland) Act 1874 and the Conveyancing (Scotland) Act 1924) of such part; and in such a case the court shall decern for such adjustment (if any) as it thinks fit (to take effect on the termination of the lease of such part in terms of the decree) in the rent of the remaining part of the property and in the conditions of the lease, including the addition of new conditions, but not including any provision for the payment of money.

(6) Subject to the provisions of this Part of this Act and of section 37(1) of the Sheriff Courts (Scotland) Act 1971, and notwithstanding section 35(1)(c) of that Act, the procedure in an action of removing under this section shall be that in an ordinary cause; and on the granting of a decree to the pursuer in such an action, or at any time before the decree is extracted, the court may sist extract of the decree for such period or periods as it thinks fit to enable any facts to be established which (if the action were still pending) would constitute a defence thereto, and if the court is satisfied that any such facts are established it may vary or rescind the decree, subject to such conditions (if any) with regard to payment of arrears of rent and otherwise as the court thinks fit.

(7) Notwithstanding the provisions of section 24 of the Court of Session Act 1868, Rule 63(b) of the Rules of Court 1965 or Rule 25 of Schedule 1 to the Sheriff Courts (Scotland) Act 1907, a decree granted in an action under this section shall, as in a question with third parties who have acted onerously and in good faith in reliance on the records, be final and not subject to challenge when an extract thereof shall have been recorded in the Register of Sasines.

(8) The provisions of this section and of section 10 of this Act shall apply in relation to a grant (not being a lease) mentioned in section 8(4) of this Act as they apply in relation to a lease, and any reference to a lease, over-lease or sub-lease, to the parties thereto, or to rent, shall be construed accordingly.

10 Modification of s 9 where lease subject to sub-lease or heritable security

(1) For the avoidance of doubt, it is hereby declared that (subject to the provisions of this section) sections 8 and 9 of this Act shall apply, as between the parties to any over-lease or sub-lease executed after the commencement of this Act, as they apply as between the parties to any other lease so executed.

(2) The pursuer in an action under section 9 of this Act shall give such intimation thereof as the court may direct—

(a) to every person appearing, from a search in the Register of Sasines for a period of 20 years immediately prior to the raising of the action, to hold for the time being the interest of creditor in a heritable security over the lease which is the subject of the action; and

(b) where the said lease is, in relation to any part of the property which is subject to the use constituting the ground of action, subject to any sub-lease, to every person appearing from such a search and from examination of the valuation roll or otherwise to be the lessee in any such sublease (of whatever duration) or the creditor in a heritable security over any such sub-lease;

and any such creditor or lessee as aforesaid shall, subject to the provisions of this section, be titled to plead in the action any defence which could be pleaded by the defender in the action.

(3) The defence provided under section 9(4) of this Act shall not be available to the lessee in a lease in respect of the use of property subject to a sub-lease derived from that lease.

(4) A sub-lessee, provided that he could have pleaded the defence provided by section 9(4) of this Act in an action by the lessor in the sub-lease, may, on

being sisted to an action under the said section 9 by the lessor in any overlease, plead
that defence in relation to the approval by the lessor in that overlease or in any sub-
lease under that over-lease of property which is subject to the use constituting the
ground of action; and the court, on being satisfied that the defence is established to
that effect, shall be entitled to decern in terms of the said section 9(4) as if the action
had been brought by the lessor in the sub-lease first mentioned.

(5)   The right provided by subsection (4) above shall be available to a sublessee
whose lease is not a long lease to the same extent as if it had been a long lease.

PART III
MISCELLANEOUS

11   Right to redeem heritable security after 20 years where security subjects used as private dwelling-house

(1)   The provisions of this section shall apply in relation to a heritable security
executed after the commencement of this Act, including a heritable security in relation to a debenture described in [section 739 of the Companies Act 2006] (perpetual
debentures, etc).

(2)   The debtor in a heritable security to which this section applies, or, where the
debtor is not the proprietor, the proprietor of the security subjects shall, subject to the
provisions of this section, be entitled, on giving two months' notice of his intention
so to do, to redeem the security at any time not less than 20 years after the execution
thereof, if, at the time when he gives such notice, the security subjects or any part
thereof are used as or as part of a private dwelling-house.

In determining for the purposes of this section whether such use has occurred,
subsection (2) of section 8 of this Act shall apply as it applies for the purposes
of that section, and the ancillary use described in subsection (3) of that section shall not render the security subjects subject to the provisions of this
section.

(3)   The right to redeem a heritable security conferred by this section shall
not apply where the use of the security subjects which is purported to constitute
the ground of the right, in terms of subsection (2) above, was, at the time of the
notice aforesaid, in contravention of a conventional condition of or relating to
the security, unless the person in right of the creditor at any time had approved
that use expressly or by his actings, and the said use had not subsequently been
discontinued.

[(3A)   The right to redeem a heritable security conferred by this section does not
apply to a heritable security where—
    (a)   the debtor (or where the debtor is not the proprietor, the proprietor of the
    security subjects) has in writing renounced the right to redeem conferred by this
    section; and
    (b)   at the time of doing so that body is—
        (i)   a social landlord (within the meaning of section 165 of the Housing
        (Scotland) Act 2010);
        (ii)   a body connected to a social landlord (within the meaning of section 164
        of the Housing (Scotland) Act 2010);
        (iii)   a rural housing body (within the meaning of section 122(1) of the Title
        Conditions (Scotland) Act 2003) [; or
        (iv)   a body prescribed, or of a type prescribed, by the Scottish Ministers by
        order made by statutory instrument].]
[(3B)   An order under subsection (3A)(b)(iv) may—
    (a)   prescribe a body or type of body subject to conditions or restrictions,

(b) prescribe conditions which a body or type of body must meet for the purposes of subsection (3A),

(c) restrict the application of subsection (3A) to specified heritable securities, or heritable securities of specified descriptions,

(d) prescribe circumstances in which subsection (3A) is to apply or cease to apply in relation to a body or type of body or any heritable security.

(3C) A statutory instrument containing an order under subsection (3A)(b)(iv) is subject to annulment in pursuance of a resolution of the Scottish Parliament.]

[(3D) The right to redeem a heritable security conferred by this section does not apply to a heritable security which is in security of a debt of a description specified in an order made by the Scottish Ministers.

(3E) An order under subsection (3D) may—

(a) disapply the right to redeem conferred by this section subject to conditions or restrictions,

(b) restrict the disapplication of the right to redeem conferred by this section to—

(i) specified descriptions of debt,

(ii) specified creditors, or creditors of specified descriptions,

(iii) specified heritable securities, or heritable securities of specified descriptions,

(c) prescribe circumstances in which the disapplication of the right to redeem conferred by this section is to apply or cease to apply.

(3F) An order under subsection (3D) is subject to the negative procedure.]

(4) Subject to the provisions of subsection (5) below, the whole amount due to the creditor in a heritable security on redemption under this section, including any sums due thereunder by way of interest or otherwise, shall not exceed the amount remaining unredeemed of—

(a) where the security constituted to any extent (whether expressly or otherwise) the consideration for the acquisition of the security subjects by the debtor or proprietor or his predecessor in title, any excess of the value of the security subjects at the date of the execution of the security over the amount of money paid for the subjects, and

(b) any money advanced under the security to the debtor or proprietor and his predecessors in title, and

(c) any expense or charge reasonably incurred by the creditor in the exercise of a right to perform any obligation imposed on the debtor, which the debtor has failed to perform, and which was reasonably necessary for the protection of the security,

together with interest outstanding at the date of the said notice of redemption and interest due for the period between the date of that notice and the date of redemption, at the rate applicable in terms of the security immediately before that date.

(5) In the application of paragraph (a) of subsection (4) above to security subjects which are burdened with two or more heritable securities to which this section applies, the maximum amount determined in accordance with that paragraph shall be apportioned among the securities according to the rights and preferences of the creditors in the securities; and the amount so apportioned in respect of each of the securities shall, on the redemption of any of the securities, be the maximum amount due in terms of that paragraph on the redemption at any time of all such securities.

[. . .]

12 Restriction to 20 years of period within which certain rights of redemption and reversion are exercisable

A right of redemption or reversion of land (other than the right of a lessor to the reversion of a lease), created in a deed executed after the commencement of this

Act, which purports to be exercisable on the happening of an event which is bound to occur, or the occurrence of which is within the control of the person for the time being entitled to exercise the right or of a third party, shall be exercisable only within 20 years of the date of its creation.

16   No casualties in future leases
In leases executed after the commencement of this Act, it shall not be lawful to stipulate for the payment of any casualty, but this provision shall be without prejudice to the right to stipulate for review of rent or for a permanent or periodical variation of rent in accordance with any condition of or relating to the lease.

17   Interposed leases
(1)   It shall be competent, and shall be deemed always to have been competent, for the person in right of the lessor of a lease to grant, during the subsistence of that lease, a lease of or including his interest in the whole or part of the land subject to the lease first mentioned, and whether longer or shorter than or of the same duration as that lease, and the said grant shall be effectual (or, as the case may be, shall be deemed to have been effectual) for all purposes as a lease of land; and the grantee or person in his right shall be deemed (whether before or after the commencement of this Act) to have entered into the possession of the land leased under the grant at the date of that grant: Provided that, in the case of a lease which is registrable under the Registration of Leases (Scotland) Act 1857, or which (being a lease granted before the commencement of this Act) would have been so registrable if this Act had been in force, the rights of parties shall be determined by reference to that Act, as amended by any other enactment, including this Act.

(2)   Subject to any agreement to the contrary, as from the date of the grant of a lease in terms of subsection (1) above, the lessee under the lease so granted shall become (or, as the case may be, shall be deemed to have become) the lessor of the lessee in the subsisting lease, on the same terms and conditions as if the subsisting lease had, in respect of the property subject to the lease granted as aforesaid, been assigned to the grantee of the lease so granted; and, on the determination, for any reason, of the lease so granted, any remaining rights and obligations of the person in right of the said grantee, in relation to the said subsisting lease, shall vest (or as the case may be, shall be deemed to have vested) in the person in right of the grantor of the lease granted as aforesaid, on the same terms and conditions as if that lease had not been granted.

PART IV
GENERAL

21   Provisions for contracting out to be void
Subject to the provisions of [sections 8(3A), 8(6), 11(3), 11(3A) and 11(3D)] of this Act, any agreement or other provision, however constituted, which is made after the commencement of this Act, shall be void in so far as it purports to exclude or limit the operation of any enactment contained in this Act.

22   Application to Crown
This Act shall apply to land [. . .] belonging to Her Majesty in right of the Crown or to a Government department, or held on behalf of Her Majesty for the purposes of a Government department, in like manner as it applies to other land.

23   Interpretation and repeals
(1)   In this Act, unless the context otherwise requires—

'deed' has the meaning assigned to it in section 3 of the Titles to Land Consolidation (Scotland) Act 1868, section 3 of the Conveyancing (Scotland) Act 1874 and section 2 of the Conveyancing (Scotland) Act 1924;

'heritable security' (except in relation to sections 4(5), 5(10) and 10(2)), does not include any security for the purpose of securing the payment of a periodical sum payable in respect of land, and 'heritable creditors' shall be construed accordingly;

'land' has the meaning assigned to it in section 2 of the said Act of 1924.

(2)   Unless the context otherwise requires, any reference in this Act to any other enactment is a reference thereto as amended, and includes a reference thereto as extended or applied, by or under a any other enactment, including this Act.

(3)   The enactments specified in Schedule 7 to this Act are hereby repealed to the extent specified in relation thereto in that Schedule.

24   Short title, commencement and extent

(1)   This Act may be cited as the Land Tenure Reform (Scotland) Act 1974.
(2)   This Act shall come into operation on 1st September 1974.
(3)   This Act shall extend to Scotland only.

SCHEDULES

[. . .]

Section 9   SCHEDULE 5
              FORM OF NOTICE PRESCRIBED UNDER SECTION 9

'NOTICE

under subsection (1) of section 9 of the Land Tenure Reform (Scotland) Act 1974 (consequences of use as dwelling-house of property subject to long lease, etc)

To Terminate Use as or as part of Private Dwelling-House of
Property subject to [Lease]
[Liferent]
[Right of Occupancy]
                                    [*Address of person sending notice, and Date*]
To [*name and address of addressee*]

You are required to terminate the use as or as part of a private dwelling-house of [*give sufficient identification of the property by reference to the lease, etc. or otherwise: if the notice relates to the use of part only of the property subject to the lease, etc., the identification should be a particular description or a description by reference of that part, in terms of section 9(5) of this Act*] within 28 days from the date of this notice, under pain of action of removing in terms of section 9 of the Land Tenure Reform (Scotland) Act 1974.

(Signed) AB.
or CD,
Agent for AB.'

Note to be appended to Notice

'The reason for giving this notice is contravention of the condition contained in subsection (1) of section 8 of the Land Tenure Reform (Scotland) Act 1974 (property let under long lease, etc. not to be used as private dwelling-house).

Without prejudice to any other rights, obligations or defences which you may have under section 8, 9 or 10 of the said Act or otherwise, your attention is directed to the following provisions of the Act:—

Section 9(3):
[*Here quote the subsection verbatim*]
Section 9(4):
[*Here quote the subsection verbatim*]
Section 10(3):
[*Here quote the subsection verbatim*]

If you are in doubt about your position in law you should obtain legal advice promptly.'

LAND REGISTRATION (SCOTLAND) ACT 1979
(1979, c 33)

15 Simplification of deeds relating to registered interests
[. . .]

(4)   It shall not be necessary, in connection with any deed relating to a [plot of land or lease registered in the Land Register of Scotland], to include an assignation of any obligation or right of relief or to narrate the series of writs by which the grantor of the deed became entitled to enforce that obligation or exercise that right if the obligation or right has been entered in the title sheet of [the plot or lease] and, accordingly, in such a case—

(a)   section 50 of and Schedule M to the Conveyancing (Scotland) Act 1874 (form and effect of assigning right of relief or other right affecting land) shall not apply to such a deed; and

(b)   such a deed shall for all purposes import a valid and complete assignation of that obligation or right.

16 Omission of certain clauses in deeds

(1)   It shall not be necessary to insert in any deed executed after the commencement of this Act which conveys an interest in land a clause of assignation of writs and any such deed shall, unless specially qualified, import an assignation to the grantee of the title deeds and searches and all deeds not duly recorded, and shall—

(a)   impose on the grantor or any successor an obligation—

(i)   to deliver to the grantee all title deeds and searches relating exclusively to the interest conveyed;

(ii)   to make forthcoming to the grantee and his successors at his or their expense on all necessary occasions any title deeds and searches which remain in the possession of the grantor or any successor and which relate partly to the interest conveyed; and

(b)   import an assignation to the grantee by the grantor of his right to require any person having custody thereof to exhibit or deliver any title deeds and searches remaining undelivered; and

(c)   impose on the grantee or any successor an obligation to make forthcoming on all necessary occasions to any party having an interest therein any deeds and searches which have been delivered to the grantee but which relate partly to interests other than the interest conveyed to the grantee.

(2)   [. . .]

(3)   It shall not be necessary to insert in any deed conveying an interest in land executed after the commencement of this Act a clause of assignation of rents or a clause of obligation of relief, and any such deed so executed shall, unless specially qualified, import—

(a)   an assignation of the rents payable—

(i)   in the case of backhand rents, at the legal terms following the date of entry, and

(ii)   in the case of forehand rents, at the conventional terms following that date;

(b)   an obligation on the grantor to relieve the grantee of all [. . .] annuities and public, parochial and local burdens exigible in respect of the interest prior to the date of entry [. . .].

SALE OF GOODS ACT 1979
(1979, c 54)

PART II
FORMATION OF THE CONTRACT

Contract of sale

2   Contract of sale

(1)   A contract of sale of goods is a contract by which the seller transfers or agrees to transfer the property in goods to the buyer for a money consideration, called the price.

(2)   There may be a contract of sale between one part owner and another.

(3)   A contract of sale may be absolute or conditional.

(4)   Where under a contract of sale the property in the goods is transferred from the seller to the buyer the contract is called a sale.

(5)   Where under a contract of sale the transfer of the property in the goods is to take place at a future time or subject to some condition later to be fulfilled the contract is called an agreement to sell.

(6)   An agreement to sell becomes a sale when the time elapses or the conditions are fulfilled subject to which the property in the goods is to be transferred.

Subject matter of contract

5   Existing or future goods

(1)   The goods which form the subject of a contract of sale may be either existing goods, owned or possessed by the seller, or goods to be manufactured or acquired by him after the making of the contract of sale, in this Act called future goods.

(2)   There may be a contract for the sale of goods the acquisition of which by the seller depends on a contingency which may or may not happen.

(3)   Where by a contract of sale the seller purports to effect a present sale of future goods, the contract operates as an agreement to sell the goods.

[Implied terms etc]

12   Implied terms about title, etc

(1)   In a contract of sale, other than one to which subsection (3) below applies, there is an implied [term] on the part of the seller that in the case of a sale he has a right to sell the goods, and in the case of an agreement to sell he will have such a right at the time when the property is to pass.

(2)   In a contract of sale, other than one to which subsection (3) below applies, there is also an implied [term] that—

(a)   the goods are free, and will remain free until the time when the property is to pass, from any charge or encumbrance not disclosed or known to the buyer before the contract is made, and

(b)   the buyer will enjoy quiet possession of the goods except so far as it may be disturbed by the owner or other person entitled to the benefit of any charge or encumbrance so disclosed or known.

(3)   This subsection applies to a contract of sale in the case of which there appears from the contract or is to be inferred from its circumstances an intention that the seller should transfer only such title as he or a third person may have.

(4)   In a contract to which subsection (3) above applies there is an implied [term] that all charges or encumbrances known to the seller and not known to the buyer have been disclosed to the buyer before the contract is made.

(5)   In a contract to which subsection (3) above applies there is also an implied [term] that none of the following will disturb the buyer's quiet possession of the goods, namely—

(a)   the seller;

(b)   in a case where the parties to the contract intend that the seller should transfer only such title as a third person may have, that person;

(c)   anyone claiming through or under the seller or that third person otherwise than under a charge or encumbrance disclosed or known to the buyer before the contract is made.

. . .

[(7)   This section does not apply to a contract to which Chapter 2 of Part 1 of the Consumer Rights Act 2015 applies (but see the provision made about such contracts in section 11 of that Act).]

PART III
EFFECTS OF THE CONTRACT

Transfer of property as between seller and buyer

16   Goods must he ascertained
[Subject to section 20A below] where there is a contract for the sale of unascertained goods no property in the goods is transferred to the buyer unless and until the goods are ascertained.

17   Property passes when intended to pass
(1)   Where there is a contract for the sale of specific or ascertained goods the property in them is transferred to the buyer at such time as the parties to the contract intend it to be transferred.

(2)   For the purpose of ascertaining the intention of the parties regard shall be had to the terms of the contract, the conduct of the parties and the circumstances of the case.

18   Rules for ascertaining intention
Unless a different intention appears, the following are rules for ascertaining the intention of the parties as to the time at which the property in the goods is to pass to the buyer.

Rule 1.—Where there is an unconditional contract for the sale of specific goods in a deliverable state the property in the goods passes to the buyer when the contract is made, and it is immaterial whether the time of payment or the time of delivery, or both, be postponed.

Rule 2.—Where there is a contract for the sale of specific goods and the seller is bound to do something to the goods for the purpose of putting them into a deliverable state, the property does not pass until the thing is done and the buyer has notice that it has been done.

Rule 3.—Where there is a contract for the sale of specific goods in a deliverable state but the seller is bound to weigh, measure, test, or do some other act or thing with reference to the goods for the purpose of ascertaining the price, the property does not pass until the act or thing is done and the buyer has notice that it has been done.

Rule 4.—When goods are delivered to the buyer on approval or on sale or return or other similar terms the property in the goods passes to the buyer:—

(a)   when he signifies his approval or acceptance to the seller or does any other act adopting the transaction;

(b)   if he does not signify his approval or acceptance to the seller but retains the goods without giving notice of rejection, then, if a time has been fixed for the return of the goods, on the expiration of that time, and, if no time has been fixed, on the expiration of a reasonable time.

Rule 5.—(1)   Where there is a contract for the sale of unascertained or future goods by description, and goods of that description and in a deliverable state are unconditionally appropriated to the contract, either by the seller with the assent of the buyer or by the buyer with the assent of the seller, the property in the goods then passes to the buyer; and the assent may be express or implied, and may be given either before or after the appropriation is made.

(2)   Where, in pursuance of the contract, the seller delivers the goods to the buyer or to a carrier or other bailee or custodier (whether named by the buyer or not) for the purpose of transmission to the buyer, and does not reserve the right of disposal, he is to be taken to have unconditionally appropriated the goods to the contract.

[(3)   Where there is a contract for the sale of a specified quantity of unascertained goods in a deliverable state forming part of a bulk which is identified either in the contract or by subsequent agreement between the parties and the bulk is reduced to (or to less than) that quantity, then, if the buyer under that contract is the only buyer to whom goods are then due out of the bulk—

(a)   the remaining goods are to be taken as appropriated to that contract at the time when the bulk is so reduced; and

(b)   the property in those goods then passes to that buyer.

(4)   Paragraph (3) above applies also (with the necessary modifications) where a bulk is reduced to (or to less than) the aggregate of the quantities due to a single buyer under separate contracts relating to that bulk and he is the only buyer to whom goods are then due out of that bulk.]

19   Reservation of right of disposal

(1)   Where there is a contract for the sale of specific goods or where goods are subsequently appropriated to the contract, the seller may, by the terms of the contract or appropriation, reserve the right of disposal of the goods until certain conditions are fulfilled; and in such a case, notwithstanding the delivery of the goods to the buyer, or to a carrier or other bailee or custodier for the purpose of transmission to the buyer, the property in the goods does not pass to the buyer until the conditions imposed by the seller are fulfilled.

(2)   Where goods are shipped, and by the bill of lading the goods are deliverable to the order of the seller or his agent, the seller is prima facie to be taken to reserve the right of disposal.

(3)   Where the seller of goods draws on the buyer for the price, and transmits the bill of exchange and bill of lading to the buyer together to secure acceptance or payment of the bill of exchange, the buyer is bound to return the bill of lading if he does not honour the bill of exchange, and if he wrongfully retains the bill of lading the property in the goods does not pass to him.

20   [Passing of risk]

(1)   Unless otherwise agreed, the goods remain at the seller's risk until the property in them is transferred to the buyer, but when the property in them is transferred to the buyer the goods are at the buyer's risk whether delivery has been made or not.

(2)   But where delivery has been delayed through the fault of either buyer or seller the goods are at the risk of the party at fault as regards any loss which might not have occurred but for such fault.

(3)   Nothing in this section affects the duties or liabilities of either seller or buyer as a bailee or custodier of the goods of the other party.

[(4)   This section does not apply to a contract to which Chapter 2 of Part 1 of the Consumer Rights Act 2015 applies (but see the provision made about such contracts in section 29 of that Act).]

[20A   Undivided shares in goods forming part of a bulk

(1)   This section applies to a contract for the sale of a specified quantity of unascertained goods if the following conditions are met—

(a)   the goods or some of them form part of a bulk which is identified either in the contract or by subsequent agreement between the parties; and

(b)   the buyer has paid the price for some or all of the goods which are the subject of the contract and which form part of the bulk.

(2)   Where this section applies, then (unless the parties agree otherwise), as soon as the conditions specified in paragraphs (a) and (b) of subsection (1) above are met or at such later time as the parties may agree—

(a)   property in an undivided share in the bulk is transferred to the buyer; and

(b)   the buyer becomes an owner in common of the bulk.

(3)   Subject to subsection (4) below, for the purposes of this section, the undivided share of a buyer in a bulk at any time shall be such share as the quantity of goods paid for and due to the buyer out of the bulk bears to the quantity of goods in the bulk at that time.

(4)   Where the aggregate of the undivided shares of buyers in a bulk determined under subsection (3) above would at any time exceed the whole of the bulk at that time, the undivided share in the bulk of each buyer shall be reduced proportionately so that the aggregate of the undivided shares is equal to the whole bulk.

(5)   Where a buyer has paid the price for only some of the goods due to him out of a bulk, any delivery to the buyer out of the bulk shall, for the purposes of this section, be ascribed in the first place to the goods in respect of which payment has been made.

(6)   For the purpose of this section payment of part of the price for any goods shall be treated as payment for a corresponding part of the goods.]

[20B   Deemed consent by co-owner to dealings in bulk goods

(1)   A person who has become an owner in common of a bulk by virtue of section 20A above shall be deemed to have consented to—

(a)   any delivery of goods out of the bulk to any other owner in common of the bulk, being goods which are due to him under his contract;

(b)   any removal, dealing with, delivery or disposal of goods in the bulk by any other person who is an owner in common of the bulk in so far as the goods fall within that co-owner's undivided share in the bulk at the time of the removal, dealing, delivery or disposal.

(2)   No cause of action shall accrue to anyone against a person by reason of that person having acted in accordance with paragraph (a) or (b) of subsection (1) above in reliance on any consent deemed to have been given under that subsection.

(3)   Nothing in this section or section 20A above shall—

(a)   impose an obligation on a buyer of goods out of a bulk to compensate any other buyer of goods out of that bulk for any shortfall in the goods received by that other buyer;

(b)   affects any contractual arrangement between buyers of goods out of a bulk for adjustments between themselves; or

(c)   affect the rights of any buyer under his contract.]

Transfer of title

21   Sale by person not the owner

(1)   Subject to this Act, where goods are sold by a person who is not their owner, and who does not sell them under the authority or with the consent of the owner, the buyer acquires no better title to the goods than the seller had, unless the owner of the goods is by his conduct precluded from denying the seller's authority to sell.

(2)   Nothing in this Act affects—

(a)   the provisions of the Factors Acts or any enactment enabling the apparent owner of goods to dispose of them as if he were their true owner;

(b)   the validity of any contract of sale under any special common law or statutory power of sale or under the order of a court of competent jurisdiction.

22   [*Does not apply to Scotland.*]

23   Sale under voidable title

When the seller of goods has a voidable title to them, but his title has not been avoided at the time of the sale, the buyer acquires a good title to the goods, provided he buys them in good faith and without notice of the seller's defect of title.

24　Seller in possession after sale

Where a person having sold goods continues or is in possession of the goods, or of the documents of title to the goods, the delivery or transfer by that person, or by a mercantile agent acting for him, of the goods or documents of title under any sale, pledge, or other disposition thereof, to any person receiving the same in good faith and without notice of the previous sale, has the same effect as if the person making the delivery or transfer were expressly authorised by the owner of the goods to make the same.

25　Buyer in possession after sale

(1)　Where a person having bought or agreed to buy goods obtains, with the consent of the seller, possession of the goods or the documents of title to the goods, the delivery or transfer by that person, or by a mercantile agent acting for him, of the goods or documents of title, under any sale, pledge, or other disposition thereof, to any person receiving the same in good faith and without notice of any lien or other right of the original seller in respect of the goods, has the same effect as if the person making the delivery or transfer were a mercantile agent in possession of the goods or documents of title with the consent of the owner.

(2)　For the purposes of subsection (1) above—

(a)　the buyer under a conditional sale agreement is to be taken not to be a person who has bought or agreed to buy goods, and

(b)　'conditional sale agreement' means an agreement for the sale of goods which is a consumer credit agreement within the meaning of the Consumer Credit Act 1974 under which the purchase price or part of it is payable by instalments, and the property in the goods is to remain in the seller (notwithstanding that the buyer is to be in possession of the goods) until such conditions as to the payment of instalments or otherwise as may be specified in the agreement are fulfilled.

(3)　Paragraph 9 of Schedule 1 below applies in relation to a contract under which a person buys or agrees to buy goods and which is made before the appointed day.

(4)　In subsection (3) above and paragraph 9 of Schedule 1 below references to the appointed day are to the day appointed for the purposes of those provisions by an order of the Secretary of State made by statutory instrument.

62　Savings: rules of law etc

(1)　The rules in bankruptcy relating to contracts of sale apply to those contracts, notwithstanding anything in this Act.

(2)　The rules of the common law, including the law merchant, except in so far as they are inconsistent with the provisions of [legislation including this Act and the Consumer Rights Act 2015], and in particular the rules relating to the law of principal and agent and the effect of fraud, misrepresentation, duress or coercion, mistake, or other invalidating cause, apply to contracts for the sale of goods.

(3)　Nothing in this Act or the Sale of Goods Act 1893 affects the enactments relating to bills of sale, or any enactment relating to the sale of goods which is not expressly repealed or amended by this Act or that.

(4)　The provisions of this Act about contracts of sale do not apply to a transaction in the form of a contract of sale which is intended to operate by way of mortgage, pledge, charge, or other security.

(5)　Nothing in this Act prejudices or affects the landlord's right of hypothec [. . .] in Scotland.

MATRIMONIAL HOMES (FAMILY PROTECTION) (SCOTLAND) ACT 1981
(1981, c 59)

Protection of occupancy rights of one spouse against the other

1　Right of spouse without title to occupy matrimonial home

(1)　Where, apart from the provisions of this Act, one spouse is entitled, or permitted by a third party, to occupy a matrimonial home (an 'entitled spouse') and the other spouse is not so entitled or permitted (a 'non-entitled spouse'), the nonentitled spouse shall, subject to the provisions of this Act, have the following rights—

(a) if in occupation, a right [. . .] to [continue to occupy] the matrimonial home or any part of it by the entitled spouse;

(b) if not in occupation, a right to enter into and occupy the matrimonial home.

[(1A)   The rights conferred by subsection (1) above to continue to occupy or, as the case may be, to enter and occupy the matrimonial home include, without prejudice to their generality, the right to do so together with any child of the family.]

(2)   In subsection (1) above, an 'entitled spouse' includes a spouse who is entitled, or permitted by a third party, to occupy a matrimonial home along with an individual who is not the other spouse only if that individual has waived his or her right of occupation in favour of the spouse so entitled or permitted.

(3)   If the entitled spouse refuses to allow the non-entitled spouse to exercise the right conferred by subsection (1)(b) above, the non-entitled spouse may exercise that right only with the leave of the court under section 3(3) or (4) of this Act.

(4)   In this Act, the rights mentioned in paragraphs (a) and (b) of subsection (1) above are referred to as occupancy rights.

(5)   A non-entitled spouse may renounce in writing his or her occupancy rights only—

(a) in a particular matrimonial home; or

(b) in a particular property which it is intended by the spouses will become a matrimonial home.

(6)   A renunciation under subsection (5) above shall have effect only if at the time of making the renunciation, the non-entitled spouse has sworn or affirmed before a notary public that it was made freely and without coercion of any kind.

[In this subsection, 'notary public' includes any person duly authorised by the law of the country (other than Scotland) in which the swearing or affirmation takes place to administer oaths or receive affirmations in that other country.]

[(7)   Subject to subsection (5), if—

(a)   there has been no cohabitation between an entitled spouse and a nonentitled spouse during a continuous period of two years; and

(b)   during that period the non-entitled spouse has not occupied the matrimonial home,

the non-entitled spouse shall, on the expiry of that period, cease to have occupancy rights in the matrimonial home.

(8)   A non-entitled spouse who has ceased to have occupancy rights by virtue of subsection (7) may not apply to the court for an order under section 3(1).]

2   Subsidiary and consequential rights

(1)   For the purpose of securing the occupancy rights of a non-entitled spouse, that spouse shall, in relation to a matrimonial home, be entitled without the consent of the entitled spouse—

(a)   to make any payment due by the entitled spouse in respect of rent, rates, secured loan instalments, interest or other outgoings (not being outgoings on repairs or improvements);

(b)   to perform any other obligation incumbent on the entitled spouse (not being an obligation in respect of non-essential repairs or improvements);

(c)   to enforce performance of an obligation by a third party which that third party has undertaken to the entitled spouse to the extent that the entitled spouse may enforce such performance;

(d)   to carry out such essential repairs as the entitled spouse may carry out;

(e)   to carry out such non-essential repairs or improvements as may be authorised by an order of the court, being such repairs or improvements as the entitled spouse may carry out and which the court considers to be appropriate for the reasonable enjoyment of the occupancy rights;

(f)   to take such other steps, for the purpose of protecting the occupancy rights of the non-entitled spouse, as the entitled spouse may take to protect the occupancy rights of the entitled spouse.

(2)   Any payment made under subsection (1)(a) above or any obligation performed under subsection (1)(b) above shall have effect in relation to the rights of a third party as if the payment were made or the obligation were performed by the entitled spouse; and the performance of an obligation which has been enforced under subsection (1)(c) above shall have effect as if it had been enforced by the entitled spouse.

(3)   Where there is an entitled and a non-entitled spouse, the court, on the application of either of them, may, having regard in particular to the respective financial circumstances of the spouses, make an order apportioning expenditure incurred or to be incurred by either spouse—

(a)   without the consent of the other spouse, on any of the items mentioned in paragraphs (a) and (d) of subsection (1) above;

(b)   with the consent of the other spouse, on anything relating to a matrimonial home.

(4)   Where both spouses are entitled, or permitted by a third party, to occupy a matrimonial home—

(a)   either spouse shall be entitled, without the consent of the other spouse, to carry out such non-essential repairs or improvements as may be authorised by an order of the court, being such repairs or improvements as the court considers to be appropriate for the reasonable enjoyment of the occupancy rights;

(b)   the court, on the application of either spouse, may, having regard in particular to the respective financial circumstances of the spouses, make an order apportioning expenditure incurred or to be incurred by either spouse, with or without the consent of the other spouse, on anything relating to the matrimonial home.

(5)   Where one spouse owns or hires, or is acquiring under a hire-purchase or conditional sale agreement, furniture and plenishings in a matrimonial home—

(a)   the other spouse may, without the consent of the first mentioned spouse—

(i)   make any payment due by the first mentioned spouse which is necessary, or take any other step which the first mentioned spouse is entitled to take to secure the possession or use of any such furniture and plenishings (and any such payment shall have effect in relation to the rights of a third party as if it were made by the first mentioned spouse); or

(ii)   carry out such essential repairs to the furniture and plenishings as the first mentioned spouse is entitled to carry out;

(b)   the court, on the application of either spouse, may, having regard in particular to the respective financial circumstances of the spouses, make an order apportioning expenditure incurred or to be incurred by either spouse—

(i)   without the consent of the other spouse, in making payments under a hire, hire-purchase or conditional sale agreement, or in paying interest charges in respect of the furniture and plenishings, or in carrying out essential repairs to the furniture and plenishings; or

(ii)   with the consent of the other spouse, on anything relating to the furniture and plenishings.

(6)   An order under subsection (3), (4)(b) or (5)(b) above may require one spouse to make a payment to the other spouse in implementation of the apportionment.

(7)   Any application under subsection (3), (4)(b) or (5)(b) above shall be made within five years of the date on which any payment in respect of such incurred expenditure was made.

(8)   Where—

(a)   the entitled spouse is a tenant of a matrimonial home; and

(b)   possession thereof is necessary in order to continue the tenancy; and

(c)   the entitled spouse abandons such possession,

the tenancy shall be continued by such possession by the non-entitled spouse.

(9)   In this section 'improvements' includes alterations and enlargement.

3   Regulation by court of rights of occupancy of matrimonial home

(1)   [Subject to section 1(7) of this Act] where there is an entitled and a nonentitled spouse, or where both spouses are entitled, or permitted by a third party, to occupy a matrimonial home, either spouse may apply to the court for an order—

(a)   declaring the occupancy rights of the applicant spouse;

(b)   enforcing the occupancy rights of the applicant spouse;

(c)   restricting the occupancy rights of the non-applicant spouse;

(d)   regulating the exercise by either spouse of his or her occupancy rights;

(e)   protecting the occupancy rights of the applicant spouse in relation to the other spouse.

(2)   Where one spouse owns or hires, or is acquiring under a hire-purchase or conditional sale agreement, furniture and plenishings in a matrimonial home, the other spouse, if he or she has occupancy rights in that home, may apply to the court for an order granting to the applicant the possession or use in the matrimonial home of any such furniture and plenishings; but, subject to section 2 of this Act, an order under this subsection shall not prejudice the rights of any third party in relation to the non-performance of any obligation under such hire-purchase or conditional sale agreement.

(3)   The court shall grant an application under subsection (1)(a) above if it appears to the court that the application relates to a matrimonial home; and, on an application under any of paragraphs (b) to (e) of subsection (1) or under subsection (2) above, the court may make such order relating to the application as appears to it to be just and reasonable having regard to all the circumstances of the case including—

(a)   the conduct of the spouses in relation to each other and otherwise;

(b)   the respective needs and financial resources of the spouses;

(c)   the needs of any child of the family;

(d)   the extent (if any) to which—

(i)   the matrimonial home; and

(ii)   in relation only to an order under subsection (2) above, any item of furniture and plenishings referred to in that subsection,

is used in connection with a trade, business or profession of either spouse; and

(e)   whether the entitled spouse offers or has offered to make available to the non-entitled spouse any suitable alternative accommodation.

(4)   Pending the making of an order under subsection (3) above, the court, on the application of either spouse, may make such interim order as it may consider necessary or expedient in relation to—

(a)   the residence of either spouse in the home to which the application relates;

(b)   the personal effects of either spouse or of any child of the family; or

(c)   the furniture and plenishings:

Provided that an interim order may be made only if the non-applicant spouse has been afforded an opportunity of being heard by or represented before the court.

(5)   The court shall not make an order under subsection (3) or (4) above if it appears that the effect of the order would be to exclude the non-applicant spouse from the matrimonial home.

(6)   If the court makes an order under subsection (3) or (4) above which requires the delivery to one spouse of anything which has been left in or removed from the matrimonial home, it may also grant a warrant authorising a messengerat-arms or sheriff officer to enter the matrimonial home or other premises occupied by the other spouse and to search for and take possession of the thing required to be delivered, if need be by opening shut and lockfast places, and to deliver the thing in accordance with the said order:

Provided that a warrant granted under this subsection shall be executed only after expiry of the period of a charge, being such period as the court shall specify in the order for delivery.

(7)   Where it appears to the court—

(a)   on the application of a non-entitled spouse, that that spouse has suffered a loss of occupancy rights or that the quality of the non-entitled spouse's occupation of a matrimonial home has been impaired; or

(b)   on the application of a spouse who has been given the possession or use of furniture and plenishings by virtue of an order under subsection (3) above, that the applicant has suffered a loss of such possession or use or that the quality of the applicant's possession or use of the furniture and plenishings has been impaired,

in consequence of any act or default on the part of the other spouse which was intended to result in such loss or impairment, it may order that other spouse to pay to the applicant such compensation as the court in the circumstances considers just and reasonable in respect of that loss or impairment.

(8)   A spouse may renounce in writing the right to apply under subsection (2) above for the possession or use of any item of furniture and plenishings.

[. . .]

5   Duration of orders under ss 3 and 4

(1)   The court may, on the application of either spouse, vary or recall any order made by it under section 3 or 4 of this Act, but, subject to subsection (2) below, any such order shall, unless previously so varied or recalled, cease to have effect—

(a)   on the termination of the marriage; or

(b)   subject to section 6(1) of this Act, where there is an entitled and a non-entitled spouse, on the entitled spouse ceasing to be an entitled spouse in respect of the matrimonial home to which the order relates; or

(c)   where both spouses are entitled, or permitted by a third party, to occupy the matrimonial home, on both spouses ceasing to be so entitled or permitted.

(2)   Without prejudice to the generality of subsection (1) above, an order under section 3(3) or (4) of this Act which grants the possession or use of furniture and plenishings shall cease to have effect if the furniture and plenishings cease to be permitted by a third party to be retained in the matrimonial home.

Occupancy rights in relation to dealings with third parties

6   Continued exercise of occupancy rights after dealing

(1)   Subject to subsection (3) below—

(a)   the continued exercise of the rights conferred on a non-entitled spouse by the provisions of this Act in respect of a matrimonial home shall not be prejudiced by reason only of any dealing of the entitled spouse relating to that home; and

(b)   a third party shall not by reason only of such a dealing be entitled to occupy that matrimonial home or any part of it.

[(1A)   The occupancy rights of a non-entitled spouse in relation to a matrimonial home shall not be exercisable in relation to the home where, following a dealing of the entitled spouse relating to the home—

(a)   a person acquires the home, or an interest in it, in good faith and for value from a person other than the person who is or, as the case may be, was the entitled spouse; or

(b)   a person derives title to the home from a person who acquired title as mentioned in paragraph (a).]

(2)   In this section and section 7 of this Act—

'dealing' includes the grant of a heritable security and the creation of a trust but does not include a conveyance under section 80 of the Lands Clauses Consolidation (Scotland) Act 1845;

'entitled spouse' does not include a spouse who, apart from the provisions of this Act,—

(a)   is permitted by a third party to occupy a matrimonial home; or

(b)   is entitled to occupy a matrimonial home along with an individual who is not the other spouse, whether or not that individual has waived his or her right of occupation in favour of the spouse so entitled;

and 'non-entitled spouse' shall be construed accordingly.

(3)   This section shall not apply in any case where—

(a)   the non-entitled spouse in writing either—

(i)   consents or has consented to the dealing, and any consent shall be in such form as the Secretary of State may, by regulations made by statutory instrument, prescribe; or

(ii)   renounces or has renounced his or her occupancy rights in relation to the matrimonial home or property to which the dealing relates;

(b)   the court has made an order under section 7 of this Act dispensing with the consent of the non-entitled spouse to the dealing;

(c)   the dealing occurred, or implements, a binding obligation entered into by the entitled spouse before his or her marriage to the non-entitled spouse;

(d)   the dealing occurred, or implements, a binding obligation entered into before the commencement of this Act; . . .

(e)   the dealing comprises a [transfer for value] to a third party who has acted in good faith if, [. . .] there is produced to the third party by the [transferor—

(i)   a written declaration signed by the transferor, or a person acting on behalf of the transferor under a power of attorney or as a guardian (within the meaning of the Adults with Incapacity (Scotland) Act 2000 (asp 4)), that the subjects of the transfer are not, or were not at the time of the dealing, a matrimonial home in relation to which a spouse of the transferor has or had occupancy rights; or

(ii)   a renunciation of occupancy rights or consent to the dealing which bears to have been properly made or given by the non-entitled spouse or a person acting on behalf of the non-entitled spouse under a power of attorney or as a guardian (within the meaning of the Adults with Incapacity (Scotland) Act 2000 (asp 4)).]

(f)   the entitled spouse has permanently ceased to be entitled to occupy the matrimonial home, and at any time thereafter a continuous period of [2] years has elapsed, during which the non-entitled spouse has not occupied the matrimonial home.

(4)   [Amends Land Registration (Scotland) Act 1979.]

7   Dispensation by court with spouse's consent to dealing

(1)   [Subject to subsections (1A) to (1D) below] the court may, on the application of an entitled spouse or any other person having an interest, make an order dispensing with the consent of a non-entitled spouse to a dealing which has taken place or a proposed dealing, if—

(a)   such consent is unreasonably withheld;

(b)   such consent cannot be given by reason of physical or mental disability;

(c)   the non-entitled spouse cannot be found after reasonable steps have been taken to trace him or her; or

(d)   the non-entitled spouse is [under legal disability by reason of nonage].

[(1A)   Subsection (1B) applies if, in relation to a proposed sale—

(a)   negotiations with a third party have not begun; or

(b)   negotiations have begun but a price has not been agreed.

(1B)   An order under subsection (1) dispensing with consent may be made only if—

(a)   the price agreed for the sale is no less than such amount as the court specifies in the order; and

(b)   the contract for the sale is concluded before the expiry of such period as may be so specified.

(1C)   Subsection (1D) applies if the proposed dealing is the grant of a heritable security.

(1D)   An order under subsection (1) dispensing with consent may be made only if—

(a)   the heritable security is granted for a loan of no more than such amount as the court specifies in the order; and

(b)   the security is executed before the expiry of such period as may be so specified.]

(2)   For the purposes of subsection (1)(a) above, a non-entitled spouse shall have unreasonably withheld consent to a dealing which has taken place or a proposed dealing, where it appears to the court—

(a)   that the non-entitled spouse has led the entitled spouse to believe that he or she would consent to the dealing and that the non-entitled spouse would not be prejudiced by any change in the circumstances of the case since such apparent consent was given; or

(b)   that the entitled spouse has, having taken all reasonable steps to do so, been unable to obtain an answer to a request for consent.

(3)   The court, in considering whether to make an order under subsection (1) above, shall have regard to all the circumstances of the case including the matters specified in paragraphs (a) to (e) of section 3(3) of this Act.

[(3A)   If the court refuses an application for an order under subsection (1), it may make an order requiring a non-entitled spouse who is or becomes the occupier of the matrimonial home—

(a)   to make such payments to the owner of the home in respect of that spouse's occupation of it as may be specified in the order;

(b)   to comply with such other conditions relating to that spouse's occupation of the matrimonial home as may be so specified.]

(4)   Where—

(a)   an application is made for an order under this section; and

(b)   an action is or has been raised by a non-entitled spouse to enforce occupancy rights,

the action shall be sisted until the conclusion of the proceedings on the application.

(5)   [. . .]

8   Interests of heritable creditors

(1)   The rights of a third party with an interest in the matrimonial home as a creditor under a secured loan in relation to the non-performance of any obligation under the loan shall not be prejudiced by reason only of the occupancy rights of the non-entitled spouse; but where a non-entitled spouse has or obtains occupation of a matrimonial home and—

(a)   the entitled spouse is not in occupation; and

(b)   there is a third party with such an interest in the matrimonial home,

the court may, on the application of the third party, make an order requiring the non-entitled spouse to make any payment due by the entitled spouse in respect of the loan.

(2)   This section shall not apply [to secured loans in respect of which the security was granted prior to the commencement of section 13 of the Law Reform (Miscellaneous Provisions) (Scotland) Act 1985] unless the third party in granting the secured loan acted in good faith and . . . there was produced to the third party by the entitled spouse—

(a)   [a written declaration signed] by the entitled spouse declaring that there is no non-entitled spouse; or

(b)   a renunciation of occupancy rights or consent to the taking of the loan which bears to have been properly made or given by the non-entitled spouse.

[(2A)   This section shall not apply to secured loans in respect of which the security was granted after the commencement of section 13 of the Law Reform (Miscellaneous Provisions) (Scotland) Act 1985 unless the third party in granting the secured loan acted in good faith and . . . there was produced to the third party by the grantor—

(a)   [a written declaration signed] by the grantor declaring that the security subjects are not or were not at the time of the granting of the security a matrimonial home in relation to which a spouse of the grantor has or had occupancy rights; or

(b)   a renunciation of occupancy rights or consent to the granting of the security which bears to have been properly made or given by the non-entitled spouse.

(2B)   for the purposes of subsections (2) and (2A) above, the time of granting a security, in the case of a heritable security, is the date of delivery of the deed creating the security.]

9   Provisions where both spouses have title

(1)   Subject to subsection (2) below, where, apart from the provisions of this Act, both spouses are entitled to occupy a matrimonial home—

(a)   the rights in that home of one spouse shall not be prejudiced by reason only of any dealing of the other spouse; and

(b)   a third party shall not by reason only of such a dealing be entitled to occupy that matrimonial home or any part of it.

(2)   The definition of 'dealing' in section 6(2) of this Act and sections 6(3) and 7 of this Act shall apply for the purposes of subsection (1) above as they apply for the purposes of section 6(1) of this Act subject to the following modifications—

(a)   any reference to the entitled spouse and to the non-entitled spouse shall be construed as a reference to a spouse who has entered into or, as the case may be, proposes to enter into a dealing and to the other spouse respectively; and

(b)   in paragraph (b) of section 7(4) the reference to occupancy rights shall be construed as a reference to any rights in the matrimonial home.

[Reckoning of non-cohabitation periods in sections 1 and 6]

[9A   Effect of court action under section 3, 4 or 5 on reckoning of periods in sections 1 and 6

(1)   Subsection (2) applies where an application is made under section 3(1), 4(1) or 5(1) of this Act.

(2)   In calculating the period of two years mentioned in section 1(7)(a) or 6(3)(f) of this Act, no account shall be taken of the period mentioned in subsection (3) below.

(3)   The period is the period beginning with the date on which the application is made and—

(a)   in the case of an application under section 3(1) or 4(1) of this Act, ending on the date on which—

(i)   an order under section 3(3) or, as the case may be, 4(2) of this Act is made; or

(ii)   the application is otherwise finally determined or abandoned;

(b)   in the case of an application under section 5(1) of this Act, ending on the date on which—

(i)   the order under section 3(3) or, as the case may be, 4(2) is varied or recalled; or

(ii)   the application is otherwise finally determined or abandoned.]

[. . .]

11   Poinding

Where [an attachment] has been executed of furniture and plenishings of which the debtor's spouse has the possession or use by virtue of an order under section 3(3) or

(4) of this Act, the sheriff, on the application of that spouse within 40 days of the date of execution of [the attachment], may—

(a)   declare that [the attachment] is null; or

(b)   make such order as he thinks appropriate to protect such possession or use by that spouse,

if he is satisfied that the purpose of the diligence was wholly or mainly to prevent such possession or use.

12   Adjudication

(1)   Where a matrimonial home of which there is an entitled spouse and a non-entitled spouse is adjudged, the Court of Session, on the application of the non-entitled spouse within 40 days of the date of the decree of adjudication, may—

(a)   order the reduction of the decree; or

(b)   make such order as it thinks appropriate to protect the occupancy rights of the non-entitled spouse,

if it is satisfied that the purpose of the diligence was wholly or mainly to defeat the occupancy rights of the non-entitled spouse.

(2)   In this section, 'entitled spouse' and 'non-entitled spouse' have the same meanings respectively as in section 6(2) of this Act.

Transfer of tenancy

13   Transfer of tenancy

(1)   The court may, on the application of a non-entitled spouse, make an order transferring the tenancy of a matrimonial home to that spouse and providing, subject to subsection (11) below, for the payment by the non-entitled spouse to the entitled spouse of such compensation as seems just and reasonable in all the circumstances of the case.

[(2)   In an action—

(a)   for divorce, the Court of Session or a sheriff;

(b)   for nullity of marriage, the Court of Session,

may, on granting decree or within such period as the court may specify on granting decree, make an order granting an application under subsection (1) above.]

(3)   In determining whether to grant an application under subsection (1) above, the court shall have regard to all the circumstances of the case including the matters specified in paragraphs (a) to (e) of section 3(3) of this Act and the suitability of the applicant to become the tenant and the applicant's capacity to perform the obligations under the lease of the matrimonial home.

(4)   The non-entitled spouse shall serve a copy of an application under subsection (1) above on the landlord and, before making an order under subsection (1) above, the court shall give the landlord an opportunity of being heard by it.

(5)   On the making of an order granting an application under subsection (1) above, the tenancy shall vest in the non-entitled spouse without intimation to the landlord, subject to all the liabilities under the lease (other than any arrears of rent for the period before the making of the order, which shall remain the liability of the original entitled spouse).

(6)   The clerk of court shall notify the landlord of the making of an order granting an application under subsection (1) above.

(7)   It shall not be competent for a non-entitled spouse to apply for an order under subsection (1) above where the matrimonial home—

(a)   is let to the entitled spouse by his or her employer as an incident of employment, and the lease is subject to a requirement that the entitled spouse must reside therein;

(b)   [is on or pertains to land comprised in an agricultural lease];

(c)   is on or pertains to a croft or the subject of a cottar or the holding of a landholder or a statutory small tenant;

(d) is let on a long lease;

(e) is part of the tenancy land of a tenant-at-will.

(8)   In subsection (7) above—

['agricultural lease' means a lease constituting a 1991 Act tenancy within the meaning of the Agricultural Holdings (Scotland) Act 2003 (asp 11) or a lease constituting a limited duration tenancy [, a short limited duration tenancy, a modern limited duration tenancy or a repairing tenancy] (within the meaning of that Act);]

'cottar' has the same meaning as in section 28(4) of the [Crofters (Scotland) Act 1993];

'croft' has the same meaning as in the [Crofters (Scotland) Act 1993];

'holding', in relation to a landholder and a statutory small tenant, 'landholder' and 'statutory small tenant' have the same meanings respectively as in sections 2(1), 2(2) and 32(1) of the Small Landholders (Scotland) Act 1911;

'long lease' has the same meaning as in [section 9(2) of the Land Registration etc (Scotland) Act 2012 (asp 5)];

'tenant-at-will' has the same meaning as in section 20(8) of the Land Registration (Scotland) Act 1979.

(9)   Where both spouses are joint or common tenants of a matrimonial home, the court may, on the application of one of the spouses, make an order vesting the tenancy in that spouse solely and providing, subject to subsection (11) below, for the payment by the applicant to the other spouse of such compensation as seems just and reasonable in the circumstances of the case.

(10)   Subsections (2) to (8) above shall apply for the purposes of an order under subsection (9) above as they apply for the purposes of an order under subsection (1) above subject to the following modifications—

(a) in subsection (3) for the word 'tenant' there shall substituted the words 'sole tenant';

(b) in subsection (4) for the words 'non-entitled' there should be substituted the word 'applicant';

(c) in subsection (5) for the words 'non-entitled' and 'liability of the original entitled spouse' there shall substituted respectively the words 'applicant' and 'joint and several liability of both spouses';

(d) in subsection (7)—

(i) for the words 'a non-entitled' there shall substituted the words 'an applicant';

(ii) for paragraph (a) there shall be substituted the following paragraph—

'(a) is let to both spouses by their employer as an incident of employment, and the lease is subject to a requirement that both spouses must reside there;';

(iii) paragraphs (c) and (e) shall be omitted.

[. . .]

(12)   In the Tenants' Rights, Etc (Scotland) Act 1980—

(a) paragraph 6 of Part I of Schedule 2 is repealed.

[. . .]

Cohabiting couples

18 Occupancy rights of cohabiting couples

(1)   If a man and a woman are living with each other as if they were man and wife [or two persons of the same sex are living together as if they were civil partners] ([in either case] 'a cohabiting couple') in a house which, apart from the provisions of this section—

(a) one of them (an 'entitled partner') is entitled, or permitted by a third party, to occupy; and

(b) the other (a 'non-entitled partner') is not so entitled or permitted to occupy,

the court may, on the application of the non-entitled partner, if it appears that the [entitled partner and non-entitled partner] are a cohabiting couple in that house, grant occupancy rights therein to the applicant for such period, not exceeding [6] months, as the court may specify:

Provided that the court may extend the said period for a further period or periods, no such period exceeding 6 months.

(2)   In determining whether for the purpose of subsection (1) above [two persons] are a cohabiting couple the court shall have regard to all the circumstances of the case including—

(a)   the time for which it appears they have been living together; and

(b)   whether there [is any child—

(i)   of whom they are the parents; or

(ii)   who they have treated as a child of theirs.]

(3)   While an order granting an application under subsection (1) above or an extension of such an order is in force, or where both partners of a cohabiting couple are entitled, or permitted by a third party, to occupy the house where they are cohabiting, the following provisions of this Act shall subject to any necessary modifications—

(a)   apply to the cohabiting couple as they apply to parties to a marriage; and

(b)   have effect in relation to any child residing with the cohabiting couple as they have effect in relation to a child of the family,

section 2;

section 3, except subsection (1)(a);

section 4;

in section 5(1), the words from the beginning to 'Act' where it first occurs;

[section 13 . . .]; and

section 22,

and any reference in these provisions to a matrimonial home shall be construed as a reference to a house.

(4)   Any order under section 3 or 4 of this Act as applied to a cohabiting couple by subsection (3) above shall have effect—

(a)   if one of them is a non-entitled partner, for such a period, not exceeding the period or periods which from time to time may be specified in any order under subsection (1) above for which occupancy rights have been granted under that subsection, as may be specified in the order;

(b)   if they are both entitled, or permitted by a third party, to occupy the house, until a further order of the court.

(5)   Nothing in this section shall prejudice the rights of any third party having an interest in the house referred to in subsection (1) above.

(6)   In this section—

'house' includes a caravan, houseboat or other structure in which the couple are cohabiting and any garden or other ground or building attached to, and usually occupied with, or otherwise required for the amenity or convenience of, the house, caravan, houseboat or other structure;

'occupancy rights' means the following rights of a non-entitled partner—

(a)   if in occupation, a right to [continue to occupy] the house [and, without prejudice to the generality of these rights, includes the right to continue to occupy or, as the case may be, to enter and occupy the house together with any child residing with the cohabiting couple];

(b)   if not in occupation, a right to enter into and occupy the house;

'entitled partner' includes a partner who is entitled, or permitted by a third party, to occupy the house along with an individual who is not the other partner only if that individual has waived his or her right of occupation in favour of the partner so entitled or permitted.

[. . .]

Miscellaneous and general

19   Rights of occupancy in relation to division and sale

Where a spouse brings an action for the division and sale of a matrimonial home which the spouses own in common, the court, after having regard to all the circumstances of the case including—

(a) the matters specified in paragraphs (a) to (d) of section 3(3) of this Act; and

(b) whether the spouse bringing the action offers or has offered to make available to the other spouse any suitable alternative accommodation,

may refuse to grant decree in that action or may postpone the granting of decree for such period as it may consider reasonable in the circumstances or may grant decree subject to such conditions as it may prescribe.

20   Spouse's consent in relation to calling up of standard securities over matrimonial homes

Section 19(10) of the Conveyancing and Feudal Reform (Scotland) Act 1970 shall have effect as if at the end there were added the following proviso—

'Provided that, without prejudice to the foregoing generality, if the standard security is over a matrimonial home as defined in section 22 of the Matrimonial Homes (Family Protection) (Scotland) Act 1981, the spouse on whom the calling-up notice has been served may not dispense with or shorten the said period without the consent in writing of the other spouse.'.

[. . .]

22   Interpretation

[(1)] In this Act—

'caravan' means a caravan which is mobile or affixed to the land;

'child of the family' includes any child or grandchild of either spouse, and any person who has been brought up or [treated] by either spouse as if he or she were a child of that spouse, whatever the age of such a child, grandchild or person may be;

'the court' means the Court of Session or the sheriff;

'furniture and plenishings' means any article situated in a matrimonial home which—

(a) is owned or hired by either spouse or is being acquired by either spouse under a hire-purchase agreement or conditional sale agreement; and

(b) is reasonably necessary to enable the home to be used as a family residence,

but does not include any vehicle, caravan or houseboat, or such other structure as is mentioned in the definition of 'matrimonial home';

'matrimonial home' means [subject to subsection (2),] any house, caravan, houseboat or other structure which has been provided or has been made available by one or both of the spouses as, or has become, a family residence and includes any garden or other ground or building [. . .] usually occupied with, or otherwise required for the amenity or convenience of, the house, caravan, houseboat or other structure [but does not include a residence provided or made available by [a person for one] spouse to reside in, whether with any child of the family or not, separately from the other spouse];

'occupancy rights' has, subject to section 18(6) of this Act, the meaning assigned by section 1(4) of this Act;

'the sheriff' includes the sheriff having jurisdiction in the district where the matrimonial home is situated;

'tenant' includes sub-tenant and a statutory tenant as defined in section 3 of the Rent (Scotland) Act [1984 and a statutory assured tenant as defined in section 16(1) of the Housing (Scotland) Act 1988] and 'tenancy' shall be construed accordingly;

'entitled spouse' and 'non-entitled spouse', subject to sections 6(2) and 12(2) of this Act, have the meanings respectively assigned to them by section 1 of this Act.

[(2)   If—

(a)   the tenancy of a matrimonial home is transferred from one spouse to the other by agreement or under any enactment; and

(b)   following the transfer, the spouse to whom the tenancy was transferred occupies the home but the other spouse does not,

the home shall, on such transfer, cease to be a matrimonial home.]

23   Short title, commencement and extent

(1)   This Act may be cited as the Matrimonial Homes (Family Protection) (Scotland) Act 1981.

(2)   This Act (except this section) shall come into operation on such day as the Secretary of State may by order made by statutory instrument appoint, and different days may be so appointed for different provisions and for different purposes.

(3)   This Act extends to Scotland only.

Equivalent provisions for civil partners are contained in the Civil Partnership Act 2004, ss 101–112.

FAMILY LAW (SCOTLAND) ACT 1985
(1985, c 37)

Matrimonial property, etc

24   Marriage not to affect property rights or legal capacity

(1)   Subject to the provisions of any enactment (including this Act), marriage [or civil partnership] shall not of itself affect—

(a)   the respective rights of the parties to the marriage [or as the case may be the partners in a civil partnership] in relation to their property;

(b)   the legal capacity of [those parties or partners].

(2)   Nothing in subsection (1) above affects the law of succession.

25   Presumption of equal shares in household goods

(1)   If any question arises (whether during or after a marriage [or civil partnership]) as to the respective rights of ownership of the parties to a marriage [or the partners in a civil partnership] in any household goods obtained in prospect of or during the marriage [or civil partnership] other than by gift or succession from a third party, it shall be presumed, unless the contrary is proved, that each has a right to an equal share in the goods in question.

(2)   For the purposes of subsection (1) above, the contrary shall not be treated as proved by reason only that while [—

(a)]   the parties were married;

[(b)   the partners were in a civil partnership],

and living together the goods in question were purchased from a third party by either party alone or by both in unequal shares.

(3)   In this section 'household goods' means any goods (including decorative or ornamental goods) kept or used at any time during the marriage [or civil partnership in any family] home for the joint domestic purposes of the parties to the marriage [or the partners], other than—

(a)   money or securities;

(b)   any motor car, caravan or other road vehicle;

(c)   any domestic animal.

26   Presumption of equal shares in money and property derived from housekeeping allowance

If any question arises (whether during or after a marriage [or civil partnership]) as to the right of a party to a marriage [or as the case may be of a partner in a civil partnership] to money derived from any allowance made by either party [or partner] for their joint household expenses or for similar purposes, or to any property acquired out of such money, the money or property shall, in the absence of any agreement between them to the contrary, be treated as belonging to each party [or partner] in equal shares.

COMPANIES ACT 1985
(1985, c 6)

PART XVIII
FLOATING CHARGES AND RECEIVERS (SCOTLAND)

CHAPTER I
FLOATING CHARGES

462   Power of incorporated company to create floating charge

(1)   It is competent under the law of Scotland for an incorporated company (whether a company within the meaning of this Act or not), for the purpose of securing any debt or other obligation (including a cautionary obligation) incurred or to be incurred by, or binding upon, the company or any other person, to create in favour of the creditor in the debt or obligation a charge, in this Part referred to as a floating charge, over all or any part of the property (including uncalled capital) which may from time to time be comprised in its property and undertaking.

[. . .]

(4)   References in this Part to the instrument by which a floating charge was created are, in the case of a floating charge created by words in a bond or other written acknowledgment, references to the bond or, as the case may be, the other written acknowledgment.

(5)   Subject to this Act, a floating charge has effect in accordance with this Part [and Part III of the Insolvency Act 1986] in relation to any heritable property in Scotland to which it relates, notwithstanding that the instrument creating it is not recorded in the Register of Sasines or, as appropriate, registered in accordance with the Land Registration (Scotland) Act 1979.

463   Effect of floating charge on winding up

(1)   [Where a company goes into liquidation within the meaning of section 247(2) of the Insolvency Act 1986], a floating charge created by the company attaches to the property then comprised in the company's property and undertaking or, as the case may be, in part of that property and undertaking, but does so subject to the rights of any person who—

(a)   has effectually executed diligence on the property or any part of it; or

(b)   holds a fixed security over the property or any part of it ranking in priority to the floating charge; or

(c)   holds over the property or any part of it another floating charge so ranking.

(2)   The provisions of [Part IV of the Insolvency Act (except section 185)] have effect in relation to a floating charge, subject to subsection (1), as if the charge were a fixed security over the property to which it has attached in respect of the principal of the debt or obligation to which it relates and any interest due or to become due thereon.

[(3)   Nothing in this section derogates from the provisions of sections 53(7) and 54(6) of the Insolvency Act (attachment of floating charge on appointment of receiver), or prejudices the operation of sections 175 and 176 of that Act (payment of preferential debts in winding up).]

(4) Interest accrues, in respect of a floating charge which after 16th November 1972 attaches to the property of the company, until payment of the sum due under the charge is made.

464 Ranking of floating charges

(1) Subject to subsection (2), the instrument creating a floating charge over all or any part of the company's property under section 462 may contain—

(a) provisions prohibiting or restricting the creation of any fixed security or any other floating charge having priority over, or ranking *pari passu* with, the floating charge; or

(b) [with the consent of the holder of any subsisting floating charge or fixed security which would be adversely affected] provisions regulating the order in which the floating charge shall rank with any other subsisting or future floating charges or fixed securities over that property or any part of it.

[(1A) Where an instrument creating a floating charge contains any such provision as is mentioned in subsection (1)(a), that provision shall be effective to confer priority on the floating charge over any fixed security or floating charge created after the date of the instrument.]

(2) Where all or any part of the property of a company is subject both to a floating charge and to a fixed security arising by operation of law, the fixed security has priority over the floating charge.

[(3) The order of ranking of the floating charge with any other subsisting or future floating charges or fixed securities over all or any part of the company's property is determined in accordance with the provisions of subsections (4) and (5) except where it is determined in accordance with any provision such as is mentioned in paragraph (a) or (b) of subsection (1).]

(4) Subject to the provisions of this section—

(a) a fixed security, the right to which has been constituted as a real right before a floating charge has attached to all or any part of the property of the company, has priority of ranking over the floating charge;

(b) floating charges rank with one another according to the time of registration accordance with Chapter II of Part XII;

(c) floating charges which have been received by the registrar for registration by the same postal delivery rank with one another equally.

(5) Where the holder of a floating charge over all or any part of the company's property which has been registered in accordance with Chapter II of Part XII has received, intimation in writing of the subsequent registration in accordance with that Chapter of another floating charge over the same property or any part thereof, the preference in ranking of the first-mentioned floating charge is restricted to security for—

(a) the holder's present advances;

(b) future advances which he may be required to make under the instrument creating the floating charge or under any ancillary document;

(c) interest due or to become due on all such advances;

(d) any expenses or outlays which may reasonably be incurred by the holder [; and]

[(e) (in the case of a floating charge to secure a contingent liability other than a liability arising under any further advances made from time to time) the maximum sum to which that contingent liability is capable of amounting whether or not it is contractually limited.]

(6) This section is subject to [Part XII and to sections 175 and 176 of the Insolvency Act].

LAW REFORM (MISCELLANEOUS PROVISIONS) (SCOTLAND) ACT 1985
(1985 c 73)

4 Irritancy clauses etc relating to monetary breaches of lease

(1) A landlord shall not, for the purpose of treating a lease as terminated or terminating it, be entitled to rely—

(a) on a provision in the lease which purports to terminate it, or to enable him to terminate it, in the event of a failure of the tenant to pay rent, or to make any other payment, on or before the due date therefor or such later date or within such period as may be provided for in the lease; or

(b) on the fact that such a failure is, or is deemed by a provision of the lease to be, a material breach of contract,

unless subsection (2) or (5) below applies.

(2) This subsection applies if—

(a) the landlord has, at any time after the payment of rent or other payment mentioned in subsection (1) above has become due, served a notice on the tenant—

(i) requiring the tenant to make payment of the sum which he has failed to pay together with any interest thereon in terms of the lease within the period specified in the notice; and

(ii) stating that, if the tenant does not comply with the requirement mentioned in sub-paragraph (i) above, the lease may be terminated; and

(b) the tenant has not complied with that requirement.

(3) The period to be specified in any such notice shall be not less than—

(a) a period of 14 days immediately following the service of the notice; or

(b) if any period remaining between the service of the notice and the expiry of any time provided for in the lease or otherwise for the late payment of the sum which the tenant has failed to pay is greater than 14 days, that greater period.

(4) Any notice served under subsection (2) above shall be sent by recorded delivery and shall be sufficiently served if it is sent to the tenant's last business or residential address in the United Kingdom known to the landlord or to the last address in the United Kingdom provided to the landlord by the tenant for the purpose of such service.

(5) This subsection applies if the tenant does not have an address in the United Kingdom known to the landlord and has not provided an address in the United Kingdom to the landlord for the purpose of service.

5 Irritancy clauses etc not relating to monetary breaches of leases

(1) Subject to subsection (2) below, a landlord shall not, for the purpose of treating a lease as terminated or terminating it, be entitled to rely—

(a) on a provision in the lease which purports to terminate it, or to enable the landlord to terminate it, in the event of an act or omission by the tenant (other than such a failure as is mentioned in section 4(1)(a) of this Act) or of a change in the tenant's circumstances; or

(b) on the fact that such act or omission or change is, or is deemed by a provision of the lease to be, a material breach of contract,

if in all the circumstances of the case a fair and reasonable landlord would not seek so to rely.

(2) No provision of a lease shall of itself, irrespective of the particular circumstances of the case, be held to be unenforceable by virtue of subsection (1) above.

(3) In the consideration, for the purposes of subsection (1)(a) or (b) above, of the circumstances of a case where—

(a) an act, omission or change is alleged to constitute a breach of a provision of the lease or a breach of contract; and

(b) the breach is capable of being remedied in reasonable time,

regard shall be had to whether a reasonable opportunity has been afforded to the tenant to enable the breach to be remedied.

. . .

8   Rectification of defectively expressed documents

(1)   Subject to section 9 of this Act, where the court is satisfied, on an application made to it, that—

(a)   a document intended to express or to give effect to an agreement fails to express accurately the common intention of the parties to the agreement at the date when it was made; or

(b)   a document intended to create, transfer, vary or renounce a right, not being a document falling within paragraph (a) above, fails to express accurately the intention of the grantor of the document at the date when it was executed,

it may order the document to be rectified in any manner that it may specify in order to give effect to that intention.

(2)   For the purposes of subsection (1) above, the court shall be entitled to have regard to all relevant evidence, whether written or oral.

(3)   Subject to section 9 of this Act, in ordering the rectification of a document under subsection (1) above (in this subsection referred, to as 'the original document'), the court may, at its own instance or on an application made to it [and in either case after calling all parties who appear to it to have an interest], order the rectification of any other document intended for any of the purposes mentioned in paragraph (a) or (b) of subsection (1) above which is defectively expressed by reason of the defect in the original document.

[(3A)   If a document is registered in the Land Register of Scotland in favour of a person acting in good faith then, unless the person consents to rectification of the document, it is not competent to order its rectification under subsection (3) above.]

(4)   Subject to [sections 8A and 9(4)] of this Act, a document ordered to be rectified under this section shall have effect as if it had always been so rectified.

(5)   Subject to section 9(5) of this Act, where a document recorded in the Register of Sasines is ordered to be rectified under this section and the order is likewise recorded, the document shall be treated as having been always so recorded as rectified.

(6)   Nothing in this section shall apply to a document of a testamentary nature.

(7)   It shall be competent to register in the Register of Inhibitions and Adjudications a notice of an application under this section for the rectification of a deed relating to land, being an application in respect of which authority for service or citation has been granted; and the land to which the application relates shall be rendered litigious as from the date of registration of such a notice [except that this subsection is subject to subsection (8A) below].

(8)   A notice under subsection (7) above shall specify the names and designations of the parties to the application and the date when authority for service or citation was granted and contain a description of the land to which the application relates.

[(8A)   A notice under subsection (7) above registered on or after the date on which section 67 of the Land Registration etc (Scotland) Act 2012 (asp 5) (warrant to place a caveat) comes into force shall not have any effect in rendering litigious any land for which there is a title sheet in the Land Register of Scotland or in placing in bad faith any person acquiring such land.]

(9)   In this section and section 9 of this Act 'the court' means the Court of Session or the sheriff.

[8A   Registration of order for rectification

An order for rectification made under section 8 of this Act in respect of a document which has been registered in the Land Register of Scotland—

(a)   may be registered in that register, and

(b)   does not have real effect until so registered.]

9   Provisions supplementary to section 8: protection of other interest

(1)   The court shall order a document to be rectified under section 8 of this Act only where it is satisfied—

(a)   that the interests of a person to whom this section applies would not be adversely affected to a material extent by the rectification; or

(b)   that that person has consented to the proposed rectification.

(2)   Subject to subsection (3) below, this section applies to a person (other than a party to the agreement or the grantor of the document) who has acted or refrained from acting in reliance on the terms of the document [. . .], with the result that his position has been affected to a material extent.

[(2A)   This section does not apply where the document to be rectified is a deed registered in the Land Register of Scotland.]

(3)   This section does not apply to a person—

(a)   who, at the time when he acted or refrained from acting as mentioned in subsection (2) above, knew, or ought in the circumstances known to him at that time to have been aware, that the document [. . .] failed accurately to express the common intention of the parties to the agreement or, as the case may be, the intention of the grantor of the document; or

(b)   whose reliance on the terms of the document [. . .] was otherwise unreasonable.

(4)   Notwithstanding subsection (4) of section 8 of this Act and without prejudice to subsection (5) below, the court may, for the purpose of protecting the interests of a person to whom this section applies, order that the rectification of a document shall have effect as at such date as it may specify, being a date later than that as at which it would have effect by virtue of the said subsection (4).

(5)   Notwithstanding subsection (5) of section 8 of this Act and without prejudice to subsection (4) above, the court may, for the purpose of protecting the interests of a person to whom this section applies, order that a document as rectified shall be treated as having been recorded as mentioned in the said subsection (5) at such date as it may specify, being a date later than that as at which it would be treated by virtue of that subsection as having been so recorded.

[. . .]

(7)   Where a person to whom this section applies was unaware, before a document was ordered to be rectified under section 8 of this Act, that an application had been made under that section for the rectification of the document, the Court of Session, on an application made by that person within the time specified in subsection (8) below, may—

(a)   reduce the rectifying order; or

(b)   order the applicant for the rectifying order to pay such compensation to that person as it thinks fit in respect of his reliance on the terms of the document or on the title sheet.

(8)   The time referred to in subsection (7) above is whichever is the earlier of the following—

(a)   the expiry of 5 years after the making of the rectifying order;

(b)   the expiry of 2 years after the making of that order first came to the notice of the person referred to in that subsection.

INSOLVENCY ACT 1986
(1986, c 45)

53 Mode of appointment by holder of charge

(1)–(6) [deal with powers of receivers]

(7) On the appointment of a receiver under this section, the floating charge by virtue of which he was appointed attaches to the property then subject to the charge; and such attachment has effect as if the charge was a fixed security over the property to which it has attached.

60 Distribution of moneys

(1) Subject to the next section, and to the rights of any of the following categories of persons (which rights shall, except to the extent otherwise provided in any instrument, have the following order of priority), namely—

(a) the holder of any fixed security which is over property subject to the floating charge and which ranks prior to, or *pari passu* with, the floating charge;

(b) all persons who have effectually executed diligence on any part of the property of the company which is subject to the charge by virtue of which the receiver was appointed;

(c) creditors in respect of all liabilities, charges and expenses incurred by or on behalf of the receiver;

(d) the receiver in respect of his liabilities, expenses and remuneration, and any indemnity to which he is entitled out of the property of the company; and

(e) the preferential creditors entitled to payment under section 59,

the receiver shall pay moneys received by him to the holder of the floating charge by virtue of which the receiver was appointed in or towards satisfaction of the debt secured by the floating charge.

(2) Any balance of moneys remaining after the provisions of subsection (1) and section 61 below have been satisfied shall be paid in accordance with their respective rights and interests to the following persons, as the case may require—

(a) any other receiver;

(b) the holder of a fixed security which is over property subject to the floating charge;

(c) the company or its liquidator, as the case may be.

(3) Where any question arises as to the person entitled to a payment under this section, or where a receipt or a discharge of a security cannot be obtained in respect of any such payment, the receiver shall consign the amount of such payment in any joint stock bank of issue in Scotland in name of the Accountant of Court for behoof of the person or persons entitled thereto.

REQUIREMENTS OF WRITING (SCOTLAND) ACT 1995
(1995, c 7)

[Note—*The text of this Act reflects the amendments made by the Land Registration etc (Scotland) Act 2012. Note that as a result of the Schedule to the Land Registration etc (Scotland) Act 2012 (Commencement No 2 and Transitional Provisions) Order 2014 (SSI 2014/41) these amendments do not apply where the relevant document is a will, codicil, or testamentary trust, disposition and settlement. In such cases the text of this Act as it appears in the 9th edition (2012) of these Statutes continues to apply.*]

[PART 1
WHEN WRITING IS REQUIRED]

1 Writing required for certain contracts, obligations, trusts, conveyances and wills

(1) Subject to subsection (2) below and any other enactment, writing shall not be required for the constitution of a contract, unilateral obligation or trust.

(2) Subject to [subsection (3)] below, a written document [which is a traditional document] complying with section 2 [or an electronic document complying with section 9B] of this Act shall be required for—

(a) the constitution of—

(i) a contract or unilateral obligation for the creation, transfer, variation or extinction of [a real right] in land;

(ii) a gratuitous unilateral obligation except an obligation undertaken in the course of business; and

(iii) a trust whereby a person declares himself to be sole trustee of his own property or any property which he may acquire;

(b) the creation, transfer, variation or extinction of [a real right] in land otherwise than by the operation of a court decree, enactment or rule of law; and

[(ba) the constitution of an agreement under section 66(1) of the Land Registration etc (Scotland) Act 2012 (asp 5),]

(c) the making of any will, testamentary trust disposition and settlement or codicil.

(3) Where a contract, obligation or trust mentioned in [subsection (2)(a)] above is not constituted in a [. . .] document complying with section 2 [or, as the case may be, section 9B], of this Act but one of the parties to the contract, a creditor in the obligation or a beneficiary under the trust ('the first person') has acted or refrained from acting in reliance on the contract, obligation or trust with the knowledge and acquiescence of the other party to the contract, the debtor in the obligation or the truster ('the second person')—

(a) the second person shall not be entitled to withdraw from the contract, obligation or trust; and

(b) the contract, obligation or trust shall not be regarded as invalid,

on the ground that it is not so constituted, if the condition set out in subsection (4) below is satisfied.

(4) The condition referred to in subsection (3) above is that the position of the first person—

(a) as a result of acting or refraining from acting as mentioned in that subsection has been affected to a material extent; and

(b) as a result of such a withdrawal as is mentioned in that subsection would be adversely affected to a material extent.

(5) In relation to the constitution of any contract, obligation or trust mentioned in [subsection (2)(a)] above, subsections (3) and (4) above replace the rules of law known as *rei interventus* and homologation.

(6) This section shall apply to the variation of a contract, obligation or trust as it applies to the constitution thereof but as if in subsections (3) and (4) for the references to acting or refraining from acting in reliance on the contract, obligation

or trust and withdrawing therefrom there were substituted respectively references to acting or refraining from acting in reliance on the variation of the contract, obligation or trust and withdrawing from the variation.

(7) In this section ['real right in land' means any real] right in or over land, including any right to occupy or to use land or to restrict the occupation or use of land, but does not include—

    (a) a tenancy;

    (b) a right to occupy or use land; or

    (c) a right to restrict the occupation or use of land,

if the tenancy or right is not granted for more than one year, unless the tenancy or right is for a recurring period or recurring periods and there is a gap of more than one year between the beginning of the first, and the end of the last, such period.

(8) For the purposes of subsection (7) above 'land' does not include—

    (a) growing crops; or

    (b) a moveable building or other moveable structure.

[PART 2
TRADITIONAL DOCUMENTS]

[1A   Application of Part 2

This Part of this Act applies to documents written on paper, parchment or some similar tangible surface ('traditional documents').]

2   Type of writing required for formal validity of certain [traditional] documents

(1) No [traditional] document required by section 1(2) of this Act shall be valid in respect of the formalities of execution unless it is subscribed by the granter of it or, if there is more than one granter, by each granter, but nothing apart from such subscription shall be required for the document to be valid as aforesaid.

(2) A contract mentioned in section 1(2)(a)(i) of this Act may be regarded as constituted or varied (as the case may be) if the offer is contained in one or more [traditional documents] and the acceptance is contained in another [traditional document] or other [traditional documents], and each [such] document is subscribed by the granter or granters thereof.

(3) Nothing in this section shall prevent a [traditional document] which has not been subscribed by the granter or granters of it from being used as evidence in relation to any right or obligation to which the document relates.

(4) This section is without prejudice to any other enactment which makes different provision in respect of the formalities of execution of a document to which this section applies.

[. . .]

3   Presumption as to granter's subscription or date or place of subscription

(1) Subject to subsections (2) to (7) below, where—

    (a) a [traditional document] bears to have been subscribed by a granter of it;

    (b) the document bears to have been signed by a person as a witness of that granter's subscription and the document, or the testing clause or its equivalent, bears to state the name and address of the witness; and

    (c) nothing in the document, or in the testing clause or its equivalent, indicates—

        (i) that it was not subscribed by that granter as it bears to have been so subscribed; or

        (ii) that it was not validly witnessed for any reason specified in paragraphs (a) to (e) of subsection (4) below,

the document shall be presumed to have been subscribed by that granter.

(2)   Where a [traditional document is a testamentary document consisting] of more than one sheet, it shall not be presumed to have been subscribed by a granter as mentioned in subsection (1) above unless, in addition to it bearing to have been subscribed by him and otherwise complying with that subsection, it bears to have been signed by him on every sheet.

(3)   For the purposes of subsection (1)(b) above—

(a)   the name and address of a witness may be added at any time before the document is—

(i)   founded on in legal proceedings; or

(ii)   registered for preservation in the Books of Council and Session or in sheriff court books; and

(b)   the name and address of a witness need not be written by the witness himself.

(4)   Where, in any proceedings relating to a [traditional document] in which a question arises as to a granter's subscription, it is established—

(a)   that a signature bearing to be the signature of the witness of that granter's subscription is not such a signature, whether by reason of forgery or otherwise;

(b)   that the person who signed the document as the witness of that granter's subscription is a person who is named in the document as a granter of it;

(c)   that the person who signed the document as the witness of that granter's subscription, at the time of signing—

(i)   did not know the granter;

(ii)   was under the age of 16 years; or

(iii)   was mentally incapable of acting as a witness;

(d)   that the person who signed the document, purporting to be the witness of that granter's subscription, did not witness such subscription;

(e)   that the person who signed the document as the witness of that granter's subscription did not sign the document after him or that the granter's subscription or, as the case may be, acknowledgement of his subscription and the person's signature as witness of that subscription were not one continuous process;

(f)   that the name or address of the witness of that granter's subscription was added after the document was founded on or registered as mentioned in subsection (3)(a) above or is erroneous in any material respect; or

(g)   in the case of a testamentary document consisting of more than one sheet, that a signature on any sheet bearing to be the signature of the granter is not such a signature, whether by reason of forgery or otherwise,

then, for the purposes of those proceedings, there shall be no presumption that the document has been subscribed by that granter.

(5)   For the purposes of subsection (4)(c)(i) above, the witness shall be regarded as having known the person whose subscription he has witnessed at the time of witnessing if he had credible information at that time of his identity.

(6)   For the purposes of subsection (4)(e) above, where—

(a)   a document is granted by more than one granter; and

(b)   a person is the witness to the subscription of more than one granter,

the subscription or acknowledgement of any such granter and the signature of the person witnessing that granter's subscription shall not be regarded as not being one continuous process by reason only that, between the time of that subscription or acknowledgement and that signature, another granter has subscribed the document or acknowledged his subscription.

(7)   For the purposes of the foregoing provisions of this section a person witnesses a granter's subscription of a document—

(a)   if he sees the granter subscribe it; or

(b)   if the granter acknowledges his subscription to that person.

(8)   Where—

(a) by virtue of subsection (1) above a document to which this subsection applies is presumed to have been subscribed by a granter of it;

(b) the document, or the testing clause or its equivalent, bears to state the date or place of subscription of the document by that granter; and

(c) nothing in the document, or in the testing clause or its equivalent, indicates that that statement as to date or place is incorrect,

there shall be a presumption that the document was subscribed by that granter on the date or at the place as stated.

(9) Subsection (8) above applies to any [traditional document] other than a testamentary document.

(10) Where—

(a) a [traditional document is a testamentary document bearing] to have been subscribed and the document, or the testing clause or its equivalent, bears to state the date or place of subscription (whether or not it is presumed under subsections (1) to (7) above to have been subscribed by a granter of it); and

(b) nothing in the document, or in the testing clause or its equivalent, indicates that that statement as to date or place is incorrect,

there shall be a presumption that the statement as to date or place is correct.

[. . .]

4 Presumption as to granter's subscription or date or place of subscription when established in court proceedings

(1) Where a [traditional document] bears to have been subscribed by a granter of it, but there is no presumption under section 3 of this Act that the document has been subscribed by that granter, then, if the court, on an application being made to it by any person who has an interest in the document, is satisfied that the document was subscribed by that granter, it shall—

(a) cause the document to be endorsed with a certificate to that effect; or

(b) where the document has already been registered in the Books of Council and Session or in sheriff court books, grant decree to that effect.

(2) Where a [traditional document] bears to have been subscribed by a granter of it, but there is no presumption under section 3 of this Act as to the date or place of subscription, then, if the court, on an application being made to it by any person who has an interest in the document, is satisfied as to the date or place of subscription, it shall—

(a) cause the document to be endorsed with a certificate to that effect; or

(b) where the document has already been registered in the Books of Council and Session or in sheriff court books, grant decree to that effect.

(3) On an application under subsection (1) or (2) above evidence shall, unless the court otherwise directs, be given by affidavit.

(4) An application under subsection (1) or (2) above may be made either as a summary application or as incidental to and in the course of other proceedings.

(5) The effect of a certificate or decree—

(a) under subsection (1) above shall be to establish a presumption that the document has been subscribed by the granter concerned;

(b) under subsection (2) above shall be to establish a presumption that the statement in the certificate or decree as to date or place is correct.

(6) In this section 'the court' means—

(a) in the case of a summary application—

(i) the sheriff in whose sheriffdom the applicant resides; or

(ii) if the applicant does not reside in Scotland, the sheriff at Edinburgh; and

(b) in the case of an application made in the course of other proceedings, the court before which those proceedings are pending.

5 Alterations to [traditional documents]: formal validity and presumptions

(1) An alteration made to a [traditional document] required by section 1(2) of this Act—

(a) before the document is subscribed by the granter or, if there is more than one granter, by the granter first subscribing it, shall form part of the document as so subscribed;

(b) after the document is so subscribed shall, if the alteration has been signed by the granter or (as the case may be) by all the granters, have effect as a formally valid alteration of the document as so subscribed,

but an alteration made to such a document otherwise than as mentioned in paragraphs (a) and (b) above shall not be formally valid.

(2) Subsection (1) above is without prejudice to—

(a) any rule of law enabling any provision in a testamentary document to be revoked by deletion or erasure without authentication of the deletion or erasure by the testator;

(b) the Erasures in Deeds (Scotland) Act 1836 and section 54 of the Conveyancing (Scotland) Act 1874.

(3) The fact that an alteration to a [traditional document] was made before the document was subscribed by the granter of it, or by the granter first subscribing it, may be established by all relevant evidence, whether written or oral.

(4) Where a [traditional document] bears to have been subscribed by the granter or, if there is more than one granter, by all the granters of it, then, if subsection (5) or (6) below applies, an alteration made to the document shall be presumed to have been made before the document was subscribed by the granter or, if there is more than one granter, by the granter first subscribing it, and to form part of the document as so subscribed.

(5) This subsection applies where—

(a) the document is presumed under section 3 of this Act to have been subscribed by the granter or granters (as the case may be);

(b) it is stated in the document, or in the testing clause or its equivalent, that the alteration was made before the document was subscribed; and

(c) nothing in the document, or in the testing clause or its equivalent, indicates that the alteration was made after the document was subscribed.

(6) This subsection applies where subsection (5) above does not apply, but the court is satisfied, on an application being made to it, that the alteration was made before the document was subscribed by the granter or, if there is more than one granter, by the granter first subscribing it, and causes the document to be endorsed with a certificate to that effect or, where the document has already been registered in the Books of Council and Session or in sheriff court books, grants decree to that effect.

(7) Subsections (3), (4) and (6) of section 4 of this Act shall apply in relation to an application under subsection (6) above as they apply in relation to an application under subsection (1) of that section.

(8) Where an alteration is made to a [traditional document] after the document has been subscribed by a granter, Schedule 1 to this Act (presumptions as to granter's signature and date and place of signing in relation to such alterations) shall have effect.

6 Registration of [traditional documents]

(1) Subject to subsection (3) below, it shall not be competent—

(a) to record a [traditional document] in the Register of Sasines; or

(b) to register a [traditional document] for execution or preservation in the Books of Council and Session or in sheriff court books, [(ba)   to register a traditional document in the Land Register of Scotland,] unless subsection (2) below applies in relation to the document.

(2)   This subsection applies where—

(a)   the document is presumed under section 3 or 4 of this Act to have been subscribed by the granter; or

(b)   if there is more than one granter, the document is presumed under section 3 or 4 or partly under the one section and partly under the other to have been subscribed by at least one of the granters.

(3)   Subsection (1) above shall not apply in relation to—

[(a)   a document's—

(i)   being recorded in the Register of Sasines, or

(ii)   being registered in the Land Register of Scotland, in the Books of Council and Session or in sheriff court books,

if an enactment requires or expressly permits such recording or registration notwithstanding that the document is not presumed to have been subscribed by the granter or by at least one of the granters,]

(b)   the recording of a court decree in the Register of Sasines [or the registering of such a decree in the Land Register of Scotland];

(c)   the registration in the Books of Council and Session or in sheriff court books of—

(i)   a testamentary document;

(ii)   a document which is directed by the Court of Session or (as the case may be) the sheriff to be so registered;

(iii)   a document whose formal validity is governed by a law other than Scots law, if the Keeper of the Registers of Scotland or (as the case may be) the sheriff clerk is satisfied that the document is formally valid according to the law governing such validity;

(iv)   a court decree granted under section 4 or 5 of this Act in relation to a document already registered in the Books of Council and Session or in sheriff court books (as the case may be); or

(d)   the registration of a court decree in a separate register maintained for that purpose.

(4)   A [traditional document] may be registered for preservation in the Books of Council and Session or in sheriff court books without a clause of consent to registration.

[. . .]

7   Subscription and signing

(1)   Except where an enactment expressly provides otherwise, a [traditional document] is subscribed by a granter of it if it is signed by him at the end of the last page (excluding any annexation, whether or not incorporated in the document as provided for in section 8 of this Act).

(2)   Subject to paragraph 2(2) of Schedule 2 to this Act, a [traditional document], or an alteration to [such a document], is signed by an individual natural person as a granter or on behalf of a granter of it if it is signed by him—

(a)   with the full name by which he is identified in the document or in any testing clause or its equivalent; or

(b)   with his surname, preceded by at least one forename (or an initial or abbreviation or familiar form of a forename); or

(c)   except for the purposes of section 3(1) to (7) of this Act, with a name (not in accordance with paragraph (a) or (b) above) or description or an initial or mark if it is established that the name, description, initial or mark—

(i)   was his usual method of signing, or his usual method of signing documents or alterations of the type in question; or

(ii)   was intended by him as his signature of the document or alteration.

(3)   Where there is more than one granter, the requirement under subsection (1) above of signing at the end of the last page of a document shall be regarded as complied with if at least one granter signs at the end of the last page and any other granter signs on an additional page.

(4)   Where a person grants a [traditional document] in more than one capacity, one subscription of the document by him shall be sufficient to bind him in all such capacities.

(5)   A [traditional document], or an alteration to [such a document], is signed by a witness if it is signed by him—

(a)   with the full name by which he is identified in the document or in any testing clause or its equivalent; or

(b)   with his surname, preceded by at least one forename (or an initial or abbreviation or familiar form of a forename),

and if the witness is witnessing the signature of more than one granter, it shall be unnecessary for him to sign the document or alteration more than once.

(6)   This section is without prejudice to any rule of law relating to the subscription or signing of documents by members of the Royal Family, by peers or by the wives or the eldest sons of peers.

(7)   Schedule 2 to this Act (special rules relating to subscription and signing of [traditional documents] etc by partnerships, companies, [limited liability partnerships,] local authorities, other bodies corporate and Ministers) shall have effect.

8   Annexations to [traditional documents]

(1)   Subject to subsection (2) below and except where an enactment expressly otherwise provides, any annexation to a [traditional document] shall be regarded as incorporated in the document if it is—

(a)   referred to in the document; and

(b)   identified on its face as being the annexation referred to in the document, without the annexation having to be signed or subscribed.

(2)   Where a document relates to land and an annexation to it describes or shows all or any part of the land to which the document relates, the annexation shall be regarded as incorporated in the document if and only if—

(a)   it is referred to in the document; and

(b)   it is identified on its face as being the annexation referred to in the document; and

(c)   it is signed on—

(i)   each page, where it is a plan, drawing, photograph or other representation; or

(ii)   the last page, where it is an inventory, appendix, schedule or other writing.

(3)   Any annexation referred to in subsection (2) above which bears to have been signed by a granter of the document shall be presumed to have been signed by the person who subscribed the document as that granter.

(4)   Section 7(2) of this Act shall apply in relation to any annexation referred to in subsection (2) above as it applies in relation to a [traditional document] as if for any reference to a document (except the reference in paragraph (a)) there were substituted a reference to an annexation.

(5)   It shall be competent to sign any annexation to a [traditional document] at any time before the document is—

(a)   founded on in legal proceedings;

(b)   registered for preservation in the Books of Council and Session or in sheriff court books;

(c)   recorded in the Register of Sasines;

(d)   registered in the Land Register of Scotland.

(6)   Where there is more than one granter, the requirement under subsection (2) (c)(ii) above of signing on the last page shall be regarded as complied with (provided that at least one granter signs at the end of the last page) if any other granter signs on an additional page.

9   Subscription on behalf of blind granter or granter unable to write

(1)   Where a granter of a [traditional document] makes a declaration to a relevant person that he is blind or unable to write, the relevant person—

  (a)   having read the document to that granter; or

  (b)   if the granter makes a declaration that he does not wish him to do so, without having read it to the granter,

shall, if authorised by the granter, be entitled to subscribe it and, if it is a testamentary document, sign it as mentioned in section 3(2) of this Act, on the granter's behalf.

(2)   Subscription or signing by a relevant person under subsection (1) above shall take place in the presence of the granter.

(3)   This Act shall have effect in relation to subscription or signing by a relevant person under subsection (1) above subject to the modifications set out in Schedule 3 to this Act.

(4)   A document subscribed by a relevant person under subsection (1) above which confers on the relevant person or his spouse, son or daughter a benefit in money or money's worth (whether directly or indirectly) shall be invalid to the extent, but only to the extent, that it confers such benefit.

(5)   This section and Schedule 3 to this Act apply in relation to the signing of—

  (a)   an annexation to a [traditional document] as mentioned in section 8(2) of this Act;

  (b)   an alteration made to a [traditional document as mentioned in section 5(1)] or to any such annexation to a document, as they apply in relation to the subscription of a document; and for that purpose, any reference to reading a document includes a reference to describing a plan, drawing, photograph or other representation in such an annexation or in an alteration to such an " annexation.

(6)   In this Act [(other than section 10A)] 'relevant person' means a solicitor who has in force a practising certificate as defined in section 4(c) of the Solicitors (Scotland) Act 1980, an advocate, a justice of the peace or a sheriff clerk and, in relation to the execution of documents outwith Scotland, includes a notary public or any other person with official authority under the law of the place of execution to execute documents on behalf of persons who are blind or unable to write.

(7)   Nothing in this section shall prevent the granter of a document who is blind from subscribing or signing the document as mentioned in section 7 of this Act.

[PART 3
ELECTRONIC DOCUMENTS

[9A   Application of Part 3

This Part applies to documents which, rather than being written on paper, parchment or some similar tangible surface are created in electronic form ('electronic documents').]

[9B   Validity of electronic documents

(1)   No electronic document required by section 1(2) is valid in respect of the formalities of execution unless—

  (a)   it is authenticated by the granter, or if there is more than one granter by each granter, in accordance with subsection (2), and

  (b)   it meets such other requirements (if any) as may be prescribed by the Scottish Ministers in regulations.

(2)   An electronic document is authenticated by a person if the electronic signature of that person—

(a)   is incorporated into, or logically associated with, the electronic document,

(b)   was created by the person by whom it purports to have been created, and

(c)   is of such type, and satisfies such requirements (if any), as may be prescribed by the Scottish Ministers in regulations.

(3)   A contract mentioned in section 1(2)(a) may be regarded as constituted or varied (as the case may be) if—

(a)   the offer is contained in one or more electronic documents,

(b)   the acceptance is contained in another electronic document or in other such documents, and

(c)   each of the documents is authenticated by its granter or granters.

(4)   Where a person grants an electronic document in more than one capacity, authentication by the person of the document, in accordance with subsection (3), is sufficient to bind the person in all such capacities.

(5)   Nothing in this section prevents an electronic document which has not been authenticated by the granter or granters of it from being used as evidence in relation to any right or obligation to which the document relates.

(6)   Regulations under subsection (1)(b) or (2)(c) are subject to the negative procedure.]

[9C   Presumption as to authentication of electronic documents

(1)   Where—

(a)   an electronic document bears to have been authenticated by the granter,

(b)   nothing in the document or in the authentication indicates that it was not so authenticated, and

(c)   the conditions set out in subsection (2) are satisfied,

the document is to be presumed to have been authenticated by the granter.

(2)   The conditions are that the electronic signature incorporated into, or logically associated with, the document—

(a)   is of such type and satisfies such requirements as may be prescribed by the Scottish Ministers in regulations, and

(b)   (either or both)—

(i)   is used in such circumstances as may be so prescribed,

(ii)   bears to be certified,

and that if the electronic signature bears to be certified (and does not conform with paragraph (b)(i)) the certification is of such type and satisfies such requirements as may be so prescribed.

(3)   Regulations under subsection (2) are subject to the negative procedure.]

[9D   Presumptions as to granter's authentication etc when established in court proceedings

(1)   Where—

(a)   an electronic document bears to have been authenticated by a granter of it, and

(b)   there is no presumption under section 9C that the document has been authenticated by that granter,

the court must, on an application being made to it by any person who has an interest in the document, if satisfied that the document was authenticated by that granter, grant decree to that effect.

(2)   Where—

(a)   an electronic document bears to have been authenticated by a granter of it, and

    (b)   there is no presumption by virtue of section 9E(1) as to the time, date or place of authentication,
the court must, on an application being made to it by any person who has an interest in the document, if satisfied as to that time, date or place, grant decree to that effect.

    (3)   On an application under subsection (1) or (2), evidence is, unless the court otherwise directs, to be given by affidavit.

    (4)   An application under subsection (1) or (2) may be made either as a summary application or as incidental to, and in the course of, other proceedings.

    (5)   The effect of a decree—

        (a)   under subsection (1), is to establish a presumption that the document has been authenticated by the granter concerned, or

        (b)   under subsection (2), is to establish a presumption that the statement in the decree as to time, date or place is correct.

    (6)   In this section, 'the court' means—

        (a)   in the case of a summary application—

            (i)   the sheriff in whose sheriffdom the applicant resides, or

            (ii)   if the applicant does not reside in Scotland, the sheriff at Edinburgh, or

        (b)   in the case of an application made in the course of other proceedings, the court before which those proceedings are pending.]

[9E   Further provision by Scottish Ministers about electronic documents

    (1)   The Scottish Ministers may, in regulations, make provision as to the effectiveness or formal validity of, or presumptions to be made with regard to—

        (a)   any alteration made, whether before or after authentication, to an electronic document,

        (b)   the authentication, by or on behalf of the granter, of such a document,

        (c)   the authentication, by or on behalf of a person with a disability, of such a document, or

        (d)   any annexation to such a document,
(including, without prejudice to the generality of this subsection, presumptions to be made with regard to the time, date and place of authentication of such a document).

    (2)   Regulations under subsection (1) may make such incidental, supplemental, consequential, transitional, transitory or saving provision as the Scottish Ministers consider necessary or expedient for the purposes of, or in consequence of the regulations.

    (3)   Subject to subsection (4), regulations under subsection (1) are subject to the negative procedure.

    (4)   Regulations which—

        (a)   make provision of the kind mentioned in subsection (1)(b), or

        (b)   add to, replace or omit any part of an Act (including this Act), are subject to the affirmative procedure.]

[9F   Delivery of electronic documents

    (1)   An electronic document may be delivered electronically or by such other means as are reasonably practicable.

    (2)   But such a document must be in a form, and such delivery must be by a means—

        (a)   the intended recipient has agreed to accept, or

        (b)   which it is reasonable in all the circumstances for the intended recipient to accept.]

[9G   Registration and recording of electronic documents

(1)   Subject to subsection (6), it is not competent—

(a)   to record an electronic document in the Register of Sasines,

(b)   to register such a document in the Land Register of Scotland,

(c)   to register such a document for execution or preservation in the Books of Council and Session, or

(d)   to record or register such a document in any other register under the management and control of the Keeper of the Registers of Scotland,

unless both subsection (2) and subsection (3) apply in relation to the document.

(2)   This subsection applies where—

(a)   the document is presumed under section 9C or 9D or by virtue of section 9E(1) to have been authenticated by the granter, or

(b)   if there is more than one granter, the document is presumed by virtue of any of those provisions to have been authenticated by at least one of the granters.

(3)   This subsection applies where—

(a)   the document,

(b)   the electronic signature authenticating it, and

(c)   if the document bears to be certified, the certification,

are in such form and of such type as are prescribed by the Scottish Ministers in regulations.

(4)   Before making regulations under subsection (3), the Scottish Ministers must consult with—

(a)   the Keeper of the Registers of Scotland,

(b)   the Keeper of the Records of Scotland, and

(c)   the Lord President of the Court of Session.

(5)   Regulations under subsection (3)—

(a)   may make different provision for different cases or classes of case, and

(b)   are subject to the negative procedure.

(6)   Subsection (1) above does not apply in relation to—

(a)   a document's—

(i)   being recorded in the Register of Sasines,

(ii)   being registered in the Land Register of Scotland or in the Books of Council and Session, or

(iii)   being recorded or registered in any other register under the management and control of the Keeper of the Registers of Scotland,

if an enactment requires or expressly permits such recording or registration notwithstanding that the document is not presumed to have been authenticated by the granter or by at least one of the granters,

(b)   the recording of a court decree in the Register of Sasines or the registering of such a decree in the Land Register of Scotland,

(c)   the registering in the Books of Council and Session of—

(i)   a document registration of which is directed by the Court of Session,

(ii)   a document the formal validity of which is governed by a law other than Scots law, provided that the Keeper of the Registers of Scotland is satisfied that the document is formally valid according to that other law,

(iii)   a court decree granted under section 9D, or by virtue of section 9E(1), of this Act in relation to a document already registered in the Books of Council and Session, or

(d)   the registration of a court decree in a separate register maintained for that purpose.

(7)   An electronic document may be registered for preservation in the Books of Council and Session without a clause of consent to registration.]]

[PART 4
GENERAL PROVISIONS]

10   Forms of testing clause

(1)   Without prejudice to the effectiveness of any other means of providing information relating to the execution of a document, this information may be provided in such form of testing clause as may be prescribed in regulations made by the Secretary of State.

(2)   Regulations under subsection (1) above shall be made by statutory instrument which shall be subject to annulment in pursuance of a resolution of either House of Parliament and may prescribe different forms for different cases or classes of case.

[10A   Disapplication of physical presence requirements

(1)   The following requirements (however expressed) do not apply—

(a)   a requirement for a relevant person to be physically in the same place as another person when that person—

(i)   signs or subscribes a document or an alteration of a document,

(ii)   takes an oath, or

(iii)   makes an affirmation or declaration,

(b)   a requirement for another person to be physically in the same place as a relevant person when the relevant person signs or subscribes a document or an alteration of a document.

(2)   In this section—

'relevant person' means—

(a)   a solicitor,

(b)   an advocate,

(c)   a notary public,

'requirement' means a requirement arising from an enactment or rule of law.

(3)   For the avoidance of doubt—

(a)   the requirements described by subsection (1)(a) include a requirement that may be fulfilled by the physical presence of a professional of a type not mentioned in the definition of "relevant person" as well as by a professional of a type that is (for example, it includes a requirement for the physical presence of a solicitor or a registered medical practitioner), but

(b)   subsection (1) only causes such a requirement not to apply in relation to a professional of a type that is mentioned in the definition of 'relevant person.']

[. . .]

12   Interpretation

(1)   In this Act, except where the context otherwise requires—

'alteration' includes interlineation, marginal addition, deletion, substitution, erasure or anything written on erasure;

'annexation' includes any inventory, appendix, schedule, other writing, plan, drawing, photograph or other representation annexed to a document;

[. . .]

'authorised' means expressly or impliedly authorised and any reference to a person authorised to sign includes a reference to a person authorised to sign generally or in relation to a particular document;

['certification', in relation to an electronic signature incorporated into or logically associated with an electronic document, means confirming in a statement that—

(a) the electronic signature,

(b) a means of producing, communicating or verifying that signature, or

(c) a procedure applied to that signature,

is, either alone or combined with other factors, a valid means of establishing the authenticity of the electronic document, its integrity or both its authenticity and its integrity (it being immaterial, in construing this definition, whether the statement is made before or after the authentication of an electronic document to which the statement relates),]

'company' has the same meaning as in [section 1(1) of the Companies Act 2006];

[. . .]

'decree' includes a judgment or order, or an official certified copy, abbreviate or extract of a decree;

[. . .]

'director' includes any person occupying the position of director, by whatever name he is called;

'document' includes [, in the case of a traditional document,] any annexation which is incorporated in it under section 8 of this Act and any reference, however expressed, to the signing of a document includes a reference to the signing of an annexation;

[. . .]

['electronic document' has the meaning given by section 9A,]

['electronic signature' means so much of anything in electronic form as—

(a) is incorporated into, or logically associated with, an electronic document, and

(b) purports to be so incorporated or associated for the purpose of being used in establishing the authenticity of the electronic document, its integrity or both its authenticity and its integrity,]

'enactment' includes an enactment contained in a statutory instrument [and an enactment comprised in, or in an instrument made under, an Act of the Scottish Parliament];

'governing board', in relation to a body corporate to which paragraph 5 of Schedule 2 to this Act applies, means any governing body, however described;

'local authority' means a local authority within the meaning of section 235(1) of the Local Government (Scotland) Act 1973 and a council constituted under section 2 of the Local Government etc. (Scotland) Act 1994;

'Minister' has the same meaning as 'Minister of the Crown' has in section 8 of the Ministers of the Crown Act 1975 [and also includes a Member of the Scottish Government];

'office-holder' does not include a Minister but, subject to that, means—

(a) the holder of an office created or continued in existence by a public general Act of Parliament;

(b) the holder of an office the remuneration in respect of which is paid out of money provided by Parliament [or out of the Scottish Consolidated Fund];

(c) the registrar of companies [. . .];

'officer'—

(a) in relation to a Minister, means any person in the civil service of the Crown who is serving in his Department [or as the case may be, as a member of the staff of the Scottish Ministers or the Lord Advocate];

(b) in relation to an office-holder, means any member of his staff, or any person in the civil service of the Crown who has been assigned or appointed to assist him in the exercise of his functions;

'proper officer', in relation to a local authority, has the same meaning as in section 235(3) of the Local Government (Scotland) Act 1973; and

'secretary' means, if there are two or more joint secretaries, any one of them.
[...]
['traditional document' has the meaning given by section 1A].

(2)   Any reference in this Act to subscription or signing by a granter of a document or an alteration made to a document, in a case where a person is subscribing or signing under a power of attorney on behalf of the granter, shall be construed as a reference to subscription or signing by that person of the document or alteration.

[(3)   In a case where a person is authenticating an electronic document on behalf of a granter, any reference in this Act to authentication by a granter of an electronic document shall be construed as a reference to authentication by that person.]

[(4)   In relation to an electronic document—
    (a)   references to authenticity—
        (i)   are references to whether the document has been electronically signed by a particular person, and
        (ii)   may include references to whether the document is accurately timed or dated, and
    (b)   references to integrity are references as to whether there has been any tampering with, or other modification of, the document.]

13   Application of Act to Crown
(1)   Nothing in this Act shall—
    (a)   prevent Her Majesty from authenticating—
        (i)   a document by superscription; or
        (ii)   a document relating to her private estates situated or arising in Scotland in accordance with section 6 of the Crown Private Estates Act 1862;
    (b)   prevent authentication under the Writs Act 1672 of a document passing the seal appointed by the Treaty of Union to be kept and used in Scotland in place of the Great Seal of Scotland formerly in use; or
    (c)   prevent any document mentioned in paragraph (a) or (b) above authenticated as aforesaid from being recorded in the Register of Sasines [, registered in the Land Register of Scotland] or registered for execution or preservation in the Books of Council and Session or in sheriff court books.
(2)   [...]
(3)   Subject to subsections (1) and (2) above, this Act binds the Crown.

14   Minor and consequential amendments, repeals, transitional provisions and savings
(1)   The enactments mentioned in Schedule 4 to this Act shall have effect subject to the minor and consequential amendments specified in that Schedule.
(2)   The enactments mentioned in Schedule 5 to this Act are hereby repealed to the extent specified in the third column of that Schedule.
(3)   Subject to subsection (4) below and without prejudice to subsection (5) below and section 11(4) of this Act, nothing in this Act shall—
    (a)   apply to any document executed or anything done before the commencement of this Act; or
    (b)   affect the operation, in relation to any document executed before such commencement, of any procedure for establishing the authenticity of such a document.
(4)   In the repeal of the Blank Bonds and Trusts Act 1696 (provided for in Schedule 5 to this Act), the repeal of the words from 'And farder' to the end—
    (a)   shall have effect in relation to a deed of trust, whether executed before or after the commencement of this Act; but

(b)   notwithstanding paragraph (a) above, shall not have effect in relation to proceedings commenced before the commencement of this Act in which a question arises as to the deed of trust.

(5)   The repeal of certain provisions of the Lyon King of Arms Act 1672 (provided for in Schedule 5 to this Act) shall not affect any right of a person to add a territorial designation to his signature or the jurisdiction of the Lord Lyon King of Arms in relation to any such designation.

(6)   For the purposes of this Act, if it cannot be ascertained whether a document was executed before or after the commencement of this Act, there shall be a presumption that it was executed after such commencement.

15   Short title, commencement and extent

(1)   This Act may be cited as the Requirements of Writing (Scotland) Act 1995.

(2)   This Act shall come into force at the end of the period of three months beginning with the date on which it is passed.

(3)   This Act extends to Scotland only.

SCHEDULES

Section 5(8)   SCHEDULE 1
ALTERATIONS MADE TO A [TRADITIONAL DOCUMENT] AFTER IT HAS
BEEN SUBSCRIBED

Presumption as to granter's signature or date or place of signing

1.—(1)   Subject to sub-paragraphs (2) to (7) below, where—

(a)   an alteration to a [traditional document] bears to have been signed by a granter of the document;

(b)   the alteration bears to have been signed by a person as a witness of that granter's signature and the alteration, or the testing clause or its equivalent, bears to state the name and address of the witness; and

(c)   nothing in the document or alteration, or in the testing clause or its equivalent, indicates—

(i)   that the alteration was not signed by that granter as it bears to have been so signed; or

(ii)   that it was not validly witnessed for any reason specified in paragraphs (a) to (e) of sub-paragraph (4) below,

the alteration shall be presumed to have been signed by that granter.

(2)   Where an alteration to a testamentary document consists of more than one sheet, the alteration shall not be presumed to have been signed by a granter as mentioned in sub-paragraph (1) above unless, in addition to it bearing to have been signed by him on the last sheet and otherwise complying with that subparagraph, it bears to have been signed by him on every other sheet.

(3)   For the purposes of sub-paragraph (1)(b) above—

(a)   the name and address of a witness may be added at any time before the alteration is—

(i)   founded on in legal proceedings; or

(ii)   registered for preservation in the Books of Council and Session or in sheriff court books; and

(b)   the name and address of a witness need not be written by the witness himself.

(4)   Where, in any proceedings relating to an alteration to a document in which a question arises as to a granter's signature, it is established—

(a)   that a signature bearing to be the signature of the witness of that granter's signature is not such a signature, whether by reason of forgery or otherwise;

(b)   that the person who signed the alteration as the witness of that granter's signature is a person who is named in the document as a granter of the document;

(c)   that the person who signed the alteration as the witness of that granter's signature, at the time of signing—

(i)   did not know the granter;

(ii)   was under the age of 16 years; or

(iii)   was mentally incapable of acting as a witness;

(d)   that the person who signed the alteration, purporting to be the witness of that granter's signature, did not witness such signature;

(e)   that the person who signed the alteration as the witness of that granter's signature did not sign the alteration after him or that the signing of the alteration by the granter or, as the case may be, the granter's acknowledgement of his signature and the signing by the person as witness were not one continuous process;

(f)   that the name or address of the witness of that granter's signature was added after the alteration was founded on or registered as mentioned in subparagraph (3)(a) above or is erroneous in any material respect; or

(g)   in the case of an alteration to a testamentary document consisting of more than one sheet, that a signature on any sheet of the alteration bearing to be the signature of the granter is not such a signature, whether by reason of forgery or otherwise,

then, for the purposes of those proceedings, there shall be no presumption that the alteration has been signed by that granter.

(5)   For the purposes of sub-paragraph (4)(c)(i) above, the witness shall be regarded as having known the person whose signature he has witnessed at the time of witnessing if he had credible information at that time of his identity.

(6)   For the purposes of sub-paragraph (4)(e) above, where—

(a)   an alteration to a document is made by more than one granter; and

(b)   a person is the witness to the signature of more than one granter,

the signing of the alteration by any such granter or the acknowledgement of his signature and the signing by the person witnessing that granter's signature shall not be regarded as not being one continuous process by reason only that, between the time of signing or acknowledgement by that granter and of signing by that witness, another granter has signed the alteration or acknowledged his signature.

(7)   For the purposes of the foregoing provisions of this paragraph a person witnesses a granter's signature of an alteration—

(a)   if he sees the granter sign it; or

(b)   if the granter acknowledges his signature to that person.

(8)   Where—

(a)   by virtue of sub-paragraph (1) above an alteration to a document to which this sub-paragraph applies is presumed to have been signed by a granter of the document;

(b)   the alteration, or the testing clause or its equivalent, bears to state the date or place of signing of the alteration by that granter; and

(c)   nothing in the document or alteration, or in the testing clause or its equivalent, indicates that that statement as to date or place is incorrect,
there shall be a presumption that the alteration was signed by that granter on the date or at the place as stated.

(9)   Sub-paragraph (8) above applies to any document other than a testamentary document.

(10)   Where—

(a)   an alteration to a testamentary document bears to have been signed and the alteration, or the testing clause or its equivalent, bears to state the date or place of signing (whether or not it is presumed under sub-paragraphs (1) to (7) above to have been signed by a granter of the document); and

(b)   nothing in the document or alteration, or in the testing clause or its equivalent, indicates that that statement as to date or place is incorrect,
there shall be a presumption that the statement as to date or place is correct.

Presumption as to granter's signature or date or place of signing when established in court proceedings

2.—(1)   Where an alteration to a [traditional document] bears to have been signed by a granter of the document, but there is no presumption under paragraph 1 above that the alteration has been signed by that granter, then, if the court, on an application being made to it by any person having an interest in the document, is satisfied that the alteration was signed by that granter, it shall—

(a)   cause the document to be endorsed with a certificate to that effect; or

(b)   where the document has already been registered in the Books of Council and Session or in sheriff court books, grant decree to that effect.

(2)   Where an alteration to a [traditional document] bears to have been signed by a granter of the document, but there is no presumption under paragraph 1 above as to the date or place of signing, then, if the court, on an application being made to it by any person having an interest in the document, is satisfied as to the date or place of signing, it shall—

(a)   cause the document to be endorsed with a certificate to that effect; or

(b)   where the document has already been registered in the Books of Council and Session or in sheriff court books, grant decree to that effect.

(3)   In relation to an application under sub-paragraph (1) or (2) above evidence shall, unless the court otherwise directs, be given by affidavit.

(4)   An application under sub-paragraph (1) or (2) above may be made either as a summary application or as incidental to and in the course of other proceedings.

(5)   The effect of a certificate or decree—

(a)   under sub-paragraph (1) above shall be to establish a presumption that the alteration has been signed by the granter concerned;

(b)   under sub-paragraph (2) above shall be to establish a presumption that the statement in the certificate or decree as to date or place is correct.

(6)   In this paragraph 'the court' means—

(a)   in the case of a summary application—

(i)   the sheriff in whose sheriffdom the applicant resides; or

(ii)   if the applicant does not reside in Scotland, the sheriff at Edinburgh; and

(b)   in the case of an application made in the course of other proceedings, the court before which those proceedings are pending.

Section 7(7)   SCHEDULE 2
                    SUBSCRIPTION AND SIGNING: SPECIAL CASES

General

1.   Any reference in this Act to subscription or signing by a granter of a [traditional document] or an alteration to a document, in a case where the granter is a person to whom any of paragraphs 2 to 6 of this Schedule applies shall, unless the context otherwise requires, be construed as a reference to subscription or, as the case may be, signing of the document or alteration by a person in accordance with that paragraph.

Partnerships

2.—(1)   Except where an enactment expressly provides otherwise, where a granter of a [traditional document] is a partnership, the document is signed by the partnership if it is signed on its behalf by a partner or by a person authorised to sign the document on its behalf.
   (2)   A person signing on behalf of a partnership under this paragraph may use his own name or the firm name.
   (3)   Sub-paragraphs (1) and (2) of this paragraph apply in relation to the signing of an alteration made to a document as they apply in relation to the signing of a document.
   (4)   In this paragraph 'partnership' has the same meaning as in section 1 of the Partnership Act 1890.

Companies

3.—(1)   Except where an enactment expressly provides otherwise, where a granter of a [traditional document] is a company, the document is signed by the company if it is signed on its behalf by a director, or by the secretary, of the company or by a person authorised to sign the document on its behalf.
   (2)   This Act is without prejudice to—
      (a)   [sections 270(3) and 274 of the Companies Act 2006; and]
      (b)   paragraph 9 of Schedule 1, paragraph 9 of Schedule 2, and paragraph 7 of Schedule 4, to the Insolvency Act 1986.
   (3)   Sub-paragraphs (1) and (2) of this paragraph apply in relation to the signing of an alteration made to a document as they apply in relation to the signing of a document.
   (4)   Where a granter of a [traditional document] is a company, section 3 of and Schedule 1 to this Act shall have effect subject to the modifications set out in subparagraphs (5) and (6) below.
   (5)   In section 3—
      (a)   for subsection (1) there shall be substituted the following subsections—
         '(1) Subject to subsections (1A) to (7) below, where—
            (a)   a [traditional document] bears to have been subscribed on behalf of a company by a director, or by the secretary, of the company or by a person bearing to have been authorised to subscribe the document on its behalf;
            (b)   the document bears to have been signed by a person as a witness of the subscription of the director, secretary or other person subscribing on behalf of the company and to state the name and address of the witness; and
            (c)   nothing in the document, or in the testing clause or its equivalent, indicates—
               (i)   that it was not subscribed on behalf of the company as it bears to have been so subscribed; or

(ii)   that it was not validly witnessed for any reason specified in paragraphs (a) to (e) of subsection (4) below,

the document shall be presumed to have been subscribed by the company.

(1A)   Where a document does not bear to have been signed by a person as a witness of the subscription of the director, secretary or other person subscribing on behalf of the company it shall be presumed to have been subscribed by the company if it bears to have been subscribed on behalf of the company by—

(a)   two directors of the company; or

(b)   a director and secretary of the company; or

(c)   two persons bearing to have been authorised to subscribe the document on its behalf.

(1B)   For the purposes of subsection (1)(b) above, the name and address of the witness may bear to be stated in the document itself or in the testing clause or its equivalent.

(1C)   A presumption under subsection (1) or (1A) above as to subscription of a document does not include a presumption—

(a)   that a person bearing to subscribe the document as a director or the secretary of the company was such director or secretary; or

(b)   that a person subscribing the document on behalf of the company bearing to have been authorised to do so was authorised to do so.';

(b)   in subsection (4) after paragraph (g) there shall be inserted the following paragraph—

'(h)   if the document does not bear to have been witnessed, but bears to have been subscribed on behalf of the company by two of the directors of the company, or by a director and secretary of the company, or by two authorised persons, that a signature bearing to be the signature of a director, secretary or authorised person is not such a signature, whether by reason of forgery or otherwise;'.

(6)   In paragraph 1 of Schedule 1—

(a)   for sub-paragraph (1) there shall be substituted the following sub-paragraphs—

'(1) Subject to sub-paragraphs (1A) to (7) below, where—

(a)   an alteration to a [traditional document] bears to have been signed on behalf of a company by a director, or by the secretary, of the company or by a person bearing to have been authorised to sign the alteration on its behalf;

(b)   the alteration bears to have been signed by a person as a witness of the signature of the director, secretary or other person signing on behalf of the company and to state the name and address of the witness; and

(c)   nothing in the document or alteration, or in the testing clause or its equivalent, indicates—

(i)   that the alteration was not signed on behalf of the company as it bears to have been so signed; or

(ii)   that the alteration was not validly witnessed for any reason specified in paragraphs (a) to (e) of sub-paragraph (4) below,

the alteration shall be presumed to have been signed by the company.

(1A) Where an alteration does not bear to have been signed by a person as a witness of the signature of the director, secretary or other person signing on behalf of the company it shall be presumed to have been signed by the company if it bears to have been signed on behalf of the company by—

(a)   two directors of the company; or

(b)   a director and secretary of the company; or

(c)   two persons bearing to have been authorised to sign the alteration on its behalf.

(1B) For the purposes of sub-paragraph (1)(b) above, the name and address of the witness may bear to be stated in the alteration itself or in the testing clause or its equivalent.

(1C) A presumption under sub-paragraph (1) or (1A) above as to signing of an alteration to a document does not include a presumption—

    (a) that a person bearing to sign the alteration as a director or the secretary of the company was such director or secretary; or

    (b) that a person signing the alteration on behalf of the company bearing to have been authorised to do so was authorised to do so.';

(b) in sub-paragraph (4) after paragraph (g) there shall be inserted the following paragraph—

    '(h) if the alteration does not bear to have been witnessed, but bears to have been signed on behalf of the company by two of the directors of the company, or by a director and secretary of the company, or by two authorised persons, that a signature bearing to be the signature of a director, secretary or authorised person is not such a signature, whether by reason of forgery or otherwise;'.

[Limited liability partnerships

3A. (1) Except where an enactment expressly provides otherwise, where a granter of a [traditional document] is a limited liability partnership, the document is signed by the limited liability partnership if it is signed on its behalf by a member of the limited liability partnership.

(2) This Act is without prejudice to paragraph 9 of Schedule 1, paragraph 9 of Schedule 2, and paragraph 7 of Schedule 4, to the Insolvency Act 1986.

(3) Sub-paragraphs (1) and (2) of this paragraph apply in relation to the signing of an alteration made to a document as they apply in relation to the signing of a document.

(4) Where a granter of a [traditional document] is a limited liability partnership, section 3 of and Schedule 1 to this Act shall have effect subject to the modifications set out in sub-paragraphs (5) and (6) below.

(5) In section 3—

    (a) for subsection (1) there shall be substituted the following sub-sections—

    '(1) Subject to subsections (1A) to (7) below, where—

      (a) a [traditional document] bears to have been subscribed on behalf of a limited liability partnership by a member of the limited liability partnership;

      (b) the document bears to have been signed by a person as a witness of the subscription of the member of the limited liability partnership and to state the name and address of the witness; and

      (c) nothing in the document, or in the testing clause or its equivalent, indicates—

        (i) that it was not subscribed on behalf of the limited liability partnership as it bears to have been so subscribed; or

        (ii) that it was not validly witnessed for any reason specified in paragraphs (a) to (e) of subsection (4) below,

the document shall be presumed to have been subscribed by the limited liability partnership.

(1A) Where a document does not bear to have been signed by a person as a witness of the subscription of the member of the limited liability partnership it shall be presumed to have been subscribed by the limited liability partnership if it bears to have been subscribed on behalf of the limited liability partnership by two members of the limited liability partnership.

(1B) A presumption under subsection (1) or (1A) above as to subscription of a document does not include a presumption that a person bearing to subscribe the document as a member of the limited liability partnership was such member.'

(b) in subsection (4) after paragraph (g) there shall be inserted the following paragraph—

'(h) if the document does not bear to have been witnessed, but bears to have been subscribed on behalf of the limited liability partnership by two of the members of the limited liability partnership, that a signature bearing to be the signature of a member is not such a signature, whether by reason of forgery or otherwise;'

(6) In paragraph 1 of Schedule 1—

(a) for sub-paragraph (1) there shall be substituted the following sub-paragraphs—

'(1) Subject to sub-paragraphs (1A) to (7) below, where—

(a) an alteration to a [traditional document] bears to have been signed on behalf of a limited liability partnership by a member of the limited liability partnership;

(b) the alteration bears to have been signed by a person as a witness of the signature of the member of the limited liability partnership and to state the name and address of the witness; and

(c) nothing in the document or alteration, or in the testing clause or its equivalent, indicates—

(i) that the alteration was not signed on behalf of the limited liability partnership as it bears to have been so signed; or

(ii) that the alteration was not validly witnessed for any reason specified in paragraphs (a) to (e) of sub-paragraph (4) below,

the alteration shall be presumed to have been signed by the limited liability partnership.

(1A) Where an alteration does not bear to have been signed by a person as a witness of the signature of the member of the limited liability partnership it shall be presumed to have been signed by the limited liability partnership if it bears to have been signed on behalf of the limited liability partnership by two members of the limited liability partnership.

(1B) For the purposes of sub-paragraph (1)(b) above, the name and address of the witness may bear to be stated in the alteration itself or in the testing clause or its equivalent.

(1C) A presumption under sub-paragraph (1) or (1A) above as to signing of an alteration to a document does not include a presumption that a person bearing to sign the alteration as a member of the limited liability partnership was such member';

(b) in sub-paragraph (4) after paragraph (g) there shall be inserted the following—

'; or

(h) if the alteration does not bear to have been witnessed, but bears to have been signed on behalf of the limited liability partnership by two of the members of the limited liability partnership, that a signature bearing to be the signature of a member is not such a signature, whether by reason of forgery or otherwise;']

Local authorities

4.—(1) Except where an enactment expressly provides otherwise, where a granter of a [traditional document] is a local authority, the document is signed by the authority if it is signed on their behalf by the proper officer of the authority.

(2)   For the purposes of the signing of a document under this paragraph, a person purporting to sign on behalf of a local authority as an officer of the authority shall be presumed to be the proper officer of the authority.

(3)   Sub-paragraphs (1) and (2) of this paragraph apply in relation to the signing of an alteration made to a document as they apply in relation to the signing of a document.

(4)   Where a granter of a [traditional document] is a local authority, section 3 of and Schedule 1 to this Act shall have effect subject to the modifications set out in sub-paragraphs (5) to (8) below.

(5)   For section 3(1) there shall be substituted the following subsections—

'(1)   Subject to subsections (1A) to (7) below, where—

(a)   a [traditional document] bears to have been subscribed on behalf of a local authority by the proper officer of the authority;

(b)   the document bears—

(i)   to have been signed by a person as a witness of the proper officer's subscription and to state the name and address of the witness; or

(ii)   (if the subscription is not so witnessed), to have been sealed with the common seal of the authority; and

(c)   nothing in the document, or in the testing clause or its equivalent, indicates—

(i)   that it was not subscribed on behalf of the authority as it bears to have been so subscribed; or

(ii)   that it was not validly witnessed for any reason specified in paragraphs (a) to (e) of subsection (4) below or that it was not sealed as it bears to have been sealed or that it was not validly sealed for the reason specified in subsection (4)(h) below,

the document shall be presumed to have been subscribed by the proper officer and by the authority.

(1A)   For the purposes of subsection (1)(b)(i) above, the name and address of the witness may bear to be stated in the document itself or in the testing clause or its equivalent.'.

(6)   In section 3(4) after paragraph (g) there shall be inserted the following paragraph—

'(h)   if the document does not bear to have been witnessed, but bears to have been sealed with the common seal of the authority, that it was sealed by a person without authority to do so or was not sealed on the date on which it was subscribed on behalf of the authority;'.

(7)   For paragraph 1(1) of Schedule 1 there shall be substituted the following sub-paragraphs—

'(1)   Subject to sub-paragraphs (1A) to (7) below, where—

(a)   an alteration to a [traditional document] bears to have been signed on behalf of a local authority by the proper officer of the authority;

(b)   the alteration bears—

(i)   to have been signed by a person as a witness of the proper officer's signature and to state the name and address of the witness; or

(ii)   (if the signature is not so witnessed), to have been sealed with the common seal of the authority; and

(c)   nothing in the document or alteration, or in the testing clause or its equivalent, indicates—

(i)   that the alteration was not signed on behalf of the authority as it bears to have been so signed; or

(ii)   that the alteration was not validly witnessed for any reason specified in paragraphs (a) to (e) of sub-paragraph (4) below or that it was not sealed as it bears to have been sealed or that it was not validly sealed for the reason specified in sub-paragraph (4)(h) below,

the alteration shall be presumed to have been signed by the proper officer and by the authority.

(1A)   For the purposes of sub-paragraph (1)(b)(i) above, the name and address of the witness may bear to be stated in the alteration itself or in the testing clause or its equivalent.'.

(8)   In paragraph 1(4) of Schedule 1 after paragraph (g) there shall be inserted the following paragraph—

'(h)   if the alteration does not bear to have been witnessed, but bears to have been sealed with the common seal of the authority, that it was sealed by a person without authority to do so or was not sealed on the date on which it was signed on behalf of the authority;'.

Other bodies corporate

5.—(1)   This paragraph applies to any body corporate other than a company or a local authority.

(2)   Except where an enactment expressly provides otherwise, where a granter of a [traditional document] is a body corporate to which this paragraph applies, the document is signed by the body if it is signed on its behalf by—

(a)   a member of the body's governing board or, if there is no governing board, a member of the body;

(b)   the secretary of the body by whatever name he is called; or

(c)   a person authorised to sign the document on behalf of the body.

(3)   Sub-paragraphs (1) and (2) of this paragraph apply in relation to the signing of an alteration made to a document as they apply in relation to the signing of a document.

(4)   Where a granter of a [traditional document] is a body corporate to which this paragraph applies, section 3 of and Schedule 1 to this Act shall have effect subject to the modifications set out in sub-paragraphs (5) to (8) below.

(5)   For section 3(1) there shall be substituted the following subsections—

'(1)   Subject to subsections (1A) to (7) below, where—

(a)   a [traditional document] bears to have been subscribed on behalf of a body corporate to which paragraph 5 of Schedule 2 to this Act applies by—

(i)   a member of the body's governing board or, if there is no governing board, a member of the body;

(ii)   the secretary of the body; or

(iii)   a person bearing to have been authorised to subscribe the document on its behalf;

(b)   the document bears—

(i)   to have been signed by a person as a witness of the subscription of the member, secretary or other person signing on behalf of the body and to state the name and address of the witness; or

(ii)   (if the subscription is not so witnessed), to have been sealed with the common seal of the body; and

(c)   nothing in the document, or in the testing clause or its equivalent, indicates—

(i)   that it was not subscribed on behalf of the body as it bears to have been so subscribed; or

(ii)   that it was not validly witnessed for any reason specified in

paragraphs (a) to (e) of subsection (4) below or that it was not sealed as it bears to have been sealed or that it was not validly sealed for the reason specified in subsection (4)(h) below,
the document shall be presumed to have been subscribed by the member, secretary or authorised person (as the case may be) and by the body.

(1A)   For the purposes of subsection (1)(b)(i) above, the name and address of the witness may bear to be stated in the document itself or in the testing clause or its equivalent.

(1B)   A presumption under subsection (1) above as to subscription of a document does not include a presumption—

(a)   that a person bearing to subscribe the document as a member of the body's governing board, a member of the body or the secretary of the body was such member or secretary; or

(b)   that a person subscribing the document on behalf of the body bearing to have been authorised to do so was authorised to do so.'.

(6)   In section 3(4) after paragraph (g) there shall be inserted the following paragraph—

'(h)   if the document does not bear to have been witnessed, but bears to have been sealed with the common seal of the body, that it was sealed by a person without authority to do so or was not sealed on the date on which it was subscribed on behalf of the body;'.

(7)   For paragraph 1(1) of Schedule 1 there shall be substituted the following sub-paragraphs—

'(1)   Subject to sub-paragraphs (1A) to (7) below, where—

(a)   an alteration to a [traditional document] bears to have been signed on behalf of a body corporate to which paragraph 5 of Schedule 2 to this Act applies by—

(i)   a member of the body's governing board or, if there is no governing board, a member of the body;

(ii)   the secretary of the body; or

(iii)   a person bearing to have been authorised to sign the alteration on its behalf,

(b)   the alteration bears—

(i)   to have been signed by a person as a witness of the signature of the member, secretary or other person signing on behalf of the body and to state the name and address of the witness; or

(ii)   (if the signature is not so witnessed), to have been sealed with the common seal of the body; and

(c)   nothing in the document or alteration, or in the testing clause or its equivalent, indicates—

(i)   that the alteration was not signed on behalf of the body as it bears to have been so signed; or

(ii)   that the alteration was not validly witnessed for any reason specified in paragraphs (a) to (e) of sub-paragraph (4) below or that it was not sealed as it bears to have been sealed or that it was not validly sealed for the reason specified in sub-paragraph (4)(h) below,
the alteration shall be presumed to have been signed by the member, secretary or authorised person (as the case may be) and by the body.

(1A)   For the purposes of sub-paragraph (1)(b)(i) above, the name and address of the witness may bear to be stated in the alteration itself or in the testing clause or its equivalent.

(1B)   A presumption under sub-paragraph (1) above as to signing of an alteration to a document does not include a presumption—

(a)   that a person bearing to sign the alteration as a member of the body's governing board, a member of the body or the secretary of the body was such member or secretary; or

(b)   that a person signing the alteration on behalf of the body bearing to have been authorised to do so was authorised to do so.'.

(8)   In paragraph 1(4) of Schedule 1 after paragraph (g) there shall be inserted the following paragraph—

'(h)   if the alteration does not bear to have been witnessed, but bears to have been sealed with the common seal of the body, that it was sealed by a person without authority to do so or was not sealed on the date on which it was signed on behalf of the body;'.

Ministers of the Crown and office-holders

6.—(1)   Except where an enactment expressly provides otherwise, where a granter of a [traditional document] is a Minister or an office-holder, the document is signed by the Minister or office-holder if it is signed—

(a)   by him personally; or

(b)   in a case where by virtue of any enactment or rule of law a document by a Minister may be signed by an officer of his or by any other Minister, by that officer or by that other Minister as the case may be; or

(c)   in a case where by virtue of any enactment or rule of law a document by an office-holder may be signed by an officer of his, by that officer; or

(d)   by any other person authorised to sign the document on his behalf.

(2)   For the purposes of the signing of a document under this paragraph, a person purporting to sign—

(a)   as an officer as mentioned in sub-paragraph (1)(b) or (1)(c) above;

(b)   as another Minister as mentioned in sub-paragraph (1)(b) above;

(c)   as a person authorised as mentioned in sub-paragraph (1)(d) above,

shall be presumed to be the officer, other Minister or authorised person, as the case may be.

(3)   Sub-paragraphs (1) and (2) of this paragraph are without prejudice to section 3 of and Schedule 1 to the Ministers of the Crown Act 1975.

(4)   Sub-paragraphs (1) to (3) of this paragraph apply in relation to the signing of an alteration made to a document as they apply in relation to the signing of a document.

(5)   Where a granter of a [traditional document] is a Minister or office-holder, section 3 of and Schedule 1 to this Act shall have effect subject to the modifications set out in sub-paragraphs (6) and (7) below.

(6)   For section 3(1) there shall be substituted the following subsections—

'(1)   Subject to subsections (1A) to (7) below, where—

(a)   a [traditional document] bears to have been subscribed—

(i)   by a Minister or, in a case where by virtue of any enactment or rule of law a document by a Minister may be signed by an officer of his or by any other Minister, by that officer or by that other Minister; or

(ii)   by an office-holder or, in a case where by virtue of any enactment or rule of law a document by an office-holder may be signed by an officer of his, by that officer; or

(iii)   by any other person bearing to have been authorised to subscribe the document on behalf of the Minister or office-holder;

(b)   the document bears to have been signed by a person as a witness of the subscription mentioned in paragraph (a) above and to state the name and address of the witness; and

(c)   nothing in the document, or in the testing clause or its equivalent, indicates—

(i)   that it was not subscribed as it bears to have been subscribed; or

(ii)   that it was not validly witnessed for any reason specified in paragraphs (a) to (e) of subsection (4) below, the document shall be presumed to have been subscribed by the officer, other Minister or authorised person and by the Minister or office-holder, as the case may be.

(1A)   For the purposes of subsection (1)(b) above, the name and address of the witness may bear to be stated in the document itself or in the testing clause or its equivalent.'.

(7)   For paragraph 1(1) of Schedule 1 there shall be substituted the following sub-paragraphs—

'(1)   Subject to sub-paragraphs (1A) to (7) below, where—

(a)   an alteration to a [traditional document] bears to have been signed by—

(i)   a Minister or, in a case where by virtue of any enactment or rule of law a document by a Minister may be signed by an officer of his or by any other Minister, by that officer or by that other Minister; or

(ii)   an office-holder or, in a case where by virtue of any enactment or rule of law a document by an office-holder may be signed by an officer of his, by that officer; or

(iii)   any other person bearing to have been authorised to sign the alteration on behalf of the Minister or office-holder;

(b)   the alteration bears to have been signed by a person as a witness of the signature mentioned in paragraph (a) above and to state the name and address of the witness; and

(c)   nothing in the document or alteration, or in the testing clause or its equivalent, indicates—

(i)   that the alteration was not signed as it bears to have been signed; or

(ii)   that the alteration was not validly witnessed for any reason specified in paragraphs (a) to (e) of sub-paragraph (4) below,

the alteration shall be presumed to have been signed by the officer, other Minister or authorised person and by the Minister or office-holder, as the case may be.

(1A)   For the purposes of sub-paragraph (1)(b) above, the name and address of the witness may bear to be stated in the alteration itself or in the testing clause or its equivalent.'.

SCHEDULE 3   Section 9(3)
MODIFICATIONS OF THIS ACT IN RELATION TO SUBSCRIPTION OR SIGNING BY RELEVANT PERSON UNDER SECTION 9

1.   For any reference to the subscription or signing of a document by a granter there shall be substituted a reference to such subscription or signing by a relevant person under section 9(1).

2.   For section 3(1) there shall be substituted the following subsection—

'(1) Subject to subsections (2) to (6) below, where—

(a)   a [traditional document] bears to have been subscribed by a relevant person with the authority of a granter of it;

(b)   the document, or the testing clause or its equivalent, states that the document was read to that granter by the relevant person before such subscription or states that it was not so read because the granter made a declaration that he did not wish him to do so;

(c)   the document bears to have been signed by a person as a witness of the relevant person's subscription and the document, or the testing clause or its equivalent, bears to state the name and address of the witness; and

(d)   nothing in the document, or in the testing clause or its equivalent, indicates—

(i)   that it was not subscribed by the relevant person as it bears to have been so subscribed;

(ii)   that the statement mentioned in paragraph (b) above is incorrect; or

(iii)   that it was not validly witnessed for any reason specified in paragraphs (a) to (e) of subsection (4) below (as modified by paragraph 4 of Schedule 3 to this Act),

the document shall be presumed to have been subscribed by the relevant person and the statement so mentioned shall be presumed to be correct.'.

3.   In section 3(3) for the words 'subsection (1)(b)' there shall be substituted the words 'subsection (1)(c)'.

4.   For section 3(4) there shall be substituted the following subsection—

'(4)   Where, in any proceedings relating to a [traditional document] in which a question arises as to a relevant person's subscription on behalf of a granter under section 9(1) of this Act, it is established—

(a)   that a signature bearing to be the signature of the witness of the relevant person's subscription is not such a signature, whether by reason of forgery or otherwise;

(b)   that the person who signed the document as the witness of the relevant person's subscription is a person who is named in the document as a granter of it;

(c)   that the person who signed the document as the witness of the relevant person's subscription, at the time of signing—

(i)   did not know the granter on whose behalf the relevant person had so subscribed;

(ii)   was under the age of 16 years; or

(iii)   was mentally incapable of acting as a witness;

(d)   that the person who signed the document, purporting to be the witness of the relevant person's subscription, did not see him subscribe it;

(dd)   that the person who signed the document as the witness of the relevant person's subscription did not witness the granting of authority by the granter concerned to the relevant person to subscribe the document on his behalf or did not witness the reading of the document to the granter by the relevant person or the declaration that the granter did not wish him to do so;

(e)   that the person who signed the document as the witness of the relevant person's subscription did not sign the document after him or that such subscription and signature were not one continuous process;

(f)   that the name or address of such a witness was added after the document was founded on or registered as mentioned in subsection (3)(a) above or is erroneous in any material respect; or

(g)   in the case of a testamentary document consisting of more than one sheet, that a signature on any sheet bearing to be the signature of the relevant person is not such a signature, whether by reason of forgery or otherwise,

then, for the purposes of those proceedings, there shall be no presumption that the document has been subscribed by the relevant person on behalf of the granter concerned.'.

5.   In section 3(6) the words 'or acknowledgement' in both places where they occur shall be omitted.

6. Section 3(7) shall be omitted.

7. For section 4(1) there shall be substituted the following subsection—
'(1) Where—
(a)   a [traditional document] bears to have been subscribed by a relevant person under section 9(1) of this Act on behalf of a granter of it; but
(b)   there is no presumption under section 3 of this Act (as modified by paragraph 2 of Schedule 3 to this Act) that the document has been subscribed by that person or that the procedure referred to section 3(1)(b) of this Act as so modified was followed,
then, if the court, on an application being made to it by any person who has an interest in the document, is satisfied that the document was so subscribed by the relevant person with the authority of the granter and that the relevant person read the document to the granter before subscription or did not so read it because the granter declared that he did not wish him to do so, it shall—
(i)   cause the document to be endorsed with a certificate to that effect; or
(ii)   where the document has already been registered in the Books of Council and Session or in sheriff court books, grant decree to that effect.'.

8. At the end of section 4(5)(a) there shall be added the following words—
'and that the procedure referred to in section 3(1)(b) of this Act as modified by paragraph 2 of Schedule 3 to this Act was followed.'.

9. For paragraph 1(1) of Schedule 1 there shall be substituted the following subparagraph—
'(1) Subject to sub-paragraphs (2) to (6) below, where—
(a)   an alteration to a [traditional document] bears to have been signed by a relevant person with the authority of a granter of the document;
(b)   the document or alteration, or the testing clause or its equivalent, states that the alteration was read to that granter by the relevant person before such signature or states that the alteration was not so read because the granter made a declaration that he did not wish him to do so;
(c)   the alteration bears to have been signed by a person as a witness of the relevant person's signature and the alteration, or the testing clause or its equivalent, bears to state the name and address of the witness; and
(d)   nothing in the document or alteration, or in the testing clause or its equivalent, indicates—
(i)   that the alteration was not signed by the relevant person as it bears to have been so signed;
(ii)   that the statement mentioned in paragraph (b) above is incorrect; or
(iii) that the alteration was not validly witnessed for any reason specified in paragraphs (a) to (e) of sub-paragraph (4) below (as modified by paragraph 11 of Schedule 3 to this Act),
the alteration shall be presumed to have been signed by the relevant person and the statement so mentioned shall be presumed to be correct.'.

10. In paragraph 1(3) of Schedule 1 for the words 'sub-paragraph (1)(b)' there shall be substituted the words 'sub-paragraph (1)(c)'.

11. For paragraph 1(4) of Schedule 1 there shall be substituted the following subparagraph—
'(4) Where, in any proceedings relating to an alteration to a document in which a question arises as to a relevant person's signature on behalf of a granter under section 9(1) of this Act, it is established—

(a)   that a signature bearing to be the signature of the witness of the relevant person's signature is not such a signature, whether by reason of forgery or otherwise;

(b)   that the person who signed the alteration as the witness of the relevant person's signature is a person who is named in the document as a granter of it;

(c)   that the person who signed the alteration as the witness of the relevant person's signature, at the time of signing—

(i)   did not know the granter on whose behalf the relevant person had so signed;

(ii)   was under the age of 16 years; or

(iii)   was mentally incapable of acting as a witness;

(d)   that the person who signed the alteration, purporting to be the witness of the relevant person's signature, did not see him sign it;

(dd)   that the person who signed the alteration as the witness of the relevant person's signature did not witness the granting of authority by the granter concerned to the relevant person to sign the alteration on his behalf or did not witness the reading of the alteration to the granter by the relevant person or the declaration that the granter did not wish him to do so;

(e)   that the person who signed the alteration as the witness of the relevant person's signature did not sign the alteration after him or that the signing of the alteration by the granter and the witness was not one continuous process;

(f)   that the name or address of such a witness was added after the alteration was founded on or registered as mentioned in sub-paragraph (3)(a) above or is erroneous in any material respect; or

(g)   in the case of an alteration to a testamentary document consisting of more than one sheet, that a signature on any sheet of the alteration bearing to be the signature of the relevant person is not such a signature, whether by reason of forgery or otherwise,

then, for the purposes of those proceedings, there shall be no presumption that the alteration has been signed by the relevant person on behalf of the granter concerned.'.

12.   In paragraph 1(6) of Schedule 1 the words 'or the acknowledgement of his signature' and the words 'or acknowledgement' shall be omitted.

13.   Paragraph 1(7) of Schedule 1 shall be omitted.

14.   For paragraph 2(1) of Schedule 1 there shall be substituted the following subparagraph—

'(1)   Where—

(a)   an alteration to a [traditional document] bears to have been signed by a relevant person under section 9(1) of this Act on behalf of a granter of the document; but

(b)   there is no presumption under paragraph 1 of Schedule 1 to this Act (as modified by paragraph 9 of Schedule 3 to this Act) that the alteration has been signed by that person or that the procedure referred to in paragraph 1(1)(b) of Schedule 1 to this Act as so modified was followed,

then, if the court, on an application being made to it by any person who has an interest in the document, is satisfied that the alteration was so signed by the relevant person with the authority of the granter and that the relevant person read the alteration to the granter before signing or did not so read it because the granter declared that he did not wish him to do so, it shall—

(i)   cause the document to be endorsed with a certificate to that effect; or

(ii)   where the document has already been registered in the Books of Council and Session or in sheriff court books, grant decree to that effect.'.

15. At the end of paragraph 2(5)(a) of Schedule 1 there shall be added the following words—

'and that the procedure referred to in paragraph 1(1)(b) of Schedule 1 to this Act as modified by paragraph 9 of Schedule 3 to this Act was followed.'.

CONTRACT (SCOTLAND) ACT 1997
(1997, c 34)

1   Extrinsic evidence of additional contract term etc

(1)   Where a document appears (or two or more documents appear) to comprise all the express terms of a contract or unilateral voluntary obligation, it shall be presumed, unless the contrary is proved, that the document does (or the documents do) comprise all the express terms of the contract or unilateral voluntary obligation.

(2)   Extrinsic oral or documentary evidence shall be admissible to prove, for the purposes of subsection (1) above, that the contract or unilateral voluntary obligation includes additional express terms (whether or not written terms).

(3)   Notwithstanding the foregoing provisions of this section, where one of the terms in the document (or in the documents) is to the effect that the document does (or the documents do) comprise all the express terms of the contract or unilateral voluntary obligation, that term shall be conclusive in the matter.

(4)   This section is without prejudice to any enactment which makes provision as respects the constitution, or formalities of execution, of a contract or unilateral voluntary obligation.

2   Supersession

(1)   Where a deed is executed in implement, or purportedly in implement, of a contract, an unimplemented, or otherwise unfulfilled, term of the contract shall not be taken to be superseded by virtue only of that execution or of the delivery and acceptance of the deed.

(2)   Subsection (1) above is without prejudice to any agreement which the parties to a contract may reach (whether or not an agreement incorporated into the contract) as to supersession of the contract.

3   Damages for breach of contract of sale

Any rule of law which precludes the buyer in a contract of sale of property from obtaining damages for breach of that contract by the seller unless the buyer rejects the property and rescinds the contract shall cease to have effect.

4   Short title, extent etc

(1)   This Act may be cited as the Contract (Scotland) Act 1997.

(2)   This Act shall come into force at the end of that period of three months which begins with the day on which the Act is passed.

(3)   Section 1 of this Act applies only for the purposes of proceedings commenced on or after, and sections 2 and 3 only as respects contracts entered into on or after, the date on which this Act comes into force.

(4)   This Act extends to Scotland only.

ABOLITION OF FEUDAL TENURE ETC (SCOTLAND) ACT 2000
(2000, asp 5)

PART 1
ABOLITION OF FEUDAL TENURE

1   Abolition on appointed day
The feudal system of land tenure, that is to say the entire system whereby land is held by a vassal on perpetual tenure from a superior is, on the appointed day, abolished.

2   Consequences of abolition
(1)   An estate of dominium utile of land shall, on the appointed day, cease to exist as a feudal estate but shall forthwith become the ownership of the land and, in so far as is consistent with the provisions of this Act, the land shall be subject to the same subordinate real rights and other encumbrances as was the estate of dominium utile.

(2)   Every other feudal estate in land shall, on that day, cease to exist.

(3)   It shall, on that day, cease to be possible to create a feudal estate in land.

PART 2
LAND TRANSFERS ETC ON AND AFTER APPOINTED DAY

[. . .]

5   Form of application for recording deed in Register of Sasines
(1)   Any application for the recording of a deed in the Register of Sasines shall be made by, or on behalf of, the person in whose favour the deed is granted; and it shall not be necessary to endorse on any deed a warrant of registration.

(2)   The Scottish Ministers may, after consultation with the Lord President of the Court of Session, make rules—

(a)   prescribing the form to be used for the purposes of subsection (1) above; and

(b)   regulating the procedure relating to applications for recording.

6   Deduction of title for unregistered land etc
In respect of any land—

(a)   a real right in which has never been registered in the Land Register of Scotland; and

(b)   title to which has never been constituted by the recording of a deed in the Register of Sasines,

title may be deduced from any person having ownership of the land.

PART 4
REAL BURDENS

Extinction of superior's rights

17   Extinction of superior's right
(1)   Subject to sections 18 [to 18C], 19, 20, 23, 27, [27A,] 28, [28A] and 60 of this Act [and to sections 52 to 56 (which make provision as to common schemes, facility burdens and service burdens) and 63 (which makes provision as to manager burdens) of the Title Conditions (Scotland) Act 2003 (asp 9)]—

(a)   a real burden which, immediately before the appointed day, is enforceable by, and only by, a superior shall on that day be extinguished; and

(b)   any other real burden shall, on and after that day, not be enforceable by a former superior [other than in that person's capacity as owner of land or as holder of a conservation burden, health care burden or economic development burden].

(2)   Subject to subsection (3) below and to the provision made by section 20 of this Act for there to be a transitional period during which a real burden shall yet be enforceable—

(a)   on or after the appointed day, no proceedings for such enforcement shall be commenced;

(b)   any proceedings already commenced for such enforcement shall be deemed to have been abandoned on that day and may, without further process and without any requirement that full judicial expenses shall have been paid by the pursuer, be dismissed accordingly; and

(c)   any decree or interlocutor already pronounced in proceedings for such enforcement shall be deemed to have been reduced, or as the case may be recalled, on that day.

(3)   Subsection (2) above shall not affect any proceedings, decree or interlocutor in relation to—

(a)   a right of irritancy held by a superior;

[(aa) a right of enforcement held by virtue of any of the provisions mentioned in subsection (1) above;] or

(b)   a right to recover damages or to the payment of money.

Reallotment etc

18   Reallotment of real burden by nomination of new dominant tenement

(1)   [Without prejudice to sections 18A to 18C of this Act,] where—

(a)   a feudal estate of dominium utile of land is subject to a real burden enforceable by a superior of the feu or which would be so enforceable were the person in question to complete title to the dominium directum; and

(b)   at least one of the conditions set out in subsection (7) below is met, the superior may, before the appointed day, prospectively nominate other land (being land of which he has right to the sole dominium utile or sole allodial ownership), or any part of that other land, as a dominant tenement by duly executing and registering a notice in, or as nearly as may be in, the form contained in schedule 5 to this Act.

(2)   The notice shall—

(a)   set out the title of the superior;

(b)   describe, sufficiently to enable identification by reference to the Ordnance Map, both the land the dominium utile of which is subject to the real burden (or any part of that land) and the land (or part) nominated;

(c)   specify which of the conditions set out in subsection (7) below is (or are) met;

(d)   set out the terms of the real burden; and

(e)   set out the terms of any counter-obligation to the real burden if it is a counter-obligation enforceable against the superior.

(3)   For the purposes of subsection (1) above a notice is duly registered only when registered against both tenements described in pursuance of subsection (2)(b) above.

(4)   Before submitting any notice for registration under this section, the superior shall swear or affirm before a notary public that to the best of the knowledge and belief of the superior all the information contained in the notice is true.

(5)   For the purposes of subsection (4) above, if the superior is—

(a)   an individual unable by reason of legal disability, or incapacity, to swear or affirm as mentioned in that subsection, then a legal representative of the superior may swear or affirm;

(b)   not an individual, then any person authorised to sign documents on its behalf may swear or affirm;

and any reference in that subsection to a superior shall be construed accordingly.

(6)   [Subject to subsection (6A) below,] if subsections (1) to (5) above are complied with and immediately before the appointed day the real burden is still enforceable by the superior (or by his successor) or would be so enforceable, or still so enforceable, were the person in question to complete title to the dominium directum then, on that day—

(a)   the land (or part) nominated shall become a dominant tenement; and

(b)   the land the dominium utile of which was subject to the real burden (or if part only of that land is described in pursuance of subsection (2)(b) above, that part) shall be the servient tenement.

[(6A)   Such compliance as is mentioned in subsection (6) above shall not be effective to preserve any right to enforce a manager burden ('manager burden' being construed in accordance with section 63(1) of the Title Conditions (Scotland) Act 2003 (asp 9)).]

(7)   The conditions are—

(a)   that the land which by virtue of this section would become the dominant tenement has on it a permanent building which is in use wholly or mainly as a place of human—

(i)   habitation; or

(ii)   resort,

and that building is, at some point, within one hundred metres (measuring along a horizontal plane) of the land which would be the servient tenement;

(b)   that the real burden comprises—

(i)   a right [(other than any sporting rights, as defined by section 65A(9) of this Act)] to enter, or otherwise make use of, the servient tenement; or

(ii)   a right of pre-emption or of redemption; or

(c)   that the land which by virtue of this section would become the dominant tenement comprises—

(i)   minerals; or

(ii)   salmon fishings or some other incorporeal property, and it is apparent from the terms of the real burden that it was created for the benefit of such land.

(8)   This section is subject to sections 41 and 42 of this Act.

[18A   Personal pre-emption burdens and personal redemption burdens

(1)   Without prejudice to section 18 of this Act, where a feudal estate of dominium utile of land is subject to a real burden which comprises a right of preemption or redemption and is enforceable by a superior of the feu or would be so enforceable were the person in question to complete title to the dominium directum the superior may, before the appointed day, by duly executing and registering against the dominium utile a notice in, or as nearly as may be in, the form contained in schedule 5A to this Act, prospectively convert that burden into a personal pre-emption burden or as the case may be into a personal redemption burden.

(2)   The notice shall—

(a)   set out the title of the superior;

(b)   describe, sufficiently to enable identification by reference to the Ordnance Map, the land the dominium utile of which is subject to the real burden (or any part of that land);

(c)   set out the terms of the real burden; and

(d)   set out the terms of any counter-obligation to the real burden if it is a counter-obligation enforceable against the superior.

(3)   Before submitting any notice for registration under this section, the superior shall swear or affirm as is mentioned in subsection (4) of section 18 of this Act.

(4)   Subsection (5) of that section applies for the purposes of subsection (3) above as it applies for the purposes of subsection (4) of that section.

(5)   If subsections (1) to (3) above are, with subsection (4) of that section, complied with and immediately before the appointed day the real burden is still enforceable by the superior (or his successor) or would be so enforceable, or still so enforceable, were the person in question to complete title to the dominium directum then, on that day—

(a)   the real burden shall be converted into a real burden in favour of that person, to be known as a 'personal pre-emption burden' or as the case may be as a 'personal redemption burden'; and

(b)   the land the dominium utile of which was subject to the real burden (or if part only of that land is described in pursuance of subsection (2)(b) above, that part) shall become the servient tenement.

(6)   Title to enforce the burden against the land to which the notice relates shall be subject to any such counter-obligation as was set out by virtue of subsection (2) (d) above.

(7)   The right to a personal pre-emption burden or personal redemption burden may be assigned or otherwise transferred to any person; and any such assignation or transfer shall take effect on registration.

(8)   Where the holder of a personal pre-emption burden or personal redemption burden does not have a completed title—

(a)   title may be completed by the holder registering a notice of title; or

(b)   without completing title, the holder may grant a deed—

(i)   assigning the right to; or

(ii)   discharging, in whole or in part,

the burden; but unless the deed is one to which section [101 of the Land Registration etc (Scotland) Act 2012 (asp 5)] (circumstances where unnecessary to deduce title) applies, it shall be necessary, in the deed, to deduce title to the burden through the midcouples linking the holder to the person who had the last completed title.

(9)   This section is subject to sections 41 and 42 of this Act.]

[18B   Conversion into economic development burden

(1)   Without prejudice to section 18 of this Act, where a feudal estate of dominium utile of land is subject to a real burden which is imposed for the purpose of promoting economic development and is enforceable by the Scottish Ministers or a local authority, being in either case the superior of the feu, or would be so enforceable were the Scottish Ministers or as the case may be the local authority to complete title to the dominium directum, the superior may, before the appointed day, by duly executing and registering against the dominium utile a notice in, or as nearly as may be in, the form contained in schedule 5B to this Act, prospectively convert that burden into an economic development burden.

(2)   The notice shall—

(a)   set out the title of the superior;

(b)   describe, sufficiently to enable identification by reference to the Ordnance Map, the land the dominium utile of which is subject to the real burden (or any part of that land);

(c)   set out the terms of the real burden;

(d)   set out the terms of any counter-obligation to the real burden if it is a counter-obligation enforceable against the superior; and

(e)   state that the burden was imposed for the purpose of promoting economic development and provide information in support of that statement.

(3)   If subsections (1) and (2) above are complied with and immediately before the appointed day the real burden is still enforceable by the superior or would be so enforceable were the Scottish Ministers or as the case may be the local authority to complete title to the dominium directum then on that day the real burden shall

be converted into an economic development burden and on and after that day the Scottish Ministers or, as the case may be, the authority, shall—

    (a) have title to enforce the burden against the land to which the notice relates; and

    (b) be presumed to have an interest to enforce it.

(4) Title to enforce the burden against the land to which the notice relates shall be subject to any such counter-obligation as was set out by virtue of subsection (2) (d) above.

(5) This section is subject to sections 41 and 42 of this Act.]

[18C Conversion into health care burden

(1) Without prejudice to section 18 of this Act, where a feudal estate of dominium utile of land is subject to a real burden which is imposed for the purpose of promoting the provision of facilities for health care and is enforceable by [. . .] the Scottish Ministers, being [. . .] the superior of the feu, or would be so enforceable were the trust or as the case may be the Scottish Ministers to complete title to the dominium directum, the superior may,-before the appointed day, by duly executing and registering against the dominium utile a notice in, or as nearly as may be in, the form contained in schedule 5C to this Act, prospectively convert that burden into a health care burden.

(2) The notice shall—

    (a) set out the title of the superior;

    (b) describe, sufficiently to enable identification by reference to the Ordnance Map, the land the dominium utile of which is subject to the real burden (or any part of that land);

    (c) set out the terms of the real burden;

    (d) set out the terms of any counter-obligation to the real burden if it is a counter-obligation enforceable against the superior; and

    (e) state that the burden was imposed for the purpose of promoting the provision of facilities for health care and provide information in support of that statement.

(3) If subsections (1) and (2) are complied with and immediately before the appointed day the real burden is still enforceable by the superior or would be so enforceable were [. . .] the Scottish Ministers to complete title to the dominium directum then on that day the real burden shall be converted into a health care burden and on and after that day [. . .] the Scottish Ministers, shall—

    (a) have title to enforce the burden against the land to which the notice in question relates; and

    (b) be presumed to have an interest to enforce it.

(4) Title to enforce the burden against the land to which the notice relates shall be subject to any such counter-obligation as was set out by virtue of subsection (2) (d) above.

(5) In subsections (1) and (2) above, 'facilities for health care' includes facilities ancillary to health care; as for example (but without prejudice to that generality) accommodation for staff employed to provide health care.

(6) This section is subject to sections 41 and 42 of this Act.]

19 Reallotment of real burden by agreement

(1) Where a feudal estate of dominium utile of land is subject to a real burden enforceable by a superior of the feu or which would be so enforceable were the person in question to complete title to the dominium directum the superior may, before the appointed day—

    (a) serve notice in, or as nearly as may be in, the form contained in schedule 6 to this Act, on the person who has right to the feu that he seeks to enter into an agreement with that person under this section prospectively nominating other land (being land of which the superior has right to the sole dominium utile or sole allodial ownership), or any part of that other land, as a dominant tenement;

    (b) enter into such an agreement with that person; and

    (c) duly register that agreement;

but if they think fit they may, by the agreement, modify the real burden or any counter-obligation to the real burden if it is a counter-obligation enforceable against the superior (or both the real burden and any such counter-obligation).

(2) The notice shall—

    (a) set out the title of the superior;

    (b) describe both the land the dominium utile of which is subject to the real burden (or any part of that land) and the land (or part) nominated;

    (c) set out the terms of the real burden; and

    (d) set out the terms of any such counter-obligation as is mentioned in subsection (1) above.

(3) An agreement such as is mentioned in paragraph (b) of subsection (1) above shall be a written agreement—

    (a) which expressly states that it is made under this section; and

    (b) which includes all the information, other than that relating to service, required to be set out in completing the notice the form of which is contained in schedule 6 to this Act.

(4) For the purposes of subsection (1)(c) above an agreement is duly registered only when registered against both tenements described in pursuance of subsection (2)(b) above.

(5) If subsections (1)(b) and (c), (3) and (4) above are complied with and immediately before the appointed day the real burden is still enforceable by the superior (or by his successor) or would be so enforceable, or still so enforceable, were the person in question to complete title to the dominium directum then on that day—

    (a) the land (or part) nominated shall become a dominant tenement; and

    (b) the land the dominium utile of which was subject to the real burden (or if part only of that land is described in pursuance of subsection (2)(b) above, that part) shall be the servient tenement.

(6) A person may enter into an agreement under this section even if he has not completed title to the dominium utile of the land subject to the real burden, or as the case may be title to the dominium directum of that land or to the dominium utile of the land nominated (or, if the land nominated is allodial land, to the land nominated), provided that, in any case to which section 15(3) of the Land Registration (Scotland) Act 1979 (c 33) (simplification of deeds relating to registered interests) does not apply, he deduces title, in the agreement, from the person who appears in the Register of Sasines as having the last recorded title to the interest in question.

(7) This section is subject to section 42 of this Act.

[Sections 20 and 21 were transitional provisions, now spent.]

22 *[Amends Tribunals and Inquiries Act 1992.]*

[. . .]

24 **Interest to enforce real burden**
Sections 18 to 20 and 23 of this Act are without prejudice to any requirement that a dominant proprietor have an interest to enforce a real burden (and such interest shall not be presumed).

25 **Counter-obligations on reallotment**
Where a real burden is reallotted under section 18, 19, [or 20] of this Act [or under section 56 or 63 of the Title Conditions (Scotland) Act 2003 (asp 9) (which makes provision, respectively, as to facility burdens and service burdens and as to

manager burdens)], the right to enforce the burden shall be subject to any counter-obligation (modified as the case may be by the agreement or by the order of the Lands Tribunal) enforceable against the superior immediately before [reallotment is effected].

Conservation burdens

[. . .]

27 Notice preserving right to enforce conservation burden

(1)   Where a conservation body has, or the Scottish Ministers have, the right as superior to enforce a real burden of the class described in subsection (2) below or would have that right were it or they to complete title to the dominium directum, it or they may, before the appointed day, preserve for the benefit of the public the right to enforce the burden in question after that day by executing and registering against the dominium utile of the land subject to the burden a notice in, or as nearly as may be in, the form contained in schedule 8 to this Act; and [, without prejudice to section 27A(1) of this Act,] any burden as respects which such a right is so preserved shall, on and after the appointed day, be known as a 'conservation burden'.

(2)   The class is those real burdens which are enforceable against a feudal estate of dominium utile of land for the purpose of preserving, or protecting—

(a)   the architectural or historical characteristics of the land; or

(b)   any other special characteristics of the land (including, without prejudice to the generality of this paragraph, a special characteristic derived from the flora, fauna or general appearance of the land).

(3)   The notice shall—

(a)   state that the superior is a conservation body by virtue of section [38 of the Title Conditions (Scotland) Act 2003 (asp 9) (which makes provision generally as respects conservation burdens)] or that the superior is the Scottish Ministers;

(b)   set out the title of the superior;

(c)   describe, sufficiently to enable identification by reference to the Ordnance Map, the land subject to the real burden (or any part of that land);

(d)   set out the terms of the real burden; and

(e)   set out the terms of any counter-obligation to the real burden if it is a counter-obligation enforceable against the superior.

(4)   This section is subject to sections 41 and 42 of this Act.

[27A Nomination of conservation body or Scottish Ministers to have title to enforce conservation burden

(1)   Where a person other than a conservation body or the Scottish Ministers has the right as superior to enforce a real burden of the class described in section 27(2) of this Act or would have that right were he to complete title to the dominium directum, he may, subject to subsection (2) below, before the appointed day nominate for the benefit of the public, by executing and registering against the dominium utile of the land subject to the burden a notice in, or as nearly as may be in, the form contained in schedule 8A to this Act, a conservation body or the Scottish Ministers to have title on or after that day to enforce the burden against that land; and, without prejudice to section 27(1) of this Act, any burden as respects which such title to enforce is by virtue of this subsection so obtained shall, on and after the appointed day, be known as a 'conservation burden'.

(2)   Subsection (1) above applies only where the consent of the nominee to being so nominated is obtained—

(a)   in a case where sending a copy of the notice, in compliance with section 41(3) of this Act, is reasonably practicable, before that copy is so sent; and

(b)   in any other case, before the notice is executed.

(3)   The notice shall—
  (a)   state that the nominee is a conservation body (identifying it) or the Scottish Ministers, as the case may be; and
  (b)   do as mentioned in paragraphs (b) to (e) of section 27(3) of this Act.
(4)   This section is subject to sections 41 and 42 of this Act except that, in the application of subsection (1)(i) of section 42 for the purposes of this subsection, such discharge as is mentioned in that subsection shall be taken to require the consent of the nominated person.]

28   Enforcement of conservation burden

(1)   If a notice has been executed and registered in accordance with section 27 of this Act and, immediately before the appointed day, the burden to which the notice relates is still enforceable by the conservation body or the Scottish Ministers as superior or would be so enforceable, or still so enforceable, were the body in question or they to complete title to the dominium directum then, on and after the appointed day, the conservation body or as the case may be the Scottish Ministers shall—
  (a)   subject to any counter-obligation, have title to enforce the burden against the land to which the notice in question relates; and
  (b)   be presumed to have an interest to enforce that burden.
(2)   The references in subsection (1) above to—
  (a)   the conservation body include references to—
    (i)   any conservation body which is; or
    (ii)   the Scottish Ministers where they are, its successor as superior;
  (b)   the Scottish Ministers include references to a conservation body which is their successor as superior.

[28A   Effect of section 27A nomination

If a notice has been executed and registered in accordance with section 27A of this Act and, immediately before the appointed day, the burden to which the notice relates is still enforceable by the nominating person as superior (or by such person as is his successor) or would be so enforceable, or still so enforceable, were the person in question to complete title to the dominium directum then, on and after the appointed day, the conservation body or as the case may be the Scottish Ministers shall—
  (a)   subject to any counter-obligation, have title to enforce the burden against the land to which the notice in question relates; and
  (b)   be presumed to have an interest to enforce that burden.]

[. . .]

Compensation

33   Notice reserving right to claim compensation where land subject to development value burden

(1)   Where—
  (a)   before the appointed day, land was feued subject to a real burden enforceable by a superior (or so enforceable if the person in question were to complete title to the dominium directum) which reserved for the superior the benefit (whether wholly or in part) of any development value of the land (such a real burden being referred to in this Part of this Act as a ('development value burden'); and
  (b)   either—
    (i)   the consideration paid, or payable, under the grant in feu was significantly lower than it would have been had the feu not been subject to the real burden; or
    (ii)   no consideration was paid, or payable, under the grant in feu, the

superior may, before that day, reserve the right to claim (in accordance with section 35 of this Act) compensation by executing and registering against the dominium utile of the land subject to the burden a notice in, or as nearly as may be in, the form contained in schedule 9 to this Act.

(2) A notice under this section shall—

(a) set out the title of the superior;

(b) describe, sufficiently to enable identification by reference to the Ordnance Map, the land the dominium utile of which is subject to the development value burden;

(c) set out the terms of the burden;

(d) state that the burden reserves development value and set out any information relevant to that statement;

(e) set out, to the best of the superior's knowledge and belief, the amount by which the consideration was reduced because of the imposition of the burden; and

(f) the superior reserves the right to claim compensation in accordance with section 35 of this Act.

(3) Before submitting any notice for registration under this section, the superior shall swear or affirm before a notary public that to the best of the knowledge and belief of the superior all the information contained in the notice is true.

(4) For the purposes of subsection (3) above, if the superior is—

(a) an individual unable by reason of legal disability, or incapacity, to swear or affirm as mentioned in that subsection, then a legal representative of the superior may swear or affirm;

(b) not an individual, then any person authorised to sign documents on its behalf may swear or affirm;

and any reference in that subsection to a superior shall be construed accordingly.

(5) In this Part of this Act, 'development value' (except in the expression 'development value burden') means any significant increase in the value of the land arising as a result of the land becoming free to be used, or dealt with, in some way not permitted under the grant in feu.

(6) This section is subject to sections 41 and 42 of this Act.

34 Transmissibility of right to claim compensation

A right to claim compensation reserved in accordance with section 33 of this Act is transmissible.

35 Claiming compensation

(1) Where the conditions mentioned in subsection (2) below are satisfied, any person who has, by or by virtue of a notice executed and registered in accordance with section 33 of this Act, a reserved right to claim compensation shall be entitled, subject to any order under section 44(2) of this Act, to compensation from the person who is the owner.

(2) The conditions are that—

(a) the real burden set out in the notice was, immediately before the appointed day, enforceable by the superior or would have been so enforceable immediately before that day had the person in question completed title to the dominium directum;

(b) on that day the burden, or as the case may be any right (or right on completion of title) of the superior to enforce the burden, was extinguished, or rendered unenforceable, by section 17(1) of this Act; and

(c) at any time—

(i) during the period of five years ending immediately before the appointed day, there was a breach of the burden; or

(ii) during the period of twenty years beginning with the appointed day, there was an occurrence, which, but for the burden becoming extinct, or unenforceable, as mentioned in paragraph (b) above, would have been a breach of the burden.

(3)   Where a person is entitled, by virtue of subsection (1) above, to compensation, he shall make any claim for such compensation by notice in writing duly served on the owner; and any such notice shall specify, in accordance with section 37 of this Act, the amount of compensation claimed.

(4)   Where, in relation to a claim made under subsection (3) above, the condition mentioned in—

(a)   sub-paragraph (i) of subsection (2)(c) above applies, any such claim may not be made more than three years after the appointed day;

(b)   sub-paragraph (ii) of subsection (2)(c) above applies, any such claim may not be made more than three years after the date of the occurrence.

(5)   For the purposes of this section, if a breach, or occurrence, such as is mentioned in subsection (2)(c) above is continuing, the breach or, as the case may be, occurrence shall be taken to occur when it first happens.

(6)   The reference in subsection (3) above to a notice being duly served shall be construed in accordance with section 36 of this Act.

36   Service under section 35(3)

(1)   Due service under section 35(3) of this Act is effected by delivering the notice in question to the owner or by sending it by registered post, or the recorded delivery service, addressed to him at an appropriate place.

(2)   An acknowledgement, signed by the owner, which conforms to Form A of schedule 10 to this Act, or as the case may be a certificate which conforms to Form B of that schedule and is accompanied by the postal receipt, shall be sufficient evidence of such due service; and if the notice in question is, under subsection (1) above, sent by post but is returned to the person who is entitled to compensation with an intimation that it could not be delivered, the notice may be delivered or sent by post, with that intimation, to the Extractor of the Court of Session, the delivery or sending to the Extractor being taken to be equivalent to the service of that notice on the owner.

(3)   For the purposes of subsection (2) above, an acknowledgement of receipt by the Extractor on a copy of that notice shall be sufficient evidence of its receipt by him.

(4)   The date on which notice under section 35(3) of this Act is served on an owner is the date of delivery, or as the case may be of posting, in compliance with subsection (1) or (2) above.

(5)   A reference in this section to an 'appropriate place' is, for any owner, to be construed as a reference to—

(a)   his place of residence;

(b)   his place of business; or

(c)   a postal address which he ordinarily uses,

or, if none of those is known at the time of delivery or posting, as a reference to whatever place is at that time his most recently known place of residence or place of business or postal address which he ordinarily used.

37   Amount of compensation

(1)   The amount of any compensation payable on a claim made under section 35(3) of this Act shall, subject to subsections (2) and (3) below, be such sum as represents, at the time of the breach or occurrence in question, any development value which would have accrued to the owner had the burden been modified to the extent necessary to permit the land to be used, or dealt with, in the way that constituted the breach or, as the case may be, occurrence on which the claim is based.

(2)   The amount payable as compensation (or, where more than one claim is made in relation to the same development value burden, the total compensation payable) under subsection (1) above shall not exceed such sum as will make up for

any effect which the burden produced, at the time when it was imposed, in reducing the consideration then paid or made payable for the feu.

(3)   In assessing for the purposes of subsection (1) above an amount of compensation payable—

(a)   any entitlement of the claimant to recover any part of the development value of the land subject to the development value burden shall be taken into account; and

(b)   a claimant to whom the reserved right was assigned or otherwise transferred shall be entitled to no greater sum than the former superior would have been had there been no such assignation or transfer.

(4)   The reference in subsection (1) above to a burden shall, in relation to an occurrence, be construed as a reference to the burden which would have been breached but for its becoming, by section 17(1) of this Act, extinct or unenforceable.

38   Duty to disclose identity of owner

Where a person ('the claimant') purports duly to serve notice under section 35(3) of this Act and the person on whom it is served, being a person who had right, before the time of the breach (or, as the case may be, occurrence) founded on by the claimant, to the dominium utile (or the ownership) of the land, is not the owner, that person shall forthwith disclose to the claimant—

(a)   the identity and address of the owner; or

(b)   (if he cannot do that) such other information as he has that might enable the claimant to discover the identity and address;

and the notice shall refer to that requirement for disclosure.

39   The expression 'owner' for purposes of sections 35 to 38

(1)   In sections 35 to 38 of this Act, "owner' means the person who, at the time of the breach or, as the case may be, occurrence, mentioned in section 35(2)(c) of this Act, has right to—

(a)   the dominium utile; or

(b)   the ownership,

of the land which, immediately before the appointed day, was subject to the development value burden, whether or not he has completed title; and if more than one person comes within that description, then the owner is the person who has most recently acquired such right.

(2)   Where the land in question is held by two or more such owners as common property, they shall be severally liable to make any compensatory payment (but as between, or as the case may be among, themselves they shall be liable in the proportions in which they hold the land).

40   Assignation, discharge, or restriction, of reserved right to claim compensation

A reserved right to claim, in accordance with section 35 of this Act, compensation may be—

(a)   assigned, whether wholly or to such extent (expressed as a percentage of each claim which may come to be made) as may be specified in the assignation; or

(b)   discharged or restricted,

by execution and registration of an assignation, or as the case may be a discharge, or restriction, in the form, or as nearly as may be in the form, contained in schedule 11 to this Act.

Miscellaneous

41   Notices: pre-registration requirements etc

(1)   This section applies in relation to any notice which is to be submitted for registration under this Act.

(2)   It shall not be necessary to endorse on the notice a warrant of registration.

(3)   Except where it is not reasonably practicable to do so, a superior shall, before he executes the notice, send by post to the person who has the estate of dominium utile of the land to which the burden relates (addressed to 'The Proprietor' where the name of that person is not known) a copy of—

(a)   the notice; and

(b)   the explanatory note set out in whichever schedule to this Act relates to the notice.

(4)   A superior shall, in the notice, state either—

(a)   that a copy of the notice has been sent in accordance with subsection (3) above; or

(b)   that it was not reasonably practicable for such a copy to be sent.

42   Further provision as respects sections 18 to 20, 27 and 33

(1)   Where—

(a)   a notice relating to a real burden has been registered under section 18, [18A, 18B, 18C,] 20, 27 [, 27A] or 33 of this Act; or

(b)   an agreement relating to a real burden has been registered under section 19 of this Act,

against the dominium utile of any land which is subject to the burden, it shall not be competent to register under any of those sections against that dominium utile another such notice or agreement relating to the same real burden; but nothing in this subsection shall prevent registration where—

(i)   the discharge of any earlier such notice has been registered by the person who registered that notice (or by his successor); or

(ii)   as the case may be, the discharge of any earlier such agreement has been registered, jointly, by the parties to that agreement (or by their successors).

(2)   Where the dominium utile of any land comprises parts each held by a separate vassal, each part shall be taken to be a separate feudal estate of dominium utile.

(3)   Where more than one feudal estate of dominium utile is subject to the same real burden enforceable by a superior of the feu, he shall, if he wishes to execute and register a notice under section 18, [18A, 18B, 18C,] 20, 27 [, 27A] or 33 of this Act against those feudal estates in respect of that real burden, require to do so against each separately.

(4)   Where a feudal estate of dominium utile is subject to more than one real burden enforceable by a superior of the feu, he may if he wishes to—

(a)   execute and register a notice under section 18, [18A, 18B, 18C,] 20, 27 [, 27A] or 33 of this Act against that feudal estate in respect of those real burdens, do so by a single notice; or

(b)   enter into and register an agreement under section 19 of this Act against that feudal estate in respect of those real burdens, do so by a single agreement.

[(5)   Nothing in this Part requires registration against land prospectively nominated as a dominant tenement but outwith Scotland.]

43   Notices and agreements under certain sections: extent of Keeper's duty

(1)   In relation to any notice submitted for registration under section 18, [18A, 18B, 18C,] 20, 27 [, 27A] or 33 of this Act, the Keeper of the Registers of Scotland shall not be required to determine whether the superior has complied with the terms of section 41(3) of this Act.

(2)   In relation to any notice, or as the case may be any agreement, submitted for registration under—

(a)   section 18, [18A, 18B, 18C,] 19, 20, 27 [, 27A] or 33 of this Act, the Keeper shall not be required to determine whether, for the purposes of subsection (1) of the section in question, a real burden is enforceable by a superior;

(b)   section 18 of this Act, the Keeper shall not be required to determine, where, in pursuance of subsection (2)(c) of that section, the condition specified is that mentioned in subsection (7)(a) of that section, whether the terms of that condition are satisfied;

[(bb)   section 18B or 18C of this Act, the Keeper shall not be required to determine whether—

(i)   the requirements of subsection (1) of the section in question are satisfied; or

(ii)   the statement made in pursuance of subsection (2)(e) of the section in question is correct;]

(c)   paragraph (c) of subsection (1) of section 19 of this Act, the Keeper shall not be required to determine whether the requirements of paragraph (a) of that subsection are satisfied;

(d)   section 20 of this Act, the Keeper shall not be required to determine—

(i)   whether the description provided in pursuance of subsection (2) of that section is correct;

(ii)   whether the notice has been executed, and is being registered, timeously; or

(iii)   any matter as to which the Lands Tribunal must be satisfied before making an order under that section;

(e)   section 33 of this Act, the Keeper shall not be required to determine whether—

(i)   the requirements of subsection (1)(a) and (b) of that section are satisfied; or

(ii)   the statements made or information provided, in pursuance of subsection (2)(d) or (e) of that section, are correct.

(3)   The Keeper shall not be required to determine—

(a)   for the purposes of section 18(6), [18A(5), 18B(3), 18C(3),] 19(5), 20(5) or (8) (a)(i), 28 [, 28A] or 60(1) of this Act, whether immediately before the appointed day a real burden is, or is still, enforceable, or by whom; or

(b)   for the purposes of subsection (8)(a)(ii) of section 20 of this Act, whether immediately before the day of registration of an order of the Lands Tribunal under subsection (7) of that section a real burden is, or is still, enforceable, or by whom.

44   Referral to Lands Tribunal of notice dispute

(1)   Any dispute arising in relation to a notice registered under this Act may be referred to the Lands Tribunal; and, in determining the dispute, the Tribunal may make such order as it thinks fit discharging or, to such extent as may be specified in the order, restricting the notice in question.

(2)   Any dispute arising in relation to a claim made under section 35(3) of this Act may be referred to the Lands Tribunal; and, in determining the dispute, the Tribunal may make such order as it thinks fit (including an order fixing the amount of any compensation payable under the claim in question).

(3)   In any referral under subsection (1) or (2) above, the burden of proving any disputed question of fact shall be on the person relying on the notice or, as the case may be, making the claim.

(4)   An extract of any order made under subsection (1) or (2) above may be registered and the order shall take effect as respects third parties on such registration.

45   Circumstances where certain notices may be registered after appointed day

(1)   Subject to subsection (2) below, where—

(a)   a notice submitted, before the appointed day, for registration under this Act, or an agreement so submitted for registration under section 19 of this Act, is rejected by the Keeper of the Registers of Scotland; but

(b)   a court or the Lands Tribunal then determines that the notice or agreement is registrable,
the notice or agreement may, if not registered before the appointed day, be registered—

(i)   within two months after the determination is made; but

(ii)   before such date after the appointed day as the Scottish Ministers may by order prescribe,

and any notice or agreement registered under this subsection on or after the appointed day shall be treated as if it had been registered before that day.

(2)   For the purposes of subsection (1) above, the application to the court, or to the Lands Tribunal, which has resulted in the determination shall require to have been made within such period as the Scottish Ministers may by order prescribe.

(3)   In subsection (1)(b) above, 'court' means any court having jurisdiction in questions of heritable right or title.

[. . .]

47   Extinction of counter-obligation

Without prejudice to any other way in which a counter-obligation to a real burden may be extinguished, any such counter-obligation is extinguished on the extinction of the real burden.

48   No implication as to dominant tenement where real burden created in grant in feu

Where a real burden is created (or has at any time been created) in a grant in feu, the superior having the dominium utile, or allodial ownership, of land (the 'superior's land') in the vicinity of the land feued, no implication shall thereby arise that the superior's land is a dominant tenement.

Interpretation

49   Interpretation of Part 4

In this Part of this Act, unless the context otherwise requires—

'conservation body' means a body prescribed [by order under section 38(4) of the Title Conditions (Scotland) Act 2003 (asp 9)];

'conservation burden' shall be construed in accordance with [sections 27(1) and 27A(1)] of this Act;

'development value burden' and 'development value' shall be construed in accordance with section 33 of this Act;

['economic development burden' shall be construed in accordance with section 18B(3) of this Act;

'health care burden' shall be construed in accordance with section 18C(3) of this Act;

'local authority' means a council constituted under section 2 of the Local Government etc (Scotland) Act 1994 (c 39);]

'notary public' includes any person duly authorised by the law of the country (other than Scotland) in which the swearing or affirmation takes place to administer oaths or receive affirmations in that other country;

['personal pre-emption burden' and 'personal redemption burden' shall be construed in accordance with section 18A(5) of the Act;]

'real burden'—

(a)   includes—

(i)   a right of pre-emption;

(ii)   a right of redemption; [. . .] but

(b)   does not include a pecuniary real burden [or sporting rights (as defined by section 65A(9) of this Act)];

'registering' means registering an interest in land (or information relating to such an interest) in the Land Register of Scotland or, as the case may be, recording a document in the Register of Sasines; and cognate expressions shall be construed accordingly; and

'superior' means a person who has right to the immediate superiority or to any over-superiority, whether or not he has completed title (and if more than one person comes within either of those descriptions then, in relation to that description, the person who has most recently acquired such right) and 'former superior' shall be construed accordingly.

. . .

PART 6
MISCELLANEOUS

Discharge of certain rights and extinction of certain obligations and payments

. . .

54   Extinction of superior's rights and obligations qua superior

(1)   Subject to section 13, to Part 4, and to [sections 60(1) and 65A], of this Act, a right or obligation which, immediately before the appointed day, is enforceable by, or as the case may be against, a superior qua superior [(including, without prejudice to that generality, sporting rights as defined by subsection (9) of that section 65A)] shall, on that day, be extinguished.

(2)   Subject to subsection (3) below—

(a)   on or after the appointed day, no proceedings for such enforcement shall be commenced;

(b)   any proceedings already commenced for such enforcement shall be deemed to have been abandoned on that day and may, without further process and without any requirement that full judicial expenses shall have been paid by the pursuer, be dismissed accordingly; and

(c)   any decree, or interlocutor, already pronounced in proceedings for such enforcement shall be deemed to have been reduced, or as the case may be recalled, on that day.

(3)   Subsection (2) above shall not affect any proceedings, decree or interlocutor in relation to—

(a)   a right of irritancy held by a superior;

[(aa)   a right of enforcement held by virtue of section 13, 33, 60(1) or 65A of this Act;] or

(b)   a right to recover damages or to the payment of money.

. . .

The Crown, the Lord Lyon and Barony

58   Crown application

(1)   This Act binds the Crown and accordingly such provision as is made by section 2 of this Act as respects feudal estates of dominium shall apply to the superiority of the Prince and Steward of Scotland and to the ultimate superiority of the Crown; but nothing in this Act shall be taken to supersede or impair any power exercisable by Her Majesty by virtue of Her prerogative.

(2)   Without prejudice to the generality of subsection (1) above, in that subsection —

(a)   Her Majesty's prerogative includes the prerogative of honour; and

(b) 'any power exercisable by Her Majesty by virtue of Her prerogative' includes—

    (i) prerogative rights as respects ownerless or unclaimed property; and

    (ii) the regalia majora.

59 Crown may sell or otherwise dispose of land by disposition

It shall be competent for the Crown, in selling or otherwise disposing of any land, to do so by granting a disposition of that land.

60 Preserved right of Crown to maritime burdens

(1) Where, immediately before the appointed day, the Crown has the right as superior to enforce a real burden against part of the sea bed or part of the foreshore, then, on and after that day, the Crown shall—

    (a) subject to any counter-obligation, have title to enforce; and

    (b) be presumed to have an interest to enforce,

the burden; and any burden as respects which the Crown has such title and interest shall, on and after the appointed day, be known as a 'maritime burden'.

(2) [. . .]

(3) For the purposes of this section—

'sea bed' means the bed of the territorial sea adjacent to Scotland; and

territorial sea' includes any tidal waters.

(4) In this section, 'real burden' has the same meaning as in Part 4 of this Act.

61 Mines of gold and silver

The periodical payment to the Crown, in respect of the produce of a mine which by the Royal Mines Act 1424 (c 12) belongs to the Crown, of an amount which is not fixed but is calculated as a proportion of that produce is not—

    (a) a payment to the Crown qua superior for the purposes of section 54 of this Act;

    (b) a perpetual periodical payment for the purposes of section 56 of this Act; or

    (c) a feuduty for the purposes of Part 3 of this Act.

62 Jurisdiction and prerogative of Lord Lyon

Nothing in this Act shall be taken to supersede or impair the jurisdiction or prerogative of the Lord Lyon King of Arms.

63 Baronies and other dignities and offices

(1) Any jurisdiction of, and any conveyancing privilege incidental to, barony shall on the appointed day cease to exist; but nothing in this Act affects the dignity of baron or any other dignity or office (whether or not of feudal origin).

(2) When, by this Act, an estate held in barony ceases to exist as a feudal estate, the dignity of baron, though retained, shall not attach to the land; and on and after the appointed day any such dignity shall be, and shall be transferable only as, incorporeal heritable property (and shall not be [a right as respects which a deed can be registered in the Land Register of Scotland] recorded in the Register of Sasines).

(3) Where there is registered, before the appointed day, a heritable security over an estate to which is attached the dignity of baron, the security shall on and after that day (until discharge) affect—

    (a) in the case of an estate of dominium utile, both the dignity of baron and the land; and

    (b) in any other case, the dignity of baron.

(4) In this section—

'conveyancing privilege' includes any privilege in relation to prescription;

'dignity' includes any quality or precedence associated with, and any heraldic privilege incidental to, a dignity; and

'registered' has the same meaning as in Part 4 of this Act.

Kindly Tenants of Lochmaben

64   Abolition of Kindly Tenancies

(1)   The system of land tenure whereby the persons known as the Kindly Tenants of Lochmaben hold land on perpetual tenure without requiring to procure infeftment is, on the appointed day, abolished.

(2)   On the appointed day the interest of a Kindly Tenant shall forthwith become the ownership of the land (which shall be taken to include any right of salmon fishing inseverable from the kindly tenancy); and, in so far as is consistent with the provisions of this Act, the land shall be subject to the same subordinate real rights and other encumbrances as was the kindly tenancy.

(3)   A right of salmon fishing inseverable from a kindly tenancy shall on and after the appointed day be inseverable from the ownership of the land in question.

Miscellaneous

[. . .]

[65A   Sporting rights

(1)   Where a feudal estate of dominium utile of land is subject to sporting rights which are enforceable by a superior of the feu or which would be so enforceable were the person in question to complete title to the dominium directum the superior may, before the appointed day, by duly executing and registering against the dominium utile a notice in, or as nearly as may be in, the form contained in schedule 11A to this Act, prospectively convert those rights into a tenement in land.

(2)   The notice shall—

(a)   set out the title of the superior;

(b)   describe, sufficiently to enable identification by reference to the Ordnance Map, the land the dominium utile of which is subject to the sporting rights (or any part of that land);

(c)   describe those rights; and

(d)   set out the terms of any counter-obligation to those rights if it is a counter-obligation enforceable against the superior.

(3)   Before submitting any notice for registration under this section, the superior shall swear or affirm as is mentioned in subsection (4) of section 18 of this Act.

(4)   Subsection (5) of that section applies for the purposes of subsection (3) above as it applies for the purposes of subsection (4) of that section.

(5)   If subsections (1) to (3) above are, with subsection (4) of that section, complied with and immediately before the appointed day the sporting rights are still enforceable by the superior (or his successor) or would be so enforceable, or still so enforceable, were the person in question to complete title to the dominium directum then, on that day, the sporting rights shall be converted into a tenement in land.

(6)   No greater, or more exclusive, sporting rights shall be enforceable by virtue of such conversion than were (or would have been) enforceable as mentioned in subsection (5) above.

(7)   Where the dominium utile comprises parts each held by a separate vassal, each part shall be taken to be a separate feudal estate of dominium utile.

(8)   Where sporting rights become, under subsection (5) above, a tenement in land, the right to enforce those rights shall be subject to any counter-obligation enforceable against the superior immediately before the appointed day; and section 47 of this Act shall apply in relation to any counter-obligation to sporting rights as it applies in relation to any counter-obligation to a real burden.

(9)   In this section, 'sporting rights' means a right of fishing or game.

(10)   This section is subject to section 41 of this Act.

(11)   Subsections (1) and (2)(a) of section 43 of this Act apply in relation to a

notice submitted for registration under this section as they apply in relation to a notice so submitted under any of the provisions mentioned in those subsections; and paragraph (a) of subsection (3) of that section applies in relation to a determination for the purposes of subsection (5) of this section as it applies in relation to a determination for the purposes of any of the provisions mentioned in that paragraph.

[...]

66   Obligation to make title deeds and searches available

A possessor of title deeds or searches which relate to any land shall make them available to a person who has (or is entitled to acquire) a real right in the land, on all necessary occasions when the person so requests, at the person's expense.

67   Prohibition on leases for periods of more than 175 years

(1)   Notwithstanding any provision to the contrary in any lease, no lease of land executed on or after the coming into force of this section (in this section referred to as the 'commencement date') may continue for a period of more than 175 years; and any such lease which is still subsisting at the end of that period shall, by virtue of this subsection, be terminated forthwith.

(2)   If a lease of land so executed includes provision (however expressed) requiring the landlord or the tenant to renew the lease then the duration of any such renewed lease shall be added to the duration of the original lease for the purposes of reckoning the period mentioned in subsection (1) above.

(3)   Nothing in subsection (1) above shall prevent—

(a)   any lease being continued by tacit relocation; or

(b)   the duration of any lease being extended by, under or by virtue of any enactment.

(4)   Subsections (1) and (2) above do not apply—

(a)   to a lease executed on or after the commencement date in implement of an obligation entered into before that date;

(b)   to a lease executed after the commencement date in implement of an obligation contained in a lease such as is mentioned in paragraph (a) above; or

(c)   where—

(i)   a lease for a period of more than 175 years has been executed before the commencement date; or

(ii)   a lease such as is mentioned in paragraph (a) or (b) above is executed on or after that date,

to a sub-lease executed on or after that date of the whole, or part, of the land subject to the lease in question.

(5)   For the purposes of this section 'lease' includes sub-lease.

68   [*Amends the Titles to Land Consolidation (Scotland) Act 1868.*]

69   Application of 1970 Act to earlier forms of heritable security

(1)   Sections 14 to 30 of the Conveyancing and Feudal Reform (Scotland) Act 1970 (c 35) (which provisions relate to the assignation, variation, discharge and calling-up etc of standard securities) shall apply (with the substitution of the word 'heritable' for 'standard' and subject to such other modifications as may be necessary) as respects any heritable security granted before 29th November 1970 as those provisions apply as respects a standard security.

(2)   For the purposes of the said sections 14 to 30 (as modified by, or by virtue of, subsection (1) above), 'heritable security' shall, with the modification mentioned in subsection (3) below, include a pecuniary real burden but shall not include a security constituted by ex facie absolute disposition.

(3)   The modification is that the reference to the date in subsection (1) above shall be disregarded.

70 Ownership of land by a firm
A firm may, if it has a legal personality distinct from the persons who compose it, itself own land.

PART 7
GENERAL

71 The appointed day
The Scottish Ministers may, for the purposes of this Act, by order appoint a day (in this Act referred to as the 'appointed day'), being a day which—
    (a) falls not less than six months after the order is made; and
    (b) is one or other of the terms of Whitsunday and Martinmas.

72 Interpretation
In this Act, unless the context otherwise requires—
    'land' includes all subjects of heritable property which, before the appointed day, are, or of their nature might be, held of a superior according to feudal tenure;
    'Lands Tribunal' means Lands Tribunal for Scotland; and
    [. . .]

73 Feudal terms in enactments and documents: construction after abolition of feudal system
(1) Where a term or expression, which before the appointed day would ordinarily, or in the context in which it is used, depend for its meaning on there being a feudal system of land tenure, requires to be construed, in relation to any period from that day onwards—
    (a) in an enactment (other than this Act) passed [before that day];
    (b) in an enactment contained in subordinate legislation made [before that day];
    (c) in a document executed [before that day;
    (d) in the Land Register of Scotland or in—
        (i) a land certificate;
        (ii) a charge certificate; or
        (iii) an office copy, [or
    (e) in an extract or certified copy issued under section 104 of the Land Registration etc (Scotland) Act 2012 (asp 5),]
issued, whether or not before that day, under the Land Registration (Scotland) Act 1979 (c 33), then]
in so far as the context admits, where the term or expression is, or contains, a reference to—
        (i) the dominium utile of the land, that reference shall be construed either as a reference to the land or as a reference to the ownership of that land;
        (ii) an estate in land, that reference shall be construed as a reference to a right in land and as including ownership of land;
        (iii) a vassal in relation to land, that reference shall be construed as a reference to the owner of the land;
        (iv) feuing, that reference shall be construed as a reference to disponing;
        (v) a feu disposition, that reference shall be construed as a reference to a disposition;
        (vi) taking infeftment, that reference shall be construed as a reference to completing title,
analogous terms and expressions being construed accordingly.
(2) On and after the appointed day, any reference
    [(a)] in any document executed before that day [or
    (b) in the Land Register of Scotland or in any certificate or copy such as is mentioned in [paragraph (d) of, or extract or certified copy such as is mentioned in paragraph (e) of, subsection (1)] above (whenever issued),]

to a superior shall, where that reference requires to be construed in relation to a real burden which a person is entitled, by virtue of section 18, [18A, 18B, 18C, 19, 20, 28, 28A or 60 of this Act or section 56 of the Title Conditions (Scotland) Act 2003 (asp 9) (facility burdens and service burdens)] to enforce on and after that day, be construed as a reference to that person.

[(2A)   In construing, after the appointed day and in relation to a right enforceable on or after that day, a document, or entry in the Land Register, which—

(a)   sets out the terms of a real burden; and

(b)   is not a document or entry references in which require to be construed as mentioned in subsection (2) above,

any provision of the document or entry to the effect that a person other than the person entitled to enforce the burden may waive compliance with, or mitigate or otherwise vary a condition of, the burden shall be disregarded].

(3)   Subsection (1) above is without prejudice to section 76 of, and schedules 12 and 13 to, this Act or to any order made under subsection (3) of that section.

(4)   In subsection (1) above—

(a)   in paragraph (a), 'enactment' includes a local and personal or private Act; and

(b)   in paragraph (b), 'subordinate legislation' has the same meaning as in the Interpretation Act 1978 (c 30) (but includes subordinate legislation made under an Act of the Scottish Parliament).

74   Orders, regulations and rules

(1)   Any power of the Scottish Ministers under this Act to make orders, regulations or rules shall be exercisable by statutory instrument; and a statutory instrument containing any such orders, regulations or rules, other than an order under section 71, 76(3) or 77(4), shall be subject to annulment in pursuance of a resolution of the Scottish Parliament.

(2)   A statutory instrument containing an order under section 76(3) of this Act shall not be made unless a draft of the instrument has been—

(a)   laid before; and

(b)   approved by a resolution of,

the Scottish Parliament.

75   Saving for contractual rights

[(1)]   As respects any land granted in feu before the appointed day, nothing in this Act shall affect any right (other than a right to feuduty) included in the grant in so far as that right is contractual as between the parties to the grant (or, as the case may be, as between one of them and a person to whom any such right is assigned).

[(2)   In construing the expression 'parties to the grant' in subsection (1) above, any enactment or rule of law whereby investiture is deemed renewed when the parties change shall be disregarded.]

76   Minor and consequential amendments, repeals and power to amend or repeal enactments

(1)   Schedule 12 to this Act, which contains minor amendments and amendments consequential upon the provisions of this Act, shall have effect.

(2)   The enactments mentioned in schedule 13 to this Act are hereby repealed to the extent specified in the second column of that schedule.

(3)   The Scottish Ministers may by order make such further amendments or repeals, in such enactments as may be specified in the order, as appear to them to be necessary or expedient in consequence of any provision of this Act.

(4)   In this section 'enactment' has the same meaning as in section 73(1)(a) of this Act.

77   Short title and commencement

(1)   This Act—

(a) may be cited as the Abolition of Feudal Tenure etc (Scotland) Act 2000; and

(b) subject to subsections (2) and (4) below, comes into force on Royal Assent.

(2) [. . .] There shall come into force on the appointed day—

(a) sections 1 and 2, 4 to 13, 32, 35 to 37, 46, 50 and 51, 54 to 57, 59 to 61, [64, 65,] 66, 68 to 70, 73, 75 and 76(1) (except in so far as relating to paragraph 30(23)(a) of schedule 12) and (2);

(b) schedules 1 to 3;

(c) subject to paragraph 46(3) of schedule 12, that schedule, except paragraph 30(23)(a); and

(d) schedule 13.

(3) Note 1 to Schedule 2 to the Conveyancing and Feudal Reform (Scotland) Act 1970 (c 35) shall be deemed to have been originally enacted as amended by the said paragraph 30(23)(a).

(4) There shall come into force on such day as the Scottish Ministers may by order appoint—

(a) sections 17 to 31, 33, 34, 38 to 45 [, 47 to 49, 63 and 65A];

(b) schedules 5 to 11.

[. . .]

MORTGAGE RIGHTS (SCOTLAND) ACT 2001
(2001, asp 11)

[. . .]

4 Notices to debtors, proprietors and occupiers

[. . .]

(7) The Scottish Ministers may, by order made by statutory instrument, amend—

(a) the Notes inserted in Forms A and B in Schedule 6 to the 1970 Act by Part 1 of the schedule to this Act,

(b) Forms BB, E and F in Schedule 6 to the 1970 Act,

(c) the Forms set out in Part 2 of the schedule to this Act.

(8) A statutory instrument containing an order under subsection (7) is subject to annulment in pursuance of a resolution of the Scottish Parliament.

5 Crown application
This Act binds the Crown.

6 Interpretation
Except so far as the context otherwise requires, expressions used in this Act and in Part II of the 1970 Act have the same meanings in this Act as they have in that Part.

7 Commencement and short title
(1) The preceding provisions of this Act come into force on such day as the Scottish Ministers may by order made by statutory instrument appoint.

(2) An order under subsection (1) may include such transitional and transitory provisions and savings as the Scottish Ministers think expedient.

(3) This Act may be cited as the Mortgage Rights (Scotland) Act 2001.

Section 4   SCHEDULE
               NOTICES TO DEBTORS, PROPRIETORS AND OCCUPIERS

                                    PART 2
               FORMS RELATING TO PROCEEDINGS UNDER SECTION 5 OF THE
                                   1894 ACT

                                  [FORM 1
                          NOTICE OF PROCEEDINGS

**IT IS IMPORTANT THAT YOU READ THIS LETTER—YOUR HOME MAY BE
AT RISK OF REPOSSESSION**

To AB (*address*)

CD (*designation*), the creditor in a security by you (or by EF) in favour of CD (or of
GH to which CD now has right) recorded in the Register for. (*or, as the* case may
be, registered in the Land Register for Scotland) on (*date*) has commenced proceedings against you under section 5 of the Heritable Securities (Scotland) Act
1894 to eject you from (*address of security subjects*) in consequence of the following
default—

(specify in detail the default in respect of which the application is made)

A copy of the application is attached.

Dated this .... day of ....

(*Signature of CD, or signature and designation of CD's agent followed by the words Agent
of CD*)

IT IS STRONGLY RECOMMENDED THAT YOU SEEK ADVICE:
You can get advice about this Notice and what it means for you from a solicitor,
Citizens Advice Bureau or other advice agency or an approved lay representative. A
Citizens Advice Bureau or other advice agency may also be able to give you advice
about how to manage debt. Take this Notice with you when seeking advice. You may
be eligible for legal aid depending on your circumstances. You can get information
about legal aid from a solicitor.

A solicitor or approved lay representative may represent you in any court proceedings in relation to an application by CD for possession and sale of your home. You
can find out more about approved lay representatives from the housing department
of your local authority or from a Citizens Advice Bureau or other advice agency.

**YOUR RIGHTS IN RELATION TO RESIDENTIAL PROPERTY ARE
PROTECTED BY LAW:**
CD's application is not valid and can be challenged by you (or by EF) if CD has failed
to comply with certain pre-action requirements. These requirements include providing specified information and to contacting you (or the debtor) to discuss alternatives
to repossession. It is important to discuss with your solicitor or advisor if you have
doubts about whether CD has complied with these requirements.

YOU HAVE THE RIGHT TO BE HEARD IN COURT:
You are (or the debtor is) entitled to intervene in the court proceedings following from CD's application. You (or the debtor) can appear personally or be represented by a solicitor or approved lay representative. For example, you (or the
debtor) might want to argue that the pre-action requirements have not been complied with or that it would not be reasonable for the sheriff to grant the applica-

tion. Even if they have, you have (or the debtor has) the right to ask the sheriff to continue the proceedings or make any other order. The sheriff will take into account matters such as the nature of and reasons for the default, your (or the debtor's) ability to fulfil your (or the) obligations under the security within a reasonable time, any action taken by CD to assist you (or the debtor) to fulfil your (or the) obligations, your (or the debtor's) participation in a relevant debt payment programme and your (or the debtor's) ability, or the ability of any other person residing in the property, to secure reasonable alternative accommodation.

YOU MAY WISH TO VOLUNTARILY SURRENDER YOUR HOME:
It is open to you (or the debtor), in certain circumstances, to voluntarily surrender the property to CD if all entitled residents in it consent. If you wish to consider voluntary surrender you should discuss with your solicitor or advisor whether this option is right for you. You should not proceed with voluntary surrender unless you understand the consequences of doing so, for example that you may still owe money to CD.

WHAT IF AN ORDER FOR REPOSSESSION HAS ALREADY BEEN GRANTED AND I HAVE JUST BECOME AWARE OF THE APPLICATION?
It may not be too late to intervene so you should urgently seek advice. You have the right to apply to the court to ask for the order to be recalled at any time before repossession has taken place. If the court recalls the order it will fix a hearing, giving you (or the debtor) the opportunity to appear or be represented.

FORM 2
NOTICE OF PROCEEDINGS TO THE OCCUPIER

IT IS IMPORTANT THAT YOU READ THE LETTER—YOUR HOME MAY BE AT RISK OF REPOSSESSION

To the Occupier (including any Tenant) (*address*)

CD (designation) has commenced proceedings under section 5 of the Heritable Securities (Scotland) Act 1894 to eject AB from (*address of security subjects*). A copy of the initial writ is attached.

Dated this .... day of ....

(*Signature of CD, or signature and designation of CD's agent followed by the words Agent of CD*)

IT IS STRONGLY RECOMMENDED THAT YOU SEEK ADVICE:
You can get advice about this Notice and what it means for you from a solicitor, Citizens Advice Bureau or other advice agency or, in certain cases, an approved lay representative. Take this Notice with you when seeking advice. You may be eligible for legal aid depending on your circumstances. You can get information about legal aid from a solicitor.

YOUR RIGHTS IN RELATION TO RESIDENTIAL PROPERTY ARE PROTECTED BY LAW:
CD must comply with statutory pre-action requirements before being allowed to apply to the court. These requirements include providing AB with specified information and contacting AB to discuss alternatives to repossession. It is important to discuss with your solicitor or advisor any doubts you have about whether CD has complied with these requirements.

IF YOU ARE OR WERE THE SPOUSE, CIVIL PARTNER OR PARTNER OF AB OR
ARE THE OWNER OF THE HOUSE:

You may be an ENTITLED RESIDENT and should discuss this with your solicitor
or advisor. This means that AB cannot voluntarily surrender the property if you or
anyone else is living there or without your written consent. You may be asked to give
your consent—it is recommended that you do not do so until you have discussed this
with a solicitor or other advisor.

You have the RIGHT TO BE HEARD IN COURT. You are entitled to intervene to ask
the court to continue the proceedings or to make any other order (for example an
order suspending CD's rights or refusing CD's application). For example, you might
want to argue that the pre-action requirements have not been complied with or that
it would not be reasonable for the sheriff to grant the application. Even if they have,
you have the right to ask the sheriff to continue the proceedings or make any other
order. The sheriff will take into account matters such as the nature of and reasons for
the default, your or the debtor's ability to fulfil the obligations under the security
within a reasonable time, any action taken by CD to assist the debtor to fulfil the obligations, the debtor's participation in a relevant debt payment programme and your
ability, or the ability of any other person residing in the property (including you), to
secure reasonable alternative accommodation.

You may represent yourself, or be represented by a solicitor or approved lay representative. You can find out more about approved lay representatives from the housing department of your local authority or from a Citizens Advice Bureau or other
advice agency.

IF YOU ARE A TENANT OF AB:

You should contact CD to let them know about your tenancy as soon as possible as
they may not be aware that you live in the property.

If you have an assured or short assured tenancy you may have rights under the
Housing (Scotland) Act 1988—in certain circumstances CD cannot take possession of
the property or evict you without making a separate application to court under that
Act. The sheriff may also permit you to intervene in the proceedings for possession
as an interested party. Whatever your type of tenancy, you should obtain legal advice
about your rights as a tenant.

**WHAT IF AN ORDER FOR REPOSSESSION HAS ALREADY BEEN
GRANTED AND I HAVE JUST BECOME AWARE OF THE APPLICATION?**
If you are an ENTITLED RESIDENT it may not be too late to intervene so you should
urgently seek advice. You have the right to apply to court to ask for the order to be
recalled at any time before repossession has taken place. If the court recalls the order
it will fix a hearing, giving you the opportunity to appear or be represented.

If you are a TENANT, CD may need to obtain a separate order for eviction, depending on your tenancy type. You should urgently obtain legal advice about your rights
as a tenant.]

LAND REFORM (SCOTLAND) ACT 2003
(2003, asp 2)

PART 1
ACCESS RIGHTS

CHAPTER 1
NATURE AND EXTENT OF ACCESS RIGHTS

1   Access rights
(1)   Everyone has the statutory rights established by this Part of this Act.
(2)   Those rights (in this Part of this Act called 'access rights') are—
(a)   the right to be, for any of the purposes set out in subsection (3) below, on land; and
(b)   the right to cross land.
(3)   The right set out in subsection (2)(a) above may be exercised only—
(a)   for recreational purposes;
(b)   for the purposes of carrying on a relevant educational activity; or
(c)   for the purposes of carrying on, commercially or for profit, an activity which the person exercising the right could carry on otherwise than commercially or for profit.
(4)   The reference—
(a)   in subsection (2)(a) above to being on land for any of the purposes set out in subsection (3) above is a reference to—
(i)   going into, passing over and remaining on it for any of those purposes and then leaving it; or
(ii)   any combination of those;
(b)   in subsection (2)(b) above to crossing land is a reference to going into it, passing over it and leaving it all for the purpose of getting from one place outside the land to another such place.
(5)   A 'relevant educational activity' is, for the purposes of subsection (3) above, an activity which is carried on by a person for the purposes of—
(a)   furthering the person's understanding of natural or cultural heritage; or
(b)   enabling or assisting other persons to further their understanding of natural or cultural heritage.
(6)   Access rights are exercisable above and below (as well as on) the surface of the land.
(7)   The land in respect of which access rights are exercisable is all land except that specified in or under section 6 below.

2   Access rights to be exercised responsibly
(1)   A person has access rights only if they are exercised responsibly.
(2)   In determining whether access rights are exercised responsibly a person is to be presumed to be exercising access rights responsibly if they are exercised so as not to cause unreasonable interference with any of the rights (whether access rights, rights associated with the ownership of land or any others) of any other person, but—
(a)   a person purporting to exercise access rights who, at the same time—
(i)   engages in any of the conduct within section 9 below or within any byelaw made under section 12(1)(a)(i) below; or
(ii)   does anything which undoes anything done by Scottish Natural Heritage under section 29 below,
is to be taken as not exercising those rights responsibly; and
(b)   regard is to be had to whether the person exercising or purporting to exercise access rights is, at the same time—
(i)   disregarding the guidance on responsible conduct set out in the Access Code and incumbent on persons exercising access rights; or

(ii)   disregarding any request included or which might reasonably be implied in anything done by Scottish Natural Heritage under section 29 below.

(3)   In this section the references to the responsible exercise of access rights are references to the exercise of these rights in a way which is lawful and reasonable and takes proper account of the interests of others and of the features of the land in respect of which the rights are exercised.

3   Reciprocal obligations of owners

(1)   It is the duty of every owner of land in respect of which access rights are exercisable—

(a)   to use and manage the land; and

(b)   otherwise to conduct the ownership of it,

in a way which, as respects those rights, is responsible.

(2)   In determining whether the way in which land is used, managed or the ownership of it is conducted is responsible an owner is to be presumed to be using, managing and conducting the ownership of land in a way which is responsible if it does not cause unreasonable interference with the access rights of any person exercising or seeking to exercise them, but—

(a)   an owner who contravenes section 14(1) or (3) or 23(2) of this Act or any byelaw made under section 12(1)(a)(ii) below is to be taken as not using, managing or conducting the ownership of the land in a responsible way;

(b)   regard is to be had to whether any act or omission occurring in the use, management or conduct of the ownership of the land disregards the guidance on responsible conduct set out in the Access Code and incumbent on the owners of land.

(3)   In this section the references to the use, management and conduct of the ownership of land in a way which is responsible are references to the use, management and conduct of the ownership of it in a way which is lawful and reasonable and takes proper account of the interests of persons exercising or seeking to exercise access rights.

4   Modification of sections 9, 14 and 23

(1)   Ministers may by order modify, for the purposes of sections 2 and 3 above, any of the provisions of sections 9, 14 and 23 below.

(2)   They may do so generally (that is to say in terms similar to those in sections 2 and 3 above as enacted) or by making provision which relates to particular areas, locations or classes of land or to particular access rights or particular activities which may take place in the exercise of access rights or to particular ways of using, managing or conducting the ownership of land or any combination of those.

(3)   Before doing so, they shall consult such persons whom they consider to have a particular interest in the effect of the proposed modification (or associations representing such persons) and such other persons as they think fit.

5   Access rights, reciprocal obligations and other rules and rights

(1)   The exercise of access rights does not of itself constitute trespass.

(2)   The extent of the duty of care owed by an occupier of land to another person present on the land is not, subject to section 22(4) below, affected by this Part of this Act or by its operation.

(3)   The existence or exercise of access rights does not diminish or displace any other rights (whether public or private) of entry, way, passage or access.

(4)   The existence or exercise of access rights does not diminish or displace any public rights under the guardianship of the Crown in relation to the foreshore.

(5)   The exercise of access rights does not of itself amount to the exercise or possession of any right for the purpose of any enactment or rule of law relating to the circumstances in which a right of way or servitude or right of public navigation may be constituted.

(6)   Access rights do not constitute a public right of passage for the purposes of the definition of 'road' in section 151(1) (interpretation) of the Roads (Scotland) Act 1984 (c 54).

(7)   A person exercising access rights is to be regarded as being in a public place for the purposes of section 53 (obstruction by pedestrians) of the Civic Government (Scotland) Act 1982 (c 45).

CHAPTER 2
NATURE AND EXTENT OF ACCESS RIGHTS: FURTHER PROVISIONS

6   Land over which access rights not exercisable

(1)   The land in respect of which access rights are not exercisable is land—

  (a)   to the extent that there is on it—

    (i)   a building or other structure or works, plant or fixed machinery;

    (ii)   a caravan, tent or other place affording a person privacy or shelter;

  (b)   which—

    (i)   forms the curtilage of a building which is not a house or of a group of buildings none of which is a house;

    (ii)   forms a compound or other enclosure containing any such structure, works, plant or fixed machinery as is referred to in paragraph (a)(i) above;

    (iii)   consists of land contiguous to and used for the purposes of a school; or

    (iv)   comprises, in relation to a house or any of the places mentioned in paragraph (a)(ii) above, sufficient adjacent land to enable persons living there to have reasonable measures of privacy in that house or place and to ensure that their enjoyment of that house or place is not unreasonably disturbed;

  (c)   to which, not being land within paragraph (b)(iv) above, two or more persons have rights in common and which is used by those persons as a private garden;

  (d)   to which public access is, by or under any enactment other than this Act, prohibited, excluded or restricted;

  (e)   which has been developed or set out—

    (i)   as a sports or playing field; or

    (ii)   for a particular recreational purpose;

  (f)   to which—

    (i)   for not fewer than 90 days in the year ending on 31st January 2001, members of the public were admitted only on payment; and

    (ii)   after that date, and for not fewer than 90 days in each year beginning on 1st February 2001, members of the public are, or are to be, so admitted;

  (g)   on which—

    (i)   building, civil engineering or demolition works; or

    (ii)   works being carried out by a statutory undertaker for the purposes of the undertaking,

are being carried out;

  (h)   which is used for the working of minerals by surface workings (including quarrying);

  (i)   in which crops have been sown or are growing;

  (j)   which has been specified in an order under section 11 or in byelaws under section 12 below as land in respect of which access rights are not exercisable.

(2)   For the purposes of subsection (1)(a)(i) above, a bridge, tunnel, causeway, launching site, groyne, weir, boulder weir, embankment of a canalised waterway, fence, wall or anything designed to facilitate passage is not to be regarded as a structure.

7   Provisions supplementing and qualifying section 6

(1)   Section 6 above does not prevent or restrict the exercise of access rights over any land which is a core path [unless it is land—

(a)   to which public access is prohibited or restricted by or under any enactment in consequence of an outbreak of animal disease; or

(b)   in respect of which access rights are not exercisable, having been specified (whether as part of a larger area or not) in an order under section 11].

(2)   Land which bears to be within section 6 above by virtue of a development or change of use for which planning permission was or is required under the Town and Country Planning (Scotland) Act 1997 (c 8) shall, if—

(a)   such planning permission has not been granted; or

(b)   such permission was granted subject to a condition which has not been complied with,

be regarded, for the purposes of that section, as if that development or change of use had not occurred.

(3)   Where planning permission for such a development or change of use of land has been granted, the land shall, for the purposes of section 6 above, be regarded, while that development or change of use is taking place in accordance with the permission, as having been developed or having had its use changed accordingly.

(4)   In section 6(1)(b)(iii) above, 'school' means not only a school within the meaning of section 135(1) of the Education (Scotland) Act 1980 (c 44) but also any other institution which provides education for children below school age within the meaning of that provision.

(5)   There are included among the factors which go to determine what extent of land is sufficient for the purposes mentioned in section 6(1)(b)(iv) above, the location and other characteristics of the house or other place.

(6)   For the purposes of section 6(1)(d) above, access rights do not extend to the land to which public access is prohibited, excluded or restricted only to the extent of the prohibition, exclusion or restriction.

(7)   Section 6(1)(e) above prevents the exercise of access rights over land to which it applies only if—

(a)   the land is being used for the purpose for which it has been developed or set out and, in the case of land which is not a sports or playing field, the exercise of those rights would interfere with the recreational use to which the land is being put;

(b)   the land is a golf green, bowling green, cricket square, lawn tennis court or other similar area on which grass is grown and prepared for a particular recreational purpose; or

(c)   in the case of land which is a sports or playing field, the surface of the land is comprised of synthetic grass, acrylic, resin or rubber granule.

(8)   For the purposes of section 6(1)(e) above, land which has been developed or set out for a particular recreational purpose does not include land on which groynes have been constructed, deepening of pools has been undertaken, fishing platforms have been erected, or where other works for the purposes of fishing have taken place.

(9)   Section 6(1)(f) above does not prevent or restrict the exercise of access rights over land to which it applies by any person who forms part of a class of persons who are not, on the days taken into account for the purposes of determining whether that provision applies in relation to the land, required to pay to gain admittance to the land.

(10)   For the purposes of section 6(1)(i) above land on which crops are growing—

(a)   includes land on which grass is being grown for hay and silage which is at such a late stage of growth that it is likely to be damaged by the exercise of access rights in respect of the land in which it is growing, but otherwise does not include grassland;

(b)   does not include headrigs, endrigs or other margins of fields in which crops are growing,
   [(c)   does not include land used wholly or mainly—
      (i)   as woodland or an orchard, or
      (ii)   for the growing or trees;
but does include land used wholly for the cultivation of tree seedlings in beds,] and 'crops' means plants which are cultivated for agricultural [. . .] or commercial purposes.

8   Adjustment of land excluded from access rights

(1)   Ministers may by order modify any of the provisions of sections 6 and 7 above.

(2)   They may do so generally (that is to say, in terms similar to those in sections 6 and 7 above as enacted) or by making provision which relates to particular areas, locations or classes of land.

(3)   Before doing so, they shall consult such persons whom they consider to have a particular interest in the effect of the proposed modification (or associations representing such persons) and such other persons as they think fit.

9   Conduct excluded from access rights

The conduct which is within this section is—
   (a)   being on or crossing land in breach of an interdict or other order of a court;
   (b)   being on or crossing land for the purpose of doing anything which is an offence or a breach of an interdict or other order of a court;
   (c)   hunting, shooting or fishing;
   (d)   being on or crossing land while responsible for a dog or other animal which is not under proper control;
   (e)   being on or crossing land for the purpose of taking away, for commercial purposes or for profit, anything in or on the land;
   (f)   being on or crossing land in or with a motorised vehicle or vessel (other than a vehicle or vessel which has been constructed or adapted for use by a person who has a disability and which is being used by such a person);
   (g)   being, for any of the purposes set out in section 1(3) above, on land which is a golf course.

CHAPTER 3
THE SCOTTISH OUTDOOR ACCESS CODE

10   The Scottish Outdoor Access Code

(1)   It is the duty of Scottish Natural Heritage to draw up and issue a code, to be known as the Scottish Outdoor Access Code, setting out, in relation to access rights, guidance as to the circumstances in which—
   (a)   those exercising these rights are to be regarded as doing so in a way which is or is not responsible;
   (b)   persons are to be regarded as carrying on activities, otherwise than in the course of exercising access rights, in a way which is likely to affect the exercise of these rights by other persons;
   (c)   owners of land in respect of which these rights are exercisable are to be regarded as using and managing, or otherwise conducting the ownership of it, in a way which is or is not responsible;
   (d)   owners of land in respect of which these rights are not exercisable are to be regarded as using and managing, or otherwise conducting the ownership of it, in a way which is likely to affect the exercise of these rights on land which is contiguous to that land.

(2)   Scottish Natural Heritage shall consult local authorities and such other persons or bodies as they think appropriate about the proposed Access Code and

then submit it (with or without modifications) to Ministers together with copies of any objections or representations made in response to that consultation.

(3)   On receiving a proposed Access Code, Ministers may—

(a)   approve it, with or without modifications; or

(b)   reject it.

(4)   Where Ministers reject a proposed Access Code under subsection (3)(b) above they may either instruct Scottish Natural Heritage to submit a new Code or they may substitute a Code of their own devising.

(5)   Where Ministers approve an Access Code with or without modification under subsection (3)(a) above or devise a Code themselves under subsection (4) above, they shall lay the proposed Code before the Scottish Parliament and Scottish Natural Heritage shall not issue the Code unless it has been approved by resolution of the Parliament.

(6)   The Access Code comes into operation on such date as Ministers fix.

(7)   It is the duty of—

(a)   Scottish Natural Heritage and local authorities to publicise the Access Code;

(b)   Scottish Natural Heritage to promote understanding of it.

(8)   Scottish Natural Heritage shall keep the Access Code under review and may modify it from time to time.

(9)   In reviewing the Access Code, Scottish Natural Heritage shall consult such persons or bodies as they think appropriate about the operation of the Code.

(10)   Subsections (2) to (6) above apply to modifications of the Access Code as they apply to the Code.

CHAPTER 4
REGULATION AND PROTECTION OF ACCESS RIGHTS

11   Power to exempt particular land from access rights

(1)   The local authority may (whether on application made to them or not) by order under this section made in respect of a particular area of land specified in the order exempt it for a particular purpose specified in the order from the access rights which would otherwise be exercisable in respect of it during such times as may be specified in the order.

(2)   Before making an order under this section which would have effect for a period of six or more days, the local authority shall—

(a)   consult the owner of the land to which it would relate, the local access forum established by them and such other persons as they think appropriate; and

(b)   give public notice of the intended purpose and effect of the proposed order, inviting objections to be sent to them within such reasonable time as is specified in the notice; and shall consider any such objections and any other representations made to them.

(3)   An order under this section which would have effect for such a period requires confirmation by Ministers.

(4)   It is the duty of the local authority to send to Ministers—

(a)   copies of any objections made in response to the invitation under subsection (2) above; and

(b)   any other representations made to them,

in relation to an order requiring such confirmation.

(5)   Ministers—

(a)   shall not confirm such an order without considering any objections or representations sent to them under subsection (4) above; and

(b)   may cause an inquiry to be held for the purposes of enabling them to decide whether to confirm the order.

(6)   Subsections (2) to (13) of section 265 (local inquiries) of the Town and

Country Planning (Scotland) Act 1997 (c 8) apply to an inquiry held under subsection (5)(b) above as they apply to one held under that section.

(7) Ministers may—

(a) confirm the order, with or without modifications; or

(b) refuse to confirm it.

(8) An order under this section takes effect—

(a) where the order does not require to be confirmed by Ministers, from the date on which it is made or such other date as may be specified in it for the purpose; or

(b) where the order requires to be so confirmed, from such date as is specified in it for the purpose or such other date as Ministers may direct when confirming it.

(9) The local authority shall give public notice of their making an order under this section as soon as practicable after it is made or, where the order requires to be confirmed by Ministers, the authority receive notice of such confirmation.

(10) The power of a local authority to make an order under this section includes power to revoke, amend or re-enact any such order.

(11) Where a revoked, amended or re-enacted order would—

(a) but for the revocation or amendment; or, as the case may be

(b) by virtue of the amendment or re-enactment,

have effect for a period of six or more days beginning on or after the date on which it is revoked, amended or re-enacted, subsections (2) to (9) above apply in relation to the revocation, amendment or, as the case may be, re-enactment.

(12) An order under this section has effect, subject to subsection (13) below—

(a) for the period of two years beginning on the day on which the order takes effect;

(b) where the order specifies that it is to cease to have effect for such shorter period as may be specified in the order, for that shorter period; or

(c) where the order is revoked with effect from a day which falls before the end of that period or, as the case may be, that shorter period, until that day.

(13) If, at any time before an order under this section ceases to have effect, the local authority which made the order re-enacts it, the order continues to have effect—

(a) for the period of two years beginning on the day on which the order would otherwise have ceased to have effect under subsection (12)(a) or (b) above (or, as the case may be, under this paragraph or paragraph (b) below);

(b) where the order (as amended or re-enacted) specifies that it is to cease to have effect for such shorter period as may be specified in the order, for that shorter period; or

(c) where the order is revoked with effect from a day which falls before the end of that period or, as the case may be, that shorter period, until that day.

12 Byelaws in relation to land over which access rights are exercisable

(1) The local authority may, in relation to land in respect of which access rights are exercisable, make byelaws—

(a) making provision further or supplementary to that made—

(i) by sections 2 and 9 and under section 4 above as to the responsible exercise of access rights; and

(ii) by section 3(2) and under section 4 above as to the responsible use, management and conduct of the ownership of the land;

(b) specifying land for the purposes of section 6(j) above;

(c) providing for—

(i) the preservation of public order and safety;

(ii) the prevention of damage;

(iii) the prevention of nuisance or danger;

(iv) the conservation or enhancement of natural or cultural heritage.

(2) Byelaws made under section (1)(c) above may, in particular—

(a) prohibit, restrict or regulate the exercise of access rights;

(b) facilitate their exercise;

(c) so as to protect and further the interests of persons who are exercising or who might exercise access rights, prohibit or regulate—

(i) the use of vehicles or vessels;

(ii) the taking place of sporting and recreational activities;

(iii) the conduct of any trade or business;

(iv) the depositing or leaving of rubbish or litter; and

(v) the lighting of fires and the doing of anything likely to cause a fire,

on the land.

(3) Byelaws made under this section shall not interfere with the exercise of—

(a) any public right of way or navigation; or

(b) the functions of a statutory undertaker.

(4) Sections 202 to 204 (byelaws) of the Local Government (Scotland) Act 1973 (c 65) apply to byelaws made under this section as they apply to byelaws made under that Act, but with the following modifications and further provisions.

(5) The references to one month in subsections (4), (5) and (7) of section 202 shall be read as references to such period of not less than 12 weeks as the local authority determine.

(6) The local authority shall, at the same time as they first make the proposed byelaws open to public inspection, consult the persons and bodies mentioned in subsection (7) below on the proposed byelaws.

(7) Those persons and bodies are—

(a) every community council whose area includes an area to which the proposed byelaws would apply;

(b) the owners of land to which the proposed byelaws would apply;

(c) such persons as appear to them to be representative of the interests of those who live, work, carry on business or engage in recreational activities on any land affected by the proposed byelaws;

(d) the local access forum established by them;

(e) every statutory undertaker which carries on its undertaking on land to which the proposed byelaws would apply;

(f) Scottish Natural Heritage; and

(g) such other persons as they think fit.

(8) The local authority are, for the purposes of subsection (6) above, to be taken as having consulted a person of whom or a body of which they have no knowledge or whom or which they cannot find if they have taken reasonable measures to ascertain whether the person or body exists or, as the case may be, the person's or body's whereabouts.

CHAPTER 5
LOCAL AUTHORITY FUNCTIONS: ACCESS AND OTHER RIGHTS

13 Duty of local authority to uphold access rights

(1) It is the duty of the local authority to assert, protect and keep open and free from obstruction or encroachment any route, waterway or other means by which access rights may reasonably be exercised.

(2) A local authority is not required to do anything in pursuance of the duty imposed by subsection (1) above which would be inconsistent with the carrying on of any of the authority's other functions.

(3) The local authority may, for the purposes set out in subsection (1) above, institute and defend legal proceedings and generally take such steps as they think expedient.

14 Prohibition signs, obstructions, dangerous impediments etc

(1) The owner of land in respect of which access rights are exercisable shall

not, for the purpose or for the main purpose of preventing or deterring any person entitled to exercise these rights from doing so—

(a) put up any sign or notice;

(b) put up any fence or wall, or plant, grow or permit to grow any hedge, tree or other vegetation;

(c) position or leave at large any animal;

(d) carry out any agricultural or other operation on the land; or

(e) take, or fail to take, any other action.

(2) Where the local authority consider that anything has been done in contravention of subsection (1) above they may, by written notice served on the owner of the land, require that such remedial action as is specified in the notice be taken by the owner of the land within such reasonable time as is so specified.

(3) If the owner fails to comply with such a notice, the local authority may—

(a) remove the sign or notice; or, as the case may be,

(b) take the remedial action specified in the notice served under subsection (2) above,

and, in either case, may recover from the owner such reasonable costs as they have incurred by acting under this subsection.

(4) An owner on whom a notice has been so served may, by summary application made to the sheriff, appeal against it.

(5) Rules of Court shall provide—

(a) for public notice of the making of summary applications for the purposes of this section;

(b) for enabling persons interested in the exercise of access rights over the land to which a summary application relates, and persons or bodies representative of such persons, to be parties to the proceedings;

(c) for limiting the number of persons and bodies who may be such parties.

15 Measures for safety, protection, guidance and assistance

(1) The local authority may take such steps (which may include the putting up and maintenance of notices and fences) as appear to them appropriate—

(a) to warn the public of and protect the public from danger on any land in respect of which access rights are exercisable;

(b) to indicate or enclose, or to give directions to, any such land.

(2) Where the local authority consider that a fence, wall or other erection is so constructed or adapted (whether by the use of barbed wire or other sharp material or by being electrified or otherwise) as to be likely to injure a person exercising access rights, they may by written notice served on the owner of the land on which it is placed, require the owner to take, within such reasonable time as is specified in the notice, such reasonable action as is so specified, being action calculated to remove the risk of injury.

(3) Subsections (3)(b), (4) and (5) of section 14 above apply in respect of a notice served under subsection (2) above as they apply to a notice served under those subsections.

(4) The local authority may install and maintain, in any land in respect of which access rights are exercisable, gates, stiles, moorings, launching sites or other means of facilitating the exercise of these rights, and seats, lavatories and other means of contributing to the comfort and convenience of persons exercising them.

(5) The local authority may, in relation to inland waters in respect of which access rights are exercisable, provide staff for life saving and any boats or equipment which are appropriate for life saving.

(6) In exercising their powers under this section, the local authority shall—

(a) have regard to the extent to which there are existing facilities in their area for the purposes of assisting persons to exercise access rights; and

(b) have regard to the needs of persons with disabilities.

(7) The local authority may carry out the operations authorised by subsections

(4) and (5) above within the land over which the access rights are exercisable only with the consent of the owner.

16 Acquisition by local authority of land to enable or facilitate exercise of access rights

(1) Where it appears to the local authority to be necessary or expedient for the purpose of enabling or facilitating the exercise of access rights in respect of any land to which this section applies that the land be acquired by them, the authority may—

(a) acquire it by agreement (whether by purchase, feu, lease or excambion); or

(b) with the consent of Ministers, acquire it compulsorily.

(2) The land to which this section applies is land other than—

(a) land in respect of which access rights do not extend by virtue of section 6(1) (a)(ii), (d), (e) or (f) above;

(b) land which has been exempted by order made by the local authority under section 11(1) of this Act.

(3) A local authority shall hold and manage any land acquired by them under this section so as best to facilitate the exercise of access rights.

(4) The Acquisition of Land (Authorisation Procedure) (Scotland) Act 1947 (c 42) shall apply in relation to a compulsory purchase under this section as if this section had been in force immediately before that Act.

17 Core paths plan

(1) It is the duty of the local authority, not later than 3 years after the coming into force of this section, to draw up a plan for a system of paths ('core paths') sufficient for the purpose of giving the public reasonable access throughout their area.

(2) Such a system of paths may include—

(a) rights of way by foot, horseback, pedal cycle or any combination of those, being rights which are or may be established by or under any enactment or rule of law;

(b) paths, footways, footpaths, cycle tracks or other means of access (however described but not falling within paragraph (a) above) which are or may be provided by or under any enactment other than this Act;

(c) paths which are or may be delineated by a path agreement under section 21 or a path order under section 22 below;

(d) other routes, waterways or other means by which persons may cross land.

(3) In drawing up the plan, the local authority shall have regard to—

(a) the likelihood that persons exercising rights of way and access rights will do so by using core paths;

(b) the desirability of encouraging such persons to use core paths; and

(c) the need to balance the exercise of those rights and the interests of the owner of the land in respect of which those rights are exercisable.

(4) The plan may consist of or include maps showing core paths and, where it does not, shall refer to such maps.

18 Core paths plan: further procedure

(1) The local authority shall—

(a) give public notice of the plan drawn up by them under section 17 above and any maps it refers to;

(b) make the plan and any such maps available thereafter for public inspection for a period of not less than 12 weeks; and

(c) consult—

(i) the local access forum for their area;

(ii) persons representative of those who live, work, carry on business or engage (or would be likely to engage) in recreational activities on the land on which it is proposed that there be core paths;

 (iii) Scottish Natural Heritage; and

 (iv) such other persons as the local authority think fit,

in each case inviting objections and representations to be made to them within such period as they specify.

(2) If no objections are made or any made are withdrawn, the local authority shall adopt the plan.

(3) If an objection is made and not withdrawn, the local authority shall not adopt the plan unless Ministers direct them to do so.

(4) Where an objection remains unwithdrawn, Ministers shall not make such a direction without first causing a local inquiry to be held into whether the plan will, if adopted, fulfil the purpose mentioned in section 17(1) above.

(5) Ministers may, in any other case, cause such an inquiry to be held.

(6) Subsections (2) to (13) of section 265 (local inquiries) of the Town and Country Planning (Scotland) Act 1997 (c 8) apply to an inquiry held under subsection (4) or (5) above as they apply to one held under that section.

(7) Following the publication of the report by the person appointed to hold the inquiry, Ministers may (but need not) direct the local authority to adopt the plan either as drawn up under section 17 above or with such modification as Ministers specify in the direction.

(8) On adopting the plan, the local authority shall—

 (a) give public notice of its adoption;

 (b) compile a list of core paths;

 (c) keep the plan, any maps it refers to and the list available for public inspection and for sale at a reasonable price; and

 (d) send a copy of each of those documents to Ministers.

(9) Where Ministers decline to make a direction under subsection [. . .] (7) above, the local authority shall draw up a revised plan and shall do so in accordance with such procedure and within such time limits as Ministers specify.

(10) Such specification shall include provision under which Ministers may (but need not) direct the local authority to [adopt] the revised plan.

19 Power to maintain core paths etc

The local authority may do anything which they consider appropriate for the purposes of—

 (a) maintaining a core path;

 (b) keeping a core path free from obstruction or encroachment;

 (c) providing the public with directions to, or with an indication of the extent of, a core path.

20 Review and amendment of core paths plan

[(1) A local authority—

 (a) must review the plan adopted under section 18 (or that plan as amended under this section or section 20C) if Ministers require them to do so,

 (b) may review such a plan if they consider it appropriate to do so for the purpose of ensuring that the core paths plan continues to give the public reasonable access throughout their area.]

(2) Where, following a review of a plan under subsection (1) above, the local authority consider that—

 (a) a core path should be removed from the plan; or

 (b) the line of a core path, or part of that line, should be diverted,

the authority may amend the plan by removing the core path from the plan or, as the case may be, by diverting the line of the core path on the plan.

(3) The local authority may not amend the plan under subsection (2) above unless they are satisfied that it is expedient so to do having regard to—

(a) the extent to which it appears to them that persons would, but for the amendment, be likely to exercise access rights using the core path; and

(b) the effect which the amendment of the plan would have as respects land served by the core path.

(4) Where the local authority stop up, or divert, a core path by order under section 208 of the Town and Country Planning (Scotland) Act 1997 (c 8) they shall amend their plan accordingly.

[(5) On adopting the amended plan under subsection (4), the local authority must—

(a) amend the list of core paths compiled under section 18(8) to show the effect of the stopping up or diversion,

(b) keep the amended plan, any maps it refers to and the list available for public inspection and for sale at a reasonable price, and

(c) send a copy of each of those documents to Ministers.]

(6) Where, following a review of a plan under subsection (1) above, the local authority consider that the plan should be amended so as to include a further path, waterway or other means of crossing land such as is mentioned in section 17(2) above, the authority shall draw up an amended plan.

(7) [Subsections (3) and (4) of section 17] apply in relation to a plan drawn up under subsection (6) above as they apply to a plan drawn up under section 17(1) above.

[20A Review and amendment of core paths plan: further procedure

(1) Where, following a review of a plan under section 20(1), the local authority consider that a plan should be amended, the local authority must—

(a) give public notice of the amended plan and any maps it refers to,

(b) make the original plan and the amended plan and any such maps available for public inspection for a period of not less than 12 weeks, and

(c) consult—

(i) the local access forum for their area,

(ii) persons representative of those who live, work, carry on business or engage (or would be likely to engage) in recreational activities on the land affected by the amendment to the plan,

(iii) Scottish Natural Heritage, and

(iv) such other persons as the local authority think fit,

in each case inviting objections and representations in relation to the amendment to the plan to be made to them within such period as they specify.

(2) If no objections are made or any made are withdrawn, the local authority must adopt the amended plan.

(3) If an objection is made and not withdrawn, the local authority must not adopt the amended plan unless Ministers direct them to do so.

(4) If, after complying with subsection (1), the local authority modify the amended plan, they must notify and consult such persons as they consider appropriate on the modified amended plan.

(5) Where an objection remains unwithdrawn, Ministers must not make a direction without first causing a local inquiry to be held into whether the amended plan (or, as the case may be, the modified amended plan) will, if adopted, fulfil the purpose mentioned in section 17(1).

(6) Ministers may, in any other case, cause such an inquiry to be held.

(7) Subsections (2) to (13) of section 265 (local inquiries) of the Town and Country Planning (Scotland) Act 1997 apply to an inquiry held under subsection (5) or (6) as they apply to one held under that section.

(8) Following the publication of the report by the person appointed to hold the inquiry, Ministers may (but need not) direct the local authority to adopt the amended plan (or, as the case may be, the modified amended plan) either as

drawn up under section 20 or with such modification as Ministers specify in the direction.

(9)   On adopting the amended plan, the local authority must—

(a)   give public notice of the adoption of the amended plan,

(b)   amend the list of core paths compiled under section 18(8),

(c)   keep the amended plan, any maps it refers to and the list available for public inspection and for sale at a reasonable price, and

(d)   send a copy of each of those documents to Ministers.

(10)   Where Ministers decline to make a direction under subsection (8), the local authority must draw up a revised amended plan and must do so in accordance with such procedure and within such time limits as Ministers specify.

(11)   Such specification must include provision under which Ministers may (but need not) direct the local authority to adopt the revised amended plan.

20B   Review and amendment of core paths plan: notice to owners and occupiers of land

(1)   Where, following a review of a plan under section 20(1), the local authority consider that a plan should be amended, the local authority must, at the same time as complying with section 20A(1), serve a written notice on the owner and occupier of any land which is, as a result of the amendment of the plan, being included in a plan for the first time (the 'affected land').

(2)   Notice under subsection (1) must—

(a)   explain the potential effect of the amended plan on the affected land,

(b)   set out where the original plan and the amended plan may be inspected, and

(c)   specify the period within which any objections and representations in relation to the amendment to the plan may be made.

(3)   Where it is not possible, after reasonable enquiry, to identify the owner or occupier of the affected land, notice under subsection (1) may be given instead by leaving a copy of the notice in a prominent place on the affected land.

20C   Single amendment of core paths plan: procedure

If the local authority consider that it would be appropriate to make a single amendment of a core paths plan, the local authority must—

(a)   consult such persons as the local authority think fit on the amendment, inviting objections and representations in relation to the amendment to be made to them within such period as they specify, and

(b)   give such notice of the amendment as the local authority think fit.

20D   Single amendment of core paths plan: further procedure

(1)   Section 17(3) applies to an amendment under section 20C which includes a further path, waterway or other means of crossing land such as is mentioned in section 17(2) as it applies to a plan drawn up under section 17(1).

(2)   Section 20(3) applies to an amendment under section 20C which removes a core path from the plan or diverts the line of a core path on the plan as it applies to an amendment of a plan under section 20(2).

(3)   The following provisions apply to an amendment under section 20C as they apply to an amendment of a plan under section 20(1)—

(a)   subsections (2) to (9) of section 20A,

(b)   section 20B, subject to the modification that the reference in section 20B(1) to section 20A(1) is to be read as a reference to section 20C.]

21   Delineation by agreement of paths in land in respect of which access rights exercisable

(1)   The local authority may enter an agreement (a 'path agreement') with a person having the necessary power for the delineation and maintenance or, as the case may be, for the delineation, creation and maintenance of a path within land in respect of which access rights are exercisable.

(2)   A path agreement shall be on such terms and conditions as to payment or otherwise as may be specified in it.

22   Compulsory powers to delineate paths in land in respect of which access rights exercisable

(1)   Where, in the circumstances set out in subsection (2) below, it appears to the local authority that, having regard to the rights and interests of the owner of land in respect of which access rights are exercisable and persons likely to exercise these rights, it is expedient to delineate a path within that land, the authority may, by order (a 'path order'), do so.

(2)   These circumstances are that it appears to the local authority to be impracticable to delineate the path by means of a path agreement.

(3)   Where the local authority make a path order—

(a)   delineating an existing path, they have the duty of maintaining it;

(b)   delineating a new path, they have the duty of creating and maintaining it.

(4)   Regard may be had, in determining whether a local authority has control of a path for the purposes of the Occupiers' Liability (Scotland) Act 1960 (c 30), to the duties imposed by subsection (3) above.

(5)   A path order may be revoked by the local authority.

(6)   A path order shall be in such form as is prescribed but shall contain a map showing the delineation of the path.

(7)   Where access rights—

(a)   have, by virtue of any provision of this Part of this Act, not been exercisable over any land consisting of a public path created under sections 30 to 36 of the Countryside (Scotland) Act 1967 (c 86); but

(b)   become exercisable over that land,

the public path creation agreement or the public path creation order or public path diversion order by which the public path was created shall, for the purposes of the exercise of access rights, be treated as a path agreement or, as the case may be, a path order.

(8)   Schedule 1 to this Act has effect for the purposes of providing further as to path orders.

[. . .]

23   Ploughing etc

(1)   Where land is, in accordance with good husbandry, being ploughed or having its surface otherwise disturbed and it is convenient to plough, or otherwise disturb the surface of, a core path or a right of way which forms part of the land, nothing in this Part of this Act prevents that path or, as the case may be, right of way from being ploughed or from having its surface otherwise disturbed.

(2)   The owner of land being a path or, as the case may be, right of way which has been ploughed or which has had its surface otherwise disturbed in accordance with subsection (1) above shall, however, within the period of 14 days beginning on the day on which the path or, as the case may be, right of way is ploughed or has its surface otherwise disturbed or such longer period as the local authority may allow, reinstate the path or, as the case may be, right of way.

(3)   An owner who fails to comply with subsection (2) above shall be guilty of an offence and liable on summary conviction to a fine not exceeding level 3 on the standard scale.

(4)   If the owner fails to comply with subsection (2) above, the local authority may, after giving the owner 14 days' notice of their intention to do so—

(a)   take all necessary steps to reinstate the path or, as the case may be, right of way; and

(b)   recover from the owner their reasonable expenses in doing so.

(5) Nothing in this section prejudices any limitation or condition having effect otherwise.

24 Rangers

(1) The local authority may appoint persons to act as rangers in relation to any land in respect of which access rights are exercisable.

(2) The purposes for which such rangers may be so appointed are—

(a) to advise and assist the owner of the land and other members of the public as to any matter relating to the exercise of access rights in respect of the land; and

(b) to perform such other duties in relation to the exercise of those rights in respect of that land as the local authority determine.

(3) A person appointed under this section as a ranger may, for the purpose of exercising any function conferred by or under subsection (2) above, enter any land in respect of which access rights are exercisable.

25 Local access forums

(1) Each local authority shall establish for its area a body, to be known as the 'local access forum', to carry out the functions set out in subsection (2) below.

(2) Those functions are—

(a) to advise the local authority and any other person or body consulting the forum on matters having to do with the exercise of access rights, the existence and delineation of rights of way or the drawing up and adoption of a plan for a system of core paths under sections 17 and 18 above;

(b) to offer and, where the offer is accepted, to give assistance to the parties to any dispute about—

(i) the exercise of access rights;

(ii) the existence and delineation of rights of way;

(iii) the drawing up and adoption of the plan referred to in paragraph (a) above; or

(iv) the use of core paths, towards the resolution of the dispute.

(3) A local access forum consists of such persons as are appointed to it by the local authority.

(4) The matters to which the local authority have regard when making appointments to the local access forum shall include—

(a) ensuring reasonable representation in the forum of—

(i) bodies representative of persons with an interest in any of the matters mentioned in subsection (2)(b)(i) to (iv) above;

(ii) persons having such an interest;

(iii) bodies representative of the owners of land in respect of which access rights are exercisable or in which there is a core path; and

(iv) owners of such land, and

(b) ensuring a reasonable balance among those mentioned in sub-paragraphs (i) to (iv) of paragraph (a) above.

(5) The local authority may appoint one or more of its own members to a local access forum.

(6) More than one local access forum may be established for the area of a local authority.

(7) The local authority may pay to members of the local access forum such expenses and allowances as the local authority determine.

(8) Ministers may give guidance to local authorities to assist them in the performance of their functions under this section.

26 Power of entry

(1) Any person authorised by the local authority to do so may enter any land

for a purpose connected with the exercise or proposed exercise of any of the authority's functions under this Part of this Act.

    (2)   A person so authorised may, subject to subsection (3) below, enter land only—

        (a)   at a reasonable time; and

        (b)   on giving reasonable notice to the owner of the land.

    (3)   Subsection (2) above does not apply—

        (a)   in case of emergency; or

        (b)   in relation to the exercise by a local authority of any of their powers under sections 15(1)(a) and (4) and 19 above in relation to land which is a core path.

    (4)   A person may, on entering any land by virtue of subsection (1) above, take onto the land any machinery, other equipment or materials required for the purpose for which the power of entry is being exercised.

27   Guidance

    (1)   Ministers may give guidance to local authorities on the performance of any of their functions under this Part of this Act.

    (2)   Such guidance may be given generally or to a particular local authority.

    (3)   A local authority to which such guidance is given shall have regard to it.

    (4)   Before giving such guidance, Ministers shall—

        (a)   consult each (or the) local authority to whom they propose to give it; and

        (b)   lay a draft of the proposed guidance before the Scottish Parliament;

and the guidance shall not be given until after a period of 40 days beginning with the day on which the draft was so laid.

    (5)   If, within that period, the Parliament resolves that the guidance proposed should not be given, Ministers shall not give it.

    (6)   In calculating any period of 40 days for the purposes of subsection (4) or (5) above, no account is to be taken of any time during which the Parliament is dissolved or is in recess for more than 4 days.

CHAPTER 6

GENERAL AND MISCELLANEOUS PROVISIONS

28 Judicial determination of existence and extent of access rights and rights of way

    (1)   It is competent, on summary application made to the sheriff, for the sheriff—

        (a)   to declare that the land specified in the application is or, as the case may be, is not land in respect of which access rights are exercisable;

        (b)   to declare—

            (i)   whether a person who has exercised or purported to exercise access rights has exercised those rights responsibly for the purposes of section 2 above;

           (ii)   whether the owner of land in respect of which access rights are exercisable is using, managing or conducting the ownership of the land in a way which is, for the purposes of section 3 above, responsible.

    (2)   It is competent, on summary application made to the sheriff, for the sheriff to declare whether a path, bridleway or other means of crossing land specified in the application is, or is not, a right of way by foot, horseback, pedal cycle or any combination of those.

    (3)   The proceedings for a declaration under subsection (1) or (2) above are those for an action of declarator initiated by summary application to the sheriff.

    (4)   A summary application for a declaration shall be served on the local authority.

(5)   The local authority are entitled to be a party to proceedings for a declaration.

(6)   Where the person seeking a declaration is the owner of the land, it is not necessary to serve the application on any person but the local authority [unless subsection (7A) applies].

(7)   In any other case, the person seeking the declaration shall serve the application on the owner of the land.

[(7A)   Where a declaration is being sought under subsection (1)(b)(i), the person seeking the declaration must also serve the application on the person whose exercise or purported exercise of access rights is in question.]

(8)   Rules of court shall provide—

(a)   for the circumstances in which (including any time periods within which) a summary application may be made for the purposes of this section;

(b)   for public notice of the making of summary applications for the purposes of this section;

(c)   for enabling persons interested in the exercise of access rights over specific land or, as the case may be, in the existence of a right of way over specific land and persons or bodies representative of such persons to be parties to the proceedings;

(d)   for limiting the number of persons and bodies who may be such parties.

(9)   This section is without prejudice to any remedy otherwise available in respect of rights conferred and duties imposed by or under this Part of this Act.

29   Powers to protect natural and cultural heritage etc

(1)   Scottish Natural Heritage may put up and maintain notices for the purposes of protecting the natural heritage of land in respect of which access rights are exercisable.

(2)   The Scottish Ministers may put up and maintain notices for the purposes of protecting the cultural heritage of land in respect of which access rights are exercisable.

(3)   Any notice put up under subsection (1) or (2) above may warn persons of any adverse effect that their presence on the land or any activities they might conduct there might have on the natural or, as the case may be, cultural heritage sought to be protected.

30   Existing byelaws providing for public access to land

It is the duty of every person, body or authority having power under any enactment to make byelaws which may provide for or relate to public access to land in respect of which access rights are exercisable and which is owned or managed by that person, body or authority—

(a)   within 2 years of the coming into force of this section, to review those of its byelaws which so provide or relate and are in force at the time of the review; and

(b)   to modify any of those byelaws which are inconsistent with the provisions of this Act (including any made under it) as they apply to that land so as to make them consistent.

31   Application of sections 14 and 15 to rights of way

Sections 14 and 15 above apply in relation to rights of way by foot, horseback, pedal cycle or any combination of those as they apply in relation to access rights.

32   Interpretation of Part 1

In this Part of this Act—

'Access Code' means the Scottish Outdoor Access Code issued by Scottish Natural Heritage under section 10 above;

'canals' means inland waterways within the meaning of section 92 (interpretation) of the Transport Act 1962 (c 46);

'core path' means a path, waterway or any other means of crossing land such as is mentioned in section 17(2) above which is set out in a plan adopted under section 18 above or, as the case may be, such a plan as amended under section 20 above;

'cultural heritage' includes structures and other remains resulting from human activity of all periods, traditions, ways of life and the historic, artistic and literary associations of people, places and landscapes;

'inland waters' means any inland, non-tidal loch, river (to the extent that it is non-tidal), lake or reservoir, whether natural or artificial and whether navigable or not, and includes the bed and the shores or banks thereof;

'land' includes—

(a)   bridges and other structures built on or over land;

(b)   inland waters;

(c)   canals; and

(d)   the foreshore, that is to say, the land between the high and low water marks of ordinary spring tides;

'local authority' in relation to specific land in respect of which access rights are or would, but for a provision of or order made under this Act, be exercisable means—

(a)   where the land is, on the day on which this section comes into force, within an area designated as a National Park under the National Parks (Scotland) Act 2000 (asp 10), the National Park authority for that National Park; and

(b)   in any other case, the council (being a council constituted under section 2 of the Local Government etc (Scotland) Act 1994 (c 39)) whose area includes that land;

'natural heritage' includes the flora and fauna of land, its geological and physiographical features and its natural beauty and amenity;

'owner', in relation to land, means—

(a)   the owner of the land; and

(b)   where the owner is not in natural possession of the land, the person who is entitled to such natural possession;

'statutory undertaker' means—

(a)   a person authorised by any enactment to carry on any railway, light railway, tramway, road transport, water transport, canal, inland navigation, dock, harbour, pier or lighthouse undertaking or any undertaking for the supply of hydraulic power;

(b)   the operator of a telecommunications code system;

(c)   an airport operator (within the meaning of the Airports Act 1986 (c 31)) operating an airport to which Part V of that Act applies;

(d)   a gas transporter, within the meaning of Part I of the Gas Act 1986 (c 44);

(e)   Scottish Water;

(f)   a holder of a licence under section 6(1) of the Electricity Act 1989 (c 29);

(g)   the Civil Aviation Authority or a holder of a licence under Chapter I of Part I of the Transport Act 2000 (c 38) (to the extent that the person holding the licence is carrying out activities authorised by it);

(h)   the Scottish Environment Protection Agency; or

(i)   a universal postal service provider within the meaning of the Postal Services Act 2000 (c 26);

and 'undertaking' means the undertaking of such a statutory undertaker; and

'telecommunications code system' and 'operator', in relation to such a system, have the same meanings in this Part of this Act as they have in the Telecommunications Act 1984 (c 12).

TITLE CONDITIONS (SCOTLAND) ACT 2003
(2003, asp 9)

PART 1
REAL BURDENS: GENERAL

Meaning and creation

1 The expression 'real burden'
(1)   A real burden is an encumbrance on land constituted in favour of the owner of other land in that person's capacity as owner of that other land.

(2)   In relation to a real burden—

(a)   the encumbered land is known as the 'burdened property'; and

(b)   the other land is known as the 'benefited property'.

(3)   Notwithstanding subsections (1) and (2) above, the expression 'real burden' includes a personal real burden; that is to say a conservation burden, a rural housing burden, a maritime burden, an economic development burden, a health care burden, a manager burden, a personal pre-emption burden and a personal redemption burden (being burdens constituted in favour of a person other than by reference to the person's capacity as owner of any land).

2 Affirmative, negative and ancillary burdens
(1)   Subject to subsection (3) below, a real burden may be created only as—

(a)   an obligation to do something (including an obligation to defray, or contribute towards, some cost); or

(b)   an obligation to refrain from doing something.

(2)   An obligation created as is described in—

(a)   paragraph (a) of subsection (1) above is known as an 'affirmative burden'; and

(b)   paragraph (b) of that subsection is known as a 'negative burden'.

(3)   A real burden may be created which—

(a)   consists of a right to enter, or otherwise make use of, property; or

(b)   makes provision for management or administration,

but only for a purpose ancillary to those of an affirmative burden or a negative burden.

(4)   A real burden created as is described in subsection (3) above is known as an 'ancillary burden'.

(5)   In determining whether a real burden is created as is described in subsection (1) or (3) above, regard shall be had to the effect of a provision rather than to the way in which the provision is expressed.

3 Other characteristics
(1)   A real burden must relate in some way to the burdened property.

(2)   The relationship may be direct or indirect but shall not merely be that the obligated person is the owner of the burdened property.

(3)   In a case in which there is a benefited property, a real burden must, unless it is a community burden, be for the benefit of that property.

(4)   A community burden may be for the benefit of the community to which it relates or of some part of that community.

(5)   A real burden may consist of a right of pre-emption; but a real burden created on or after the appointed day must not consist of—

(a)   a right of redemption or reversion; or

(b)   any other type of option to acquire the burdened property.

(6)   A real burden must not be contrary to public policy as for example an unreasonable restraint of trade and must not be repugnant with ownership (nor must it be illegal).

(7)   Except in so far as expressly permitted by this Act, a real burden must not

have the effect of creating a monopoly (as for example, by providing for a particular person to be or to appoint—

    (a) the manager of property; or

    (b) the supplier of any services in relation to property).

  (8) It shall not be competent—

    (a) to make in the constitutive deed provision; or

    (b) to import under section 6(1) of this Act terms which include provision,

to the effect that a person other than [a holder] of the burden may waive compliance with, or mitigate or otherwise vary, a condition of the burden.

  (9) Subsection (8) above is without prejudice to section 33(1)(a) of this Act.

4   Creation

  (1) A real burden is created by duly registering the constitutive deed except that [. . .] the constitutive deed may provide for the postponement of the effectiveness of the real burden to—

    (a) a date specified in that deed (the specification being of a fixed date and not, for example, of a date determinable by reference to the occurrence of an event); or

    (b) the date of registration of some other deed so specified.

  (2) The reference in subsection (1) above to the constitutive deed is to a deed which—

    (a) sets out (employing, unless subsection (3) below is invoked, the expression 'real burden') the terms of the prospective real burden;

    (b) is granted by or on behalf of the owner of the land which is to be the burdened property; and

    (c) except in the case mentioned in subsection (4) below, nominates and identifies—

      (i) that land;

      (ii) the land (if any) which is to be the benefited property; and

      (iii) any person in whose favour the real burden is to be constituted (if it is to be constituted other than by reference to the person's capacity as owner of any land).

  (3) Where the constitutive deed relates, or purports to relate, to the creation of a nameable type of real burden (such as, for example, a community burden), that deed may, instead of employing the expression 'real burden', employ the expression appropriate to that type.

  (4) Where the constitutive deed relates to the creation of a community burden, that deed shall nominate and identify the community.

  (5) For the purposes of this section, a constitutive deed is duly registered in relation to a real burden only when registered against the land which is to be the burdened property and (except where there will be no benefited property or the land in question is outwith Scotland) the land which is to be the benefited property.

  (6) A right of ownership held pro indiviso shall not in itself constitute a property against which a constitutive deed can be duly registered.

  (7) This section is subject to sections [53(3A),] 73(2) and 90(8) [and (8A)] of this Act and is without prejudice to section 6 of this Act.

5   Further provision as respects constitutive deed

  (1) It shall not be an objection to the validity of a real burden (whenever created) that—

    (a) an amount payable in respect of an obligation to defray some cost is not specified in the constitutive deed; or

    (b) a proportion or share payable in respect of an obligation to contribute towards some cost is not so specified provided that the way in which that proportion or share can be arrived at is so specified.

  (2) Without prejudice to the generality of subsection (1) above, such specification may be by making reference to another document the terms of which are

not reproduced in the deed; but for reference to be so made the other document must be a public document (that is to say, an enactment or a public register or some record or roll to which the public readily has access).

6 Further provision as respects creation

(1) A real burden is created by registering against the land which is to be the burdened property a deed which—

(a) is granted by or on behalf of the owner of that land; and

(b) imports the terms of the prospective burden.

(2) 'Imports' in subsection (1)(b) above means imports into itself from a deed of conditions; and importation in, or as near as may be in, the form set out in schedule 1 to this Act shall suffice in that regard.

(3) A right of ownership held pro indiviso shall not in itself constitute a property against which a deed such as is mentioned in subsection (1) above can be duly registered.

(4) This section is without prejudice to section 4 of this Act.

Duration, enforceability and liability

7 Duration

Subject to any enactment (including this Act) or to any rule of law, the duration of a real burden is perpetual unless the constitutive deed provides for a duration of a specific period.

8 Right to enforce

(1) A real burden is enforceable by any person who has both title and interest to enforce it.

(2) A person has such title if an owner of the benefited property; but the following persons also have such title—

(a) a person who has a real right of lease or proper liferent in the benefited property (or has a pro indiviso share in such right);

(b) a person who—

(i) is the non-entitled spouse [or non-entitled partner] of an owner of the benefited property or of a person mentioned in paragraph (a) above; and

(ii) has occupancy rights in that property; and

(c) if the real burden was created as mentioned in subsection (3)(b) below, a person who was, at the time the cost in question was incurred—

(i) an owner of the benefited property; or

(ii) a person having such title by virtue of paragraph (a) or (b) above.

(3) A person has such interest if—

(a) in the circumstances of any case, failure to comply with the real burden is resulting in, or will result in, material detriment to the value or enjoyment of the person's ownership of, or right in, the benefited property; or

(b) the real burden being an affirmative burden created as an obligation to defray, or contribute towards, some cost, that person seeks (and has grounds to seek) payment of, or as respects, that cost.

(4) A person has title to enforce a real burden consisting of—

(a) a right of pre-emption, redemption or reversion; or

(b) any other type of option to acquire the burdened property,

only if the owner of the benefited property.

(5) In subsection (2)(b) above—

'non-entitled partner' shall be construed in accordance with section 101(1) of the Civil Partnership Act 2004 (c 33) (right of civil partner without title to occupy family home);

'non-entitled spouse' shall be construed in accordance with section 1 of the Matrimonial Homes (Family Protection) (Scotland) Act 1981 (c 59) (right of spouse without title to occupy matrimonial home); and 'occupancy rights' shall be construed, in relation to non-entitled partners, in accordance with section 135 of the 2004 Act and, in relation to non-entitled spouses, in accordance with section 1 of the 1981 Act.

(6)　Subsections (2) to (5) above do not apply in relation to a personal real burden.

9　Persons against whom burdens are enforceable

(1)　An affirmative burden is enforceable against the owner of the burdened property.

(2)　A negative burden or an ancillary burden is enforceable against—

    (a)　the owner, or tenant, of the burdened property; or

    (b)　any other person having the use of that property.

10　Affirmative burdens: continuing liability of former owner

(1)　An owner of burdened property shall not, by virtue only of ceasing to be such an owner, cease to be liable for the performance of any relevant obligation.

(2)　[Subject to subsection (2A) below,] a person who becomes an owner of burdened property (any such person being referred to in this section as a 'new owner') shall be severally liable with any former owner of the property for any relevant obligation for which the former owner is liable.

[(2A)　A new owner shall be liable as mentioned in subsection (2) above for any relevant obligation consisting of an obligation to pay a share of costs relating to maintenance or work (other than local authority work) carried out before the acquisition date only if—

    (a)　notice of the maintenance or work—

        (i)　in, or as near as may be in, the form set out in schedule 1A to this Act; and

        (ii)　containing the information required by the notes for completion set out in that schedule,

(such a notice being referred to in this section and section 10A of this Act as a 'notice of potential liability for costs') was registered in relation to the burdened property at least 14 days before the acquisition date; and

    (b)　the notice had not expired before the acquisition date.

(2B)　In subsection (2A) above—

'acquisition date' means the date on which the new owner acquired right to the burdened property; and

'local authority work' means work carried out by a local authority by virtue of any enactment.']

(3)　A new owner who incurs expenditure in the performance of any relevant obligation for which a former owner of the property is liable may recover an amount equal to such expenditure from that former owner.

(4)　For the purposes of subsections (1) to (3) above, 'relevant obligation' means any obligation under an affirmative burden which is due for performance; and such an obligation becomes due—

    (a)　in a case where—

        (i)　the burden is a community burden; and

        (ii)　a binding decision to incur expenditure is made,

on the date on which that decision is made; or

    (b)　in any other case, on—

        (i)　such date; or

        (ii)　the occurrence of such event,

as may be stipulated for its performance (whether in the constitutive deed or otherwise).

[(5)　This section does not apply in any case where section 12 of the Tenements (Scotland) Act 2004 (asp 11) applies.]

[10A Notice of potential liability for costs: further provision

(1) A notice of potential liability for costs—

 (a) may be registered in relation to burdened property only on the application of—

  (i) an owner of the burdened property;

  (ii) an owner of the benefited property; or

  (iii) any manager; and

 (b) shall not be registered unless it is signed by or on behalf of the applicant.

(2) A notice of potential liability for costs may be registered—

 (a) in relation to more than one burdened property in respect of the same maintenance or work; and

 (b) in relation to any one burdened property, in respect of different maintenance or work.

(3) A notice of potential liability for costs expires at the end of the period of 3 years beginning with the date of its registration, unless it is renewed by being registered again before the end of that period.

[(3A) The owner of a burdened property may apply to register a notice (a 'notice of discharge') if—

 (a) a notice of potential liability for costs in relation to the property has not expired,

 (b) the liability for costs under section 10(2) to which the notice of potential liability relates has, in relation to the property which is the subject of the application, been fully discharged, and

 (c) the person who registered the notice of potential liability for costs consents to the application.

(3B) A notice of discharge—

 (a) must be in the form prescribed by order made by the Scottish Ministers, and

 (b) on being registered, discharges the notice of potential liability for costs as it applies to the property which is the subject of the application.]

(4) This section applies to a renewed notice of potential liability for costs as it applies to any other such notice.

(5) The Keeper of the Registers of Scotland shall not be required to investigate or determine whether the information contained in any notice of potential liability for costs submitted for registration is accurate.

(6) The Scottish Ministers may by order amend schedule 1A to this Act.]

11 Affirmative burdens: shared liability

(1) If a burdened property as respects which an affirmative burden is created is divided (whether before or after the appointed day) into two or more parts then, subject to subsections (2) and (4) below, the owners of the parts—

 (a) are severally liable in respect of the burden; and

 (b) as between (or among) themselves, are liable in the proportions which the areas of their respective parts bear to the area of the burdened property.

(2) 'Part' in subsection (1) above does not include a part to which the affirmative burden cannot relate.

(3) In the application of subsection (1) above to parts which are flats in a tenement, the reference in paragraph (b) of that subsection to the areas of the respective parts shall be construed as a reference to the floor areas of the respective flats.

[(3A) For the purposes of subsection (3) above, the floor area of a flat is calculated by measuring the total floor area (including the area occupied by any internal wall or other internal dividing structure) within its boundaries; but no account shall be taken of any pertinents or any of the following parts of a flat—

 (a) a balcony; and

(b) except where it is used for any purpose other than storage, a loft or basement.]

(4)   Paragraph (a) of subsection (1) above shall not apply if, in the constitutive deed, it is provided that liability as between (or among) the owners of the parts shall be otherwise than is provided for in that paragraph; and paragraph (b) of that subsection shall not apply if, in the constitutive deed or in the conveyance effecting the division, it is provided that liability as between (or among) them shall be otherwise than is provided for in that paragraph.

(5)   If two or more persons own in common a burdened property as respects which an affirmative burden is created then, unless the constitutive deed otherwise provides—

(a)   they are severally liable in respect of the burden; and

(b)   as between (or among) themselves, they are liable in the proportions in which they own the property.

Division of benefited or burdened property

12   Division of a benefited property

(1)   Where part of a benefited property is conveyed, then on registration of the conveyance the part conveyed shall cease to be a benefited property unless in the conveyance some other provision is made, as for example—

(a)   that the part retained and the part conveyed are separately to constitute benefited properties; or

(b)   that it is the part retained which is to cease to be a benefited property.

(2)   Different provision may, under subsection (1) above, be made in respect of different real burdens.

(3)   For the purposes of subsection (1) above, any such provision as is referred to in that subsection shall—

(a)   identify the constitutive deed, say where it is registered and give the date of registration;

(b)   identify the real burdens; and

(c)   be of no effect in so far as it relates to—

(i)   a right of pre-emption, redemption or reversion; or

(ii)   any other type of option to acquire the burdened property,

if it is other than such provision as is mentioned in paragraph (b) of that subsection.

(4)   Subsection (1) above does not apply where—

(a)   the property, part of which is conveyed, is a benefited property only by virtue of any of sections 52 to 56 of this Act [or sections 29 or 31 of the Long Leases (Scotland) Act 2012 (asp 9)];

(b)   the real burdens are community burdens; or

(c)   the real burdens are set out in a common deed of conditions, that is to say in a deed which sets out the terms of the burdens imposed on the part conveyed, that part being one of two or more properties on which they are or will be imposed under a common scheme.

13   Division of a burdened property

Where part of a burdened property is conveyed (whether before or after the appointed day), then on registration of the conveyance the part retained and the part conveyed shall separately constitute burdened properties unless the real burden cannot relate to one of the parts, in which case that part shall, on that registration, cease to be a burdened property.

Construction

14   Construction

Real burdens shall be construed in the same manner as other provisions of deeds which relate to land and are intended for registration.

Extinction

15   Discharge

(1)   A real burden is discharged as respects a benefited property by registering against the burdened property a deed of discharge granted by or on behalf of the owner of the benefited property.

(2)   In subsection (1) above, 'discharged' means discharged—

(a)   wholly; or

(b)   to such extent as may be specified in the deed of discharge.

16   Acquiescence

(1)   Where—

(a)   a real burden is breached in such a way that material expenditure is incurred;

(b)   any benefit arising from such expenditure would be substantially lost were the burden to be enforced; and

(c)   in the case of—

(i)   a burden other than a conservation burden, economic development burden or health care burden, the owner of the benefited property (if any) has an interest to enforce the burden in respect of the breach and consents to the carrying on of the activity which results in that breach, or every person by whom the burden is enforceable and who has such an interest, either so consents or, being aware of the carrying on of that activity (or, because of its nature, being in a position where that person ought to be aware of it), has not, by the expiry of such period as is in all the circumstances reasonable (being in any event a period which does not exceed that of twelve weeks beginning with the day by which that activity has been substantially completed), objected to its being carried on; or

(ii)   a conservation burden, economic development burden or health care burden, the person by whom the burden is enforceable consents to the carrying on of that activity,

the burden shall, to the extent of the breach, be extinguished.

(2)   Where the period of twelve weeks following the substantial completion of an activity has expired as mentioned in sub-paragraph (i) of subsection (1)(c) above, it shall be presumed, unless the contrary is shown, that the person by whom the real burden was, at the time in question, enforceable (or where a burden is enforceable by more than one person, each of those persons) was, or ought to have been, aware of the carrying on of the activity and did not object as mentioned in that sub-paragraph.

17   Further provision as regards extinction where no interest to enforce

Where at any time a real burden is breached but at that time no person has an interest to enforce it in respect of the breach, the burden shall, to the extent of the breach, be extinguished.

18   Negative prescription

(1)   Subject to subsection (5) below, if—

(a)   a real burden is breached to any extent; and

(b)   during the period of five years beginning with the breach neither—

(i)   a relevant claim; nor

(ii)   a relevant acknowledgement,

is made,

then, subject to subsection (2) below, the burden shall, to the extent of the breach, be extinguished on the expiry of that period.

(2) Subject to subsections (5) and (6) below, where, in relation to a real burden which consists of—

    (a) a right of pre-emption, redemption or reversion; or

    (b) any other type of option to acquire the burdened property,

the owner of the burdened property fails to comply with an obligation to convey (or, as the case may be, to offer to convey) the property (or part of the property) and paragraph (b) of subsection (1) above is satisfied, the burden shall be extinguished in relation to the property (or part) on the expiry of the period mentioned in the said paragraph (b).

(3) Sections 9 and 10 of the Prescription and Limitation (Scotland) Act 1973 (c 52) (which define the expressions 'relevant claim' and 'relevant acknowledgement' for the purposes of sections 6, 7 and 8A of that Act) shall apply for the purposes of subsections (1) and (2) above as those sections apply for the purposes of sections 6, 7 and 8A of that Act but subject to the following modifications—

    (a) in each of sections 9 and 10 of that Act—

        (i) subsection (2) shall not apply;

        (ii) for any reference to an obligation there shall be substituted a reference to a real burden; and

        (iii) for any reference to a creditor there shall be substituted a reference to any person by whom a real burden is enforceable;

    (b) in section 9 of that Act, for the reference to a creditor in an obligation there shall be substituted a reference to any person by whom a real burden is enforceable; and

    (c) in section 10 of that Act, for any reference to a debtor there shall be substituted a reference to any person against whom the real burden is enforceable.

(4) Section 14 of the said Act of 1973 (which makes provision as respects the computation of prescriptive periods) shall apply for the purposes of subsections (1) and (2) above as that section applies for the purposes of Part I of that Act except that paragraph (a) of subsection (1) of that section shall for the purposes of those subsections be disregarded.

(5) In relation to a breach occurring before the appointed day, subsections (1) and (2) above apply with the substitution in paragraph (b) of subsection (1), for the words 'period of five years beginning with the breach', of the words 'appropriate period'.

(6) In the case of a right of pre-emption constituted as a rural housing burden, subsection (2) above shall apply with the modification that for the words 'the burden shall be extinguished in relation to the property (or part) on' there shall be substituted 'it shall not be competent to commence any action in respect of that failure after'.

(7) The reference, in subsection (5) above, to the 'appropriate period' is to whichever first expires of—

    (a) the period of five years beginning with the appointed day; and

    (b) the period of twenty years beginning with the breach.

19   Confusio not to extinguish real burden

A real burden is not extinguished by reason only that—

    (a) the same person is the owner of the benefited property and the burdened property; or

    (b) in a case in which there is no benefited property, the person in whose favour the real burden is constituted is the owner of the burdened property.

Termination

20 Notice of termination

(1)   Subject to section 23 of this Act, if at least one hundred years have elapsed since the date of registration of the constitutive deed (whether or not the real burden has been varied or renewed since that date), an owner of the burdened property, or any other person against whom the burden is enforceable, may, after intimation under section 21(1) of this Act, execute and register, in (or as nearly as may be in) the form contained in schedule 2 to this Act, a notice of termination as respects the real burden.

(2)   It shall be no objection to the validity of a notice of termination that it is executed or registered by a successor in title of the person who has given such intimation; and any reference in this Act to the 'terminator' shall be construed as a reference to—

(a)   except where paragraph (b) below applies, the person who has given such intimation; or

(b)   where that person no longer has the right or obligation by virtue of which intimation was given, the person who has most recently acquired that right or obligation.

(3)   Subsections (1) and (2) above do not apply in relation to—

(a)   a conservation burden;

(b)   a maritime burden;

(c)   a facility burden;

(d)   a service burden; or

(e)   a real burden which is a title condition of a kind specified in schedule 11 to this Act.

(4)   The notice of termination shall—

(a)   identify the land which is the burdened property;

(b)   describe the terminator's connection with the property (as for example by identifying the terminator as an owner or as a tenant);

(c)   set out the terms of the real burden and (if it is not wholly to be terminated) specify the extent of the termination;

(d)   specify a date on or before which any application under paragraph (b) of section 90(1) of this Act will require to be made if the real burden is to be renewed or varied under that paragraph (that date being referred to in this Act as the 'renewal date');

(e)   specify the date on which, and the means by which, intimation was given under subsection (1) of section 21 of this Act; and

(f)   set out the name (in so far as known) and the address of each person to whom intimation is sent under subsection (2)(a) of that section.

(5)   Any date may be specified under paragraph (d) of subsection (4) above provided that it is a date not less than eight weeks after intimation is last given under subsection (1) of the said section 21 (intimation by affixing being taken, for the purposes of this subsection, to be given when first the notice is affixed).

(6)   Where a property is subject to two or more real burdens, it shall be competent to execute and register a single notice of termination in respect of both (or all) the real burdens.

[(7)   This section applies to a real burden created by the conversion of a qualifying condition under Part 2 of the Long Leases (Scotland) Act 2012 (asp 9) as if the reference to the 'constitutive deed' were a reference to the deed setting out the qualifying condition.]

21 Intimation

(1)   A proposal to execute and register a notice of termination shall be intimated—

(a)   to the owner of each benefited property;

(b)   in the case of a personal real burden, to the holder; and

(c) to the owner (or, if the terminator is an owner, to any other owner) of the burdened property.

(2) Subject to subsection (3) below, such intimation may be given—

(a) by sending a copy of the proposed notice of termination, completed as respects all the matters which must, in pursuance of paragraphs (a) to (d) and (f) of section 20(4) of this Act, be identified, described, set out or specified in the notice and with the explanatory note which immediately follows the form of notice of termination in schedule 2 to this Act;

(b) by affixing to the burdened property and to—

(i) in a case (not being one mentioned in paragraph (c)(ii) below) where there exists one, and only one, lamp post which is situated within one hundred metres of that property, that lamp post; or

(ii) in a case (not being one so mentioned) where there exists more than one lamp post so situated, each of at least two such lamp posts,

a conspicuous notice in the form set out in schedule 3 to this Act; or

(c) in a case where—

(i) it is not possible to comply with paragraph (b) above; or

(ii) the burdened property is minerals or salmon fishings,

by advertisement in a newspaper circulating in the area of the burdened property.

(3) Such intimation shall, except where it is impossible to do so, be given by the means described in subsection (2)(a) above if it is given—

(a) under subsection (1)(b) or (c) above; or

(b) under subsection (1)(a) above in relation to a benefited property which is at some point within four metres of the burdened property.

(4) An advertisement giving intimation under subsection (2)(c) above shall—

(a) identify the land which is the burdened property;

(b) set out the terms of the real burden either in full or by reference to the constitutive deed;

(c) specify the name and address of a person from whom a copy of the proposed notice of termination may be obtained; and

(d) state that any owner of a benefited property, or as the case may be any holder of a personal real burden, may apply to the Lands Tribunal for Scotland for the real burden to be renewed or varied but that if no such application is received by a specified date (being the renewal date) the consequence may be that the real burden is extinguished.

(5) The terminator shall provide a person with a copy of the proposed notice of termination (completed as is mentioned in subsection (2)(a) above and with the explanatory note referred to in that subsection) if so requested by that person.

(6) A person—

(a) is entitled to affix a notice to a lamp post in compliance with subsection (2)(b) above regardless of who owns the lamp post but must—

(i) take all reasonable care not to damage the lamp post in doing so; and

(ii) remove the notice no later than one week after the date specified in it as the renewal date; and

(b) must, until the day immediately following the date so specified, take all reasonable steps to ensure that the notice continues to be displayed and remains conspicuous and readily legible.

(7) Section 184 of the Town and Country Planning (Scotland) Act 1997 (c 8) (planning permission not needed for advertisements complying with regulations) applies in relation to a notice affixed in compliance with subsection (2)(b) above as that section applies in relation to an advertisement displayed in accordance with regulations made under section 182 of that Act (regulations controlling display of advertisements).

22   Oath or affirmation before notary public

(1) Before submitting a notice of termination for registration, the terminator

shall swear or affirm before a notary public that, to the best of the terminator's knowledge and belief, all the information contained in the notice is true and that section 21 of this Act has been complied with.

(2) For the purposes of subsection (1) above, if the terminator is—

(a) an individual unable by reason of legal disability, or incapacity, to swear or affirm as mentioned in that subsection, then a legal representative of the terminator may swear or affirm;

(b) not an individual, then any person authorised to sign documents on its behalf may swear or affirm;

and any reference in that subsection to a terminator shall be construed accordingly.

23 Prerequisite certificate for registration of notice of termination

(1) A notice of termination shall not be registrable unless, after the renewal date, there is endorsed on the notice (or on an annexation to it referred to in an endorsement on it and identified, on the face of the annexation, as being the annexation so referred to) a certificate executed by a member of the Lands Tribunal, or by their clerk, to the effect that no application in relation to the proposal to execute and register the notice has been received under section 90(1)(b) (and (4)) of this Act or that any such application which has been received—

(a) has been withdrawn; or

(b) relates (either or both)—

(i) to one or more but not to all of the real burdens the terms of which are set out in the notice (any real burden to which it relates being described in the certificate);

(ii) to one or more but not to all (or probably or possibly not to all) of the benefited properties (any benefited property to which it relates being described in the certificate),

and where more than one such application has been received the certificate shall relate to both (or as the case may be all) applications.

(2) At any time before endorsement under subsection (1) above, a notice of termination, whether or not it has been submitted for such endorsement, may be withdrawn, by intimation in writing to the Lands Tribunal, by the terminator; and it shall not be competent to endorse under that subsection a notice in respect of which such intimation is given.

24 Effect of registration of notice of termination

(1) Subject to subsection (2) below, a notice of termination, when registered against the burdened property, extinguishes the real burden in question wholly or as the case may be to such extent as may be described in that notice.

(2) A notice of termination registrable by virtue of a certificate under paragraph (b) of section 23(1) of this Act shall not, on being registered, extinguish a real burden which is the subject of an application disclosed by the certificate in so far as that burden—

(a) is constituted in favour of the property of which the applicant is owner; or

(b) is a personal real burden of which the applicant is holder,

but if under that section a further certificate is endorsed on the notice (or on an annexation to the notice) the notice may be registered again, the effect of the later registration being determined by reference to the further certificate rather than to the certificate by virtue of which the notice was previously registered.

PART 2
COMMUNITY BURDENS

Meaning, creation etc

25 The expression 'community burdens'

(1)   Subject to subsection (2) below, where—

(a)   real burdens are imposed under a common scheme on [two] or more units; and

(b)   each of those units is, in relation to some or all of those burdens, both a benefited property and a burdened property,

the burdens shall, in relation to the units, be known as 'community burdens'.

(2)   Any real burdens such as are mentioned in section 54(1) of this Act are community burdens.

26 Creation of community burdens: supplementary provision

(1)   Without prejudice to section 2 of this Act, community burdens may make provision as respects any of the following—

(a)   the appointment by the owners of a manager;

(b)   the dismissal by the owners of a manager;

(c)   the powers and duties of a manager;

(d)   the nomination of a person to be the first manager;

(e)   the procedures to be followed by the owners in making decisions about matters affecting the community;

(f)   the matters on which such decisions may be made; and

(g)   the resolution of disputes relating to community burdens.

(2)   In this Act 'community' means—

(a)   the units subject to community burdens; and

(b)   any unit in a sheltered or retirement housing development which is used in some special way as mentioned in section 54(1) of this Act.

27 Effect on units of statement that burdens are community burdens

Where, in relation to any real burdens, the constitutive deed states that the burdens are to be community burdens, each unit shall, in relation to those burdens, be both a benefited property and a burdened property.

Management of community

28 Power of majority to appoint manager etc

(1)   Subject to sections 54(5)(a) and 63(8)(a) of this Act and to any provision made by community burdens, the owners of a majority of the units in a community may—

(a)   appoint a person to be the manager of the community on such terms as they may specify;

(b)   confer on any such manager the right to exercise such of their powers as they may specify;

(c)   revoke, or vary, the right to exercise such of the powers conferred under paragraph (b) above as they may specify; and

(d)   dismiss any such manager.

(2)   Without prejudice to the generality of subsection (1)(b) above, the powers mentioned there include—

(a)   power to carry out maintenance;

(b)   power to enforce community burdens; and

(c)   power to vary or discharge such burdens.

(3)   If a unit is owned by two or more persons in common, then, for the purposes of voting on any proposal to exercise a power conferred by subsection (1)

above, the vote allocated as respects the unit shall only be counted for or against the proposal if it is the agreed vote of those of them who together own more than a half share of the unit.

(4)   The powers conferred by paragraphs (b) to (d) of subsection (1) above may be exercised whether or not the manager was appointed by virtue of paragraph (a) of that subsection.

29   Power of majority to instruct common maintenance

(1)   This section applies where—

(a)   community burdens impose an obligation on the owners of all or some of the units to maintain, or contribute towards the cost of maintaining, particular property; and

(b)   the obligation so imposed accounts for the entire liability for the maintenance of such property.

(2)   Subject to any provision made by community burdens, the owners of a majority of the units subject to the obligation may—

(a)   decide that maintenance should be carried out;

(b)   [subject to subsection (3A) below, require each] owner to deposit—

(i)   by such date as they may specify (being a date not less than twenty-eight days after the requirement is made of that owner); and

(ii)   [with such person as they may nominate for the purpose,]

a sum of money (being a sum not exceeding that owner's apportioned share, in accordance with the terms of the community burdens, of a reasonable estimate of the cost of maintenance);

[. . .]

(d)   instruct or carry out such maintenance; and

(e)   modify or revoke anything done by them by virtue of paragraphs (a) to (d) above.

(3)   If a unit is owned by two or more persons in common, then, for the purposes of voting on any proposal to exercise a power conferred by subsection (2) above, the vote allocated as respects the unit shall only be counted for or against the proposal if it is the agreed vote of those of them who together own more than a half share of the unit.

[(3A)   A requirement under subsection (2)(b) above that each owner deposit a sum of money—

(a)   exceeding £100; or

(b)   of £100 or less where the aggregate of that sum taken together with any other sum or sums required (otherwise than by a previous notice under this subsection) in the preceding 12 months to be deposited under that subsection by each owner exceeds £200,

shall be made by written notice to each owner and shall require the sum to be deposited into such account (the 'maintenance account') as the owners may nominate for the purpose.

(3B)   The owners may authorise a manager or at least two other persons (whether or not owners) to operate the maintenance account on their behalf.]

(4)   Any notice given under subsection [(3A)] above shall contain, or to it shall be attached, a note comprising a summary of the nature and extent of the maintenance to be carried out together with the following information—

(a)   the estimated cost of carrying out that maintenance;

(b)   why the estimate is considered a reasonable estimate;

(c)   how—

(i)   the sum required from the owner in question; and

(ii)   the apportionment among the owners,

have been arrived at;

(d)   what the apportioned shares of the other owners are;

(e)   the date on which the decision to carry out the maintenance was taken and the names of those by whom it was taken;

(f)   a timetable for the carrying out of the maintenance, including the dates by which it is proposed the maintenance will be—

(i)   commenced; and

(ii)   completed;

(g)   the location and number of the maintenance account; and

(h)   the names and addresses of the persons who will be authorised to operate that account on behalf of the community.

(5)   The maintenance account shall be a bank or building society account which is interest bearing; and the authority of at least two persons, or of a manager on whom has been conferred the right to give authority, shall be required for any payment from it.

(6)   If modification or revocation under paragraph (e) of subsection (2) above affects the information contained in a notice or note under subsection (4) above, that information shall forthwith be sent again, modified accordingly, to the owners.

[(6A)   The notice given under subsection (2)(b) above may specify a date as a refund date for the purposes of subsection (7)(b)(i) below.]

(7)   An owner shall be entitled—

(a)   to inspect, at any reasonable time, any tender received in connection with the maintenance to be carried out;

(b)   if—

(i)   that maintenance is not commenced by [—

(A)   where the notice under subsection (2)(b) above specifies a refund date, that date; or

(B)   where that notice does not specify such a date, the twenty-eighth] day after the date specified by virtue of subsection (4)(f)(i) above; and

(ii)   the owner demands, by written notice, from the persons authorised under subsection [(3B)] above repayment (with accrued interest) of such sum as has been deposited by that owner in compliance with the requirement under subsection (2)(b) above,

to be repayed accordingly; except that no requirement to make repayment in compliance with a notice under paragraph (b)(ii) above shall arise if the persons so authorised do not receive that notice before the maintenance is commenced.

[(7A)   A former owner who, before ceasing to be an owner, deposited sums in compliance with a requirement under subsection (2)(b) above, shall have the same entitlement as an owner has under subsection (7)(b) above.]

(8)   Such sums as are held in the maintenance account by virtue of subsection [(3A)] above are held in trust for all the depositors, for the purpose of being used by the persons authorised to make payments from the account as payment for the maintenance.

(9)   Any sums held in the maintenance account after all sums payable in respect of the maintenance carried out have been paid shall be shared among the owners—

(a)   by repaying each depositor, with any accrued interest and after deduction of that person's apportioned share of the actual cost of the maintenance, the sum which the person deposited; or

(b)   in such other way as the depositors agree in writing.

[(10)   The Scottish Ministers may by order substitute for the sums for the time being specified in subsection (3A) above such other sums as appear to them to be justified by a change in the value of money appearing to them to have occurred since the last occasion on which the sums were fixed.]

30   Owners' decision binding

Anything done (including any decision made) by—

(a)   the owners in accordance with such provision as is made in community burdens; or

(b)   a majority of them, in accordance with section 28 or 29 of this Act,

is binding on all the owners and their successors as owners.

31   Remuneration of manager

Subject to any provision made by community burdens, liability for any remuneration due to a manager of the community (however appointed) shall be shared equally among the units in a community and each owner shall be liable accordingly; but if two or more persons have common ownership of a unit then—

(a)   they are severally liable for any share payable in respect of that unit; and

(b)   as between (or among) themselves, they are liable in the proportions in which they own the unit.

[31A   Disapplication of provisions of sections 28, 29 and 31 in certain cases

(1)   Sections 28(1)(a) and (d) and (2)(a), 29 and 31 of this Act shall not apply in relation to a community consisting of one tenement.

(2)   Sections 28(1)(a) and (d) and 31 of this Act shall not apply to a community in any period during which the development management scheme applies to the community.]

Variation, discharge etc

32   The expressions 'affected unit' and 'adjacent unit'

In this Part of this Act a unit in respect of which a community burden is to be varied ('varied' including imposed), or discharged, is referred to as an 'affected unit'; and 'adjacent unit' means, in relation to an affected unit, any unit which is at some point within four metres of the unit.

33   Majority etc variation and discharge of community burdens

(1)   A community burden may be varied ('varied' including imposed), or discharged, by registering against each affected unit a deed of variation, or discharge, granted—

(a)   where provision is made in the constitutive deed for it to be granted by the owners of such units in the community as may be specified, by or on behalf of the owners of those units; or

(b)   [. . .] in accordance with subsection (2) below.

(2)   A deed is granted in accordance with this subsection if granted—

(a)   [where no such provision as is mentioned in subsection (1)(a) above is made,] by or on behalf of the owners of a majority of the units in the community (except that, where one person owns a majority of those units, the deed must also be granted by at least one other owner); or

(b)   where the manager of the community is authorised to do so (whether in the constitutive deed or otherwise), by that manager.

(3)   An affected unit may, for the purposes of subsection (1)(a) or (2)(a) above, be included in any calculation of the number of units.

(4)   For the purposes of this section, where a unit is owned by two or more persons in common a deed is granted by or on behalf of the owners of the unit if—

(a)   granted in accordance with such provision as is made in that regard in the constitutive deed; or

(b)   where no such provision is made, granted by or on behalf of those of them who together own more than a half share of the unit.

(5)   This section is subject to section 54(5)(b) and (c) of this Act.

34   Variation or discharge under section 33: intimation

(1)   Where a deed of variation or discharge is granted under section 33(2) of this Act, a proposal to register that deed shall be intimated to such other owners of the units in the community as have not granted the deed.

(2)   Such intimation shall be given by sending a copy of the deed, together
with—
(a)   a notice in, or as near as may be in, the form set out in schedule 4 to this Act;
and
(b)   the explanatory note which immediately follows that form in that schedule.
(3)   Where a deed has been granted as mentioned in subsection (1) above, any person to whom intimation is given under subsection (2) above may, during the period
of eight weeks beginning with the latest date on which intimation of the proposal to
register the deed is so given, apply to the Lands Tribunal for preservation, unvaried,
of the community burden in so far as constituted in favour of, or against, any unit not
all of whose owners have granted the deed.
(4)   Subsections (2) to (4) of section 37 of this Act apply to a deed granted as mentioned in subsection (1) above as they apply in relation to a deed granted as mentioned in section 35 of this Act but with the modifications specified in subsection (5)
below.
(5)   The modifications are that—
(a)   references in the said subsections (2) and (4) to subsection (1) of that section
are to be construed as references to subsection (3) above;
(b)   the reference in the former of those said subsections to no application having been received under section 37 is to be construed as a reference to none having
been received under this section; and
(c)   the reference in the latter of those said subsections to section 36 of this Act is
to be construed as a reference to subsections (1) and (2) above.
(6)   For the purposes of subsection (4) of section 37 of this Act as so applied, if the
person proposing to submit for registration a deed granted as mentioned in subsection (1) above is—
(a)   an individual unable by reason of legal disability, or incapacity, to swear or
affirm as mentioned in the said subsection (4), then a legal representative of that
person may swear or affirm;
(b)   not an individual, then any person authorised to sign documents on its
behalf may swear or affirm,
and any reference in the said subsection (4) to the person so proposing shall be construed accordingly.

35 Variation and discharge of community burdens by owners of adjacent units
(1)   A community burden may be varied or discharged by registering against
each affected unit a deed of variation, or discharge, granted, [. . .] by or on behalf
of the owners of the affected units and by or on behalf of the owners of all units (if
any) which in relation to any of the affected units are adjacent units, except that this
subsection—
(a)   shall not apply where the burden is a facility burden or a service burden or
where the units constitute a sheltered or retirement housing development;
(b)   may expressly be disapplied by the constitutive deed; and
(c)   is subject to sections 36 and 37 of this Act and to any determination of the
Lands Tribunal.
(2)   Subsection (4) of section 33 of this Act applies for the purposes of this section
as it applies for the purposes of that section.

36 Variation and discharge under section 35: intimation
(1)   A proposal to register under section 35 of this Act a deed of variation or discharge shall be intimated to such owners of the units in the community as have not
granted the deed.
(2)   Such intimation may be given—
(a)   by sending a copy of the deed together with—
(i)   a notice in, or as near as may be in, the form set out in schedule 5 to this
Act; and

(ii) the explanatory note which immediately follows that form in that schedule;

(b) by affixing to each affected unit and to—

(i) in a case where there exists one, and only one, lamp post which is situated within one hundred metres of that unit, that lamp post; or

(ii) in a case where there exists more than one lamp post so situated, each of at least two such lamp posts,

a conspicuous notice in the form set out in schedule 6 to this Act; or

(c) in a case where it is not possible to comply with paragraph (b) above, by advertisement in a newspaper circulating in the area of the affected unit.

(3) An advertisement giving intimation under subsection (2)(c) above shall—

(a) identify the land which is the affected unit;

(b) set out the terms of the community burden either in full or by reference to the constitutive deed;

(c) specify the name and address of the person who proposes to register the deed and state that from that person (or from some other person whose name and address are specified in the advertisement) a copy of that deed may be obtained;

(d) state that any owner of a unit who has not granted the deed may apply to the Lands Tribunal for Scotland for the community burden to be preserved but that if no such application is received by a specified date (being the date on which the period mentioned in section 37(1) of this Act expires) the consequence may be that the community burden is varied or discharged in relation to the affected unit.

(4) The person proposing to register the deed shall provide any other person with a copy of that deed if so requested by that other person.

(5) Subsections (6) and (7) of section 21 of this Act apply in relation to affixing, and to a notice affixed, under subsection (2)(b) above as they apply in relation to affixing, and to a notice affixed, under subsection (2)(b) of that section (the reference in paragraph (a)(ii) of the said subsection (6) to the date specified in the notice as the renewal date being construed as a reference to the date so specified by virtue of subsection (2)(b) above).

37 Preservation of community burden in respect of which deed of variation or discharge has been granted as mentioned in section 35(1)

(1) Where a deed of variation or, as the case may be, of discharge has been granted as mentioned in section 35(1) of this Act, any owner of a unit in the community who has not granted the deed may, during the period of eight weeks beginning with the latest date on which intimation of the proposal to register that deed is given under section 36(2) of this Act, apply to the Lands Tribunal for preservation, unvaried, of the community burden in so far as constituted in favour of, or against, any unit not all of whose owners have granted the deed.

(2) A deed of variation or discharge granted as so mentioned shall not, on registration, vary or discharge a community burden in so far as constituted in favour of, or against, any unit not all of whose owners have granted the deed unless, after the expiry of the period mentioned in subsection (1) above, there is endorsed on it (or on an annexation to it referred to in an endorsement on it and identified, on the face of the annexation, as being the annexation so referred to) a certificate executed by a member of the Lands Tribunal, or by their clerk, to the effect that no application in relation to the proposal to register the deed has been received under this section or that any such application which has been received—

(a) has been withdrawn; or

(b) relates to one or more but not to all of the community burdens the terms of which are set out [or referred to] in the deed (any community burden to which it relates being described in the certificate), and where more than one such application has been received the certificate shall relate to both (or as the case may be all) applications.

(3)   A deed of variation or discharge granted as so mentioned does not vary or discharge, in so far as constituted in favour of, or against, any unit not all of whose owners have granted the deed, a burden described by virtue of subsection (2)(b) above.

(4)   A person who proposes to submit a deed of variation or discharge granted as so mentioned for registration shall, before doing so, swear or affirm before a notary public (the deed being endorsed accordingly)—

(a)   that section 36 of this Act has been complied with; and

(b)   as to the date on which the period mentioned in subsection (1) above expires,

but if more than one person so proposes only one of them need so swear or affirm.

(5)   Subsection (2) of section 22 of this Act applies in relation to such a person and for the purposes of subsection (4) above as it applies in relation to a terminator and for the purposes of subsection (1) of that section.

(6)   For the purposes of subsection (1) above, intimation by affixing shall be taken to be given when first the notice is affixed.

PART 3
CONSERVATION AND OTHER PERSONAL REAL BURDENS

Conservation burdens

38   Conservation burdens

(1)   On and after the day on which this section comes into force it shall, subject to subsection (2) below, be competent to create a real burden in favour of a conservation body, or of the Scottish Ministers, for the purpose of preserving, or protecting, for the benefit of the public—

(a)   the architectural or historical characteristics of any land; or

(b)   any other special characteristics of any land (including, without prejudice to the generality of this paragraph, a special characteristic derived from the flora, fauna or general appearance of the land);

and any such burden shall be known as a 'conservation burden'.

(2)   If under subsection (1) above the conservation burden is to be created other than by the conservation body or the Scottish Ministers, the consent of—

(a)   that body to the creation of the burden in its favour; or

(b)   those Ministers to the creation of the burden in their favour,

must be obtained before the constitutive deed is registered.

(3)   It shall not be competent to grant a standard security over a conservation burden.

(4)   The Scottish Ministers may, subject to subsection (5) below, by order, prescribe such body as they think fit to be a conservation body.*

(5)   The power conferred by subsection (4) above may be exercised in relation to a body only if the object, or function, of the body (or, as the case may be, one of its objects or functions) is to preserve, or protect, for the benefit of the public such characteristics of any land as are mentioned in paragraph (a) or (b) of subsection (1) above.

(6)   Where the power conferred by subsection (4) above is exercised in relation to a trust, the conservation body shall be the trustees of the trust.

---

* Prescribed conservation bodies are listed in the Title Conditions (Scotland) Act 2003 (Conservation Bodies) Order 2003 (SSI 2003/453): see p 421 below.

(7)   The Scottish Ministers may, by order, determine that such conservation body as may be specified in the order shall cease to be a conservation body.

39   Assignation
The right to a conservation burden may be assigned or otherwise transferred to any conservation body or to the Scottish Ministers; and any such assignation or transfer takes effect on registration.

40   Enforcement where no completed title
A conservation burden is enforceable by the holder of the burden irrespective of whether the holder has completed title to the burden.

41   Completion of title
Where the holder of a conservation burden does not have a completed title—
  (a)   title may be completed by the holder registering a notice of title; or
  (b)   without completing title, the holder may grant—
      (i)   under section 39 of this Act, a deed assigning the right to the burden; or
      (ii)   under section 48 of this Act, a deed discharging, in whole or in part, the burden,
but unless the deed is one to which section [101 of the Land Registration etc (Scotland) Act 2012 (asp 5)] (circumstances where unnecessary to deduce title) applies, it shall be necessary, in the deed, to deduce title to the burden through the midcouples linking the holder to the person who had the last completed title.

42   Extinction of burden on body ceasing to be conservation body
Where—
  (a)   the holder of a conservation burden is a conservation body or, as the case may be, two or more such bodies; and
  (b)   that body ceases to be such a body, or those bodies cease to be such bodies (whether because an order under section 38(7) of this Act so provides or because the body in question has ceased to exist),
the conservation burden shall, on the body or bodies so ceasing, forthwith be extinguished.

Rural housing burdens

43   Rural housing burdens
(1)   On and after the day on which this section comes into force it shall, subject to subsections (2) and (3) below, be competent to create a real burden [over rural land] which comprises a right of pre-emption in favour of a rural housing body other than by reference to the body's capacity as owner of any land; and any such burden shall be known as a 'rural housing burden'.
(2)   If under subsection (1) above the rural housing burden is to be created other than by the rural housing body, the consent of that body to the creation of the burden in its favour must be obtained before the constitutive deed is registered.
(3)   It shall not be competent to create a rural housing burden on the sale of a property by virtue of section 61 of the Housing (Scotland) Act 1987 (c 26) (secure tenant's right to purchase).
(4)   It shall not be competent to grant a standard security over a rural housing burden.
(5)   The Scottish Ministers may, subject to subsection (6) below, by order, prescribe such body as they think fit to be a rural housing body.*
(6)   The power conferred by subsection (5) above may be exercised in relation

---
* Prescribed rural housing bodies are listed in the Title Conditions (Scotland) Act 2003 (Rural Housing Bodies) Order 2004 (SSI 2004/477): see p 422 below.
---

to a body only if the object, or function, of the body (or, as the case may be one of its principal objects or functions) is to provide housing [or] land for housing.

(7)   Where the power conferred by subsection (5) above is exercised in relation to a trust, the rural housing body shall be the trustees of the trust.

(8)   The Scottish Ministers may, by order, determine that such rural housing body as may be specified in the order shall cease to be a rural housing body.

(9)   In this section, 'rural land' means land other than excluded land ('excluded land' having the same meaning as in Part 2 of the Land Reform (Scotland) Act 2003 (asp 2)).

(10)   Sections 39 to 42 of this Act apply in relation to a rural housing burden and a rural housing body as they apply in relation to a conservation burden and a conservation body but with the modifications that in section 39 the words 'or to the Scottish Ministers' shall be disregarded and in section 42(b) the reference to an order under section 38(7) of this Act shall be construed as a reference to an order under subsection (8) above.

Maritime burdens

44   Maritime burdens

(1)   On and after the day on which this section comes into force, it shall be competent to create a real burden over the sea bed or foreshore in favour of the Crown for the benefit of the public; and any such burden shall be known as a 'maritime burden'.

(2)   The right of the Crown to a maritime burden may not be assigned or otherwise transferred.

(3)   For the purposes of this section—
    (a)   'sea bed' means the bed of the territorial sea adjacent to Scotland; and
    (b)   'territorial sea' includes any tidal waters.

Economic development burdens

45   Economic development burdens

(1)   On and after the day on which this section comes into force it shall, subject to subsection (2) below, be competent to create a real burden in favour of a local authority, or of the Scottish Ministers, for the purpose of promoting economic development; and any such burden shall be known as an 'economic development burden'.

(2)   If under subsection (1) above the economic development burden is to be created other than by the local authority or the Scottish Ministers, the consent of that body or those Ministers to the creation of the burden in their favour must be obtained before the constitutive deed is registered.

(3)   An economic development burden may comprise an obligation to pay a sum of money (the sum or the method of determining it being specified in the constitutive deed) to the local authority or the Scottish Ministers as the case may be.

(4)   It shall not be competent—
    (a)   to grant a standard security over; or
    (b)   to assign the right to,
an economic development burden.

(5)   Sections 40 and 41(a) and (b)(ii) of this Act apply in relation to an economic development burden as they apply in relation to a conservation burden.
    [. . .]

Health care burdens

46   Health care burdens

(1)   On and after the day on which this section comes into force it shall, subject to subsection (2) below, be competent to create a real burden in favour of [. . .] the Scottish Ministers, for the purpose of promoting the provision of

facilities for health care; and any such burden shall be known as a 'health care burden'.

(2) If under subsection (1) above the health care burden is to be created other than by [. . .] the Scottish Ministers, the consent of [. . .] those Ministers to the creation of the burden in [. . .] their favour must be obtained before the constitutive deed is registered.

(3) A health care burden may comprise an obligation to pay a sum of money (the sum or the method of determining it being specified in the constitutive deed) to [. . .] the Scottish Ministers [. . .].

(4) It shall not be competent—
  (a) to grant a standard security over; or
  (b) to assign the right to,
a health care burden.

(5) Sections 40 and 41(a) and (b)(ii) of this Act apply in relation to a health care burden as they apply in relation to a conservation burden.

(6) In subsection (1) above, 'facilities for health care' includes facilities ancillary to health care; as for example (but without prejudice to that generality) accommodation for staff employed to provide health care.

[Climate change burdens]

[46A Climate change burdens
(1) On and after the day on which this section comes into force, it shall be competent to create a real burden in favour of a public body or trust, or of the Scottish Ministers, for the purpose of reducing greenhouse gas emissions; and any such burden shall be known as a 'climate change burden'.

(2) A climate change burden may only consist of an obligation, in the event of the burdened property being developed, for the property to meet specified mitigation and adaptation standards.

(3) For the purposes of this section, a 'public body' means a body listed in Part I or II of the Schedule to the Title Conditions (Scotland) Act 2003 (Conservation Bodies) Order 2003 (SSI 2003/453).]

General

47 Interest to enforce
The holder of a personal real burden is presumed to have an interest to enforce the burden.

48 Discharge
(1) A personal real burden is discharged by registering against the burdened property a deed of discharge granted by or on behalf of the holder of the burden.

(2) In subsection (1) above, 'discharged' means discharged—
  (a) wholly; or
  (b) to such extent as may be specified in the deed of discharge.

PART 4
TRANSITIONAL: IMPLIED RIGHTS OF ENFORCEMENT

Extinction of implied rights of enforcement

49 Extinction
(1) Any rule of law whereby land may be the benefited property, in relation to a real burden, by implication (that is to say, without being nominated in the constitutive deed as the benefited property and without being so nominated in any deed into which the constitutive deed is incorporated) shall cease to have effect on

the appointed day and a real burden shall not, on and after that day, be enforceable by virtue of such rule; but this subsection is subject to subsection (2) below.

(2)   In relation to a benefited property as respects which, on the appointed day, it is competent (taking such rule of law as is mentioned in subsection (1) above still to be in effect) to register a notice of preservation or of converted servitude, subsection (1) above shall apply with the substitution, for the reference to the appointed day, of a reference to the day immediately following the expiry of the period of ten years beginning with the appointed day.

50   Preservation

(1)   Subject to subsection (6) below, an owner of land which is a benefited property by virtue of such rule of law as is mentioned in section 49(1) of this Act may, during the period of ten years beginning with the appointed day, execute and duly register, in (or as nearly as may be in) the form contained in schedule 7 to this Act, a notice of preservation as respects the land; and if the owner does so then the land shall continue to be a benefited property after the expiry of that period (in so far as the burdened property, the benefited property and the real burden are the burdened property, the benefited property, and the real burden identified in the notice of preservation).

(2)   The notice of preservation shall—
   (a)   identify the land which is the burdened property (or any part of that land);
   (b)   identify the land which is the benefited property (or any part of that land);
   (c)   where the person registering the notice does not have a completed title to the benefited property, set out the midcouples linking that person to the person who last had such completed title;
   (d)   set out the terms of the real burden; and
   (e)   set out the grounds, both factual and legal, for describing as a benefited property the land identified in pursuance of paragraph (b) above.

(3)   For the purposes of subsection (1) above, a notice is, subject to section 116 of this Act, duly registered only when registered against both properties identified in pursuance of subsection (2)(a) and (b) above.

(4)   A person submitting any notice for registration under this section shall, before doing so, swear or affirm before a notary public that to the best of the knowledge and belief of the person all the information contained in the notice is true.

(5)   For the purposes of subsection (4) above, if the person is—
   (a)   an individual unable by reason of legal disability, or incapacity, to swear or affirm as mentioned in that subsection, then a legal representative of the person may swear or affirm;
   (b)   not an individual, then any person authorised to sign documents on its behalf may swear or affirm;
and any reference in that subsection to a person shall be construed accordingly.

(6)   Subsection (1) above does not apply as respects a real burden which has been imposed under a common scheme affecting both the burdened and the benefited property.

(7)   This section is subject to section 115 of this Act.

[. . .]

New implied rights of enforcement

52   Common schemes: general

(1)   Where real burdens are imposed under a common scheme and the deed by which they are imposed on any unit, being a deed registered before the appointed day, expressly refers to the common scheme or is so worded that the existence of the common scheme is to be implied (or a constitutive deed incorporated into that

deed so refers or is so worded) then, subject to subsection (2) below, any unit subject to the common scheme by virtue of—

(a) that deed; or

(b) any other deed so registered,

shall be a benefited property in relation to the real burdens.

(2) Subsection (1) above applies only in so far as no provision to the contrary is impliedly (as for example by reservation of a right to vary or waive the real burdens) or expressly made in the deed mentioned in paragraph (a) of that subsection (or in any such constitutive deed as is mentioned in that subsection).

(3) This section confers no right of pre-emption, redemption or reversion.

(4) This section is subject to sections 57(1) and 122(2)(ii) of this Act.

53 Common schemes: related properties

(1) Where real burdens are imposed under a common scheme, the deed by which they are imposed on any unit comprised within a group of related properties being a deed registered before the appointed day, then all units comprised within that group and subject to the common scheme (whether or not by virtue of a deed registered before the appointed day) shall be benefited properties in relation to the real burdens.

(2) Whether properties are related properties for the purposes of subsection (1) above is to be inferred from all the circumstances; and without prejudice to the generality of this subsection, circumstances giving rise to such an inference might include—

(a) the convenience of managing the properties together because they share—

(i) some common feature; or

(ii) an obligation for common maintenance of some facility;

(b) there being shared ownership of common property;

(c) their being subject to the common scheme by virtue of the same deed of conditions; or

(d) the properties each being a flat in the same tenement.

(3) This section confers no right of pre-emption, redemption or reversion.

[(3A) Section 4 of this Act shall apply in relation to any real burden to which subsection (1) above applies as if—

(a) in subsection (2), paragraph (c)(ii);

(b) subsection (4); and

(c) in subsection (5), the words from 'and' to the end,

were omitted.]

(4) This section is subject to sections 57 and 122(2)(ii) of this Act.

54 Sheltered housing

(1) Where by a deed (or deeds) registered before the appointed day real burdens are imposed under a common scheme on all the units in a sheltered or retirement housing development or on all such units except a unit which is used in some special way, each unit shall be a benefited property in relation to the real burdens.

(2) Subsection (1) above is subject to section 122(2)(ii) of this Act.

(3) In this section, 'sheltered or retirement housing development' means a group of dwelling-houses which, having regard to their design, size and other features, are particularly suitable for occupation by elderly people (or by people who are disabled or infirm or in some other way vulnerable) and which, for the purposes of such occupation, are provided with facilities substantially different from those of ordinary dwelling-houses.

(4) Any real burden which regulates the use, maintenance, reinstatement or management—

(a) of—

(i) a facility; or

(ii) a service,

which is one of those which make a sheltered or retirement housing development particularly suitable for such occupation as is mentioned in subsection (3) above; or

(b) of any other facility if it is a facility such as is mentioned in that subsection ,

is in this section referred to as a 'core burden'.

(5)   In relation to a sheltered or retirement housing development—

(a)   section 28 of this Act applies with the following modifications—

(i)   in subsection (1), the reference to the owners of a majority of the units in a community shall, for the purposes of paragraphs (b) and (c) of that subsection, be construed as a reference to the owners of at least two thirds of the units in the development; and

(ii)   in paragraph (c) of subsection (2), the reference to varying or discharging shall be construed as a reference only to varying and that to community burdens as a reference only to real burdens which are not core burdens (the words 'Without prejudice to the generality of subsection (1)(b) above,' which begin the subsection being, for the purposes of that modification, disregarded except in so far as they give meaning to the words 'the powers mentioned there' which immediately follow them);

(b)   section 33 of this Act, in relation to core burdens, applies with the following modifications—

(i)   in subsection (1), the reference to varying or discharging shall, in relation to a deed granted in accordance with subsection (2) of the section, be construed as a reference only to varying; and

(ii)   in subsection (2)(a) the reference to the owners of a majority of the units shall be construed as a reference to the owners of at least two thirds of the units of the development; and

(c)   no real burden relating to a restriction as to any person's age may be varied or discharged by virtue of section 33(2) of this Act.

(6)   This section confers no right of pre-emption, redemption or reversion and is subject to section 57 of this Act.

55   Grant of deed of variation or discharge of community burdens relating to sheltered or retirement housing: community consultation notice

(1)   Where in relation to a sheltered or retirement housing development it is proposed to grant, under section 33(1)(a) or (2) of this Act, a deed of variation or discharge, the proposal shall be intimated to all the owners of the units of the community.

(2)   Such intimation shall be given by sending a notice (a 'community consultation notice') in, or as near as may be in, the form set out in schedule 8 to this Act together with the explanatory note which immediately follows that form in that schedule.

(3)   The deed of variation or discharge shall not be granted before the date specified in the community consultation notice as that by which any comments are to be made, being a date no earlier than that on which expires the period of three weeks beginning with the latest date on which such intimation is given.

(4)   Subsection (4) of section 37 of this Act shall apply in relation to a deed of variation or discharge granted as mentioned in subsection (1) above and to the person giving intimation as it applies in relation to such a deed granted as mentioned in section 35(1) of this Act and to the person proposing to submit the deed but with the modifications that the reference—

(a)   in paragraph (a) of the said subsection (4), to section 36 of this Act is to be construed as a reference to this section; and

(b)   in paragraph (b) of that subsection, to subsection (1) of section 37 of this Act is to be construed as a reference to subsection (3) above.

(5)   For the purposes of subsection (4) of section 37 as so applied, if the person giving intimation is—

(a)   an individual unable by reason of legal disability, or incapacity, to swear or affirm as mentioned in the said subsection (4), then a legal representative of that person may swear or affirm;

(b)   not an individual, then any person authorised to sign documents on its behalf may swear or affirm,

and any reference in the said subsection (4) (as so applied) to the person giving intimation shall be construed accordingly.

56   Facility burdens and service burdens

(1)   Where by a deed registered before the appointed day—

(a)   a facility burden is imposed on land, then—

(i)   any land to which the facility is (and is intended to be) of benefit; and

(ii)   the heritable property which constitutes the facility,

shall be benefited properties in relation to the facility burden;

(b)   a service burden is imposed on land, then any land to which the services are provided shall be a benefited property in relation to the service burden.

(2)   Subsection (1) above is subject to section 57 of this Act; and in paragraph (a) of that subsection 'facility burden' does not include a manager burden.

57   Further provisions as respects rights of enforcement

(1)   Nothing in sections 52 to 56 revives a right of enforcement waived or otherwise lost as at the day immediately preceding the appointed day.

(2)   Where there is a common scheme, and a deed, had it nominated and identified a benefited property, would have imposed under that scheme the real burdens whose terms the deed sets out, the deed shall, for the purposes of sections 25 and 53 to 56 of this Act, be deemed so to have imposed them.

(3)   Sections 53 to 56 do not confer a right of enforcement in respect of anything done, or omitted to be done, in contravention of the terms of a real burden before the appointed day.

[. . .]

PART 5
REAL BURDENS: MISCELLANEOUS

59   Effect of extinction etc on court proceedings

Where by virtue of this Act, a real burden is to any extent discharged, extinguished or made unenforceable, then on and after the day on which that happens (but only to the extent in question)—

(a)   no proceedings for enforcement shall be commenced;

(b)   any such proceedings already commenced shall, in so far as they do not relate to the payment of money, be deemed to have been abandoned on that day and may, without further process and without any requirement that full judicial expenses shall have been paid by the pursuer, be dismissed accordingly; and

(c)   any decree or interlocutor already pronounced in proceedings for such enforcement shall, in so far as it does not relate to the payment of money, be deemed to have been reduced, or as the case may be recalled, on that day.

60   Grant of deed where title not completed: requirements

(1)   Subject to subsection (2) below, where an owner who does not have a completed title to land is to grant, as respects a real burden—

(a)   a constitutive deed;

(b)   a deed of discharge; or

(c)   a deed of variation,

then unless the deed is one to which section [101 of the Land Registration etc (Scotland) Act 2012 (asp 5)] (circumstances where unnecessary to deduce title) applies, it shall be necessary in the deed to deduce title to the land through the midcouples linking the owner to the person who had the last completed title to the land.

(2)   Where, under section 33 of this Act, a manager is to grant a deed of variation or discharge, it shall not be necessary to comply with subsection (1) above [. . .].

61   Contractual liability incidental to creation of real burden

Incidental contractual liability which a constitutive deed (or a deed into which a constitutive deed is incorporated) gives rise to as respects a prospective real burden, ends when the deed has been duly registered and the real burden has become effective.

62   Real burdens of combined type

(1)   Where an obligation is constituted both as a nameable type of real burden (such as, for example, a community burden) and as a real burden which is not of that nameable type, then in so far as a provision of this Act relates specifically to real burdens of the nameable type the obligation shall be taken, for the purpose of determining the effect of that provision, to be constituted as two distinct real burdens.

(2)   The owner of a benefited property which is a unit of a community shall not be entitled to enforce that obligation against the community constituted other than as a community burden or as a burden mentioned in section 1(3) of this Act.

63   Manager burdens

(1)   A real burden (whenever created) may make provision conferring on such person as may be specified in the burden power to—
  (a)   act as the manager of related properties;
  (b)   appoint some other person to be such manager; and
  (c)   dismiss any person appointed by virtue of paragraph (b) above,
a real burden making any such provision being referred to in this Act as a 'manager burden'.

(2)   A power conferred by a manager burden is exercisable only if the person on whom the power is conferred is the owner of one of the related properties.

(3)   The right to a manager burden may be assigned or otherwise transferred; and any such assignation or transfer shall take effect on the sending of written intimation to the owners of the related properties.

(4)   A manager burden shall be extinguished on the earliest of the following dates—
  (a)   the date on which such period as may be specified in the burden expires;
  (b)   the relevant date;
  (c)   the ninetieth day of any continuous period throughout which, by virtue of subsection (2) above, the burden is not exerciseable; and
  (d)   if a manager is dismissed under section 64 of this Act (in [either of the cases mentioned in subsection (6) or (6A)] below), the date of dismissal.

(5)   In this section, the 'relevant date'—
  (a)   in [either of the cases] so mentioned means the date thirty years after the day specified in subsection (7) below;
  (b)   in a case where the manager burden is imposed under a common scheme on any unit of a sheltered or retirement housing development, means the date three years after the day so specified; and
  (c)   in any other case, means the date five years after the day so specified.

(6)   The case is where the manager burden is imposed on the sale, by virtue of section 61 of the Housing (Scotland) Act 1987 (c 26) (secure tenant's right to purchase), of a property by—

(a)   a person such as is mentioned in any of the sub-paragraphs of sub-section (2)(a) of that section; or

(b)   a predecessor of any such person,

to a tenant of such a person.

[(6A)   he case is where—

(a)   a leasehold condition is imposed on the disposal, by virtue of section 61 of the Housing (Scotland) Act 1987 as modified by section 84A of that Act (application of right to buy in cases where landlord is lessee), of a landlord's interest in a property by—

(i)   a person such as is mentioned in any of the sub-paragraphs of subsection (2)(a) of section 61; or

(ii)   a predecessor of such a person, to a tenant of such a person; and

(b)   that condition is converted into a manager burden under section 30 of the Long Leases (Scotland) Act 2012 (asp 9) (conversion of qualifying conditions into manager burdens).]

(7)   The day is that on which the constitutive deed setting out the terms of the burden is registered (and if there is more than one day on which such a constitutive deed is registered in respect of the related properties, then the first such day).

(8)   Where a power conferred by a manager burden is exercisable, any person who is, by virtue of that burden, a manager may not be dismissed—

(a)   under section 28(1)(d) of this Act; or

(b)   in a case other than [those] mentioned in [subsections (6) or (6A)] above, under section 64 of this Act.

(9)   Section 17(1) of the 2000 Act (extinction on appointed day of certain rights of superior) shall not apply to manager burdens.

64   Overriding power to dismiss and appoint manager

(1)   Where a person is the manager of related properties, the owners of two thirds of those properties may—

(a)   dismiss that person; and

(b)   where they do so, appoint some other person to be such manager,

and such actings shall be effective notwithstanding the terms of any real burden affecting those properties; but this section is subject to section 63(8)(b) of this Act.

(2)   If a property is owned by two or more persons in common, then, for the purposes of voting on any proposal to exercise a power conferred by subsection (1) above, the vote allocated as respects the property shall only be counted for or against the proposal if it is the agreed vote of those of them who together own more than a half share of the property.

65   Manager: transitory provisions

Where, immediately before the appointed day, any person is, by virtue of any real burden or purported real burden, ostensibly the manager of related properties that person shall be deemed to have been validly appointed as such.

66   The expression 'related properties'

(1)   Whether properties are related properties for the purposes of sections 63 to 65 of this Act is, subject to subsection (2) below, to be inferred from all the circumstances; and without prejudice to the generality of this section circumstances giving rise to such an inference might include—

(a)   the convenience of managing the properties together because they share—

(i)   some common feature; or

(ii)   an obligation for common maintenance of some facility;

(b) it being evident that the properties constitute a group of properties on which real burdens are imposed under a common scheme; or

(c) there being shared ownership of common property.

(2) For the purposes of section 63(2) of this Act, the following are not related properties—

(a) any property which, being a unit in a sheltered or retirement housing development, is used in some special way (that is to say, is the unit mentioned as an exception in section 54(1) of this Act);

(b) any property to which a development management scheme applies; or

(c) any facility which benefits two or more properties (examples of such a facility being, without prejudice to the generality of this paragraph, a private road and a common area for recreation).

67 Discharge of rights of irritancy

(1) All rights of irritancy in respect of a breach of a real burden are, on the day on which this section comes into force, discharged; and on and after that day—

(a) it shall not be competent to create any such right; and

(b) any proceedings already commenced to enforce any such right shall be deemed abandoned and may, without further process and without any requirement that full judicial expenses shall have been paid by the pursuer, be dismissed accordingly.

(2) Subsection (1)(b) above shall not affect any cause in which final decree (that is to say, any decree or interlocutor which disposes of the cause and is not subject to appeal or review) is granted before the coming into force of this section.

68 Requirement for repetition etc of terms of real burden in future deed

In any deed (whenever executed) a requirement to the effect that the terms of a real burden shall be repeated or referred to in any subsequent deed shall be of no effect.

69 Further provision as respects deeds of variation and of discharge

(1) Where a deed of variation or deed of discharge is granted under this Act, it is not requisite that there be a grantee.

(2) Any such deed so granted may be registered by an owner of the burdened property or by any other person against whom the real burden is enforceable.

(3) Without prejudice to subsection (2) above, a deed of variation or deed of discharge granted under section 33 or 35 of this Act may be registered by a granter.

70 Duty to disclose identity of owner

A person who has title to enforce a real burden (the 'entitled person') may require any person who, at any time, was an owner of the burdened property (the 'second person') to disclose to the entitled person—

(a) the name and address of the owner, for the time being, of such property; or

(b) (if the second person cannot do that) such other information as the second person has which might enable the entitled person to discover that name and address.

PART 6

DEVELOPMENT MANAGEMENT SCHEME

71 Development management scheme

(1) The development management scheme may be applied to any land by registering against the land (in this Part of this Act referred to as 'the development') a deed of application granted by, or on behalf of, the owner of the land or, if and in so far as the terms of the order mentioned in subsection (3) below so admit, may be thus applied with such variations as may be specified in the deed;

and the scheme shall take effect in relation to the development on the date of registration or [. . .]—

    (a) on such later date as may be so specified (the specification being of a fixed date and not, for example, of a date determinable by reference to the occurrence of an event); or

    (b) on the date of registration of such other deed as may be so specified,

and different provision for the taking effect of the scheme may be made for different parts of the development.

(2) The deed of application shall include specification or description of the matters which the scheme requires shall be specified or described and shall in any event include—

    (a) the meaning, in the scheme, of such expressions as 'the development', 'scheme property' and 'unit';

    (b) the name by which any owners' association established by the scheme is to be known, being a name which either ends with the words 'Owners Association' or begins with those words preceded by the definite article;

    (c) the name and address of the first manager of any association so established.

(3) In this Act, 'the development management scheme' means such scheme of rules for the management of land as is set out in an order made, in consequence of this section, under section 104 of the Scotland Act 1998 (c 46) (power to make provision consequential on legislation of, or scrutinised by, the Scottish Parliament) or, in relation to a particular development, that scheme as applied to the development.

72 Application of other provisions of this Act to rules of scheme

In so far as the terms of the order mentioned in section 71(3) of this Act so admit, sections 2, 3, 5, 10 (except subsection (4)(a)), 11, 13, 14, 16, 18, 59 to 61, 67 to 70, 98, 100, 104 and 105 of this Act apply in relation to the rules of the development management scheme as those sections apply in relation to community burdens; except that, for the purposes of that application, in those sections any reference—

    (a) to an owner of a benefited property shall be construed as to the manager of any owners' association established by the scheme;

    (b) to a benefited property shall be construed as to a unit of the development in so far as advantaged by those rules;

    (c) to a burdened property shall be construed as to a unit of the development in so far as constrained by those rules;

    (d) to a community shall be construed as to the development; and

    (e) to a constitutive deed shall be construed as to the deed of application.

73 Disapplication

(1) The development management scheme may be disapplied to the development, or to any part of the development, by an owners' association established by the scheme registering against the development or as the case may be the part, a deed of disapplication granted by that association in accordance with the scheme; and subject to subsection (3) below the disapplication shall take effect—

    (a) on the date of registration; or

    (b) [. . .] on such later date as may be specified in the deed (the specification being of a fixed date and not, for example, of a date determinable by reference to the occurrence of an event).

(2) The deed of disapplication may by means of real burdens provide for the future management and regulation—

    (a) in the case of disapplication to the development, of the development or of any part of the development; or

    (b) in the case of disapplication to a part of the development, of that part or of any part of that part, and section 4 of this Act shall apply accordingly except that paragraph (b) of subsection (2) of that section shall, for the purposes of this subsection, apply with the substitution, for the reference to the owner of the land which is to be the burdened property, of a reference to the owners' association.

(3) The deed of disapplication shall not, on registration, disapply the development management scheme or impose a real burden unless, after the expiry of the period mentioned in subsection (3) of section 74 of this Act, there is endorsed on the deed (or on an annexation to it referred to in an endorsement on it and identified, on the face of the annexation, as being the annexation so referred to) a certificate executed by a member of the Lands Tribunal, or by their clerk, to the effect that no application for preservation of the scheme has been received under that subsection or that any such application which has been received has been withdrawn; and where more than one such application has been received the certificate shall relate to both (or as the case may be all) applications.

(4) An owners' association proposing to submit a deed of disapplication granted as mentioned in subsection (1) above for registration shall, before doing so, swear or affirm before a notary public (the deed being endorsed accordingly)—

(a) that section 74 of this Act has been complied with; and
(b) as to the date on which the period mentioned in subsection (3) of that section expires.

(5) Subsection (2)(b) of section 22 of this Act applies in relation to the owners' association and for the purposes of subsection (4) above as it applies in relation to a terminator and for the purposes of subsection (1) of that section.

74 Intimation of proposal to register deed of disapplication

(1) Where a deed of disapplication is granted as mentioned in section 73(1) of this Act, any proposal to register that deed shall be intimated by the owners' association to every person who is the owner of a unit of the development.

(2) Such intimation to an owner shall be given by sending a copy of the deed, together with a notice stating—

(a) what the effect of registering the deed would be; and
(b) that an owner who has not agreed to the granting of the deed and who wishes to apply to the Lands Tribunal for preservation of the development management scheme must do so by a date specified in the notice (being the date on which the period mentioned in subsection (3) below expires).

(3) A person to whom intimation is given under subsection (2) and who has not so agreed may, during the period of eight weeks beginning with the date by which subsection (1) above has been complied with fully, apply to the Lands Tribunal for preservation of the scheme.

PART 7

SERVITUDES

Positive servitudes

75 Creation of positive servitude by writing: deed to be registered

(1) A deed is not effective to create a positive servitude by express provision unless it is registered against both the benefited property and the burdened property.

(2) It shall be no objection to the validity of a positive servitude that, at the time when the deed was registered as mentioned in subsection (1) above, the same person owned the benefited property and the burdened property; but [. . .] the servitude shall not be created while that person remains owner of both those properties.

(3) Subsection (1) above—

(a) is subject to section 3(1) of the Prescription and Limitation (Scotland) Act

1973 (c 52) (creation of positive servitude by 20 years' possession following execution of deed); and

   (b) does not apply to servitudes such as are mentioned in section 77(1) of this Act.

76   Disapplication of requirement that positive servitude created in writing be of a known type

(1) Any rule of law that requires that a positive servitude be of a type known to the law shall not apply in relation to any servitude created in accordance with section 75(1) of this Act.

(2) Nothing in subsection (1) above permits the creation of a servitude that is repugnant with ownership.

77   Positive servitude of leading pipes etc over or under land

(1) A right to lead a pipe, cable, wire or other such enclosed unit over or under land for any purpose may be constituted as a positive servitude.

(2) It shall be deemed always to have been competent to constitute a right such as is mentioned in subsection (1) above as a servitude.

78   Discharge of positive servitude

A positive servitude—

   (a) which has been registered against the burdened property; or

   (b) which has been noted in, or otherwise appears in, the title sheet of that
   property,

is discharged by deed only on registration of the deed against the burdened property.

Negative servitudes

79   Prohibition on creation of negative servitude

On the appointed day it shall cease to be competent to create a negative servitude.

Transitional

80   Negative servitudes to become real burdens

(1) A negative servitude shall, on the appointed day, cease to exist as such but shall forthwith become a real burden (such a real burden being, for the purposes of this section, referred to as a 'converted servitude').

(2) Subject to subsections (3) and (4) below, a converted servitude shall be extinguished on the expiry of the period of ten years beginning with the appointed day.

(3) If, before the appointed day, a negative servitude was registered against the burdened property or was noted in, or otherwise appeared in, the title sheet of that property the converted servitude shall not be extinguished as mentioned in subsection (2) above.

(4) If, during the period mentioned in subsection (2) above, an owner of the benefited property executes and duly registers, in (or as nearly as may be in) the form contained in schedule 9 to this Act, a notice of converted servitude, the converted servitude shall not be extinguished as mentioned in subsection (2) above (in so far as the burdened property, the benefited property and the converted servitude are, respectively, the burdened property, the benefited property, and the converted servitude identified in the notice of converted servitude).

(5) The notice of converted servitude shall—

   (a) identify the land which is the burdened property (or any part of that land);

   (b) identify the land which is the benefited property (or any part of that land);

   (c) where the person registering the notice does not have a completed title to the benefited property, set out the midcouples linking that person to the person who last had such completed title;

(d) set out the terms of the converted servitude;

(e) include as an annexation the constitutive deed, if any (or a copy of such deed); and

(f) if the land identified for the purposes of paragraph (b) above is not nominated in the constitutive deed, set out the grounds, both factual and legal, for describing that land as a benefited property.

(6) For the purposes of subsection (4) above, a notice is, subject to section 116 of this Act, duly registered only when registered against both properties identified in pursuance of subsection (5)(a) and (b) above.

(7) Subsections (4) and (5) of section 50 of this Act shall apply in respect of a notice of converted servitude as they apply in respect of a notice of preservation.

(8) This section is subject to section 115 of this Act.

81 Certain real burdens to become positive servitudes

(1) A real burden consisting of a right to enter, or otherwise make use of, the burdened property shall, on the appointed day, cease to exist as such but shall forthwith become a positive servitude.

(2) Subsection (1) above—

(a) is subject to section 17(1) of the 2000 Act (extinction on appointed day of certain rights of superior);

(b) does not apply to real burdens such as are mentioned in section 2(3)(a) of this Act.

PART 8
PRE-EMPTION AND REVERSION

Pre-emption

82 Application and interpretation of sections 83 and 84

Sections 83 and 84 of this Act apply to any subsisting right of pre-emption constituted as a title condition which—

(a) was originally created in favour of a feudal superior; or

(b) was created in a deed executed after 1st September 1974,

and for the purposes of sections 83(1)(a) and 84(1)(b) of this Act the person last registered as having title to a personal pre-emption burden or rural housing burden shall be taken to be the holder for a right of pre-emption which that burden comprises.

83 Extinction following pre-sale undertaking

(1) Where, in relation to any burdened property (or, as the case may be, part of such property)—

(a) the holder of a right of pre-emption to which this section applies gives an undertaking (in the form, or as nearly as may be in the form, contained in schedule 10 to this Act) that, subject to such conditions (if any) as the holder may specify in the undertaking, the holder will not exercise that right during such period as may be so specified;

(b) a conveyance in implement of the sale of the burdened property (or part) is registered before the end of that period; and

(c) any conditions specified under paragraph (a) above have been satisfied, such right shall, on registration of such a conveyance, be extinguished unless the right is constituted as a rural housing burden in which case the title condition shall be taken to have been complied with as respects that sale only.

(2) Any undertaking given under subsection (1) above—

(a) is binding on the holder of the right of pre-emption; and

(b) if registered is binding on any successor as holder provided that the undertaking was registered before the successor completed title.

84 Extinction following offer to sell

(1) If in relation to a right of pre-emption to which this section applies—

(a) an event specified in the constitutive deed as an event on the occurrence of which such right may be exercised occurs; and

(b) the owner of the burdened property makes, in accordance with subsections (2) to (6) below, an offer to sell that property (or, as the case may be, part of that property) to the holder of such right,

then such right shall, in relation to that property (or part), be extinguished unless it is constituted as a rural housing burden in which case the title condition shall be taken to have been complied with as respects that event only.

(2) An offer shall be in writing and shall comply with section 2 or 9B of the Requirements of Writing (Scotland) Act 1995 (c 7) (requirements for formal validity of certain documents).

(3) An offer shall be open for acceptance during whichever is the shorter of—

(a) the period of 21 days, or where the right is constituted as a rural housing burden 42 days, beginning with the day on which the offer is sent;

(b) such number of days beginning with that day as may be specified in the constitutive deed.

(4) An offer shall be made on such terms as may be set out, or provided for, in the constitutive deed; but in so far as no such terms are set out, an offer shall be made on such terms (including any terms so provided for) as are reasonable in the circumstances.

(5) Where—

(a) an offer is sent in accordance with this section; and

(b) the holder of the right does not, within the time allowed by virtue of subsection (3) above for acceptance of the offer, inform (in writing, whether or not transmitted by electronic means) the owner of the burdened property that the holder considers, giving reasons for so considering, that the terms on which the offer is made are unreasonable,

the terms of the offer shall, for the purposes of subsection (4) above, be deemed to be reasonable.

(6) If the holder of a right cannot by reasonable inquiry be identified or found, an offer may be sent to the Extractor of the Court of Session; and for the purposes of this section an offer so sent shall be deemed to have been sent to the holder.

85 Ending of council's right of pre-emption as respects certain churches

In a scheme framed under subsection (1) of section 22 of the Church of Scotland (Property and Endowments) Act 1925 (c 33) (schemes for the ownership, maintenance and administration of churches etc), any provision made in accordance with subsection (2)(h) of that section (council's right of pre-emption) shall cease to have effect.

Reversion

86 Reversions under School Sites Act 1841

(1) In a case where—

(a) land would, under the third proviso to section 2 of the School Sites Act 1841 (4 & 5 Vict c 38) (the '1841 Act') revert (but for this section) to any person or has so reverted; but

(b) the person has not, before the day on which this section comes into force, completed title to the land, subsections (2) to (9) below shall (to the extent that subsection (9) admits) apply in place of that proviso and be deemed always to have applied and nothing shall be void or challengeable by virtue of that proviso.

(2)   If the circumstances are that a contract of sale of the land has been concluded by, or on behalf of, the education authority, the authority shall pay to the person, where the cessation of use by virtue of which the land would (but for this section) revert, or has reverted, occurred—

(a)   before the day on which this section comes into force, an amount equal to the open market value of the land as at that day;

(b)   on or after that day, an amount equal to the open market value of the land as at the date of cessation less any improvement value as at that date.

(3)   If the circumstances are other than is mentioned in subsection (2) above—

(a)   the person may specify an obligation mentioned in paragraph (a), or as the case may be (b), of subsection (4) below and require the authority to comply therewith, which subject to paragraph (b) below the authority shall do;

(b)   the authority may, if the person requires under paragraph (a) above performance of the obligation mentioned in paragraph (a)(i), or as the case may be (b)(i), of that subsection, instead elect to make payment to the person of such amount as is mentioned in paragraph (a)(ii), or as the case may be (b)(ii), of that subsection provided that such election is timeous.

(4)   The obligations are, where the cessation of use by virtue of which the ownership of the land would (but for this section) revert, or has reverted, occurred—

(a)   before the day on which this section comes into force—

(i)   to convey the land to the person;

(ii)   to make a payment to the person of an amount equal to the open market value of the land as at that day; or

(b)   on or after that day—

(i)   on payment by the person of any improvement value as at the date of cessation, to convey the land to the person;

(ii)   to make a payment to the person of an amount equal to the open market value of the land as at the date of cessation less any improvement value as at that date.

(5)   Any dispute arising in relation to the assessment of the value for the purposes of this section of any land, buildings or structures may be referred to, and determined by, the Lands Tribunal.

(6)   For the purposes of this section—

'education authority' has the meaning given by section 135(1) of the Education (Scotland) Act 1980 (c 44) except that if title to the land has been transferred to any person by any enactment it means that person; and

'improvement value' means such part of the value of the land as is attributable to any building (or other structure) on the land other than any such building (or other structure) erected by or at the expense of—

(a)   the person who made the gift, sale or exchange of the land under section 2 of the 1841 Act; or

(b)   any predecessor, as owner of such land, of that person.

(7)   References in subsection (1) above to the third proviso to section 2 of the 1841 Act shall be construed as including references to that proviso as applied by virtue of any other enactment; and for the purposes of that construction, the reference in paragraph (a) of the definition of 'improvement value' in subsection (6) above to the said section 2 shall be construed as a reference to the provision corresponding to that section in such other enactment.

(8)   The reference in subsection (3)(b) above to an election being timeous is to its being notified to the person within three months after the requirement in question is made.

(9)   Subsections (2) to (8) above do not apply where the person has, before the day on which this section comes into force, accepted an offer of compensation in respect of the land or concluded a contract for, or accepted, a conveyance of the land.

(10)   Subsections (1)(b) and (2) of section 67 of this Act shall apply in relation to any proceedings already commenced by virtue of the proviso mentioned in subsection (1)(a) above as they apply in relation to any proceedings already commenced as mentioned in the said subsection (1)(b).

87   Right to petition under section 7 of Entail Sites Act 1840

(1)   In a case where—

(a)   it would be competent but for this section, section 50(1) of the 2000 Act (disentailment on appointed day) and the repeal of the Entail Sites Act 1840 by that Act for a person to apply by petition under section 7 of that Act of 1840 (petition praying to have feu charter or other right or lease declared to be forfeited etc); but

(b)   the person has not, before the day on which this section comes into force, accepted an offer of compensation in respect of the right so to apply,

subsections (2) to (6) and (8) of section 86 of this Act shall, in place of the said section 7 but with the modifications specified in subsection (2) below, apply.

(2)   The modifications are that—

(a)   for any reference to the education authority there shall be substituted a reference to the parties in whose favour the feu charter or lease was granted, or the successors other than by purchase for value of those parties;

(b)   in each of subsections (2) and (4), for the word 'revert' there shall be substituted 'be forfeit' and for the word 'reverted' there shall be substituted 'have been forfeit'; and

(c)   in subsection (6), for paragraph (a) of the definition of 'improvement value' there shall be substituted—

'(a)   the person who granted the feu or lease under section 1 of the Entail Sites Act 1840 (3 & 4 Vict c 48) (grants for sites of churches etc);'.

(3)   After such obligations as arise by virtue of this section are met or prescribe, the purposes for which the land in question was feued or leased under the said Act of 1840 need no longer be given effect.

(4)   Subsections (1)(b) and (2) of section 67 of this Act shall apply in relation to any application already made by petition as mentioned in subsection (1)(a) above as they apply in relation to any proceedings already commenced as mentioned in the said subsection (1)(b).

88–89 [*Amendment provisions*]

PART 9
TITLE CONDITIONS: POWERS OF LANDS TRIBUNAL

90   Powers of Lands Tribunal as respects title conditions

(1)   Subject to sections 97, 98 and 104 of this Act and to subsections (3) to (5) below, the Lands Tribunal may by order, on the application of—

(a)   an owner of a burdened property or any other person against whom a title condition (or purported title condition) is enforceable (or bears to be enforceable)—

(i)   discharge it, or vary it, in relation to that property; or

(ii)   if the title condition is a real burden or a rule of a development management scheme, determine any question as to its validity, applicability or enforceability or as to how it is to be construed;

(b)   an owner of a benefited property, renew or vary, in relation to that property, a title condition which is—

(i)   a real burden in respect of which intimation of a proposal to execute and register a notice of termination has been given under section 21 of this Act; or

    (ii)   a real burden or servitude affected by a proposal to register a conveyance, being a proposal of which notice has been given under section 107(4) of this Act; or

    (c) an owner of a unit in a community, preserve as mentioned in section 34(3) or 37(1) of this Act, a community burden in respect of which intimation of a proposal to register a deed of variation or discharge has been given under section 34(1) or 36(1) of this Act;

    (d) an owner of a unit of the development to which applies a development management scheme in respect of which intimation of a proposal to register a deed of disapplication has been given under subsection (1) of section 74 of this Act, preserve the scheme;

    (e) the owners' association of a development to which applies a development management scheme in respect of which intimation of a proposal to register a conveyance, being a proposal of which notice has been given as mentioned in subsection (b)(ii) above, preserve the scheme;

but where the Lands Tribunal refuse an application under paragraph (b) or (c) above wholly, or an application under paragraph (b) partly, they shall in relation to the benefited property discharge the title condition, wholly or partly, accordingly or as the case may be shall in relation to the units not all of whose owners have granted the deed vary or discharge the community burden accordingly and where they refuse an application under paragraph (d) or (e) above, they shall disapply the development management scheme.

(2)   Paragraph (b) of subsection (1) above applies in relation to the application of a holder of a personal real burden as it applies to the application of an owner of a benefited property except that, for the purposes of any application made by virtue of this subsection, the words 'in relation to that property' in paragraph (b) shall be disregarded as shall the words 'in relation to the benefited property' in what follows paragraph (e) in that subsection.

(3)   It shall not be competent to make an application under subsection (1) above in relation to a title condition of a kind specified in schedule 11 to this Act.

(4)   It shall not be competent to make an application under subsection (1)(b), (c), (d) or (e) above—

    (a) after the renewal date, or as the case may be the date specified by virtue of section 107(6)(d)(ii) of, or the expiry of the period mentioned in section 34(3), 37(1) or 74(3) of, this Act, except with the consent of the terminator or as the case may be of—

        (i) the person proposing to register the conveyance or the deed of variation or discharge, or

        (ii) the owners' association; or

    (b) after there has been, in relation to the proposal, endorsement under section 23(1) or, as the case may be, execution of a relevant certificate applied for by virtue of section 107(1)(b), or endorsement under section 37(2) or 73(3), of this Act.

(5)   Variation which would impose a new obligation or would result in a property becoming a benefited property shall not be competent on an application—

    (a) under subsection (1)(a)(i) above unless the owner of the burdened property consents; or

    (b) under subsection (1)(b) above.

(6)   Subject to section 97(1) of this Act and to subsections (9) and (10) below, an order discharging [. . .] or varying a title condition may—

    (a) where made under paragraph (a)(i) of subsection (1) above, direct the applicant; or

    (b) where made by virtue of the refusal of an application under paragraph (b) or (c) of that subsection, direct the terminator or, as the case may be,

the person proposing to register the conveyance or deed of variation or discharge,
to pay to any person who in relation to the title condition was an owner of the benefited property or, where there is no benefited property, to any holder of the title condition, such sum as the Lands Tribunal may think it just to award under one, but not both, of the heads mentioned in subsection (7) below.

(7)   The heads are—

(a)   a sum to compensate for any substantial loss or disadvantage suffered by, as the case may be—

(i)   the owner, as owner of the benefited property; or

(ii)   the holder of the title condition,

in consequence of the discharge [or variation];

(b)   a sum to make up for any effect which the title condition produced, at the time when it was created, in reducing the consideration then paid or made payable for the burdened property.

(8)   Subject to section 97(1) of this Act and to subsection (11) below, an order discharging, renewing or varying a title condition may impose on the burdened property a new title condition or vary a title condition extant at the time the order is made.

[(8A)   An order disapplying the development management scheme shall, where the deed of [disapplication] makes such provision as is mentioned in section 73(2) of this Act, impose the real burdens in question.]

(9)   A direction under subsection (6) above shall be made only if the person directed consents.

(10)   Where an application under subsection (1)(b)(ii) above is refused, wholly or partly, any direction under subsection (6) above for payment to that person may be made only if that application was made by virtue of subsection (2) above.

(11)   An imposition under subsection (8) above shall be made only if the owner of the burdened property consents.

(12)   The jurisdiction conferred by subsection (1) above includes power, in relation to an application under paragraph (a)(ii) only of that subsection, to decline (with reason stated) to proceed to determine the question.

91   Special provision as to variation or discharge of community burdens

(1)   Without prejudice to section 90(1)(a)(i) of this Act, an application may be made to the Lands Tribunal under this section by owners of at least one quarter of the units in a community for the variation ('variation' including imposition) or discharge of a community burden as it affects, or as the case may be would affect, all or some of the units in the community.

(2)   In the case of an application made by owners of some only of the units in the community, the units affected need not be the units which they own.

(3)   Subsections (6), (7) and (9) of section 90 of this Act shall apply in relation to an order made by virtue of subsection (1) above varying or discharging a community burden as they apply to an order under subsection (1)(a)(i) of that section discharging a title condition.

92   Early application for discharge: restrictive provisions

In the constitutive deed, provision may be made to the effect that there shall be no application under section 90(1)(a)(i) or 91(1) of this Act in respect of a title condition before such date as may be specified in the deed (being a date not more than five years after the creation of the title condition); and if such provision is so made it shall not be competent to make an application under the section in question before that date.

93   Notification of application

(1)   The Lands Tribunal shall, on receipt of an application under—

(a) section 90(1)(a) or 91(1) of this Act, give notice of that application to any person who, not being the applicant, appears to them to fall within any of the following descriptions—
    (i)   an owner of the burdened property;
    (ii) an owner of any benefited property;
    (iii) a holder of the title condition;
(b) section 90(1)(b) of this Act, give such notice to any person who appears to them to fall within any of the following descriptions—
    (i)   in the case mentioned in sub-paragraph (i) of that provision, the terminator;
    (ii) an owner of the burdened property; or
    (iii) in the case mentioned in sub-paragraph (ii) of that provision, the person proposing to register the conveyance;
(c) section 90(1)(c) of this Act, give such notice to the person proposing to register the deed of variation or discharge;
(d) section 90(1)(d) of this Act, give such notice to the owners' association; or
(e) section 90(1)(e) of this Act, give notice to the person proposing to register the conveyance,
and subject to subsection (2) below shall do so by sending the notice.
(2) Notice under subsection (1) above may be given by advertisement, or by such other method as the Lands Tribunal think fit, if—
(a) given to a person who cannot, by reasonable inquiry, be identified or found;
(b) the person to whom it is given, being a person given notice by virtue of paragraph (a)(ii) of that subsection, does not appear to them to have any interest to enforce the title condition; or
(c) so many people require to be given notice that, in the opinion of the Lands Tribunal, it is not reasonably practicable to send it.
(3) The Lands Tribunal may also give notice of the application, by such means as they think fit, to any other person.

94 Content of notice
The Lands Tribunal shall—
(a) in any notice given by them under section 93 of this Act—
    (i)   summarise or reproduce the application;
    (ii) set a date (being a date no earlier than twenty-one days after the notice is given) by which representations to them as respects the application may be made;
    (iii) state the fee which must accompany any such representations; and
    (iv) in the case of an application for the discharge, renewal or variation of a real burden, or for the preservation of a real burden or development management scheme, state that if the application is not opposed it may be granted without further inquiry; and
(b) in any notice so given (other than by advertisement) in respect of an application under section 90(1)(a) or 91(1) of this Act, also set out the name and address of every person to whom the notice is being sent.

95 Persons entitled to make representations
The persons entitled to make representations as respects an application under section 90(1) or 91(1) of this Act are—
(a) any person who has title to enforce the title condition;
(b) any person against whom the title condition is enforceable;
(c) in the case mentioned in paragraph (b)(ii) or (e) of section 90(1), the person proposing to register the conveyance; and
(d) in the case mentioned in paragraph (d) of that section, the owners' association and the owner of any unit of the development.

96   Representations

(1)   Representations made by any person to the Lands Tribunal as respects an application under section 90(1) or 91(1) of this Act shall be in writing and shall comprise a statement of the facts and contentions upon which the person proposes to rely.

(2)   For the purposes of this Act, representations are made when they are received by the Lands Tribunal with the requisite fee; and a person sending such representations shall forthwith send a copy of them to the applicant.

(3)   Notwithstanding section 94(a)(ii) of this Act, the Lands Tribunal may if they think fit accept representations made after the date set under that section.

97   Granting unopposed application for discharge or renewal of real burden

(1)   Subject to subsection (2) below, an unopposed application duly made for—
(a)   the discharge or variation;
(b)   the renewal or variation; or
(c)   the preservation,
of a real burden shall be granted as of right; and as respects an application under paragraph (a) above neither subsection (6)(a) nor subsection (8) of section 90 of this Act shall apply in relation to the order discharging or as the case may be varying the real burden.

(2)   Subsection (1) above does not apply as respects an application—
(a)   for the discharge or variation of a facility burden;
(b)   for the discharge or variation of a service burden; or
(c)   under section 91(1) of this Act for the discharge or variation of a community burden imposed on any unit of a sheltered or retirement housing development.

(3)   An application is unopposed for the purposes of—
(a)   subsection (1)(a) above if, as at the date on which the application falls to be determined, no representations opposing it have been made under section 96 of this Act either by an owner of any benefited property or by a holder of a personal real burden;
(b)   subsection (1)(b) above if, as at that date, no representations opposing the application have been made under that section by the terminator or as the case may be the person proposing to register the conveyance; or
(c)   subsection (1)(c) above if, as at that date, no representations opposing the application have been made under that section by the person proposing to register the deed of variation or discharge, or all such representations which have been so made have been withdrawn.

(4)   In granting an application under subsection (1)(b) or (c) above, the Lands Tribunal may, as they think fit, order either—
(a)   the person who intimated the proposal to execute and register the notice of termination or as the case may be the deed of variation or discharge or the conveyance; or
(b)   any other person who succeeded that person as terminator or proposer,
to pay to the applicant a specific sum in respect of the expenses incurred by the applicant or such proportion of those expenses as the Tribunal think fit.

98   Granting other applications for variation, discharge, renewal or preservation of title condition

An application for the variation, discharge, renewal or preservation, of a title condition shall, unless it falls to be granted as of right under section 97(1) of this Act, be granted by the Lands Tribunal only if they are satisfied, having regard to the factors set out in section 100 of this Act, that—
(a)   except in the case of an application under subsection (3) of section 34 or, in respect of a deed of variation or discharge granted by the owner of an adjacent unit, subsection (1) of section 37 of this Act, it is reasonable to grant the application; or

(b) in such a case, the variation or discharge in question—
  (i) is not in the best interests of [all the owners (taken as a group) of] the units in the community; or
  (ii) is unfairly prejudicial to one or more of those owners.

99 Granting applications as respects development management schemes

(1) An unopposed application for preservation of a development management scheme shall be granted as of right.

(2) An application is unopposed for the purposes of subsection (1) above if, as at the date on which the application falls to be determined, no representations opposing it have been made under section 96 of this Act by the owners' association or, as the case may be, by the person proposing to register the conveyance.

(3) In granting an application under subsection (1) above, the Lands Tribunal may order the owners' association to pay to the applicant a specific sum in respect of the expenses incurred by the applicant or such proportion of those expenses as the Tribunal think fit.

(4) An application for the preservation of a development management scheme shall, unless it falls to be granted as of right under subsection (1) above, be granted by the Lands Tribunal only if they are satisfied, in the case of an application—

(a) under paragraph (d) of section 90(1) of this Act, that the disapplication of the development management scheme [or a real burden imposed by the deed of disapplication] is not in the best interests of [all the owners (taken as a group)] of the units of the development or is unfairly prejudicial to one or more of those owners; or

(b) under paragraph (e) of that section, that having regard to the purpose for which the land is being acquired by the person proposing to register the conveyance it is reasonable to grant the application.

100 Factors to which the Lands Tribunal are to have regard in determining applications etc

The factors mentioned in section 98 of this Act are—

(a) any change in circumstances since the title condition was created (including, without prejudice to that generality, any change in the character of the benefited property, of the burdened property or of the neighbourhood of the properties);

(b) the extent to which the condition—
  (i) confers benefit on the benefited property; or
  (ii) where there is no benefited property, confers benefit on the public;

(c) the extent to which the condition impedes enjoyment of the burdened property;

(d) if the condition is an obligation to do something, how—
  (i) practicable; or
  (ii) costly,
it is to comply with the condition;

(e) the length of time which has elapsed since the condition was created; (f) the purpose of the title condition;

(g) whether in relation to the burdened property there is the consent, or deemed consent, of a planning authority, or the consent of some other regulatory authority, for a use which the condition prevents;

(h) whether the owner of the burdened property is willing to pay compensation;

(i) if the application is under section 90(1)(b)(ii) of this Act, the purpose for which the land is being acquired by the person proposing to register the conveyance; and

(j) any other factor which the Lands Tribunal consider to be material.

101   Regulation of applications to Lands Tribunal

The Scottish Ministers may make rules regulating any application under this Act to the Lands Tribunal and may in particular make provision, in those rules, as to the evidence which may be required for such an application.

102   Referral to Lands Tribunal of notice dispute

(1)   Any dispute arising in relation to a notice registered under section 50 or 80 of this Act may be referred to the Lands Tribunal; and in determining the dispute the Tribunal may make such order as they think fit discharging or, to such extent as may be specified in the order, restricting the notice in question.

(2)   In any referral under subsection (1) above, the burden of proving any disputed question of fact shall be on the person relying on the notice.

(3)   An extract of any order made under subsection (1) above may be registered and the order shall take effect as respects third parties on such registration.

103   Expenses

(1)   The Lands Tribunal may, in determining an application made under this Part of this Act, make such order as to expenses as they think fit but shall have regard, in particular, to the extent to which the application, or any opposition to the application, is successful.

(2)   Subsection (1) above is without prejudice to sections 97(4) and 99(3) of this Act.

104   Taking effect of orders of Lands Tribunal etc

(1)   The Scottish Ministers may, after consultation with the Scottish Committee of the [Administrative Justice and Tribunals Council], make rules as to when an order of the Lands Tribunal on an application under section 90(1) or 91(1) of this Act shall take effect.

(2)   An order under subsection (1)(a)(i), (b) or (c) of section 90, under subsection (1) of that section on the refusal (wholly or partly as the case may be) of an application under paragraph (b) or (c) of that subsection or under section 91(1) of this Act which has taken effect in accordance with rules made under subsection (1) above may be registered against the burdened property by any person who was a party to the application or who was, under section 95 of this Act, entitled to make representations as respects the application; and on the order being so registered the title condition to which it relates is discharged (wholly or partly), renewed (wholly or partly), imposed, preserved or varied according to the terms of the order.

(3)   An order—

(a)   which disapplies a development management scheme, being an order under subsection (1) of section 90 of this Act, or preserves it under paragraph (d) or (e) of that subsection; and

(b)   which has taken effect in accordance with rules so made,

may be registered against the units of the development by the owners' association or as the case may be by an owner of a unit of the development or the person proposing to register the conveyance; and on the order being so registered the scheme [whether or not it imposes new burdens] is disapplied or preserved [and the burdens imposed] as the case may be.

(4)   Any enforceability which the obligation in question has as a contractual obligation shall be unaffected by such an order.

PART 10

MISCELLANEOUS

Consequential alterations to Land Register

105   Alterations to Land Register consequential upon registering certain deeds

(1)   Subject to subsection (2) below, in registering in the Register of Sasines a document mentioned in subsection (3) below the Keeper of the Registers of

Scotland may make such consequential alterations to the Land Register of Scotland as the Keeper considers requisite.

(2)   In so registering such a document, or in registering it in the Land Register, by virtue of [—

(a)   section 18, 19 or 20 of the 2000 Act;

(b)   section 15 or 18 of the Long Leases (Scotland) Act 2012 (asp 9); or

(c)   section 4(5), 50, 75 or 80 of this Act,]

the Keeper shall make such consequential alterations as are mentioned in subsection (1) above.

(3)   The documents are—

(a)   any decree, deed or other document which varies, discharges, renews, real-lots, preserves or imposes a real burden or servitude; and

[(aa)   any—

(i)   notice under section 14 of the Long Leases (Scotland) Act 2012; or

(ii)   agreement under section 17 of that Act,

which converts a qualifying condition (within the meaning of that Act) into a real burden;]

(b)   any deed which comprises a conveyance of part of—

(i)   the benefited property; or

(ii)   the burdened property.

Compulsory acquisition of land

106   Extinction of real burdens and servitudes etc on compulsory acquisition of land

(1)   If land is acquired compulsorily by virtue of a compulsory purchase order [to which this section applies] then, except in so far as the terms of—

(a)   the order; or

(b)   the conveyance in implement of such acquisition,

provide otherwise, on registration of the conveyance, any real burden, or servitude, over the land shall be extinguished and any development management scheme applying as respects the land disapplied.

(2)   Without prejudice to the generality of the exception in subsection (1) above, such terms as are mentioned in that exception may provide—

(a)   for the variation of any of the real burdens or servitudes;

(b)   that there shall be such extinction only—

(i)   of certain of the real burdens and servitudes;

(ii)   in relation to certain parts of the burdened property; or

(iii)   in respect of the enforcement rights of the owners of certain of the benefited properties.

(3)   If the compulsory purchase order provides for an exception such as is mentioned in subsection (1) above, the conveyance in implement of the acquisition shall not, unless the owners of the benefited properties consent, or as the case may be the owners' association or the holder of any personal real burden consents, be registrable if its terms do not conform in that regard.

(4)   Where a personal real burden is extinguished by virtue of subsection (1) above, such person as immediately before the extinction held the right to enforce the burden shall be entitled to receive compensation from the acquiring authority in question for any loss thereby occasioned that person.

[4A)   This section applies to a compulsory purchase order in respect of which notice is given under—

(a)   paragraph 3 of the First Schedule to the Acquisition of Land (Authorisation Procedure) (Scotland) Act 1947 (c 42) on or after the day of which section 109; or

(b)   paragraph 2 of Schedule 5 to the Forestry Act 1967 (c 10) on or after the day on which section 110,

of this Act comes into force.]

(5)   In this section—

'compulsory purchase order' has the meaning given by section 1(1) of the Acquisition of Land (Authorisation Procedure) (Scotland) Act 1947 (c 42) (procedure for compulsory purchase of land by local authorities etc) except that it includes a compulsory purchase order made under the Forestry Act 1967 (c 10); and

'conveyance' means—

(a)   a—

(i)   disposition;

(ii)   notice of title; or

(iii)   notarial instrument,

which includes a reference to the application of subsection (1) above;

(b)   a conveyance in the form set out in Schedule A to the Lands Clauses Consolidation (Scotland) Act 1845 (c 19); or

(c)   a general vesting declaration (as defined in paragraph 1(1) of Schedule 15 to the Town and Country Planning (Scotland) Act 1997 (c 8)).

107   Extinction of real burdens and servitudes etc where land acquired by agreement

(1)   If—

(a)   land acquired by a person by agreement could have been so acquired by that person compulsorily by virtue of any enactment; and

(b)   the person, having complied with subsection (4) below, registers a conveyance in implement of such acquisition together with a relevant certificate,

then, except in so far as the terms of the conveyance provide otherwise, on such registration any real burden, or servitude, over the land shall be extinguished and any development management scheme applying as respects the land disapplied.

(2)   Registration under subsection (1) above shall not vary or extinguish a title condition which is the subject of an application disclosed by the certificate in so far as that title condition—

(a)   is constituted in favour of the property of which the applicant is owner; or

(b)   is a personal real burden of which the applicant is holder, or disapply a development management scheme, described in the certificate; but the conveyance may be registered again, together with a further such certificate, under that subsection, the effect of the later registration being determined by reference to the further certificate rather than to the earlier certificate.

(3)   Subsection (2) of section 106 of this Act shall apply in relation to the exception in subsection (1) above as it applies in relation to the exception in subsection (1) of that section.

(4)   The person proposing to register the conveyance shall, before doing so in accordance with subsection (1)(b) above—

(a)   if such registration would extinguish a title condition, give notice to the owner of the benefited property (or in the case of a personal real burden to the holder of that burden); and

(b)   if it would disapply a development management scheme, give notice to the owners' association,

of the matters mentioned in subsection (6) below.

(5)   Any person to whom notice is given under subsection (4) above may, on or before the date specified by virtue of subsection (6)(d)(ii) below, apply to the Lands Tribunal for renewal or variation of the title condition or as the case may be preservation of the development management scheme.

(6)   The matters are—

(a)   a description of the land;

(b)   the name and address of the person proposing to register the conveyance;

(c)   the fact that, by virtue of this section (and subject to the terms of the conveyance), real burdens and servitudes over the land may be extinguished and any development management scheme disapplied;

(d)   that the person given notice—

    (i)   may obtain information from the person acquiring the land about any entitlement to compensation; and

    (ii)   will require to apply to the Lands Tribunal for Scotland, by a date specified in the notice, if the title condition is to be renewed or varied under paragraph (b) of section 90(1) of this Act or as the case may be the development management scheme preserved under paragraph (e) of that section.

(7)   The date so specified may be any date which is not fewer than twenty-one days after the notice is given (intimation by affixing being taken, for the purposes of this subsection, to be given when first the notice is affixed).

(8)   Notice under subsection (4)(a) above may be given—

(a)   by sending;

(b)   by advertisement;

(c)   by affixing a conspicuous notice to the burdened property and to—

    (i)   in a case where there exists one, and only one, lamp post within one hundred metres of that property, that lamp post; or

    (ii)   in a case where there exists more than one lamp post so situated, each of at least two such lamp posts; or

(d)   by such other method as the person acquiring the land thinks fit,

and notice under subsection (4)(b) above may be given by sending or by such other means as that person thinks fit.

(9)   Subsections (6) and (7) of section 21 of this Act apply in relation to affixing, and to a notice affixed, under subsection (8)(c) above as they apply in relation to affixing, and to a notice affixed, under subsection (2)(b) of that section (the reference in paragraph (a)(ii) of the said subsection (6) to the date specified in the notice as the renewal date being construed as a reference to the date specified by virtue of subsection (6)(d)(ii) above).

(10)   In this section—

'conveyance' has the same meaning as in section 106(5) of this Act except that the reference, in paragraph (a) of the definition of that expression in that section, to subsection (1) of that section shall be read as a reference to that subsection of this section and paragraph (c) of that definition shall be disregarded; and

'relevant certificate' means a certificate executed, on or after the date specified by virtue of subsection (6)(d)(ii) above, by a member of the Lands Tribunal, or by their clerk, to the effect that no application in relation to the proposal to register the conveyance has been received under section 90(1)(b)(ii) or (e) of this Act or that any such application which has been received—

(a)   has been withdrawn; or

(b)   relates, in the case of an application under section 90(1)(b)(ii), (either or both)—

    (i)   to one or more but not to all of the title conditions over the land (any title condition to which it relates being described in the certificate);

    (ii)   to one or more but not to all (or probably or possibly not to all) of the benefited properties (any benefited property to which it relates being described in the certificate),

and where more than one such application has been received the certificate shall relate to both (or as the case may be to all) applications.

(11)   Any application for a relevant certificate shall be made in the form set out in schedule 12 to this Act.

Miscellaneous

115 Further provision as respects notices of preservation or of converted servitude

(1) This section applies in relation to a notice of preservation or of converted servitude.

(2) Except where it is not reasonably practicable to do so, the owner of the benefited property shall, before executing the notice, send to the owner of the burdened property a copy of—

(a) the notice;

(b) the explanatory note set out in whichever schedule to this Act relates to the notice; and

(c) in the case of a notice of converted servitude, the constitutive deed (if any).

(3) The owner of the benefited property shall, in the notice, state either—

(a) that a copy of the notice has been sent in accordance with subsection (2) above; or

(b) that it was not reasonably practicable for such a notice to be so sent.

(4) However many the benefited or burdened properties may be, if the terms of the real burdens or converted servitudes are set out in a single constitutive deed, execution and registration may be accomplished in a single notice.

(5) The Keeper of the Registers of Scotland shall not be required to determine whether a person submitting a notice for registration has complied with subsection (2) above.

(6) Where—

(a) a notice submitted before the expiry of the period of ten years which commences immediately after the appointed day is rejected by the Keeper; but

(b) a court or the Lands Tribunal then determines that the notice is registrable, the notice may, if not registered before that expiry, be registered—

(i) within two months after the determination is made; but

(ii) before such date after that expiry as the Scottish Ministers may by order prescribe;

and any notice registered under this subsection shall be treated as if it had been registered before that expiry.

(7) For the purposes of subsection (6) above, the application to the court, or to the Lands Tribunal, which has resulted in the determination shall require to have been made within such period as the Scottish Ministers may by order prescribe.

(8) In subsection (6)(b) above, 'court' means Court of Session or sheriff.

116 Benefited property outwith Scotland

As respects a real burden or servitude, the benefited property need not be in Scotland; but where it is not then nothing in this Act requires registration against that property.

117 Pecuniary real burdens

On and after the day on which this section comes into force, it shall not be competent to create a pecuniary real burden (that is to say, to constitute a heritable security by reservation in a conveyance).

118 Common interest

On and after the day on which this section comes into force—

(a) it shall not be competent to create a right of common interest; and

(b) no such right shall arise otherwise than by implication of law.

PART 11
SAVINGS, TRANSITIONAL AND GENERAL

Savings and transitional provisions etc

119 Savings and transitional provisions etc

(1)   Nothing in this Act shall be taken to impair the validity of creating, varying or discharging a real burden by the registering of a deed before the appointed day.
[. . .]
(3)   The repeal by this Act of section 32 of the Conveyancing (Scotland) Act 1874 (c 94) does not affect the construction of the expression 'deed of conditions' provided for in section 122(1) of this Act.
(4)   Sections 8 and 14 of this Act do not affect proceedings commenced before the appointed day.
(5)   Section 10 of this Act does not apply where a person ceases to be, or becomes, an owner before the appointed day.
(6)   Section 16 of this Act does not apply as respects a breach of a real burden which occurs before the appointed day.
(7)   Section 61 of this Act does not apply as respects a constitutive deed (or a deed into which the constitutive deed is incorporated) registered before the appointed day except in so far as a real burden the terms of which are set out in the constitutive deed is a community burden.
(8)   Sections 75 and 78 of this Act do not apply as respects a deed executed before the appointed day.
[. . .]
(10) Except where the contrary intention appears, this Act applies to all real burdens, whenever created.

General

120 Requirement for dual registration

A deed which, to be duly registered for the purposes of any provision of this Act, requires to be registered against both a benefited property and a burdened property, shall not be registrable against one only of the properties; nor shall a document which includes but does not wholly consist of such a deed.

121 Crown application

This Act binds the Crown.

122 Interpretation

(1)   In this Act, unless the context otherwise requires—
'the 1979 Act' means the Land Registration (Scotland) Act 1979 (c 33);
'the 2000 Act' means the Abolition of Feudal Tenure etc (Scotland) Act 2000 (asp 5);
'affirmative burden' shall be construed in accordance with section 2(2)(a) of this Act;
'ancillary burden' shall be construed in accordance with section 2(4) of this Act;
'appointed day' means the day appointed under section 71 of the 2000 Act;
'benefited property'—
    (a) in relation to a real burden, shall be construed in accordance with section 1(2)(b) of this Act; and
    (b) in relation to a title condition other than a real burden, means the land, or real right in land, to which the right to enforce the title condition is attached; 'burdened property'—
    (a) in relation to a real burden, shall be construed in accordance with section 1(2)(a) of this Act; and
    (b) in relation to a title condition other than a real burden, means the land, or real right in land, which is subject to the title condition;

'community' has the meaning given by section 26(2) of this Act;

'community burdens' shall be construed in accordance with section 25 of this Act;

'conservation body' means any body prescribed by order under subsection (4) of section 38 of this Act;

'conservation burden' shall be construed in accordance with subsection (1) of that section and includes (other than in subsections (1) and (2) of that section) a reference to a real burden the right to enforce which was—

(a)   preserved by virtue of section 27(1) of the 2000 Act (preservation of right to enforce conservation burden); or

(b)   obtained by virtue of section 27A(1) of that Act (nomination of conservation body or Scottish Ministers to have title to enforce conservation burden);

[(c)   obtained by virtue of section 27 of the Long Leases (Scotland) Act 2012 (asp 9) (conversion of qualifying condition to conservation burden); or

(d)   obtained by virtue of section 28 of that Act (conversion of qualifying condition to conservation burden where conservation body or Scottish Ministers nominated to enforce);]

'constitutive deed' is [, subject to subsection (4) below,] the deed which sets out the terms of a title condition (or of a prospective title condition) but the expression includes any document in which the terms of the title condition in question are varied;

'deed of conditions' means a deed mentioned in section 32 of the Conveyancing (Scotland) Act 1874 (c 94) (importation by reference) and registered before the appointed day having been executed in accordance with that section;

'the development management scheme' has the meaning given by section 71(3) of this Act;

'economic development burden' shall be construed in accordance with subsection (1) of section 45 of this Act and includes (other than in subsections (1) to (3) of that section) a reference to a real burden which was converted under section 18B of the 2000 Act (conversion into economic development burden) [and to a real burden created under section 24 of the Long Leases (Scotland) Act 2012 (asp 9) (conversion of qualifying condition to economic development burden)];

'enactment' includes a local and personal or private Act;

'facility burden' means, subject to subsection (2) below, a real burden which regulates the maintenance, management, reinstatement or use of heritable property which constitutes, and is intended to constitute, a facility of benefit to other land (examples of property which might constitute such a facility being without prejudice to the generality of this definition, set out in subsection (3) below);

[. . .]

'health care burden' shall be construed in accordance with subsection (1) of section 46 of this Act and includes (other than in subsections (1) to (3) of that section) a reference to a real burden which was converted under section 18C of the 2000 Act (conversion into health care burden) [and to a real burden created under section 25 of the Long Leases (Scotland) Act 2012 (asp 9) (conversion of qualifying condition to health care burden)];

'holder', in relation to a title condition, means the person who has right to the title condition [but does not include a person who has title to enforce it only by virtue of any of the paragraphs (a), (b) and (c) of section 8(2) of this Act];

'land' includes—

(a)   heritable property, whether corporeal or incorporeal, held as a separate tenement; and

(b)   land covered with water,

but does not include any estate of dominium directum;

'Lands Tribunal' means Lands Tribunal for Scotland;

['local authority' means a council constituted under section 2 of the Local Government etc (Scotland) Act 1994 (c 39);]

'maintenance' includes (cognate expressions being construed accordingly)—

    (a) repair or replacement; and

    (b) such demolition, alteration or improvement as is reasonably incidental to maintenance;

'manager', in relation to related properties, means any person (including an owner of one of those properties or a firm) who is authorised (whether by virtue of this Act or otherwise) to act generally, or for such purposes as may be applicable in relation to a particular authorisation, in respect of those properties;

'manager burden' shall be construed in accordance with section 63(1) of this Act;

'maritime burden' shall be construed in accordance with subsection (1) of section 44 of this Act and includes (other than in that subsection) a reference to any real burden in relation to which the Crown has title and interest under section 60(1) of the 2000 Act (preserved right of Crown to maritime burdens);

'midcouple' means such midcouple or link in title as it is competent to specify, under section 5(1) of the Conveyancing (Scotland) Act 1924 (14 & 15 Geo 5, c 27), in a deduction of title in terms of that Act;

'negative burden' shall be construed in accordance with section 2(2)(b) of this Act;

'notary public' includes, in a case where swearing or affirmation is to take place outwith Scotland, any person duly authorised by the law of the country or territory in question to administer oaths or receive affirmations in that country or territory;

'notice of converted servitude' shall be construed in accordance with section 80(4) and (5) of this Act;

'notice of preservation' shall be construed in accordance with section 50 of this Act;

'notice of termination' shall be construed in accordance with section 20 of this Act;

'owner' shall be construed in accordance with section 123 of this Act;

'personal pre-emption burden' and 'personal redemption burden' shall be construed in accordance with section 18A(5) of the 2000 Act [and section 23(1) of the Long Leases (Scotland) Act 2012 (asp 9)];

'personal real burden' shall be construed in accordance with section 1(3) of this Act;

'property' includes unit;

'real burden' has the meaning given by section 1 of this Act except that in construing that section for the purposes of this definition 'land' shall be taken to include an estate of dominium directum;

'registering', in relation to any document, means registering an interest in land or information relating to an interest in land (being an interest or information for which that document provides) in the Land Register of Scotland or, as the case may be, recording the document in the Register of Sasines (cognate expressions being construed accordingly);

'renewal date' has the meaning given by section 20(4)(d) of this Act;

'road' has the meaning given by section 151(1) of the Roads (Scotland) Act 1984 (c 54) (interpretation);

'rural housing body' means any body prescribed by order under subsection (5) of section 43 of this Act;

'rural housing burden' shall be construed in accordance with subsection (1) of that section and includes a personal pre-emption burden the holder of which is a rural housing body;

'send' shall be construed in accordance with section 124 of this Act (cognate expressions being construed accordingly);

'service burden' means a real burden which relates to the provision of services to land other than the burdened property;

'sheltered or retirement housing development' has the meaning given by section 54(3) of this Act;

['tenement' has the meaning given by section 26 of the Tenements (Scotland) Act 2004 (asp 11); and references to a flat in a tenement shall be construed accordingly;]

'terminator' shall be construed in accordance with section 20(2) of this Act;

'title condition' means—

   (a)   a real burden;

   (b)   a servitude;

   (c)   an affirmative obligation imposed, in a servitude, on the person who is in right of the servitude;

   (d)   a condition in a registrable lease if it is a condition which relates to the land (but not a condition which imposes either an obligation to pay rent or an obligation of relief relating to the payment of rent);

   (e)   a condition or stipulation—

      (i)   imposed under subsection (2) of section 3 of the Registration of Leases (Scotland) Act 1857 (c 26) ([assignations of registered or] recorded leases) in an assignation which has been duly registered; or

      (ii)   contained in a deed registered under subsection (2A) or (5) of that section;

   (f)   a condition in an agreement entered into under section 7 of the National Trust for Scotland Order Confirmation Act 1938 (c iv); or

   (g)   such other condition relating to land as the Scottish Ministers may, for the purposes of this paragraph, prescribe by order;

'unit' means any land which is designed to be held in separate ownership (whether it is so held or not); and

'variation', in relation to a title condition, includes both—

   (a)   imposition of a new obligation; and

   (b)   provision that a property becomes a benefited property,

(cognate expressions being construed accordingly).

(2)   In so far as it constitutes an obligation to maintain or reinstate which has been assumed—

   (a)   by a local or other public authority; or

   (b)   by virtue of any enactment, by a successor body to any such authority, a real burden is neither—

      (i)   a facility burden; nor

      (ii)   for the purposes of sections 52 to 54(1) of this Act, to be regarded as imposed as mentioned in any of those sections.

(3)   The examples referred to in the definition of 'facility burden' in subsection (1) above are—

   (a)   a common part of a tenement;

   (b)   a common area for recreation;

   (c)   a private road;

   (d)   private sewerage; and

   (e)   a boundary wall.

[(4)   If title is completed in the manner provided for in section 4 or 4A of the Conveyancing (Scotland) Act 1924 (c 27) (completion of title) and a midcouple relevant to the title sets out the terms of a title condition (or of a prospective title condition), then for the purposes of this Act the midcouple and notice of title are together the constitutive deed of the title condition.]

123   The expression 'owner'

(1)   Subject to subsections (2) and (3) below, in this Act 'owner', in relation to any property, means a person who has right to the property whether or not that person has completed title; but if, in relation to the property (or, if the property is

held pro indiviso, any pro indiviso share in the property) more than one person comes within that description of owner, then 'owner'—

(a) for the purposes of sections 4(2)(b), 6(1)(a), 15, 16, 19, 33(1) and (2) and 35 of this Act, means any person having such right; and

(b) for any other purposes means such person as has most recently acquired such right.

(2) Where a heritable creditor is in lawful possession of security subjects which comprise the property, then 'owner'—

(a) for the purposes of the sections mentioned in paragraph (a) of subsection (1) above includes, in addition to any such person as is there mentioned, that heritable creditor; and

(b) for any other purposes (other than of construing section 1 of this Act) means the heritable creditor.

(3) In section 60(1) of this Act, 'owner' in relation to any property has the meaning given by subsection (1) above except that, for the purposes of this subsection , in that subsection—

(a) the words 'Subject to subsections (2) and (3) below, in this Act' shall be disregarded; and

(b) paragraph (a) shall be construed as if section 60(1) were one of the sections mentioned.

124 Sending

(1) Where a provision of this Act requires that a thing be sent—

(a) to a person it shall suffice, for the purposes of that provision, that the thing be sent to an agent of the person;

(b) to an owner of property but only the property is known and not the name of the owner, it shall suffice, for the purposes of that provision, that the thing be sent there addressed to 'The Owner' (or using some other such expression, as for example 'The Proprietor').

(2) Except in subsection (3) below, in this Act any reference to a thing being sent shall be construed as a reference to its being—

(a) posted;

(b) delivered; or

(c) transmitted by electronic means.

(3) For the purposes of any provision of this Act, a thing posted shall be taken to be sent on the day of posting; and a thing transmitted by electronic means, to be sent on the day of transmission.

125 References to distance

Where a provision of this Act refers to a property being within a certain distance of another property, the reference is to distance along a horizontal plane, there being disregarded—

(a) the width of any intervening road if of less than twenty metres; and

(b) any pertinent of either property.

126 Fees chargeable by Lands Tribunal in relation to functions under this Act

The Scottish Ministers may, after consultation with the Scottish Committee of the [Administrative Justice and Tribunals Council], make rules as to the fees chargeable by the Lands Tribunal in respect of that tribunal's functions under this Act.

127 Orders, regulations and rules

(1) Any power of the Scottish Ministers under this Act to make orders, regulations or rules shall be exercisable by statutory instrument; and a statutory instrument containing any such orders, regulations or rules, other than an order under section 128(4) or 129(4), shall be subject to annulment in pursuance of a resolution of the Scottish Parliament.

(2) A statutory instrument containing an order under section 128(4) of this Act shall not be made unless a draft of the instrument has been—

(a) laid before; and
(b) approved by a resolution of,
the Scottish Parliament.

128 Minor and consequential amendments, repeals and power to amend forms

(1)   Schedule 14 to this Act, which contains minor amendments and amendments consequential upon the provisions of this Act, shall have effect.

(2)   The enactments mentioned in schedule 15 to this Act are repealed to the extent specified.

(3)   The Scottish Ministers may by order amend any of schedules—
(a) [1A] to 10 and 12 to this Act; and
(b) 1 to 11A to the 2000 Act.

(4)   The Scottish Ministers may by order make such incidental, supplemental, consequential, transitional, transitory or saving provision as they consider necessary or expedient for the purposes, or in consequence, of this Act or of any order, regulations or rules made under this Act.

(5)   An order under subsection (4) above may amend or repeal any enactment (including any provision of this Act).

129 Short title and commencement

(1)   This Act may be cited as the Title Conditions (Scotland) Act 2003.

(2)   Subject to subsections (3) to (5) below, this Act, except this section, shall come into force on the appointed day.

(3)   Sections 63, 66, 67, 86 and 88, except in so far as it inserts a sub-paragraph (ab) (ii) into paragraph 1 of Schedule 1 to the Prescription and Limitation (Scotland) Act 1973 (c 52), Part 9 for the purposes of any application under section 107(5) of this Act, sections 111, 113, 114, 117, 118, 122 to 124, 126, 127, 128(3) to (5), schedules 12 and 13 and, in schedule 14, paragraph 7(1), (3) and (6) come into force on the day after Royal Assent.

(4)   There shall come into force on such day as the Scottish Ministers may by order appoint, Parts 3 and 6 and sections 106 to 110; and different days may be so appointed for different provisions.

(5)   In so far as—
(a) it relates to paragraph 7(1), (3) and (6) of schedule 14, section 128(1);
(b) it relates to the 2000 Act, section 128(2);
(c) it relates to the 2000 Act, schedule 15;
(d) is necessary for the purposes of Part 3 and section 63, Part 1,
shall come into force on the day after Royal Assent.

SCHEDULES

Section 6(2)   SCHEDULE 1
FORM IMPORTING TERMS OF TITLE CONDITIONS

There are imported the terms of the title conditions specified in [*refer to the deed of conditions in such terms as shall be sufficient to identify it and specify the register in which it is registered and the date of registration*].

[SCHEDULE 1A
FORM OF NOTICE OF POTENTIAL LIABILITY FOR COSTS
(introduced by section 10(2A))

'NOTICE OF POTENTIAL LIABILITY FOR COSTS

This notice gives details of certain maintenance or work carried out [or to be carried out] in relation to the property specified in the notice. The effect of the notice is that a person may, on becoming the owner of the property, be liable by virtue of section 10(2A) of the Title Conditions (Scotland) Act 2003 (asp 9) for any outstanding costs relating to the maintenance or work.

Property to which the notice relates:
(*see note 1 below*)

Description of the maintenance or work to which notice relates:
(*see note 2 below*)

Person giving notice:
(*see note 3 below*)

Signature:
(*see note 4 below*)

Date of signing:'

Notes for completion

(*These notes are not part of the notice*)
    1   Describe the property in a way that is sufficient to identify it. Where the property has a postal address, the description must include that address. Where title to the property has been registered in the Land Register of Scotland, the description must refer to the title number of the property or of the larger subjects of which it forms part. Otherwise, the description should normally refer to and identify a deed recorded in a specified division of the Register of Sasines.
    2   Describe the maintenance or work in general terms.
    3   Give the name and address of the person applying for registration of the notice ('the applicant') or the applicant's name and the name and address of the applicant's agent.
    4   The notice must be signed by or on behalf of the applicant.]

Section 20(1)   SCHEDULE 2
                         FORM OF NOTICE OF TERMINATION

'NOTICE OF TERMINATION

Name and address of terminator:
(see note for completion 1)

Description of burdened property:
(see note for completion 2)

Terminator's connection with burdened property:
(see note for completion 3)

Terms of real burden(s):
(see note for completion 4)

Extent of termination:
(see note for completion 5)

Renewal date:
(see note for completion 6)

An application to the Lands Tribunal for Scotland for renewal or variation of the real burden(s) must be made by not later than the renewal date.

Persons to whom a copy of the notice sent:
(see note for completion 7)

Date and method of intimation:
(see note for completion 8)

I swear [or affirm] that the information contained in this notice is, to the best of my knowledge and belief, true, and that this notice has been duly intimated.

Signature of person so swearing [or affirming]:
(see note for completion 9)

Signature of notary public:

Date:

Certificate by Lands Tribunal for Scotland
(see note for completion 10).'

Explanatory note

(This explanation has no legal effect)

This notice, given under section 20(1) of the Title Conditions (Scotland) Act 2003, concerns real burdens which affect a [*neighbouring*] property (referred to in the notice as the 'burdened property'), and is sent to you by the owner of that property or by some other person affected by the burdens. The sender (who is referred to in the notice and in these notes as the 'terminator') wishes to free the property of the real burdens listed in the notice.

The burdens are more than 100 years old.

If you are opposed to the freeing, you can apply to the Lands Tribunal for Scotland for the burdens to be renewed or varied. The address of the Lands Tribunal is [*insert address*] and their telephone number is [*insert telephone number*]. However, you can only apply if you are an owner of a property which, in a legal sense, takes benefit from the burden and which carries enforcement rights or if the burden is a personal real burden. For further guidance you may wish to consult a solicitor or other adviser.

[A list of other people who have been sent this notice is given in the notice itself.

It is possible to make an application to the Lands Tribunal jointly with other people.]

An application to the Lands Tribunal must be made by the renewal date stated in the notice. If no application is made by then, you may lose any right which you may currently hold to enforce the burdens.

Notes for completion of the notice

(These notes have no legal effect)

1   The 'terminator' is the person who, at any time, is seeking to terminate the real burden. Where the person who proposes to execute and register the notice of termination and so intimates is not the terminator when the notice comes to be executed, the name and address of the person executing should be appended after the name and address of the person who so intimated.

2   Describe the property in a way that is sufficient to identify it. Where the property has a postal address the description should include that address. Where the title has been registered in the Land Register the description should refer to the title number of the property or of the larger subjects of which the property forms part. Otherwise it should normally refer to and identify a deed recorded in a specified division of the Register of Sasines.

3   Describe the terminator's connection with the burdened property, as for example by identification as owner or tenant or by setting out the midcouple which links (or midcouples which link) the terminator to the person who last had a completed title as owner. Where the circumstances mentioned in note for completion 1 arise, the description should be extended accordingly.

4   Identify the constitutive deed by reference to the appropriate Register, and set out the real burden in full. A single notice may be used for two or more real burdens.

5   If the real burden is wholly to be terminated say so; otherwise describe the extent of termination.

6   Insert the date by which applications for renewal or variation must be made. This can be any date, provided that it is not less than 8 weeks after the last date on which this notice is intimated (intimation by affixing being taken to be given when first the notice is affixed).

7   This notice (and the explanatory note) must be intimated to (a) the owner of any benefited property, (b) the holder of any personal real burden and (c) the owner of the burdened property (or, if the terminator is such an owner, any other owner of that property). Intimation can be by sending (or delivering) the notice, by affixing a conspicuous notice to the burdened property and also to a lamp post within 100 metres of that property (or to at least two lamp posts if there is more than one within that distance of that property) or by newspaper advertisement. However, affixing or advertisement cannot be used for the owner of a benefited property which lies within 4 metres of the burdened property (disregarding roads less than 20 metres wide) or for the owner of the burdened property or for any such person as is mentioned in paragraph (b) of this note and advertisement cannot be used where affixing can. Where sending or delivery is used, state (i) the name of the person concerned (if known) (ii) the address to which the notice is sent or delivered, and (iii) the address of the benefited (or burdened) property owned by that person, if different from (ii). Since evidence of sending may be required at the time of registration in the Land Register, it is recommended that the notice be sent by recorded delivery or registered post.

8   State the date and method of intimation. By way of example—

(a) if notices were posted, to the persons listed in the previous note, on 25th March 2003 and advertised in the Inverness Courier on 4th April 2003, insert:

'(a)   Intimation by post on 25th March 2003; (b) Advertisement in the Inverness Courier on 4th April 2003.'; or

(b)   if on 12th July a notice was posted to the owner of the burdened property and otherwise intimation was given by affixing notices on that date, insert: '(a) Intimation by post on 12th July 2005; (b) Notices affixed to the burdened property and to each of two lamp posts within 100 metres of that property on 12th July 2005.'.

9   The terminator should not swear or affirm, or sign, until the notice has been completed (except for the certificate by the Lands Tribunal for Scotland) and duly intimated. Before signing, the terminator should swear or affirm before a notary public (or, if the notice is being completed outwith Scotland, before a person duly authorised under the local law to administer oaths or receive affirmations) that, to the best of the terminator's knowledge and belief, all the information contained in the notice is true and that the notice has been duly intimated. The notary public should also sign. Swearing or affirming a statement which is known to be false or which is believed not to be true is a criminal offence under the False Oaths (Scotland) Act 1933 (c 20). Normally the terminator should swear or affirm, and sign, personally. If, however, the terminator is legally disabled or incapable (for example because of mental disorder) a legal representative should swear or affirm, and sign. If the terminator is not an individual (for example, if it is a company) a person entitled by law to sign formal documents on its behalf should swear or affirm, and sign.

10   There is to be endorsed before registration the certificate required by section 23(1) of the Title Conditions (Scotland) Act 2003 (asp 9).

Section 21(2)(b)   SCHEDULE 3
FORM OF AFFIXED NOTICE RELATING TO TERMINATION

'TERMINATION OF REAL BURDEN

This notice is intimation that the person who is described below as terminator wishes to free the property which is described below as the burdened property from a real burden which affects that property. The terminator proposes to register a notice of termination so as to extinguish the real burden. A copy of that notice of termination (which among other things describes the real burden fully) is available from the terminator on request.

Name and address of terminator:
(see note for completion 1)

Description of burdened property:
(see note for completion 2)

The real burden and the extent of termination:
(see note for completion 3)

Renewal date:
(see note for completion 4)

If you wish to apply to the Lands Tribunal for Scotland for renewal or variation of the real burden you must do so by not later than the renewal date. If no application is made by then, you may lose any right which you may currently hold to enforce the burden. For further guidance you may wish to consult a solicitor or other adviser.

Signature of terminator:

Date affixed: .'

Notes for completion of the notice

(These notes have no legal effect)

1   The 'terminator' is the person who, at any time, is seeking to terminate the real burden. Give the terminator's name and address (or the terminator's name and the name and address of the terminator's agent).
2   Describe the property in a way that is sufficient to identify it. Where the property has a postal address the description should include that address. Where the title has been registered in the Land Register the description should refer to the title number of the property or of the larger subjects of which the property forms part. Otherwise it should normally refer to and identify a deed recorded in a specified division of the Register of Sasines.
3   Provide briefly a description of the real burden. If the burden is wholly to be terminated say so; otherwise describe the extent of termination.
4   Insert the date by which applications for renewal or variation must be made. This can be any date, provided that it is not less than 8 weeks after the last date on which the notice of termination is intimated (intimation by affixing being taken to be given when first the notice is affixed).

SCHEDULE 4   Section 34(2)(a)

FORM OF NOTICE OF PROPOSAL TO REGISTER DEED OF VARIATION OR DISCHARGE

'NOTICE OF PROPOSAL TO REGISTER DEED OF VARIATION OR DISCHARGE

Proposer:
(see note for completion 1)

Description of affected unit(s):
(see note for completion 2)

Terms of community burden(s):
(see note for completion 3)

Effect of registration of deed on burden(s):
(see note for completion 4)

An application to the Lands Tribunal for Scotland for preservation of the community burden(s) must be made not later than [specify the date on which the period mentioned in section 34(3) of this Act expires].

Signature of proposer:

Date: .'

Explanatory note

(This explanation has no legal effect)

This notice is given under section 34(2)(a) of the Title Conditions (Scotland) Act 2003. The sender (who is referred to in the notice and in these notes as the 'proposer') wishes [to free a property of a community burden] or [to vary a community burden].

A deed of [discharge] or [variation] has already been granted. A copy of the deed in question is attached. If the deed is duly registered the burden will be [discharged] or [varied] in relation to the affected unit.

If you want to preserve such rights as you may have, you can apply to the

Lands Tribunal for Scotland in that regard. The address of the Lands Tribunal is [insert address] and their telephone number is [insert telephone number]. For further guidance you may wish to consult a solicitor or other adviser.

An application to the Lands Tribunal must be made by the date stated in the notice. If no application is made by then, you may lose any right which you may currently hold to enforce the burdens.

Notes for completion of the notice

(These notes have no legal effect)

1   The 'proposer' is the person who is seeking to discharge or vary the community burden. Give the proposer's name and address (or the proposer's name and the name and address of the proposer's agent).

2   Describe the unit in a way that is sufficient to identify it. Where the unit has a postal address the description should include that address. Where the title has been registered in the Land Register the description should refer to the title number of the property or of the larger subjects of which the unit forms part. Otherwise it should normally refer to and identify a deed recorded in a specified division of the Register of Sasines.

3   Identify the constitutive deed by reference to the appropriate Register, and set out the community burden in full.

4   State whether the deed is of variation or of discharge. If the community burden is wholly to be discharged say so; otherwise describe the extent of variation or discharge.

5   Intimation is by sending (or delivering) the notice. Since evidence of sending may be required at the time of registration in the Land Register, it is recommended that the notice be sent by recorded delivery or registered post.

6   There is to be endorsed on the deed before registration the certificate required by subsection (2) of section 37 of the Title Conditions (Scotland) Act 2003 (asp 9) (as applied by section 34 of that Act).

Section 36(2)(a)   SCHEDULE 5
FURTHER FORM OF NOTICE OF PROPOSAL TO REGISTER DEED OF
VARIATION OR DISCHARGE OF COMMUNITY BURDEN: SENT VERSION

'NOTICE OF PROPOSAL TO REGISTER DEED OF VARIATION OR
DISCHARGE OF COMMUNITY BURDEN

Proposer:
(see note for completion 1)

Description of affected unit:
(see note for completion 2)

Terms of community burden(s):
(see note for completion 3)

Nature of deed:
(see note for completion 4)

An application to the Lands Tribunal for Scotland for preservation of the community burden(s) must be made not later than [specify the date on which the period mentioned in section 37(1) of this Act expires].

Signature of proposer:

Date: .'

Explanatory note

(This explanation has no legal effect)
This notice is given under section 36(2)(a) of the Title Conditions (Scotland) Act 2003. The sender (who is referred to in the notice and in these notes as the 'proposer') wishes [to free a property of a community burden] or [to vary a community burden].

A deed of [discharge] or [variation] has already been granted by the owners of adjacent properties and a copy of it is attached. If the deed is duly registered the burden will be [discharged] or [varied] in relation to the affected property.

If you want to preserve such rights as you may have, you can apply to the Lands Tribunal for Scotland in that regard. The address of the Lands Tribunal is *[insert address]* and their telephone number is *[insert telephone number]*. However, you can only apply if you are an owner of a property which, in a legal sense, takes benefit from the burden and which carries enforcement rights. For further guidance you may wish to consult a solicitor or other adviser.

An application to the Lands Tribunal must be made by the date stated in the notice. If no application is made by then, you may lose any right which you may currently hold to enforce the burdens.

Notes for completion of the notice

(These notes have no legal effect)

1   The 'proposer' is the person who is seeking to discharge or vary the community burden. Give the proposer's name and address (or the proposer's name and the name and address of the proposer's agent.)

2   Describe the affected unit in a way that is sufficient to identify it. Where the unit has a postal address the description should include that address. Where the title has been registered in the Land Register the description should refer to the title number of the property or of the larger subjects of which the unit forms part. Otherwise it should normally refer to and identify a deed recorded in a specified division of the Register of Sasines.

3   Identify the constitutive deed by reference to the appropriate Register and set out the community burden in full.

4   State whether the deed is of variation or of discharge. If the community burden is wholly to be discharged say so; otherwise describe the extent of variation or discharge.

5   This notice requires to be sent. Since evidence of sending may be required at the time of registration in the Land Register, it is recommended that the notice be sent by recorded delivery or registered post.

6   There is to be endorsed on the deed before registration the certificate required by subsection (2) of section 37 of the Title Conditions (Scotland) Act 2003 (asp 9).

Section 36(2)(b)   SCHEDULE 6
FURTHER FORM OF NOTICE OF PROPOSAL TO REGISTER DEED OF
VARIATION OR DISCHARGE OF COMMUNITY BURDEN: AFFIXED VERSION

'NOTICE OF PROPOSAL TO REGISTER DEED OF VARIATION OR
DISCHARGE OF COMMUNITY BURDEN

This notice is intimation that the person who is described below as proposer wishes to vary or discharge a community burden which affects a property described below as the affected unit. The proposer intends to register a deed already granted by certain other owners of units. A copy of the deed in question can be obtained from the proposer on request as can a description of the community burden. If the deed is registered the community burden will be varied or discharged in so far as it affects the property.

Proposer:
(see note for completion 1)

Description of affected unit:
(see note for completion 2)

The community burden and the extent of termination:
(see note for completion 3)

An application to the Lands Tribunal for Scotland for preservation of the community burden(s) must be made not later than [specify the date on which the period mentioned in section 37(1) of this Act expires]. If no application is made by then, you may lose any right you may currently hold to enforce the community burden. For further guidance you may wish to consult a solicitor or other adviser.

Signature of proposer:

Date affixed: .'

Notes for completion of the notice

(These notes have no legal effect)

   1   The 'proposer' is the person who is seeking to discharge or vary the community burden. Give the proposer's name and address (or the proposer's name and the name and address of the proposer's agent).
   2   Describe the affected unit in a way that is sufficient to identify it. Where the unit has a postal address the description should include that address. Where the title has been registered in the Land Register the description should refer to the title number of the property or of the larger subjects of which the unit forms part. Otherwise it should normally refer to and identify a deed recorded in a specified division of the Register of Sasines.
   3   Provide a brief description of the community burden. If the burden is wholly to be discharged say so; otherwise describe the extent of variation or discharge.
   4   This notice requires to be affixed conspicuously to the affected unit and also to a lamp post within 100 metres of that unit (or to at least two lamp posts if there is more than one within that distance of that unit).
   5   There is to be endorsed on the deed before registration the statement required by subsection (2) of section 37 of the Title Conditions (Scotland) Act 2003 (asp 9).

SCHEDULE 7   Section 50(1)
FORM OF NOTICE OF PRESERVATION

'NOTICE OF PRESERVATION

Name and address of person sending notice:

Description of burdened property:
(see note for completion 1)

Description of benefited property:
(see note for completion 1)

[Links in title:]
(see note for completion 2)

Terms of real burden(s):
(see note for completion 3)

Explanation of why the property described as a benefited property is such a property:
(see note for completion 4)

Service:
(see note for completion 5)

I swear [or affirm] that the information contained in this notice is, to the best of my knowledge and belief, true.

Signature of person sending notice:
(see note for completion 6)

Signature of notary public:

Date: .'

Explanatory note for owner of burdened property

(This explanation has no legal effect)

This notice is sent by a person who asserts that the use of your property is affected by the real burden [or real burdens] whose terms are described in the notice and that that person is one of the people entitled to the benefit of the real burden [or real burdens] and can, if necessary, enforce it [or them] against you. In this notice your property (or some part of it) is referred to as the 'burdened property' and the property belonging to that person is referred to as the 'benefited property'.

The grounds for the assertion are given in the notice. By section 50 of the Title Conditions (Scotland) Act 2003 (asp 9) that person's rights will be lost unless this notice is registered in the Land Register or Register of Sasines by not later than [insert date ten years after the appointed day]. Registration preserves the rights and means that the burden [or burdens] can continue to be enforced by that person and by anyone succeeding as owner of that person's property.

This notice does not require you to take any action; but if you think there is a mistake in it, or if you wish to challenge it, you are advised to contact your solicitor or other adviser. A notice can be challenged even after it has been registered.

Notes for completion of the notice

(These notes have no legal effect)

   1   A single notice may be used for any properties covered by the same constitutive deed. Describe the property in a way that is sufficient to identify it. Where

the title has been registered in the Land Register the description should refer to the title number of the property or of the larger subjects of which the property forms part. Otherwise it should normally refer to and identify a deed recorded in a specified division of the Register of Sasines.

2   Include the section 'Links in Title' only if the person sending the notice does not have a completed title to the benefited property. Set out the midcouple (or midcouples) linking that person with the person who had the last completed title.

3   A single notice may be used for any real burdens created in the same constitutive deed. Identify the constitutive deed by reference to the appropriate Register, and set out the real burden in full or refer to the deed in such a way as to identify the real burden.

4   Explain the legal and factual grounds on which the land described as a benefited property is a benefited property in relation to the burdened property and the burden described in the notice.

5   Do not complete until a copy of the notice, together with the explanatory note, has been sent (or delivered) to the owner of the burdened property (except in a case where that is not reasonably practicable). Then insert whichever is applicable of the following:

'A copy of this notice has been sent by [state method and if by post specify whether by recorded delivery, by registered post or by ordinary post] on [date] to the owner of the burdened property at [address].'; or

'It has not been reasonably practicable to send a copy of this notice to the owner of the burdened property for the following reason: [specify the reason]'.

6   The person sending the notice should not swear or affirm, or sign, until a copy of the notice has been sent (or otherwise) as mentioned in note 5. Before signing, the sender should swear or affirm before a notary public (or, if the notice is being completed outwith Scotland, before a person duly authorised under the local law to administer oaths or receive affirmations) that, to the best of the sender's knowledge and belief, all the information contained in the notice is true. The notary public should also sign. Swearing or affirming a statement which is known to be false or which is believed not to be true is a criminal offence under the False Oaths (Scotland) Act 1933 (c 20). Normally the sender should swear or affirm, and sign, personally. If, however, the sender is legally disabled or incapable (for example because of mental disorder) a legal representative should swear or affirm, and sign. If the sender is not an individual (for example, if it is a company) a person entitled by law to sign formal documents on its behalf should swear or affirm, and sign.

Section 55(2)   SCHEDULE 8
                        COMMUNITY CONSULTATION NOTICE

'NOTICE INVITING COMMENTS IN RELATION TO PROPOSAL TO VARY OR
DISCHARGE COMMUNITY BURDEN AFFECTING SHELTERED OR
RETIREMENT HOUSING

Person to whom comments should be sent:
(see note for completion 1)

Description of development:
(see note for completion 2)

Terms of community burden to be varied or discharged:
(see note for completion 3)

Effect of registration of proposed deed on that burden:
(see note for completion 4)

Date by which any comments are to be made:
(see note for completion 5)

Date of intimation:
(see notes for completion 6)

Signature of a person who proposes to grant the deed:

Date: .'

Explanatory note

(This explanation has no legal effect)

This notice, which is sent under section 55 of the Title Conditions (Scotland) Act 2003, concerns a community burden which affects the sheltered or retirement housing development of which your property is part. The sender is intimating to you a proposal to grant a deed of [variation] or [discharge] in respect of the burden and invites your comments.

If such a deed is granted and duly registered (which cannot be before the date specified, in the notice, as that by which any comments are to be made) the burden [may be varied] or [may be discharged] as described in the notice.

For further guidance you may wish to consult a solicitor or other adviser.

Notes for completion of the notice

(These notes have no legal effect)

1   This should ordinarily be a person who proposes to grant the deed. Give the person's name and address.

2   Describe the sheltered or retirement housing development in a way that is sufficient to identify it.

3   Set out the community burden in question in full.

4   State whether the proposed deed is of variation or of discharge. If the community burden is wholly to be discharged say so; otherwise describe the extent of variation or discharge.

5   Specify a date no earlier than three weeks after the latest date mentioned in section 55(3) of the Title Conditions (Scotland) Act 2003 (asp 9).

6   Intimation is by sending (or delivering) the notice. Since evidence of sending may be required at the time of registration in the Land Register of any deed granted, it is recommended that the notice be sent by recorded delivery or registered post.

SCHEDULE 9   Section 80(4)
FORM OF NOTICE OF CONVERTED SERVITUDE

'NOTICE OF CONVERTED SERVITUDE

Name and address of person sending notice:

Description of burdened property:
(see note for completion 1)

Description of benefited property:
(see note for completion 1)

[Links in title:]
(see note for completion 2)

Terms of converted servitude:
(see note for completion 3)

Explanation of why the property described as a benefited property is such a property:
(see note for completion 4)

Service:
(see note for completion 5)

I swear [or affirm] that the information contained in this notice is, to the best of my knowledge and belief, true. The constitutive deed [or A copy of the constitutive deed] is annexed to the notice.
(see note for completion 6)

Signature of person sending notice:
(see note for completion 7)

Signature of notary public:

Date: .'

Explanatory note for owner of burdened property

(This explanation has no legal effect)

This notice is sent by a person who asserts that the use of your property is affected by a converted servitude which the sender is entitled to enforce. In this notice your property (or some part of it) is referred to as the 'burdened property' and the property belonging to the sender is referred to as the 'benefited property'. The 'converted servitude' is a condition which may affect the use of your property. Formerly a servitude, the condition was converted into a real burden by subsection

(1) of section 80 of the Title Conditions (Scotland) Act 2003 (asp 9).

At the moment the converted servitude is not disclosed against your title on the property registers. By subsection (2) of that section the sender's right will be lost unless this notice is registered in the Land Register of Scotland or the Register of Sasines by not later than [insert date ten years after the appointed day]. Registration preserves the right and means that the converted servitude can continue to be enforced by the sender, and by anyone succeeding the sender as owner of that property.

This notice does not require you to take any action; but if you think there is a mistake in it, or if you wish to challenge it, you are advised to contact your solicitor or other adviser. A notice can be challenged even after it has been registered.

Notes for completion of the notice

(These notes have no legal effect)

1   A single notice may be used for any properties covered by the same constitutive deed. Describe the property in a way that is sufficient to identify it. Where the title has been registered in the Land Register the description should refer to the title number of the property or of the larger subjects of which the property forms part. Otherwise it should normally refer to and identify a deed recorded in a specified division of the Register of Sasines.

2   Include the section 'Links in Title' only if the person sending the notice does not have a completed title to the benefited property. List the midcouple (or midcouples) linking that person with the person who had the last completed title.

3   A single notice may be used for any converted servitudes created in the same constitutive deed. Set out the converted servitude in full or refer to the constitutive deed in such a way as to identify the servitude. If there is no such deed, explain the factual and legal circumstances in which the servitude was created.

4   Complete this part only if the land described as the benefited property is not

nominated as such by the constitutive deed. Explain the legal and factual grounds on which that land is a benefited property in relation to the burdened property and the converted servitude described in the notice.

5   Do not complete until a copy of the notice, together with the constitutive deed and the explanatory note, has been sent (or delivered) to the owner of the burdened property (except in a case where that is not reasonably practicable). Then insert whichever is applicable of the following:

'A copy of this notice has been sent by [state method and if by post specify whether by recorded delivery, by registered post or by ordinary post] on [date] to the owner of the burdened property at [address].'; or

'It has not been reasonably practicable to send a copy of this notice to the owner of the burdened property for the following reason: [specify the reason]'.

6   Endorse on the constitutive deed (or copy) words to the effect of:

'This is the constitutive deed referred to in the notice of converted servitude by [give name of person sending the notice] dated [give date].'

The endorsement need not be signed.

7   The person sending the notice should not swear or affirm, or sign, until a copy of the notice has been sent (or otherwise) as mentioned in note 5. Before signing, the sender should swear or affirm before a notary public (or, if the notice is being completed outwith Scotland, before a person duly authorised under the local law to administer oaths or receive affirmations) that, to the best of the sender's knowledge and belief, all the information contained in the notice is true. The notary public should also sign. Swearing or affirming a statement which is known to be false or which is believed not to be true is a criminal offence under the False Oaths (Scotland) Act 1933 (c 20). Normally the sender should swear or affirm, and sign, personally. If, however, the sender is legally disabled or incapable (for example because of mental disorder) a legal representative should swear or affirm, and sign. If the sender is not an individual (for example, if it is a company) a person entitled by law to sign formal documents on its behalf should swear or affirm, and sign.

SCHEDULE 10   Section 83(1)(a)
FORM OF UNDERTAKING

'UNDERTAKING NOT TO EXERCISE RIGHT OF PRE-EMPTION

Property benefited by right of pre-emption:
(see note for completion 1)

Holder of right of pre-emption:
(see note for completion 2)

Property subject to right of pre-emption:
(see note for completion 3)

Deed in which right of pre-emption imposed:
(see note for completion 4)

I hereby undertake that I will not exercise my right of pre-emption in respect of a sale occurring before (insert date) [if (insert any conditions to be satisfied)— see note for completion 5]

Signature by or on behalf of holder of right of pre-emption:

Signature of witness:

Date: .'

Notes for completion of the undertaking

(These notes have no legal effect)

1   Describe the property in a way that is sufficient to enable it to be identified. Where the title has been registered in the Land Register the description should refer to the title number. Otherwise it should normally refer to and identify a deed recorded in a specified division of the Register of Sasines.

Where the right of pre-emption is a personal pre-emption burden or rural housing burden, insert (only) 'Personal pre-emption burden' or 'Rural housing burden'.

2   Insert the holder's name and address. The holder is the owner of the benefited property or, in the case of a personal pre-emption burden or rural housing burden, the person in whose favour the burden is constituted. (The person last registered as having title to such a burden is taken to be the holder of the right of pre-emption which the burden comprises.)

3   Describe the property in a way that is sufficient to enable it to be identified. Where the title has been registered in the Land Register the description should refer to the title number. Otherwise it should normally refer to and identify a deed recorded in a specified division of the Register of Sasines. If part only of the burdened property is to be sold, describe that part only.

4   Give the name of the deed and the particulars of its registration or recording.

5   Insert any conditions concerning the type of sale in respect of which the right of pre-emption will not be exercised (for example, 'if the consideration for the sale is £100,000 or more').

Section 90(3)   SCHEDULE 11
TITLE CONDITIONS NOT SUBJECT TO DISCHARGE BY LANDS TRIBUNAL

1   An obligation, however constituted, relating to the right to work minerals or to any ancillary rights in relation to minerals ('minerals' and 'ancillary rights' having the same meanings as in the Mines (Working Facilities and Support) Act 1966 (c 4)).

2   In so far as enforceable by or on behalf of—
(a)   the Crown, an obligation created or imposed for naval, military or air force purposes; or
(b)   the Crown or any public or international authority, an obligation created or imposed—
(i)   for civil aviation purposes; or
(ii)   in connection with the use of land as an aerodrome.

3   An obligation created or imposed in or in relation to a lease of—
(a)   an agricultural holding (as defined in section 1(1) of the Agricultural Holdings (Scotland) Act 1991 (c 55));
(b)   a holding (within the meaning of the Small Landholders (Scotland) Acts 1886 to 1931); or
(c)   a croft (within the meaning of the Crofters (Scotland) Act 1993 (c 44)).

Section 107(11)   SCHEDULE 12
FORM OF APPLICATION FOR RELEVANT CERTIFICATE

'APPLICATION BY ACQUIRING AUTHORITY FOR RELEVANT CERTIFICATE

Acquiring authority:

Description of land acquired:
(see note for completion 1)

Proposed effect of registering conveyance:
(see note for completion 2)

Date and method of intimation:
(see note for completion 3)

Date by which any application to Lands Tribunal must be made:
(see note for completion 4)

Signature:
(see note for completion 5)
Date: *.'*

Notes for completion of the application

(These notes have no legal effect)

1   Give the postal address if there is one, then describe the land in a way that is sufficient to enable the Keeper to identify it by reference to the Ordnance Map. Where the title to the land has been registered in the Land Register the description should refer to the title number of the land or the larger subjects of which the land forms part. Otherwise it should normally refer to and identify a deed recorded in a specified division of the Register of Sasines.

2   If it is proposed that all real burdens and servitudes be extinguished, and any development management scheme disapplied, say so. If the terms of the conveyance are to provide otherwise, annex a copy of the draft conveyance to the application.

3   Intimation can be by sending, by advertisement or by such other method as the acquiring authority thinks fit.

4   Specify a date no fewer than 21 days after the date of intimation.

5   The signature is to be that of a person entitled by law to sign formal documents on behalf of the acquiring authority.

TENEMENTS (SCOTLAND) ACT 2004
(2004, asp 11)

Boundaries and pertinents

1   Determination of boundaries and pertinents

(1)   Except in so far as any different boundaries or pertinents are constituted by virtue of the title to the tenement, or any enactment, the boundaries and pertinents of sectors of a tenement shall be determined in accordance with sections 2 and 3 of this Act.

(2)   In this Act, 'title to the tenement' means—
    (a)   any conveyance, or reservation, of property which affects—
        (i)   the tenement; or
        (ii)   any sector in the tenement; and
    (b)   where [. . .]—
        (i)   the tenement; or
        (ii)   any sector in the tenement,
has been registered in the Land Register of Scotland, the [relevant title sheet].

2   Tenement boundaries

(1)   Subject to subsections (3) to (7) below, the boundary between any two contiguous sectors is the median of the structure that separates them; and a sector—
    (a)   extends in any direction to such a boundary; or
    (b)   if it does not first meet such a boundary—

(i) extends to and includes the solum or any structure which is an outer surface of the tenement building; or

(ii) extends to the boundary that separates the sector from a contiguous building which is not part of the tenement building.

(2) For the purposes of subsection (1) above, where the structure separating two contiguous sectors is or includes something (as for example, but without prejudice to the generality of this subsection, a door or window) which wholly or mainly serves only one of those sectors, the thing is in its entire thickness part of that sector.

(3) A top flat extends to and includes the roof over that flat.

(4) A bottom flat extends to and includes the solum under that flat.

(5) A close extends to and includes the roof over, and the solum under, the close.

(6) Where a sector includes the solum (or any part of it) the sector shall also include, subject to subsection (7) below, the airspace above the tenement building and directly over the solum (or part).

(7) Where the roof of the tenement building slopes, a sector which includes the roof (or any part of it) shall also include the airspace above the slope of the roof (or part) up to the level of the highest point of the roof.

3 Pertinents

(1) Subject to subsection (2) below, there shall attach to each of the flats, as a pertinent, a right of common property in (and in the whole of) the following parts of a tenement—

(a) a close;

(b) a lift by means of which access can be obtained to more than one of the flats.

(2) If a close or lift does not afford a means of access to a flat then there shall not attach to that flat, as a pertinent, a right of common property in the close or, as the case may be, lift.

(3) Any land (other than the solum of the tenement building) pertaining to a tenement shall attach as a pertinent to the bottom flat most nearly adjacent to the land (or part of the land); but this subsection shall not apply to any part which constitutes a path, outside stair or other way affording access to any sector other than that flat.

(4) If a tenement includes any part (such as, for example, a path, outside stair, fire escape, rhone, pipe, flue, conduit, cable, tank or chimney stack) that does not fall within subsection (1) or (3) above and that part—

(a) wholly serves one flat, then it shall attach as a pertinent to that flat;

(b) serves two or more flats, then there shall attach to each of the flats served, as a pertinent, a right of common property in (and in the whole of) the part.

(5) For the purposes of this section, references to rights of common property being attached to flats as pertinents are references to there attaching to each flat equal rights of common property; except that where the common property is a chimney stack the share allocated to a flat shall be determined in direct accordance with the ratio which the number of flues serving it in the stack bears to the total number of flues in the stack.

Tenement Management Scheme

4 Application of the Tenement Management Scheme

(1) The Tenement Management Scheme (referred to in this section as 'the Scheme'), which is set out in schedule 1 to this Act, shall apply in relation to a tenement to the extent provided by the following provisions of this section.

(2) The Scheme shall not apply in any period during which the development

management scheme applies to the tenement by virtue of section 71 of the Title Conditions (Scotland) Act 2003 (asp 9).

(3)   The provisions of rule 1 of the Scheme shall apply, so far as relevant, for the purpose of interpreting any other provision of the Scheme which applies to the tenement.

(4)   Rule 2 of the Scheme shall apply unless—

(a)   a tenement burden provides procedures for the making of decisions by the owners; and

(b)   the same such procedures apply as respects each flat.

(5)   The provisions of rule 3 of the Scheme shall apply to the extent that there is no tenement burden enabling the owners to make scheme decisions on any matter on which a scheme decision may be made by them under that rule.

(6)   Rule 4 of the Scheme shall apply in relation to any scheme costs incurred in relation to any part of the tenement unless a tenement burden provides that the entire liability for those scheme costs (in so far as liability for those costs is not to be met by someone other than an owner) is to be met by one or more of the owners.

(7)   The provisions of rule 5 of the Scheme shall apply to the extent that there is no tenement burden making provision as to the liability of the owners in the circumstances covered by the provisions of that rule.

(8)   The provisions of rule 6 of the Scheme shall apply to the extent that there is no tenement burden making provision as to the effect of any procedural irregularity in the making of a scheme decision on—

(a)   the validity of the decision; or

(b)   the liability of any owner affected by the decision.

(9)   Rule 7 of the Scheme shall apply to the extent that there is no tenement burden making provision—

(a)   for an owner to instruct or carry out any emergency work as defined in that rule; or

(b)   as to the liability of the owners for the cost of any emergency work as so defined.

(10)   The provisions of—

(a)   rule 8; and

(b)   subject to subsection (11) below, rule 9,

of the Scheme shall apply, so far as relevant, for the purpose of supplementing any other provision of the Scheme which applies to the tenement.

(11)   The provisions of rule 9 are subject to any different provision in any tenement burden.

(12)   The Scottish Ministers may by order substitute for the sums for the time being specified in rule 3.3 of the Scheme such other sums as appear to them to be justified by a change in the value of money appearing to them to have occurred since the last occasion on which the sums were fixed.

(13)   Where some but not all of the provisions of the Scheme apply, references in the Scheme to 'the scheme' shall be read as references only to those provisions of the Scheme which apply.

(14)   In this section [and section 4A], 'scheme costs' and 'scheme decision' have the same meanings as they have in the Scheme.

[4A   Power of local authority to pay share of scheme costs

(1)   The local authority for the area in which a tenement is situated may pay a sum representing an owner's share of scheme costs if that owner—

(a)   is unable or unwilling to do so, or

(b)   cannot, by reasonable inquiry, be identified or found.

(2)   But a local authority may not pay a sum representing an owner's share of scheme costs which are attributable to a scheme decision mentioned in rule 3.1(e) of the Tenement Management Scheme.

(3) For the purposes of this section an owner's share of any scheme costs is to be determined in accordance with—

(a) the Tenement Management Scheme as it applies to the owner's tenement, or

(b) where a tenement burden provides that the entire liability for those scheme costs (in so far as liability for those costs is not to be met by someone other than an owner) is to be met by one or more of the owners, that burden.

(4) Before making a payment under this section, the local authority must give notice to the owner who has failed to pay a share of any scheme costs.

(5) The local authority may recover from the owner who failed to pay a share of any scheme costs any—

(a) payments made under this section, and

(b) administrative expenses incurred by it in connection with the making of the payment.

(6) This section is without prejudice to any entitlement to recover sums in accordance with section 11 or 12.]

Resolution of disputes

5 Application to sheriff for annulment of certain decisions

(1) Where a decision is made by the owners in accordance with the management scheme which applies as respects the tenement (except where that management scheme is the development management scheme), an owner mentioned in subsection (2) below may, by summary application, apply to the sheriff for an order annulling the decision.

(2) That owner is—

(a) any owner who, at the time the decision referred to in subsection (1) above was made, was not in favour of the decision; or

(b) any new owner, that is to say, any person who was not an owner at that time but who has since become an owner.

(3) For the purposes of any such application, the defender shall be all the other owners.

(4) An application under subsection (1) above shall be made—

(a) in a case where the decision was made at a meeting attended by the owner making the application, not later than 28 days after the date of that meeting; or

(b) in any other case, not later than 28 days after the date on which notice of the making of the decision was given to the owner for the time being of the flat in question.

(5) The sheriff may, if satisfied that the decision—

(a) is not in the best interests of all (or both) the owners taken as a group; or

(b) is unfairly prejudicial to one or more of the owners,

make an order annulling the decision (in whole or in part).

(6) Where such an application is made as respects a decision to carry out maintenance, improvements or alterations, the sheriff shall, in considering whether to make an order under subsection (5) above, have regard to—

(a) the age of the property which is to be maintained, improved or, as the case may be, altered;

(b) its condition;

(c) the likely cost of any such maintenance, improvements or alterations; and

(d) the reasonableness of that cost.

(7) Where the sheriff makes an order under subsection (5) above annulling a decision (in whole or in part), the sheriff may make such other, consequential, order as the sheriff thinks fit (as, for example, an order as respects the liability of owners for any costs already incurred).

(8)   A party may not later than fourteen days after the date of—

(a)   an order under subsection (5) above; or

(b)   an interlocutor dismissing such an application,

appeal to the Court of Session on a point of law.

(9)   A decision of the Court of Session on an appeal under subsection (8) above shall be final.

(10)   Where an owner is entitled to make an application under subsection (1) above in relation to any decision, no step shall be taken to implement that decision unless—

(a)   the period specified in subsection (4) above within which such an application is to be made has expired without such an application having been made and notified to the owners; or

(b)   where such an application has been so made and notified—

(i)   the application has been disposed of and either the period specified in subsection (8) above within which an appeal against the sheriff's decision may be made has expired without such an appeal having been made or such an appeal has been made and disposed of; or

(ii)   the application has been abandoned.

(11)   Subsection (10) above does not apply to a decision relating to work which requires to be carried out urgently.

6   Application to sheriff for order resolving certain disputes

(1)   Any owner may by summary application apply to the sheriff for an order relating to any matter concerning the operation of—

(a)   the management scheme which applies as respects the tenement (except where that management scheme is the development management scheme); or

(b)   any provision of this Act in its application as respects the tenement.

(2)   Where an application is made under subsection (1) above the sheriff may, subject to such conditions (if any) as the sheriff thinks fit—

(a)   grant the order craved; or

(b)   make such other order under this section as the sheriff considers necessary or expedient.

(3)   A party may not later than fourteen days after the date of—

(a)   an order under subsection (2) above; or

(b)   an interlocutor dismissing such an application,

appeal to the Court of Session on a point of law.

(4)   A decision of the Court of Session on an appeal under subsection (3) above shall be final.

Support and shelter

7   Abolition as respects tenements of common law rules of common interest

Any rule of law relating to common interest shall, to the extent that it applies as respects a tenement, cease to have effect; but nothing in this section shall affect the operation of any such rule of law in its application to a question affecting both a tenement and—

(a)   some other building or former building (whether or not a tenement); or

(b)   any land not pertaining to the tenement.

8   Duty to maintain so as to provide support and shelter etc

(1)   Subject to subsection (2) below, the owner of any part of a tenement building, being a part that provides, or is intended to provide, support or shelter to any other part, shall maintain the supporting or sheltering part so as to ensure that it provides support or shelter.

(2)   An owner shall not by virtue of subsection (1) above be obliged to maintain any part of a tenement building if it would not be reasonable to do so, having

regard to all the circumstances (and including, in particular, the age of the tenement building, its condition and the likely cost of any maintenance).

(3) The duty imposed by subsection (1) above on an owner of a part of a tenement building may be enforced by any other such owner who is, or would be, directly affected by any breach of the duty.

(4) Where two or more persons own any such part of a tenement building as is referred to in subsection (1) above in common, any of them may, without the need for the agreement of the others, do anything that is necessary for the purpose of complying with the duty imposed by that subsection.

9 Prohibition on interference with support or shelter etc

(1) No owner or occupier of any part of a tenement shall be entitled to do anything in relation to that part which would, or would be reasonably likely to, impair to a material extent—

    (a) the support or shelter provided to any part of the tenement building; or

    (b) the natural light enjoyed by any part of the tenement building.

(2) The prohibition imposed by subsection (1) above on an owner or occupier of a part of a tenement may be enforced by any other such owner who is, or would be, directly affected by any breach of the prohibition.

10 Recovery of costs incurred by virtue of section 8
Where—

    (a) by virtue of section 8 of this Act an owner carries out maintenance to any part of a tenement; and

    (b) the management scheme which applies as respects the tenement provides for the maintenance of that part,

the owner shall be entitled to recover from any other owner any share of the cost of the maintenance for which that other owner would have been liable had the maintenance been carried out by virtue of the management scheme in question.

Repairs: costs and access

11 Determination of when an owner's liability for certain costs arise

(1) An owner is liable for any relevant costs (other than accumulating relevant costs) arising from a scheme decision from the date when the scheme decision to incur those costs is made.

(2) For the purposes of subsection (1) above, a scheme decision is, in relation to an owner, taken to be made on—

    (a) where the decision is made at a meeting, the date of the meeting; or

    (b) in any other case, the date on which notice of the making of the decision is given to the owner.

(3) An owner is liable for any relevant costs arising from any emergency work from the date on which the work is instructed.

(4) An owner is liable for any relevant costs of the kind mentioned in rule 4.1(d) of the Tenement Management Scheme from the date of any statutory notice requiring the carrying out of the work to which those costs relate.

(5) An owner is liable for any accumulating relevant costs (such as the cost of an insurance premium) on a daily basis.

(6) Except where subsection (1) above applies in relation to the costs, an owner is liable for any relevant costs arising from work instructed by a manager from the date on which the work is instructed.

(7) An owner is liable in accordance with section 10 of this Act for any relevant costs arising from maintenance carried out by virtue of section 8 of this Act from the date on which the maintenance is completed.

(8) An owner is liable for any relevant costs other than those to which subsections (1) to (7) above apply from—

    (a) such date; or

(b) the occurrence of such event,
as may be stipulated as the date on, or event in, which the costs become due.
(9) For the purposes of this section and section 12 of this Act, 'relevant costs'
means, as respects a flat—
    (a) the share of any costs for which the owner is liable by virtue of the manage-
ment scheme which applies as respects the tenement (except where that management scheme is the development management scheme); and
    (b) any costs for which the owner is liable by virtue of this Act.
(10) In this section, 'emergency work', 'manager' and 'scheme decision' have the
same meanings as they have in the Tenement Management Scheme.

12 Liability of owner and successors for certain costs

(1) Any owner who is liable for any relevant costs shall not, by virtue only of
ceasing to be such an owner, cease to be liable for those costs.
(2) Subject to subsection (3) below, where a person becomes an owner (any such
person being referred to in this section as a 'new owner'), that person shall be severally liable with any former owner of the flat for any relevant costs for which the
former owner is liable.
(3) A new owner shall be liable as mentioned in subsection (2) above for relevant
costs relating to any maintenance or work (other than local authority work) carried
out before the acquisition date only if—
    (a) notice of the maintenance or work—
        (i) in, or as near as may be in, the form set out in schedule 2 to this Act;
and
        (ii) containing the information required by the notes for completion set out
in that schedule,
(such a notice being referred to in this section and section 13 of this Act as a 'notice
of potential liability for costs') was registered in relation to the new owner's flat at
least 14 days before the acquisition date; and
    (b) the notice had not expired before the acquisition date.
(4) In subsection (3) above—
'acquisition date' means the date on which the new owner acquired right to
the flat; and
'local authority work' means work carried out by a local authority by virtue of
any enactment.
(5) Where a new owner pays any relevant costs for which a former owner of the
flat is liable, the new owner may recover the amount so paid from the former owner.
(6) This section applies as respects any relevant costs for which an owner becomes
liable on or after the day on which this section comes into force.

13 Notice of potential liability for costs: further provision

(1) A notice of potential liability for costs—
    (a) may be registered in relation to a flat only on the application of—
        (i) the owner of the flat;
        (ii) the owner of any other flat in the same tenement; or
      [(iia) a local authority entitled to recover costs under section 4A(5),]
        (iii) any manager (within the meaning of the Tenement Management
Scheme) of the tenement; and
    (b) shall not be registered unless it is signed by or on behalf of the applicant.
(2) A notice of potential liability for costs may be registered—
    (a) in relation to more than one flat in respect of the same maintenance or work;
and
    (b) in relation to any one flat, in respect of different maintenance or work.
(3) A notice of potential liability for costs expires at the end of the period of 3
years beginning with the date of its registration, unless the notice is renewed by
being registered again before the end of that period.

[(3A)   The owner of a flat may apply to register a notice (a 'notice of discharge') if—

(a)   a notice of potential liability for costs in relation to the flat has not expired,

(b)   the liability for costs under section 12(2) to which the notice of potential liability relates has, in relation to the flat which is the subject of the application, been fully discharged, and

(c)   the person who registered the notice of potential liability for costs consents to the application.

(3B)   A notice of discharge—

(a)   must be in the form prescribed by order made by the Scottish Ministers, and

(b)   on being registered, discharges the notice of potential liability for costs as it applies to the flat which is the subject of the application.]

(4)   This section applies to a renewed notice of potential liability for costs as it applies to any other such notice.

(5)   The Keeper of the Registers of Scotland shall not be required to investigate or determine whether the information contained in any notice of potential liability for costs submitted for registration is accurate.

(6)   The Scottish Ministers may by order amend schedule 2 to this Act.

(7)   [Amended Land Registration (Scotland) Act 1979.]

14   Former owner's right to recover costs

An owner who is entitled, by virtue of the Tenement Management Scheme or any other provision of this Act, to recover any costs or a share of any costs from any other owner shall not, by virtue only of ceasing to be an owner, cease to be entitled to recover those costs or that share.

15   [Amends Prescription and Limitation (Scotland) Act 1973.]

16   Common property: disapplication of common law right of recovery

Any rule of law which enables an owner of common property to recover the cost of necessary maintenance from the other owners of the property shall not apply in relation to any common property in a tenement where the maintenance of that property is provided for in the management scheme which applies as respects the tenement.

17   Access for maintenance and other purposes

(1)   Where an owner gives reasonable notice to the owner or occupier of any other part of the tenement that access is required to, or through, that part for any of the purposes mentioned in subsection (3) below, the person given notice shall, subject to subsection (5) below, allow access for that purpose.

(2)   Without prejudice to subsection (1) above, where the development management scheme applies, notice under that subsection may be given by any owners' association established by the scheme to the owner or occupier of any part of the tenement.

(3)   The purposes are—

(a)   carrying out maintenance or other work by virtue of the management scheme which applies as respects the tenement;

(b)   carrying out maintenance to any part of the tenement owned (whether solely or in common) by the person requiring access;

(c)   carrying out an inspection to determine whether it is necessary to carry out maintenance;

(d)   determining whether the owner of the part is fulfilling the duty imposed by section 8(1) of this Act;

(e)   determining whether the owner or occupier of the part is complying with the prohibition imposed by section 9(1) of this Act;

(f)   doing anything which the owner giving notice is entitled to do by virtue of section 19(1) of this Act;

(g)   where floor area is relevant for the purposes of determining any liability of owners, measuring floor area; and

(h)   where a power of sale order has been granted in relation to the tenement building or its site, doing anything necessary for the purpose of or in connection with any sale in pursuance of the order (other than complying with paragraph 4(3) of schedule 3 to this Act).

(4)   Reasonable notice need not be given as mentioned in subsection (1) above where access is required for the purpose specified in subsection (3)(a) above and the maintenance or other work requires to be carried out urgently.

(5)   An owner or occupier may refuse to allow—

(a)   access under subsection (1) above; or

(b)   such access at a particular time,

if, having regard to all the circumstances (and, in particular, whether the requirement for access is reasonable), it is reasonable to refuse access.

(6)   Where access is allowed under subsection (1) above for any purpose, such right of access may be exercised by—

(a)   the owner who or owners' association which gave notice that access was required; or

(b)   such person as the owner or, as the case may be, owners' association may authorise for the purpose (any such person being referred to in this section as an 'authorised person').

(7)   Where an authorised person acting in accordance with subsection (6) above is liable by virtue of any enactment or rule of law for damage caused to any part of a tenement, the owner who or owners' association which authorised that person shall be severally liable with the authorised person for the cost of remedying the damage; but an owner or, as the case may be, owners' association making any payment as respects that cost shall have a right of relief against the authorised person.

(8)   Where access is allowed under subsection (1) above for any purpose, the owner who or owners' association which gave notice that access was required (referred to as the 'accessing owner or association') shall, so far as reasonably practicable, ensure that the part of the tenement to or through which access is allowed is left substantially in no worse a condition than that which it was in when access was taken.

(9)   If the accessing owner or association fails to comply with the duty in subsection (8) above, the owner of the part to or through which access is allowed may—

(a)   carry out, or arrange for the carrying out of, such work as is reasonably necessary to restore the part so that it is substantially in no worse a condition than that which it was in when access was taken; and

(b)   recover from the accessing owner or association any expenses reasonably incurred in doing so.

Insurance

18   Obligation of owner to insure

(1)   It shall be the duty of each owner to effect and keep in force a contract of insurance against the prescribed risks for the reinstatement value of that owner's flat and any part of the tenement building attaching to that flat as a pertinent.

(2)   The duty imposed by subsection (1) above may be satisfied, in whole or in part, by way of a common policy of insurance arranged for the entire tenement building.

(3)   The Scottish Ministers may by order prescribe risks against which an owner shall require to insure (in this section referred to as the 'prescribed risks').

(4)   Where, whether because of the location of the tenement or otherwise, an owner—

(a)   having made reasonable efforts to do so, is unable to obtain insurance against a particular prescribed risk; or

(b)   would be able to obtain such insurance but only at a cost which is unreasonably high,

the duty imposed by subsection (1) above shall not require an owner to insure against that particular risk.

(5)   Any owner may by notice in writing request the owner of any other flat in the tenement to produce evidence of—

(a)   the policy in respect of any contract of insurance which the owner of that other flat is required to have or to effect; and

(b)   payment of the premium for any such policy,

and not later than 14 days after that notice is given the recipient shall produce to the owner giving the notice the evidence requested.

(6)   The duty imposed by subsection (1) above on an owner may be enforced by any other owner.

Installation of service pipes etc

19   Installation of service pipes etc

(1)   Subject to subsections (2) and (3) below and to section 17 of this Act, an owner shall be entitled—

(a)   to lead through any part of the tenement such pipe, cable or other equipment; and

(b)   to fix to any part of the tenement, and keep there, such equipment,

as is necessary for the provision to that owner's flat of such service or services as the Scottish Ministers may by regulations prescribe.

(2)   The right conferred by subsection (1) above is exercisable only in accordance with such procedure as the Scottish Ministers may by regulations prescribe; and different procedures may be so prescribed in relation to different services.

(3)   An owner is not entitled by virtue of subsection (1) above to lead anything through or fix anything to any part which is wholly within another owner's flat.

(4)   This section is without prejudice to any obligation imposed by virtue of any enactment relating to—

(a)   planning;

(b)   building; or

(c)   any service prescribed under subsection (1) above.

Demolition and abandonment of tenement building

20   Demolition of tenement building not to affect ownership

(1)   The demolition of a tenement building shall not alone effect any change as respects any right of ownership.

(2)   In particular, the fact that, as a consequence of demolition of a tenement building, any land pertaining to the building no longer serves, or affords access to, any flat or other sector shall not alone effect any change of ownership of the land as a pertinent.

21   Cost of demolishing tenement building

(1)   Except where a tenement burden otherwise provides, the cost of demolishing a tenement building shall, subject to subsection (2) below, be shared equally among all (or both) the flats in the tenement, and each owner is liable accordingly.

(2)   Where the floor area of the largest (or larger) flat in the tenement is more than one and a half times that of the smallest (or smaller) flat the owner of each flat shall be liable to contribute towards the cost of demolition of the tenement

building in the proportion which the floor area of that owner's flat bears to the total floor area of all (or both) the flats.

(3)   An owner is liable under this section for the cost of demolishing a tenement building—

(a)   in the case where the owner agrees to the proposal that the tenement building be demolished, from the date of the agreement; or

(b)   in any other case, from the date on which the carrying out of the demolition is instructed.

(4)   This section applies as respects the demolition of part of a tenement building as it applies as respects the demolition of an entire tenement building but with any reference to a flat in the tenement being construed as a reference to a flat in the part.

(5)   In this section references to flats in a tenement include references to flats which were comprehended by the tenement before its demolition.

(6)   This section is subject to section 123 of the Housing (Scotland) Act 1987 (c 26) (which makes provision as respects demolition of buildings in pursuance of local authority demolition orders and recovery of expenses by local authorities etc).

22   Use and disposal of site where tenement building demolished

(1)   This section applies where a tenement building is demolished and after the demolition two or more flats which were comprehended by the tenement building before its demolition (any such flat being referred to in this section as a 'former flat') are owned by different persons.

(2)   Except in so far as—

(a)   the owners of all (or both) the former flats otherwise agree; or

(b)   those owners are subject to a requirement (whether imposed by a tenement burden or otherwise) to erect a building on the site or to rebuild the tenement,

no owner may build on, or otherwise develop, the site.

(3)   Except where the owners have agreed, or are required, to build on or develop the site as mentioned in paragraphs (a) and (b) of subsection (2) above, any owner of a former flat shall be entitled to apply for power to sell the entire site in accordance with schedule 3.

(4)   Except where a tenement burden otherwise provides, the net proceeds of any sale in pursuance of subsection (3) above shall, subject to subsection (5) below, be shared equally among all (or both) the former flats and the owner of each former flat shall be entitled to the share allocated to that flat.

(5)   Where—

(a)   evidence of the floor area of each of the former flats is readily available; and

(b)   the floor area of the largest (or larger) former flat was more than one and a half times that of the smallest (or smaller) former flat,

the net proceeds of any sale shall be shared among (or between) the flats in the proportion which the floor area of each flat bore to the total floor area of all (or both) the flats and the owner of each former flat shall be entitled to the share allocated to that flat.

(6)   The prohibition imposed by subsection (2) above on an owner of a former flat may be enforced by any other such owner.

(7)   In subsections (4) and (5) above, 'net proceeds of any sale' means the proceeds of the sale less any expenses properly incurred in connection with the sale.

(8)   In this section references to the site are references to the solum of the tenement building that occupied the site together with the airspace that is directly above the solum and any land pertaining, as a means of access, to the tenement building immediately before its demolition.

23 Sale of abandoned tenement building

(1) Where—

(a) because of its poor condition a tenement building has been entirely un-occupied by any owner or person authorised by an owner for a period of more than six months; and

(b) it is unlikely that any such owner or other person will occupy any part of the tenement building,

any owner shall be entitled to apply for power to sell the tenement building in accordance with schedule 3.

(2) Subsections (4) and (5) of section 22 of this Act shall apply as respects a sale in pursuance of subsection (1) above as those subsections apply as respects a sale in pursuance of subsection (3) of that section.

(3) In this section any reference to a tenement building includes a reference to its solum and any land pertaining, as a means of access, to the tenement building.

Liability for certain costs

24 Liability to non owner for certain damage costs

(1) Where—

(a) any part of a tenement is damaged as the result of the fault of any person (that person being in this subsection referred to as 'A'); and

(b) the management scheme which applies as respects the tenement makes pro-vision for the maintenance of that part,

any owner of a flat in the tenement (that owner being in this subsection referred to as 'B') who is required by virtue of that provision to contribute to any extent to the cost of maintenance of the damaged part but who at the time when the damage was done was not an owner of the part shall be treated, for the purpose of determining whether A is liable to B as respects the cost of maintenance arising from the damage, as having been such an owner at that time.

(2) In this section 'fault' means any wrongful act, breach of statutory duty or negligent act or omission which gives rise to liability in damages.

Miscellaneous and general

26 Meaning of 'tenement'

(1) In this Act, 'tenement' means a building or a part of a building which com-prises two related flats which, or more than two such flats at least two of which—

(a) are, or are designed to be, in separate ownership; and

(b) are divided from each other horizontally,

and, except where the context otherwise requires, includes the solum and any other land pertaining to that building or, as the case may be, part of the building; and the expression 'tenement building' shall be construed accordingly.

(2) In determining whether flats comprised in a building or part of a building are related for the purposes of subsection (1), regard shall be had, among other things, to—

(a) the title to the tenement; and

(b) any tenement burdens,

treating the building or part for that purpose as if it were a tenement.

27 Meaning of 'management scheme'

References in this Act to the management scheme which applies as respects any tene-ment are references to—

(a) if the Tenement Management Scheme applies in its entirety as respects the tenement, that Scheme;

(b) if the development management scheme applies as respects the tenement, that scheme; or

(c) in any other case, any tenement burdens relating to maintenance, management or improvement of the tenement together with any provisions of the Tenement Management Scheme which apply as respects the tenement.

28 Meaning of 'owner', determination of liability etc

(1) In this Act, references to 'owner' without further qualification are, in relation to any tenement, references to the owner of a flat in the tenement.

(2) Subject to subsection (3) below, in this Act 'owner' means, in relation to a flat in a tenement, a person who has right to the flat whether or not that person has completed title; but if, in relation to the flat (or, if the flat is held pro indiviso, any pro indiviso share in it) more than one person comes within that description of owner, then 'owner' means such person as has most recently acquired such right.

(3) Where a heritable security has been granted over a flat and the heritable creditor has entered into lawful possession, 'owner' means the heritable creditor in possession of the flat.

(4) Subject to subsection (5) below, if two or more persons own a flat in common, any reference in this Act to an owner is a reference to both or, as the case may be, all of them.

(5) Any reference to an owner in sections 5(1) and (2), 6(1), 8(3), 9, 10, 12 to 14, 17(1), (6) and (7), 18(5) and (6), 19, 22, 23 and 24 of, and schedule 3 to, this Act shall be construed as a reference to any person who owns a flat either solely or in common with another.

(6) Subsections (2) to (5) above apply to references in this Act to the owner of a part of a tenement as they apply to references to the owner of a flat, but as if references in them to a flat were to the part of the tenement.

(7) Where two or more persons own a flat in common—

(a) they are severally liable for the performance of any obligation imposed by virtue of this Act on the owner of that flat; and

(b) as between (or among) themselves they are liable in the proportions in which they own the flat.

29 Interpretation

(1) In this Act, unless the content otherwise requires—

'chimney stack' does not include flue or chimney pot;

'close' means a connected passage, stairs and landings within a tenement building which together constitute a common access to two or more of the flats;

'demolition' includes destruction and cognate expressions shall be construed accordingly; and demolition may occur on one occasion or over any period of time;

'the development management scheme' has the meaning given by section 71(3) of the Title Conditions (Scotland) Act 2003 (asp 9);

'door' includes its frame;

'flat' includes any premises whether or not—

(a) used or intended to be used for residential purposes; or

(b) on the one floor;

'lift' includes its shaft and operating machinery;

'local authority' means a council constituted under section 2 of the Local Government etc. (Scotland) Act 1994 (c 39);

'owner' shall be construed in accordance with section 28 of this Act;

'power of sale order' means an order granted under paragraph 1 of schedule 3 to this Act;

'register', in relation to a notice of potential liability for costs [, a notice of discharge] or power of sale order, means register the information contained in the notice or order in the Land Register of Scotland or, as appropriate, record the notice or order in the Register of Sasines, and 'registered' and other related expressions shall be construed accordingly;

'sector' means—

(a) a flat;

(b) any close or lift; or

(c) any other three dimensional space not comprehended by a flat, close or lift,

and the tenement building shall be taken to be entirely divided into sectors;

'solum' means the ground on which a building is erected;

'tenement' shall be construed in accordance with section 26 of this Act;

'tenement burden' means, in relation to a tenement, any real burden (within the meaning of the Title Conditions (Scotland) Act 2003 (asp 9)) which affects—

(a) the tenement; or

(b) any sector in the tenement;

'Tenement Management Scheme' means the scheme set out in schedule 1 to this Act;

'title to the tenement' shall be construed in accordance with section 1(2) of this Act; and

'window' includes its frame.

(2) The floor area of a flat is calculated for the purposes of this Act by measuring the total floor area (including the area occupied by any internal wall or other internal dividing structure) within its boundaries; but no account shall be taken of any pertinents or any of the following parts of a flat—

(a) a balcony; and

(b) except where it is used for any purpose other than storage, a loft or basement.

30 Giving of notice to owners

(1) Any notice which is to be given to an owner under or in connection with this Act (other than under or in connection with the Tenement Management Scheme) may be given in writing by sending the notice to—

(a) the owner; or

(b) the owner's agent.

(2) The reference in subsection (1) above to sending a notice is to its being—

(a) posted;

(b) delivered; or

(c) transmitted by electronic means.

(3) Where an owner cannot by reasonable inquiry be identified or found, a notice shall be taken for the purposes of subsection (1)(a) above to be sent to the owner if it is posted or delivered to the owner's flat addressed to 'The Owner' or using some similar expression such as 'The Proprietor'.

(4) For the purposes of this Act—

(a) a notice posted shall be taken to be given on the day of posting; and

(b) a notice transmitted by electronic means shall be taken to be given on the day of transmission.

31 Ancillary provision

(1) The Scottish Ministers may by order make such incidental, supplemental, consequential, transitional, transitory or saving provision as they consider necessary or expedient for the purposes, or in consequence, of this Act.

(2) An order under this section may modify any enactment (including this Act), instrument or document.

32 Orders and regulations

(1) Any power of the Scottish Ministers to make orders or regulations under this Act shall be exercisable by statutory instrument.

(2) A statutory instrument containing an order or regulations under this Act (except an order under section 34(2) or, where subsection (3) applies, section

31) shall be subject to annulment in pursuance of a resolution of the Scottish Parliament.

(3)   Where an order under section 31 contains provisions which add to, replace or omit any part of the text of an Act, the order shall not be made unless a draft of the statutory instrument containing the order has been laid before, and approved by a resolution of, the Parliament.

33   Crown application
This Act, except section 18, binds the Crown.

34   Short title and commencement
(1)   This Act may be cited as the Tenements (Scotland) Act 2004.

(2)   This Act (other than this section, section 25 and schedule 4) shall come into force on such day as the Scottish Ministers may by order appoint; and different days may be appointed for different purposes.

(3)   Section 25 and schedule 4 shall come into force on the day after Royal Assent.

SCHEDULES

SCHEDULE 1
TENEMENT MANAGEMENT SCHEME
(introduced by section 4)

RULE 1—SCOPE AND INTERPRETATION

1.1   Scope of scheme
This scheme provides for the management and maintenance of the scheme property of a tenement.

1.2   Meaning of 'scheme property'
For the purposes of this scheme, 'scheme property' means, in relation to a tenement, all or any of the following—

(a)   any part of the tenement that is the common property of two or more of the owners,

(b)   any part of the tenement (not being common property of the type mentioned in paragraph (a) above) the maintenance of which, or the cost of maintaining which, is, by virtue of a tenement burden, the responsibility of two or more of the owners,

(c)   with the exceptions mentioned in rule 1.3, the following parts of the tenement building (so far as not scheme property by virtue of paragraph (a) or (b) above)—

(i)   the ground on which it is built,

(ii)   its foundations,

(iii)   its external walls,

(iv)   its roof (including any rafter or other structure supporting the roof),

(v)   if it is separated from another building by a gable wall, the part of the gable wall that is part of the tenement building, and

(vi)   any wall (not being one falling within the preceding sub-paragraphs), beam or column that is load bearing.

1.3   Parts not included in rule 1.2(c)
The following parts of a tenement building are the exceptions referred to in rule 1.2(c)—

(a)   any extension which forms part of only one flat,

(b)   any—

(i)   door,

(ii)   window,
(iii)   skylight,
(iv)   vent, or
(v)   other opening,
which serves only one flat,
(c)   any chimney stack or chimney flue.

1.4   Meaning of 'scheme decision'
A decision is a 'scheme decision' for the purposes of this scheme if it is made in accordance with—
(a)   rule 2, or
(b)   where that rule does not apply, the tenement burden or burdens providing the procedure for the making of decisions by the owners.

1.5   Other definitions
In this scheme—
'maintenance' includes repairs and replacement, [the installation of insulation,] cleaning, painting and other routine works, gardening, the day to day running of a tenement and the reinstatement of a part (but not most) of the tenement building, but does not include demolition, alteration or improvement unless reasonably incidental to the maintenance,
'manager' means, in relation to a tenement, a person appointed (whether or not by virtue of rule 3.1(c)(i)) to manage the tenement, and
'scheme costs' has the meaning given by rule 4.1.

1.6   Rights of co owners
If a flat is owned by two or more persons, then one of them may do anything that the owner is by virtue of this scheme entitled to do.

RULE 2—PROCEDURE FOR MAKING SCHEME DECISIONS

2.1   Making scheme decisions
Any decision to be made by the owners shall be made in accordance with the following provisions of this rule.

2.2   Allocation and exercise of votes
Except as mentioned in rule 2.3, for the purpose of voting on any proposed scheme decision one vote is allocated as respects each flat, and any right to vote is exercisable by the owner of that flat or by someone nominated by the owner to vote as respects the flat.

2.3   Qualification on allocation of votes
No vote is allocated as respects a flat if—
(a)   the scheme decision relates to the maintenance of scheme property, and
(b)   the owner of that flat is not liable for maintenance of, or the cost of maintaining, the property concerned.

2.4   Exercise of vote where two or more persons own flat
If a flat is owned by two or more persons the vote allocated as respects that flat may be exercised in relation to any proposal by either (or any) of them, but if those persons disagree as to how the vote should be cast then the vote is not to be counted unless—
(a)   where one of those persons owns more than a half share of the flat, the vote is exercised by that person, or
(b)   in any other case, the vote is the agreed vote of those who together own more than a half share of the flat.

2.5   Decision by majority
A scheme decision is made by majority vote of all the votes allocated.

2.6   Notice of meeting
If any owner wishes to call a meeting of the owners with a view to making a scheme decision at that meeting that owner must give the other owners at least 48 hours' notice of the date and time of the meeting, its purpose and the place where it is to be held.

2.7   Consultation of owners if scheme decision not made at meeting
If an owner wishes to propose that a scheme decision be made but does not wish to call a meeting for the purpose that owner must instead—
    (a)   unless it is impracticable to do so (whether because of absence of any owner or for other good reason) consult on the proposal each of the other owners of flats as respects which votes are allocated, and
    (b)   count the votes cast by them.

2.8   Consultation where two or more persons own flat
For the purposes of rule 2.7, the requirement to consult each owner is satisfied as respects any flat which is owned by more than one person if one of those persons is consulted.

2.9   Notification of scheme decisions
A scheme decision must, as soon as practicable, be notified—
    (a)   if it was made at a meeting, to all the owners who were not present when the decision was made, by such person as may be nominated for the purpose by the persons who made the decision, or
    (b)   in any other case, to each of the other owners, by the owner who proposed that the decision be made.

2.10   Case where decision may be annulled by notice
Any owner (or owners) who did not vote in favour of a scheme decision to carry out, or authorise, maintenance to scheme property and who would be liable for not less than 75 per cent of the scheme costs arising from that decision may, within the time mentioned in rule 2.11, annul that decision by giving notice that the decision is annulled to each of the other owners.

2.11   Time limits for rule 2.10
The time within which a notice under rule 2.10 must be given is—
    (a)   if the scheme decision was made at a meeting attended by the owner (or any of the owners), not later than 21 days after the date of that meeting, or
    (b)   in any other case, not later than 21 days after the date on which notification of the making of the decision was given to the owner or owners (that date being, where notification was given to owners on different dates, the date on which it was given to the last of them).

RULE 3—MATTERS ON WHICH SCHEME DECISIONS MAY BE MADE

3.1   Basic scheme decisions
The owners may make a scheme decision on any of the following matters—
    (a)   to carry out maintenance to scheme property,
    (b)   to arrange for an inspection of scheme property to determine whether or to what extent it is necessary to carry out maintenance to the property,
    (c)   except where a power conferred by a manager burden (within the meaning of the Title Conditions (Scotland) Act 2003 (asp 9)) is exercisable in relation to the tenement—
        (i)   to appoint on such terms as they may determine a person (who may be an owner or a firm) to manage the tenement,
        (ii)   to dismiss any manager,

(d) to delegate to a manager power to exercise such of their powers as they may specify, including, without prejudice to that generality, any power to decide to carry out maintenance and to instruct it,

(e) to arrange for the tenement a common policy of insurance complying with section 18 of this Act and against such other risks (if any) as the owners may determine and to determine on an equitable basis the liability of each owner to contribute to the premium,

(f) to install a system enabling entry to the tenement to be controlled from each flat,

(g) to determine that an owner is not required to pay a share (or some part of a share) of such scheme costs as may be specified by them,

(h) to authorise any maintenance of scheme property already carried out,

(i) to modify or revoke any scheme decision.

3.2 Scheme decisions relating to maintenance

If the owners make a scheme decision to carry out maintenance to scheme property or if a manager decides, by virtue of a scheme decision, that maintenance needs to be carried out to scheme property, the owners may make a scheme decision on any of the following matters—

(a) to appoint on such terms as they may determine a person (who may be an owner or a firm) to manage the carrying out of the maintenance,

(b) to instruct or arrange for the carrying out of the maintenance,

(c) subject to rule 3.3, to require each owner to deposit—

(i) by such date as they may decide (being a date not less than 28 days after the requirement is made of that owner), and

(ii) with such person as they may nominate for the purpose,

a sum of money (being a sum not exceeding that owner's apportioned share of a reasonable estimate of the cost of the maintenance),

(d) to take such other steps as are necessary to ensure that the maintenance is carried out to a satisfactory standard and completed in good time.

3.3 Scheme decisions under rule 3.2(c) requiring deposits exceeding certain amounts

A requirement, in pursuance of a scheme decision under rule 3.2(c), that each owner deposit a sum of money—

(a) exceeding £100, or

(b) of £100 or less where the aggregate of that sum taken together with any other sum or sums required (otherwise than by a previous notice under this rule) in the preceding 12 months to be deposited by each owner by virtue any scheme decision under rule 3.2(c) exceeds £200,

shall be made by written notice to each owner and shall require the sum to be deposited into such account (the 'maintenance account') as the owners may nominate for the purpose.

3.4 Provision supplementary to rule 3.3

Where a requirement is, or is to be, made in accordance with rule 3.3—

(a) the owners may make a scheme decision authorising a manager or at least two other persons (whether or not owners) to operate the maintenance account on behalf of the owners,

(b) there must be contained in or attached to the notice to be given under rule 3.3 a note comprising a summary of the nature and extent of the maintenance to be carried out together with the following information—

(i) the estimated cost of carrying out that maintenance,

(ii) why the estimate is considered a reasonable estimate,

(iii) how the sum required from the owner in question and the apportionment among the owners have been arrived at,

(iv) what the apportioned shares of the other owners are,

(v)   the date on which the decision to carry out the maintenance was made and the names of those by whom it was made,

(vi)   a timetable for the carrying out of the maintenance, including the dates by which it is proposed the maintenance will be commenced and completed,

(vii)   the location and number of the maintenance account, and

(viii)   the names and addresses of the persons who will be authorised to operate that account on behalf of the owners,

(c)   the maintenance account to be nominated under rule 3.3 must be a bank or building society account which is interest bearing, and the authority of at least two persons or of a manager on whom has been conferred the right to give authority, must be required for any payment from it,

(d)   if a modification or revocation under rule 3.1(i) affects the information contained in the notice or the note referred to in paragraph (b) above, the information must be sent again, modified accordingly, to the owners,

(e)   an owner is entitled to inspect, at any reasonable time, any tender received in connection with the maintenance to be carried out,

(f)   the notice to be given under rule 3.3 may specify a date as a refund date for the purposes of paragraph (g)(i) below,

(g)   if—

(i)   the maintenance is not commenced by—

(A)   where the notice under rule 3.3 specifies a refund date, that date, or

(B)   where that notice does not specify such a date, the twenty-eighth day after the proposed date for its commencement as specified in the notice by virtue of paragraph (b)(vi) above, and

(ii)   a depositor demands, by written notice, from the persons authorised under paragraph (a) above repayment (with accrued interest) of such sum as has been deposited by that person in compliance with the scheme decision under rule 3.2(c),

the depositor is entitled to be repaid accordingly, except that no requirement to make repayment in compliance with a notice under sub-paragraph (ii) arises if the persons so authorised do not receive that notice before the maintenance is commenced,

(h)   such sums as are held in the maintenance account by virtue of rule 3.3 are held in trust for all the depositors, for the purpose of being used by the persons authorised to make payments from the account as payment for the maintenance,

(i)   any sums held in the maintenance account after all sums payable in respect of the maintenance carried out have been paid shall be shared among the depositors—

(i)   by repaying each depositor, with any accrued interest and after deduction of that person's apportioned share of the actual cost of the maintenance, the sum which the person deposited, or

(ii)   in such other way as the depositors agree in writing.

3.5   Scheme decisions under rule 3.1(g): votes of persons standing to benefit not to be counted

A vote in favour of a scheme decision under rule 3.1(g) is not to be counted if—

(a)   the owner exercising the vote, or

(b)   where the vote is exercised by a person nominated by an owner—

(i)   that person, or

(ii)   the owner who nominated that person,

is the owner or an owner who, by virtue of the decision, would not be required to pay as mentioned in that rule.

RULE 4—SCHEME COSTS: LIABILITY AND APPORTIONMENT

4.1 Meaning of 'scheme costs'

Except in so far as rule 5 applies, this rule provides for the apportionment of liability among the owners for any of the following costs—

(a) any costs arising from any maintenance or inspection of scheme property where the maintenance or inspection is in pursuance of, or authorised by, a scheme decision,

(b) any remuneration payable to a person appointed to manage the carrying out of such maintenance as is mentioned in paragraph (a),

(c) running costs relating to any scheme property (other than costs incurred solely for the benefit of one flat),

(d) any costs recoverable by a local authority in respect of work relating to any scheme property carried out by them by virtue of any enactment,

(e) any remuneration payable to any manager,

(f) the cost of any common insurance to cover the tenement,

(g) the cost of installing a system enabling entry to the tenement to be controlled from each flat,

(h) any costs relating to the calculation of the floor area of any flat, where such calculation is necessary for the purpose of determining the share of any other costs for which each owner is liable,

(i) any other costs relating to the management of scheme property,

and a reference in this scheme to 'scheme costs' is a reference to any of the costs mentioned in paragraphs (a) to (i).

4.2 Maintenance and running costs

Except as provided in rule 4.3, if any scheme costs mentioned in rule 4.1(a) to (d) relate to—

(a) the scheme property mentioned in rule 1.2(a), then those costs are shared among the owners in the proportions in which the owners share ownership of that property,

(b) the scheme property mentioned in rule 1.2(b) or (c), then—

(i) in any case where the floor area of the largest (or larger) flat is more than one and a half times that of the smallest (or smaller) flat, each owner is liable to contribute towards those costs in the proportion which the floor area of that owner's flat bears to the total floor area of all (or both) the flats,

(ii) in any other case, those costs are shared equally among the flats,

and each owner is liable accordingly.

4.3 Scheme costs relating to roof over the close

Where—

(a) any scheme costs mentioned in rule 4.1(a) to (d) relate to the roof over the close, and

(b) that roof is common property by virtue of section 3(1)(a) of this Act,

then, despite the fact that the roof is scheme property mentioned in rule 1.2(a), paragraph (b) of rule 4.2 shall apply for the purpose of apportioning liability for those costs.

4.4 Insurance premium

Any scheme costs mentioned in rule 4.1(f) are shared among the flats—

(a) where the costs relate to common insurance arranged by virtue of rule 3.1(e), in such proportions as may be determined by the owners by virtue of that rule, or

(b) where the costs relate to common insurance arranged by virtue of a tenement burden, equally,

and each owner is liable accordingly.

4.5   Other scheme costs
Any scheme costs mentioned in rule 4.1(e), (g), (h) or (i) are shared equally among the flats, and each owner is liable accordingly.

RULE 5—REDISTRIBUTION OF SHARE OF COSTS

Where an owner is liable for a share of any scheme costs but—
    (a)   a scheme decision has been made determining that the share (or a portion of it) should not be paid by that owner, or
    (b)   the share cannot be recovered for some other reason such as that—
        (i)   the estate of that owner has been sequestrated, or
        (ii)   that owner cannot, by reasonable inquiry, be identified or found,
then [(unless that share has been paid by the local authority under section 4A)] that share must be paid by the other owners who are liable for a share of the same costs (the share being divided equally among the flats of those other owners), but where paragraph (b) applies that owner is liable to each of those other owners for the amount paid by each of them.

RULE 6—PROCEDURAL IRREGULARITIES

6.1   Validity of scheme decisions
Any procedural irregularity in the making of a scheme decision does not affect the validity of the decision.

6.2   Liability for scheme costs where procedural irregularity
If any owner is directly affected by a procedural irregularity in the making of a scheme decision and that owner—
    (a)   was not aware that any scheme costs relating to that decision were being incurred, or
    (b)   on becoming aware as mentioned in paragraph (a), immediately objected to the incurring of those costs,
that owner is not liable for any such costs (whether incurred before or after the date of objection), and, for the purposes of determining the share of those scheme costs due by each of the other owners, that owner is left out of account.

RULE 7—EMERGENCY WORK

7.1   Power to instruct or carry out
Any owner may instruct or carry out emergency work.

7.2   Liability for cost
The owners are liable for the cost of any emergency work instructed or carried out as if the cost of that work were scheme costs mentioned in rule 4.1(a).

7.3   Meaning of 'emergency work'
For the purposes of this rule, 'emergency work' means work which, before a scheme decision can be obtained, requires to be carried out to scheme property—
    (a)   to prevent damage to any part of the tenement, or
    (b)   in the interests of health or safety.

RULE 8—ENFORCEMENT

8.1   Scheme binding on owners
This scheme binds the owners.

8.2 Scheme decision to be binding
A scheme decision is binding on the owners and their successors as owners.

8.3 Enforceability of scheme decisions
Any obligation imposed by this scheme or arising from a scheme decision may be enforced by any owner.

8.4 Enforcement by third party
Any person authorised in writing for the purpose by the owner or owners concerned [and a local authority entitled to recover costs under section 4A(5)] may—
    (a) enforce an obligation such as is mentioned in rule 8.3 on behalf of one or more owners, and
    (b) in doing so, may bring any claim or action in that person's own name.

RULE 9—GIVING OF NOTICE

9.1 Giving of notice
Any notice which requires to be given to an owner under or in connection with this scheme may be given in writing by sending the notice to—
    (a) the owner, or
    (b) the owner's agent.

9.2 Methods of 'sending' for the purposes of rule 9.1
The reference in rule 9.1 to sending a notice is to its being—
    (a) posted,
    (b) delivered, or
    (c) transmitted by electronic means.

9.3 Giving of notice to owner where owner's name is not known
Where an owner cannot by reasonable inquiry be identified or found, a notice shall be taken for the purposes of rule 9.1(a) to be sent to the owner if it is posted or delivered to the owner's flat addressed to 'The Owner' or using some other similar expression such as 'The Proprietor'.

9.4 Day on which notice is to be taken to be given
For the purposes of this scheme—
    (a) a notice posted shall be taken to be given on the day of posting, and
    (b) a notice transmitted by electronic means shall be taken to be given on the day of transmission.

SCHEDULE 2
FORM OF NOTICE OF POTENTIAL LIABILITY FOR COSTS
(introduced by section 12(3))

'NOTICE OF POTENTIAL LIABILITY FOR COSTS

This notice gives details of certain maintenance or work carried out [or to be carried out] in relation to the flat specified in the notice. The effect of the notice is that a person may, on becoming the owner of the flat, be liable by virtue of section 12(3) of the Tenements (Scotland) Act 2004 (asp 11) for any outstanding costs relating to the maintenance or work.

Flat to which notice relates:
(see note 1 below)

Description of the maintenance or work to which notice relates:
(see note 2 below)

Person giving notice:
(see note 3 below)

Signature:
(see note 4 below)

Date of signing:'

Notes for completion

(These notes are not part of the notice)
   1   Describe the flat in a way that is sufficient to identify it. Where the flat has a postal address, the description must include that address. Where title to the flat has been registered in the Land Register of Scotland, the description must refer to the title number of the flat or of the larger subjects of which it forms part. Otherwise, the description should normally refer to and identify a deed recorded in a specified division of the Register of Sasines.
   2   Describe the maintenance or work in general terms.
   3   Give the name and address of the person applying for registration of the notice ('the applicant') or the applicant's name and the name and address of the applicant's agent.
   4   The notice must be signed by or on behalf of the applicant.

SCHEDULE 3
SALE UNDER SECTION 22(3) OR 23(1)
(introduced by sections 22(3) and 23(1)

1   Application to sheriff for power to sell
   (1)   Where an owner is entitled to apply—
      (a)   under section 22(3), for power to sell the site; or
      (b)   under section 23(1), for power to sell the tenement building, the owner may make a summary application to the sheriff seeking an order (referred to in this Act as a 'power of sale order') conferring such power on the owner.
   (2)   The site or tenement building in relation to which an application or order is made under sub-paragraph (1) is referred to in this schedule as the 'sale subjects'.
   (3)   An owner making an application under sub-paragraph (1) shall give notice of it to each of the other owners of the sale subjects.
   (4)   The sheriff shall, on an application under sub-paragraph (1)—
      (a)   grant the power of sale order sought unless satisfied that to do so would—
         (i)   not be in the best interests of all (or both) the owners taken as a group;
   or

(ii)   be unfairly prejudicial to one or more of the owners; and

(b)   if a power of sale order has previously been granted in respect of the same sale subjects, revoke that previous order.

(5)   A power of sale order shall contain—

(a)   the name and address of the owner in whose favour it is granted;

(b)   the postal address of each flat or, as the case may be, former flat comprised in the sale subjects to which the order relates; and

(c)   a sufficient conveyancing description of each of those flats or former flats.

(6)   A description of a flat or former flat is a sufficient conveyancing description for the purposes of sub-paragraph (5)(c) if—

[(a)   where the flat or former flat has been registered in the Land Register of Scotland, the description refers to the number of the title sheet]; or

(b)   in relation to any other flat or former flat, the description is by reference to a deed recorded in the Register of Sasines.

(7)   An application under sub-paragraph (1) shall state the applicant's conclusions as to—

(a)   which of subsections (4) and (5) of section 22 applies for the purpose of determining how the net proceeds of any sale of the sale subjects in pursuance of a power of sale order are to be shared among the owners of those subjects; and

(b)   if subsection (5) of that section is stated as applying for that purpose—

(i)   the floor area of each of the flats or former flats comprised in the sale subjects; and

(ii)   the proportion of the net proceeds of sale allocated to that flat.

2   Appeal against grant or refusal of power of sale order

(1)   A party may, not later than 14 days after the date of—

(a)   making of a power of sale order; or

(b)   an interlocutor refusing an application for such an order, appeal to the Court of Session on a point of law.

(2)   The decision of the Court of Session on any such appeal shall be final.

3   Registration of power of sale order

(1)   A power of sale order has no effect—

(a)   unless it is registered within the period of 14 days after the relevant day; and

(b)   until the beginning of the forty-second day after the day on which it is so registered.

(2)   In sub-paragraph (1)(a) above, 'the relevant day' means, in relation to a power of sale order—

(a)   the last day of the period of 14 days within which an appeal against the order may be lodged under paragraph 2(1) of this schedule; or

(b)   if such an appeal is duly lodged, the day on which the appeal is abandoned or determined.

4   Exercise of power of sale

(1)   An owner in whose favour a power of sale order is granted may exercise the power conferred by the order by private bargain or by exposure to sale.

(2)   However, in either case, the owner shall—

(a)   advertise the sale; and

(b)   take all reasonable steps to ensure that the price at which the sale subjects are sold is the best that can reasonably be obtained.

(3)   In advertising the sale in pursuance of sub-paragraph (2)(a) above, the owner shall, in particular, ensure that there is placed and maintained on the sale subjects a conspicuous sign—

(a)   advertising the fact that the sale subjects are for sale; and (b)　giving the name and contact details of the owner or of any agent acting on the owner's behalf in connection with the sale.

(4)　So far as may be necessary for the purpose of complying with sub-paragraph (3) above, the owner or any person authorised by the owner shall be entitled to enter any part of the sale subjects not owned, or not owned exclusively, by that owner.

5　Distribution of proceeds of sale

(1)　An owner selling the sale subjects (referred to in this paragraph as the 'selling owner') shall, within seven days of completion of the sale—

(a)　calculate each owner's share; and

(b)　apply that share in accordance with sub-paragraph (2) below.

(2)　An owner's share shall be applied—

(a)　first, to repay any amounts due under any heritable security affecting that owner's flat or former flat;

(b)　next, to defray any expenses properly incurred in complying with paragraph (a) above; and

(c)　finally, to pay to the owner the remainder (if any) of that owner's share.

(3)　If there is more than one heritable security affecting an owner's flat or former flat, the owner's share shall be applied under paragraph (2)(a) above in relation to each security in the order in which they rank.

(4)　If any owner cannot by reasonable inquiry be identified or found, the selling owner shall consign the remainder of that owner's share in the sheriff court.

(5)　On paying to another owner the remainder of that owner's share, the selling owner shall also give to that other owner—

(a)　a written statement showing—

(i)　the amount of that owner's share and of the remainder of it; and

(ii)　how that share and remainder were calculated; and

(b)　evidence of—

(i)　the total amount of the proceeds of sale; and

(ii)　any expenses properly incurred in connection with the sale and in complying with sub-paragraph (2)(a) above.

(6)　In this paragraph—

'remainder', in relation to an owner's share, means the amount of that share remaining after complying with sub-paragraph (2)(a) and (b) above;

'share', in relation to an owner, means the share of the net proceeds of sale to which that owner is entitled in accordance with subsection (4) or, as the case may be, subsection (5) of section 22.

6　Automatic discharge of heritable securities

Where—

(a)　an owner—

(i)　sells the sale subjects in pursuance of a power of sale order; and

(ii)　grants a disposition of those subjects to the purchaser or the purchaser's nominee; and

(b)　that disposition is duly registered in the Land Register of Scotland or recorded in the Register of Sasines,

all heritable securities affecting the sale subjects or any part of them shall, by virtue of this paragraph, be to that extent discharged.

HOUSING (SCOTLAND) ACT 2006
(2006 asp 1)

50 Power of majority to recover maintenance costs

(1) Subsection (3) applies where—

(a) the owners of two or more houses which form part of the same premises are responsible by virtue of a real burden or otherwise for maintaining any part of those premises and—

(i) those owners are required to carry out any such maintenance (whether in implementation of a maintenance plan or otherwise), or

(ii) a majority of those owners agree to carry out any such maintenance,

(b) notice has been served on each owner responsible for that maintenance requiring the owner to deposit a sum into a maintenance account representing the apportioned share of the estimated costs for which that owner will be liable,

(c) an owner on whom such a notice is served has not complied with such a requirement, and

(d) the local authority is satisfied as to the matters set out in subsection (2).

(2) Those matters are—

(a) that the maintenance proposed is, having regard to the state of repair of the premises, reasonable,

(b) that the share of estimated costs apportioned to the owner who has not complied with the requirement does not conflict with any provision about liability for or apportionment of costs contained in—

(i) any real burdens encumbering the houses concerned,

(ii) the development management scheme in so far as it applies to those houses or any decision made under that scheme, or

(iii) the tenement management scheme in so far as it applies to those houses or any decision made under that scheme, and

(c) that—

(i) the owner who has not complied with the requirement is unable to do so,

(ii) it is unreasonable to require that owner to deposit the sum in question, or

(iii) that owner cannot, by reasonable inquiry, be identified or found.

(3) Where this subsection applies the local authority may, on the application of any of the owners concerned, deposit in the maintenance account a sum representing the share of the estimated costs of any owner who has not complied with a requirement to make such a deposit.

(4) Before deciding to make a deposit under subsection (3), the local authority may request the owner who has failed to comply to make representations to the authority, by such date as the authority may specify, about the owner's financial circumstances.

(5) A notice of the type referred to in subsection (1)(b) must set out—

(a) the maintenance which is to be carried out,

(b) the timetable for carrying out the maintenance, including proposed commencement and completion dates,

(c) the date of any requirement or agreement to carry out the maintenance; and, in the case of an agreement, the names of those by whom it was agreed,

(d) the estimated cost of the maintenance,

(e) why the estimate is considered reasonable,

(f) the apportioned share of the estimated costs attributable to each of the owners,

(g) how that apportionment is arrived at,

(h) the location and number of the maintenance account, and

(i) the date by which the owners are required to deposit the sum representing their respective apportioned shares in the maintenance account.

(7)   This section is without prejudice to any other entitlement of the owner of any house to recover sums from an owner who has not complied with a requirement set out in a notice of the type mentioned in subsection (1)(b).

(8)   The local authority must have regard to any guidance issued by the Scottish Ministers about the exercise of its functions under this section.

(9)   The Scottish Ministers may vary or revoke any such guidance.

98   Duty to have information about a house which is on the market

A person who is responsible for marketing a house which is on the market must possess the prescribed documents in relation to the house.

99   Duty to provide information to potential buyer

(1)   A person who is responsible for marketing a house which is on the market must comply with any request by a potential buyer for a copy of any or all of the prescribed documents in relation to the house.

(2)   Such a request must be complied with within such period as the Scottish Ministers may by regulations specify ('the permitted period').

(3)   The duty under subsection (1) does not apply if the person responsible for marketing the house reasonably believes that the person making the request—

(a)   is unlikely to have sufficient means to buy the house in question,

(b)   is not genuinely interested in buying the house, or

(c)   is not a person to whom the seller is likely to be prepared to sell the house.

(4)   Nothing in subsection (3) authorises the doing of anything which is an unlawful act of discrimination.

(5)   Subsection (3) does not apply if the person responsible for marketing the house knows or suspects that the person making the request is an officer of an enforcement authority.

(6)   The person responsible for marketing the house may charge a sum not exceeding the reasonable cost of making and, if requested, sending a paper copy of any prescribed documents requested under subsection (1).

(7)   If the person responsible for marketing the house ceases to be so responsible before the end of the permitted period (whether because the house has been sold, taken off the market or for any other reason), that person ceases to be under any duty to comply with a request made under subsection (1).

(8)   A person does not comply with the duty under subsection (1) by providing a copy in electronic form unless the potential buyer consents in writing to receiving it in that form.

100   Imposition of conditions on provision of information

(1)   A potential buyer who has made a request to which section 99(1) applies may be required to comply with either or both of the following conditions before a copy is provided.

(2)   The potential buyer may be required to pay a charge authorised by section 99(6).

(3)   The potential buyer may be required to accept any terms specified in writing which—

(a)   are proposed by the seller or in pursuance of the seller's instructions, and

(b)   relate to the use or disclosure of the copy (or any information contained in or derived from it).

(4)   A condition is effective only if it is notified to the potential buyer before the end of the permitted period.

(5)   Where the potential buyer has been so notified of either or both of the conditions authorised by this section, the permitted period for the purposes of section 99(2) is to run afresh beginning with—

(a)   where one condition only is involved, the day on which the potential buyer complies with it by making the payment demanded or, as the case may be, accepting the terms proposed (or such other terms as may be agreed between the seller and the potential buyer in substitution for those proposed), or

(b)   where both conditions are involved, the day on which the potential buyer complies with them or, where each condition is complied with on a different day, the later of those days.

101   Other duties of person acting as agent for seller

(1)   This section applies to a person acting as agent for the seller of a house where—

(a)   the house is not on the market, or

(b)   the house is on the market but the person so acting is not responsible for marketing the house.

(2)   A person to whom this section applies must possess the prescribed documents in relation to a house when any qualifying action is taken by or on behalf of that person.

(3)   In subsection (2) 'qualifying action' means action taken with the intention of marketing the house which—

(a)   communicates to any person the fact that the house is or may become available for sale, but

(b)   does not put the house on the market.

102   Acting as agent

(1)   A person acts as agent for the seller of a house if the person does anything in the course of a business in pursuance of marketing instructions from the seller.

(2)   In subsection (1) 'marketing instructions' means instructions to carry out any activities with a view to—

(a)   effecting the introduction to the seller of a person wishing to buy the house, or

(b)   selling the house by auction.

103   Duty to ensure authenticity of documents held under section 98 or 101

(1)   This section applies to a person who is subject to the duty in section 98 or 101(2).

(2)   Where such a person—

(a)   provides a potential buyer with, or

(b)   allows a potential buyer to inspect,

a copy of a prescribed document (or a part of such a document), that person must ensure that the copy is authentic.

Prescribed documents

104   Information to be held or provided to potential buyers

(1)   The Scottish Ministers may by regulations—

(a)   prescribe documents for the purposes of section 98, 99(1) or 101(2), and

(b)   make such further provision about those documents as they think fit.

(2)   A document may be prescribed under subsection (1) only if the Scottish Ministers consider that it discloses information about—

(a)   the physical condition of a house (including any characteristics or features of the house),

(b)   the value of a house, or

(c)   any other matter connected with a house, or the sale of a house, that would be of interest to potential buyers.

(3)   Regulations under subsection (1) may, in particular, make provision—

(a)   about the form of, and the information to be included in, or excluded from, a prescribed document,

(b)   requiring that a prescribed document be prepared by a person of a description specified in the regulations,

(c) requiring that the date to which information in a prescribed document relates is no earlier than the beginning of such period as the regulations may specify before the date on which the house was put on the market,

(d) requiring that a prescribed document is to be valid for such period of time, or is to be invalidated in such circumstances, as the regulations may specify.

(4) Regulations under subsection (1) may also make provision for and in connection with the registration of prescribed documents and may, in particular, make provision—

(a) for a register of prescribed documents to be kept by the Scottish Ministers or such other person as the regulations may specify (or for the keeping of 2 or more such registers),

(b) authorising the Scottish Ministers to make payments or to give other assistance in connection with the creation, administration or operation of such a register,

(c) requiring persons of such type as may be so specified to register prescribed documents in such circumstances as may be so specified,

(d) about the circumstances and manner in which, and the purposes for which, information contained in such a register may be inspected, copied or otherwise obtained,

(e) setting the amount, or the maximum amount, of any fee which may be charged in connection with registering documents or with inspecting or obtaining information contained in such a register,

(f) for enforcement by enforcement authorities of any requirement to register prescribed documents.

Exceptions from duty

105 Exceptions from duty to have or provide information

The Scottish Ministers may by regulations—

(a) exempt persons of such description as the regulations may specify from any of the duties in section 98, 99(1) or 101(2),

(b) specify periods of time during which or circumstances under which—

(i) a person need not possess any prescribed document under section 98 or section 101(2), or

(ii) a person need not comply with a request under section 99(1),

(c) set out such other exceptions to the duties mentioned in paragraph (a) as may be so specified.

Responsibility for marketing houses

106 Responsibility for marketing: general

(1) Only the seller or a person acting as agent for the seller may be responsible for marketing the house.

(2) A seller is not so responsible if any person is acting as agent for the seller.

(3) But a seller who—

(a) is not responsible because of subsection (2), and

(b) reasonably believes that the person acting as agent for the seller possesses the prescribed documents,

must take reasonable steps to inform a potential buyer that a request under section 99(1) should be made to the person acting as agent.

(4) A person may be responsible for marketing the house on more than one occasion.

107 Responsibility of person acting as agent

(1) A person acting as agent becomes responsible for marketing the house when action taken by or on behalf of that person results in the house being on the market.

(2) That responsibility ceases when—

(a) the house is sold or taken off the market, or

(b) each of the conditions in subsection (3) is satisfied.

(3) Those conditions are that—

(a) the contract between the person acting as agent and the seller is terminated (whether by withdrawal of marketing instructions or otherwise),

(b) the person acting as agent has ceased to take any action which makes public the fact that the house is on the market, and

(c) any such action being taken on behalf of the person acting as agent has ceased.

108 Responsibility of seller

(1) A seller becomes responsible for marketing the house when action taken by or on behalf of the seller results in the house being on the market.

(2) That responsibility ceases when—

(a) the house is sold or taken off the market, or

(b) the conditions in subsection (3) are satisfied.

(3) Those conditions are that—

(a) the seller has ceased to take any action which makes public the fact that the house is on the market, and

(b) any such action being taken on behalf of the seller has ceased.

(4) In this section references to action taken on behalf of the seller exclude action taken by or on behalf of a person acting as the seller's agent.

Enforcement

109 Enforcement authorities

(1) Every local weights and measures authority is an enforcement authority for the purposes of this Part.

(2) It is the duty of each enforcement authority to enforce this Part in their area.

110 Power to require production of prescribed documents

(1) An authorised officer of an enforcement authority may require a person who appears to the officer to be or to have been subject to the duty under section 98, 99(1) or 101(2) in relation to a house to produce for inspection a copy of any prescribed document in relation to the house.

(2) The power conferred by subsection (1) includes power—

(a) to require the production in a legible documentary form of any document which is held in electronic form, and

(b) to take copies of any document produced for inspection.

(3) A requirement under this section may not be made more than 6 months after the last day on which the person concerned appeared to the officer to be subject to the duty under section 98, 99(1) or 101(2) in relation to the house.

(4) A person subject to a requirement under this section must comply with it within the period of 7 days beginning with the day after that on which it is made.

(5) But a person need not comply with the requirement if the person has a reasonable excuse for not complying with it.

111 Penalty charge notices

(1) An authorised officer of an enforcement authority may, if the officer believes that a person has breached any duty under section 98, 99(1), 101(2) or 103(2), give a penalty charge notice to that person.

(2) A penalty charge notice may not be given after the end of the period of 6 months beginning with the day on which it appeared to the officer that the duty was breached.

(3) Schedule 3 (which makes further provision about penalty charge notices) has effect.

(4)   The Scottish Ministers may by regulations make further provision about penalty charge notices or any other notice mentioned in schedule 3.

(5)   Such regulations may, in particular, include provision prescribing—

(a)   the form of penalty charge notices or any other notice mentioned in that schedule,

(b)   circumstances in which penalty charge notices may not be given,

(c)   the methods by which penalty charge notices or any other notice must be given,

(d)   the method or methods by which penalty charges may be paid.

112   Offences relating to enforcement officers

(1)   A person who obstructs an authorised officer of an enforcement authority acting in pursuance of section 110 is guilty of an offence.

(2)   A person who, not being an authorised officer of an enforcement authority, purports to act as such in pursuance of section 110 or 111 is guilty of an offence.

(3)   A person guilty of an offence under this section is liable on summary conviction to a fine not exceeding level 5 on the standard scale.

113   [*Amends Housing (Scotland) Act 1987.*]

Supplementary

114   Grants for development of proposals

(1)   The Scottish Ministers may make grants towards expenditure incurred by any person in connection with the development of proposals for any provision to be made by regulations under section 104(1).

(2)   A grant under this section may be made on conditions, which may include (among other things)—

(a)   conditions as to the purposes for which the grant or any part of it may be used,

(b)   conditions requiring the repayment of the grant or any part of it in such circumstances as may be specified in the conditions.

115   Disapplication for houses not available with vacant possession

(1)   The duties under sections 98, 99, 101 and 103 apply in relation to a house only when it is available for sale with vacant possession.

(2)   For the purposes of this Part, a house being marketed is presumed to be available with vacant possession unless the contrary appears from the manner in which the house is being marketed.

116   Application of Part to sub-divided buildings

(1)   This section applies where—

(a)   two or more houses in a sub-divided building are marketed for sale as a single property, and

(b)   any one or more of those houses—

(i)   is not available for sale separately from the others, but

(ii)   is available with vacant possession.

(2)   The provisions of this Part (but not section 115) apply to the house mentioned in subsection (1)(a) as if it were a single house.

(3)   Subsection (2) does not affect the application of this Part to any of those houses which are available for sale as a separate house.

(4)   In this section 'sub-divided building' means a building originally constructed or adapted for use as a single dwelling which has been divided (on one or more occasions) into separate houses.

117   Notification of breach of duty

(1)   An enforcement authority may notify—

(a)   the Office of Fair Trading,

(b)   any other person or body having an interest,

of any breach of duty under this Part appearing to the authority to have been committed by a person acting as agent for the seller of a house.

(2)   An enforcement authority must notify the Office of Fair Trading of—

(a) any penalty charge notice given by an officer of the authority under section 111,

(b) any notice given by the authority confirming or withdrawing a penalty charge notice, and

(c) the result of any appeal from the confirmation of a penalty charge notice.

118   Possession of documents

(1)   For the purposes of this Part, 'possession' includes civil possession; and 'possess' and 'possesses' are to be construed accordingly.

(2)   A document held in electronic form is to be treated for the purposes of this Part as being in a person's possession if the person is readily able (using equipment available to that person)—

(a) to view the document in a form that is legible, and

(b) to produce copies of it in a legible documentary form.

119   Meaning of 'on the market', 'sale' and related expressions

(1)   In this Part references to 'the market' are to the market for houses in Scotland.

(2)   A house is on the market when the fact that it is or may become available for sale is, with a view to marketing the house, made public in Scotland by or on behalf of the seller.

(3)   A house is to be regarded as remaining on the market until it is sold or taken off the market.

(4)   A fact is made public when it is advertised or otherwise communicated (in whatever form and by whatever means) to the public or a section of the public.

(5)   In this Part—

'long lease' means a probative lease—

(a) granted for a period exceeding 20 years, or

(b) which contains an obligation on the landlord to renew the lease from time to time at fixed periods, upon the termination of a life or lives, or otherwise so that the total duration could (in terms of the lease, as renewed, and without any subsequent agreement, express or implied, between the persons holding the interests of the landlord and the tenant) endure for a period exceeding 20 years,

'potential buyer' means a person who claims to be interested, or that the person may become interested, in buying a house,

'sale', in relation to a house, means a disposal, or agreement to dispose, by way of sale of—

(a) the ownership of the house,

(b) the interest of the tenant under a long lease of a house, and

'seller' means a person contemplating such a disposal (and related expressions are to be construed accordingly).

FAMILY LAW (SCOTLAND) ACT 2006
(2006, asp 2)

Cohabitation

25 Meaning of 'cohabitant' in sections 26 to 29

(1) In sections 26 to 29, 'cohabitant' means either member of a couple consisting of—

    (a) a man and a woman who are (or were) living together as if they were husband and wife; or

    (b) two persons of the same sex who are (or were) living together as if they were civil partners.

(2) In determining for the purposes of any of sections 26 to 29 whether a person ('A') is a cohabitant of another person ('B'), the court shall have regard to—

    (a) the length of the period during which A and B have been living together (or lived together);

    (b) the nature of their relationship during that period; and

    (c) the nature and extent of any financial arrangements subsisting, or which subsisted, during that period.

(3) In subsection (2) and section 28, 'court' means Court of Session or sheriff.

26 Rights in certain household goods

(1) Subsection (2) applies where any question arises (whether during or after the cohabitation) as to the respective rights of ownership of cohabitants in any household goods.

(2) It shall be presumed that each cohabitant has a right to an equal share in household goods acquired (other than by gift or succession from a third party) during the period of cohabitation.

(3) The presumption in subsection (2) shall be rebuttable.

(4) In this section, 'household goods' means any goods (including decorative or ornamental goods) kept or used at any time during the cohabitation in any residence in which the cohabitants are (or were) cohabiting for their joint domestic purposes; but does not include—

    (a) money;

    (b) securities;

    (c) any motor car, caravan or other road vehicle; or

    (d) any domestic animal.

27 Rights in certain money and property

(1) Subsection (2) applies where, in relation to cohabitants, any question arises (whether during or after the cohabitation) as to the right of a cohabitant to—

    (a) money derived from any allowance made by either cohabitant for their joint household expenses or for similar purposes; or

    (b) any property acquired out of such money.

(2) Subject to any agreement between the cohabitants to the contrary, the money or property shall be treated as belonging to each cohabitant in equal shares.

(3) In this section 'property' does not include a residence used by the co-habitants as the sole or main residence in which they live (or lived) together.

Private International Law

. . .

39 Matrimonial property

(1) Any question in relation to the rights of spouses to each other's immoveable property arising by virtue of the marriage shall be determined by the law of the place in which the property is situated.

(2)   Subject to subsections (4) and (5), if spouses are domiciled in the same country, any question in relation to the rights of the spouses to each other's moveable property arising by virtue of the marriage shall be determined by the law of that country.

(3)   Subject to subsections (4) and (5), if spouses are domiciled in different countries then, for the purposes of any question in relation to the rights of the spouses to each other's moveable property arising by virtue of the marriage, the spouses shall be taken to have the same rights to such property as they had immediately before the marriage.

(4)   Any question in relation to—

(a) the use or occupation of a matrimonial home which is moveable; or

(b) the use of the contents of a matrimonial home (whether the home is moveable or immoveable),

shall be determined by the law of the country in which the home is situated.

(5)   A change of domicile by a spouse (or both spouses) shall not affect a right in moveable property which, immediately before the change, has vested in either spouse.

(6)   This section shall not apply—

(a) in relation to the law on aliment, financial provision on divorce, transfer of property on divorce or succession;

(b) to the extent that spouses agree otherwise.

(7)   In this section, 'matrimonial home' has the same meaning as in section 22 of the 1981 Act.

COMPANIES ACT 2006
(2006 c 46)

PART 25
COMPANY CHARGES

[CHAPTER A1
REGISTRATION OF COMPANY CHARGES

Company charges

[859A   Charges created by a company

(1)   Subject to subsection (6), this section applies where a company creates a charge.

(2)   The registrar must register the charge if, before the end of the period allowed for delivery, the company or any person interested in the charge delivers to the registrar for registration a section 859D statement of particulars.

(3)   Where the charge is created or evidenced by an instrument, the registrar is required to register it only if a certified copy of the instrument is delivered to the registrar with the statement of particulars.

(4)   'The period allowed for delivery' is 21 days beginning with the day after the date of creation of the charge (see section 859E), unless an order allowing an extended period is made under section 859F(3).

(5)   Where an order is made under section 859F(3) a copy of the order must be delivered to the registrar with the statement of particulars.

(6)   This section does not apply to—

(a) a charge in favour of a landlord on a cash deposit given as a security in connection with the lease of land;

(b) a charge created by a member of Lloyd's (within the meaning of the Lloyd's Act 1982) to secure its obligations in connection with its underwriting business at Lloyd's;

(c) a charge excluded from the application of this section by or under any other Act.

(7) In this Part—

'cash' includes foreign currency,

'charge' includes—

(a) a mortgage;

(b) a standard security, assignation in security, and any other right in security constituted under the law of Scotland, including any heritable security, but not including a pledge, and

'company' means a UK-registered company.]

[859B Charge in series of debentures

(1) This section applies where—

(a) a company creates a series of debentures containing a charge, or giving a charge by reference to another instrument, and

(b) debenture holders of that series are entitled to the benefit of the charge pari passu.

(2) The registrar must register the charge if, before the end of the period allowed for delivery, the company or any person interested in the charge delivers to the registrar for registration, a section 859D statement of particulars which also contains the following—

(a) either—

(i) the name of each of the trustees for the debenture holders, or

(ii) where there are more than four such persons, the names of any four persons listed in the charge instrument as trustees for the debenture holders, and a statement that there are other such persons;

(b) the dates of the resolutions authorising the issue of the series;

(c) the date of the covering instrument (if any) by which the series is created or defined.

(3) Where the charge is created or evidenced by an instrument, the registrar is required to register it only if a certified copy of the instrument is delivered to the registrar with the statement of particulars.

(4) Where the charge is not created or evidenced by an instrument, the registrar is required to register it only if a certified copy of one of the debentures in the series is delivered to the registrar with the statement of particulars.

(5) For the purposes of this section a statement of particulars is taken to be a section 859D statement of particulars even if it does not contain the names of the debenture holders.

(6) 'The period allowed for delivery' is—

(a) if there is a deed containing the charge, 21 days beginning with the day after the date on which the deed is executed;

(b) if there is no deed containing the charge, 21 days beginning with the day after the date on which the first debenture of the series is executed.

(7) Where an order is made under section 859F(3) a copy of the order must be delivered to the registrar with the statement of particulars.

(8) In this section 'deed' means—

(a) a deed governed by the law of England and Wales or Northern Ireland, or

(b) an instrument governed by a law other than the law of England and Wales or Northern Ireland which requires delivery under that law in order to take effect.]

[859C Charges existing on property or undertaking acquired

(1) This section applies where a company acquires property or undertaking which is subject to a charge of a kind which would, if it had been created by the company after the acquisition of the property or undertaking, have been capable of being registered under section 859A.

(2) The registrar must register the charge if the company or any person

interested in the charge delivers to the registrar for registration a section 859D statement of particulars.

(3)   Where the charge is created or evidenced by an instrument, the registrar is required to register it only if a certified copy of the instrument is delivered to the registrar with the statement of particulars.]

[859D   Particulars to be delivered to registrar

(1)   A statement of particulars relating to a charge created by a company is a 'section 859D statement of particulars' if it contains the following particulars—
  (a)   the registered name and number of the company;
  (b)   the date of creation of the charge and (if the charge is one to which section 859C applies) the date of acquisition of the property or undertaking concerned;
  (c)   where the charge is created or evidenced by an instrument, the particulars listed in subsection (2);
  (d)   where the charge is not created or evidenced by an instrument, the particulars listed in subsection (3).

(2)   The particulars referred to in subsection (1)(c) are—
  (a)   any of the following—
    (i)   the name of each of the persons in whose favour the charge has been created or of the security agents or trustees holding the charge for the benefit of one or more persons; or,
    (ii)   where there are more than four such persons, security agents or trustees, the names of any four such persons, security agents or trustees listed in the charge instrument, and a statement that there are other such persons, security agents or trustees;
  (b)   whether the instrument is expressed to contain a floating charge and, if so, whether it is expressed to cover all the property and undertaking of the company;
  (c)   whether any of the terms of the charge prohibit or restrict the company from creating further security that will rank equally with or ahead of the charge;
  (d)   whether (and if so, a short description of) any land, ship, aircraft or intellectual property that is registered or required to be registered in the United Kingdom, is subject to a charge (which is not a floating charge) or fixed security included in the instrument;
  (e)   whether the instrument includes a charge (which is not a floating charge) or fixed security over—
    (i)   any tangible or corporeal property, or
    (ii)   any intangible or incorporeal property,
not described in paragraph (d).

(3)   The particulars referred to in subsection (1)(d) are—
  (a)   a statement that there is no instrument creating or evidencing the charge;
  (b)   the names of each of the persons in whose favour the charge has been created or the names of any security agents or trustees holding the charge for the benefit of one or more persons;
  (c)   the nature of the charge;
  (d)   a short description of the property or undertaking charged;
  (e)   the obligations secured by the charge.

(4)   In this section 'fixed security' has the meaning given in section 486(1) of the Companies Act 1985.

(5)   In this section 'intellectual property' includes—
  (a)   any patent, trade mark, registered design, copyright or design right;
  (b)   any licence under or in respect of any such right.]

[859E   Date of creation of charge

(1)   For the purposes of this Part, a charge of the type described in column 1 of

the Table below is taken to be created on the date given in relation to it in column 2 of that Table.

1. Type of charge	2. When charge created
Standard security	The date of its recording in the Register of Sasines or its registration in the Land Register of Scotland
Charge other than a standard security, where created or evidenced by an instrument	Where the instrument is a deed that has been executed and has immediate effect on execution and delivery, the date of delivery
	Where the instrument is a deed that has been executed and held in escrow, the date of delivery into escrow
	Where the instrument is a deed that has been executed and held as undelivered, the date of delivery
	Where the instrument is not a deed and has immediate effect on execution, the date of execution
	Where the instrument is not a deed and does not have immediate on execution, the date on which the instrument takes effect
Charge other than a standard security, where not created or evidenced by an instrument	The date on which the charge comes into effect

(2)   Where a charge is created or evidenced by an instrument made between two or more parties, references in the Table in subsection (1) to execution are to execution by all the parties to the instrument whose execution is essential for the instrument to take effect as a charge.

(3)   This section applies for the purposes of this Chapter even if further forms, notices, registrations or other actions or proceedings are necessary to make the charge valid or effectual for any other purposes.

(4)   For the purposes of this Chapter, the registrar is entitled without further enquiry to accept a charge as created on the date given as the date of creation of the charge in a section 859D statement of particulars.

(5)   In this section 'deed' means—

(a)   a deed governed by the law of England and Wales or Northern Ireland, or

(b)   an instrument governed by a law other than the law of England and Wales or Northern Ireland which requires delivery under that law in order to take effect.

(6)   References in this section to delivery, in relation to a deed, include delivery as a deed where required.]

[859F   Extension of period allowed for delivery

(1)   Subsection (3) applies if the court is satisfied that—

(a)   neither the company nor any other person interested in the charge has delivered to the registrar the documents required under section 859A or (as the case may be) 859B before the end of the period allowed for delivery under the section concerned, and

(b)   the requirement in subsection (2) is met.

(2)   The requirement is—

(a)   that the failure to deliver those documents—

(i)   was accidental or due to inadvertence or to some other sufficient cause, or

(ii) is not of a nature to prejudice the position of creditors or shareholders of the company, or

(b) that on other grounds it is just and equitable to grant relief.

(3)   The court may, on the application of the company or a person interested, and on such terms and conditions as seem to the court just and expedient, order that the period allowed for delivery be extended.]

[859G   Personal information etc in certified copies

(1)   The following are not required to be included in a certified copy of an instrument or debenture delivered to the registrar for the purposes of any provision of this Chapter—

(a) personal information relating to an individual (other than the name of an individual);

(b) the number or other identifier of a bank or securities account of a company or individual;

(c) a signature.

(2)   The registrar is entitled without further enquiry, to accept the certified copy of an instrument whether or not any of the information in subsection (1) is contained within the instrument.]

[Consequence of non-delivery]

[859H   Consequence of failure to deliver charges

(1)   This section applies if—

(a) a company creates a charge to which section 859A or 859B applies, and

(b) the documents required by section 859A or (as the case may be) 859B are not delivered to the registrar by the company or another person interested in the charge before the end of the relevant period allowed for delivery.

(2)   'The relevant period allowed for delivery' is—

(a) the period allowed for delivery under the section in question, or

(b) if an order under section 859F(3) has been made, the period allowed by the order.

(3)   Where this section applies, the charge is void (so far as any security on the company's property or undertaking is conferred by it) against—

(a) a liquidator of the company,

(b) an administrator of the company, and

(c) a creditor of the company.

(4)   Subsection (3) is without prejudice to any contract or obligation for repayment of the money secured by the charge; and when a charge becomes void under this section, the money secured by it immediately becomes payable.]

[The register]

[859I   Entries on the register

(1)   This section applies where a charge is registered in accordance with a provision of this Chapter.

(2)   The registrar must—

(a) allocate to the charge a unique reference code and place a note in the register recording that reference code; and

(b) include in the register any documents delivered under section 859A(3) or (5), 859B(3), (4) or (7), or 859C(3).

(3)   The registrar must give a certificate of the registration of the charge to the person who delivered to the registrar a section 859D statement of particulars relating to the charge.

(4)   The certificate must state—

(a) the registered name and number of the company in respect of which the charge was registered; and

(b) the unique reference code allocated to the charge.

(5) The certificate must be signed by the registrar or authenticated by the registrar's official seal.

(6) In the case of registration under section 859A or 859B, the certificate is conclusive evidence that the documents required by the section concerned were delivered to the registrar before the end of the relevant period allowed for delivery.

(7) 'The relevant period allowed for delivery' is—

(a) the period allowed for delivery under the section in question, or

(b) if an order under section 859F(3) has been made, the period allowed by the order.]

[859J Company holding property or undertaking as trustee

(1) Where a company is acting as trustee of property or undertaking which is the subject of a charge delivered for registration under this Chapter, the company or any person interested in the charge may deliver to the registrar a statement to that effect.

(2) A statement delivered after the delivery for registration of the charge must include—

(a) the registered name and number of the company; and

(b) the unique reference code allocated to the charge.]

[859K Registration of enforcement of security

(1) Subsection (2) applies where a person—

(a) obtains an order for the appointment of a receiver or manager of a company's property or undertaking, or

(b) appoints such a receiver or manager under powers contained in an instrument.

(2) The person must, within 7 days of the order or of the appointment under those powers—

(a) give notice to the registrar of that fact, and

(b) if the order was obtained, or the appointment made, by virtue of a registered charge held by the person give the registrar a notice containing—

(i) in the case of a charge created before 6th April 2013, the information specified in subsection (4);

(ii) in the case of a charge created on or after 6th April 2013, the unique reference code allocated to the charge.

(3) Where a person appointed receiver or manager of a company's property or undertaking under powers contained in an instrument ceases to act as such a receiver or manager, the person must, on so ceasing—

(a) give notice to the registrar of that fact, and

(b) give the registrar a notice containing—

(i) in the case of a charge created before 6th April 2013, the information specified in subsection (4), or

(ii) in the case of a charge created on or after 6th April 2013, the unique reference code allocated to the charge.

(4) The information referred to in subsections (2)(b)(i) and (3)(b)(i) is—

(a) the date of the creation of the charge;

(b) a description of the instrument (if any) creating or evidencing the charge;

(c) short particulars of the property or undertaking charged.

(5) The registrar must include in the register—

(a) a fact of which notice is given under subsection (2)(a), and

(b) a fact of which notice is given under subsection (3)(a).

(6) A person who makes default in complying with the requirements of subsections (2) or (3) of this section commits an offence.

(7) A person guilty of an offence under this section is liable on summary conviction to a fine not exceeding level 3 on the standard scale and, for continued contravention, a daily default fine not exceeding one-tenth of level 3 on the standard scale.

(8) This section applies only to a receiver or manager appointed—

(a) by a court in England and Wales or Northern Ireland, or

(b) under an instrument governed by the law of England and Wales or Northern Ireland.

(9) This section does not apply to a receiver appointed under Chapter 2 of Part 3 of the Insolvency Act 1986 (receivers (Scotland)).]

[859L Entries of satisfaction and release

(1) Subsection (5) applies if the statement set out in subsection (2) and the particulars set out in subsection (4) are delivered to the registrar with respect to a registered charge.

(2) The statement referred to in subsection (1) is a statement to the effect that—

(a) the debt for which the charge was given has been paid or satisfied in whole or in part, or

(b) all or part of the property or undertaking charged—

(i) has been released from the charge, or

(ii) has ceased to form part of the company's property or undertaking.

(3) Where a statement within subsection (2)(b) relates to part only of the property or undertaking charged, the statement must include a short description of that part.

(4) The particulars referred to in subsection (1) are—

(a) the name and address of the person delivering the statement and an indication of their interest in the charge;

(b) the registered name and number of the company that—

(i) created the charge (in a case within section 859A or 859B), or

(ii) acquired the property or undertaking subject to the charge (in a case within section 859C);

(c) in respect of a charge created before 6th April 2013—

(i) the date of creation of the charge;

(ii) a description of the instrument (if any) by which the charge is created or evidenced;

(iii) short particulars of the property or undertaking charged;

(d) in respect of a charge created on or after 6th April 2013, the unique reference code allocated to the charge.

(5) The registrar must include in the register—

(a) a statement of satisfaction in whole or in part, or

(b) a statement of the fact that all or part of the property or undertaking has been released from the charge or has ceased to form part of the company's property or undertaking (as the case may be).]

[859M Rectification of register

(1) Subsection (3) applies if the court is satisfied that—

(a) there has been an omission or mis-statement in any statement or notice delivered to the registrar in accordance with this Chapter, and

(b) the requirement in subsection (2) is met.

(2) The requirement is that the court is satisfied—

(a) that the omission or mis-statement—

(i) was accidental or due to inadvertence or to some other sufficient cause, or

(ii) is not of a nature to prejudice the position of creditors or shareholders of the company, or

(b) that on other grounds it is just and equitable to grant relief.

(3) The court may, on the application of the company or a person interested,

and on such terms and conditions as seem to the court just and expedient, order that the omission or mis-statement be rectified.

(4)   A copy of the court's order must be sent by the applicant to the registrar for registration.]

[859N   Replacement of instrument or debenture

(1)   Subsection (2) applies if the court is satisfied that—

(a)   a copy of an instrument or debenture delivered to the registrar under this Chapter contains material which could have been omitted under section 859G;

(b)   the wrong instrument or debenture was delivered to the registrar; or

(c)   the copy was defective.

(2)   The court may, on the application of the company or a person interested, and on such terms and conditions as seem to the court just and expedient, order that the copy of the instrument or debenture be removed from the register and replaced.

(3)   A copy of the court's order must be sent by the applicant to the registrar for registration.]

[859O   Notification of addition to or amendment of charge

(1)   This section applies where, after the creation of a charge, the charge is amended by adding or amending a term that—

(a)   prohibits or restricts the creation of any fixed security or any other charge having priority over, or ranking pari passu with, the charge; or

(b)   varies, or otherwise regulates the order of, the ranking of the charge in relation to any fixed security or any other charge.

(2)   Either the company that created the charge or the person taking the benefit of the charge (or another charge referred to in subsection (1)(b)) may deliver to the registrar for registration—

(a)   a certified copy of the instrument effecting the amendment, variation or regulation, and

(b)   a statement of the particulars set out in subsection (3).

(3)   The particulars to be included in the statement are—

(a)   the registered name and number of the company;

(b)   in the case of a charge created before 6th April 2013—

(i)   the date of creation of the charge;

(ii)   a description of the instrument (if any) by which the charge was created or evidenced;

(iii)   short particulars of the property or undertaking charged as set out when the charge was registered;

(c)   in the case of a charge created on or after 6th April 2013, (where allocated) the unique reference code allocated to the charge.

(4)   Subsections (1) to (3) do not affect the continued application of section 466 of the Companies Act 1985.

(5)   In this section 'fixed security' has the meaning given in section 486(1) of the Companies Act 1985.]

[Companies' records and registers]

[859P   Companies to keep copies of instruments creating and amending charges

(1)   A company must keep available for inspection a copy of every—

(a)   instrument creating a charge capable of registration under this Chapter, and

(b)   instrument effecting any variation or amendment of such a charge.

(2)   In the case of a charge contained in a series of uniform debentures, a copy

of one of the debentures of the series is sufficient for the purposes of subsection (1)(a).

(3)   If the particulars referred to in section 859D(1) or the particulars of the property or undertaking charged are not contained in the instrument creating the charge, but are instead contained in other documents which are referred to in or otherwise incorporated into the instrument, then the company must also keep available for inspection a copy of those other documents.

(4)   It is sufficient for the purposes of subsection (1)(a) if the company keeps a copy of the instrument in the form delivered to the registrar under section 859A(3), 859B(3) or (4) or 859C(3).

(5)   Where a translation has been delivered to the registrar in accordance with section 1105, the company must keep available for inspection a copy of the translation.]

[859Q   Instruments creating charges to be available for inspection

(1)   This section applies to documents required to be kept available for inspection under section 859P (copies of instruments creating and amending charges).

(2)   The documents must be kept available for inspection—
  (a)   at the company's registered office, or
  (b)   at a place specified in regulations under section 1136.

(3)   The company must give notice to the registrar—
  (a)   of the place at which the documents are kept available for inspection, and
  (b)   of any change in that place,
unless they have at all times been kept at the company's registered office.

(4)   The documents must be open to the inspection—
  (a)   of any creditor or member of the company, without charge, and
  (b)   of any other person, on payment of such fee as may be prescribed.

(5)   If default is made for 14 days in complying with subsection (3) or an inspection required under subsection (4) is refused, an offence is committed by—
  (a)   the company, and
  (b)   every officer of the company who is in default.

(6)   A person guilty of an offence under this section is liable on summary conviction to a fine not exceeding level 3 on the standard scale and, for continued contravention, a daily default fine not exceeding one-tenth of level 3 on the standard scale.

(7)   If an inspection required under subsection (4) is refused the court may by order compel an immediate inspection.

(8)   Where the company and a person wishing to carry out an inspection under subsection (4) agree, the inspection may be carried out by electronic means.]

CHAPTER 3
POWERS OF SECRETARY OF STATE

893   Power to make provision for effect of registration in special register

(1)   In this section a 'special register' means a register, other than [the register], in which a charge to which [Chapter A1] applies is required or authorised to be registered.

(2)   The Secretary of State may by order make provision for facilitating the making of information-sharing arrangements between the person responsible for maintaining a special register ('the responsible person') and the registrar that meet the requirement in subsection (4).

'Information-sharing arrangements' are arrangements to share and make use of information held by the registrar or by the responsible person.

(3)   If the Secretary of State is satisfied that appropriate information-sharing arrangements have been made, he may by order provide that—

(a) the registrar is authorised not to register a charge of a specified description under [Chapter A1],

(b) a charge of a specified description that is registered in the special register within a specified period is to be treated as if it had been registered (and certified by the registrar as registered) in accordance with the requirements of [Chapter A1], and

(c) the other provisions of [Chapter A1] apply to a charge so treated with specified modifications.

(4) The information-sharing arrangements must ensure that persons inspecting the [register]—

(a) are made aware, in a manner appropriate to the inspection, of the existence of charges in the special register which are treated in accordance with provision so made, and

(b) are able to obtain information from the special register about any such charge.

(5) An order under this section may—

(a) modify any enactment or rule of law which would otherwise restrict or prevent the responsible person from entering into or giving effect to information-sharing arrangements,

(b) authorise the responsible person to require information to be provided to him for the purposes of the arrangements,

(c) make provision about—

(i) the charging by the responsible person of fees in connection with the arrangements and the destination of such fees (including provision modifying any enactment which would otherwise apply in relation to fees payable to the responsible person), and

(ii) the making of payments under the arrangements by the registrar to the responsible person,

(d) require the registrar to make copies of the arrangements available to the public (in hard copy or electronic form).

(6) In this section 'specified' means specified in an order under this section.

(7) A description of charge may be specified, in particular, by reference to one or more of the following—

(a) the type of company by which it is created,

(b) the form of charge which it is,

(c) the description of assets over which it is granted,

(d) the length of the period between the date of its registration in the special register and the date of its creation.

(8) Provision may be made under this section relating to registers maintained under the law of a country or territory outside the United Kingdom.

(9) An order under this section is subject to negative resolution procedure.

BANKRUPTCY AND DILIGENCE ETC (SCOTLAND) ACT 2007
(2007, asp 3)

PART 11
MAILLS AND DUTIES, SEQUESTRATION FOR RENT AND LANDLORD'S
HYPOTHEC

[Landlord's hypothec and sequestration for rent]

208   Abolition of sequestration for rent and restriction of landlord's hypothec

(1)   The diligence of sequestration for rent is abolished and any enactment or rule of law enabling an action of sequestration for rent to be raised ceases to have effect.

(2)   Notwithstanding that abolition, the landlord's hypothec—

(a)   continues, subject to subsections (3) to (9) below, as a right in security over corporeal moveable property kept in or on the subjects let; and—

(b)   ranks accordingly in any—

(i)   sequestration;

(ii)   insolvency proceedings; or

(iii)   other process in which there is ranking, in respect of that property.

(3)   The landlord's hypothec no longer arises in relation to property which is kept—

(a)   in a dwellinghouse;

(b)   on agricultural land; or

(c)   on a croft.

(4)   It no longer arises in relation to property which is owned by a person other than the tenant.

(5)   Property which is acquired by a person from the tenant—

(a)   in good faith; or

(b)   where the property is acquired after an interdict prohibiting the tenant from disposing of or removing items secured by the hypothec has been granted in favour of the landlord, in good faith and for value,

ceases to be subject to the hypothec upon acquisition by the person.

(6)   Subsection (5)(b) above does not affect the tenant's liability for breach of the interdict.

(7)   Where property is owned in common by the tenant and a third party, any right of hypothec arises only to the extent of the tenant's interest in that property.

(8)   The landlord's hypothec—

(a)   is security for rent due and unpaid only; and

(b)   subsists for so long as that rent remains unpaid.

(9)   Any enactment or rule of law relating to the landlord's hypothec ceases to have effect in so far as it is inconsistent with subsections (2) to (8) above.

(10)   Subsections (1) to (3), (8) and (9) above do not affect an action of sequestration for rent brought before this section comes into force.

(11)   Subsection (3) above does not affect a landlord's right of hypothec which arose before and subsists on the coming into force of this section.

(12)   In subsection (2) above, 'insolvency proceedings' means—

(a)   winding up;

(b)   receivership;

(c)   administration; and

(d)   proceedings in relation to a company voluntary arrangement,

within the meaning of the Insolvency Act 1986 (c 45).

(13)   In subsection (3) above—

'agricultural land' has the same meaning as in section 1(2) of the Agricultural Holdings (Scotland) Act 1991 (c 55);

'croft' has the same meaning as in section 3(1) of the Crofters (Scotland) Act 1993 (c 44); and

'dwellinghouse' includes—
  (a) a mobile home or other place used as a dwelling; and
  (b) any other structure or building used in connection with the dwelling-house.

LAND REGISTRATION ETC (SCOTLAND) ACT 2012
(2012 asp 5)

PART 1
THE LAND REGISTER

The Land Register of Scotland

1 The Land Register of Scotland
  (1)   There is to continue to be a public register of rights in land in Scotland (which is to continue to be known as the 'Land Register of Scotland').
  (2)   The register is to continue to be under the management and control of the Keeper of the Registers of Scotland.
  (3)   The register is to continue to have a seal.
  (4)   Subject to the provisions of this Act, the register is to be in such form (which may be, or be in part, an electronic form) as the Keeper considers appropriate.
  (5)   The Keeper must take such steps as appear reasonable to the Keeper to protect the register from—
  (a) interference,
  (b) unauthorised access, and
  (c) damage.

Structure and contents of the register

2 The parts of the register
The Keeper must make up and maintain, as parts of the register—
  (a)   the title sheet record,
  (b)   the cadastral map,
  (c)   the archive record, and
  (d)   the application record.

Title sheets and the title sheet record

3 Title sheets and the title sheet record
  (1)   The Keeper must make up and maintain a title sheet for each registered plot of land.
  (2)   The Keeper may make up and maintain a title sheet for a registered lease.
  (3)   The title sheet record is the totality of all such title sheets.
  (4)   A plot of land is an area or areas of land all of which are owned by one person, or one set of persons.
  (5)   A separate tenement constitutes a plot of land for the purposes of this Act.
  (6)   Subject to subsections (2) and (7), there is to be only one title sheet for each plot of land.
  (7)   The Keeper need not make up and maintain a title sheet for a plot of land which is a pertinent of another plot of land (or of two or more other plots of land) but may instead include it in the title sheet of the other plot or plots of land of which it is a pertinent.

4 Title and lease title numbers
  (1)   The Keeper must assign a title number to—
  (a)   the title sheet of each registered plot of land, and

(b) where a registered lease has a title sheet, to that title sheet.

(2) A title number is an unique identifier consisting of numerals or of letters and numerals.

5   Structure of title sheets

(1) A title sheet is to comprise—
  (a) a property section,
  (b) a proprietorship section,
  (c) a securities section, and
  (d) a burdens section.

(2) A section of a title sheet may be sub-divided if and as the Keeper considers appropriate.

6   The property section of the title sheet

(1) The Keeper must enter in the property section of the title sheet—
  (a) a description—
    (i)   of the plot of land (being a description by reference to the cadastral map),
    (ii) of the nature of the proprietor's right in the plot of land, and
    (iii) if the plot is a separate tenement, of the nature of the tenement,
  (b) the particulars of any incorporeal pertinents (including, if there is a burdened property, the particulars of that property in so far as known),
  (c) any agreement registered under section 66(2),
  (d) any entry required under section 18(2)(a) or paragraph 7(a) of schedule 1,
  (e) if the title sheet is a lease title sheet, the particulars of the lease, and
  (f) where there is for the area of land another title sheet (as for example for a plot which is a separate tenement), the title number of that other title sheet.

(2) Paragraph (f) of subsection (1) does not apply where the other title sheet is the title sheet of a flat in a flatted building.

7   The proprietorship section of the title sheet

(1) The Keeper must enter in the proprietorship section of the title sheet—
  (a) the name and designation of the proprietor, and
  (b) in the case of ownership in common, the respective shares of the proprietors.

(2) Paragraph (a) of subsection (1) is subject to section 18(1)(b) and to paragraph 6(b) of schedule 1; and paragraph (b) of that subsection is subject to sections 16(2) (b) and 18(2)(b), to paragraph 7(b) of schedule 1 and to paragraphs 8(b) and 10 of schedule 4.

8   The securities section of the title sheet

(1) The Keeper must enter in the securities section of the title sheet particulars of any heritable security over the right in land to which the title sheet relates (including the name and designation of the creditor in the security).

(2) This section is subject to section 18(3)(b) and to paragraph 8(b) of schedule 1.

9   The burdens section of the title sheet

(1) The Keeper must enter in the burdens section of the title sheet—
  (a) where the right in land to which the title sheet relates is encumbered with a title condition—
    (i)   the terms of the title condition,
    (ii) a description of any benefited property (in so far as known to the Keeper), and
    (iii) if the title condition is a personal real burden, the name and designation of the person who has title to enforce it,
  (b) where there is a long lease (other than a long sub-lease) which has real effect, that fact,
  (c) in a case where the title sheet is a lease title sheet, where there is a long sub-lease (other than a long sub-sub-lease) which has real effect, that fact,

(d) in so far as known to the Keeper, any public right of way (by whatever means) over or through the land,

(e) particulars of any path order made under section 22 of the Land Reform (Scotland) Act 2003 (asp 2) (compulsory powers to delineate paths in land in respect of which access rights are exercisable), and

(f) any other encumbrance the inclusion of which in the register is permitted or required, expressly or impliedly, by an enactment and the name and designation of the person who has title to enforce that encumbrance.

(2) In subsection (1)—

'encumbrance' does not include a heritable security,

'long lease' means—

(a) a lease exceeding 20 years, or

(b) a lease which includes provision (however expressed) requiring the landlord to renew the lease at the tenant's request as a result of which (and without any subsequent agreement express or implied between the landlord and tenant) the total duration could exceed 20 years.

(3) This section is subject to section 18(4) and to paragraph 9 of schedule 1.

10 What is entered or incorporated by reference in a title sheet

(1) The Keeper must, in addition to what is to be entered under sections 6 to 9, enter the matters mentioned in subsection (2) in a title sheet.

(2) The matters are—

(a) any statement made by virtue of any of subsections (3) and (4)(b) of section 75 or subsection (5)(a) of section 76,

(b) particulars of any special destination,

(c) a reference to an entry in the Register of Inhibitions made under section 32(2),

(d) the terms of any caveat, warrant for which is granted under section 67(3), and

(e) such other information (if any) as the Keeper considers appropriate.

(3) The Keeper may incorporate by reference in a title sheet—

(a) a document in the archive record, or

(b) a deed in any other register under the management and control of the Keeper or of the Keeper of the Records of Scotland.

(4) The Keeper must not enter or incorporate by reference in a title sheet any rights or obligations except in so far as their entry is authorised by an enactment.

(5) The entry or incorporation by reference in a title sheet of any right or obligation, in so far as not so authorised—

(a) does not constitute notice of that right or obligation, and

(b) is without any other effect.

(6) Subsection (2)(b) is subject to section 18(3)(c) and to paragraph 8(c) of schedule 1.

The cadastral map

11 The cadastral map

(1) The cadastral map is a map—

(a) showing the totality of registered geospatial data (other than supplementary data in individual title sheets),

(b) showing for each cadastral unit—

(i) the cadastral unit number,

(ii) the boundaries of the unit, and

(iii) the title number of any registered lease relating to the unit, and

(c) otherwise depicting registered rights in such manner as the Keeper considers appropriate.

(2) A cadastral unit which represents a separate tenement must be shown on the map in such a way as will distinguish it as a cadastral unit from other units.

(3)   The cadastral map may (but need not) show the boundaries of cadastral units on the vertical plane.

(4)   The cadastral map may contain such other information as the Keeper considers appropriate.

(5)   The cadastral map must be based upon the base map.

(6)   The base map is—

(a)   the Ordnance Map,

(b)   another system of mapping, being a system which accords with such requirements as the Scottish Ministers may, by order, prescribe, or

(c)   a combination of the Ordnance map and such other system.

(7)   On the base map being updated, the Keeper must make any changes to the register which are necessary in consequence of the updating.

(8)   For the purposes of subsection (1)(a), the Keeper may determine what data is supplementary data.

(9)   This section and sections 12 and 13 are without prejudice to section 16.

12   Cadastral units

(1)   A cadastral unit is a unit which represents a single registered plot of land.

(2)   Subject to subsection (3), the same area of land cannot be represented by more than one cadastral unit.

(3)   The Keeper need not represent a plot of land such as is mentioned in section 3(7) as a separate cadastral unit but may instead include it in the cadastral unit representing the plot or plots of land of which it is a pertinent.

(4)   The Keeper must assign a cadastral unit number to each cadastral unit.

(5)   The cadastral unit number is to be the title number of the plot of land which that unit represents.

13   The cadastral map: further provision

(1)   Where a plot of land—

(a)   lies wholly outwith the base map, or

(b)   extends partly outwith the base map,

the Keeper may adopt such means of representing the boundaries on the cadastral map as the Keeper considers appropriate.

(2)   The Keeper may—

(a)   combine cadastral units,

(b)   remove a cadastral unit from the map, or

(c)   divide a cadastral unit.

(3)   On dividing a cadastral unit under subsection (2)(c), the Keeper may combine any of the resultant parts with a different cadastral unit.

(4)   The Keeper must make such changes to the register as are necessary in consequence of anything done under subsections (2) and (3).

The archive record

14   The archive record

(1)   The archive record is to consist of—

(a)   copies of all documents submitted to the Keeper,

(b)   copies of all documents which the Keeper is required to include under land register rules, and

(c)   copies of such other documents as the Keeper considers appropriate.

(2)   The Keeper must also include in the archive record such information as is required for the purposes of section 104.

(3)   But the Keeper need not include in the archive record a copy of—

(a)   any enactment, or

(b)   any document comprised in any other register under the management and control of the Keeper or of the Keeper of the Records of Scotland.

(4)   A fact which can be discovered from the archive record is not, by reason only of that circumstance, a fact which a person ought to know.

The application record

15   The application record
The application record is to consist of all—
  (a)   applications for registration as are for the time being pending, and
  (b)   advance notices as are for the time being extant.

Tenements etc

16   Tenements and other flatted buildings
  (1)   Where the Keeper considers it appropriate in relation to a flatted building to do so, the Keeper may, instead of representing each registered flat in the building as a separate cadastral unit, represent the building and all the registered flats in it as a single cadastral unit.
  (2)   Where a flatted building and the registered flats in it are represented as a single cadastral unit—
  (a)   the cadastral map must show, for that cadastral unit, the title numbers of each registered flat, and
  (b)   the respective pro indiviso shares in the pertinents of the registered flats need not be entered in the proprietorship section of the title sheet of any of those flats.
  (3)   But subsections (1) and (2) do not apply in relation to land pertaining to the flatted building which—
  (a)   extends more than 25 metres from the building in so far as it so extends, or
  (b)   is further than 25 metres from the building (measuring along a horizontal plane from whatever point of that building is nearest to the land).
  (4)   In this Act a 'flatted building' means—
  (a)   a tenement, or
  (b)   any other subdivided building.
  (5)   A 'subdivided building'—
  (a)   means a building or part of a building, not being a tenement, which comprises two or more related flats, at least two of which—
      (i)   are, or are designed to be, in separate ownership, and
      (ii)   are divided from each other vertically, and
  (b)   includes the solum and any other land pertaining to the building or part of the building.
  (6)   In determining whether flats comprised in a subdivided building are related, the Keeper must have regard, among other things, to—
  (a)   the title to the building, and
  (b)   any real burdens.
  (7)   In subsection (6), 'title to the building' means—
  (a)   any conveyance, or reservation, of property which affects the subdivided building, any flat in the building or any pertinent of the building or of any such flat, and
  (b)   the relevant title sheet of the building, any flat in it or any pertinent of the building or of any such flat.
  (8)   Expressions used in this section and in sections 26 and 29 of the Tenements (Scotland) Act 2004 (asp 11) have the meanings given in that Act.

Shared plots

17   Shared plots
  (1)   This section applies where a plot of land—
  (a)   is owned in common by the proprietors of two or more other plots of land by virtue of their ownership of those other plots,
  (b)   is not owned in common by anyone else.

(2)   The Keeper may, if the Keeper considers it appropriate, designate the title sheet of the plot of land to be a 'shared plot title sheet'.

(3)   In this section and in sections 18 and 19—

(a)   references to a 'shared plot' are to a plot of land the title sheet of which is designated under subsection (2),

(b)   references to the 'sharing plots' are to the other plots of land the proprietors of which own the shared plot in common.

(4)   Unless the context otherwise requires, any reference in a document to a sharing plot is to be taken to include a reference to the share in the shared plot which pertains to the sharing plot.

(5)   Registration has the same effect in relation to a share in a shared plot which pertains to a sharing plot as it has in relation to the sharing plot (except in so far as may otherwise be provided in the deed registered).

18   Shared plot and sharing plot title sheets

(1)   The Keeper must enter—

(a)   in the property section of the title sheet of each of the sharing plots, the title number of the shared plot title sheet,

(b)   in the proprietorship section of the shared plot title sheet, the title numbers of the title sheets of each of the sharing plots.

(2)   The Keeper must also enter—

(a)   in the property section of the title sheet of each sharing plot, the quantum of the share which the proprietor of that sharing plot has in the shared plot,

(b)   in the proprietorship section of the shared plot title sheet, in relation to the information required by section 7(1)(b), the respective share each sharing plot has in the shared plot,

(c)   in the securities section of that title sheet, a statement to the effect that the shared plot may be subject to a heritable security registered against a sharing plot,

(d)   in the burdens section of that title sheet, a statement to the effect that the shared plot may be subject to some other encumbrance so registered.

(3)   The Keeper must not enter in or, if entered, must omit from—

(a)   the proprietorship section of the shared plot title sheet, the information that would otherwise be required under section 7(1)(a),

(b)   the securities section of that title sheet, the information that would otherwise be required under section 8(1) unless the security is over the shared plot only,

(c)   that title sheet, any matter that would otherwise be required under section 10(2)(b).

(4)   The Keeper may, if the condition mentioned in subsection (5) is satisfied and the Keeper considers it appropriate, omit from the burdens section of the shared plot title sheet any entry which would otherwise be required under section 9(1).

(5)   The condition is that the encumbrance to which the entry would relate is (or falls to be) registered against each of the sharing plots.

19   Conversion of shared plot title sheet to ordinary title sheet

(1)   The Keeper may at any time revoke a designation under section 17(2) of a title sheet as a shared plot title sheet.

(2)   Where the Keeper revokes a designation, the Keeper must make such changes to the title sheets of the plots of land that were, in relation to the shared plot title sheet, the shared plot and the sharing plots as are consequential upon the revocation.

20   Shared plot title sheets in relation to registered leases

Schedule 1 makes provision for registered leases tenanted in common similar to that made by sections 17 to 19 for plots of land owned in common.

PART 2

REGISTRATION

Applications for registration

21 Application for registration of deed

(1)   A person may apply to the Keeper for registration of a registrable deed.

(2)   The Keeper must accept an application under subsection (1) to the extent the applicant satisfies the Keeper that, as at the date of application, the general application conditions are met and—

(a)   where the application is made in respect of a disposition of, or a notice of title to, an unregistered plot, the conditions set out in section 23 are met,

(b)   where section 25 applies, the conditions set out in that section are met,

(c)   in any other case, the conditions set out in section 26 are met.

(3)   To the extent the applicant does not so satisfy the Keeper, the Keeper must reject the application.

(4)   Subsection (2) is subject to section 45(5) [and paragraphs 1 to 5 of schedule 1A].

[(5)   Schedule 1A makes provision about certain land transactions involving overseas entities.]*

[(5)   For the purposes of this section, submission by electronic means of a copy of the deed is sufficient evidence of the original for the purposes of accepting an application for registration.

(6)   But subsection (5) applies only where submission of the copy is by a means (and in a form) which is specified on the Keeper's website as being acceptable.

(7)   In subsection (5), the reference to submission by electronic means is to submission—

(a)   by means of an electronic communications network (for example as an attachment to an email), or

(b)   by other means but in a form which requires the use of electronic apparatus by the recipient to render the thing delivered intelligible.

(8)   In this section—

'electronic communications network' has the meaning given by section 32 of the Communications Act 2003,

'the Keeper's website' means the website maintained by, or on behalf of, the Keeper of the Registers of Scotland.]

22 General application conditions

(1)   The general application conditions are—

(a)   the application is such that the Keeper is able to comply, in respect of it, with such duties as the Keeper has under Part 1,

(b)   the application does not relate to a souvenir plot,

(c)   the application does not fall to be rejected by virtue of section 6 or 9G of the Requirements of Writing (Scotland) Act 1995 (c 7) (registration of document) or of a prohibition in an enactment,

(d)   the application is in the form (if any) prescribed by land register rules, and

(e)   either—

---

* At the time the proofs for this edition were revised the House of Lords had just passed an amendment in the Economic Crime and Corporate Transparency Bill which would renumber this subsection as subsection (4A).

    (i)   such fee as is payable for registration is paid, or

    (ii) arrangements satisfactory to the Keeper are made for payment of that fee.

(2) In subsection (1)(b), 'souvenir plot' means a plot of land which—

    (a) is of inconsiderable size and of no practical utility, and

    (b) is neither—

       (i)   a registered plot, nor

       (ii) a plot the ownership of which has, at any time, separately been constituted or transferred by a document recorded in the Register of Sasines.

23 Conditions of registration: transfer of unregistered plot

(1) The conditions are that—

    (a) the application is made by the grantee of the disposition or as the case may be the person in whose favour is the notice of title,

    (b) the deed is valid,

    (c) the deed so describes the plot as to enable the Keeper to delineate its boundaries on the cadastral map,

    (d) where within the plot there is a lesser area in respect of which a registrable encumbrance is constituted there is included in, or submitted with, the application a plan or description sufficient to enable the Keeper to delineate the boundaries of the lesser area on the cadastral map,

    (e) there is included in the application a description of every public right of way (by whatever means) over or through the plot in so far as known to the applicant.

(2) Subsection (1)(c) and (d) do not apply—

    (a) if the plot to which the application relates is a flat in a flatted building, and

    (b) either—

       (i)   the flatted building is, by virtue of section 16, represented as a single cadastral unit on the cadastral map, or

       (ii) the Keeper has indicated that the flatted building is, by virtue of that section, to be so represented.

(3) Despite subsection (2), subsection (1)(c) and (d) apply in so far as the plot includes a pertinent outwith the flatted building, being a pertinent only of the plot.

(4) Subsection (1)(d) does not apply in relation to an encumbrance which consists of—

    (a) a right to lead a pipe, cable, wire or other such enclosed unit over or under land,

    (b) a servitude created other than by registration.

(5) In this section, 'the deed' means the disposition or as the case may be the notice of title.

24 Circumstances in which section 25 applies

(1) Section 25 applies where any of subsections (2) to (7) apply.

(2) This subsection applies where—

    (a) the application is in respect of a grant of a lease, and

    (b) the subjects of the lease consist of or form part of an unregistered plot of land.

(3) This subsection applies where—

    (a) the application is in respect of an assignation of an unregistered lease, and

    (b) the subjects of the lease consist of or form part of an unregistered plot of land.

(4) This subsection applies where—

    (a) the application is in respect of a sublease granted by a tenant, and

    (b) the subjects of the tenant's lease consist of or form part of an unregistered plot of land.

(5) This subsection applies where—

(a)   the application is in respect of a deed registrable by virtue of section 48(4), and

(b)   the land to which the deed relates consists of or forms part of an unregistered plot of land.

(6)   This subsection applies where—

(a)   the application is in respect of a notice of title to a subordinate real right,

(b)   the notice of title is registrable by virtue of section 4A (as inserted by section 53(3)) of the Conveyancing (Scotland) Act 1924 (c 27),

(c)   the last completed title to the subordinate real right is recorded in the Register of Sasines, and

(d)   the land in respect of which the subordinate real right is constituted consists of or forms part of an unregistered plot of land.

(7)   This subsection applies where—

(a)   the application is in respect of a standard security granted over an unregistered subordinate real right, and

(b)   the land in respect of which the subordinate real right is constituted consists of or forms part of an unregistered plot of land.

25   Conditions of registration: certain deeds relating to unregistered plots

(1)   The conditions are that—

(a)   the deed is valid,

(b)   the deed so describes the plot as to enable the Keeper to delineate its boundaries on the cadastral map,

(c)   where within the plot there is a lesser area in respect of which a registrable encumbrance is constituted there is included in, or submitted with, the application a plan or description sufficient to enable the Keeper to delineate the boundaries of the lesser area on the cadastral map,

(d)   there is included in the application a description of every public right of way (by whatever means) over or through the plot in so far as known to the applicant.

(2)   Subsection (1)(b) and (c) do not apply—

(a)   if the plot to which the deed relates is a flat in a flatted building, and

(b)   either—

(i)   the flatted building is, by virtue of section 16, represented as a single cadastral unit in the cadastral map, or

(ii)   the Keeper has indicated that the flatted building is, by virtue of that section, to be so represented.

(3)   Despite subsection (2), subsection (1)(b) and (c) apply in so far as the plot includes a pertinent outwith the flatted building, being a pertinent only of the plot.

(4)   Subsection (1)(c) does not apply in relation to an encumbrance which consists of—

(a)   a right to lead a pipe, cable, wire or other such enclosed unit over or under land,

(b)   a servitude created other than by registration.

(5)   In this section and sections 30 and 41 in so far as they apply by virtue of this section, references to the plot are to be read as references to—

(a)   where this section applies by virtue of section 24(2), (3) or (4), the area of land which forms the subjects of the lease,

(b)   where this section applies by virtue of section 24(5), the area of land to which the deed relates,

(c)   where this section applies by virtue of section 24(6) or (7), the area of land in respect of which the subordinate real right is constituted.

26   Conditions of registration: deeds relating to registered plots

(1)   The conditions are that—

(a)   the deed is valid,

(b)   the deed relates to a registered plot of land,

(c)   the deed narrates the title number of each title sheet to which the application relates, and

(d)   the deed, in so far as it relates to part only of a plot of land or of the subjects of a lease, so describes the part as to enable the Keeper to delineate on the cadastral map the boundaries of the part.

(2)   Where the title number of the title sheet of a sharing plot is narrated in the deed, subsection (1)(c) does not require the narration of the title number of the title sheet of the shared plot.

(3)   Subsection (1)(d) does not apply if—

(a)   the part to which the deed relates is a flat in a flatted building, and

(b)   either—

(i)   the flatted building is, by virtue of section 16, represented as a single cadastral unit in the cadastral map, or

(ii)   the Keeper has indicated that the flatted building is, by virtue of that section, to be so depicted.

(4)   Despite subsection (3), subsection (1)(d) applies in so far as the part includes a pertinent outwith the flatted building, being a pertinent only of the part.

(5)   Subsection (1)(d) does not apply in the case of an application which relates to registration to create as a servitude a right to lead a pipe, cable, wire or other such enclosed unit over or under land.

Registration without deed

27   Application for voluntary registration

(1)   A person mentioned in subsection (2) may apply for registration of an unregistered plot of land or any part of that plot.

(2)   The person is the owner (or, in the case of ownership in common, any of the owners) of the plot.

(3)   The Keeper must accept an application under subsection (1) to the extent—

(a)   the applicant satisfies the Keeper that, as at the date of the application, the following are met—

(i)   the general application conditions, and

(ii)   the conditions mentioned in section 28, and

(b)   the Keeper is satisfied that it is expedient that the plot (or the part of the plot) should be registered.

(4)   To the extent the applicant does not so satisfy the Keeper, the Keeper must reject the application.

[(4A)   Subsection (3) is subject to paragraph 6 of schedule 1A.]

(5)   Where the application is in respect of a part of a plot of land, references to the plot in section 28 and section 30 in so far as it applies by virtue of this section are to be read as references to the part.

(6)   The Scottish Ministers may by order repeal subsection (3)(b).

(7)   Before making such an order, the Scottish Ministers must consult the Keeper.

(8)   An order under subsection (6) may make different provision for different areas.

28   Conditions of registration: voluntary registration

(1)   The conditions are that—

(a)   there is submitted with the application a plan or description of the plot sufficient to enable the Keeper to delineate the plot's boundaries in the cadastral map,

(b)   where within the plot there is a lesser area in respect of which a registrable encumbrance is constituted there is included in, or submitted with, the application a plan or description sufficient to enable the Keeper to delineate the boundaries of the lesser area in the cadastral map.

(2)   Subsection (1)(a) and (b) does not apply—

(a) if the plot to which the application relates is a flat in a flatted building, and

(b) either—

   (i) the flatted building is, by virtue of section 16, represented as a single cadastral unit on the cadastral map, or

   (ii) the Keeper has indicated that the flatted building is, by virtue of that section, to be so depicted.

(3) Despite subsection (2), subsection (1)(a) and (b) applies in so far as the plot includes a pertinent outwith the flatted building, being a pertinent only of the plot.

(4) Subsection (1)(b) does not apply in relation to an encumbrance which consists of—

(a) a right to lead a pipe, cable, wire or other such enclosed unit over or under land, or

(b) a servitude created other than by registration.

29 Keeper-induced registration

(1) Other than on application and irrespective of whether the proprietor or any other person consents, the Keeper may register an unregistered plot of land or part of that plot.

(2) Where the Keeper decides under this section to register a part of a plot, references to the plot in section 30 are to be read as references to the part.

Completion of registration

30 Completion of registration of plot

(1) This section applies where—

(a) the Keeper accepts—

   (i) an application under section 21 in respect of a disposition of, or a notice of title to, an unregistered plot of land,

   (ii) an application under section 21 by virtue of it meeting the conditions in section 25, or

   (iii) an application under section 27 in respect of a plot of land or a part of a plot, or

(b) the Keeper decides to register a plot of land or a part of a plot under section 29.

(2) The Keeper must—

(a) make up a title sheet for the plot,

(b) make such other changes to the title sheet record as are necessary or expedient,

(c) create a cadastral unit for the plot,

(d) make such other changes to the cadastral map as are necessary or expedient, and

(e) copy into the archive record any document which—

   (i) has been submitted to the Keeper or, where this section applies by virtue of subsection (1)(a)(ii) or (1)(b), is reasonably available to the Keeper, and

   (ii) is relevant to the accuracy of the register.

(3) Subsection (2)(e) is subject to section 14(3).

(4) Changes under paragraph (b) or (d) of subsection (2) may include—

(a) cancelling a title sheet and cadastral unit, or

(b) making up a new title sheet and creating a new cadastral unit.

(5) In a case where—

(a) this section applies by virtue of subsection (1)(a)(ii) or (1)(b), and

(b) any name or designation to be entered in the new title sheet to be made up cannot, or cannot with reasonable certainty, be determined by the Keeper, the Keeper may, in place of or as part of that entry, enter a statement that the name or designation is not known or as the case may be is not known with reasonable certainty.

31 Completion of registration of deed

(1)　This section applies where the Keeper accepts an application under section 21 other than an application to which section 30 applies.

(2)　The Keeper must as soon as reasonably practicable after accepting the application—

  (a)　make such changes to the title sheet, or each of the title sheets, to which the application relates as are necessary to give effect to the deed,

  (b)　make such other changes (if any) to the title sheet record as are necessary or expedient,

  (c)　make such changes (if any) to the cadastral map as are necessary or expedient, and

  (d)　copy into the archive record—

    (i)　the deed being given effect to by registration, and

    (ii)　any other document which has been submitted to the Keeper and is relevant to the accuracy of the register.

(3)　Subsection (2)(d)(ii) is subject to section 14(3).

(4)　Changes under paragraphs (a) to (c) of subsection (2) may include—

  (a)　cancelling a title sheet and cadastral unit, or

  (b)　making up a new title sheet and creating a new cadastral unit.

32 References to certain entries in Register of Inhibitions

(1)　Subsection (2) applies where—

  (a)　the Keeper accepts an application for registration under section 21, and

  (b)　the validity of the deed to which the application relates might be affected by an entry in the Register of Inhibitions.

(2)　The Keeper must, as soon as reasonably practicable after accepting the application, enter a reference to the entry in the title sheet.

(3)　Subsection (2) does not apply where the entry mentioned in subsection (1)(b) is—

  (a)　a notice of land attachment (within the meaning of section 83(1) of the Bankruptcy and Diligence etc (Scotland) Act 2007 (asp 3)), or

  (b)　a notice of a signeted summons in an action of reduction of a deed granted in breach of inhibition.

General provision about applications

33 Recording in application record

(1)　On receipt of an application for registration, the Keeper must—

  (a)　as soon as reasonably practicable, or

  (b)　if the application record is not open for the making of entries, as soon as reasonably practicable on the application record next opening for that purpose,

enter in the application record details of the application (including the date the entry under this subsection is made).

(2)　No such entry need be made however if, on receipt of the application, it is immediately apparent to the Keeper that the application falls to be rejected.

(3)　On an application being—

  (a)　withdrawn,

  (b)　accepted by the Keeper, or

  (c)　rejected by the Keeper,

the Keeper must remove the entry relating to it from the application record.

34 Withdrawal and amendments etc. of application

(1)　While an application for registration is pending, the applicant—

  (a)　may withdraw it, but

(b)   except with the consent of the Keeper, may not substitute it or amend it.
(2)   Land register rules may specify circumstances in which consent under subsection (1)(b) must be given.

35   Period within which decision must be made

(1)   The Keeper's decision as to whether to accept or reject an application for registration must be made within such period as may be prescribed in land register rules.
(2)   Different periods may be so prescribed for different kinds of application.
(3)   The Keeper must deal with an application without unreasonable delay.

Date of application and registration etc

36   Date of application

Any reference in this Act, however expressed, to the date of an application for registration is a reference to the date an entry in respect of the application is made in the application record under subsection (1) of section 33 (or, but for subsection (2) of that section, would fall to be made).

37   Date and time of registration

(1)   Where the Keeper accepts an application for registration, the date of registration is the date of the application.
(2)   The time of registration is deemed to be the moment at which, following the application being received by the Keeper, the application record next closes.
(3)   The Scottish Ministers may by order—
    (a)   amend subsection (2) so as to make different provision as regards time of registration, and
    (b)   make such other amendments to this Act as are consequential upon that amendment.
(4)   Before making such an order, the Scottish Ministers must consult the Keeper.

38   Power to amend section 6 of the Land Registers (Scotland) Act 1868

If, under section 37(3)(a), the Scottish Ministers amend this Act, they may, in that order, correspondingly amend section 6 of the Land Registers (Scotland) Act 1868 (c 64) (which provides for registration in the General Register of Sasines) and make such other amendments to that Act as are consequential upon that amendment to that section.

Applications in relation to the same land

39   Order in which applications are to be dealt with

(1)   The Keeper must deal with two or more applications for registration in relation to the same land in order of receipt.
(2)   In the absence of evidence to the contrary, the order of receipt is to be taken to be the order in which the details of the applications were entered in the application record.
(3)   Subsection (1) is subject to subsections (4) to (8).
(4)   Subsection (5) applies where—
    (a)   two applications ('application A' and 'application B') are received on the same date in relation to the same land,
    (b)   to accept one of the applications would require the Keeper to reject the other,
    (c)   the deed to which application A purports to give effect is a deed in relation to which a protected period is running, and
    (d)   the deed to which application B purports to give effect either—

(i)   is not such a deed, or

(ii)   is such a deed but the protected period relating to the deed to which application A purports to give effect began before the protected period relating to the deed to which application B purports to give effect.

(5)   The Keeper must deal with application A before application B.

(6)   Subsection (8) applies where—

(a)   two applications ('application C' and 'application D') are received on the same date in relation to the same land,

(b)   the deed to which one of them (application C) purports to give effect is a deed in favour of a person ('X'), and

(c)   the deed to which the other (application D) purports to give effect is a deed granted by X.

(7)   Subsection (8) also applies where—

(a)   two applications ('application C' and 'application D') are received on the same date in relation to the same land,

(b)   one application (application C) is an application under section 27, and

(c)   the other (application D) is an application under section 21.

(8)   The Keeper must deal with application C before application D.

Notification

40   Notification of acceptance, rejection or withdrawal of application

(1)   On an application for registration being accepted or rejected, the Keeper must notify—

(a)   the applicant,

(b)   the granter of the deed sought to be registered (if any),

(c)   if notification of receipt of the application was given under section 45(1), those to whom it was given, and

(d)   any other person the Keeper considers appropriate.

(2)   On an application for registration being withdrawn, the Keeper must notify—

(a)   the granter of the deed which had been sought to be registered (if any),

(b)   if such notification as is mentioned in subsection (1)(c) was given, those to whom it was given, and

(c)   any other person the Keeper considers appropriate.

(3)   The Keeper's duty to notify persons under subsections (1) and (2) only applies in so far as the Keeper considers it reasonably practicable to notify them.

(4)   Notification is to be by such means as the Keeper considers appropriate.

(5)   Land register rules may make further provision about notification under subsections (1) and (2).

(6)   A failure to comply with subsections (1) and (2) or with any rules so made does not affect the competence or validity of the acceptance, rejection or withdrawal in question.

41   Notification to proprietor

(1)   This section applies where—

(a)   the Keeper accepts an application under section 21 by virtue of it meeting the conditions in section 25, or

(b)   the Keeper registers a plot of land under section 29.

(2)   The Keeper is to notify—

(a)   the proprietor of the plot, and

(b)   any other person the Keeper considers appropriate.

(3)   The Keeper's duty to notify persons under subsection (2) only applies in so far as the Keeper considers it reasonably practicable to notify them.

(4)   Notification is to be by such means as the Keeper considers appropriate.

(5)   Land register rules may make further provision about notification under subsection (2).

(6)   A failure to comply with subsection (2) or with any rules so made does not affect the competence or validity—

(a)   of the acceptance of the application in question, or

(b)   of the registration of the plot of land in question.

42   Notification to Scottish Ministers of certain applications

(1)   This section applies where an application under section 21 is rejected on the ground that (or on grounds which include the ground that) the Keeper is not satisfied that the application does not relate to a transfer prohibited—

(a)   by section 40(1) of the Land Reform (Scotland) Act 2003 (asp 2) (effect of registration of community interest in land), or

(b)   under section 37(5)(e) of that Act (prohibition pending determination as to whether a community interest in land is to be registered).

(2)   However, this section does not apply where the only reason for the Keeper not being satisfied as mentioned in subsection (1) is that the application is not accompanied by a declaration required under section 43(2) of that Act (incorporation of certain declarations into deed giving effect to transfer).

(3)   The Keeper must—

(a)   notify the Scottish Ministers, and

(b)   provide them with a copy of the application.

Prescriptive claimants etc

43   Prescriptive claimants

(1)   For the purposes of sections 23(1)(b), and 26(1)(a), a disposition is to be treated as being valid despite not being so if the conditions mentioned in subsection s (2) to (4) are met.

(2)   It appears to the Keeper that the disposition is not valid (or, as regards part of the land to which the application relates, is not valid) for the reason only that the person who granted it had no title to do so.

(3)   The applicant satisfies the Keeper that the land to which the application relates (or as the case may be the part in question) has been possessed openly, peaceably and without judicial interruption—

(a)   by the disponer or the applicant for a continuous period of 1 year immediately preceding the date of application, or

(b)   first by the disponer and then by the applicant for periods which together constitute such a period.

(4)   The applicant satisfies the Keeper that the following person has been notified of the application—

(a)   the proprietor,

(b)   if there is no proprietor (or none can be identified), any person who appears to be able to take steps to complete title as proprietor, or

(c)   if there is no proprietor and no such person (or, in either case, none can be identified), the Crown.

(5)   For the purposes of section 26(1)(a), a deed is to be treated as being valid despite not being so if—

(a)   the deed is granted by or is directed against a prescriptive claimant, and

(b)   the application would be accepted were the prescriptive claimant's title valid.

(6)   In subsection (5), a 'prescriptive claimant' is—

(a)   a person whose name is entered as proprietor in the proprietorship section of a title sheet, on an application being accepted by virtue of subsection (1),

(b)   a person whose name is entered as holder of a right, in the appropriate section of a title sheet, the entry in relation to the right being one marked provisional under section 81(3)(a)(i),

(c)   any person in right of a person mentioned in paragraph (a) or (b).

(7) Land register rules may make further provision about notification under sub-section (4).

(8) The Scottish Ministers may, by order, amend subsection (3) so as to substitute for the period for the time being mentioned there a different period.

(9) Before making such an order, the Scottish Ministers must consult the Keeper.

44 Provisional entries on title sheet

(1) Where the Keeper accepts an application under section 21 by virtue of section 43(1) or (5), the Keeper is to mark any resulting entry in the title sheet as provisional.

(2) The Keeper is to remove the provisional marking from an entry if and when the real right to which the entry relates becomes, under section 1 of the Prescription and Limitation (Scotland) Act 1973 (c 52) (validity of right), exempt from challenge.

(3) While an entry remains provisional—

(a) it does not affect any right held by any person in the land to which the entry relates, and

(b) rights set out in the register are not to be altered or deleted by virtue only of the entry.

45 Notification of prescriptive applications

(1) Before accepting an application under section 21 which is received by virtue of section 43(1), the Keeper must notify—

(a) the proprietor,

(b) if there is no proprietor (or none can be identified), any person who appears to the Keeper able to take steps to complete title as proprietor, or

(c) if there is no proprietor and no such person (or, in either case, none can be identified), the Crown.

(2) The Keeper's duty to notify persons under subsection (1) only applies in so far as the Keeper considers it reasonably practicable to notify them.

(3) Notification is to be by such means as the Keeper considers appropriate.

(4) A person to whom notice is given under subsection (1) may object in writing to the application being accepted.

(5) If the Keeper receives such an objection within 60 days of the notice, the Keeper must reject the application.

(6) Land register rules may make further provision about notification under sub-section (1).

(7) The Scottish Ministers may, by order, amend subsection (5) so as to substitute for the number of days for the time being mentioned there a different number of days.

(8) Before making such an order, the Scottish Ministers must consult the Keeper.

Further provision

46 [Meaning of 'disposition' in certain provisions]

In the application of sections 21, 23, 30 and 48 [and schedule 1A] to a case in which transfer of ownership is by virtue of compulsory acquisition, any reference in those sections [or that schedule] to a 'disposition' includes a reference to—

(a) a conveyance the form of which is provided for by an enactment,

(b) a notarial instrument, or

(c) a general vesting declaration.

47 Effect of death or dissolution

(1) The Keeper must reject an application if the applicant dies, or as the case may be is dissolved, before the date of the application.

(2)   An application is not incompetent by reason only that the person who granted the deed sought to be registered dies, or as the case may be is dissolved, after the delivery of the deed.

Closure of Register of Sasines etc

48   Closure of Register of Sasines etc

(1)   The recording of any of the following in the Register of Sasines has no effect—

    (a)   a disposition,

    (b)   a lease,

    (c)   an assignation of a lease,

    (d)   any other deed in so far as it relates to a registered plot of land or to a registered lease.

(2)   The recording, on or after such day as is prescribed, of a standard security in the Register of Sasines has no effect.

(3)   The recording, on or after such day as is prescribed, of a deed other than one mentioned in subsection (1) or (2) in the Register of Sasines has no effect.

(4)   On and after the day prescribed under subsection (3), any deed the recording of which would, by virtue of that subsection, have no effect is (subject to the provisions of this Act) registrable in the Land Register.

(5)   Where by virtue of this section the recording of a deed, disposition, lease, assignation or standard security in the Register of Sasines would have no effect, the Keeper is to reject any application to record it.

(6)   Subsection (1)(a) is without prejudice to sections 4 (creation of real burden) and 75 (creation of positive servitude by writing: deed to be registered) of the Title Conditions (Scotland) Act 2003 (asp 9).

(7)   Any day prescribed under subsection (2) or (3) is to be a day no earlier than the day subsection (3)(b) of section 27 is repealed by virtue of subsection (6) of that section.

(8)   In subsections (2) and (3), 'prescribed' means prescribed by the Scottish Ministers by order.

(9)   An order under subsection (2) or (3) may make different provision for different areas.

(10)   Before making an order under subsection (2) or (3), the Scottish Ministers must consult—

    (a)   the Keeper, and

    (b)   such other persons appearing to have an interest in the closure of the Register of Sasines to the recording of deeds as the Scottish Ministers consider appropriate.

PART 3
COMPETENCE AND EFFECT OF REGISTRATION

Registrable deeds

49   Registrable deeds

(1)   A deed is registrable only if and in so far as its registration is authorised (whether expressly or not) by—

    (a)   this Act,

    (b)   an enactment mentioned in subsection (3), or

    (c)   any other enactment.

(2)   Registration of such a deed has the effect provided for (whether expressly or not) by—

    (a)   this Act,

    (b)   an enactment mentioned in subsection (3),

    (c)   any other enactment, or

(d) any rule of law.
(3)   The enactments referred to in subsections (1) and (2) are—
    (a) the Registration of Leases (Scotland) Act 1857 (c 26),
    (b) the Conveyancing (Scotland) Act 1924 (c 27),
    (c) the Conveyancing and Feudal Reform (Scotland) Act 1970 (c 35),
    (d) the Law Reform (Miscellaneous Provisions) (Scotland) Act 1985 (c 73).
(4)   Registration of an invalid deed confers real effect only to the extent that an enactment so provides.

Specific provisions on competence and effect of registration

50 Transfer by disposition
(1)   A disposition of land may be registered.
(2)   Registration of a valid disposition transfers ownership.
(3)   An unregistered disposition does not transfer ownership.
(4)   Subsections (1) to (3) are subject to—
    (a) sections 43 and 86, and
    (b) any other enactment or rule of law by or under which ownership of land may pass.
(5)   In subsection (1), 'land' includes land held on udal title.

51 Proper liferents
(1)   A deed creating a proper liferent over land may be—
    (a) registered, or
    (b) recorded in the Register of Sasines.
(2)   The proper liferent is not created before the deed is so registered or recorded.
(3)   Subsections (1) and (2) are subject to any other enactment or any rule of law by or under which a proper liferent over land may be created.
(4)   References in this section to the recording of a deed include references to the recording of a notice of title deducing title through a deed.

52–55 *[Amending provisions]*

PART 4
ADVANCE NOTICES

56 Advance notices
(1)   An advance notice is a notice—
    (a) stating that a person intends to grant a deed to another person,
    (b) stating the name and designation of both persons,
    (c) describing the nature of the intended deed (as for example whether it is to be a disposition),
    (d) where the intended deed relates to a registered lease or a registered plot of land—
        (i) stating the title number of the title sheet to which the deed is to relate,
        (ii) where the deed is to relate to a registered lease which does not have a lease title sheet, stating the particulars of the lease, and
        (iii) where the deed is to relate to part only of the subjects of the lease, or to part only of the plot, describing the part so as to enable the Keeper to delineate on the cadastral map the boundaries of the part, and
    (e) where the intended deed relates to an unregistered lease or unregistered plot of land, describing the lease or, as the case may be, plot.
(2)   Subsection (1)(d)(iii) does not apply if—
    (a) the part to which the deed relates is a flat in a flatted building, and
    (b) either—

(i)   the flatted building is, by virtue of section 16, represented as a single cadastral unit on the cadastral map, or

(ii)   the Keeper has indicated that the flatted building is, by virtue of that section, to be so depicted.

(3)   Despite subsection (2), subsection (1)(d)(iii) applies in so far as the part includes a pertinent outwith the flatted building, being a pertinent only of the part.

(4)   The Scottish Ministers may by regulations make provision about the description to be contained in an advance notice by virtue of subsection (1)(e).

57   Application for advance notice

(1)   A person falling within subsection (2) may apply to the Keeper for an advance notice in relation to a registrable deed which the person intends to grant.

(2)   A person falls within this subsection if—

(a)   the person may validly grant the intended deed, or

(b)   the person has the consent of such a person to apply.

(3)   The Keeper may accept an application under subsection (1) only if—

(a)   such fee as is payable in respect of the application is paid, or

(b)   arrangements satisfactory to the Keeper are made for payment of that fee.

(4)   If the Keeper accepts an application under subsection (1), the Keeper must—

(a)   where the intended deed relates to [a registered lease or] a registered plot of land—

(i)   as soon as reasonably practicable or, if the application record is not open for the making of entries, as soon as reasonably practicable on the application record next opening for that purpose, enter an advance notice in the application record, and

(ii)   where (and to the extent that) section 56(1)(d)(iii) applies in relation to the notice, delineate the boundaries of the part on the cadastral map,

(b)   in any other case, record an advance notice in the Register of Sasines.

58   Period of effect of advance notice

(1)   An advance notice has effect for the period of 35 days beginning with the day after the notice is entered in the application record or, as the case may be, recorded in the Register of Sasines.

(2)   Subsection (1) is subject to section 63.

(3)   The period during which an advance notice has effect is referred to in this Act as the 'protected period'.

(4)   Subsection (5) applies where two advance notices in relation to the same plot of land or lease are entered into the application record or recorded in the Register of Sasines on the same date.

(5)   The protected period in relation to the advance notice which is first to be entered in the application record, or as the case may be recorded in the Register of Sasines, is deemed to begin before the protected period in relation to the other advance notice.

(6)   The Scottish Ministers may, by order amend subsection (1) so as to substitute for the period for the time being mentioned there a different period.

(7)   Before making such an order, the Scottish Ministers must consult the Keeper.

59   Effect of advance notice: registered deeds

(1)   Subsections (2) and (3) apply in relation to any two deeds ('deed Y' and 'deed Z') relating to the same plot of land where—

(a)   during a protected period relating to deed Y—

(i)   an application is made for registration of deed Z, and

(ii)   on or after the date of that application, an application is made for registration of deed Y, and

(b)   deed Z either—

(i)   is not a deed in relation to which a protected period is running, or

(ii)   is such a deed, but the protected period relating to deed Y began before the protected period relating to deed Z.

(2)   If deed Z is registered before the Keeper comes to make any decision as to whether or not to accept the application for registration of deed Y, that decision is to be taken as if deed Z had not been registered.

(3)   If the decision mentioned in subsection (2) is to accept the application—

(a)   deed Y has on registration the same effect as if deed Z had not been registered, and

(b)   the Keeper must amend the register so that it gives effect (if any) to deed Z as if it were registered after deed Y.

60   Effect of advance notice: recorded deeds

(1)   Subsections (2) and (3) apply in relation to any two deeds ('deed Y' and 'deed Z') relating to the same plot of land where, during a protected period relating to deed Y—

(a)   deed Z is recorded in the Register of Sasines, and

(b)   on or after the date of recording, an application is made for registration of deed Y.

(2)   The decision as to whether or not to accept the application for registration of deed Y is to be taken as if deed Z had not been recorded.

(3)   If the decision mentioned in subsection (2) is to accept the application—

(a)   deed Y has on registration the same effect as if deed Z had not been recorded, and

(b)   in making up the title sheet for the plot, the Keeper must give effect (if any) to deed Z as if it were not recorded but registered after deed Y.

61   Effect of advance notice: further provision

(1)   A deed to which an advance notice relates, if registered on a date which falls within the protected period, is not subject to—

(a)   an inhibition registered in the Register of Inhibitions against the granter and taking effect before that date but during that period, or

(b)   anything registered or recorded in that register and taking effect, before that date but during that period, as if an inhibition registered against the granter.

(2)   Sections 59 and 60 apply irrespective of whether a deed is voluntary or involuntary.

(3)   Sections 59 and 60 do not apply in relation to—

(a)   a notice registered, or intended or sought to be registered, under—

(i)   section 10(2A) of the Title Conditions (Scotland) Act 2003 (asp 9), or

(ii)   section 12(3) of the Tenements (Scotland) Act 2004 (asp 11), and

(b)   such other deeds as the Scottish Ministers may by order specify.

(4)   Before making an order under subsection (3)(b), the Scottish Ministers must consult the Keeper.

62   Removal of advance notice etc

(1)   After the protected period in relation to an advance notice has elapsed, the Keeper must, if the notice was entered in the application record—

(a)   remove it from there, and

(b)   if the notice has not already been entered in the archive record, enter it in that record.

(2)   After such period in relation to an advance notice as may be prescribed in land register rules the Keeper must, if the intended deed has not been registered, remove from the cadastral map any delineation effected under section 57(4)(a)(ii).

63 Discharge of advance notice

(1)   A person who applied for an advance notice may apply to the Keeper for the discharge of that notice.

(2)   An application under subsection (1) may be made only during the protected period.

(3)   The Keeper may accept an application under subsection (1) only if—

    (a)   the person to whom the intended deed would be granted consents, and

    (b)   either—

        (i)   such fee as is payable in respect of the application is paid, or

        (ii)   arrangements satisfactory to the Keeper are made for payment of that fee.

(4)   If the Keeper accepts the application, the Keeper must—

    (a)   if the advance notice was entered in the application record—

        (i)   remove it from there, and

        (ii)   if the notice has not already been entered in the archive record, enter it in that record,

    (b)   if the advance notice was recorded in the Register of Sasines, record a notice of discharge in relation to the advance notice.

(5)   On the advance notice being removed from the application record or, as the case may be, a notice of discharge being recorded, the advance notice ceases to have effect.

64 Application of Part to specific deeds

(1)   The Scottish Ministers may by order modify the application of this Part in relation to any deed of a kind specified in the order.

(2)   Before making such an order, the Scottish Ministers must consult the Keeper.

PART 5

INACCURACIES IN THE REGISTER

65 Meaning of 'inaccuracy'

(1)   A title sheet is inaccurate in so far as it—

    (a)   misstates what the position is in law or in fact,

    (b)   omits anything required, by or under an enactment, to be included in it, or

    (c)   includes anything the inclusion of which is not expressly or impliedly permitted by or under an enactment.

(2)   The cadastral map is inaccurate in so far as it—

    (a)   wrongly depicts or shows what the position is in law or in fact,

    (b)   omits anything required, by or under an enactment, to be depicted or shown on it, or

    (c)   depicts or shows anything the depiction or showing of which is not expressly or impliedly permitted by or under an enactment.

(3)   The cadastral map is not inaccurate in so far as it does not depict something correctly by reason only of an inexactness in the base map which is within the published accuracy tolerances relevant to the scale of map involved.

(4)   Neither a title sheet nor the cadastral map is inaccurate by reason only that a deed which gave rise to the acquisition, variation or discharge of a real right—

    (a)   was voidable and has been reduced, or

    (b)   has been rectified under section 8 of the Law Reform (Miscellaneous Provisions) (Scotland) Act 1985 (c 73) (rectification of defectively expressed documents).

(5)   This section is subject to section 66(3).

66 Shifting boundaries

(1) This section applies where the proprietors of adjacent plots of land affected by alluvion agree that their common boundary (or part of it) is not to be so affected.

(2) Such an agreement may, on the joint application of both proprietors, be registered in the title sheets of both plots of land.

(3) Where such an agreement is registered, the cadastral map and the title sheets of the plots do not become inaccurate as a result of alluvion affecting the boundary (or part of it) occurring after registration.

PART 6

CAVEATS

67 Warrant to place a caveat

(1) This section applies to civil proceedings—

(a) for the reduction of a registered deed on the ground that it is voidable,

(b) which could result in a judicial determination that the register is inaccurate, or

(c) for an order which, if granted, would be registrable under section 8A of the Law Reform (Miscellaneous Provisions) (Scotland) Act 1985 (c 73) (registration of order for rectification).

(2) A party to the proceedings may, at any time while the proceedings are in dependence, apply to the court for warrant to place a caveat on the title sheet of a plot of land to which the proceedings relate.

(3) The court may, if satisfied as to the matters mentioned in subsection (4), make an order granting the warrant applied for.

(4) The matters are that—

(a) the applicant has a prima facie case on the merits of the proceedings,

(b) were warrant for placing the caveat not granted, there is a real and substantial risk that enforcement of any decree or order in the proceedings granted in favour of the applicant would be defeated or prejudiced by reason of the other party being likely to deal with the plot of land, and

(c) in all the circumstances, including the effect which granting the warrant may have on any person having an interest, it is reasonable to make the order granting it.

(5) The onus is on the applicant to satisfy the court that the order granting the warrant should be made.

68 Duration of caveat

(1) A caveat, warrant for which is granted under section 67(3), expires 12 months after it is placed on the title sheet unless renewed, recalled or discharged before the expiry of that period.

(2) Subsection (1) applies to a caveat renewed under section 69(2) as it applies to a caveat, warrant for which is granted under section 67(3).

(3) The Scottish Ministers may, by order, amend subsection (1) so as to substitute for the period for the time being mentioned in the subsection a different period.

(4) Before making such an order, the Scottish Ministers must consult the Keeper.

69 Renewal of caveat

(1) The applicant may apply to the court which granted the warrant to place the caveat for warrant to renew it.

(2) The court may, if satisfied as to the matters mentioned in subsection (3), make an order granting warrant to renew the caveat.

(3) The matters are that—

(a) the applicant has a prima facie case on the merits of the proceedings,

(b) were warrant to renew the caveat not granted, there is a real and substantial risk that enforcement of any decree or order in the proceedings granted in favour of the applicant would be defeated or prejudiced by reason of the other party being likely to deal with the plot of land, and

(c) in all the circumstances, including the effect which renewing the caveat may have on any person having an interest, it is reasonable to make the order renewing it.

(4) The onus is on the applicant to satisfy the court that the order renewing the caveat should be made.

(5) The court may renew a caveat on more than one occasion.

(6) In this section and in sections 70 and 71, 'the applicant' means the person who has placed a caveat on the title sheet.

70 Restriction of caveat

(1) Any person with an interest, other than the applicant, may at any time apply to the court which granted the warrant to place the caveat for an order restricting the caveat.

(2) The court may, if satisfied—

(a) as to the matters mentioned in subsection (3), and

(b) that it is reasonable in all the circumstances to do so, make an order restricting the caveat.

(3) The matters are that—

(a) the applicant has a prima facie case on the merits of the proceedings,

(b) there is a real and substantial risk that enforcement of any decree or order in the proceedings granted in favour of the applicant would be defeated or prejudiced by reason of the other party being likely to deal with the plot of land, and

(c) in all the circumstances, including the effect which granting the warrant to place the caveat may have on any person having an interest, it is reasonable for the caveat to continue to have effect.

(4) The onus is on the applicant to satisfy the court that the order restricting the caveat should not be made.

71 Recall of caveat

(1) Any person with an interest, other than the applicant, may at any time apply to the court which granted the warrant to place the caveat for the caveat to be recalled.

(2) The court must, if no longer satisfied as to the matters mentioned in subsection (3), make an order recalling the caveat.

(3) The matters are that—

(a) the applicant has a prima facie case on the merits of the proceedings,

(b) there is a real and substantial risk that enforcement of any decree or order in the proceedings granted in favour of the applicant would be defeated or prejudiced by reason of the other party being likely to deal with the plot of land, and

(c) in all the circumstances, including the effect which granting the warrant to place the caveat may have on any person having an interest, it is reasonable for the caveat to continue to have effect.

(4) The onus is on the applicant to satisfy the court that the order recalling the caveat should not be made.

72 Discharge of caveat

A person—

(a) in whose favour warrant to place a caveat has been granted, or

(b) who has renewed a caveat under section 69(2),

may at any time discharge the caveat.

PART 7
KEEPER'S WARRANTY

Keeper's warranty

73 Keeper's warranty

(1) The Keeper, in accepting an application for registration, warrants to the applicant that, as at the time of registration, the title sheet to which the application relates—

(a) is accurate—

(i) in so far as it shows an acquisition, variation or discharge in favour of the applicant, or

(ii) in the case of an application under section 27, in so far as it shows the applicant to be the proprietor or proprietor in common, and

(b) is not inaccurate in so far as there is omitted from it any encumbrance the inclusion of which is permitted or required by or under an enactment.

(2) But the Keeper does not warrant that—

(a) the plot of land to which the application relates is unencumbered by any public right of way,

(b) the land is unencumbered by a path delineated in an order under section 22 of the Land Reform (Scotland) Act 2003 (asp 2) (compulsory powers to delineate paths in land in respect of which access rights are exercisable),

(c) the land is unencumbered by a servitude created other than by registration in accordance with section 75(1) of the Title Conditions (Scotland) Act 2003 (asp 9) (creation of positive servitude by writing: deed to be registered),

(d) a right appearing on the title sheet as a pertinent is of a kind capable of being a valid pertinent,

(e) a pertinent appearing on the title sheet and of a kind extinguishable or variable without registration against the title of the benefited property has not been extinguished, or varied, without registration,

(f) the applicant has by registration acquired a right to mines or minerals,

(g) a registered lease has not been varied or terminated without the variation or termination having been registered,

(h) the title sheet to which the application relates is accurate—

(i) in so far as it shows an acquisition, variation or discharge more extensive than the deed registered bore to effect, or

(ii) in the case of an application under section 27, in so far as it shows the applicant to be the proprietor or proprietor in common of a plot of land more extensive than the plot registration of which the application bore to effect, or

(i) alluvion has not had an effect on a boundary.

(3) The benefit of warranty extends to persons to whom the benefit of warrandice by the granter of a deed would extend.

(4) In relation to an application for registration of a deed relating to a title condition, references in subsections (1) and (2) and in section 78 to the applicant are to be read as references to the person benefiting from the deed given effect to.

(5) The Keeper does not warrant as provided for in subsections (1) and (2) where the application for registration is accepted by virtue of section 43.

(6) This section is subject to sections 75 and 76.

74 Keeper's warranty on registration under sections 25 and 29

(1) The Keeper, on registering a plot of land by virtue of section 25 or under section 29, warrants to the owner that, as at the time of registration, the title sheet of the plot—

(a) is accurate in so far as it shows the owner to be the proprietor or proprietor in common, and

(b) is not inaccurate in so far as there is omitted from it any encumbrance the inclusion of which is permitted or required by or under an enactment.

(2)   Subsections (2), (3) and (5) of section 73 apply to warranty under this section as they apply to warranty under that section.

(3)   Subsection (2) of section 73 is subject to the following modifications—

(a) for paragraph (h) substitute—

'(h) in the case of registration by virtue of section 25, the title sheet is accurate in so far as it shows the owner to be the proprietor or proprietor in common of a plot of land more extensive than the area of land which forms the subjects of the lease, to which the deed relates or, as the case may be, in respect of which the subordinate real right is constituted,

(ha) in the case of registration under section 29, the title sheet is accurate in so far as it shows the owner to be the proprietor or proprietor in common of a plot of land more extensive than the plot the Keeper sought to register, or',

(b) references in that subsection to—

(i)   the application are to be read as references to the registration by virtue of section 25 or under section 29,

(ii)   to the applicant are to be construed as references to the owner.

(4)   This section is subject to sections 75 and 76.

75 Extension, limitation or exclusion of warranty

(1)   The Keeper may—

(a) if satisfied (having regard to sufficiency of evidence as to title) that it is appropriate to do so, grant more extensive warranty than is provided for in section 73 or 74, or

(b) if not satisfied as to the validity of the acquisition, variation or discharge mentioned in section 73(1)(a)(i) or that the applicant or owner is the proprietor as mentioned in section 73(1)(a)(ii) or 74(1)(a)—

(i)   grant less extensive warranty than is so provided for, or

(ii)   exclude warranty.

(2)   For the purposes of subsection (1), the Keeper must have regard to any relevant caveat placed on the title sheet by virtue of section 67.

(3)   Where warranty is granted or excluded under subsection (1), the Keeper must give effect to the grant or exclusion by entering a statement describing it in the title sheet.

(4)   If an entry made in the title sheet on an application being accepted by virtue of section 43 ceases to be provisional, the Keeper may—

(a) grant such warranty as the Keeper (having regard to sufficiency of evidence as to title) considers appropriate, and

(b) give effect to the grant by entering a statement describing it in the title sheet.

76 Variation of warranty

(1)   This section applies where warranty is—

(a) as provided for in section 73 or 74,

(b) granted under section 75(1)(a), (b)(i) or (4)(a), or

(c) excluded under section 75(1)(b)(ii).

(2)   The Keeper may, if the Keeper comes to be satisfied (having regard to sufficiency of evidence as to title) that it is appropriate to do so, grant—

(a) warranty as provided for in section 73,

(b) less extensive warranty than as so provided, or

(c) more extensive warranty than as so provided.

(3)   The Keeper may not, under subsection (2), grant warranty that is less extensive than the warranty which was originally provided for or granted as mentioned in subsection (1)(a) or (b).

(4)   For the purposes of subsection (2), the Keeper must have regard to any relevant caveat placed on the title sheet by virtue of section 67.

(5)   Where the Keeper grants warranty or more extensive warranty under subsection (2), the Keeper must—

(a)   unless the warranty granted is warranty only as provided for in section 73, give effect to the grant by entering a statement describing it on the title sheet, and

(b)   remove any statement previously entered under section 75(3) or (4)(b).

Claims under warranty

77   Claims under Keeper's warranty

(1)   The Keeper must pay compensation for loss incurred as a result of a breach of the Keeper's warranty.

(2)   Liability to pay such compensation arises only if and when the inaccuracy giving rise to the claim for compensation is rectified.

(3)   A claimant is not required to exhaust other remedies before making a claim to such compensation.

(4)   Payment by the Keeper under this section does not extinguish any rights which the claimant may have against another person in respect of the loss compensated.

(5)   But it is a condition of any such payment that the claimant assign any such rights to the Keeper.

78   Claims under warranty: circumstances where liability excluded

The Keeper has no liability to pay compensation by virtue of section 77(1)—

(a)   if the inaccuracy is consequent upon an error in the cadastral map and that error was made in reasonable reliance upon the base map,

(b)   if the existence of the inaccuracy was, or ought to have been, known to—

(i)   the applicant, or

(ii)   any person acting as solicitor or other legal adviser to the applicant, at the time of registration,

(c)   in so far as the inaccuracy is attributable to a failure of—

(i)   the applicant, or

(ii)   any person acting as solicitor or other legal adviser to the applicant, to comply with the duty owed to the Keeper under section 111,

(d)   in so far as the claimant's loss could have been avoided by the applicant, owner or claimant taking certain measures which it would have been reasonable for the applicant, owner or claimant to take,

(e)   in so far as the connection between the claimant's loss and the inaccuracy is too remote, or

(f)   for non-patrimonial loss.

79   Claims under warranty: quantification of compensation

(1)   Compensation payable by virtue of section 77(1)—

(a)   is, in so far as it is not compensation mentioned in paragraph (b), to be quantified as at the date on which the inaccuracy giving rise to the claim is rectified, and

(b)   is to include—

(i)   reimbursement of reasonable extra-judicial legal expenses, and

(ii)   compensation for any other consequential loss.

(2)   Interest on a sum so payable runs from the date mentioned in subsection (3) until the sum in question is paid.

(3)   The date is—

(a)   where the sum is payable other than by virtue of subsection (1)(b), the date mentioned in subsection (1)(a),

(b)   where the sum is payable by virtue of subsection (1)(b)(i), the date on which the claimant paid the sum in question, and

(c)   where the sum is payable by virtue of subsection (1)(b)(ii), the date on which the loss was sustained.

(4)   The Scottish Ministers may by regulations make provision as to the rate of interest payable by virtue of subsection (2).

PART 8
RECTIFICATION OF THE REGISTER

Rectification

80   Rectification of the register

(1)   This section applies where the Keeper becomes aware of a manifest inaccuracy in a title sheet or in the cadastral map.

(2)   The Keeper must rectify the inaccuracy if what is needed to do so is manifest.

(3)   Where what is so needed is not manifest, the Keeper must enter a note identifying the inaccuracy in the title sheet or, as the case may be, in the cadastral map.

(4)   Where the Keeper rectifies an inaccuracy, the Keeper must—

(a)   include in the archive record a copy of any document which discloses, or contributes to disclosing, the inaccuracy, and

(b)   give notice of the rectification to any person who appears to the Keeper to be affected by it materially.

(5)   Land register rules may make provision about—

(a)   the persons to be notified by the Keeper, and

(b)   the method by which such notice is to be given.

(6)   A failure to comply with subsection (4) or with any rules so made does not affect the validity of a rectification under subsection (2).

81   Rectification where registration provisional etc

(1)   This section applies where it appears to the Keeper that rectification of an inaccuracy would interrupt a period of possession—

(a)   which is current, and

(b)   which, if uninterrupted, would, under section 1(1) or 2(1) of the Prescription and Limitation (Scotland) Act 1973 (c 52) (sections which provide for positive prescription), affect a real right.

(2)   If the inaccuracy is in an entry marked provisional by virtue of section 44, the Keeper—

(a)   may rectify the register if all those affected consent,

(b)   where there is no such consent, must not rectify the register before the existence of the inaccuracy is judicially determined.

(3)   In any other case, the Keeper—

(a)   must—

(i)   mark the relevant entry in the title sheet provisional,

(ii)   enter in the appropriate section of the title sheet the name and designation of the true holder of the right affected by the inaccuracy (if any such person can be identified),

(b)   may rectify the register if all those affected consent,

(c)   where there is no such consent, must not rectify the register before the existence of the inaccuracy is judicially determined.

Referral of questions to Lands Tribunal

82   Referral to the Lands Tribunal for Scotland

(1)   A person with an interest may refer a question relating to—

(a) the accuracy of the register, or
(b) what is needed to rectify an inaccuracy in the register,
to the Lands Tribunal for Scotland.
(2) The Lands Tribunal must, on determining the question, give notice to—
(a) the applicant,
(b) any other person appearing to them to have an interest, and
(c) the Keeper.
(3) This section is without prejudice to any other right of recourse, whether under an enactment or under a rule of law.

Keeper's right to be heard in proceedings

83 Proceedings involving the accuracy of the register
The Keeper is entitled to appear and be heard in any civil proceedings, whether before a court or tribunal, in which—
(a) the accuracy of the register, or
(b) what is needed to rectify an inaccuracy in the register,
is put in question.

Compensation in consequence of rectification

84 Rectification: compensation for certain expenses and losses
(1) The Keeper must pay compensation for—
(a) reimbursement of reasonable extra-judicial legal expenses incurred by a person in securing rectification of the register, and
(b) any loss sustained by the person in consequence of the inaccuracy rectified.
(2) A claimant is not required to exhaust other remedies before making a claim to such compensation.
(3) Payment by the Keeper under this section does not extinguish any rights which the claimant may have against another person in respect of the loss compensated.
(4) But it is a condition of any such payment that the claimant assigns any such rights to the Keeper.
(5) Interest on a sum payable under this section runs from the date mentioned in subsection (6) until the sum in question is paid.
(6) The date is—
(a) where the sum is payable by virtue of subsection (1)(a), the date on which the claimant paid the sum in question,
(b) where the sum is payable by virtue of subsection (1)(b), the date on which the loss was sustained.
(7) The Scottish Ministers may by regulations make provision as to the rate of interest payable by virtue of subsection (5).

85 Rectification: circumstances where liability excluded
The Keeper has no liability to pay compensation under section 84—
(a) if the inaccuracy is caused other than by a change made by the Keeper to a title sheet or the cadastral map,
(b) if the inaccuracy is consequent on an error in the cadastral map and that error was made in reasonable reliance on the base map,
(c) in so far as the inaccuracy is in an entry made on an application being accepted by virtue of section 43(1) or under section 43(5),
(d) in so far as the inaccuracy is caused by some act or omission on the part of the claimant,
(e) in so far as the claimant's loss could have been avoided by the claimant taking certain measures which it would have been reasonable for the claimant to take,
(f) in so far as the connection between the claimant's loss and the inaccuracy is too remote, or
(g) for non-patrimonial loss.

PART 9

RIGHT OF PERSONS ACQUIRING ETC IN GOOD FAITH

Ownership

86 Acquisition from disponer without valid title

(1)   This section applies where a person ('A'), who is not the proprietor of a registered plot of land but—

(a)   is entered in the proprietorship section of the title sheet as proprietor, and

(b)   is in possession of the land,

purports to dispone the land.

(2)   The disponee ('B') acquires ownership of the land provided that the conditions in subsection (3) are met.

(3)   The conditions are that—

(a)   the land has been in the possession, openly, peaceably and without judicial interruption—

(i)   of A for a continuous period of at least 1 year, or

(ii)   of A and then of B for periods which together constitute such a period,

(b)   at no time during that period did the Keeper become aware that the register was inaccurate as a result of A (or B) not being the proprietor,

(c)   B is in good faith,

(d)   the disposition would have conferred ownership on B had A been proprietor when the land was disponed,

(e)   at no time during the period mentioned in paragraph (a)—

(i)   was the title sheet subject, by virtue of section 67, to a caveat relevant to the acquisition by B,

(ii)   did the title sheet contain a statement under section 30(5), and

(f)   the Keeper warrants (or is to be taken to warrant) A's title.

(4)   The date on which ownership is acquired by virtue of subsection (2) is—

(a)   where subsection (5) applies, the date on which the disposition is registered,

(b)   where subsection (6) applies, the date on which the period of possession mentioned in that subsection expires.

(5)   This subsection applies where, as at the date of registration, the land has been in the possession, openly, peaceably and without judicial interruption—

(a)   of A for a continuous period of at least 1 year, or

(b)   of A and then of B for periods which together constitute such a period.

(6)   This subsection applies where there is a continuous period of possession such as is mentioned in subsection (5) but that period, though it commences before registration on the application of B, does not expire until a date later than the date of registration.

87 Acquisition from representative of disponer without valid title

(1)   Section 86 also applies where a person ('P'), who is not entered in the proprietorship section of the title sheet as proprietor but who would have power to dispone the land—

(a)   were A the proprietor, or

(b)   (where A has died) had A been the proprietor, purports to dispone it.

(2)   For the purposes of section 86, possession of the plot of land by P is to be treated as if it were possession of the land by A.

Leases

88 Acquisition from assigner without valid title

(1)   This section applies where a person ('A'), who is not the tenant under a registered lease but—

(a)   is shown in the title sheet as tenant, and

(b) is in possession of the subjects of the lease, purports to assign the lease.

(2) The assignee ('B') acquires the lease provided that the conditions in subsection (3) are met.

(3) The conditions are that—

(a) the subjects of the lease have been in the possession, openly, peaceably and without judicial interruption—

(i) of A for a continuous period of at least 1 year, or

(ii) of A and then of B for periods which together constitute such a period,

(b) at no time during that period did the Keeper become aware that the register was inaccurate as a result of A (or B) not being the tenant,

(c) B is in good faith,

(d) the lease is extant,

(e) B would have acquired the lease had A been tenant when the lease was assigned,

(f) at no time during the period mentioned in paragraph (a) was the title sheet subject, by virtue of section 67, to a caveat relevant to the acquisition by B, and

(g) the Keeper warrants (or is to be taken to warrant) A's title.

(4) The date on which the lease is acquired by virtue of subsection (2) is—

(a) where subsection (5) applies, the date on which the deed of assignation is registered,

(b) where subsection (6) applies, the date on which the period of possession mentioned in that subsection expires.

(5) This subsection applies where, as at the date of registration, the subjects of the lease have been in the possession, openly, peaceably and without judicial interruption—

(a) of A for a continuous period of at least 1 year, or

(b) of A and then of B for periods which together constitute such a period.

(6) This subsection applies where there is a continuous period of possession such as is mentioned in subsection (5) but that period, though it commences before registration on the application of B, does not expire until a date later than the date of registration.

89 Acquisition from representative of assigner without valid title

(1) Section 88 also applies where a person ('P'), who is not entered in the title sheet as tenant but who would have power to assign the lease—

(a) were A the tenant, or

(b) (where A has died) had A been the tenant,

purports to assign it.

(2) For the purposes of section 88, possession of the subjects of the lease by P is to be treated as if it were possession of the subjects by A.

Servitudes

90 Grant of servitude by person not proprietor

(1) This section applies where a person ('A'), who is not the proprietor of a registered plot of land but—

(a) is entered in the proprietorship section of the title sheet as proprietor, and

(b) is in possession of the land,

purports to create a servitude, with the land as the burdened property.

(2) The servitude is created provided that the conditions mentioned in subsection (3) are met.

(3) The conditions are that—

(a) the land has been in the possession of A, openly, peaceably and without judicial interruption, for a continuous period of at least 1 year,

(b) at no time during that period did the Keeper become aware that the register was inaccurate as a result of A not being the proprietor,

(c) the proprietor of what is to be the benefited property is in good faith,

(d) at no time during the period mentioned in paragraph (a) was the title sheet subject, by virtue of section 67, to a caveat relevant to the creation of the servitude, and

(e) the Keeper warrants (or is to be taken to warrant) A's title.

(4) The date on which the servitude is created by virtue of subsection (2) is—

(a) where subsection (5) applies, the date of registration,

(b) where subsection (6) applies, the date on which the period mentioned in that subsection expires.

(5) This subsection applies where, as at the date of registration, the land has been in the possession of A, openly, peaceably and without judicial interruption, for a continuous period of at least 1 year.

(6) This subsection applies where there is a continuous period of possession such as is mentioned in subsection (5) but that period, though it commences before registration, does not expire until a date later than the date of registration.

(7) This section is subject to section 75 of the Title Conditions (Scotland) Act 2003 (asp 9) (creation of positive servitude by writing: deed to be registered).

Extinction of encumbrances etc

91 Extinction of encumbrance when land disponed

(1) Where the conditions mentioned in subsection (2) are met, a person ('A') who acquires ownership of land on registration or on a later date by virtue of section 86(4) (b)—

(a) takes the land free of an encumbrance which is not entered in the title sheet as at the date on which A acquires ownership of the land, and

(b) any such encumbrance is extinguished.

(2) The conditions are that, as at the date on which ownership is acquired—

(a) A is in good faith, and

(b) the title sheet is not, by virtue of section 67, subject to a caveat relevant to such acquisition by A.

(3) Subsection (1) does not apply to an heritable security which is not entered in the securities section of a shared plot title sheet by virtue of section 18(3)(b).

(4) 'Encumbrance' in subsection (1) does not include—

(a) a public right of way,

(b) a path delineated in an order under section 22 of the Land Reform (Scotland) Act 2003 (asp 2) (compulsory powers to delineate paths in land in respect of which access rights are exercisable),

(c) a servitude created other than under section 75(1) of the Title Conditions (Scotland) Act 2003 (asp 9),

(d) a lease, or

(e) an encumbrance the creation of which does not require registration of the constitutive deed.

92 Extinction of encumbrance when lease assigned

(1) Where the conditions mentioned in subsection (2) are met, a person ('A') who acquires a registered lease on registration or on a later date by virtue of section 88(4) (b)—

(a) takes that lease free of an encumbrance—

(i) of a kind mentioned in subsection (4), and

(ii) which is not entered in the title sheet as at the date on which A acquires the registered lease, and

(b) any such encumbrance is extinguished.

(2) The conditions are that, as at the date on which the lease is acquired—

(a) A is in good faith, and

(b)   the title sheet is not, by virtue of section 67, subject to a caveat relevant to such acquisition by A.

(3)   Subsection (1) does not apply to an heritable security which is not entered in the securities section of a shared lease title sheet by virtue of paragraph 8(b) of schedule 1.

(4)   The encumbrances are—

(a)   a heritable security over the lease,

(b)   a title condition such as is mentioned in paragraph (d) or (e) of the definition of 'title condition' in section 122(1) of the Title Conditions (Scotland) Act 2003 (asp 9).

93   Extinction of floating charge when land disponed

A person who, in good faith, acquires ownership of land from another person ('A'), takes the land free of any floating charge which was granted by a predecessor in title of A.

Compensation in consequence of this Part

94   Compensation for loss incurred in consequence of this Part

(1)   The Keeper must pay compensation for loss incurred by a person mentioned in subsection (2).

(2)   The person is one who—

(a)   is deprived of a right by virtue of this Part, or

(b)   is the proprietor of a property burdened by a servitude created by virtue of section 90.

(3)   A claimant is not required to exhaust other remedies before making a claim to such compensation.

(4)   Payment by the Keeper under this section does not extinguish any rights which the claimant may have against another person in respect of the loss compensated.

(5)   But it is a condition of any such payment that the claimant assigns any such rights to the Keeper.

(6)   The Keeper has no liability to pay compensation—

(a)   in so far as the claimant's loss could have been avoided by the claimant taking certain measures which it would have been reasonable for the claimant to take,

(b)   in so far as the claimant's loss is too remote, or

(c)   for non-patrimonial loss.

95   Quantification of compensation

(1)   Compensation payable by virtue of section 94(1)—

(a)   is, in so far as it is not compensation mentioned in paragraph (b), to be quantified as at the date on which the claimant lost the right or, as the case may be, on which the servitude was created, and

(b)   is to include—

(i)   reimbursement of reasonable extra-judicial legal expenses, and

(ii)   compensation for any other consequential loss.

(2)   Interest on a sum so payable runs from the date mentioned in subsection (3) until the sum in question is paid.

(3)   The date is—

(a)   where the sum is payable other than by virtue of subsection (1)(b), the date mentioned in subsection (1)(a),

(b)   where the sum is payable by virtue of subsection (1)(b)(i), the date on which the claimant paid the sum in question, and

(c)   where the sum is payable by virtue of subsection (1)(b)(ii), the date on which the loss was sustained.

(4)   The Scottish Ministers may by regulations make provision as to the rate of interest payable by virtue of subsection (2).

PART 10
ELECTRONIC DOCUMENTS, ELECTRONIC CONVEYANCING
AND ELECTRONIC REGISTRATION

Electronic documents

96, 97, 98 *[Amend the Requirements of Writing (Scotland) Act 1995.]*

Electronic conveyancing

99   Automated registration

(1)   The Keeper may, by means of a computer system under the Keeper's management and control, enable—

(a)   the creation of electronic documents,

(b)   the electronic generation and communication of applications for registration in the register, and

(c)   automated registration in the register.

(2)   Only a person authorised by the Keeper, whether directly or indirectly, may use the system mentioned in subsection (1) to make applications for registration.

(3)   The Scottish Ministers may, by regulations, make provision about the system mentioned in subsection (1) including—

(a)   the kinds of deeds which may be authorised for use in the system,

(b)   the persons who may be authorised to use the system,

(c)   the suspension or revocation of a person's authorisation under subsection (2),

(d)   the method of appeal against any such suspension or revocation,

(e)   the imposition of obligations on persons using the system, and

(f)   the creation of deemed warranties (whether in favour of the Keeper or of other users) by persons using the system.

(4)   Before making such regulations, the Scottish Ministers must consult the Keeper.

Electronic recording and registration

100   Power to enable electronic registration

(1)   The Scottish Ministers may, by regulations, make provision to enable the recording or registration of electronic documents in any register under the management and control of the Keeper.

(2)   Regulations under subsection (1) may, in particular, make provision—

(a)   regulating the making up and keeping of any such register,

(b)   regulating the procedure to be followed by any person applying for recording or registration in any such register,

(c)   regulating the procedure to be followed by the Keeper in relation to—

(i)   any such application, and

(ii)   the recording or registration of electronic documents to which such an application relates,

(d)   that the Scottish Ministers consider necessary or expedient to enable recording or registration of electronic documents in any such register.

(3)   Regulations under subsection (1) may modify any enactment.

(4)   Before making regulations under subsection (1), the Scottish Ministers must consult—

(a)   the Keeper,

(b)   the Keeper of the Records of Scotland, and

(c)   the Lord President of the Court of Session.

PART 11
MISCELLANEOUS AND GENERAL

Deduction of title

101   Deduction of title

(1)   Where a person applies to register a deed mentioned in subsection (2), the deed need not deduce title.

(2)   The deed is one validly granted by the unregistered holder of—

(a)   land, or

(b)   a real right in land, to which the deed relates.

Notes on register

102   Note of date on which entry in register is made

When an entry is made in the register there is to be included in that entry the date on which it is made.

Appeals

103   Appeals

(1)   An appeal may be made to the Lands Tribunal for Scotland, on a question of fact or on a point of law, against any decision of the Keeper under this Act.

(2)   Subsection (1) is without prejudice to any other right of recourse, whether under an enactment or under a rule of law.

(3)   Where a person successfully appeals against a decision of the Keeper to reject an application for registration, the application is not revived.

Extracts and certified copies

104   Extracts and certified copies: general

(1)   A person may apply to the Keeper for an extract—

(a)   of, or of any part of, a title sheet,

(b)   of any part of the cadastral map, or

(c)   of, or of any part of, a document in the archive record.

(2)   A person may apply to the Keeper for a certified copy—

(a)   of an application or advance notice in the application record,

(b)   of, or of any part of, any other document in that record.

(3)   The Keeper must issue the extract or, as the case may be the certified copy, if—

(a)   such fee as is payable for issuing it is paid, or

(b)   arrangements satisfactory to the Keeper are made for payment of that fee.

(4)   If, on application under subsection (1)(a) or (b), the applicant requests an extract in relation to a title sheet or the cadastral map as at a specific date, the Keeper need comply with the request only to the extent that it is reasonably practicable to do so.

(5)   An extract of a part of the cadastral map issued under subsection (3)—

(a)   must include the base map so far as relating to that part either—

(i)   as at the date on which the extract is issued, or

(ii)   if the Keeper considers it appropriate to do so, as at some earlier date, and

(b)   must specify the base map date opted for under paragraph (a).

(6)   The Keeper may authenticate the extract or, as the case may be the certified copy, as the Keeper considers appropriate.

(7)   The Keeper may issue the extract, or as the case may be the certified copy, as an electronic document if (and only if) the applicant requests that it be issued in that form.

105 Evidential status of extract or certified copy

(1)   An extract or certified copy issued under subsection (3) of section 104 in relation to an application under subsection (1)(a) or (b) or (2)(a) of that section is to be accepted for all purposes as sufficient evidence of the contents—

(a) of the original, and

(b) of any matter relating to the original which appears on the extract or copy.

(2)   An extract or certified copy issued under subsection (3) of that section in relation to an application under subsection (1)(c) or (2)(b) of that section is to be accepted for all purposes as sufficient evidence of the contents—

(a) of the document as submitted to the Keeper, and

(b) of any matter relating to the document as so submitted which appears on the extract or copy.

106 Liability of Keeper in respect of extracts, information and lost documents etc

(1)   A person is entitled to be compensated by the Keeper in respect of loss suffered as a consequence of—

(a) the issue of an extract or certified copy under section 104 that is not a true extract, or as the case may be a true copy,

(b) the provision (in writing or in such other manner as provision is made for in an order under section 107(1)(a)) of other information as to the contents of the register that is incorrect,

(c) a document being lost, damaged or destroyed while lodged with the Keeper.

(2)   The Keeper has no liability under subsection (1)—

(a) in so far as the claimant's loss could have been avoided by the applicant or claimant taking certain measures which it would have been reasonable for the applicant or claimant to take,

(b) in so far as a claimant's loss is too remote, or

(c) for non-patrimonial loss.

Information and access

107 Information and access

(1)   The Scottish Ministers may, by order, make further provision as regards—

(a) information to be made available by the Keeper and the manner in which it is to be made available,

(b) access to any register under the management and control of the Keeper.

(2)   In subsection (1)(a), 'information' includes information in the form of extracts and certified copies.

Keeper's functions

108 Provision of services by the Keeper

(1)   The Keeper may provide consultancy, advisory or other commercial services.

(2)   Those services need not relate to the law and practice of registration.

(3)   The terms on which those services are provided (including the fees charged for provision of them) are to be such as may be agreed between the Keeper and those provided with them.

(4)   If the Keeper considers it expedient to do so in connection with the provision of any of those services, the Keeper may (either or both)—

(a) form, or participate in the forming of, a body corporate or other entity,

(b) purchase, or invest in, a body corporate or other entity.

(5)   This section does not affect any other power or duty of the Keeper.

109　Performance of Keeper's functions during vacancy in office etc

(1)　This section applies where—

(a)　there is a vacancy in the office of the Keeper or the Keeper is incapable by reason of ill health of performing the Keeper's functions, and

(b)　no person has been authorised by the Scottish Ministers, under section 1(6) of the Public Registers and Records (Scotland) Act 1948 (c 57), to perform the functions of the Keeper.

(2)　A member of the Keeper's staff may perform the Keeper's functions.

(3)　Any function performed by a member of the Keeper's staff by virtue of subsection (2) is to be treated as if it had been performed by the Keeper.

Fees

110　Fees

(1)　The Scottish Ministers may, by order—

(a)　provide for the fees payable in relation to—

(i)　registering, recording or entering in any register under the management and control of the Keeper,

(ii)　access to such a register,

(iii)　information made available by the Keeper,

(b)　provide for the method of paying any such fees, and

(c)　authorise the Keeper to determine, in such circumstances and subject to such limitations and conditions as may be specified in the order, any such fees.

(2)　An order under this section may make different provision for different cases or for different classes of case.

(3)　Before making an order under this section, the Scottish Ministers must consult the Keeper about, among other things—

(a)　the expenses incurred by the Keeper in relation to administering and improving the systems of—

(i)　registering, recording or entering in any register under the management and control of the Keeper,

(ii)　providing access to any such register, and

(iii)　making information available,

(b)　in the case of the register, the expenses incurred by the Keeper in bringing all titles to land into it,

(c)　the desirability of encouraging registering, recording and entering in any register under the management and control of the Keeper.

(4)　In subsections (1)(a)(iii) and (3)(a)(iii), 'information'—

(a)　includes information in the form of extracts and certified copies,

(b)　does not include information provided by virtue of section 108.

Duty to take reasonable care

111　Duties of certain persons

(1)　A person mentioned in subsection (2) must take reasonable care to ensure that the Keeper does not inadvertently make the register inaccurate as a result of a change made in consequence of the grant mentioned in that subsection.

(2)　The persons are—

(a)　a person granting a deed intended to be registered,

(b)　a person who, in connection with the grant, acts as a solicitor or other legal adviser to the granter.

(3)　A person mentioned in subsection (4) must take reasonable care to ensure that the Keeper does not inadvertently make the register inaccurate as a result of a change made in consequence of the application mentioned in that subsection.

(4)　The persons are—

(a)　a person making an application for registration,

(b) a person who, in connection with the application, acts as a solicitor or other legal adviser to the applicant.

(5) The Keeper is entitled to be compensated by a person in breach of the duty under subsection (1) or (3) for any loss suffered as a consequence of that breach.

(6) But a person has no liability under subsection (5) in so far as—

(a) the Keeper's loss could have been avoided by the Keeper taking certain measures which it would have been reasonable for the Keeper to take, or

(b) the Keeper's loss is too remote.

[*Offences*]

112 Offence relating to applications for registration

(1) A person mentioned in subsection (2) commits an offence if the person—

(a) makes a materially false or misleading statement in relation to an application for registration knowing that, or being reckless as to whether, the statement is false or misleading, or

(b) intentionally fails to disclose material information in relation to such an application or is reckless as to whether all material information is disclosed.

(2) The persons are—

(a) a person making an application for registration, or

(b) a person who, in connection with such an application, acts as solicitor or other legal adviser to the applicant.

(3) It is a defence for a person charged with an offence under subsection (1) (the 'accused') that the accused took all reasonable precautions and exercised all due diligence to avoid the commission of the offence.

(4) The defence is established if the accused—

(a) acted in reliance on information supplied by another person, and

(b) did not know and had no reason to suppose that—

(i) the information was false or misleading, or

(ii) all material information had not been disclosed.

(5) Subsection (4) does not exclude other ways of establishing the defence mentioned in subsection (3).

(6) An accused may not rely on a defence involving the allegation that the commission of the offence was due to reliance on information supplied by another person unless—

(a) the accused has complied with subsection (7), or

(b) the court grants leave.

(7) The accused must serve on the prosecutor a notice giving such information identifying or assisting in the identification of the other person as is in the accused's possession—

(a) in proceedings on indictment, at least 14 clear days before the preliminary hearing (where the case is to be tried in the High Court) or the first diet (where the case is to be tried in the sheriff court),

(b) in summary proceedings—

(i) where an intermediate diet is held, at or before that diet,

(ii) where no such diet is held, at least 10 clear days before the trial diet.

(8) Subsection (6) does not apply where—

(a) the accused lodges a defence statement—

(i) under section 70A of the Criminal Procedure (Scotland) Act 1995 (c 46), or

(ii) under section 125 of the Criminal Justice and Licensing (Scotland) Act 2010 (asp 13) in accordance with the time limits mentioned in subsection (7)(b), and

(b) the accused's defence involves an allegation that the commission of the offence was due to reliance on information supplied by another person.

(9) A person guilty of an offence under subsection (1) is liable—

(a) on summary conviction, to imprisonment for a period not exceeding 12 months, to a fine not exceeding the statutory maximum, or to both,

(b) on conviction on indictment, to imprisonment for a period not exceeding 2 years, to a fine, or to both.

[112A Offence by overseas entity

(1) An overseas entity must not deliver to a person a qualifying registrable deed granted by the overseas entity if (disregarding the possibility of consent under paragraph 7(2) of schedule 1A) by virtue of paragraph 2 of schedule 1A the Keeper would be required to reject an application under section 21 for registration of the deed.

(2) A qualifying registrable deed is to be treated as having been granted for the purposes of subsection (1) even if at the time when it is delivered it has been executed by the overseas entity only.

(3) If an overseas entity breaches subsection (1), an offence is committed by—

(a) the entity, and

(b) every officer of the entity who is in default.

(4) Nothing in this section affects the validity of a qualifying registrable deed delivered in breach of subsection (1).

(5) A person guilty of an offence under subsection (3) is liable—

(a) on summary conviction, to imprisonment for a term not exceeding 12 months or a fine not exceeding the statutory maximum (or both);

(b) on conviction on indictment, to imprisonment for a term not exceeding 5 years or a fine (or both).

(6) Sections 1121 to 1123 of the Companies Act 2006 (liability of officers in default: interpretation etc.) apply for the purposes of this section as they apply for the purposes of provisions of the Companies Acts.

(7) In those sections as applied, a reference to an officer includes a person in accordance with whose directions or instructions the board of directors or equivalent management body of an overseas entity are accustomed to act.

(8) A person is not to be regarded as falling within subsection (7) by reason only that the board of directors or equivalent management body acts on advice given by the person in a professional capacity.

(9) In this section—

'overseas entity' has the meaning given by section 2 of the Economic Crime (Transparency and Enforcement) Act 2022;

'qualifying registrable deed' means a registrable deed which is—

(a) a disposition;

(b) a standard security;

(c) a lease;

(d) an assignation of a lease.]

General provisions

113 Interpretation

(1) In this Act, unless the context otherwise requires—

'1995 Act' means the Requirements of Writing (Scotland) Act 1995 (c 7),

'advance notice' has the meaning given by section 56(1),

'application for registration' means an application under section 21 or 27,

'application record' has the meaning given by section 15,

'archive record' has the meaning given by section 14(1),

'the base map' has the meaning given by section 11(6),

'benefited property' has the meaning given by section 122(1) of the Title Conditions (Scotland) Act 2003 (asp 9),

'burdened property' has the meaning given by section 122(1) of the Title Conditions (Scotland) Act 2003 (asp 9), 'cadastral map' has the meaning given by section 11(1), 'cadastral unit' has the meaning given by section 12,

'date of application' (in relation to an application for registration) has the meaning given by section 36,

'date of registration' has the meaning given by 37(1),

'deed' means a document (and includes a decree which is registrable under an enactment),

'designation' includes—

(a) where the person designated is not a natural person—

(i) the legal system under which the person is incorporated or otherwise established,

(ii) if a number has been allocated to the person under section 1066 of the Companies Act 2006 (c 46), that number, and

(iii) any other identifier (whether or not a number) peculiar to the person, and

(b) if the person designated has a right in land in a special capacity, a description of that capacity,

'the designated day' has the meaning given by section 122,

'enactment' includes—

(a) an enactment comprised in, or in an instrument made under, this Act, and

(b) a local and personal or private Act,

'existing title sheet' means a title sheet which is in existence immediately before the commencement of the designated day,

'flat' has the meaning given by section 29(1) of the Tenements (Scotland) Act 2004 (asp 11),

'flatted building' has the meaning given by section 16(4),

'heritable creditor' means the holder of a heritable security,

'heritable security' means—

(a) a standard security, or

(b) any other right in security over heritable property provided that it is not a right in security created as a floating charge,

'the Keeper' means the Keeper of the Registers of Scotland,

'land' includes—

(a) buildings and other structures,

(b) the seabed of the territorial sea of the United Kingdom adjacent to Scotland (including land within the ebb and flow of the tide at ordinary spring tides), and

(c) other land covered with water,

'land register rules' means rules made under section 115(1),

'lease' includes sub-lease,

'lease title sheet' means a title sheet for a registered lease,

'personal real burden' has the meaning given by section 122(1) of the Title Conditions (Scotland) Act 2003 (asp 9),

'plot of land' has the meaning given by section 3(4) and (5),

'possession' includes civil possession (analogous expressions being construed accordingly),

'proprietor' means a person who has a valid completed title as proprietor to a plot of land,

'protected period' has the meaning given by section 58(3),

'the register' means the Land Register of Scotland,

'registrable deed' is to be construed in accordance with section 49,

'sharing plot' and 'shared plot' are to be construed in accordance with section 17(3),

'tenement' has the meaning given by section 26 of the Tenements (Scotland) Act 2004 (asp 11), 'title condition' has the meaning given by section 122(1) of the Title Conditions (Scotland) Act 2003 (asp 9),

'title sheet record' has the meaning given by section 3(3).

(2)   A deed on which an application under section 21 is based is 'valid' for the purposes of this Act if—

(a)   by the registration applied for, a right would be acquired, varied or extinguished, or

(b)   the deed is certificatory of an acquisition, variation or extinction which has taken place.

(3)   In relation to a lease title sheet, any reference in this Act—

(a)   to a proprietor is (except in section 66) to be read as a reference to the tenant,

(b)   to a proprietorship section is to be construed as a reference to a tenancy section, and

(c)   to ownership in common is to be construed as a reference to tenancy in common.

(4)   The Scottish Ministers may, by order, amend paragraph (b) of the definition of 'designation' in subsection (1).

(5)   Before making such an order, the Scottish Ministers must consult the Keeper.

114   References to 'registering' etc in the Land Register of Scotland

(1)   In this Act (other than subsection (2)), unless the context otherwise requires—

(a)   any reference to 'registration' is to registration in the register, and

(b)   analogous expressions are to be construed accordingly.

(2)   Unless the context otherwise requires—

(a)   any reference, however expressed, in any enactment to 'registering' a document in the register, is to be construed as including a reference to giving effect to that document in accordance either with section 30 or with section 31, and

(b)   analogous expressions are to be construed accordingly.

115   Land register rules

(1)   The Scottish Ministers may, by regulations, make land register rules—

(a)   regulating the making up and keeping of the register,

(b)   regulating the procedure in relation to applications for registration,

(c)   prescribing forms to be used in relation to the register,

(d)   as to when the application record is open for the making of entries,

(e)   requiring the Keeper to enter in the title sheet record such information as may be specified in the rules or authorising or requiring the Keeper to enter in that record such rights or obligations as may be so specified,

(f)   relating to any other matter which this Act provides may or must be provided for by land register rules, or

(g)   concerning other matters and seeming to them to be necessary or expedient in order to give full effect to the purposes of this Act.

(2)   Before making land register rules, the Scottish Ministers must consult the Keeper.

116   Subordinate legislation

(1)   Any power conferred by this Act on the Scottish Ministers to make orders or regulations may be exercised to make different provision for different cases or descriptions of case or for different purposes.

(2)   Orders and regulations under the following [provisions] are subject to the negative procedure—

(a)   section 11(6)(b),

(b)   section 27(6),

    (c)   section 45(7),
    (d)   section 48(2) or (3),
    (e)   section 56(4),
    (f)   subject to subsection (4)(a), section 100(1),
    (g)   section 115(1),
    (h)   subject to subsection (4)(b), section 117(1),
    [(i)   paragraph 2(5) or 7(5) of schedule 1A.]

(3)   Orders and regulations under the following provisions are subject to the affirmative procedure—
    (a)   section 37(3),
    (b)   section 43(8),
    (c)   section 58(6),
    (d)   section 61(3)(b),
    (e)   section 64(1),
    (f)   section 68(3),
    (g)   section 79(4),
    (h)   section 84(7),
    (i)   section 95(4),
    (j)   section 99(3),
    (k)   section 107(1),
    (l)   section 110(1),
    (m) section 113(4).

(4)   Orders and regulations under the following sections which add to, replace or omit the text of any Act are subject to the affirmative procedure—
    (a)   section 100(1),
    (b)   section 117(1).

117   Ancillary provision

(1)   The Scottish Ministers may, by order, make such incidental, supplementary, consequential, transitory, transitional or saving provision as they consider appropriate for the purposes of, in consequence of, or for giving full effect to, any provision made by or under this Act.

(2)   An order under subsection (1) may modify any enactment (including this Act).

118   Transitional provisions

Schedule 4, which contains transitional provisions, has effect.

119   Minor and consequential modifications

Schedule 5, which contains minor amendments and repeals, and amendments and repeals consequential upon the provisions of this Act, has effect.

120   Saving provisions

(1)   The amendments to the Prescription and Limitation (Scotland) Act 1973 (c 52) made by paragraph 18(2) and (4) of schedule 5 do not apply in relation to a continuous period which has expired before the designated day.

(2)   Despite the repeal, by paragraph 19(5) of schedule 5, of section 28(1) of the Land Registration (Scotland) Act 1979 (c 33), that section continues to have effect for the purposes of sections 15(4), 16, 20 to 22A and 29 of and schedules 1 and 3 to the 1979 Act.

121   Crown application

(1)   No contravention by the Crown of section 112 makes the Crown criminally liable.

(2)   But the Court of Session may, on the application of the Keeper or any person authorised by the Keeper, declare unlawful any act or omission of the Crown which constitutes such a contravention.

(3)   Despite subsection (1), section 112 applies to persons in the public service of the Crown as it applies to other persons.

122   The designated day

The Scottish Ministers may, for the purposes of this Act, by order, designate a day ('the designated day'), being a day which falls not less than 6 months after the order is made.

123   Commencement

(1)   The following sections come into force on the day after Royal Assent—
  (a)   section 113,
  (b)   section 114(1),
  (c)   section 116,
  (d)   section 117,
  (e)   section 122,
  (f)   this section, and
  (g)   section 124.

(2)   The following provisions of this Act come into force on the designated day—
  (a)   Parts 1 to 9 (other than sections 53(4) and 64) and schedules 1 and 2,
  (b)   sections 101 to 106,
  (c)   section 111,
  (d)   section 112,
  (e)   section 114(2),
  (f)   section 115,
  (g)   section 118 and schedule 4,
  (h)   section 119 and schedule 5,
  (i)   section 120, and
  (j)   section 121.

(3)   The other provisions of this Act come into force on such day as the Scottish Ministers may, by order, appoint.

124   Short title

The short title of this Act is the Land Registration etc (Scotland) Act 2012.

SCHEDULE 1
REGISTERED LEASES TENANTED IN COMMON
(introduced by section 20)

Shared leases

1   This schedule applies where—
  (a)   an area of land—
    (i)   is tenanted in common by the tenants of two or more registered leases by virtue of their tenancy under those leases,
    (ii)   is not tenanted in common by anyone else,
  (b)   those registered leases have lease title sheets.

2   The Keeper may, if the Keeper considers it appropriate—
  (a)   where the area tenanted in common does not have a lease title sheet, make up such a title sheet and designate it as a 'shared lease title sheet',
  (b)   where that area is the subjects of a registered lease, make up (if necessary) a lease title sheet and designate it as a shared lease title sheet.

3   In the following provisions of this schedule—

(a)   references to a 'shared lease' are to a lease the title sheet of which is designated under paragraph 2,

(b)   references to the 'sharing leases' are to the other leases the tenants of which are tenants in common of the shared lease.

4   Unless the context otherwise requires, any reference in a document to a sharing lease is to be taken to include a reference to the share in the shared lease which pertains to the sharing lease.

5   Registration has the same effect in relation to a share in a shared lease which pertains to a sharing lease as it has in relation to the sharing lease (except in so far as may otherwise be provided in the deed registered).

Shared lease and sharing lease title sheets

6   The Keeper must enter—

(a)   in the property section of the title sheet of each of the sharing leases the title number of the shared lease title sheet,

(b)   in the proprietorship section of the shared lease title sheet, the title numbers of the title sheets of each sharing lease.

7   The Keeper must also enter—

(a)   in the property section of the title sheet of each sharing lease, the quantum of the share which the tenant of that sharing lease has in the shared lease,

(b)   in the proprietorship section of that title sheet, in relation to the information required by section 7(1)(b), the respective share each sharing lease has in the shared lease,

(c)   in the securities section of the shared lease title sheet, a statement to the effect that the shared lease may be subject to a heritable security registered against a sharing lease,

(d)   in the burdens section of that title sheet, a statement to the effect that the shared lease may be subject to some other encumbrance so registered.

8   The Keeper must not enter in or, if entered, must omit from—

(a)   the proprietorship section of the shared lease title sheet, the information that would otherwise be required under section 7(1)(a),

(b)   the securities section of that title sheet, the information that would otherwise be required under section 8(1) unless the security is over the shared lease only,

(c)   that title sheet, any matter that would otherwise be required under section 10(2)(b).

9   The Keeper may, if the condition mentioned in paragraph 10 is satisfied and the Keeper considers it appropriate, omit from the burdens section of the shared lease title sheet any entry which would otherwise be required under section 9(1).

10   The condition is that the encumbrance to which the entry would relate is (or falls to be) registered against each of the sharing leases.

Conversion of shared lease title sheet to ordinary lease title sheet

11   The Keeper may at any time revoke a designation under paragraph 2 of a lease title sheet as a shared lease title sheet.

12   Where the Keeper revokes a designation, the Keeper must make such changes to the title sheets of the leases that were, in relation to the shared lease title sheet, the shared lease and the sharing leases as are consequential upon the revocation.

[SCHEDULE 1A
LAND TRANSACTIONS: OVERSEAS ENTITIES
Section 21

Cases where Keeper must reject application under section 21

1—(1)   This paragraph applies where—
(a)   a person applies under section 21 for registration of a qualifying registrable deed, and
(b)   if the application is accepted by the Keeper—
(i)   the name of an overseas entity would be entered as proprietor in the proprietorship section of the title sheet of a registered plot of land, or
(ii)   an overseas entity would be the tenant under a registered lease.
(2)   The Keeper must reject the application unless the overseas entity is—
(a)   a registered overseas entity, or
(b)   an exempt overseas entity.
(3)   Sub-paragraph (2) does not apply where—
(a)   the application is made by a person other than the overseas entity referred to in sub-paragraph (1)(b)(i), and
(b)   the deed in respect of which the application is made is a lease or an assignation of a lease the subjects of which consist of or form part of an unregistered plot of land of which that overseas entity is the proprietor.
2—(1)   This paragraph applies where—
(a)   a person applies under section 21 for registration of a qualifying registrable deed or a registrable deed which is a standard security,
(b)   the granter of the deed is an overseas entity whose interest is registered, having been so registered on or after 8 December 2014, and
(c)   as at the date of delivery of the deed, the entity was not a registered overseas entity or an exempt overseas entity.
(2)   The Keeper must reject the application unless one of the following conditions is met—
(a)   the application is made—
(i)   in pursuance of a statutory obligation or court order, or
(ii)   in respect of a transfer of ownership or other event that occurs by operation of law,
(b)   the application is made in pursuance of a contract entered into before the later of the dates mentioned in sub-paragraph (3);
(c)   the application is made in pursuance of the exercise of a power of sale or lease by the creditor in a standard security that was registered on or after 8 December 2014;
(d)   the application is made in pursuance of the exercise of a right conferred on a body by relevant legislation to buy land or the interest of a tenant under a lease;
(e)   the Scottish Ministers give consent under paragraph 7(2) to the registration of the deed;
(f)   the deed is granted by a specified insolvency practitioner in specified circumstances.
(3)   The dates are—
(a)   the date on which the granter's interest was registered;
(b)   the commencement date.
(4)   In sub-paragraph (2)(d), 'relevant legislation' means Part 2, 3 or 3A of the Land Reform (Scotland) Act 2003 or Part 5 of the Land Reform (Scotland) Act 2016 (being provisions which confer on certain community bodies etc. the right to buy certain types of land or the interest of a tenant under a lease of certain types of land).
(5)   In sub-paragraph (2), in paragraph (f)—
'specified circumstances' means circumstances specified in regulations made by the Scottish Ministers for the purposes of that paragraph;

'specified insolvency practitioner' means an insolvency practitioner of a description specified in regulations made by the Scottish Ministers for the purposes of that paragraph.

Cases where Keeper must reject application to register notice of title

3—(1) This paragraph applies where—
    (a) by virtue of section 4A of the Conveyancing (Scotland) Act 1924, a person makes an application under section 21 for registration of a notice of title completing title in respect of a qualifying registrable deed, and
    (b) if the application is accepted by the Keeper—
        (i) the name of an overseas entity would be entered as proprietor in the proprietorship section of the title sheet of a registered plot of land, or
        (ii) an overseas entity would be the tenant under a registered lease.
  (2) The Keeper must reject the application unless the overseas entity is—
    (a) a registered overseas entity, or
    (b) an exempt overseas entity.
  (3) Sub-paragraph (2) does not apply where—
    (a) the application is made by a person other than the overseas entity referred to in sub-paragraph (1)(b)(i), and
    (b) the deed in respect of which title is being completed is a lease or an assignation of a lease the subjects of which consist of or form part of an unregistered plot of land of which that overseas entity is the proprietor.

4—(1) This paragraph applies where—
    (a) by virtue of section 4A of the Conveyancing (Scotland) Act 1924, a person makes an application under section 21 for registration of a notice of title completing title in respect of—
        (i) a qualifying registrable deed, or
        (ii) a registrable deed which is a standard security,
    (b) the granter of the deed is an overseas entity whose interest is registered, having been so registered on or after 8 December 2014, and
    (c) as at the date on which the application for registration of the notice of title was made, the entity was not a registered overseas entity or an exempt overseas entity.
  (2) The Keeper must reject the application unless one of the following conditions is met—
    (a) the application is made—
        (i) in pursuance of a statutory obligation or court order, or
        (ii) in respect of a transfer of ownership or other event that occurs by operation of law,
    (b) the application is made in pursuance of a contract entered into before the later of the dates mentioned in sub-paragraph (3);
    (c) the application is made in pursuance of the exercise of a power of sale or lease by the creditor in a standard security that was registered on or after 8 December 2014;
    (d) the application is made in pursuance of the exercise of a right conferred on a body by relevant legislation to buy land or the interest of a tenant under a lease;
    (e) the Scottish Ministers give consent under paragraph 7(4) to the registration of the notice of title;
    (f) the deed in respect of which title is being completed is granted by a specified insolvency practitioner in specified circumstances.
  (3) The dates are—
    (a) the date on which the granter's interest was registered;
    (b) the commencement date.
  (4) In sub-paragraph (2)(d), 'relevant legislation' means Part 2, 3 or 3A of the Land Reform (Scotland) Act 2003 or Part 5 of the Land Reform (Scotland) Act 2016

(being provisions which confer on certain community bodies etc. the right to buy certain types of land or the interest of a tenant under a lease of certain types of land).

(5)   In sub-paragraph (2)(f) 'specified circumstances' and 'specified insolvency practitioner' have the meanings given by paragraph 2(5).

Case where Keeper must reject prescriptive application

5—(1)   This paragraph applies where—
    (a)   an application under section 21 is received by the Keeper by virtue of section 43(1) or (5), and
    (b)   if the application is accepted by the Keeper—
        (i)   the name of an overseas entity would be entered as proprietor in the proprietorship section of the title sheet of a registered plot of land, and
        (ii)   that entry would be marked as provisional under section 44(1).
(2)   The Keeper must reject the application unless the overseas entity is—
    (a)   a registered overseas entity, or
    (b)   an exempt overseas entity.

Case where Keeper must reject voluntary application

6—(1)   This paragraph applies where—
    (a)   an application is made under section 27, and
    (b)   if the application is accepted by the Keeper, the name of an overseas entity would be entered as proprietor in the proprietorship section of the title sheet of a registered plot of land.
(2)   The Keeper must reject the application unless the overseas entity is—
    (a)   a registered overseas entity, or
    (b)   an exempt overseas entity.

Consent to registration of certain deeds that cannot otherwise be registered

7—(1)   Sub-paragraph (2) applies where the Keeper would be required by paragraph 2(2) to reject an application for registration of a qualifying registrable deed or a registrable deed which is a standard security.
(2)   The Scottish Ministers may consent to registration of the deed if satisfied—
    (a)   that at the time of delivery of the deed the person in whose favour it was granted did not know, and could not reasonably have been expected to know, of the duty imposed on the Keeper by paragraph 2(2), and
    (b)   that in all the circumstances it would be unjust for the deed not to be registered.
(3)   Sub-paragraph (4) applies where the Keeper would be required by paragraph 4(2) to reject an application for registration of a notice of title in respect of a qualifying registrable deed or a registrable deed which is a standard security.
(4)   The Scottish Ministers may consent to registration of the notice of title if satisfied—
    (a)   that at the time of delivery of the qualifying registrable deed or (as the case may be) registrable deed which is a standard security the person in whose favour the deed was granted did not know, and could not reasonably have been expected to know, of the duty imposed on the Keeper by paragraph 4(2), and
    (b)   that in all the circumstances it would be unjust for the notice of title not to be registered.
(5)   The Scottish Ministers may by regulations make provision in connection with applications for consent, and the giving of consent, under sub-paragraphs (2) and (4).
(6)   The regulations may, for example, make provision about—
    (a)   who may apply;
    (b)   evidence;
    (c)   time limits.

Partially executed deeds

8   For the purposes of paragraphs 2(1)(c) and 7(2)(a) and (4)(a), a qualifying registrable deed or registrable deed which is a standard security is to be treated, as at the date of delivery of the deed, as having been granted even if at that time it has been executed by the overseas entity only.

Interpretation

9—(1)   In this schedule—
    'the commencement date' means the day on which Part 1 of Schedule 4 to the Economic Crime (Transparency and Enforcement) Act 2022 comes into force;
    'exempt overseas entity' means an overseas entity of a description specified in regulations under section 34(6) of the Economic Crime (Transparency and Enforcement) Act 2022;
    'overseas entity' has the meaning given by section 2 of the Economic Crime (Transparency and Enforcement) Act 2022;
    'qualifying registrable deed' means a registrable deed which is—
        (a)   a disposition;
        (b)   a lease;
        (c)   an assignation of a lease;
    'register of overseas entities' means the register kept under section 3 of the Economic Crime (Transparency and Enforcement) Act 2022;
    'registered overseas entity' means an overseas entity that is registered in the register of overseas entities (but see sub-paragraphs (2) and (3)).
    (2)   For the purposes of this Schedule, an overseas entity that fails to comply with the duty in section 7 of the Economic Crime (Transparency and Enforcement) Act 2022 (updating duty) is not to be treated as being a 'registered overseas entity' until it remedies the failure.
    (3)   For the purpose of sub-paragraph (2), an overseas entity 'remedies' the failure when it delivers the statements and information mentioned in section 7(1)(a), (b) and (c) of the 2022 Act.]

SCHEDULE 4
TRANSITIONAL PROVISIONS

(introduced by section 118)

Existing title sheets

1   On the designated day an existing title sheet becomes part of the title sheet record.
2   An existing title sheet which becomes, under paragraph 1, part of the title sheet record, may be amended by the Keeper so as—
        (a)   to conform with a requirement of, or imposed by virtue of, this Act, or
        (b)   to reflect something permitted by, or by virtue of, this Act.
3   An amendment under paragraph 2 may be made on the designated day or at such later date as the Keeper considers appropriate.
4   An existing title sheet as respects an interest of ownership becomes under paragraph 1 a title sheet as respects a plot of land; and the Keeper, on or as soon as practicable after the designated day, must create a cadastral unit for that plot.
5   An existing title sheet as respects an interest of tenancy becomes under paragraph 1 a lease title sheet.
6   Section 12(2) does not apply to a cadastral unit created under paragraph 4.

Common areas: general

7   If, by reason of being owned in common, the selfsame area of land is, immediately before the designated day, included in two or more existing title sheets the Keeper may, if the Keeper considers it appropriate, make up a title sheet for that area and create a cadastral unit for it.

8   Where a title sheet is created by virtue of paragraph 7—

(a)   the Keeper is to make such changes to the other title sheets mentioned in that paragraph and to the cadastral map as are consequential upon its being so constituted, and

(b)   the respective shares of the proprietors of the area of land need only be entered in the title sheet if they were entered in the existing title sheets.

Common areas: developments begun before designated day

9   If, by reason of being owned in common, the selfsame area of land (in this paragraph and in paragraph 11 referred to as 'area A') is, immediately before the designated day, included in two or more existing title sheets and on or after that day title sheets (in this paragraph and in paragraph 10 referred to as the 'new title sheets') are to be constituted for plots of land the proprietors of which will (qua proprietors of those plots) be comprised within those who own area A in common, area A may, by reason of being owned in common, be included in the new title sheets.

10   Where the respective shares of the proprietors were not entered in the existing title sheets they need not be entered in the new title sheets.

11   The Keeper may at any time create a separate title sheet for area A.

[Common areas: Sasine arrangements

11A   For the period beginning with the designated day and ending with the day before the date prescribed by an order under section 48(3)—

(a)   section 7(1)(b) applies only to shares of proprietors whose right is registered,

(b)   in the case of ownership in common, section 8(1) applies only to heritable securities granted by a proprietor whose right is registered,

(c)   section 17(3)(b) applies to such of the plots of land mentioned in section 17(1)(a) as are registered,

(d)   section 27(2) applies also to a person whose right in the plot is registered only as proprietor of a share in the plot, and

(e)   section 48(1)(d) applies as if a registered plot of land means a registered share of a plot of land owned in common.]

[Certain deeds related to registered leases: Sasine arrangements]

11B   For the period beginning with the designated day and ending with the day before the date prescribed by an order under section 48(3), for an application under section 21(1) to register [a deed (except a sublease or a notice of title) which affects a lease title sheet] where the subjects of the lease consist of or form part of an unregistered plot of land, the conditions in section 26 apply with the effect that—

(a)   in subsection (1)(b), 'plot of land' is to be read as 'lease',

(b)   in subsection (1)(c), 'title sheet' is to be read as 'lease title sheet',

(c)   subsections (1)(d), (3), (4) and (5) do not apply, and

(d)   in subsection (2), 'plot' in both places it occurs is to be read as 'lease'.]

Archive record

12   The Keeper must include in the archive record—

(a)   all copies of documents upon which the terms of the existing title sheets are founded,

(b)   all copies of documents which relate to past states of title sheets and title plans, and

(c)   such other information, in whatever form, as so relates,

in so far as those copy documents, and as the case may be that other information, is held by the Keeper immediately before the designated day.

Pending applications

13   Nothing in this Act, other than provision made by or by virtue of section 35, affects an application under section 4 (applications for registration) of the Land Registration (Scotland) Act 1979 (c 33) (the '1979 Act') provided that the date of receipt of the application is before the designated day.

14   An application by virtue of section 9(1) of the 1979 Act (rectification of the register) falls if it has not been determined by the Keeper as at the designated day.

Claims under the 1979 Act

15   Where, immediately before the designated day, a person has an entitlement to claim indemnity under section 12(1) of the 1979 Act (indemnity in respect of loss) but either—

(a)   no such claim has been made, or

(b)   any such claim as has been made is as yet undetermined,

nothing in this Act affects the entitlement or claim.

16   Nothing in this Act affects any entitlement to reimbursement under subsection (1) of section 13 of the 1979 Act (reimbursement of certain expenditure) or any claim made by virtue of that subsection.

Bijural inaccuracies

17   If there is in the register, immediately before the designated day, an inaccuracy which the Keeper has power to rectify under section 9 of the 1979 Act (rectification of the register) then, as from that day—

(a)   any person whose rights in land would have been affected by such rectification has such rights (if any) in the land as that person would have if the power had been exercised, and

(b)   the register is inaccurate in so far as it does not show those rights as so affected.

18   For the purpose of determining whether the Keeper has the power mentioned in paragraphs 17 and 22, the person registered as proprietor of the land is to be presumed to be in possession unless the contrary is shown.

19   Where, by virtue of paragraph 17—

(a)   a right is lost, compensation is payable under Part 7 as if warranty had been granted under section 73 in accepting an application by the person in whom the right was vested, or

(b)   an encumbrance is revived, compensation is so payable as if such warranty had been granted in respect of an omission of the encumbrance.

20   Except that—

(a)   compensation is not so payable in so far as, had the Keeper rectified the inaccuracy before the designated day, either a right to indemnity under section 12 of the 1979 Act (indemnity in respect of loss) was excluded by virtue of subsection (2) of that section or there would, by virtue of subsection (3) of that section, have been no entitlement to such indemnity,

(b)   any compensation so payable is to be reduced to the extent that, had the Keeper rectified the inaccuracy before the designated day, the amount of any indemnity would have been reduced by virtue of section 13(4) of that Act (reduction proportionate to the extent to which a claimant has contributed, by fraudulent or careless act or omission, to loss), and

(c) in construing Part 7 for the purposes of paragraph 19, paragraphs (b) and (c) of section 78 are to be disregarded.

21   Section 77(4) and (5) applies in relation to a payment made by virtue of paragraph 19(a) as that section applies in relation to any other payment under Part 7.

22   If there is in the register, immediately before the designated day, an inaccuracy which the Keeper does not have power to rectify under section 9 of the 1979 Act, then on that day it ceases to be an inaccuracy.

23   Where, by virtue of paragraph 22, a person suffers loss which, had it been suffered by virtue of paragraph (b) of section 12(1) of the 1979 Act, would (after allowing for the effect of subsections (2) and (3) of that section) have given rise before the designated day to an entitlement under that section, the person is entitled to claim compensation, by virtue of this paragraph, from the Keeper in respect of that loss.

24   Sections 94(3) to (6) and 95 apply in respect of a claim by virtue of paragraph 23 as they apply in respect of a claim by virtue of section 94(1), but with the modification that, for paragraph (a) of section 95(1), there is substituted—

'(a) is, in so far as it is not compensation mentioned in paragraph (b), to be quantified as at the date on which the register became inaccurate,'.

Depiction of tenement etc

25   Section 16(3) does not apply if any of the flats comprised in the flatted building mentioned in that subsection—

(a) is recorded in the Register of Sasines, or

(b) is registered by virtue of an application accepted under section 4 of the 1979 Act.

SCHEDULE 5—Minor and consequential modifications

[...]

LEGAL WRITINGS (COUNTERPARTS AND DELIVERY) (SCOTLAND) ACT 2015
(2015, asp 4)

Execution of documents in counterpart

1   Execution of documents in counterpart

(1)   A document may be executed in counterpart.

(2)   A document is executed in counterpart if—

(a) it is executed in two or more duplicate, interchangeable, parts, and

(b) no part is subscribed by both or all parties.

(3)   On such execution, the counterparts are to be treated as a single document.

(4)   That single document may be made up of—

(a) both or all the counterparts in their entirety, or

(b) one of the counterparts in its entirety, collated with the page or pages on which the other counterpart has, or other counterparts have, been subscribed.

(5)   A document executed in counterpart becomes effective when—

(a) both or all the counterparts have been delivered in accordance with subsection (6) or (7), and

(b) any other step required by an enactment or rule of law for the document to become effective has been taken.

(6)   Each counterpart is to be delivered to the party or parties who did not subscribe the counterpart in question unless it is a counterpart which falls to be delivered under subsection (7).

(7)   If a party has, under section 2(1), nominated a person to take delivery of one or more counterparts, the counterpart in question is (or counterparts in question are) to be delivered to that person.

(8) Subsection (5) is subject to subsection (9).

(9) Where a counterpart is to be held by the recipient as undelivered, the counterpart is not to be treated as delivered for the purposes of subsection (5)(a) until—

(a) the person from whom the counterpart is received indicates to the recipient that it is to be so treated, or

(b) if a specified condition is to be satisfied before the counterpart may be so treated, the condition has been satisfied.

2 Nomination of person to take delivery of counterparts

(1) Parties to a document executed in counterpart may nominate a person to take delivery of one or more of the counterparts.

(2) Subsection (1) does not prevent one of the parties, or an agent of one or more of the parties, being so nominated.

(3) A person so nominated must, after taking delivery of a counterpart by virtue of subsection (1), hold and preserve it for the benefit of the parties.

(4) Subsection (3) does not apply in so far as the parties may agree, or be taken to have agreed, otherwise (whether before or after the document has effect).

(5) A document's having effect is not dependent on compliance with subsection (3) or (4).

3 Use of counterparts: electronic documents

(1) Sections 1 and 2 apply to traditional documents and electronic documents.

(2) In section 1 any reference to subscription is to be read, in the case of an electronic document to which section 1(2) of the Requirements of Writing (Scotland) Act 1995 ('the 1995 Act') applies, as a reference to authentication of the electronic document within the meaning of section 9B of the 1995 Act.

(3) In this section—

'electronic document' has the meaning given by section 9A of the 1995 Act,

'traditional document' has the meaning given by section 1A of the 1995 Act.

Delivery of traditional documents by electronic means

4 Delivery of traditional documents by electronic means

(1) This section applies where there is a requirement for delivery of a traditional document (whether or not a document executed in counterpart).

(2) The requirement may be satisfied by delivery by electronic means of—

(a) a copy of the document, or

(b) a part of such a copy.

(3) But the requirement may be satisfied by delivery of a part of such a copy only if the part—

(a) is sufficient in all the circumstances to show that it is part of the document, and

(b) is, or includes, the page on which the sender (or the person on whose behalf the sender has effected the delivery) has subscribed the document.

(4) Delivery under subsection (2) must be by a means (and what is delivered must be in a form) which the intended recipient has agreed to accept (the 'accepted method'), unless subsection (5) applies.

(5) If—

(a) no accepted method has been agreed,

(b) there is uncertainty about the accepted method, or

(c) the accepted method is impracticable,

delivery may be by such means (and in such form) as is reasonable in all the circumstances.

(6) Although delivery by electronic means constitutes effective delivery in relation to a traditional document, what is received by that means is not to be treated as being the traditional document itself.

(7) A traditional document, in relation to which delivery by electronic means has been effected, is to be held by the sender in accordance with whatever arrangements have been made by the sender and the recipient (or, if there is a number of recipients, have been made by the sender and the recipients as a group).

(8) Any reference in subsection (7) to a recipient is to be construed, in a case where a person takes delivery by virtue of section 2(1), as a reference to the parties who nominated that person.

(9) In this section, references to delivery by electronic means are to delivery—

(a) by means of an electronic communications network (for example as an attachment to an e-mail),

(b) by fax,

(c) by means of a device on which the thing delivered is stored electronically (such as a disc, a memory stick or other removable or portable media), or

(d) by other means but in a form which requires the use of electronic apparatus by the recipient to render the thing delivered intelligible.

(10) In this section—

'electronic communications network' has the meaning given by section 32 of the Communications Act 2003,

'traditional document' has the meaning given by section 1A of the 1995 Act.

Final provisions

5 Ancillary provision

(1) The Scottish Ministers may by order make such incidental, supplementary, consequential, transitional, transitory or saving provision as they consider appropriate for the purposes of, in connection with or for giving full effect to this Act.

(2) An order under subsection (1) may modify any enactment (including this Act).

(3) An order under subsection (1) is subject to the negative procedure, unless subsection (4) applies.

(4) An order under subsection (1) which adds to, replaces or omits the text of an Act is subject to the affirmative procedure.

6 Commencement

(1) Section 5, this section and section 7 come into force on the day after Royal Assent.

(2) The other provisions of this Act come into force on such day as the Scottish Ministers may by order appoint.

(3) An order under subsection (2) may include transitional, transitory or saving provision.

7 Short title

The short title of this Act is the Legal Writings (Counterparts and Delivery) (Scotland) Act 2015.

CONSUMER RIGHTS ACT 2015
(2015, C 15)

3 Contracts covered by this Chapter

(1) This Chapter applies to a contract for a trader to supply goods to a consumer.

(2) It applies only if the contract is one of these (defined for the purposes of this Part in sections 5 to 8)—

(a) a sales contract;

(b) a contract for the hire of goods;

(c) a hire-purchase agreement;

(d) a contract for transfer of goods.

(3) It does not apply—

(a) to a contract for a trader to supply coins or notes to a consumer for use as currency;

(b) to a contract for goods to be sold by way of execution or otherwise by authority of law;

(c) to a contract intended to operate as a mortgage, pledge, charge or other security;

(d) in relation to England and Wales or Northern Ireland, to a contract made by deed and for which the only consideration is the presumed consideration imported by the deed;

(e) in relation to Scotland, to a gratuitous contract.

(4) A contract to which this Chapter applies is referred to in this Part as a 'contract to supply goods'.

(5) Contracts to supply goods include—

(a) contracts entered into between one part owner and another;

(b) contracts for the transfer of an undivided share in goods;

(c) contracts that are absolute and contracts that are conditional.

(6) Subsection (1) is subject to any provision of this Chapter that applies a section or part of a section to only some of the kinds of contracts listed in subsection (2).

(7) A mixed contract (see section 1(4)) may be a contract of any of those kinds.

4 Ownership of goods

(1) In this Chapter ownership of goods means the general property in goods, not merely a special property.

(2) For the time when ownership of goods is transferred, see in particular the following provisions of the Sale of Goods Act 1979 (which relate to contracts of sale)—

section 16: goods must be ascertained

section 17: property passes when intended to pass

section 18: rules for ascertaining intention

section 19: reservation of right of disposal

section 20A: undivided shares in goods forming part of a bulk

section 20B: deemed consent by co-owner to dealings in bulk goods.

5 Sales contracts

(1) A contract is a sales contract if under it—

(a) the trader transfers or agrees to transfer ownership of goods to the consumer, and

(b) the consumer pays or agrees to pay the price.

(2) A contract is a sales contract (whether or not it would be one under subsection (1)) if under the contract—

(a) goods are to be manufactured or produced and the trader agrees to supply them to the consumer,

(b) on being supplied, the goods will be owned by the consumer, and

(c) the consumer pays or agrees to pay the price.

(3) A sales contract may be conditional (see section 3(5)), but in this Part 'conditional sales contract' means a sales contract under which—

(a) the price for the goods or part of it is payable by instalments, and

(b) the trader retains ownership of the goods until the conditions specified in the contract (for the payment of instalments or otherwise) are met; and it makes no difference whether or not the consumer possesses the goods.

8 Contracts for transfer of goods

A contract to supply goods is a contract for transfer of goods if under it the trader transfers or agrees to transfer ownership of the goods to the consumer and—

(a) the consumer provides or agrees to provide consideration otherwise than by paying a price, or

(b) the contract is, for any other reason, not a sales contract or a hirepurchase agreement.

17 Trader to have right to supply the goods etc

(1) Every contract to supply goods, except one within subsection (4), is to be treated as including a term—

(a) in the case of a contract for the hire of goods, that at the beginning of the period of hire the trader must have the right to transfer possession of the goods by way of hire for that period,

(b) in any other case, that the trader must have the right to sell or transfer the goods at the time when ownership of the goods is to be transferred.

(2) Every contract to supply goods, except a contract for the hire of goods or a contract within subsection (4), is to be treated as including a term that—

(a) the goods are free from any charge or encumbrance not disclosed or known to the consumer before entering into the contract,

(b) the goods will remain free from any such charge or encumbrance until ownership of them is to be transferred, and

(c) the consumer will enjoy quiet possession of the goods except so far as it may be disturbed by the owner or other person entitled to the benefit of any charge or encumbrance so disclosed or known.

(3) Every contract for the hire of goods is to be treated as including a term that the consumer will enjoy quiet possession of the goods for the period of the hire except so far as the possession may be disturbed by the owner or other person entitled to the benefit of any charge or encumbrance disclosed or known to the consumer before entering into the contract.

(4) This subsection applies to a contract if the contract shows, or the circumstances when they enter into the contract imply, that the trader and the consumer intend the trader to transfer only—

(a) whatever title the trader has, even if it is limited, or

(b) whatever title a third person has, even if it is limited.

(5) Every contract within subsection (4) is to be treated as including a term that all charges or encumbrances known to the trader and not known to the consumer were disclosed to the consumer before entering into the contract.

(6) Every contract within subsection (4) is to be treated as including a term that the consumer's quiet possession of the goods—

(a) will not be disturbed by the trader, and

(b) will not be disturbed by a person claiming through or under the trader, unless that person is claiming under a charge or encumbrance that was disclosed or known to the consumer before entering into the contract.

(7) If subsection (4)(b) applies (transfer of title that a third person has), the contract is also to be treated as including a term that the consumer's quiet possession of the goods—

(a) will not be disturbed by the third person, and

(b) will not be disturbed by a person claiming through or under the third person, unless the claim is under a charge or encumbrance that was disclosed or known to the consumer before entering into the contract.

(8) In the case of a contract for the hire of goods, this section does not affect the right of the trader to repossess the goods where the contract provides or is to be treated as providing for this.

(9) See section 19 for a consumer's rights if the trader is in breach of a term that this section requires to be treated as included in a contract.

29 Passing of risk

(1) A sales contract is to be treated as including the following provisions as terms.

(2) The goods remain at the trader's risk until they come into the physical possession of—

(a) the consumer, or

(b)   a person identified by the consumer to take possession of the goods.

(3)   Subsection (2) does not apply if the goods are delivered to a carrier who—

(a)   is commissioned by the consumer to deliver the goods, and

(b)   is not a carrier the trader named as an option for the consumer.

(4)   In that case the goods are at the consumer's risk on and after delivery to the carrier.

(5)   Subsection (4) does not affect any liability of the carrier to the consumer in respect of the goods.

(6)   See section 2(5) and (6) for the application of this section where goods are sold at public auction.

31   Liability that cannot be excluded or restricted

(1)   A term of a contract to supply goods is not binding on the consumer to the extent that it would exclude or restrict the trader's liability arising under any of these provisions—

. . .

(i)   section 17 (trader to have right to supply the goods etc);

. . .

(k) section 29 (passing of risk).

(2)   That also means that a term of a contract to supply goods is not binding on the consumer to the extent that it would—

(a)   exclude or restrict a right or remedy in respect of a liability under a provision listed in subsection (1),

(b)   make such a right or remedy or its enforcement subject to a restrictive or onerous condition,

(c)   allow a trader to put a person at a disadvantage as a result of pursuing such a right or remedy, or

(d)   exclude or restrict rules of evidence or procedure.

(3)   The reference in subsection (1) to excluding or restricting a liability also includes preventing an obligation or duty arising or limiting its extent.

(4)   An agreement in writing to submit present or future differences to arbitration is not to be regarded as excluding or restricting any liability for the purposes of this section.

(5)   Subsection (1)(i), and subsection (2) so far as it relates to liability under section 17, do not apply to a term of a contract for the hire of goods.

(6)   But an express term of a contract for the hire of goods is not binding on the consumer to the extent that it would exclude or restrict a term that section 17 requires to be treated as included in the contract, unless it is inconsistent with that term (and see also section 62 (requirement for terms to be fair)).

(7)   See Schedule 3 for provision about the enforcement of this section.

LAND REFORM (SCOTLAND) ACT 2016
(2016, asp 18)

At the time of going to press s 43 was not in force.

PART 3
INFORMATION ABOUT CONTROL OF LAND ETC

Information about persons with controlling interests in relation to land

39   Information about persons with controlling interests in owners and tenants of land

(1)   The Scottish Ministers must by regulations make provision—

(a)   requiring information to be provided about persons who have controlling interests in owners and tenants of land, and

(b) about the publication of that information in a public register kept by the Keeper of the Registers of Scotland.

(2) Regulations under subsection (1) may, in particular, include provision about—

(a) which owners and tenants of land the regulations apply to,

(b) what constitutes a controlling interest in an owner or tenant,

(c) which persons are to be treated as having a controlling interest in an owner or tenant,

(d) what information must be provided under the regulations (and the manner in which it is to be provided),

(e) the circumstances in which information must be provided under the regulations,

(f) publication of information required under the regulations (including the form of the register and the entry of the information in it),

(g) the circumstances in which the information entered in the register may be corrected or updated,

(h) the circumstances in which a person who has a controlling interest in an owner or tenant can request that information about that person not be published (including, in particular, where the publication of that information might result in the person being at a serious risk of violence or abuse, threat of violence or abuse or intimidation),

(i) the effect of providing (or failing to provide) information required under the regulations,

(j) sanctions for failure to comply with requirements imposed under the regulations,

(k) delegation of functions under the regulations,

(l) fees payable in relation to the provision, publication or accessing of information under the regulations,

(m) appeals against decisions made under the regulations.

(3) Regulations under subsection (1) may include provision for offences and civil penalties (including fixed penalties) for failure to comply with requirements imposed under the regulations.

(4) Where regulations under subsection (1) include provision creating offences—

(a) they must provide for those offences to be triable summarily only, and

(b) they must provide for the maximum penalty for those offences to be a fine, which must not exceed level 5 on the standard scale.

(5) Where regulations under subsection (1) include provision for the imposition of civil penalties, they must include provision about appeals against decisions to impose those penalties.

(6) Regulations under subsection (1) may modify any enactment (including this Act).

(7) The Scottish Ministers must, before laying a draft of any regulations under subsection (1) before the Scottish Parliament, consult—

(a) the Keeper, and

(b) such other persons as they consider appropriate.

(8) Subsection (7) does not apply if section 40 applies.

Procedure for first regulations under section 39

40 Procedure for first regulations under section 39

The Scottish Ministers may not lay a draft of the first regulations under section 39(1) before the Scottish Parliament unless—

(a) they have consulted in accordance with section 41, and

(b) following that consultation, they have laid before the Scottish Parliament—

(i) proposed draft regulations, and

(ii) an explanatory document prepared in accordance with section 42.

41   Procedure for first regulations under section 39: consultation
(1)   Before laying a draft of the first regulations under section 39(1) before the Scottish Parliament, the Scottish Ministers must consult—
(a)   the Keeper, and
(b)   such other persons as they consider appropriate.
(2)   For the purposes of any consultation required by subsection (1), the Scottish Ministers must—
(a)   lay before the Scottish Parliament—
(i)   a copy of the proposed draft regulations, and
(ii)   a copy of the proposed explanatory document referred to in section 40(b)
(ii) (except the details required by section 42(1)(b)),
(b)   send a copy of the proposed draft regulations and proposed explanatory document to any person to be consulted under subsection (1), and
(c)   have regard to any representations about the proposed draft regulations that are made to them within the period of 60 days beginning with the date on which the copy of the proposed draft regulations is laid before the Parliament under paragraph (a).
(3)   In calculating any period of 60 days for the purposes of subsection (2)(c), no account is to be taken of any time during which the Parliament is dissolved or is in recess for more than 4 days.

42   Procedure for first regulations under section 39: explanatory document
(1)   The explanatory document referred to in section 40(b)(ii) must—
(a)   give reasons for the provisions contained in the proposed draft regulations,
(b)   give details of—
(i)   any consultation undertaken under section 41,
(ii)   any representations received as a result of the consultation, and
(iii)   the changes (if any) made to the proposed draft regulations as a result of those representations.
(2)   Where a person making representations in response to consultation under section 41 has not consented to the disclosure of the representations, the Scottish Ministers must not disclose them under subsection (1)(b)(ii).
(3)   If information in representations made by a person in response to consultation under section 41 relates to another person, the Scottish Ministers must not disclose that information under subsection (1)(b)(ii) if or to the extent that—
(a)   it appears to the Scottish Ministers that the disclosure of that information could adversely affect the interests of that other person, and
(b)   the Scottish Ministers have been unable to obtain the consent of that other person to the disclosure.
(4)   Subsections (2) and (3) do not affect any disclosure that is requested by, and made to, a committee of the Parliament charged with reporting on the proposed draft regulations.

Information relating to proprietors of land etc

43   Power of Keeper to request or require information relating to proprietors of land etc
(1)   The Land Registration etc (Scotland) Act 2012 is amended as follows.
(2)   After section 48 insert—

    '*Entry of information relating to categories of owners and tenants in the register*

    48A   Power to request or require information relating to categories of owners and tenants
    (1)   The Scottish Ministers may, by regulations, make provision enabling the Keeper to request or, as the case may be, require information relating to the

category of person or body into which a person mentioned in subsection (2) falls.

(2)   The persons referred to in subsection (1) ("relevant persons") are—

    (a)   owners of plots of land,

    (b)   proprietors of registered plots of land and registered leases, and

    (c)   tenants of leases which are registered or registrable.

(3)   Regulations under subsection (1) may, in particular, make provision—

    (a)   about the persons who are owners, proprietors and tenants for the purposes of subsection (2),

    (b)   about the information, relating to the category of person or body into which a relevant person falls, provision of which may be requested or required,

    (c)   about the form in which the information is to be provided, which may consist of (or include) declarations by, or on behalf of, relevant persons about the category of person or body into which a relevant person falls,

    (d)   about the circumstances in which information may be requested,

    (e)   about the circumstances in which information requires, and does not require, to be provided,

    (f)   about the effect (if any) of providing (or not providing) information,

    (g)   about the entry of the information in the register,

    (h)   about whether the Keeper's warranty under Part 7 is to apply in relation to information obtained under the regulations,

    (i)   about the circumstances in which information obtained under the regulations may be corrected or updated,

    (j)   about the circumstances in which information obtained under the regulations may be provided to other persons,

    (k)   about the circumstances in which information obtained under the regulations may be published,

    (l)   for fees relating to the provision, correction or updating of information under the regulations.

(4)   Regulations under subsection (1) which make provision enabling the Keeper to require information may include provision relating to offences for failure to comply with requirements imposed by the regulations.

(5)   Where regulations under subsection (1) include provision creating offences—

    (a)   they must provide for those offences to be triable summarily only, and

    (b)   they must provide for the maximum penalty for those offences to be a fine, which must not exceed level 3 on the standard scale.

(6)   The Scottish Ministers must consult the Keeper before laying a draft of regulations under subsection (1) before the Scottish Parliament.

(7)   Regulations under subsection (1) may include such incidental, supplementary or consequential provision as the Scottish Ministers consider appropriate for the purposes of, or in connection with, the regulations.

(8)   Regulations under subsection (1) may modify any enactment (including this Act).

48B   Power to enter information relating to categories of owners and tenants in the register

(1)   The Scottish Ministers may, by regulations, make provision enabling the Keeper to enter, in the register, information relating to the category of person or body into which a person mentioned in subsection (2) falls.

(2)   The persons referred to in subsection (1) ("relevant persons") are—

    (a)   owners of plots of land,

    (b)   proprietors of registered plots of land and registered leases, and

    (c)   tenants of leases which are registered or registrable.

(3)   Regulations under subsection (1) may, in particular, make provision—

(a)   about the persons who are owners, proprietors and tenants for the purposes of subsection (2),

(b)   about notification by the Keeper of the intention to enter the information,

(c)   about the circumstances in which the Keeper may enter the information,

(d)   for the information that may be entered and the form in which it is to be entered,

(e)   about the effect (if any) of entering the information,

(f)   about whether the Keeper's warranty under Part 7 is to apply in relation to information entered under the regulations,

(g)   about the circumstances in which information entered under the regulations may be corrected or updated,

(h)   about the circumstances in which information entered under the regulations may be provided to other persons,

(i)   about the circumstances in which information entered under the regulations may be published,

(j)   for fees relating to the correction or updating of information under the regulations.

(4)   The Scottish Ministers must consult the Keeper before laying a draft of regulations under subsection (1) before the Scottish Parliament.

(5)   Regulations under subsection (1) may include such incidental, supplementary or consequential provision as the Scottish Ministers consider appropriate for the purposes of, or in connection with, the regulations.

(6)   Regulations under subsection (1) may modify any enactment (including this Act).'.

(3)   In section 116 (subordinate legislation), in subsection (3), after paragraph (b) insert—

'(ba)   section 48A(1),

(bb)   section 48B(1),'.

(4)   In section 121 (Crown application)—

(a)   in subsection (1), after first 'Crown' insert 'of a requirement imposed by regulations under section 48A or',

(b)   in subsection (3)—

(i)   for 'section 112 applies' substitute 'regulations under section 48A and section 112 apply',

(ii)   for 'it applies' substitute 'they apply'.

BANKRUPTCY (SCOTLAND) ACT 2016
(2016, asp 21)

78   Vesting of estate at date of sequestration

(1)   The whole estate of the debtor vests for the benefit of the creditors in the trustee in the sequestration, by virtue of the trustee's appointment, as at the date of sequestration.

(2)   But subsection (1) is subject to—

[(a)]   section 88 [, and

(b) section 4B(3)(a) of the Damages Act 1996.]

(3)   It is not competent for—

(a)   the trustee, or

(b)   any person deriving title from the trustee,

to complete title, before the expiry of the period mentioned in subsection (4), to any heritable property in Scotland vested in the trustee by virtue of the trustee's appointment.

(4)   The period is 28 days (or such other period as may be prescribed) beginning with the day on which the certified copy of—

(a)   the order of the sheriff granting warrant is recorded under subsection (1)(a) of section 26 in the Register of Inhibitions, or

(b)   the determination of AiB awarding sequestration is recorded under subsection (2) of that section in that register.

(5)   The exercise by the trustee of any power conferred on the trustee by this Act, in respect of any heritable estate vested in the trustee by virtue of that person's appointment, is not challengeable on the ground of a prior inhibition.

(6)   Where the debtor has an uncompleted title to any heritable estate in Scotland, the trustee may complete title to that estate either in the trustee's own name or in the name of the debtor.

(7)   But completion of title in the name of the debtor does not validate by accretion any unperfected right in favour of a person other than the trustee.

(8)   Moveable property in respect of which, but for this subsection—

(a)   delivery or possession, or

(b)   intimation of assignation,

would be required in order to complete title vests in the trustee, by virtue of the trustee's appointment, as if at the date of sequestration (as the case may be) the trustee had taken delivery or possession of the property or had made intimation of its assignation to the trustee.

(9)   Any non-vested contingent interest which the debtor has vests in the trustee as if an assignation of that interest had been executed by the debtor (and intimation of assignation made) at the date of sequestration.

(10)   Any non-vested contingent interest vested in the trustee by virtue of subsection (9) is, where it remains so vested as at the date which is 4 years after the date of sequestration, re-invested in the debtor as if an assignation of that interest had been executed by the trustee (and intimation of assignation made) at that date.

(11)   A person claiming a right to any estate claimed by the trustee may apply to the sheriff for the estate to be excluded from such vesting, a copy of the application being served on the trustee.

(12)   The sheriff must grant the application if satisfied that the estate should not be so vested.

(13)   Where any successor of a deceased debtor whose estate has been sequestrated has made up title to, or is in possession of, any part of that estate, the sheriff may on the application of the trustee order the successor to convey such estate to the trustee.

79   Provision supplementary to section 78 and interpretation of Part 5

(1)   In subsection (1) of section 78, the 'whole estate of the debtor' means the debtor's whole estate at the date of sequestration (wherever situated) including—

(a)   any income or estate vesting in the debtor on the date of sequestration,

(b)   any property of the debtor title to which has not been completed by another person deriving right from the debtor, and

(c)   the capacity to exercise and to take proceedings for exercising all such powers in, over or in respect of any property as—

(i)   might have been exercised by the debtor for the debtor's own benefit as at, or on, the date of sequestration, or

(ii)   might be exercised on a relevant date.

(2)   But subsection (1) is subject to subsection (3) [. . .].

(3)   The 'whole estate of the debtor' does not include any interest of the debtor as tenant under—

(a)   a tenancy which is an assured tenancy within the meaning of Part 2 of the Housing (Scotland) Act 1988,

(b)   a protected tenancy within the meaning of the Rent (Scotland) Act 1984 in respect of which, by virtue of Part 8 of that Act, no premium can lawfully be required as a condition of assignation, or

(c)   a Scottish secure tenancy within the meaning of the Housing (Scotland) Act 2001.

(4)   On the date on which the trustee serves notice to that effect on the debtor, the interest of the debtor as tenant under any of the tenancies referred to in subsection (3) forms part of the debtor's estate and vests in the trustee as if it had vested in the trustee under section 86(5).

(5)   In this Part 'relevant date' means a date after the date of sequestration and before the date which is 4 years after the date of sequestration.

87   Dealings and circumstances of debtor after sequestration

(1)   The debtor must immediately notify the trustee in the sequestration—
  (a)   of any assets acquired by the debtor on a relevant date, or
  (b)   of any other substantial change in the debtor's financial circumstances.

(2)   A debtor who fails to comply with subsection (1) commits an offence.

(3)   A debtor who commits an offence under subsection (2) is liable on summary conviction—
  (a)   to a fine not exceeding level 5 on the standard scale,
  (b)   to imprisonment for a term not exceeding 3 months, or
  (c)   both to such fine and to such imprisonment.

(4)   Any dealing of, or with, the debtor and relating to the debtor's estate vested in the trustee under section 78 or 86 is of no effect in a question with the trustee.

(5)   But subsection (4) does not apply where the person seeking to uphold the dealing establishes that the trustee—
  (a)   has abandoned to the debtor the property to which the dealing relates,
  (b)   has expressly or impliedly authorised the dealing, or
  (c)   is otherwise personally barred from challenging the dealing.

(6)   Nor does subsection (4) apply where the person seeking to uphold the dealing establishes both—
  (a)   that the dealing is—
    (i)   the performance of an obligation undertaken before the date of sequestration by a person obliged to the debtor in the obligation,
    (ii)   the purchase from the debtor of goods for which the purchaser has given value to the debtor or is willing to give value to the trustee, or
    (iii)   one which satisfies the conditions mentioned in subsection (10), and
  (b)   that the person dealing with the debtor was, at the time when the dealing occurred, unaware of the sequestration and had at that time no reason to believe that the debtor's estate had been sequestrated or was the subject of sequestration proceedings.

(7)   Nor does subsection (4) apply where the dealing is a banking transaction entered into before the receipt by the bank of a notice under section 86(9) (whether or not the bank is aware of the sequestration).

(8)   Where the trustee has abandoned heritable property to the debtor, notice (in such form as may be prescribed) given to the debtor by the trustee is sufficient evidence that the property is vested in the debtor.*

(9)   Where notice is given under subsection (8), the trustee is as soon as reasonably practicable after giving it to record a certified copy of it in the Register of Inhibitions.

(10)   The conditions are that—
  (a)   the dealing constitutes—
    (i)   the transfer of incorporeal moveable property, or
    (ii)   the creation, transfer, variation or extinguishing of a real right in heritable property,
  for which the person dealing with the debtor has given adequate consideration to the debtor or is willing to give adequate consideration to the trustee,
  (b)   the dealing requires the delivery of a deed, and
  (c)   the delivery occurs during the period beginning with the date of sequestration and ending 7 days after the day on which—
    (i)   the certified copy of the order of the sheriff granting warrant is recorded in the Register of Inhibitions under section 26(1)(a), or

(ii)   the certified copy of the determination of AiB awarding sequestration is recorded in that register under section 26(2).

---

*NOTE – See further Bankruptcy (Scotland) Regulations 2016 (SSI 2016/397) reg 24 and Sch 1, forms 15 and 16.

---

88   Limitation on vesting

(1)   The following property of the debtor does not vest in the trustee in the sequestration—

(a) any property—
  (i)   kept outside a dwellinghouse, and
  (ii)   in respect of which attachment is, by virtue of section 11(1) of the 2002 Act, incompetent,

(b) any property—
  (i)   kept inside a dwellinghouse, and
  (ii)   not a non-essential asset for the purposes of Part 3 of that Act, and

(c)   property held on trust by the debtor for any other person.

(2)   The vesting of the debtor's estate in the trustee in the sequestration does not affect the right of hypothec of a landlord.

(3)   Sections 78, 85 and 86 are without prejudice to the right of any secured creditor which is preferable to the rights of the trustee.

MOVEABLE TRANSACTIONS (SCOTLAND) ACT 2023
(2023, asp 3)

This Act is not yet in force.

PART 1
ASSIGNATION

CHAPTER 1
ASSIGNATION OF CLAIMS, PROTECTION OF
DEBTORS AND RELATED MATTERS

Assignation of claims

1 Assignation of claims: general

(1)   The assignation of a claim requires the execution or authentication of a document assigning the claim (an 'assignation document') by the person assigning it.

(2)   The assignation document must identify the claim.

(3)   But an assignation document which assigns a number of claims need not identify each claim separately provided that the document identifies the claims in terms of their constituting an identifiable class.

(4)   It is competent to assign a claim which, at the time the assignation document is granted, is not held by the assignor (whether or not the claim yet exists at that time).

(5)   For the purposes of subsection (2), the ways in which the claim can be identified in the assignation document include by making reference in the assignation document to another document, the terms of which are not reproduced.

(6)   Nothing in this Part applies to the assignation of a claim as part of a financial collateral arrangement, within the meaning of regulation 3(1) of the Financial Collateral Arrangements (No.2) Regulations 2003 (S.I. 2003/3226).

2 Assignation of claim subject to a condition

(1)   The assignation of a claim may be subject to a condition which must be satisfied before the claim is transferred.

(2)   Any such condition must be specified in the assignation document.

(3)   The condition may, for example—

(a) be the occurrence of a particular date,

(b) depend on something happening (whether or not it is certain that the thing will happen), or

(c) depend on a period of time elapsing during which something must not happen (whether or not it is certain that the thing will happen at some time).

(4)   For the purposes of subsection (2), the ways in which the condition can be specified in the assignation document include by making reference in the assignation document to another document, the terms of which are not reproduced.

3 Transfer of claims

(1)   A claim in respect of which an assignation document is granted is transferred on the requirements mentioned in subsection (2) all being met.

(2)   Those requirements are that—

(a) the assignor is the holder of the claim,

(b) either—

(i)   intimation of the assignation is effected under section 8(1), or

(ii) the assignation document is registered,

(c) the claim is identifiable as a claim to which the assignation document relates, and

(d) if the assignation is subject to a condition which must be satisfied before the claim is transferred, the condition is satisfied.

(3)   For the purposes of subsection (1), if the claim is a claim such as is mentioned in section 1(4)—

(a) the requirement mentioned in subsection (2)(a) is met when the assignor becomes the holder of the claim, and

(b) any rule of law as to accretion does not apply in relation to the claim.

(4)   Subsection (2)(b)(ii) is subject to section 27 (effective registration of assignation document) and, accordingly, the requirement of that subsection—

(a) is not met if the registration of the assignation document is ineffective in accordance with section 27(1), and

(b) is met if and when that registration becomes effective in accordance with section 27(3).

(5)   Subsection (6) applies where—

(a) an assignor grants more than one assignation document in respect of the same claim,

(b) each of the purported assignations of the claim is to a different person, and

(c) the requirements of subsection (2) are all met in relation to each of the purported assignations at the same time by virtue of—

(i)   the assignor becoming the holder of the claim,

(ii)   the claim becoming identifiable as a claim to which the assignation document relates, or

(iii)   where each of the purported assignations is subject to a condition which must be satisfied before the claim is transferred, those conditions being satisfied at the same time.

(6)   The claim transfers under subsection (1) to the person to whom it is assigned by whichever of the purported assignations of the claim first met the requirement of subsection (2)(b).

(7)   This section is subject to section 4 (assignation of claims: insolvency).

(8)   The Scottish Ministers may by regulations prescribe types of claim in relation to which sub-paragraph (i) of subsection (2)(b) is to be disregarded.

4   Assignation of claims: insolvency

(1)   This section applies where—

(a) an assignation document is granted in respect of a claim such as is mentioned in section 1(4), and

(b) after the document is granted, the assignor becomes insolvent.

(2)   The assignation is ineffective in relation to the claim if the assignor becomes the holder of the claim after becoming insolvent.

(3)   But subsection (2) does not apply in relation to a claim in respect of income from property in so far as that claim—

(a) is not attributable to anything agreed to by, or done by, the assignor after the assignor became insolvent, and

(b) relates to the use of property in existence at the time the assignor became insolvent.

(4)   Subsection (5) applies where—

(a) but for subsection (3), the assignation would be ineffective by virtue of subsection (2), and

(b) the assignor is discharged—

(i)   under section 137, 138 or 140 of the Bankruptcy (Scotland) Act 2016, or

(ii)   by virtue of section 184(3) of that Act.

(5)   The assignation is ineffective, in relation to the claim, if by the time of discharge the assignor has not become the holder of the claim.

(6)   For the purposes of this section—

(a) an assignor who is an individual, or the estate of which may be sequestrated by virtue of section 6 of the Bankruptcy (Scotland) Act 2016, becomes insolvent when—

(i)   the assignor's estate is sequestrated,

    (ii)   the assignor grants a trust deed for creditors or makes a composition or arrangement with creditors,

    (iii) the assignor is adjudged bankrupt,

    (iv) a voluntary arrangement proposed by the assignor is approved,

    (v)   the assignor's application for a debt payment programme is approved under section 2 of the Debt Arrangement and Attachment (Scotland) Act 2002, or

    (vi) the assignor becomes subject to any other order or arrangement analogous to any of those mentioned in sub-paragraphs (i) to (v) anywhere in the world, and

(b) an assignor other than is mentioned in paragraph (a) becomes insolvent when—

    (i)   a decision approving a voluntary arrangement entered into by the assignor has effect under section 4A of the Insolvency Act 1986 (the '1986 Act'),

    (ii) the assignor is wound up under Part 4 or 5 of the 1986 Act or under section 367 of the Financial Services and Markets Act 2000,

    (iii) an administrative receiver, as defined in section 251 of the 1986 Act, is appointed over all or part (being a part which includes the claim) of the property of the assignor,

    (iv) the assignor enters administration ('enters administration' being construed in accordance with paragraph 1(2) of schedule B1 of the 1986 Act),

    (v)   an order under section 901F of the Companies Act 2006 sanctioning a compromise or arrangement entered into by the assignor comes into effect over all or part of the property of the assignor, or

    (vi) the assignor becomes subject to any other order, appointment or arrangement analogous to any of those mentioned in sub-paragraphs (i) to (v) anywhere in the world.

(7)   The Scottish Ministers may by regulations modify—

  (a) subsection (4),

  (b) subsection (5),

  (c) subsection (6).

5 Assignation in part

(1)   A claim may be assigned in whole or in part.

(2)   But if the claim is not a monetary claim, the claim may be assigned in part only if the claim is divisible and either—

  (a) the debtor consents, or

  (b) the assignation is not likely to result in the obligation to which it relates becoming significantly more burdensome for the debtor.

(3)   Except in so far as the debtor agrees otherwise with the assignor, or agreed otherwise with a person who was previously the holder of the claim (when that person was the holder), the assignor is liable to the debtor for any expense incurred by the debtor which is attributable to the claim's being assigned in part rather than in whole.

6 Limitations as to assignability: general

(1)   Nothing in this Part affects any other enactment, or any rule of law, by virtue of which the assignation of a claim is of no effect.

(2)   But such an enactment or rule of law does not apply to an assignation if the grounds on which the assignation would be of no effect by virtue of that enactment or rule are grounds which this Part provides do not make the assignation of no effect.

(3)   The assignation, in whole or in part, of a claim is of no effect if and in so far as, before the assignation document in respect of the claim was granted—

  (a) the debtor and the holder of the claim had agreed that the claim was not to be so assigned, or

  (b) the person whose unilateral undertaking gives rise to the claim had stated that the claim was not to be so assigned.

(4)   For the purposes of subsection (3)(a), it does not matter whether the holder of the claim became the holder of the claim after the agreement was made.

(5)   Nothing in subsection (3) affects the operation of any other enactment concerning the effect of an agreement or statement such as is mentioned in that subsection.

7   Claim in respect of wages or salary

(1)   It is not competent for an individual to assign a claim in respect of wages or salary payable to the individual.

(2)   For the purposes of subsection (1), 'wages' and 'salary' include—

(a)   any of the following which is referable to the individual's employment (whether or not payable under the individual's contract of employment)—

(i)   a fee,

(ii)   a bonus,

(iii)   commission,

(iv)   holiday pay, or

(v)   any other emolument,

(b)   any payment in respect of expenses incurred by the individual in carrying out that employment, and

(c)   if the individual is dismissed from that employment by reason of redundancy, any payment referable to the redundancy.

(3)   Nothing in subsection (1) affects the operation of any other enactment allowing the assignation of a claim such as is mentioned in that subsection in particular circumstances.

8   Intimation of the assignation of a claim

(1)   For the purposes of section 3(2)(b)(i), intimation is effected only—

(a)   by the assignor or the assignee serving notice of the assignation on the debtor, or

(b)   on the occurrence either—

(i)   of the debtor acknowledging to the assignee that the claim is assigned, or

(ii)   of intimation to the debtor, in judicial proceedings to which the debtor is a party, that the assignation is founded on in the proceedings.

(2)   Where there are co-debtors in respect of a claim, intimation as respects any one or more of them is, for the purposes of section 3(2)(b)(i), intimation to them all.

(3)   A notice served under subsection (1)(a)—

(a)   must—

(i)   set out the name and address of both the assignor and the assignee,

(ii)   provide details of the claim assigned, and

(iii)   in the case of a claim assigned in part, provide details of the part assigned,

(b)   must be in writing and consist of, or be contained within, one or more documents,

(c)   need not be executed or authenticated, and

(d)   if the claim is a monetary claim, may (but need not) be in such form (if any) as is prescribed for the purposes of this paragraph.

(4)   Where a notice is served as mentioned in subsection (5)(c), paragraph (a) of subsection (3) may be satisfied by providing an electronic link to a website, or to a portal, in which the information mentioned in that paragraph is set out.

(5)   For the purposes of subsection (1)(a), service of a notice must be by—

(a)   delivering the notice personally to the debtor,

(b)   sending it—

(i)   by postal services, or

(ii)   by any other service which conveys postal packets from one place to another,

either to the proper address of the debtor or to an address for postal communication provided to the assignor by the debtor, or

(c)   transmitting it to an address for electronic communication so provided.

(6)   But a determination (a 'determination as to method of service') may be made in accordance with subsection (7) that, as respects the claim (either or both)—

(a) only certain paragraphs and sub-paragraphs of subsection (5), as specified in the determination, are to apply for the purposes of section 3(2)(b)(i),

(b) subsection (5) is to apply as if for the closing words of paragraph (b) there were substituted a reference to a particular address as specified in the determination.

(7)   A determination as to method of service is made in accordance with this subsection where it is made—

(a) by written agreement between the debtor and the holder of the claim, or

(b) where a unilateral undertaking gives rise to the claim, by a written statement (whether or not comprised within the undertaking) of the person whose undertaking it was.

(8) Where a determination as to method of service specifies an address as mentioned in subsection (6)(b)—

(a) the debtor may notify the holder of the claim of a different address to replace—

(i)   the address so specified, or

(ii)   an address previously notified under this paragraph, and

(b) an address notified under paragraph (a) is, until a further address is so notified, to be treated for the purposes of subsection (6)(b) as if it were specified in the determination.

(9)   Where a notice is served—

(a) as mentioned in subsection (5)(b) (including, where relevant, as modified by subsection (6)(b)), and

(b) by being sent to an address in the United Kingdom,

it is to be taken to have been received 48 hours after it is sent unless it is shown to have been received earlier.

(10)   Where a notice is served as mentioned in subsection (5)(c), it is to be taken to have been received 24 hours after it is transmitted unless it is shown to have been received earlier.

(11)   In this section—

'holder of the claim' includes a person who becomes the holder of the claim after a determination is made,

'postal packet' and 'postal services' have the meanings given by section 27(1) and (2) of the Postal Services Act 2011,

'proper address of the debtor' means—

(a) in the case of a body corporate, the address of the registered or principal office of the body,

(b) in the case of a partnership, the address of the principal office of the partnership, and

(c) in any other case, the last known address of the debtor.

(12)   Any reference in this section to—

(a) a notice being served on the debtor is to be construed as including a reference to its being served on a person authorised to receive such a notice on behalf of the debtor,

(b) the proper address of the debtor is, where a notice is served on a person so authorised, to be construed as a reference to the proper address of that person.

9   Warrandice implied in the assignation of a claim

(1)   Subsections (2) to (5) apply except in so far as the assignor and the assignee agree otherwise.

(2)   In granting, for value, an assignation document in respect of a claim, the assignor is taken to warrant to the assignee that—

(a) the assignor is entitled to, or (in the case of any such claim as is mentioned in section 1(4)) will be entitled to, transfer the claim to the assignee,

(b) the debtor is obliged to, or (when performance becomes due) will be obliged to, perform in full to the assignor, and

(c) the assignor has done nothing, and will do nothing, to prejudice the assignation.

(3)   In granting, other than for value, an assignation document in respect of a claim, the assignor is taken to warrant to the assignee that the assignor will do nothing to prejudice the assignation.

(4)   In granting an assignation document in respect of a claim (whether or not for value), the assignor is not taken to warrant to the assignee that the debtor will perform to the assignee.

(5)   Subsections (2) to (4) apply in relation to providing, in a contract or unilateral undertaking, for the assignation of a claim as they apply in relation to the granting of an assignation document in respect of a claim.

Protection of debtors

10   Protection of debtor who performs in good faith

(1)   Subsection (2) applies where, after a claim is transferred, the debtor, or any co-debtor, performs in good faith to the person last known to the debtor, or that co-debtor, to be the holder of the claim.

(2)   The debtor, or (where there are two or more co-debtors) each of the co-debtors, is discharged from the claim to the extent of the performance.

(3)   For the purpose of subsection (2), it is not to be taken that a debtor, or any co-debtor, has performed other than in good faith by reason only of (any or all of)—

(a)   an assignation document's having been registered,

(b)   the application of section 8(9),

(c)   the application of section 8(10).

11   Further provision as to protection of debtor

(1)   Subsection (2) applies where—

(a)   the holder of a claim purports to assign the claim (or the same part of the claim) by means of more than one assignation document, each in favour of a different person,

(b)   the claim (or part) is transferred to one of those persons,

(c)   the debtor, or any co-debtor, receives notice of the purported assignation to the other (or, as the case may be, another) of those persons (the 'purported assignee'), from the person who granted the purported assignation or from the purported assignee, in the manner mentioned in section 8(1)(a) or (b)(ii), and

(d)   by virtue of that notice, the debtor, or any co-debtor, performs in good faith to the purported assignee.

(2)   The debtor, or (where there are two or more co-debtors) each of the co-debtors, is discharged from the claim (or part) to the extent of the performance.

(3)   Section 10(3) applies for the purposes of subsection (2) as it applies for the purposes of section 10(2).

12   Performance in good faith where claim assigned cannot be transferred by intimation

(1)   Subsection (2) applies where—

(a)   by virtue only of being of a type prescribed under section 3(8), a claim in respect of which an assignation document is granted is not transferred, and

(b)   the debtor, or any co-debtor, performs in good faith to the assignee.

(2)   The debtor, or (where there are two or more co-debtors) each of the co-debtors, is discharged from the claim to the extent of the performance.

(3)   For the purposes of subsection (1)(b), a debtor, or co-debtor, is not to be taken to perform in good faith where that debtor or co-debtor knows—

(a)   that the assignation document has not been registered, and

(b)   that transfer of the claim requires registration.

13   Performance in good faith where claim assigned subject to condition

(1)   Subsection (2) applies where—

(a)   a claim in respect of which an assignation document is granted is subject to a condition which must be satisfied before the claim is transferred,

(b) the claim has not yet been transferred by virtue only of the condition not yet being satisfied, and

(c) the debtor, or any co-debtor, performs in good faith to the assignee.

(2) The debtor, or (where there are two or more co-debtors) each of the co-debtors, is discharged from the claim to the extent of the performance.

(3) Section 10(3) applies for the purposes of subsection (2) as it applies for the purposes of section 10(2).

14   Asserting defence or right of compensation

(1) Except in so far as the debtor and the assignor agree otherwise before an assignation document is granted in respect of the claim, the debtor, or any co-debtor, may assert against the assignee any defence which the debtor, or co-debtor, would have had the right to assert against the assignor.

(2) Nothing in subsection (1) affects the operation of any other enactment which restricts or prevents the making of such an agreement.

(3) For the purposes of any enactment or rule of law concerning compensation, set-off, retention, balancing of accounts or counterclaims, a debtor is not to be treated as receiving notice of the assignation of a claim only because an assignation document is registered in respect of the claim.

15   Right to withhold performance until information as to assignation is provided

(1) A debtor on whom a notice of assignation of a claim is served under section 8(1)(a) by an assignee may request from the assignee reasonable evidence of the granting of an assignation document in respect of the claim.

(2) For the purposes of subsection (1), 'reasonable evidence' includes, for example, the written confirmation of an assignor that the assignor granted the document.

(3) Subsection (1) applies to a purported notice of assignation as it applies to a notice of assignation, and a reference in that subsection to an assignee includes a reference to a purported assignee.

(4) If evidence is requested under subsection (1), the debtor may withhold performance until—

(a) that evidence is received, or

(b) the debtor receives notification in writing from the purported assignee or the purported assignor that an assignation document has not been granted in respect of the claim.

(5) A debtor who, other than by virtue of section 8(1), has reasonable grounds to believe that an assignation document has been granted in respect of a claim may state those grounds to the supposed assignor and request that person to provide a written statement as to whether the document has been granted.

(6) If a written statement provided by virtue of subsection (5) is to the effect that the document has been granted, that statement must include the name and last known address of the assignee.

(7) If a written statement is requested under subsection (5), the debtor may withhold performance until that statement (conforming, where it is a statement to the effect mentioned in subsection (6), with the requirements of that subsection) is received.

(8) A debtor who knows that an assignation document has been granted in respect of a claim may request the assignor or the assignee to provide a written statement as to whether (either or both)—

(a) the assignation of the claim is subject to a condition,

(b) any such condition has been satisfied.

(9) If a written statement is requested under subsection (8), the debtor may withhold performance until that statement is received.

(10) Where a debtor who makes a request under subsection (1), (5) or (8) is a co-debtor, the reference in subsection (4) or (as the case may be) (7) or (9) to the debtor is to the debtor who made the request and does not include a reference to any co-debtor of that debtor.

Accessory security rights

16   Accessory security rights
 (1)   Subsections (2) and (3)—
  (a)   apply, and apply only, in relation to any claim assigned in whole, but
  (b)   are subject to any express provision to the contrary in the assignation document.
 (2)   Subject to anything which requires to be done under subsection (3), the assignee acquires, by virtue of the transfer of the claim, any security (in so far as the security is transferable) which relates to, and only to, the claim transferred.
 (3)   Where the performance of some act by the assignor is necessary for the security to transfer to the assignee, the assignor must—
  (a)   perform that act, and
  (b)   do so as soon as reasonably practicable after the claim is transferred.
 (4)   In this section, 'security' means both—
  (a)   a right in security, and
  (b)   the correlative right in respect of a cautionary obligation.

Abolition of certain rules of law

17   Abolition of certain rules of law
 (1)   The following rules of law are abolished insofar as they apply to an assignation of a claim to which this Part applies—
  (a)   any rule whereby a mandate may operate as an assignation of a claim,
  (b)   any rule whereby an assignation is rendered ineffective by an instruction to the debtor by an assignee of a claim that the debtor perform to the assignor,
  (c)   any rule whereby an assignee of a claim may sue in the name of an assignor, and
  (d)   any rule as to warrandice to be implied—
   (i)   in assigning a claim, or
   (ii)   in providing, in a contract or unilateral undertaking, for the assignation of a claim.
 (2)   But subsection (1)(c) does not affect the application of any enactment, or any rule of law, as respects subrogation.

Saving

18   Saving as respects International Interests in Aircraft Equipment (Cape Town Convention) Regulations 2015
 (1)   This Part is without prejudice to the application, as respects the assignment and acquisition of associated rights, of the International Interests in Aircraft Equipment (Cape Town Convention) Regulations 2015 (S.I. 2015/912).
 (2)   In subsection (1)—
'assignment' has the meaning given by regulation 5, as read with regulation 35, of those regulations, and
'associated rights' has the meaning given by regulation 5 of those regulations.

CHAPTER 2
REGISTER OF ASSIGNATIONS

Register of Assignations

19   The Register of Assignations
 (1)   There is to be a public register known as the Register of Assignations.
 (2)   The register is to be under the management and control of the Keeper.
 (3)   Subject to the provisions of this Act, the register is to be in such form as the Keeper thinks fit.

(4) The Keeper must take such steps as appear reasonable to the Keeper to protect the register from—

    (a) interference,

    (b) unauthorised access, and

    (c) damage.

Structure and contents of the register

20   The parts of the register

The Keeper must make up and maintain, as parts of the register—

    (a) the assignations record, and

    (b) the archive record.

21   The assignations record

(1) An entry in the assignations record is to comprise—

    (a) the assignor's name and address,

    (b) where the assignor is an individual, the assignor's date of birth,

    (c) any identifying number which the assignor has and which, by virtue of RoA Rules, must be included in the entry,

    (d) the assignee's name and address,

    (e) any identifying number which the assignee has and which, by virtue of RoA Rules, must be included in the entry,

    (f) where the assignee is not an individual, an address (which may be an email address) to which any request for information regarding the assignation may be sent,

    (g) such description of the claim as is required, or permitted, for the purposes of this subsection by RoA Rules,

    (h) a copy of the assignation document,

    (i) the registration number allocated under section 25(1)(b) to the entry,

    (j) the date and time of registration of the assignation document,

    (k) any other information that is required under any other section of this Act, and

    (l) any other information that is specified for the purposes of this subsection by RoA Rules.

(2) The assignations record is the totality of all such entries.

22   The archive record

The archive record is the totality of—

    (a) all entries and copy documents transferred from the assignations record under section 30(1)(a) or (2)(c),

    (b) all copy documents included in the archive record under section 30(1)(c) or (2)(b),

    (c) all copies of such other documents as the Keeper considers it appropriate to include in the archive record, and

    (d) any other information that is specified for the purposes of this section by RoA Rules.

Registration process

23   Application for registration

(1) An assignee may apply to the Keeper for registration of an assignation document.

(2) The Keeper must deal with applications in the order in which they are received.

(3) The Keeper must accept the application if—

    (a) it is submitted with a copy of the assignation document,

    (b) it contains all the information the Keeper requires in accordance with section 21 to be able to make up an entry for the assignation document under section 25(1),

    (c) it conforms to such RoA Rules as relate to the application, and
    (d) either—
        (i)   such fee as is payable for the registration is paid, or
        (ii) arrangements satisfactory to the Keeper are made for payment of that
    fee.
(4)   If the requirements of subsection (3) are not satisfied, the Keeper must reject
the application and inform the applicant accordingly.

24   Application for registration where claims assigned to different assignees

(1)   Where an assignation document assigns different claims to different assignees, each assignee may apply to the Keeper for registration of the document only in
so far as it assigns a claim to that assignee ('the applicant').

(2)   A reference in this Part, in relation to an assignation document in respect of
which such an application has been accepted by the Keeper, to—
    (a) the registration of the document is a reference to the registration of the doc-
ument in so far as it assigns a claim to the applicant,
    (b) the assignee under the document is a reference to the applicant,
    (c) a claim assigned by the document is a reference to a claim assigned by the
document to the applicant.

25   Registration

(1)   On accepting an application made under section 23, the Keeper must—
    (a) make up an entry for the assignation document (from the assignation
document, the information provided in the application and the circumstances of
registration),
    (b) allocate a registration number to the entry (based on the order in which
applications are dealt with), and
    (c) maintain the entry in the assignations record.

(2)   An assignation document is taken to be registered on the date and at the time
entered for it for the purpose of section 21(1)(j).

26   Verification statement

(1)   After the registration of an assignation document under section 25, the Keeper
must issue a written statement verifying the registration to—
    (a) the assignor, and
    (b) the assignee,
but only if and to the extent that the application made under section 23 contains an
email address for those persons.

(2)   That statement must—
    (a) include—
        (i)   the date and time of the registration, and
        (ii) the registration number allocated to the entry made up for the assigna-
tion document, and
    (b) conform to such RoA Rules as relate to the statement.

(3)   Where a statement is issued under subsection (1) and is received by the
assignee but not the assignor, the assignor may request a copy of it from the assignee.

(4)   Within 21 days beginning with the day a request is made under subsection (3),
the assignee must supply the assignor with the copy requested.

Effective registration

27   Effective registration of assignation document

(1)   The registration of an assignation document is ineffective if—
    (a) the entry made up for the assignation document in the assignations record—
        (i)   does not include a copy of the assignation document, or
        (ii) is, at the time of registration, seriously misleading as a result of an inac-
curacy or inaccuracies in it, or
    (b) the assignation document is invalid.

(2)   But subsection (1)(a)(ii) is subject to section 28(1)(c) and (d).
(3)   Where the registration of an assignation document is ineffective by virtue of subsection (1), it becomes effective if and when the entry is corrected.

28   Seriously misleading inaccuracies in the assignations record

(1)   In determining for the purpose of section 27(1)(a)(ii) whether an entry in the assignations record is seriously misleading as a result of an inaccuracy or inaccuracies in it—
   (a)   the entry is seriously misleading where—
      (i)   any of subsections (2) to (5) apply, or
      (ii)   despite sub-paragraph (i) not being satisfied, the inaccuracy or inaccuracies are such that a reasonable person would be seriously misled by the entry,
   (b)   any inaccuracy is to be disregarded to the extent that it appears in the assignation document but is not replicated elsewhere in the entry,
   (c)   where the entry is seriously misleading in respect of only part of the assigned claim, that is not to be taken to affect the entry in its application to the rest of the claim,
   (d)   where the entry is seriously misleading in respect of a co-assignor or co-assignee but not in respect of both (or all) co-assignors or co-assignees, that is not to be taken to affect the entry in its application to a co-assignor or co-assignee in respect of whom the entry is not seriously misleading.
(2)   This subsection applies where—
   (a)   the assignor is a person required by RoA Rules to be identified in the assignations record by an identifying number, and
   (b)   if a search of the record were to be carried out for that number, using the search facility provided under section 33, it would not disclose the entry.
(3)   This subsection applies where—
   (a)   the assignor is not a person required by RoA Rules to be identified in the assignations record by an identifying number, and
   (b)   if a search of the record were to be carried out, using the search facility provided under section 33, for—
      (i)   the assignor's proper name at the date the application for registration was made, or
      (ii)   the assignor's proper name at that date together with the assignor's month and year of birth,
it would not disclose the entry.
(4)   This subsection applies where the entry inaccurately reflects the assignee's proper name at the date the application for registration was made in such a way that a reasonable person would be seriously misled.
(5)   This subsection applies where—
   (a)   there is a requirement, by virtue of section 21(1)(g), for an entry in the assignations record to specify the type of claim assigned, and
   (b)   the entry—
      (i)   describes the claim as being of a type that it is not, or
      (ii)   fails to allocate a type to the claim.
(6)   In the application of this section to co-assignors and co-assignees—
   (a)   subsections (2) and (3) apply in relation to a co-assignor as they apply in relation to an assignor,
   (b)   subsection (4) applies in relation to a co-assignee as it applies in relation to an assignee.
(7)   The Scottish Ministers may by regulations modify this section to make provision about what does, and what does not, make an entry seriously misleading for the purpose of section 27(1)(a)(ii) and how that is to be determined.
(8)   In this section, the 'proper name' of an assignor or assignee means the person's name in the form determined in accordance with RoA Rules.

Corrections

29   Correction of the assignations record

(1)   Where a court determines in any proceedings that the assignations record is inaccurate, the court—

(a)   must direct the Keeper to correct the record, and

(b)   may give the Keeper any further direction it considers necessary in connection with the correction.

(2)   Where the Keeper becomes aware of a manifest inaccuracy in the assignations record, other than as a result of a direction under subsection (1)—

(a)   the Keeper must correct the record if what is needed to correct it is manifest,

(b)   otherwise, the Keeper must note the inaccuracy on the entry in question.

(3)   There is an 'inaccuracy' in the assignations record where—

(a)   the information included, by virtue of section 21(1), in an entry in the record is inaccurate or incomplete,

(b)   an entry in the record—

(i)   does not include a copy of the assignation document as required by paragraph (h) of that section, or

(ii)   includes such a copy but the document copied is invalid, or

(c)   an entry has incorrectly been removed from the record.

(4)   A correction of the assignations record may involve—

(a)   the removal of an entry,

(b)   the removal of information included in an entry,

(c)   the amendment of, or an addition to, the information, or replacement of a copy document, included in an entry,

(d)   the restoration of information, or of a copy document, to an entry,

(e)   the restoration of an entry (whether or not by transferring it from the archive record to the assignations record).

(5)   A correction is taken to be made on the date and at the time entered for it in the register in pursuance of a provision of this Part.

30   Correction of the assignations record: procedure

(1)   Where the Keeper corrects the assignations record by removing an entry from the assignations record, the Keeper must—

(a)   transfer the entry to the archive record,

(b)   note on the transferred entry—

(i)   the subsection of section 29 by virtue of which the transfer is made, and

(ii)   the details of the correction (including the date and time of the removal), and

(c)   include in the archive record a copy of any document which discloses, or contributes to disclosing, the inaccuracy which is the subject of the correction.

(2)   Where the Keeper corrects the record by restoring an entry, by restoring, removing or amending information included in an entry or by restoring or replacing a copy document, the Keeper must—

(a)   note on the entry that it has been corrected and the details of the correction (including the date and time of the correction),

(b)   include in the archive record a copy of any document which discloses, or contributes to disclosing, the inaccuracy which is the subject of the correction, and

(c)   in the case of the replacement of the copy document, transfer the replaced copy to the archive record.

(3)   Having corrected the record, the Keeper must notify the following persons (in so far as it is reasonable and practicable to do so) that the correction has been made—

(a)   every person specified for the purposes of this subsection by RoA Rules, and

(b)   any other person who appears to the Keeper to be affected by it materially.

(4)   A failure to comply with subsection (1)(c), (2)(b) or (3) does not affect the validity of the correction of the record.

31 Proceedings involving the accuracy of the assignations record

The Keeper is entitled to appear and be heard in any civil proceedings, whether before a court or tribunal, in which—

(a) the accuracy of the assignations record, or

(b) what is needed to correct an inaccuracy in the record,

is put in question.

32 Power to make provision about applications for corrections

(1) The Scottish Ministers may by regulations modify this Part to make provision for or about applications to the Keeper for the correction of an entry in the assignations record.

(2) Regulations under subsection (1) may, in particular—

(a) make provision about—

(i) the persons, or descriptions of persons, who are entitled to make an application,

(ii) the circumstances in which an application is to be accepted (which may include consideration of whether there has been payment of a fee), and

(iii) the steps to be taken where an application is accepted,

(b) modify the Keeper's duty to act on becoming aware of a manifest inaccuracy in the assignations record to take account of the application process, and

(c) allow RoA Rules to make provision about the procedure in relation to applications for corrections.

Searches and extracts

33 Searching the assignations record

(1) The Keeper must provide a facility by which the assignations record may be searched.

(2) That search facility must allow the assignations record to be searched by reference to, and only by reference to—

(a) any of the following information in the entries contained in that record—

(i) the names of assignors, which must be capable of being searched with and without the months and years of birth of assignors who are individuals,

(ii) the identifying numbers of assignors required by RoA Rules to be identified in the assignations record by such a number,

(b) registration numbers allocated, under section 25(1)(b), to entries in that record, or

(c) any other factor, or characteristic, specified for the purposes of this paragraph by RoA Rules.

(3) Subject to any restrictions imposed under RoA Rules, a person may search the assignations record using the search facility provided under subsection (1) provided that either—

(a) such fee as is payable for the search is paid, or

(b) arrangements satisfactory to the Keeper are made for payment of that fee.

(4) But no fee is payable for a search of the assignations record which is carried out on behalf of an individual by a not-for-profit money adviser (being an adviser who does not charge individuals for the adviser's services).

(5) The Scottish Ministers may, by regulations, make further provision about the meaning of 'not-for-profit money adviser' for the purposes of subsection (4).

34 Admissibility and evidential status of search results

(1) A copy of a search result (in printed or electronic form) which relates to a search carried out by means of a search facility provided by the Keeper is admissible in evidence.

(2) In the absence of evidence to the contrary—

(a) where such a search result purports to show an entry in the assignations record, it is sufficient proof of—

(i) the registration of the assignation document to which the result relates,

(ii)   where applicable, a correction of the entry in the assignations record to which the result relates, and

(iii)   the date and time of such registration or, as the case may be, correction, and

(b)   where such a search result purports not to show an entry in the assignations record, it is sufficient proof of an entry in the assignations record not being disclosed at the date and time of such search by means of the search carried out.

35   Extracts and their evidential status

(1)   A person may apply to the Keeper for an extract of an entry in the register.

(2)   The Keeper must issue the extract if—

(a)   such fee as is payable for issuing it is paid, or

(b)   arrangements satisfactory to the Keeper are made for payment of that fee.

(3)   But if, on application under subsection (1), the applicant requests an extract as at a specific date and time, the Keeper need comply with the request only to the extent that it is reasonably practicable to do so.

(4)   The Keeper may validate the extract as the Keeper considers appropriate.

(5)   The Keeper may issue the extract as an electronic document unless the applicant requests that it be issued as a traditional document.

(6)   The extract is to be accepted for all purposes as sufficient evidence of the contents of the entry as at—

(a)   in the case of an extract requested as mentioned in subsection (3), the date and time to which the extract relates (being a date and time specified in the extract), and

(b)   in any other case, the date on which and the time at which the extract is issued (being a date and time specified in the extract).

Requests for information

36   Assignee's duty to respond to request for information

(1)   An entitled person may ask the person identified in an entry in the assignations record as the assignee (the 'registered assignee') to provide the entitled person with a written statement as to whether—

(a)   a claim specified by the entitled person is assigned by the assignation document,

(b)   the registered assignee has granted a further assignation document in respect of the claim, or

(c)   a condition specified by the entitled person and to which the assignation is subject has been satisfied.

(2)   The following are entitled persons for the purposes of this section—

(a)   in relation to a request under subsection (1), a person who (depending on who holds the claim) may have a right to execute diligence against the claim, or

(b)   a person not mentioned in paragraph (a) but who has the consent of the person identified in the entry as the assignor to make a request under subsection (1).

(3)   For the purposes of subsection (2)(a), a person who may have a right to execute diligence against the claim includes a person authorised to execute a charge for payment who (depending on who holds the claim) may have a right to execute diligence against the claim if and when the days of charge expire without payment.

(4)   The registered assignee must, within 21 days beginning with the day of receiving a request under subsection (1), comply with it unless—

(a)   it is manifest that the registration is ineffective in relation to the assignation of the claim to which the request relates,

(b)   in the case of a request made under subsection (1)(a), it is manifest from the entry for the assignation that the claim specified is not assigned by the assignation document,

(c) both—

(i) the registered assignee has, within the period of 3 months ending with the day of receipt of the request, complied with a request under the same paragraph of subsection (1) from the same person and in relation to the same claim, and

(ii) the information contained in the statement issued in relation to the earlier request remains correct.

(5) The registered assignee may recover from the entitled person any costs reasonably incurred in complying with the request.

(6) On the application of the registered assignee, the court may by order—

(a) exempt the registered assignee from complying with a request under subsection (1) or such part of the request as it specifies in the order, or

(b) extend the period within which the registered assignee must comply with the request by such number of days as it specifies in the order,

if satisfied that in all the circumstances it would be reasonable to do so.

(7) If, on the application of the entitled person, the court is satisfied that the registered assignee has, without reasonable excuse, failed to comply with subsection (4), it may by order require the registered assignee to comply with the request within 14 days or such other period (which may be longer or shorter than 14 days) as the court considers appropriate.

(8) The Scottish Ministers may by regulations modify this section so as to specify further persons, or descriptions of persons, who are entitled persons for the purposes of this section.

Entitlement to compensation

37 Liability of Keeper

(1) A person is entitled to be compensated by the Keeper for loss suffered in consequence of—

(a) an inaccuracy in the assignations record to the extent that it is attributable to the making up, maintenance or operation of the register (including an attempted correction of it),

(b) the issue, under section 26(1), of a written statement which is incorrect,

(c) the service, under section 30(3), of a notification which is incorrect,

(d) a search result which—

(i) relates to a search of the assignations record carried out by means of a search facility provided by the Keeper,

(ii) ought (as a result of the search terms used) to reflect accurately the contents of the assignations record at the time the search was made, and

(iii) does not accurately reflect those contents,

(e) the issue, under section 35, of an extract which is not a true extract,

(f) an application being accepted or rejected in error,

(g) an attempt to make an application, which the Keeper would otherwise have accepted, failing as a result of an error in the system the Keeper has for accepting applications, or

(h) applications being dealt with otherwise than in the order in which they are received.

(2) But the Keeper has no liability under subsection (1)—

(a) in so far as the person's loss could have been avoided had the person taken measures which it would have been reasonable for the person to take,

(b) in so far as the person's loss was not reasonably foreseeable, or

(c) for non-patrimonial loss.

(3) For the avoidance of doubt, an inaccuracy in information included in an entry in the assignations record when that entry is made up under section 25(1)(a) or corrected under section 29 does not fall within subsection (1)(a) to the extent that the Keeper—

(a) has been misled into making the inaccuracy, and

(b) reasonably believed the information to be accurate.

(4) For the purposes of subsection (3), the circumstances where the Keeper is entitled to reasonably believe information to be accurate include those where it is provided—

(a) in connection with an application to which the entry relates, or

(b) by the court.

38 Liability of certain other persons

(1) A person ('P') is entitled to be compensated in the following circumstances—

(a) where P suffers loss in consequence of an inaccuracy in an entry in the assignations record then, to the extent that it is not attributable to the Keeper, P is entitled to be compensated for that loss by—

(i) the person who made the application for registration which gave rise to the inaccurate entry if that person failed to take reasonable care in making it, or

(ii) where the inaccurate entry arises from the attempted correction of an apparent inaccuracy, the person who notified the Keeper of the apparent inaccuracy if that person failed to take reasonable care in doing so,

(b) where P suffers loss in consequence of an inaccuracy in information supplied in response to a request under section 36(1), P is entitled to be compensated for that loss by the person who supplied the information if that person failed to take reasonable care in supplying it, or

(c) where P suffers loss in consequence of a failure, without reasonable excuse, to comply with a request in accordance with section 36(4), P is entitled to be compensated for that loss by the person whose failure it was.

(2) But a person has no liability under subsection (1)—

(a) in so far as P's loss could have been avoided had P taken measures which it would have been reasonable for P to take,

(b) in so far as P's loss was not reasonably foreseeable, or

(c) for non-patrimonial loss.

Rules

39 Rules

(1) The Scottish Ministers may by regulations make rules ('RoA Rules')—

(a) about the making up and keeping of the register,

(b) about the procedure in relation to applications for registration under section 23(1),

(c) about searches in the register and the results of those searches,

(d) about the required form and content of any document or information to be used in relation to the register,

(e) requiring there to be entered in the assignations record or the archive record such information as is specified in the rules, or

(f) regarding other matters in relation to registration under this Part, being matters for which the Scottish Ministers consider it necessary or expedient to provide in order to give full effect to the purposes of this Part.

(2) RoA Rules under subsection (1) may, in particular, include provision—

(a) about the identification, in any application and in the register, of any person or claim, including—

(i) how the proper form of a person's name is to be determined, and

(ii) where the person has an identifying number (whether of numerals or of letters and numerals) allocated to the person, whether that number must be used in identifying the person,

(b) about the nature of the address of the assignor or the assignee to be included in an entry in the register,

(c) about the degree of precision with which time is to be recorded in the register,

(d) about information which, though contained in an assignation document, need not be included in a copy of that document submitted with an application under section 23(1),

(e) about whether a signature contained in an assignation document need be included in a copy of that document so submitted,

(f) about information which, though contained in the register, is not to be—

(i) available to persons searching it, or

(ii) included in any extract issued under section 35,

(g) about when the register is open for—

(i) registration,

(ii) searches.

(3) Before laying a draft of a Scottish statutory instrument containing regulations under subsection (1) before the Scottish Parliament, the Scottish Ministers must consult the Keeper.

CHAPTER 3

MISCELLANEOUS AND INTERPRETATION OF PART 1

Miscellaneous

40 Repeal of Transmission of Moveable Property (Scotland) Act 1862

The Transmission of Moveable Property (Scotland) Act 1862 is repealed.

Interpretation of Part 1

41 Interpretation of Part 1

(1) In this Part (except where the context requires otherwise)—

'the archive record' is to be construed in accordance with section 22,

'assignation' means assignation of a claim,

'assignation document' has the meaning given by section 1(1),

'the assignations record' is to be construed in accordance with section 21(2),

'assignee' means the person to whom a claim is assigned,

'assignor' means the person by whom a claim is assigned,

'claim'—

(a) means a right to the performance of an obligation (including an obligation not to do something), but

(b) does not include a non-monetary right relating to land or a negotiable instrument,

'correction', in relation to the assignations record, is to be construed in accordance with section 29(4),

'debtor' means the person against whom a claim may be enforced,

'holder', in relation to a claim, means the person who has the right to performance of an obligation under the claim,

'inaccuracy', in relation to the assignations record, is to be construed in accordance with section 29(3),

'the register' means the Register of Assignations,

'right in security'—

(a) means a right in security over property (including a floating charge), but

(b) does not include a right to execute diligence,

'RoA Rules' has the meaning given by section 39(1).

(2) Where two or more persons are co-assignors or co-assignees in relation to a claim, any reference in this Act to the assignor or assignee (as the case may be) is, unless the context requires otherwise, a reference to all of those persons.

(3) A reference (however expressed) in this Part to—

(a) an assignation document having been granted in respect of a claim is to be construed as a reference to the document having been executed or authenticated,

(b) an assignation document being registered is to be construed as a reference to the Keeper's carrying out, in respect of the document, the duties imposed on the Keeper by section 25(1)(a) and (b).

PART 2
SECURITY OVER MOVEABLE PROPERTY

CHAPTER 1
PLEDGE

Pledge, secured obligation and encumbered property

42 Pledge

(1)   A pledge is created in accordance with this section.

(2)   Where a pledge is to be created over moveable property which is corporeal only, the pledge is created—

(a) by delivery of the property to the secured creditor, provided that the property is the provider's at the time of delivery,

(b) in a case where the property is not the provider's at the time of such delivery, on the property becoming the provider's subsequent to such delivery, or

(c) by registration in accordance with section 48 or 49.

(3)   Where a pledge is to be created over moveable property which is—

(a) incorporeal only, or

(b) both corporeal and incorporeal,

the pledge is created by registration in accordance with section 48 or 49.

(4)   A pledge created by registration in accordance with section 48 or 49 is to be known as a 'statutory pledge'.

(5)   Nothing in this section affects any rule of law which existed prior to the commencement of this section whereby a pledge may be created over a negotiable instrument, and nothing in this Part applies in relation to any pledge created in accordance with such a rule.

43 Secured obligation and encumbered property

(1)   The obligation secured by a pledge ('the secured obligation')—

(a) may be any obligation owed, or which will or may become owed, to or by any person, and

(b) includes ancillary obligations owed (for example, to pay interest, damages and the reasonable expense of extra-judicial recovery of interest or damages).

(2)   The property over which a pledge is created and in respect of which the pledge subsists ('the encumbered property') includes, except in so far as the provider and the secured creditor agree otherwise, the natural fruits of the property but not its incorporeal fruits.

(3)   At the time the pledge is created, the property which is to be the encumbered property must be transferable (whether or not its transferability is restricted in some way).

Possessory pledge

44 Delivery

(1)   For the purposes of section 42(2)(a) and (b), delivery must be carried out—

(a) by physically handing over, or giving control of, the property to the relevant person,

(b) by giving control of the premises in which the property is located to the relevant person,

(c) by instructing another person who has direct possession or custody of the property to hold the property on behalf of the relevant person, or

(d) by delivering a bill of lading representing the property to the relevant person (and where that bill is to the order of a particular person, by procuring the endorsement of the bill in favour of the secured creditor).

(2)   Property which, at the time agreement is reached on the creation of the pledge, is already in the direct possession or custody of the relevant person is deemed to

have been delivered to the secured creditor for the purposes of section 42(2)(a) or, as the case may be, (b).

(3)   In this section, 'relevant person' means—

(a)   the secured creditor, or

(b)   a person authorised to accept delivery on behalf of the secured creditor or, where subsection (2) applies, authorised to hold the property on behalf of the secured creditor.

(4)   This section is without prejudice to section 2 of the Factors Act 1889.

Statutory pledge

45   Constitutive document

(1)   A statutory pledge requires a constitutive document.

(2)   The constitutive document must—

(a)   be executed or authenticated by the provider,

(b)   identify the property which is to be the encumbered property, and

(c)   identify the obligation which is to be the secured obligation.

(3)   If the encumbered property is to consist of more than one item, the constitutive document must—

(a)   identify each item separately, or

(b)   identify the items in terms of their constituting an identifiable class.

(4)   The property identified (whether separately or as a class) as the property which is to be the encumbered property may be either property of, or property to be acquired by, the provider.

(5)   For the purposes of subsections (2) and (3), the ways in which the encumbered property or the secured obligation can be identified in the constitutive document include by making reference in the constitutive document to another document, the terms of which are not reproduced.

46   Competence of individual acting as provider of a statutory pledge

(1)   It is not competent for an individual to be the provider of a statutory pledge unless—

(a)   the individual is acting in the course of—

(i)   the individual's business,

(ii)   the activities of a charity of which the individual is a trustee, or

(iii)   the activities of an unincorporated association (other than a charity) of which the individual is a member, and

(b)   the encumbered property is a permitted asset, or consists only of permitted assets.

(2)   For the purpose of subsection (1)(b), an asset is a 'permitted asset' if—

(a)   it is (as the case may be)—

(i)   used, or to be used, wholly or mainly for the purposes of the individual's business,

(ii)   an asset of the charity, or

(iii)   owned by the individual on behalf of, or jointly with the other members of, the association, and

(b)   in the case of corporeal property, it has a monetary value exceeding £3,000 immediately before the document under which it will become encumbered property is granted.

(3)   The Scottish Ministers may by regulations—

(a)   modify subsection (2)(b) so as to modify the amount for the time being specified there,

(b)   modify this section so as to specify types of property which are or are not permitted assets.

(4)   For the purposes of this section—

(a) 'charity' means—
    (i) a charity within the meaning of section 106 of the Charities and Trustee Investment (Scotland) Act 2005, or
    (ii) an organisation managed or controlled wholly or mainly outwith Scotland and which is registered in a register equivalent to the Scottish Charity Register (kept under section 3 of that Act) for the purposes of the country in which it operates,
(b) a trustee of a charity is one of the persons having the general control and management of the administration of the charity.

47 Competence of creating statutory pledge over certain kinds of property

(1) It is not competent to create a statutory pledge over corporeal property which is—
    (a) an aircraft in respect of which it is competent to register a mortgage in the register of aircraft mortgages kept by the Civil Aviation Authority,
    (b) an aircraft object (as defined in regulation 5 of the International Interests in Aircraft Equipment (Cape Town Convention) Regulations 2015 (S.I. 2015/912)), or
    (c) a ship (or a share in a ship) in respect of which it is competent to register a mortgage in the register of British ships maintained for the United Kingdom under section 8 of the Merchant Shipping Act 1995.
(2) It is not competent to create a statutory pledge over incorporeal property unless that property is—
    (a) intellectual property, or
    (b) an application for, or licence over, intellectual property.
(3) The Scottish Ministers may by regulations modify this section so as to specify further kinds of incorporeal property over which it is competent to create a statutory pledge.

48 Creation of statutory pledge by registration: general

(1) A statutory pledge is created over property which is identified in a constitutive document in accordance with section 45 on the requirements mentioned in subsection (2) all being met.
(2) Those requirements are that—
    (a) the property is the provider's,
    (b) the statutory pledge is registered, and
    (c) the property is identifiable as property to which the constitutive document relates.
(3) Subsection (2)(b) is subject to section 91 (effective registration of statutory pledge) and, accordingly, the requirement of that subsection—
    (a) is not met if the registration of the constitutive document is ineffective in accordance with section 91(1), and
    (b) is met if and when that registration becomes effective in accordance with section 91(3).
(4) This section is subject to section 50 (creation of statutory pledge: insolvency).

49 Creation of statutory pledge over added property

(1) Where a statutory pledge is amended so as to add property to the encumbered property by means of an amendment document under section 58, a statutory pledge is created over the added property on the requirements mentioned in subsection (2) all being met.
(2) Those requirements are that—
    (a) the added property is the provider's,
    (b) the amendment is registered, and
    (c) the added property is identifiable as property to which the amendment document relates.
(3) Subsection (2)(b) is subject to section 92 (effective registration of amendment to statutory pledge) and, accordingly, the requirement of that subsection—

(a) is not met if the registration of the amendment document is ineffective in accordance with section 92(1), and

(b) is met if and when that registration becomes effective in accordance with section 92(3).

(4)   This section is subject to section 50 (creation of statutory pledge: insolvency).

50　Creation of statutory pledge: insolvency

(1)   This section applies where—

(a) the property identified (whether separately or as a class) as the property which is to be the encumbered property under a statutory pledge is or includes property to be acquired by the provider, and

(b) after the pledge is granted, the provider becomes insolvent.

(2)   The statutory pledge is not created over any property which, though identified by the constitutive document or by an amendment document as property to be encumbered, is acquired by the provider after becoming insolvent.

(3)   For the purposes of subsection (2)—

(a) a provider who is an individual, or the estate of which may be sequestrated by virtue of section 6 of the Bankruptcy (Scotland) Act 2016, becomes insolvent when—

(i)   the provider's estate is sequestrated,

(ii)   the provider grants a trust deed for creditors or makes a composition or arrangement with creditors,

(iii)   the provider is adjudged bankrupt,

(iv)   a voluntary arrangement proposed by the provider is approved,

(v)   the provider's application for a debt payment programme is approved under section 2 of the Debt Arrangement and Attachment (Scotland) Act 2002, or

(vi)   the provider becomes subject to any other order or arrangement analogous to any of those mentioned in sub-paragraphs (i) to (v) anywhere in the world, and

(b) a provider other than is mentioned in paragraph (a) becomes insolvent when—

(i)   a decision approving a voluntary arrangement entered into by the provider has effect under section 4A of the Insolvency Act 1986 ('the 1986 Act'),

(ii)   the provider is wound up under Part 4 or 5 of the 1986 Act or under section 367 of the Financial Services and Markets Act 2000,

(iii)   an administrative receiver, as defined in section 251 of the 1986 Act, is appointed over all or part (being a part to which the constitutive document or any amendment document relates) of the property of the provider,

(iv)   the provider enters administration ('enters administration' being construed in accordance with paragraph 1(2) of schedule B1 of the 1986 Act),

(v)   an order under section 901F of the Companies Act 2006 sanctioning a compromise or arrangement entered into by the provider comes into effect over all or part of the property of the provider, or

(vi)   the provider becomes subject to any other order, appointment or arrangement analogous to any of those mentioned in sub-paragraphs (i) to (v) anywhere in the world.

(4)   The Scottish Ministers may by regulations modify subsection (3).

Property encumbered by statutory pledge: effect of transfer by provider

51　Property encumbered by statutory pledge: transfer by provider

(1)   If the provider of a statutory pledge transfers the encumbered property (or any part of it) to a third party, the transferred property remains encumbered by the pledge unless—

(a) the consent mentioned in subsection (2) is obtained,

(b) the third party acquires the property unencumbered under any of sections 53 to 55, or

(c)   the pledge is otherwise extinguished by the transfer, in whole or in relation to the transferred property, under section 52, 93 or 108.

(2)   The consent referred to in subsection (1)(a)—

(a)   is the prior written consent of the secured creditor—

(i)   to the particular transfer, and

(ii)   to the property in question being transferred unencumbered by the pledge, and

(b)   does not include consent granted more than 14 days before the day of the particular transfer.

(3)   Whether to grant or withhold the consent mentioned in subsection (2) must remain at the discretion of the secured creditor (that is, the secured creditor may not agree in advance how that discretion will be exercised).

(4)   The Scottish Ministers may by regulations—

(a)   modify subsection (2) (including by specifying further descriptions of consent by reference to which subsection (1) is to apply),

(b)   modify this section so as to specify further matters relevant to the granting or withholding of consent.

52   Extinction of statutory pledge where dealings inconsistent with a fixed security
If a secured creditor acquiesces, expressly or impliedly, in a provider's transfer of encumbered property (or any part of it) to a third party, other than by means of granting the consent mentioned in section 51(2), the statutory pledge under which the property (or part) was encumbered is extinguished.

53   Acquisition in good faith from seller acting in ordinary course of business

(1)   A purchaser of corporeal property which is encumbered property under a statutory pledge acquires it unencumbered by the statutory pledge, despite the consent mentioned in section 51(2) not having been obtained, if—

(a)   the person from whom the property is acquired is acting in the ordinary course of that person's business, and

(b)   at the time of acquisition, the purchaser is in good faith.

(2)   For the purposes of subsection (1)(b), a purchaser is not to be taken to be other than in good faith by reason only of the statutory pledge having been registered.

54   Acquisition in good faith for personal, domestic or household purposes

(1)   An individual who acquires corporeal property which is encumbered property under a statutory pledge acquires it unencumbered by the statutory pledge, despite the consent mentioned in section 51(2) not having been obtained, if—

(a)   the property is wholly or mainly acquired for personal, domestic or household purposes,

(b)   the acquirer gives value for the property acquired, and

(c)   at the time of acquisition, the acquirer is in good faith.

(2)   For the purposes of subsection (1)(c), an acquirer is not to be taken to be other than in good faith by reason only of the statutory pledge having been registered.

(3)   The Scottish Ministers may by regulations modify subsection (1) so as to—

(a)   limit its application to cases where the value of all that is acquired does not, at the time of acquisition, exceed a specified amount, and

(b)   modify the amount for the time being specified there by virtue of paragraph (a).

55   Acquisition in good faith of motor vehicles

(1)   Subsections (2) to (4) apply where—

(a)   there is a sale agreement (including a conditional sale agreement) or a hire-purchase agreement in respect of a motor vehicle,

(b)   the motor vehicle is encumbered property under a statutory pledge,

(c)   at the time of entering into the agreement, the purchaser or hirer is not a person carrying on a business described in section 29(2) of the Hire-Purchase Act 1964, and

(d) the purchaser or hirer is, at that time, in good faith.

(2)   On the motor vehicle being transferred to the purchaser or hirer in accordance with the agreement, that person acquires it unencumbered by the statutory pledge despite the consent mentioned in section 51(2) not having been obtained.

(3)   And the statutory pledge is not to be enforced against the motor vehicle before the motor vehicle is transferred to the purchaser or hirer in accordance with the agreement.

(4)   But if the transferor is, at the time the agreement is entered into, a person carrying on a business described in section 29(2) of the Hire-Purchase Act 1964, the secured creditor is entitled to receive from the transferor the lesser of—

(a) the amount outstanding in respect of the secured obligation, and

(b) the amount received, or to be received, by the transferor in respect of the acquisition.

(5)   Where the secured creditor receives a sum under subsection (4)—

(a) the provider's liability to the secured creditor under the secured obligation is reduced by the same amount, but

(b) the transferor has a right of relief against the provider in respect of the sum.

(6)   For the purposes of subsection (1)(d), a purchaser or hirer is not to be taken to be other than in good faith by reason only of the statutory pledge having been registered.

(7)   In this section, 'conditional sale agreement', 'hire-purchase agreement' and 'motor vehicle' have the meanings given by section 29(1) of the Hire-Purchase Act 1964.

(8)   The Scottish Ministers may by regulations specify classes of motor vehicles to which subsections (1) to (7) do not apply.

(9)   Regulations under subsection (8) may modify sections 53 and 54 to provide that either or both of those sections do not apply to some or all of the classes of motor vehicle specified under subsection (8).

Rights relating to matrimonial or family home where relevant to a statutory pledge

56 Occupancy and other rights in family home following grant of statutory pledge

(1)   The Matrimonial Homes (Family Protection) (Scotland) Act 1981 ('the 1981 Act') and the Civil Partnership Act 2004 ('the 2004 Act') are amended in accordance with this section.

(2)   After section 2(8) of the 1981 Act and section 102(8) of the 2004 Act, insert—

'(8A) In subsection (1)(a), 'secured loan' includes secured obligation (construed in accordance with section 43(1) of the Moveable Transactions (Scotland) Act 2023).'.

(3)   In section 3 of the 1981 Act and section 103 of the 2004 Act, at the end of subsection (2) insert 'or the rights of any secured creditor in relation to the non-performance of a secured obligation.'.

(4)   After section 3(8) of the 1981 Act, insert—

'(9) In subsection (2)—

'secured creditor' has the meaning given by section 113(1) of the Moveable Transactions (Scotland) Act 2023, and

'secured obligation' is to be construed in accordance with section 43(1) of the Moveable Transactions (Scotland) Act 2023.'.

(5)   After section 103(9) of the 2004 Act, insert—

'(10) In subsection (2)—

'secured creditor' has the meaning given by section 113(1) of the Moveable Transactions (Scotland) Act 2023, and

'secured obligation' is to be construed in accordance with section 43(1) of the Moveable Transactions (Scotland) Act 2023.'.

(6)   In section 6(2) of the 1981 Act and section 106(2) of the 2004 Act, in the definition of 'dealing', after the words 'heritable security' insert ', the grant of a statutory pledge'.

(7)   In section 8 of the 1981 Act, after subsection (2B) insert—

'(2C)   For the purposes of subsection (2A) above, the time of granting a security, in the case of a statutory pledge, is—

(a)   the date of delivery of the constitutive document of the statutory pledge, or

(b)   where the statutory pledge is granted in an amendment document, the date of delivery of that document.'.

(8)   In section 108 of the 2004 Act, after subsection (4) insert—

'(5)   For the purposes of subsection (3), the time of granting a security, in the case of a statutory pledge, is—

(a)   the date of delivery of the constitutive document of the statutory pledge, or

(b)   where the statutory pledge is granted in an amendment document, the date of delivery of that document.'.

(9)   The title of section 8 of the 1981 Act and section 108 of the 2004 Act becomes **'Interests of creditors'**.

Assignation, amendment, restriction or extinction of statutory pledge

57   Assignation of statutory pledge

(1)   Except in so far as the provider and the secured creditor agree otherwise, a statutory pledge may be assigned.

(2)   A statutory pledge is assigned only by the secured creditor executing or authenticating a document assigning the pledge.

(3)   Subject to the provisions of that document, the assignation conveys to the assignee entitlement to the benefit of any notice served, or enforcement procedure commenced, by the assignor in respect of the statutory pledge before the assignation (to the effect that the assignee may proceed as if the assignee served that notice or commenced those procedures).

58   Amendment of statutory pledge

(1)   Subject to section 59(a), a statutory pledge may be amended only by means of a document (an 'amendment document') executed or authenticated by the secured creditor and the provider.

(2)   But an amendment document which relates only to the addition of property to the encumbered property need not be executed or authenticated by the secured creditor.

(3)   An amendment document which relates to the addition of property to the encumbered property must identify the property to be added.

(4)   If the property to be added consists of more than one item, the amendment document must—

(a)   identify each item separately, or

(b)   identify the items in terms of their constituting an identifiable class.

(5)   The property identified (whether separately or as a class) as the property which is to be the added property may be either property of, or property to be acquired by, the provider.

(6)   Where an amendment increases the extent of the statutory pledge—

(a)   the statutory pledge is amended to give effect to the increase only when the amendment is registered effectively (see section 92), and

(b)   subject to any agreement to the contrary by the parties to the amendment document, any other amendments to the statutory pledge made by the amendment document also take effect at the time mentioned in paragraph (a).

(7)   For the purposes of subsection (6), an amendment increases the extent of the statutory pledge where—

(a)   the amendment adds property to the encumbered property, or

(b)   both—

(i)   the extent of the secured obligation is determinable from the terms alone of the entry for it in the statutory pledges record, and

(ii)   the amendment increases that extent.

(8)   For the purposes of subsections (3) and (4), the ways in which property added can be identified in the amendment document include by making reference in the amendment document to another document, the terms of which are not reproduced.

59   Restriction or discharge of statutory pledge

A statutory pledge may be—

(a)   restricted to only part of the encumbered property, or

(b)   discharged,

by means of a written statement by the secured creditor.

Ranking of pledges etc.

60   Ranking

(1)   Subject to the provisions of this section and of any other enactment, the priority in ranking of—

(a)   any two pledges, or

(b)   a pledge and a right in security other than a pledge,

is determined according to their creation, the earlier created having priority over the later.

(2)   Where a provider grants two or more statutory pledges over property which is not the property of the provider at the time the pledges are granted, the priority in ranking of the pledges is determined according to the dates on which and times at which they are registered effectively (see sections 91 and 92), the earlier having priority over the later.

(3)   Where property is subject both to a pledge and to a security arising by operation of law, the security arising by operation of law has priority over the pledge.

(4)   The priority in ranking of a pledge is the same irrespective of whether the secured obligation is an obligation owed or is an obligation which will or may become owed.

(5)   As between any two pledges, or as between a pledge and a right in security other than a pledge, the secured creditors or (as the case may be) the secured creditor and the holder of that other right may set out in a written agreement—

(a)   that there is no priority in ranking, or

(b)   that any priority in ranking is to be determined in a way other than would be the case in the absence of such an agreement.

(6)   An agreement under subsection (5)—

(a)   has effect only as between the parties to it and their successors, and

(b)   is not registrable in the register.

61   Amendment of Companies Act 1985 and Insolvency Act 1986

Both in section 486(1) of the Companies Act 1985 and in section 70(1) of the Insolvency Act 1986, in the definition of 'fixed security'—

(a)   the words from 'a heritable security' to '1970' become paragraph (a) of the definition, and

(b)   after that paragraph insert '; or

(b)   a statutory pledge within the meaning given by section 113(1) of the Moveable Transactions (Scotland) Act 2023;'.

62   Effect of diligence on pledge

(1)   Subsection (2) applies where diligence is executed in respect of property which is, or any part of which is, encumbered by a pledge.

(2)   The pledge has, in respect of the property or (as the case may be) the part, priority in ranking over the diligence except in relation to any part of the secured obligation which consists of a sum—

   (a) advanced after execution of the diligence, and
   (b) not required to be advanced by—
      (i) a contractual agreement entered into before execution of the diligence, or
      (ii) an undertaking entered into before execution of the diligence.

(3) Subsection (4) applies where a pledge is created over property in respect of which, or in respect of part of which, diligence has been executed.

(4) The diligence has, in respect of the property or (as the case may be) the part, priority in ranking over the pledge.

Enforcement of pledge

63 The expression 'pledge' in sections 64 to 77

In sections 64 to 77, the expression 'pledge' does not include a pledge as defined in section 189(1) of the Consumer Credit Act 1974 (that is to say, does not include a pawnee's rights over an article taken in pawn).

64 Enforcement of pledge: general

(1) A pledge is enforceable only in accordance with the provisions of this Part.

(2) A pledge may be enforced—
   (a) in such circumstances as are agreed between the provider and the secured creditor, or
   (b) subject to any such agreement, where there has been a failure to perform the secured obligation.

(3) Any agreement under subsection (2)(a) must be in writing.

(4) In enforcing a pledge, a secured creditor must conform to reasonable standards of commercial practice.

(5) Subsection (2) is subject to sections 55(3), 65 and 66.

65 Pledge enforcement notice

(1) Before taking any other steps to enforce a pledge, the secured creditor must serve a notice in, or as nearly as may be in, the form prescribed for the purposes of this subsection (to be known as a 'pledge enforcement notice') on—
   (a) the provider,
   (b) the debtor in the secured obligation (if a person other than the provider),
   (c) the holder of any other right in security over all or part of the encumbered property,
   (d) any creditor who has executed diligence against all or part of the encumbered property, and
   (e) in the case of a statutory pledge over property which is capable of being occupied, any occupier of all or part of the property (if a person other than the provider).

(2) But—
   (a) paragraph (c) of subsection (1) is to be disregarded if the secured creditor does not know, and cannot reasonably be expected to know, of the right in security mentioned in that paragraph, and
   (b) paragraph (d) of that subsection is to be disregarded if the secured creditor does not know, and cannot reasonably be expected to know, of the diligence executed as mentioned in that paragraph.

(3) If, by virtue of subsection (1)(e) of section 87 of the Consumer Credit Act 1974, a default notice must be served on the provider, the requirements of that section and of section 88 of that Act must be satisfied before a pledge enforcement notice is served.

(4) The Scottish Ministers may by regulations modify this section so as to specify—
   (a) further persons, or descriptions of persons, on whom the secured creditor must serve a pledge enforcement notice (being persons who have statutory duties in relation to the provider's estate),

(b)   cases when the requirement to serve a notice on a person specified by virtue of paragraph (a) is to be disregarded.

66   Whether court order required for enforcement

(1)   A court order is required for enforcing a pledge only—

(a)   as mentioned in subsections (2) and (3),

(b)   where taking possession of, or steps in relation to, encumbered property in accordance with section 67(3) or (4).

(2)   In a case where the provider of a pledge is an individual, a court order is required for enforcing the pledge if the provider is a sole trader and enforcement is against property used wholly or mainly for the purposes of the provider's business.

(3)   A court order is required for enforcing a statutory pledge in respect of property which is the sole or main residence of an individual unless, after the pledge becomes enforceable by virtue of section 64(2), the following persons agree in writing to its being enforced without such an order—

(a)   the secured creditor,

(b)   the provider, and

(c)   the individual whose sole or main residence is the property in question (if a person other than the provider).

(4)   The court is not to grant an order required by subsection (3) unless satisfied that enforcement is reasonable having had regard to all the circumstances of the case.

(5)   Those circumstances include—

(a)   the nature of, and reason for, the default by virtue of which authority to enforce is sought,

(b)   whether the person in default has the ability to remedy the default within a reasonable time,

(c)   whether the secured creditor has done anything to help the person in default remedy the default,

(d)   where it is, or was, appropriate for the person in default to take part in a debt payment programme approved under Part 1 of the Debt Arrangement and Attachment (Scotland) Act 2002, whether that person is taking part, or has taken part, in such a programme, and

(e)   whether reasonable alternative accommodation is available for (or can be expected to be available for) the individual whose sole or main residence is the property in question.

67   Secured creditor's right to take possession of, or steps in relation to, corporeal property

(1)   This section applies in relation to corporeal property in respect of which a secured creditor in a statutory pledge has served a pledge enforcement notice.

(2)   Subject to any court order that is required under section 66, the secured creditor is entitled to—

(a)   take possession of the property, and

(b)   take any reasonable steps necessary to ensure, whether or not by immobilising the property, that it is not disposed of or used in an unauthorised way,

but only in accordance with subsection (3) or, as the case may be, subsection (4).

(3)   Where the property is in the possession of a relevant person, the secured creditor may take possession or steps under subsection (2)—

(a)   with the consent of the relevant person,

(b)   with the consent of the court, through the agency of an authorised person, or

(c)   personally, if authorised to do so by the court.

(4)   Where the property is not in the possession of a relevant person, the secured creditor may take possession or steps under subsection (2)—

(a)   with the consent of—

(i)   the provider, given after the pledge becomes enforceable, and

  (ii) any third party who for the time being either is in direct possession, or has custody, of the property,

 (b) through the agency of an authorised person, or

 (c) personally, if authorised to do so by the court.

(5) For the purposes of subsections (3) and (4), a 'relevant person' is a person who, in respect of the property or of any part of it—

 (a) has a right in security which has priority in ranking over, or ranks equally with, the pledge to which the pledge enforcement notice relates, or

 (b) has executed diligence which has priority in ranking over, or ranks equally with, that pledge.

(6) In taking possession of the property under subsection (2)(a), the secured creditor is entitled to remove any individual from that property, but only through the agency of an authorised person.

(7) In this section, 'authorised person' means a messenger-at-arms or sheriff officer.

(8) The Scottish Ministers may by regulations modify this section so as to specify further persons, or descriptions of persons, who are authorised persons for the purposes of this section.

68 Secured creditor's right to sell

(1) Where a pledge enforcement notice has been served in respect of property, the secured creditor is, subject to any court order that is required under section 66, entitled to sell all or any of that property.

(2) In selling property by virtue of subsection (1), the secured creditor must take all reasonable steps to ensure that the price obtained is the best reasonably obtainable.

(3) The secured creditor is entitled to purchase all or any of the property but only—

 (a) in a sale by public auction, and

 (b) for a price no lower than one which bears a reasonable relationship to market value.

(4) Any proceeds obtained by virtue of subsection (1) are to be held in trust by the secured creditor until applied under section 77.

69 Sale: unencumbered acquisition

(1) This section applies where a secured creditor sells property by virtue of section 68(1) and transfers the property to the purchaser.

(2) The purchaser acquires the property unencumbered by—

 (a) the pledge which was the subject of the pledge enforcement notice, and

 (b) any right in security, or any diligence, ranking equally with or postponed to the pledge.

(3) The purchaser acquires the property unencumbered by—

 (a) any right in security which has priority in ranking over the pledge, or

 (b) any diligence which has priority in ranking over the pledge,

only if the holder of the right in security or, as the case may be, the creditor who executed the diligence consented to the sale.

70 Secured creditor's right to let

(1) A secured creditor who, by virtue of section 68(1), is entitled to sell corporeal property is entitled to let all or any of that property.

(2) In letting property by virtue of subsection (1), the secured creditor must take all reasonable steps to ensure that the income obtained is the best reasonably obtainable.

(3) Any rental income obtained by virtue of subsection (1) is to be held in trust by the secured creditor until applied under section 77.

(4) The provider and the secured creditor may agree, whether before or after the pledge becomes enforceable by virtue of section 64(2), that subsection (1) is not to apply in relation to the corporeal property or some part of it.

(5)   Any such agreement must be in writing.

71 Secured creditor's right to grant licence over intellectual property
(1)   A secured creditor who, by virtue of section 68(1), is entitled to sell intellectual property is entitled to grant a licence over all or any of that property, but only if and to the extent that the provider is entitled to grant such a licence.
(2)   In granting a licence by virtue of subsection (1), the secured creditor must take all reasonable steps to ensure that the income obtained is the best reasonably obtainable.
(3)   Any income obtained by virtue of subsection (1) is to be held in trust by the secured creditor until applied under section 77.
(4)   The provider and the secured creditor may agree, whether before or after the pledge becomes enforceable by virtue of section 64(2), that subsection (1) is not to apply in relation to the intellectual property or some part of it.
(5)   Any such agreement must be in writing.

72 Secured creditor's right to protect and manage the property
(1)   A secured creditor who, by virtue of section 68(1), is entitled to sell property is entitled to take reasonable steps to—
   (a) protect, maintain and manage it, and
   (b) preserve its value.
(2)   The right under subsection (1) includes, for example, the right of the secured creditor to—
   (a) effect or maintain an insurance policy in relation to the property,
   (b) settle any liability in relation to the property,
   (c) bring, defend or continue legal proceedings in relation to the property,
   (d) take such other steps as the provider has agreed (whether before or after the pledge becomes enforceable by virtue of section 64(2)) may be taken by the secured creditor.
(3)   Subsection (1) is without prejudice to section 67(2)(b).

73 Secured creditor's right to appropriate
(1)   Where a pledge enforcement notice has been served, the secured creditor is entitled to appropriate any or all of the encumbered property in accordance with section 74 or (as the case may be) 75 in satisfaction, in whole or in part, of the secured obligation.
(2)   But it is not competent to appropriate by virtue of subsection (1)—
   (a) corporeal property, unless that property is in the possession of the secured creditor, or
   (b) property with a value which exceeds the total of—
      (i)   the amount for the time being remaining due under the secured obligation, and
      (ii) such expenses as have reasonably been incurred by the secured creditor in enforcing the pledge,
   unless a sum of money equivalent to the amount by which that total is exceeded is set aside by the secured creditor and held in trust until applied under section 77.

74 Appropriation with prior agreement
(1)   A provider and a secured creditor may, before a pledge becomes enforceable by virtue of section 64(2), agree that the secured creditor is entitled to appropriate by virtue of section 73(1)—
   (a) the encumbered property, or
   (b) any part of that property.
(2)   Any agreement under subsection (1) must be in writing.
(3)   Property may only be appropriated in accordance with that agreement if it is property in relation to which the provider and the secured creditor have, in the agreement, set out a method of readily determining a reasonable market price.

(4) Property appropriated in accordance with that agreement is appropriated only for the value, at the date of appropriation, of the property's market price as determined as mentioned in subsection (3).

(5) Before exercising a right to appropriate property by virtue of subsection (1), the secured creditor must serve a notice on—
   (a) the provider,
   (b) the debtor in the secured obligation (if a person other than the provider),
   (c) the holder of any other right in security over all or part of the property, and
   (d) any creditor who has executed diligence against all or part of the property.

(6) But—
   (a) paragraph (c) of subsection (5) is to be disregarded if the secured creditor does not know, and cannot reasonably be expected to know, of the right in security mentioned in that paragraph, and
   (b) paragraph (d) of that subsection is to be disregarded if the secured creditor does not know, and cannot reasonably be expected to know, of the diligence executed as mentioned in that paragraph.

(7) A notice under subsection (5) must—
   (a) identify the property to be appropriated,
   (b) specify the amount for the time being remaining due under the secured obligation,
   (c) specify the amount expected to be obtained by the appropriation, and
   (d) state that—
      (i) the recipient (if a person other than the provider or the debtor) may give a written statement to the secured creditor objecting to the appropriation, and
      (ii) if such a statement is received by the secured creditor within 14 days beginning with the day that the person objecting received the notice, the appropriation is not to proceed.

(8) If, within the period specified in sub-paragraph (ii) of subsection (7)(d), the secured creditor receives a written statement as mentioned in that subsection from a recipient of a notice other than the provider or the debtor—
   (a) the appropriation is not to proceed, and
   (b) the secured creditor must, by written statement and without delay, inform each of the other recipients of the notice that the appropriation is not proceeding.

(9) The Scottish Ministers may by regulations modify this section so as to—
   (a) specify—
      (i) further persons, or descriptions of persons, on whom the secured creditor must serve a notice (being persons who have statutory duties in relation to the provider's estate),
      (ii) cases when the requirement to serve a notice on a person specified by virtue of sub-paragraph (i) is to be disregarded,
   (b) require a notice under subsection (5) to be in, or as nearly as may be in, such form as is for the time being prescribed (and may in consequence remove any requirements in this section as to what such a notice must contain).

75 Appropriation without prior agreement

(1) This section applies in respect of property in relation to which the provider and the secured creditor have not reached agreement under section 74(1).

(2) Property may only be appropriated by virtue of section 73(1) if the amount obtained by the appropriation bears a reasonable relationship to the market value of the property appropriated on the date of the appropriation.

(3) Before exercising a right to appropriate property by virtue of section 73(1), the secured creditor must serve a notice on—
   (a) the provider,
   (b) the debtor in the secured obligation (if a person other than the provider),
   (c) the holder of any other right in security over all or part of the property, and
   (d) any creditor who has executed diligence against all or part of the property.

(4) But—

(a) paragraph (c) of subsection (3) is to be disregarded if the secured creditor does not know, and cannot reasonably be expected to know, of the right in security mentioned in that paragraph, and

(b) paragraph (d) of that subsection is to be disregarded if the secured creditor does not know, and cannot reasonably be expected to know, of the diligence executed as mentioned in that paragraph.

(5) Any notice served under subsection (3) must—

(a) identify the property to be appropriated,

(b) specify the amount for the time being remaining due under the secured obligation,

(c) specify the amount expected to be obtained by the appropriation, and

(d) state that—

(i) the recipient may give a written statement to the secured creditor objecting to the appropriation, and

(ii) if such a statement is received by the secured creditor within 14 days beginning with the day that the person objecting received the notice, the appropriation is not to proceed.

(6) If, within the period specified in sub-paragraph (ii) of subsection (5)(d), the secured creditor receives a written statement as mentioned in that subsection from a recipient of a notice—

(a) the appropriation is not to proceed, and

(b) the secured creditor must, by written statement and without delay, inform each of the other recipients of the notice that the appropriation is not proceeding.

(7) The Scottish Ministers may by regulations modify this section so as to—

(a) specify—

(i) further persons, or descriptions of persons, on whom the secured creditor must serve a notice (being persons who have statutory duties in relation to the provider's estate),

(ii) cases when the requirement to serve a notice on a person specified by virtue of sub-paragraph (i) is to be disregarded,

(b) require a notice under subsection (3) to be in, or as nearly as may be in, such form as is for the time being prescribed (and may in consequence remove any requirements in this section as to what such a notice must contain).

76 Appropriation: unencumbered acquisition

Where a secured creditor appropriates property by virtue of section 73(1), the secured creditor acquires the property unencumbered by any right in security or any diligence.

77 Application of proceeds from enforcement of pledge

(1) Any proceeds arising from the enforcement of a pledge are to be applied—

(a) firstly, in payment of all expenses reasonably incurred by the secured creditor in connection with the enforcement (including any incurred under section 67(2) or 72), and

(b) secondly, in payment of the amount due to—

(i) the holder of any right in security over the property from which the proceeds arose, and

(ii) any creditor who has executed diligence against that property, and

(c) with the residue (if any) from the proceeds being paid to the provider.

(2) Any payment made by virtue of subsection (1)(b) is to be made in conformity with the ranking of the right in security or, as the case may be, of the diligence.

(3) But no such payment is to be made to—

(a) the holder of a right in security which has priority in ranking over the pledge enforced, or

(b) any creditor who has executed diligence which has such priority,

unless that holder or creditor consented to the enforcement in question.

(4) Where payment falls to be made, by virtue of subsection (1)(b), to more than one person with the same ranking but the proceeds are inadequate to enable those persons to be paid in full, their payments are to abate in equal proportions.

(5) Where a question arises regarding to whom a payment under this section is to be made, the secured creditor must—

(a) consign the amount of the payment (so far as ascertainable) in court for the person appearing to have the best right to that payment, and

(b) lodge in court a statement of the amount consigned.

(6) Where a consignation is made in pursuance of subsection (5)(a)—

(a) it operates as a payment of the amount due, and

(b) a certificate of the court is sufficient evidence of that payment.

(7) The secured creditor must, as soon as reasonably practicable after applying the proceeds arising from the enforcement, issue the persons mentioned in subsection (8) with a written statement of how the proceeds have been applied under this section.

(8) The persons referred to in subsection (7) are—

(a) the provider,

(b) the debtor in the secured obligation (if a person other than the provider), and

(c) any person who both—

(i) is mentioned in subsection (1)(b), and

(ii) has consented to the enforcement in question.

(9) In a case where—

(a) all or any of the property is let by the secured creditor by virtue of section 70(1), or

(b) the secured creditor grants a licence over all or any of it by virtue of section 71(1),

subsection (7) applies in relation to any proceeds of the letting or licensing as if, for the words 'as soon as reasonably practicable after applying the proceeds arising from the enforcement', there were substituted 'every month beginning with the month after the first proceeds arising from the enforcement are received'.

(10) The Scottish Ministers may by regulations modify this section so as to specify further persons, or descriptions of persons, to whom the secured creditor must issue a written statement (being persons who have statutory duties in relation to the provider's estate).

78 Mandatory application for removal of an entry from the statutory pledges record

(1) This section applies where a statutory pledge which has been registered is extinguished by virtue of—

(a) the enforcement of the statutory pledge,

(b) the enforcement of another right in security over the encumbered property of the statutory pledge, or

(c) the enforcement of diligence against the encumbered property of the statutory pledge.

(2) The secured creditor must, as soon as reasonably practicable after the enforcement of the statutory pledge or, as the case may be, becoming aware of the event mentioned in paragraph (b) or (c) of subsection (1), make an application under section 96(1) for removal of the entry for the statutory pledge from the statutory pledges record.

Liability for loss due to enforcement

79 Liability for loss suffered by virtue of enforcement

(1) A person ('P') is entitled to be compensated by a secured creditor for loss suffered in consequence of the secured creditor's failure to comply with any obligation imposed on the secured creditor by any provision of sections 64 to 78.

(2)   But the secured creditor has no liability under subsection (1)—

(a)   in so far as P's loss could have been avoided had P taken measures which it would have been reasonable for P to take, or

(b)   in so far as P's loss was not reasonably foreseeable.

Service of documents for purposes of this Chapter

80   Service of documents for purposes of this Chapter

(1)   In relation to the service of documents for the purposes of this Chapter, the provider and the secured creditor may agree (either or both)—

(a)   that the document may or must be served on a person by being sent to an address specified in the agreement (being an address other than is mentioned in subsection (4) of section 26 of the Interpretation and Legislative Reform (Scotland) Act 2010),

(b)   that service is to be by a method mentioned in subsection (2) of that section and specified in the agreement.

(2)   The agreement need not refer expressly to that section or to any provision of that section.

(3)   Any such agreement must be in writing.

(4)   Where there is such an agreement but service cannot be effected in accordance with it, the agreement is to be disregarded in applying section 26 of that Act of 2010 for the purposes of this Chapter.

CHAPTER 2

REGISTER OF STATUTORY PLEDGES

Register of Statutory Pledges

81   The Register of Statutory Pledges

(1)   There is to be a public register known as the Register of Statutory Pledges.

(2)   The register is to be under the management and control of the Keeper.

(3)   Subject to the provisions of this Act, the register is to be in such form as the Keeper thinks fit.

(4)   The Keeper must take such steps as appear reasonable to the Keeper to protect the register from—

(a)   interference,

(b)   unauthorised access, and

(c)   damage.

Structure and contents of the register

82   The parts of the register

The Keeper must make up and maintain, as parts of the register—

(a)   the statutory pledges record, and

(b)   the archive record.

83   The statutory pledges record

(1)   An entry in the statutory pledges record is to comprise—

(a)   the provider's name and address,

(b)   where the provider is an individual, the provider's date of birth,

(c)   any identifying number which the provider has and which, by virtue of RSP Rules, must be included in the entry,

(d)   the secured creditor's name and address,

(e)   any identifying number which the secured creditor has and which, by virtue of RSP Rules, must be included in the entry,

(f)   where the secured creditor is not an individual, an address (which may be an email address) to which any request for information regarding the statutory pledge may be sent,

(g) such description of the encumbered property as is required, or permitted, for the purposes of this subsection by RSP Rules,

(h) a copy of the constitutive document of the statutory pledge,

(i) the registration number allocated under section 87(1)(b) to the entry,

(j) where the statutory pledge has been amended in pursuance of section 58(6), a copy of the amendment document,

(k) the date and time of registration of—

    (i) the statutory pledge, and

    (ii) any amendment to the statutory pledge,

(l) any other information that is required under any other section of this Act, and

(m) any other information that is specified for the purposes of this subsection by RSP Rules.

(2) The statutory pledges record is the totality of all such entries.

84 The archive record

The archive record is the totality of—

(a) all entries and copy documents transferred from the statutory pledges record under section 102(2)(a) or (3)(c) or by virtue of section 95(1)(a),

(b) all copy documents included in the archive record under section 102(2)(c) or (3)(b),

(c) all copies of such other documents as the Keeper considers it appropriate to include in the archive record, and

(d) any other information that is specified for the purposes of this section by RSP Rules.

Registration process

85 Order in which applications are to be dealt with

The Keeper must deal with—

(a) applications for registration of a statutory pledge under section 86, and

(b) applications for registration of an amendment to a statutory pledge under section 88,

in the order in which they are received.

86 Application for registration of statutory pledge

(1) A secured creditor may apply to the Keeper for registration of a statutory pledge.

(2) The Keeper must accept the application if—

(a) it is submitted with a copy of the constitutive document,

(b) it contains all the information the Keeper requires in accordance with section 83 to be able to make up an entry for the statutory pledge under section 87(1),

(c) it conforms to such RSP Rules as relate to the application, and

(d) either—

    (i) such fee as is payable for the registration is paid, or

    (ii) arrangements satisfactory to the Keeper are made for payment of that fee.

(3) If the requirements of subsection (2) are not satisfied, the Keeper must reject the application and inform the applicant accordingly.

87 Registration of statutory pledge

(1) On accepting an application made under section 86, the Keeper must—

(a) make up an entry for the statutory pledge (from the constitutive document, the information provided in the application and the circumstances of registration),

(b) allocate a registration number to the entry (based on the order in which applications are dealt with), and

(c) maintain the entry in the statutory pledges record.

(2)   A statutory pledge is taken to be registered on the date and at the time entered for it for the purposes of section 83(1)(k)(i).

88   Application for registration of amendment

(1)   A secured creditor may apply to the Keeper for registration of an amendment to a statutory pledge to increase the extent of the statutory pledge within the meaning of section 58(7).

(2)   The Keeper must accept the application if—

(a)   it is submitted with a copy of the amendment document,

(b)   it contains all the information the Keeper requires in accordance with section 83 to be able to revise the entry to which the application relates,

(c)   it conforms to such RSP Rules as relate to the application, and

(d)   either—

(i)   such fee as is payable for the registration is paid, or

(ii)   arrangements satisfactory to the Keeper are made for payment of that fee.

(3)   If the requirements of subsection (2) are not satisfied, the Keeper must reject the application and inform the applicant accordingly.

89   Registration of amendment

(1)   On accepting an application made under section 88, the Keeper must revise the entry for the statutory pledge to which the application relates in accordance with the application.

(2)   An amendment to a statutory pledge is taken to be registered on the date and at the time entered for the amendment for the purposes of section 83(1)(k)(ii).

90   Verification statement as to registration of statutory pledge or amendment

(1)   After the registration of a statutory pledge under section 87 or an amendment to a statutory pledge under section 89, the Keeper must issue a written statement verifying the registration to—

(a)   the secured creditor, and

(b)   the provider,

but only if and to the extent that the application made under section 86 or (as the case may be) section 88 contains an email address for those persons.

(2)   That statement must—

(a)   include—

(i)   the date and time of the registration, and

(ii)   the registration number allocated to the entry to which the application relates, and

(b)   conform to such RSP Rules as relate to the statement.

(3)   Where a statement is issued under subsection (1) and is received by the secured creditor but not the provider, the provider may request a copy of it from the secured creditor.

(4)   Within 21 days beginning with the day a request is made under subsection (3), the secured creditor must supply the provider with the copy requested.

Effective registration

91   Effective registration of statutory pledge

(1)   The registration of a statutory pledge is ineffective if—

(a)   the entry made up for the statutory pledge in the statutory pledges record—

(i)   does not include a copy of the constitutive document, or

(ii)   is, at the time of registration, seriously misleading as a result of an inaccuracy or inaccuracies in it, or

(b)   the constitutive document is invalid.

(2)   But subsection (1)(a)(ii) is subject to section 94(1)(c) and (d).

(3)   Where the registration of a statutory pledge is ineffective by virtue of subsection (1), it becomes effective if and when the entry is corrected.

92 Effective registration of amendment to statutory pledge

(1) The registration of an amendment to a statutory pledge is ineffective if—

(a) the entry for the statutory pledge in the statutory pledges record—

(i) does not include a copy of the amendment document, or

(ii) is, in consequence of the amendment, seriously misleading as a result of an inaccuracy or inaccuracies in it, or

(b) the amendment document is invalid.

(2) But subsection (1)(a)(ii) is subject to section 94(1)(c) and (d).

(3) Where the registration of an amendment to a statutory pledge is ineffective by virtue of subsection (1), it becomes effective if and when the entry as amended is corrected.

93 Supervening inaccuracies: protection of third parties

(1) Subsection (5) applies where, at some time after a statutory pledge is registered effectively—

(a) a person acquires, for value, in good faith and exercising reasonable care—

(i) property which is encumbered under the pledge, or

(ii) a right in such property, and

(b) at the time the person acquires that property or right ('the acquired property'), any one of condition A, condition B or condition C is met.

(2) Condition A is that the entry for the pledge in the statutory pledges record has been incorrectly removed from the statutory pledges record (whether or not on transfer of that entry to the archive record) and remains incorrectly absent from the record.

(3) Condition B is that—

(a) the acquired property does not have an identifying number which, by virtue of RSP Rules, must be used in identifying it, and

(b) the entry for the pledge in the statutory pledges record is seriously misleading in respect of the acquired property.

(4) Condition C is that—

(a) the acquired property has an identifying number which, by virtue of RSP Rules, must be used in identifying it, and

(b) if a search of the statutory pledges record were to be carried out for that number using the search facility provided under section 104, it would not disclose the entry.

(5) On the acquisition, the statutory pledge is extinguished in relation to the acquired property.

(6) For the purposes of subsection (1)(a), the circumstances in which a person will not be taken to be in good faith and exercising reasonable care include where the person fails to carry out a search of the statutory pledges record in respect of the acquisition.

94 Seriously misleading inaccuracies in the statutory pledges record

(1) In determining for the purposes of sections 91(1)(a)(ii), 92(1)(a)(ii) and 93(3) whether an entry in the statutory pledges record is seriously misleading as a result of an inaccuracy or inaccuracies in it—

(a) the entry is seriously misleading where—

(i) any of subsections (2) to (6) apply, or

(ii) despite sub-paragraph (i) not being satisfied, the inaccuracy or inaccuracies are such that a reasonable person would be seriously misled by the entry,

(b) any inaccuracy is to be disregarded to the extent that it appears in the constitutive document, or in any amendment document, but is not replicated elsewhere in the entry,

(c) where the entry is seriously misleading in respect of only part of the encumbered property, that is not to be taken to affect the entry in its application to the rest of the property,

(d) where the entry is seriously misleading in respect of a co-provider or co-secured creditor but not in respect of both (or all) co-providers or co-secured creditors, that is not to be taken to affect the entry in its application to a co-provider or co-secured creditor in respect of whom the entry is not seriously misleading.

(2)   This subsection applies where—

(a)   the provider is a person required by RSP Rules to be identified in the statutory pledges record by an identifying number, and

(b)   if a search of the record were to be carried out for that number, using the search facility provided under section 104, it would not disclose the entry.

(3)   This subsection applies where—

(a)   the provider is not a person required by RSP Rules to be identified in the statutory pledges record by an identifying number, and

(b)   if a search of the record were to be carried out, using the search facility provided under section 104, for—

(i)   the provider's proper name, or

(ii)   the provider's proper name together with the provider's month and year of birth,

it would not disclose the entry.

(4)   This subsection applies—

(a)   for the purposes of sections 91(1)(a)(ii) and 92(1)(a)(ii) only, and

(b)   where the entry inaccurately reflects the secured creditor's proper name at the date the application for registration was made in such a way that a reasonable person would be seriously misled.

(5)   This subsection applies where—

(a)   the encumbered property is or includes property required by RSP Rules to be identified in the statutory pledges record by an identifying number, and

(b)   if a search of the record were to be carried out for that number, using the search facility provided under section 104, it would not disclose the entry.

(6)   This subsection applies where—

(a)   there is a requirement, by virtue of section 83(1)(g), for an entry in the statutory pledges record to specify the type of property encumbered, and

(b)   the entry—

(ia)   does not describe the property as being of a type that it is, or

(ii)   fails to allocate a type to the property.

(7)   In the application of this section to co-providers and co-secured creditors—

(a)   subsections (2) and (3) apply in relation to a co-provider as they apply in relation to a provider,

(b)   subsection (4) applies in relation to a co-secured creditor as it applies in relation to a secured creditor.

(8)   The Scottish Ministers may by regulations modify this section to make provision about what does, and what does not, make an entry seriously misleading for the purposes of sections 91(1)(a)(ii), 92(1)(a)(ii) and 93(3) and how that is to be determined.

(9)   In this section, the 'proper name' of a provider or secured creditor means the person's name in the form determined in accordance with RSP Rules.

Duration

95   Power of Scottish Ministers in relation to duration of statutory pledge

(1)   The Scottish Ministers may by regulations—

(a)   specify a period from the creation or renewal of an entry in the statutory pledges record at the end of which the statutory pledge to which the entry relates will be extinguished and the entry removed, unless during that period the entry has been—

(i)   renewed by virtue of paragraph (b), or

(ii)   removed, and

(b)   enable an application to be made by the secured creditor for the renewal of an entry which would otherwise fall to be removed by virtue of paragraph (a).

(2)   Before laying a draft of a Scottish statutory instrument containing regulations under subsection (1) before the Scottish Parliament, the Scottish Ministers must consult the Keeper.

Corrections

96   Application by secured creditor for correction of statutory pledges record
(1)   A relevant person may apply to the Keeper for an entry in the statutory pledges record to be corrected.
(2)   The Keeper must accept the application if—
  (a)   it conforms to such RSP Rules as relate to the application, and
  (b)   either—
    (i)   such fee as is payable for the correction is paid, or
    (ii)   arrangements satisfactory to the Keeper are made for payment of that fee.
(3)   If the requirements of subsection (2) are not satisfied, the Keeper must reject the application and inform the applicant accordingly.
(4)   For the purposes of subsection (1), 'relevant person'—
  (a)   means the person who is the secured creditor in relation to the entry (whether or not identified as such in the entry), and
  (b)   where the statutory pledge has been assigned, also includes the person who was the secured creditor before the assignation.

97   Correction of record in response to application under section 96
(1)   On accepting an application made under section 96, the Keeper must correct the entry in the statutory pledges record accordingly.
(2)   After the correction of an entry under subsection (1), the Keeper must issue a written statement verifying the correction to—
  (a)   the applicant, and
  (b)   the provider,
but only if and to the extent that the application contains an email address for those persons.
(3)   That statement must—
  (a)   include—
    (i)   the date and time of the correction, and
    (ii)   the registration number allocated to the entry to which the correction relates, and
  (b)   conform to such RSP Rules as relate to the statement.
(4)   Where a statement is issued under subsection (2) and is received by the applicant but not the provider, the provider may request a copy of it from the applicant.
(5)   Within 21 days beginning with the day a request is made under subsection (4), the applicant must supply the provider with the copy requested.

98   Demand that application for correction be made under section 96
(1)   A person may, where the conditions in subsection (2) or (3) are met, issue a demand to the person identified in an entry in the statutory pledges record as the secured creditor (the 'registered creditor') that the registered creditor apply to the Keeper under section 96 for the entry to be corrected.
(2)   The conditions in this subsection are that the person—
  (a)   is identified as the provider, or as a co-provider, of the statutory pledge in the entry, and
  (b)   either—
    (i)   claims not to be either the provider, or a co-provider, of the statutory pledge, or
    (ii)   considers that all or part of the property identified as the encumbered property in the entry is not encumbered property.
(3)   The conditions in this subsection are that the person—

(a) has a right in property identified as the encumbered property in the entry, and

(b) considers that all or part of the property is not encumbered property.

(4)   A demand issued under subsection (1) must—

(a) be in a prescribed form, and

(b) specify a period (being a period of not less than 21 days after it is received) within which compliance with it is sought.

(5)   A registered creditor may not charge a fee for compliance with a demand under subsection (1).

(6)   If the registered creditor fails to comply with the demand within the period specified by virtue of subsection (4)(b), the person who made the demand may apply to the Keeper for the statutory pledges record to be corrected.

99   Response to application for correction under section 98(6)

(1)   The Keeper must accept an application made under section 98(6) if—

(a) it conforms to such RSP Rules as relate to the application, and

(b) either—

(i)   such fee as is payable for the application is paid, or

(ii)   arrangements satisfactory to the Keeper are made for payment of that fee.

(2)   If the requirements of subsection (1) are not satisfied, the Keeper must reject the application and inform the applicant accordingly.

(3)   On accepting an application made under section 98(6), the Keeper must—

(a) serve a notice on the registered creditor stating that the Keeper intends to correct the statutory pledges record on a date specified in the notice (being a date no fewer than 21 days after the date of the notice),

(b) note on the entry to which the application relates that the application has been received and include in that note—

(i)   the details of the correction sought, and

(ii)   the date on which the application was received,

(c) issue a written statement to the applicant verifying that the application has been received, and

(d) notify the person identified in the entry as the provider (if a different person from the applicant) that the notice mentioned in paragraph (a) has been served on the registered creditor.

(4)   The registered creditor—

(a) may, before the date specified under subsection (3)(a), apply to the court opposing the making of the correction, and

(b) on making any such application, must notify the Keeper accordingly.

(5) Where the registered creditor is not the secured creditor in relation to the statutory pledge in the entry—

(a) the registered creditor must, in so far as it is reasonable and practicable to do so, promptly notify the secured creditor of the notice received under subsection (3)(a), and

(b) subsection (4) applies to the secured creditor as it applies to the registered creditor.

(6)   On an application under subsection (4)(a), the court may—

(a) if satisfied that the correction is not justified, direct that no change be made to the record in consequence of the application under section 98(6), or

(b) if satisfied that the correction is justified in whole or in part, direct that the record be corrected accordingly.

(7)   But the court is not to make a direction under subsection (6) unless satisfied that, before the date specified by virtue of subsection (3)(a), the Keeper received notification under subsection (4)(b) of the application to the court.

(8)   If the Keeper does not receive, before the date specified by virtue of subsection (3)(a), notification under subsection (4)(b) of an application to the court, the Keeper is on that date to make the correction.

(9)   In this section, 'registered creditor' has the same meaning as in section 98.

100   Correction of the statutory pledges record at instance of the court or the Keeper
(1)   Where a court determines in any proceedings that the statutory pledges record is inaccurate, the court—
(a)   must direct the Keeper to correct the record, and
(b)   may give the Keeper any further direction it considers necessary in connection with the correction.
(2)   Subsection (3) applies where the Keeper becomes aware of a manifest inaccuracy in the statutory pledges record other than—
(a)   as a result of a direction under subsection (1),
(b)   where an application has been made under section 96(1) or 98(6) in respect of the inaccuracy, or
(c)   where the Keeper considers that—
(i)   such an application could reasonably be made in respect of the inaccuracy, and
(ii)   the inaccuracy is not attributable to the Keeper.
(3)   The Keeper must—
(a)   correct the record if what is needed to correct it is manifest,
(b)   if what is needed to correct it is not manifest, note the inaccuracy on the entry in question.

101   Meaning of 'inaccuracy' and how a correction is made
(1)   There is an 'inaccuracy' in the statutory pledges record where the record misstates what the position is, in law or in fact, in relation to a statutory pledge.
(2)   A correction of the statutory pledges record—
(a)   may relate to an inaccuracy—
(i)   which has existed since an entry in the record was made up, or
(ii)   which has arisen due to circumstances that have occurred since the submission of the application in respect of which the entry was made up, and
(b)   may involve—
(i)   the removal of an entry,
(ii)   the removal of information included in an entry,
(iii)   the amendment of, or an addition to, the information, or replacement of a copy document, included in an entry,
(iv)   the restoration of information, or of a copy document, to an entry,
(v)   the restoration of an entry (whether or not by transferring it from the archive record to the statutory pledges record).
(3)   A correction is taken to be made on the date and at the time entered for it in the register in pursuance of a provision of this Part.

102   Correction of the statutory pledges record: procedure
(1)   This section applies where the Keeper corrects the statutory pledges record by virtue of section 97(1), 99(6)(b) or (8) or 100(1)(a) or (3)(a).
(2)   Where the Keeper corrects the statutory pledges record by removing an entry from the statutory pledges record, the Keeper must—
(a)   transfer the entry to the archive record,
(b)   note on the transferred entry—
(i)   the section by virtue of which the transfer is made, and
(ii)   the details of the correction (including the date and time of the removal), and
(c)   include in the archive record a copy of any document which discloses, or contributes to disclosing, the inaccuracy which is the subject of the correction.
(3)   Where the Keeper corrects the record by restoring an entry, by restoring, removing or amending information included in an entry or by restoring or replacing a copy document, the Keeper must—

(a) note on the entry that it has been corrected and the details of the correction (including the date and time of the correction),

(b) include in the archive record a copy of any document which discloses, or contributes to disclosing, the inaccuracy which is the subject of the correction, and

(c) in the case of the replacement of the copy document, transfer the replaced copy to the archive record.

(4)   Having corrected the record other than by virtue of section 97(1), the Keeper must notify the following persons (in so far as it is reasonable and practicable to do so) that the correction has been made—

(a) every person specified for the purposes of this subsection by RSP Rules, and

(b) any other person who appears to the Keeper to be affected by it materially.

(5)   A failure to comply with subsection (2)(c), (3)(b) or (4) does not affect the validity of the correction of the record.

103   Proceedings involving the accuracy of the statutory pledges record

The Keeper is entitled to appear and be heard in any civil proceedings, whether before a court or tribunal, in which—

(a) the accuracy of the statutory pledges record, or

(b) what is needed to correct an inaccuracy in the record,

is put in question.

Searches and extracts

104   Searching the statutory pledges record

(1)   The Keeper must provide a facility by which the statutory pledges record may be searched.

(2)   That search facility must allow the statutory pledges record to be searched by reference to, and only by reference to—

(a) any of the following information in the entries contained in that record—

(i)   the names of providers, which must be capable of being searched with and without the months and years of birth of providers who are individuals,

(ii)   the identifying numbers of providers required by RSP Rules to be identified in the statutory pledges record by such a number,

(iii)   if RSP Rules require the encumbered property to be identified (whether by an identifying number or in some other way), by reference to such identification,

(b) registration numbers allocated, under section 87(1)(b), to entries in that record, or

(c) any other factor, or characteristic, specified for the purposes of this paragraph by RSP Rules.

(3)   Subject to any restrictions imposed under RSP Rules, a person may search the statutory pledges record using the search facility provided under subsection (1) provided that either—

(a) such fee as is payable for the search is paid, or

(b) arrangements satisfactory to the Keeper are made for payment of that fee.

(4)   But no fee is payable for a search of the statutory pledges record which is carried out on behalf of an individual by a not-for-profit money adviser (being an adviser who does not charge individuals for the adviser's services).

(5)   The Scottish Ministers may, by regulations, make further provision about the meaning of 'not-for-profit money adviser' for the purposes of subsection (4).

105   Admissibility and evidential status of search results

(1)   A copy of a search result (in printed or electronic form) which relates to a search carried out by means of a search facility provided by the Keeper is admissible in evidence.

(2)   In the absence of evidence to the contrary—

(a) where such a search result purports to show an entry in the statutory pledges record, it is sufficient proof of—

(i)   the registration of the statutory pledge, or an amendment to the entry in the statutory pledges record, to which the result relates,

(ii)   where applicable, a correction of the entry in the statutory pledges record to which the result relates, and

(iii)   the date and time of such registration or, as the case may be, correction, and

(b)   where such a search result purports not to show an entry in the statutory pledges record, it is sufficient proof of an entry in the statutory pledges record not being disclosed at the date and time of such search by means of the search carried out.

106   Extracts and their evidential status

(1)   A person may apply to the Keeper for an extract of an entry in the register.

(2)   The Keeper must issue the extract if—

(a)   such fee as is payable for issuing it is paid, or

(b)   arrangements satisfactory to the Keeper are made for payment of that fee.

(3) But if, on application under subsection (1), the applicant requests an extract as at a specific date and time, the Keeper need comply with the request only to the extent that it is reasonably practicable to do so.

(4)   The Keeper may validate the extract as the Keeper considers appropriate.

(5)   The Keeper may issue the extract as an electronic document unless the applicant requests that it be issued as a traditional document.

(6)   The extract is to be accepted for all purposes as sufficient evidence of the contents of the entry as at—

(a)   in the case of an extract requested as mentioned in subsection (3), the date and time to which the extract relates (being a date and time specified in the extract), and

(b)   in any other case, the date on which and the time at which the extract is issued (being a date and time specified in the extract).

Requests for information

107   Secured creditor's duty to respond to request for information

(1)   An entitled person may ask the person identified in an entry in the statutory pledges record as the secured creditor (the 'registered creditor') to provide the entitled person with the following—

(a)   if the registered creditor is the secured creditor, with a written statement as to whether or not property specified by the entitled person is, or is part of, the encumbered property,

(b)   if the registered creditor is no longer the secured creditor, with—

(i)   information to that effect,

(ii)   the name and address of the person to whom the registered creditor assigned the statutory pledge, and

(iii)   where relevant and in so far as known, the names and addresses of subsequent assignees, or

(c)   if the registered creditor has never been the secured creditor, with information to that effect.

(2)   The following are entitled persons for the purposes of this section—

(a)   a person who has a right in the property so specified,

(b)   a person who has a right to execute diligence against the property so specified (or who is authorised to execute a charge for payment and will have the right to execute diligence against that property if and when the days of charge expire without payment), and

(c)   a person who is not mentioned in paragraph (a) or (b) but who has the consent of the person identified in the entry as the provider to make a request under subsection (1).

(3) The registered creditor must, within 21 days beginning with the day of receiving a request under subsection (1), comply with it unless—

(a) it is manifest that the registration is ineffective in relation to the statutory pledge to which the request relates,

(b) it is manifest from the entry for the statutory pledge that the property specified under subsection (1) by the entitled person is not encumbered by the pledge, or

(c) both—

(i) the registered creditor has, within the period of 3 months ending with the day of receipt of the request, complied with a request under subsection (1) from the same person and in relation to the same property, and

(ii) the information contained in the statement issued in relation to the earlier request remains correct.

(4) The registered creditor may recover from the entitled person any costs reasonably incurred in complying with the request.

(5) On the application of the registered creditor, the court may by order—

(a) exempt the registered creditor from complying with a request under subsection (1) or such part of the request as it specifies in the order, or

(b) extend the period within which the registered creditor must comply with the request by such number of days as it specifies in the order,

if satisfied that in all the circumstances it would be reasonable to do so.

(6) If, on the application of the entitled person, the court is satisfied that the registered creditor has, without reasonable excuse, failed to comply with subsection (3), it may by order require the registered creditor to comply with the request within 14 days or such other period (which may be longer or shorter than 14 days) as the court considers appropriate.

(7) This section applies in relation to any person whose name and address have been provided to an entitled person by virtue of subsection (1)(b) as it applies to the registered creditor.

(8) The Scottish Ministers may by regulations modify this section so as to specify further persons, or descriptions of persons, who are entitled persons for the purposes of this section.

108 Acquisition of property confirmed by creditor not to be encumbered property

(1) Subsection (2) applies where a person who is an entitled person for the purposes of section 107—

(a) makes a request under subsection (1) of that section,

(b) receives a response from the person of whom the request was made, in the form of a statement of the type mentioned in paragraph (a) of that subsection, advising that the property specified under that subsection by the entitled person is neither the encumbered property nor part of that property, and

(c) within 3 months beginning with the date of being so advised acquires in good faith—

(i) the property so specified (or any part of it), or

(ii) a right in that property (or part).

(2) On that acquisition, the statutory pledge is extinguished in relation to the property (or part).

Entitlement to compensation

109 Liability of Keeper

(1) A person is entitled to be compensated by the Keeper for loss suffered in consequence of—

(a) an inaccuracy in the statutory pledges record to the extent that it is attributable to the making up, maintenance or operation of the register (including an attempted correction of it),

(b) the issue, under section 90(1) or 97(2), of a written statement which is incorrect,

(c) the service, under section 102(4), of a notification which is incorrect,

(d) a search result which—

(i) relates to a search of the statutory pledges record carried out by means of a search facility provided by the Keeper,

(ii) ought (as a result of the search terms used) to reflect accurately the contents of the statutory pledges record at the time the search was made, and

(iii) does not accurately reflect those contents,

(e) the issue, under section 106, of an extract which is not a true extract,

(f) an application being accepted or rejected in error,

(g) an attempt to make an application, which the Keeper would otherwise have accepted, failing as a result of an error in the system the Keeper has for accepting applications, or

(h) applications being dealt with otherwise than in the order in which they are received.

(2) But the Keeper has no liability under subsection (1)—

(a) in so far as the person's loss could have been avoided had the person taken measures which it would have been reasonable for the person to take,

(b) in so far as the person's loss was not reasonably foreseeable, or

(c) for non-patrimonial loss.

(3) For the avoidance of doubt, an inaccuracy in information included in an entry in the statutory pledges record when that entry is made up under section 87(1)(a), revised under section 89(1) or corrected by virtue of section 97(1), 99(6)(b) or (8) or 100(1)(a) or (3)(a) does not fall within subsection (1)(a) to the extent that the Keeper—

(a) has been misled into making the inaccuracy, and

(b) reasonably believed the information to be accurate.

(4) For the purposes of subsection (3), the circumstances where the Keeper is entitled to reasonably believe information to be accurate include those where it is provided—

(a) in connection with an application to which the entry relates, or

(b) by the court.

110 Liability of certain other persons

(1) A person ('P') is entitled to be compensated in the following circumstances—

(a) where P suffers loss in consequence of an inaccuracy in an entry in the statutory pledges record then, to the extent that it is not attributable to the Keeper, P is entitled to be compensated for that loss by—

(i) the person who made the application for registration which gave rise to the inaccurate entry if that person failed to take reasonable care in making it, or

(ii) where the inaccurate entry arises from the attempted correction of an apparent inaccuracy, the person who notified the Keeper of the apparent inaccuracy if that person failed to take reasonable care in doing so,

(b) where P suffers loss in consequence of an inaccuracy in information supplied in response to a request under section 107(1), P is entitled to be compensated for that loss by the person who supplied the information if that person failed to take reasonable care in supplying it, or

(c) where P suffers loss in consequence of a failure, without reasonable excuse, to comply with a request in accordance with section 107(3), P is entitled to be compensated for that loss by the person whose failure it was.

(2) But a person has no liability under subsection (1)—

(a) in so far as P's loss could have been avoided had P taken measures which it would have been reasonable for P to take,

(b) in so far as P's loss was not reasonably foreseeable, or

(c) for non-patrimonial loss.

Rules

111 Rules
(1) The Scottish Ministers may by regulations make rules ('RSP Rules')—
   (a) about the making up and keeping of the register,
   (b) about the procedure in relation to—
      (i) applications for registration under section 86(1) or 88(1), or
      (ii) applications for corrections under section 96(1) or 98(6),
   (c) about searches in the register and the results of those searches,
   (d) about the required form and content of any document or information to be used in relation to the register,
   (e) requiring there to be entered in the statutory pledges record or the archive record such information as is specified in the rules, or
   (f) regarding other matters in relation to registration under this Part, being matters for which the Scottish Ministers consider it necessary or expedient to provide in order to give full effect to the purposes of this Part.
(2) RSP Rules under subsection (1) may, in particular, include provision—
   (a) about the identification, in any application and in the register, of any person or property, including—
      (i) how the proper form of a person's name is to be determined, and
      (ii) where the person or property has an identifying number (whether of numerals or of letters and numerals) allocated to the person or property, whether that number must be used in identifying the person or property,
   (b) about the nature of the address of the provider or the secured creditor to be included in an entry in the register,
   (c) about the degree of precision with which time is to be recorded in the register,
   (d) about information which, though contained in a constitutive document or amendment document, need not be included in a copy of that document submitted with an application under section 86(1) or 88(1),
   (e) about whether a signature contained in a constitutive document or amendment document need be included in a copy of that document so submitted,
   (f) about information which, though contained in the register, is not to be—
      (i) available to persons searching it, or
      (ii) included in any extract issued under section 106,
   (g) about when the register is open for—
      (i) registration,
      (ii) searches.
(3) Before laying a draft of a Scottish statutory instrument containing regulations under subsection (1) before the Scottish Parliament, the Scottish Ministers must consult the Keeper.

CHAPTER 3
MISCELLANEOUS AND INTERPRETATION OF PART 2

Miscellaneous

112 Competence of creating an agricultural charge
On the coming into force of this section, it ceases to be competent to create an agricultural charge ('agricultural charge' having the meaning given by section 5 of the Agricultural Credits (Scotland) Act 1929).

Interpretation of Part 2

113 Interpretation of Part 2
(1) In this Part (except where the context requires otherwise)—

'amendment document' has the meaning given by section 58(1),

'the archive record' is to be construed in accordance with section 84,

'corporeal moveable property' does not include money,

'correction', in relation to the statutory pledges record, is to be construed in accordance with section 101(2),

'encumbered property' has the meaning given by section 43(2),

'inaccuracy', in relation to the statutory pledges record, is to be construed in accordance with section 101(1),

'money' has the meaning given by section 175(1) of the Bankruptcy and Diligence etc. (Scotland) Act 2007,

'pledge', in sections 64 to 77, is to be construed in accordance with section 63,

'pledge enforcement notice' has the meaning given by section 65(1),

'provider'—

    (a)　means the person who grants a pledge, and

    (b)　includes or, as the case may be, consists of any successor in para, or representative, of a provider (unless the successor or representative is a person who, by virtue of Chapter 1, had acquired the encumbered property unencumbered by the statutory pledge in question),

'the register' means the Register of Statutory Pledges,

'right in security'—

    (a)　means a right in security over property (including a floating charge), but

    (b)　does not include a right to execute diligence,

'RSP Rules' has the meaning given by section 111(1),

'secured creditor'—

    (a)　means the person in whose favour a pledge is granted, and

    (b)　includes or, as the case may be, consists of any successor in para, or representative, of a secured creditor,

'secured obligation' is to be construed in accordance with section 43(1),

'statutory pledge' has the meaning given by section 42(4), and

'the statutory pledges record' is to be construed in accordance with section 83(2).

(2)　Where two or more persons are co-providers or co-secured creditors in relation to a statutory pledge, any reference in this Act to the provider or secured creditor (as the case may be) is, unless the context requires otherwise, a reference to all of those persons.

(3)　A reference in this Part—

    (a)　to a statutory pledge being registered (however expressed) is to be construed as a reference to the Keeper's carrying out, in respect of the pledge, the duties imposed on the Keeper by section 87(1)(a) and (b),

    (b)　to an amendment to a statutory pledge being registered (however expressed) is to be construed as a reference to the Keeper's carrying out, in respect of the amendment, the duty imposed on the Keeper by section 89(1).

PART 3
MISCELLANEOUS AND GENERAL

Computer system

114　Automated computer system

(1)　The Keeper may, by means of an automated computer system under the Keeper's management and control, carry out the duties imposed on the Keeper under Chapter 2 of Part 1 and Chapter 2 of Part 2.

(2)　The power under subsection (1) includes, for example, the power to enable—

    (a)　the electronic generation and communication of applications under this Act,

    (b)　automated registration under this Act, and

    (c)　the creation of electronic documents.

(3)   The Keeper may impose reasonable conditions for using any computer system provided for the purposes of subsection (1).

Registration of electronic documents

115   Competence of registration of electronic documents

Section 9G(1)(d) of the Requirements of Writing (Scotland) Act 1995 (registration and recording of electronic documents) does not apply in relation to the registration of a document by the Keeper under this Act.

Good faith

116   Good faith

(1)   This section applies in relation to any provision made in this Act as respects good faith.
(2)   If there is a dispute as to whether a person was in (or acted in) good faith, the burden of proof lies on whoever asserts that the person was not in (or did not act in) good faith.

Review of the Act

117   Review of Act

(1)   The Scottish Ministers must, as soon as reasonably practicable after the end of the review period—
    (a)   undertake a review of the operation of this Act, and
    (b)   prepare a report on that review.
(2)   The report must, in particular, set out—
    (a)   an assessment of—
       (i)   the impact of allowing the debtor to waive the right to assert defences as provided for in section 14(1), and
       (ii)   how well the provisions regarding statutory pledges are working in relation to sole traders and small businesses, and
    (b)   the steps (if any) that the Scottish Ministers propose to take as a result of the findings of the review.
(3)   The Scottish Ministers must, as soon as reasonably practicable after preparing the report—
    (a)   publish the report, and
    (b)   lay the report before the Scottish Parliament.
(4)   For the purposes of this section, 'the review period' is the period of 5 years beginning with the day on which sections 1 and 42 come into force or, if they come into force on different days, the earlier of those days.

General

118   Regulations

(1)   Any power of the Scottish Ministers to make regulations under this Act includes the power to make—
    (a)   incidental, supplementary, consequential, transitional, transitory or saving provision,
    (b)   different provision for different purposes.
(2)   Regulations under any of the following sections are subject to the affirmative procedure: section 3(8), 4(7), 28(7), 32(1), 36(8), 46(3), 47(3), 50(4), 51(4), 54(3), 55(8), 65(4), 67(8), 74(9)(a), 75(7)(a), 77(10), 94(8), 95(1), 107(8) and 120(3).
(3)   Regulations under section 74(9)(b), 75(7)(b) or 119 which add to, replace or omit any part of the text of an Act are subject to the affirmative procedure.
(4)   Any other regulations under this Act are subject to the negative procedure.
(5)   This section does not apply to regulations under section 121.

119 Ancillary provision

(1) The Scottish Ministers may by regulations make any incidental, supplementary, consequential, transitional, transitory or saving provision they consider appropriate for the purposes of, in connection with or for giving full effect to this Act or any provision made under it.

(2) Regulations under this section may modify any enactment (including this Act).

120 Interpretation of Act

(1) In this Act (except where the context requires otherwise)—

'court' means Court of Session or sheriff,

'electronic document' has the meaning given by section 9A of the Requirements of Writing (Scotland) Act 1995,

'electronic signature' has the meaning given by section 12(1) of the Requirements of Writing (Scotland) Act 1995,

'the Keeper' means the Keeper of the Registers of Scotland,

'prescribed' means prescribed by regulations made by the Scottish Ministers,

'registration number' means a unique identifier consisting of numerals or of letters and numerals, and

'traditional document' has the meaning given by section 1A of the Requirements of Writing (Scotland) Act 1995.

(2) In this Act, a reference (however expressed) to—

  (a) the authentication of a document by a person is a reference to the electronic signature of that person—

    (i) being incorporated into, or logically associated with, the electronic document, and

    (ii) having been created by that person,

  (b) the execution of a document is a reference to the document's being subscribed as a traditional document in compliance with section 2(1) of the Requirements of Writing (Scotland) Act 1995.

(3) The Scottish Ministers may by regulations modify (either or both) paragraph (a) or paragraph (b) of subsection (2).

(4) Where, under or by virtue of a provision of this Act, however expressed, a person ('P') is required or permitted to proceed in some way, the provision is to be construed as if any reference in it to P includes a reference to any person authorised by P to proceed in such a way on P's behalf.

121 Commencement

(1) This section and sections 118, 119 and 122 come into force on the day after Royal Assent.

(2) The other provisions of this Act come into force on such day as the Scottish Ministers may by regulations appoint.

(3) Regulations under this section may—

  (a) include transitional, transitory or saving provision,

  (b) make different provision for different purposes.

122 Short title

The short title of this Act is the Moveable Transactions (Scotland) Act 2023.

OTHER MATERIALS

MATRIMONIAL HOMES (FORM OF CONSENT) (SCOTLAND) REGULATIONS 1982*
(SI 1982/971)

1—(1) These regulations may be cited as the Matrimonial Homes (Form of Consent) (Scotland) Regulations 1982 and shall come into operation on 1st September 1982.

(2) In these regulations—

'the Act' means the Matrimonial Homes (Family Protection) (Scotland) Act 1981, and, in a case where section 9(1) of the Act applies, any references in these regulations to the entitled spouse and to the non-entitled spouse shall be construed in accordance with section 9(2)(a) of the Act.

2 The consent of the non-entitled spouse to any dealing of the entitled spouse relating to a matrimonial home shall be—

(a) where the consent is given in a deed effecting the dealing, in or as nearly as may be in the form set out in Schedule 1 to these regulation; or

(b) where the consent is given in a separate document, in or as nearly as may be in the form set out in Schedule 2 to these regulations.

SCHEDULE 1
CONSENT TO BE INSERTED IN THE DEED EFFECTING THE DEALING

(The following words should be inserted where appropriate in the deed. The consenter should sign as a party to the deed.)

... with the consent of AB (*designation*), the spouse of the said CD, for the purposes of the Matrimonial Homes (Family Protection) (Scotland) Act 1981 ... [To be attested]

SCHEDULE 2
CONSENT IN A SEPARATE DOCUMENT

I, AB (*designation*), spouse of CD (*designation*), hereby consent, for the purposes of the Matrimonial Homes (Family Protection) (Scotland) Act 1981, to the undernoted dealing of the said CD relating to (*here describe the matrimonial home or the part of it to which the dealer relates: see Note 1*).

Dealing referred to:—

(*Here describe the dealing: see Note 2.*)

[To be attested].

Note 1

The expression 'matrimonial home' is defined in section 22 of the Matrimonial Homes (Family Protection) (Scotland) Act 1981 as follows:—

'"matrimonial home" means any house, caravan, houseboat or other structure which has been provided or has been made available by one or both of the spouses as, or has become, a family residence and includes any garden or other ground or building attached to, and usually occupied with, or otherwise required for the amenity or convenience of, the house, caravan, houseboat or other structure.'

---

* A similar form of consent for civil partners is made by the Civil Partnership Family Homes (Form of Consent) (Scotland) Regulations 2006 (SSI 2006/115).

Note 2
The expression 'dealing' is defined in section 6(2) of the Matrimonial Homes (Family Protection) (Scotland) Act 1981 as follows:—
>'"dealing" includes the grant of a heritable security and the creation of a trust but does not include a conveyance under section 80 of the Lands Clauses Consolidation (Scotland) Act 1845.'

TITLE CONDITIONS (SCOTLAND) ACT 2003 (CONSERVATION BODIES) ORDER 2003
(SSI 2003/453)

(amended by SSIs 2004/400; 2004/477; 2006/110; 2006/130; 2007/533; 2008/217; 2015/239, 2016/371)

Citation and commencement
1   This Order may be cited as the Title Conditions (Scotland) Act 2003 (Conservation Bodies) Order 2003 and shall come into force on 1st November 2003.

Prescribed conservation bodies
2   The bodies listed in Parts I and II of the Schedule to this Order are prescribed to be conservation bodies under section 38(4) (conservation burdens) of the Title Conditions (Scotland) Act 2003.

SCHEDULE
CONSERVATION BODIES PRESCRIBED UNDER SECTION 38(4) OF THE TITLE CONDITIONS (SCOTLAND) ACT 2003

PART I LOCAL AUTHORITIES

Aberdeen City Council
Aberdeenshire Council
Angus Council
Argyll and Bute Council
City of Edinburgh Council
Clackmannanshire Council
Comhairle nan Eilean Siar
Dumfries and Galloway Council
Dundee City Council
East Ayrshire Council
East Dunbartonshire Council
East Lothian Council
East Renfrewshire Council
Falkirk Council
Fife Council
Glasgow City Council

Highland Council
Inverclyde Council
Midlothian Council
Moray Council
North Ayrshire Council
North Lanarkshire Council
Orkney Islands Council
Perth and Kinross Council
Renfrewshire Council
Scottish Borders Council
Shetland Islands Council
South Ayrshire Council
South Lanarkshire Council
Stirling Council
West Dunbartonshire Council
West Lothian Council

PART II OTHER BODIES

[Aberdeen City Heritage Trust]
[Alba Conservation Trust]
Castles of Scotland Preservation Trust
[Chapelton Community Interest Company]
[Dundee Historic Environment Trust]
Edinburgh World Heritage Trust
Glasgow Building Preservation Trust
[Glasgow City Heritage Trust]
[. . .]
Highland Buildings Preservation Trust
[Historic Environment Scotland]
[Inverness City Heritage Trust]
[New Lanark Trust]
[Perth and Kinross Heritage Trust]
Plantlife – The Wild-Plant Conservation Charity
Scottish Natural Heritage
[Sir Henry Wade's Pilmuir Trust]
Solway Heritage
St Vincent Crescent Preservation Trust
[Stirling City Heritage Trust]
Strathclyde Building Preservation Trust
[Tayside Building Preservation Trust]
The John Muir Trust
The National Trust [for Scotland] for Places of Historic Interest and Natural Beauty
The Royal Society for the Protection of Birds
[The Scottish Wildlife Trust]
The Trustees of The Landmark Trust
[. . .]
The Woodland Trust
[Tornagrain Conservation Trust]
[United Kingdom Historic Building Preservation Trust]

TITLE CONDITIONS (SCOTLAND) ACT 2003 (RURAL HOUSING BODIES) ORDER 2004
(SSI 2004/477)

(amended by SSIs 2006/108; 2007/58; 2007/535; 2008/391; 2013/100; 2014/220; 2017/7; 2017/301; 2019/172)

Citation and commencement
1   This Order may be cited as the Title Conditions (Scotland) Act 2003 (Rural Housing Bodies) Order 2004 and shall come into force on 28th November 2004.

Prescribed rural housing bodies
2   The bodies listed in the Schedule to this Order are prescribed to be rural housing bodies under section 43(5) (rural housing burdens) of the Title Conditions (Scotland) Act 2003.

SCHEDULE
RURAL HOUSING BODIES PRESCRIBED UNDER SECTION 43(5) OF THE TITLE CONDITIONS (SCOTLAND) ACT 2003

Albyn Housing Society Limited
[Argyll Community Housing Association] [Arran Development Trust]
Barra and Vatersay Housing Association Limited

Berneray Housing Association Limited
[Buidheann Tigheadas Loch Aillse Agus An Eilein Sgitheanaich Limited]
Buidheann Tigheadas na Meadhanan Limited
Cairn Housing Association Limited
[Colonsay Community Development Company]
Comhairle nan Eilean Siar
[Community Self-Build Scotland Limited]
[Craignish Community Company Limited]
[Dormont Passive Homes (Scotland) Ltd]
[Down to Earth Solutions Community Interest Company]
Dumfries and Galloway Small Communities Housing Trust]
Dunbritton Housing Association Limited
[Ekopia Resource Exchange Limited]
Fyne Homes Limited
[Fyne Initiatives Limited]
[HIFAR Limited]
Isle of Jura Development Trust
[Kilfinan Community Forest Company]
Lochaber Housing Association Limited
Muirneag Housing Association Limited
[Mull and Iona Community Trust]
[North West Mull Community Woodland Company Limited]
Orkney Islands Council
Pentland Housing Association Limited
[Rural Stirling Housing Association Limited]
Taighean Ceann a Tuath na'Hearadh Limited
[The Highland Housing Alliance]
The Highlands Small Communities' Housing Trust
The Isle of Eigg Heritage Trust
The Isle of Gigha Heritage Trust
The North Harris Trust
Tighean Innse Gall Limited
[West Harris Trust]
[West Highland Housing Association Limited]
[West Highland Rural Solutions Limited]
[Yuill Community Trust CIC]

TENEMENTS (SCOTLAND) ACT 2004 (PRESCRIBED RISKS) ORDER 2007
(SSI 2007/16)

Citation and commencement
1   This Order may be cited as the Tenements (Scotland) Act 2004 (Prescribed Risks) Order 2007 and shall come into force on 1st May 2007.

Prescribed risks
2   The risks prescribed for the purposes of section 18 of the Tenements (Scotland) Act 2004 (obligations of owner to insure) are those risks specified in the Schedule to this Order.

Article 2   SCHEDULE
                                      PRESCRIBED RISKS

The risk of damage to a flat or any part of a tenement building attaching to that flat as a pertinent caused by:
    (a)   fire, smoke, lightning, explosion, earthquake;
    (b)   storm or flood;

(c)   theft or attempted theft;

(d)   riot, civil commotion, labour or political disturbance;

(e)   malicious persons or vandals;

(f)   subsidence, heave or landslip;

(g)   escape of water from water tanks, pipes, apparatus and domestic appliances;

(h)   collision with the building caused by any moving object originating outside the building;

(i)   leakage of oil from fixed heating installations; and

(j)   accidental damage to underground services.

TITLE CONDITIONS (SCOTLAND) ACT 2003 (DEVELOPMENT MANAGEMENT SCHEME) ORDER 2009
(SI 2009/729)

PART I
INTRODUCTORY

1   Citation, commencement and extent

(1)   This Order may be cited as the Title Conditions (Scotland) Act 2003 (Development Management Scheme) Order 2009 and comes into force on 1st June 2009.

(2)   This Order extends only to Scotland.

2   Interpretation

In this Order—

'the Act' means the Title Conditions (Scotland) Act 2003;

'association' means the owners' association of the development established under article 4;

'benefited unit' means a unit advantaged by a rule;

'burdened unit' means a unit constrained by a rule;

'deed of application' means a deed granted pursuant to section 71 of the Act;

'deed of variation' means a deed of variation or discharge granted pursuant to article 7 or 8;

'the development' means the land to which the Development Management Scheme is applied as described in the deed of application;

'the Development Management Scheme' has the meaning given in article 3;

'Lands Tribunal' means the Lands Tribunal for Scotland;

'manager' means the person appointed to be manager of the association;

'member' means a member of the association in accordance with rule 2.3 of the Development Management Scheme;

'owner' has the meaning given in article 18;

'registering' in relation to any document, means registering an interest in land or information relating to an interest in land (being an interest or information for which that document provides) in the Land Register of Scotland or, as the case may be, recording in the Register of Sasines (cognate expressions being construed accordingly);

'road' has the meaning given by section 151(1) of the Roads (Scotland) Act 1984;

'rule' means a rule of the Development Management Scheme;

'scheme property' has the meaning given in article 20;

'send' shall be construed in accordance with article 19 (cognate expressions being construed accordingly);

'service charge' has the meaning given in the Development Management Scheme;

'tenement' and 'tenement building' have the meanings given in section 26 of the Tenements (Scotland) Act 2004;

'unit' means an individual property forming the development as described in the deed of application for that development; and

'variation' includes the imposition of a new obligation (cognate expressions being construed accordingly).

PART 2
THE DEVELOPMENT MANAGEMENT SCHEME

3   The Development Management Scheme

The Development Management Scheme is the scheme of rules for the management of land set out in Schedule 1 to this Order or, in relation to a particular development, that scheme as applied to the development with such variations as may be specified by the deed of application and any other variations as may subsequently be made to that scheme.

4   Owners' association

(1)   The owners' association for the development is established on the date on which the Development Management Scheme applied to that development takes effect under section 71(1) of the Act in respect of that development (or part of that development).

(2)   The association is, on being established, a body corporate.

5   Application of provisions of the Act to rules of Scheme

(1) Sections 2, 3, 5, 10, 11, 13, 14, 16, 18, 59 to 61, 67, 70 and 105 of the Act shall apply, as modified by section 72 of the Act, in relation to the rules of the Development Management Scheme (other than the rules set out in Part 2 of Schedule 1 to this Order) as those sections apply in relation to community burdens.

(2)   Sections 68, 69, 98, 100 and 104 of the Act shall not apply in relation to the rules of the Development Management Scheme.

(3)   In this article and subject to paragraph (4), 'community burdens' has the same meaning as in the Act.

(4)   For the purposes of the application of the sections of the Act mentioned in paragraph (1) 'unit' has the meaning given in article 2 of this Order.

PART 3
VARIATION OF THE DEVELOPMENT MANAGEMENT SCHEME

6   Variation of Scheme in deed of application

(1)   A deed of application may, subject to paragraph (2), apply the Development Management Scheme to any land with such variations as may be specified in the deed of application.

(2)   The rules in Part 2 of Schedule 1 to this Order may not be varied in a deed of application other than in accordance with paragraph (3).

(3)   The deed of application must specify (as required in the instructions in rule 2.2) the name of the association, being a name which either ends with the words 'Owners' Association' or begins with those words preceded by the definite article.

7   Variation of Scheme with agreement of owners of affected and adjacent units

(1)   A rule of the Development Management Scheme (other than any rule in Part 2 of Schedule 1 to this Order) may be varied, or discharged, in relation to a unit by registering against that unit ('the affected unit') a deed of variation granted—

(a)   by the association, in accordance with the Development Management Scheme;

(b)   by the owner of the affected unit; and

(c)   by the owner of at least one adjacent unit (if any) in relation to the affected unit.

(2)   For the purposes of paragraph (1), 'adjacent unit' means, in relation to an affected unit, any unit which is at some point within four metres of the affected unit.

(3)   The reference in paragraph (2) to an adjacent unit being within four metres of the affected unit is a reference to distance along a horizontal plane, disregarding—

(a) the width of any intervening road if of less than twenty metres; and

(b) any pertinent of either unit.

8   Variation of Scheme generally by owners' association

A rule of the Development Management Scheme (other than any rule in Part 2 of Schedule 1 to this Order) may, subject to article 9, be varied, or discharged, in relation to a unit by registering against that unit a deed of variation granted by the association in accordance with the Development Management Scheme.

9   Intimation of variation under article 8

(1)   Where a deed of variation is granted under article 8, a proposal to register that deed must be intimated by the association to the members.

(2)   Intimation under paragraph (1) is to be given by sending a copy of the deed, together with—

(a) a notice in, or as near as may be in, the form set out in Schedule 2 to this Order; and

(b) the note which immediately follows that form in that Schedule.

(3)   A member may, during the period of eight weeks beginning with the date on which intimation of the proposal to register the deed is given to that member under paragraph (1), apply under article 22(1)(b) to the Lands Tribunal for preservation, unvaried, of the Development Management Scheme or a rule thereof.

(4)   A deed of variation granted under article 8 does not, on registration, vary or discharge a rule of the Development Management Scheme unless, after the expiry of the period of eight weeks beginning with the latest date on which intimation is given under paragraph (1), there is endorsed on it (or on an annexation to it referred to in an endorsement on it and identified, on the face of the annexation, as being the annexation so referred to) a certificate executed by a member of the Lands Tribunal, or by their clerk, to the effect that no application in relation to the proposal to register the deed has been received under article 22(1)(b) or that any such application which has been received—

(a) has been withdrawn; or

(b) relates to one or more but not to all of the rules of the Development Management Scheme to be varied or discharged by the deed (any rule to which it relates being described in the certificate),

and where more than one such application has been received the certificate must relate to both or (as the case may be) all applications.

(5)   Registration of a deed of variation granted under article 8 does not vary or discharge any rule described in a certificate by virtue of paragraph (4)(b).

(6)   Before a deed of variation granted under article 8 is submitted for registration a certificate must be endorsed on the deed by the association confirming—

(a) that paragraphs (1) and (2) have been complied with; and

(b) as to the date on which the period mentioned in paragraph (4) expires.

10   Enforcement of rules by members

(1)   Notwithstanding article 6(2), 7(1) or 8, a deed of application or a deed of variation may confer a right to enforce all or some of the rules of the Development Management Scheme on a member and the right to enforce may be conferred in respect of specified units or all the units in the development.

(2)   Where a deed of application or a deed of variation confers a right to enforce a rule on a member, the member is entitled to enforce the rule only if the member has interest to enforce it.

(3)   A member has such interest if, in the circumstances of any case, failure to comply with the rule is resulting in, or will result in, material detriment to the value or enjoyment of the member's ownership of the unit.

11   Further provision as respects deeds of variation
(1)   Where a deed of variation is granted no grantee is required.
(2)   A deed of variation may be registered by an owner of a burdened unit or by a granter.

PART 4
RIGHTS OF CREDITORS

12   Rights of creditors
(1)   Where—
    (a)   a debt due by the association satisfies the conditions mentioned in article 13; or
    (b)   the association is being, or has been, wound up,
any creditor of the association shall be entitled to recover a proportion of the debt from the owner of each of the units (or, as the case may be, from the person who was at the commencement of the winding up the owner of a unit) in accordance with the provisions of paragraphs (2) to (4).
(2)   The owner of each unit is, subject to paragraph (4), liable to the creditor for the proportion of the debt attributable to the unit in accordance with paragraph (3).
(3)   The proportion of the debt attributable to each unit is—
    (a)   where service charge is payable by the owner of the unit in accordance with the Development Management Scheme, the share of the debt equal to the proportion of service charge which would have been attributable to the unit had the debt been due as service charge; or
    (b)   if there is no service charge payable, an equal share of the debt.
(4)   Where all or part of the proportion of the debt attributable to a unit ('a non-paying unit') cannot be recovered (for example, because the estate of the owner of the non-paying unit has been sequestrated or cannot by reasonable inquiry be identified or found) then the proportion of the debt recoverable by the creditor from the other units shall be increased by an amount equal to an equal share (as among such other units) of the proportion of the debt which cannot be recovered from the owner of the non paying unit.
(5)   If an owner of a unit makes a payment to a creditor in accordance with paragraph (4) that owner may recover an amount equal to the amount paid under paragraph (4) from the owner of the non-paying unit.
(6)   If two or more persons own a unit in common then, unless the Development Management Scheme otherwise provides—
    (a)   they are severally liable in respect of the proportion of the debt; and
    (b)   as between (or among) themselves, they are liable in the proportions in which they own the unit.

13   Conditions referred to in article 12
The conditions referred to in article 12(1) are that—
    (a)   the debt is constituted by—
        (i)   decree; or
        (ii)   a document which has been registered for execution in the Books of Council and Session or, as the case may be, in the appropriate sheriff court books kept for any sheriffdom; and
    (b)   either—
        (i)   the creditor has executed diligence but has not recovered the debt in full; or

(ii)   it does not appear that the association has any assets which reasonably could be recovered by diligence.

PART 5
CHALLENGES TO OPERATION OF THE SCHEME

14   Application to sheriff for annulment of decisions made under Scheme
(1)   A member may, by summary application to the sheriff, seek an order annulling a decision made by the association at a general meeting provided that the member was not, at the time the decision was made, in favour of the decision.

(2)   An application by a member under paragraph (1) is to be made—
(a)   in a case where the decision was made at a meeting attended by the member, not later than twenty eight days after the date of that meeting; or
(b)   in any other case, not later than twenty eight days after the date on which notice of the making of the decision was sent to the owner for the time being of the unit in question.

(3)   The sheriff may, if satisfied that the decision—
(a)   is not in the best interests of all the members taken as a group; or
(b)   is unfairly prejudicial to one or more of the members, make an order annulling the decision (in whole or in part).

(4)   Where an application under paragraph (1) is made as respects a decision to carry out maintenance, improvements or alterations, the sheriff is, in considering whether to make an order under paragraph (3), to have regard to—
(a)   the age of the property which is to be maintained, improved or, as the case may be, altered;
(b)   its condition;
(c)   the likely cost of any such maintenance, improvements or alterations; and
(d)   the reasonableness of that cost.

(5)   Where the sheriff makes an order under paragraph (3) annulling a decision (in whole or in part), the sheriff may make such other, consequential, order as the sheriff thinks fit (for example, an order as respects the liability of members for any costs already incurred).

(6)   A party may, not later than fourteen days after the date of—
(a)   an order under paragraph (3); or
(b)   an interlocutor dismissing an application under paragraph (1),
appeal to the Court of Session on a point of law.

(7)   A decision of the Court of Session on an appeal under paragraph (6) shall be final.

(8)   Where a member is entitled to make an application under paragraph (1) in relation to any decision, no step shall be taken to implement that decision unless—
(a)   the period specified in paragraph (2) within which such an application is to be made has expired without such an application having been made and notified to the members; or
(b)   where such an application has been so made and notified—
(i)   the application has been disposed of and either the period specified in paragraph (6) within which an appeal against the sheriff's decision has expired without such an appeal having been made or such an appeal has been made and disposed of; or
(ii)   the application has been abandoned.

(9)   Paragraph (8) does not apply to a decision relating to work which requires to be carried out urgently.

(10)   For the purposes of any application under paragraph (1) the defender shall be the association.

15   Application to sheriff for order resolving certain disputes
(1)   Any member may by summary application apply to the sheriff for an order relating to any matter concerning the operation of—
  (a)   the Development Management Scheme which applies as respects the development; or
  (b)   any provision of this Order in its application as respects the development.
(2)   Where an application is made under paragraph (1) the sheriff may, subject to such conditions (if any) as the sheriff thinks fit—
  (a)   grant the order craved; or
  (b)   make such other order as the sheriff considers necessary or expedient.
(3)   A party may not later than fourteen days after the date of—
  (a)   an order under paragraph (2); or
  (b)   an interlocutor dismissing an application under paragraph (1),
appeal to the Court of Session on a point of law.
(4)   A decision of the Court of Session on an appeal under paragraph (3) shall be final.

PART 6
GENERAL

16   Liability of successor for service charge
(1)   Where a person who becomes, or is to become, an owner of a unit in the development obtains a certificate signed by the manager stating that as at the date on which it is signed no service charge is outstanding as respects the unit or, as the case may be, that any service charge due does not exceed an amount specified in the certificate, then, apart from a service charge no greater than the amount so specified, that person shall not be liable for any service charge which was outstanding on that date.
(2)   The manager must, on the request of the person mentioned in paragraph (1), prepare and sign a certificate required for the purposes of that paragraph and provide it to that person.

17   Continued application of the rules following disapplication of the Scheme
Rules 6 and 17 and any other rule of the Development Management Scheme in so far as applicable as respects the winding up of the association, shall continue to have effect notwithstanding the disapplication of the Scheme to the development.

18   The expression 'owner'
(1)   Subject to paragraph (2), 'owner', in relation to any unit, means a person who has right to the unit whether or not that person has completed title; but if, in relation to the unit (or, if the unit is held *pro indiviso*, any *pro indiviso* share in the unit) more than one person comes within that description of owner, then 'owner'—
  (a)   for the purposes of article 7(1), means any person having such right; and
  (b)   for any other purpose, means such person as has most recently acquired such right.
(2)   Where a heritable creditor is in lawful possession of security subjects which comprise the unit, then 'owner'—
  (a)   for the purposes of article 7(1) includes, in addition to any such person as is mentioned in paragraph (1)(a), that heritable creditor; and
  (b)   for any other purposes means the heritable creditor.

19   Sending
(1)   Where a provision of this Order requires that a thing be sent—
  (a)   to a person it shall suffice, for the purposes of that provision, that the thing be sent to an agent of the person;

(b) to a member and that member cannot by reasonable inquiry be identified or found, it shall suffice, for the purposes of that provision, that the thing be sent to the member's unit addressed to 'The Owner' (or using some other such expression, as for example 'The Proprietor').

(2) Except in paragraph (3), any reference in this Order to a thing being sent is to be construed as a reference to its being—

(a) posted;

(b) delivered; or

(c) transmitted by electronic means.

(3) For the purposes of any provision of this Order, a thing posted is to be taken to be sent on the day of posting; and a thing transmitted by electronic means, to be sent on the day of transmission.

20 Scheme property

(1) Subject to paragraphs (2) and (3) 'scheme property' means the property specified or described as such in the Development Management Scheme.

(2) Where the development is, or includes, a tenement 'scheme property' includes—

(a) any part of a tenement that is the common property of the owners of two or more units;

(b) with the exceptions mentioned in paragraph (3), the following parts of a tenement building (so far as not scheme property by virtue of paragraph (a))—

(i) the ground on which it is built;

(ii) its foundations;

(iii) its external walls;

(iv) its roof (including any rafter or other structure supporting the roof);

(v) if it is separated from another building by a gable wall, the part of the gable wall that is part of the tenement building; and

(vi) any wall (not being one falling within the preceding sub paragraphs), beam or column that is load bearing.

(2) The following parts of a tenement building are the exceptions referred to in paragraph (2)(b)—

(a) any extension which forms part of only one unit;

(b) any—

(i) door;

(ii) window;

(iii) skylight;

(iv) vent; or

(v) other opening; and

(c) any chimney stack or chimney flue.

21 Tenements—emergency work, redistribution of costs

(1) Where the development is, or includes, a tenement, rule 14 of Schedule 1 to this Order applies and is to be treated as forming a rule of the Development Management Scheme as applied to that development to the extent that there is no rule in the Development Management Scheme as applied to that development making provision for a member to instruct or carry out any emergency work as defined in that rule.

(2) Where the development is, or includes, a tenement, rule 19.4 of Schedule 1 to this Order applies and is to be treated as forming a rule of the Development Management Scheme as applied to that development to the extent that there is no rule in the Development Management Scheme as applied to that development making provision as to the liability of the members in the circumstances covered by the provisions of that rule.

PART 7
POWERS OF THE LANDS TRIBUNAL FOR SCOTLAND

22   Powers of the Lands Tribunal

(1)   Subject to articles 28 and 30 and to paragraphs (3) and (4), the Lands Tribunal may by order, on the application of a member—

(a)   discharge or vary a rule of the Development Management Scheme (other than a rule in Part 2 of the Development Management Scheme) in relation to a unit owned by that member;

(b)   preserve, as mentioned in article 9(3), a rule in respect of which intimation of a proposal to register a deed of variation has been given under article 9(1); or

(c)   determine any question as to the validity, applicability or enforceability of a rule of the Development Management Scheme or as to how it is to be construed.

(2)   Where the Lands Tribunal refuse an application under paragraph (1)(b), they are to vary or discharge the rule accordingly.

(3)   It is not competent to make an application under paragraph (1)(b)—

(a)   after the expiry of the period mentioned in article 9(3), except with the consent of the association; or

(b)   after there has been, in relation to the proposal, endorsement under article 9(4).

(4)   Variation which would impose a new obligation or would result in the owner of a unit becoming entitled to enforce an obligation shall not be competent on an application under paragraph (1)(a) unless the owner of the unit subject, or to be made subject, to the obligation consents.

(5)   Subject to paragraph (7), an order discharging or varying a rule may—

(a)   where made under paragraph (1)(a) direct the applicant; or

(b)   where made by virtue of the refusal of an application under paragraph (1)(b),

direct the association, to pay to any person who was entitled to enforce the rule, such sum as the Lands Tribunal may think it just to award under one, but not both, of the heads mentioned in paragraph (6).

(6)   The heads are—

(a)   a sum to compensate for any substantial loss or disadvantage suffered by the member, as owner of a unit, in consequence of the discharge or variation;

(b)   a sum to make up for any effect which the rule produced, at the time when it was created, in reducing the consideration then paid or made payable for the burdened unit.

(7)   A direction under paragraph (5) shall be made only if the person directed consents.

(8)   Subject to paragraph (9), an order discharging or varying a rule may impose on a unit a new rule or vary a rule extant at the time the order is made.

(9)   An imposition under paragraph (8) shall be made only if the owner of the unit consents.

23   Special provision as to variation or discharge of rules

(1)   Without prejudice to article 22(1)(a), an application may be made to the Lands Tribunal under this article by owners of at least one quarter of the units for the variation or discharge of a rule (other than a rule in Part 2 of the Development Management Scheme) as it affects, or as the case may be would affect, all or some of the units forming the development.

(2)   In the case of an application made by owners of some (but not all) of the units forming the development, the units affected need not be the units which they own.

(3)   Paragraphs (5) to (7) of article 22 apply in relation to an order made by

virtue of paragraph (1) varying or discharging a rule as they apply to an order under article 22(1)(a).

24   Notification of application

   (1)   The Lands Tribunal must, on receipt of an application under—

     (a)   article 22(1)(a) or 23(1), give notice of that application to the association and the members;

     (b)   article 22(1)(b) or (c), give such notice to the association,

and subject to paragraph (2) are to do so by sending the notice.

   (2)   If the person to whom the notice is to be given cannot, by reasonable inquiry, be identified or found, notice under paragraph (1) may be given by advertisement, or by such other method as the Lands Tribunal think fit.

   (3)   The Lands Tribunal may also give notice of the application, by such means as they think fit, to any other person.

25   Content of notice

   (1)   The Lands Tribunal must in any notice given by them under article 24(1)—

     (a)   summarise or reproduce the application;

     (b)   set a date (being a date no earlier than twenty one days after the notice is given) by which representations to them as respects the application may be made;

     (c)   state the fee which must accompany any such representations; and

     (d)   state that if the application is not opposed it may be granted without further inquiry.

   (2)   Any notice given (other than by advertisement) in respect of an application under article 22(1)(a) or article 23 must also set out the name and address of every person to whom the notice is being sent.

26   Persons entitled to make representations

The persons entitled to make representations as respects an application under article 22 or 23 are—

     (a)   the association; and

     (b)   any member.

27   Representations

   (1)   Representations made by any person to the Lands Tribunal as respects an application under article 22 or 23 must be in writing and must comprise a statement of the facts and contentions upon which the person proposes to rely.

   (2)   Representations are made when they are received by the Lands Tribunal with the requisite fee; and a person sending such representations must forthwith send a copy of them to the applicant.

   (3)   Notwithstanding article 25(1)(b), the Lands Tribunal may if they think fit accept representations made after the date set under that sub paragraph.

28   Granting applications for discharge, variation or preservation of a rule

   (1)   An application for the variation, discharge or preservation of a rule is to be granted by the Lands Tribunal only if they are satisfied, having regard to the factors set out in paragraph (2) that—

     (a)   except in the case of an application under article 22(1)(b), it is reasonable to grant the application; or

     (b)   in such a case, the variation or discharge in question—

        (i)   is not in the best interests of all the members (taken as a group); or

        (ii)   is unfairly prejudicial to one or more members.

   (2)   The factors mentioned in paragraph (1) are—

     (a)   any change in circumstances since the rule was created (including, without prejudice to that generality, any change in the character of the benefited unit or burdened unit or of the neighbourhood of the units);

     (b)   the extent to which the rule confers a benefit on a benefited unit;

(c)   the extent to which the rule impedes enjoyment of the burdened unit;
(d)   if the rule is an obligation to do something, how—
    (i)   practicable; or
    (ii)   costly,
it is to comply with the rule;
(e)   the length of time which has elapsed since the rule was created;
(f)   the purpose of the rule;
(g)   whether in relation to the burdened unit there is the consent, or deemed consent of a planning authority, or consent of some other regulatory authority, for a use which the rule prevents;
(h)   whether the owner of the burdened unit is willing to pay compensation;
(i)   any other factor which the Lands Tribunal consider to be material.

29   Expenses

The Lands Tribunal may, in determining an application made under article 22 or 23, make such order as to expenses as they think fit but are to have regard, in particular, to the extent to which the application, or any opposition to the application, is successful.

30   Taking effect of orders of Lands Tribunal etc

(1)   Subject to paragraphs (2) to (4), an order made by the Lands Tribunal in respect of an application under article 22 or article 23 takes effect on the occurrence of whichever of the following events last occurs after the Lands Tribunal has made the order—
(a)   the expiry of the period of 21 days after the date when the order was made by the Lands Tribunal;
(b)   the disposal by the Court of Session of a case stated by the Lands Tribunal on appeal to that court or, if there is an appeal to the House of Lords, the disposal of the case by the House of Lords;
(c)   the abandonment or other termination of the proceedings on a case so stated without a decision having been given;
(d)   the abandonment or other termination of an appeal against the decision of the Court of Session on a case so stated or the expiry of the time for bringing any such appeal without it having been brought; or
(e)   the variation by the Lands Tribunal of the order in compliance with any directions given by the Court of Session or the House of Lords in proceedings relating to such a case.

(2)   Where the application is unopposed or all persons who have opposed or made representations in respect of the application have informed the Lands Tribunal that they consent to the order taking effect immediately, and it is so certified in the order, such order takes effect on the date on which it is made by the Lands Tribunal.

(3)   Where a rule is varied or discharged subject to the payment of any compensation awarded by the Lands Tribunal, the order of the Lands Tribunal shall not, so far as it affects such variation or discharge, take effect until the Lands Tribunal has endorsed the order to the effect either that the compensation has been paid or that all persons to whom any compensation has been awarded but who have not received payment of it have agreed to the order taking effect.

(4)   The Lands Tribunal may direct that the compensation must be paid or satisfied within a specified time and that, unless it is so paid or satisfied, the order shall be void on the expiration of the time so specified.

31   Registration of orders

(1)   An order under—
(a)   article 22(1) granting an application under article 22(1)(a) or (b);
(b)   article 22(1) on the refusal (wholly or partly as the case may be) of an application under article 22(1)(b); or

(c)   article 23(1);

which has taken effect in accordance with article 30 may be registered against the unit of the development by any person who was a party to the application or who was, under article 26, entitled to make representations as respects the application; and on the order being so registered the rule to which it relates is preserved, discharged (wholly or partly) or varied according to the terms of the order.

(2)   Any enforceability which the obligation in question has as a contractual obligation is unaffected by an order made under article 22(1) or article 23.

SCHEDULE 1
DEVELOPMENT MANAGEMENT SCHEME

Article 3

PART 1
INTERPRETATION

Rule 1—Interpretation

1   Definitions

In this scheme, unless the context otherwise requires—

'the Act' means the Title Conditions (Scotland) Act 2003;

'advisory committee' means any such committee formed in pursuance of rule 15.1;

'association' means the owners' association of the development established under article 4 of the Development Management Scheme Order;

'deed of disapplication' means a deed granted pursuant to section 73 of the Act;

'deed of variation' means a deed of variation or discharge granted pursuant to article 7 or 8 of the Development Management Scheme Order;

'the development' is [*specify the extent of the development*];

'the Development Management Scheme Order' means the Title Conditions (Scotland) Act 2003 (Development Management Scheme) Order 2009;

'general meeting' means an annual or other general meeting of the association;

'maintenance' includes repairs or replacement, cleaning, painting and other routine works, gardening and the day to day running of property; but does not include demolition, alteration or improvement unless reasonably incidental to the maintenance;

'manager' means the person appointed to be manager of the association;

'member' means a member of the association in accordance with rule 2.3;

'owner' has the meaning given in article 18 of the Development Management Scheme Order;

'regulations' means regulations made under rule 3.6;

'reserve fund' means money held on behalf of the association to meet the cost of long term maintenance, improvement or alteration of scheme property or to meet such other expenses of the association as the association may determine;

'scheme property' means [*describe the property which is subject to maintenance under the scheme*];

'service charge' means the contribution to association funds payable in accordance with Part 4 of this scheme and includes additional service charge; and

'unit' means [*specify the individual properties forming the development*].

PART 2
THE OWNERS' ASSOCIATION

Rule 2—Establishment, status etc

2.1 Establishment
The association is established on the day on which this scheme takes effect.

2.2 Status
The association is a body corporate to be known as [*specify the name of the owners' association*].

2.3 Members of the association
The members are the persons who, for the time being, are the owners of the units to which this scheme applies and has taken effect; and where two or more persons own a unit both (or all) of them are members.

2.4 Address of association
The address of the association is that of—
  (a) the development; and
  (b) the manager,
or either of them.

Rule 3—Function, powers and enforcement

3.1 Function of association
The function of the association is to manage the development for the benefit of the members.

3.2 Powers of the association
The association has, subject to rule 3.3, power to do anything necessary for or in connection with the carrying out of the function mentioned in rule 3.1 and in particular may—
  (a) own, or acquire ownership of, any part of the development;
  (b) carry out maintenance, improvements or alterations to, or demolition of, the scheme property;
  (c) enter into a contract of insurance in respect of the development or any part of it (and for that purpose the association is deemed to have an insurable interest);
  (d) purchase, or otherwise acquire or obtain the use of, moveable property;
  (e) require owners of units to contribute by way of service charge to association funds;
  (f) open and maintain an account with any bank or building society;
  (g) invest any money held by the association;
  (h) borrow money; or
  (i) engage employees or appoint agents.

3.3 Prohibited activities
The association shall not have power to—
  (a) acquire land outwith the development;
  (b) carry on any trade whether or not for profit; or
  (c) make regulations other than in accordance with rule 3.6.

3.4 Scheme to be binding
This scheme is binding on the association, the manager and the members as are any regulations which have taken effect; and a rule, or any such regulation, in the form of an obligation to refrain from doing something is binding on—
  (a) a tenant of property affected by the rule or regulation; or
  (b) any other person having the use of such property.

3.5 Enforcement of scheme

The association may enforce—

(a) the provisions of this scheme and any regulations which have taken effect; and

(b) any obligation owed by any person to the association.

3.6 Regulations

The association may, at a general meeting—

(a) make regulations as to the use of recreational facilities which are part of the scheme property; and

(b) revoke or amend regulations made under paragraph (a),

but any such regulation, revocation or amendment takes effect only after a copy of it has been delivered or sent to each member.

Rule 4—The manager

4.1 Association to have manager

The association is to have a manager who, subject to any other provision of this scheme, is a person (whether or not a member) appointed by the association at a general meeting.

4.2 Power to remove manager

The association may at a general meeting remove the manager from office before the expiry of that person's term of office.

4.3 Validity of actings of manager

Any actings of the manager are valid notwithstanding any defect in that person's appointment.

4.4 Manager to be agent

The manager is an agent of the association.

4.5 Exercise of powers

Subject to this scheme, any power conferred on the association under or by virtue of this scheme is exercisable by—

(a) the manager; or

(b) the association at a general meeting.

4.6 Duties owed to association and members

Any duty imposed on the manager under or by virtue of this scheme is owed to the association and to the members.

4.7 Manager to comply with directions

The manager must, in so far as it is reasonably practicable to do so, comply with any direction given by the association at a general meeting as respects the exercise by the manager of—

(a) powers conferred; or

(b) duties imposed,

on the association or on the manager.

4.8 Information about management

Any member may require the manager to allow that member to inspect a copy of any document, other than any correspondence with another member, which relates to the management of the development; and if the document is in the manager's possession or it is reasonably practicable for the manager to obtain a copy of it the manager must comply with the requirement.

4.9 Notice to manager on sale etc of unit

Any member who sells or otherwise disposes of a unit must, before the date on which the person to whom the unit is to be sold (or otherwise transferred) will be entitled to take entry, send a notice to the manager stating, to the extent to which the information is known by that member—

(a)   the entry date and the name and address of that person;

(b)   the name and address of the solicitor or other agent acting for that person in the acquisition of the unit; and

(c)   an address at which the member may be contacted after that date.

Rule 5—Execution of documents

5   Execution of documents by association

A document is signed by the association if signed on behalf of the association by—

(a)   the manager; or

(b)   a person nominated for the purpose by the association at a general meeting, provided that the manager or person acts within actual or ostensible authority to bind the association.

Rule 6—Winding up

6.1   Commencement of winding up

The manager must commence the winding up of the association on the day on which this scheme ceases to apply as respects the development.

6.2   Distribution of funds

The manager must, as soon as practicable after the commencement of the winding up, use any association funds to pay any debts of the association; and thereafter must distribute in accordance with this scheme any remaining funds among those who were, on the date when the winding up commenced, owners of units.

6.3   Final accounts

The manager must—

(a)   prepare the final accounts of the association showing how the winding up was conducted and the funds were disposed of; and

(b)   not later than six months after the commencement of the winding up, send a copy of those accounts to the owner of every unit.

6.4   Automatic dissolution of association

Subject to rule 6.5, the association is dissolved at the end of the period of six months beginning with the commencement of the winding up.

6.5   Delayed dissolution

At any time before the end of the period of six months mentioned in rule 6.4, the members may determine that the association is to continue for such period as they may specify; and if they so determine it is dissolved at the end of the period so specified.

PART 3
MANAGEMENT

Rule 7—Appointment of manager

7.1   First manager

The first manager is [*complete name and address of manager*] and—

(a)   acts as manager until the first annual general meeting is held;

(b)   is entitled to reasonable remuneration; and

(c)   is eligible for reappointment.

7.2   Appointment of manager

The association—

(a)   at the first annual general meeting; and

(b) where the manager's period of office expires or a vacancy occurs, at any subsequent general meeting,

is to appoint a person to be manager on such terms and conditions as the association may decide.

7.3 Certificate of appointment
Not later than one month after the date of a general meeting at which a person is appointed to be manager—
(a) that person; and
(b) on behalf of the association, a member,

must sign a certificate recording the making, and the period, of the appointment.

Rule 8—Duties of manager

8 Duties of manager
The manager must manage the development for the benefit of the members and in particular must—
(a) from time to time carry out inspections of the scheme property;
(b) arrange for the carrying out of maintenance to scheme property;
(c) fix the financial year of the association;
(d) keep, as respects the association, proper financial records and prepare the accounts of the association for each financial year;
(e) implement any decision made by the association at a general meeting;
(f) in so far as it is reasonable to do so, enforce—
 (i) any obligation owed by any person to the association; and
 (ii) the provisions of the scheme and of any regulations which have taken effect;
(g) if there are regulations, keep a copy of them (taking account of revocations and amendments); and
(h) keep a record of the name and address of each member.

Rule 9—Calling of general meetings

9.1 First annual general meeting
The first annual general meeting must be called by the manager and held not later than twelve months after the day on which, in accordance with rule 2.1, the association is established.

9.2 Annual general meetings
The manager must call an annual general meeting each year; and a meeting so called must be held no more than fifteen months after the date on which the previous annual general meeting was held.

9.3 Other general meetings
The manager may call a general meeting at any time and must call a general meeting if—
(a) a revised draft budget requires to be considered;
(b) required to call that meeting by members holding not less than twenty five per cent of the total number of votes allocated; or
(c) so required by a majority of the members of the advisory committee.

9.4 Calling of meeting
Not later than fourteen days before the date fixed for a general meeting the manager must call the meeting by sending to each member—
(a) a notice stating—
 (i) the date and time fixed for the meeting and the place where it is to be held; and
 (ii) the business to be transacted at the meeting; and
(b) if the meeting is an annual general meeting, copies of the draft budget

and (except in the case of the first annual general meeting) the accounts of the association for the last financial year.

9.5 Validity of proceedings
Any inadvertent failure to comply with rule 9.4 as respects any member does not affect the validity of proceedings at a general meeting.

9.6 Member's right to call meeting in certain circumstances
Any member may call a general meeting if—
    (a) the manager fails to call a general meeting—
        (i) in a case where paragraph (b) or (c) of rule 9.3 applies, not later than fourteen days after being required to do so as mentioned in those paragraphs; or
        (ii) in any other case, in accordance with this scheme; or
    (b) the association does not have a manager.

9.7 Procedure where member calls meeting
Where under rule 9.6 a general meeting is called by a member—
    (a) any rule imposing a procedural or other duty on the manager in relation to general meetings (other than the duty imposed by rule 9.4(b)) applies as if it imposed the duty on the member; and
    (b) if there is a manager, the member must send that person a notice stating the date and time fixed for the meeting, the business to be transacted at it and the place where it is to be held.

Rule 10—General meetings: Quorum

10.1 Number required for quorum
A quorum is—
    (a) where there are no more than thirty units in the development, members present or represented holding fifty per cent of the total number of votes allocated;
    (b) where there are more than thirty such units, members present or represented holding thirty-five per cent of the total number of votes allocated.

10.2 Quorum necessary for meeting to begin
A general meeting is not to begin unless there is a quorum; and if there is still no quorum twenty minutes after the time fixed for a general meeting then—
    (a) the meeting is to be postponed until such date, being not less than fourteen nor more than twenty-eight days later, as may be specified by the manager (or, if the manager is not present or if there is no manager, by a majority of the members present or represented); and
    (b) the manager (or any member) must send to each member a notice stating the date and time fixed for the postponed meeting and the place where it is to be held.

10.3 No quorum at postponed meeting
A meeting may be postponed only once; and if at a postponed meeting the provisions in rule 10.2 as respects a quorum are not satisfied, then the members who are present or represented are to be deemed a quorum.

10.4 Quorum need not be maintained
If a general meeting has begun, it may continue even if the number of members present or represented ceases to be a quorum.

Rule 11—General meetings: Voting

11.1 Allocation and exercise of votes
For the purpose of voting on any proposal at a general meeting one vote is allo-

cated to each unit; and any right to vote is exercisable by the owner of that unit or by someone (not being the manager) nominated in writing by the owner to vote.

11.2   Exercise of vote where two or more persons own unit
If a unit is owned by two or more persons the vote allocated to that unit may be exercised by either (or any) of them; but if those persons disagree as to how the vote should be cast then no vote is counted for that unit.

11.3   Decision by majority
Except where this scheme otherwise provides, a decision is made by the association at a general meeting by majority vote of all the votes cast.

11.4   Method of voting
Voting on any proposal is by show of hands; but the convener may determine that voting on a particular proposal is to be by ballot.

Rule 12—General meetings: Further provisions

12.1   Election of convener
The members present or represented at a general meeting are to elect one of their number or the manager to be convener of the meeting; and on being so elected the convener is to take charge of the organisation of the business of the meeting.

12.2   Additional business
Any member present or represented at a general meeting may nominate additional business to be transacted at that meeting.

12.3   Manager to attend and keep record of business transacted
Except where unable to do so because of illness or for some other good reason, the manager must attend each general meeting and—
    (a)   keep a record of the business transacted; and
    (b)   not later than twenty-one days after the date of the meeting, send a copy of the record of business to each member,
and where the manager does not attend the convener is to nominate a person present to carry out the manager's duties under paragraphs (a) and (b) of this rule in respect of the meeting.

Rule 13—Special majority decisions

13.1   Special majority required
The association may—
    (a)   make a payment out of any reserve fund which it has formed; or
    (b)   use any money held on behalf of the association to carry out improvements or alterations to, or demolition of, scheme property (not being improvements, alterations or demolition reasonably incidental to maintenance),
but only after the association have, at a general meeting, by majority vote of all the votes allocated, determined to do so.

13.2   Consent of owner to be given where not common property
Where scheme property is not the common property of the members (or not the common property of members who between them own two or more units) a determination under rule 13.1 for the purposes of paragraph (b) of that rule may be implemented only if the owner of the property consents in writing to the improvements, alterations or demolition in question.

Rule 14—Emergency work

14.1   Power to instruct etc
Any member may instruct or carry out emergency work.

14.2 Reimbursement of member
The association must reimburse any member who pays for emergency work.

14.3 Meaning of 'emergency work'
'Emergency work' means work which requires to be carried out to scheme property—
    (a) to prevent damage to any part of that or any other property; or
    (b) in the interests of health or safety,
in circumstances in which it is not practicable to consult the manager before carrying out the work.

Rule 15—Advisory committee

15.1 Power to elect advisory committee
The association may at a general meeting elect such number of the members as it may specify to form an advisory committee whose function is to provide the manager with advice relating to the manager's—
    (a) exercise of powers; and
    (b) fulfilment of duties, under or by virtue of this scheme.

15.2 Manager to consult advisory committee
Where an advisory committee is formed, the manager is from time to time to seek advice from the committee.

Rule 16—Variation

16.1 Deeds of variation under article 7
The manager may, on behalf of the association and after consulting the advisory committee (if any), grant a deed of variation under article 7 of the Development Management Scheme Order, and at the first general meeting after the granting of the deed the manager must then report that it has been so granted.

16.2 Deeds of variation under article 8 and deeds of disapplication
The manager may, on behalf of the association, grant a deed of variation under article 8 of the Development Management Scheme Order or a deed of disapplication but only after the association has, at a general meeting, by majority of all the votes allocated, determined to do so.

Rule 17—Winding up

17 Distribution of funds on winding up
Where funds are distributed under rule 6.2 the basis of distribution is that each unit receives one share.

PART 4
FINANCIAL MATTERS

Rule 18—Annual budget

18.1 Duty of manager to prepare annual budget
Before each annual general meeting the manager must prepare, and submit for consideration at that meeting, a draft budget for the new financial year.

18.2 Content of draft budget
A draft budget is to set out—
    (a) the total service charge and the date (or dates) on which the service charge will be due for payment;
    (b) an estimate of any other funds which the association is likely to receive and the source of those funds;

(c)   an estimate of the expenditure of the association; and

(d)   the amount (if any) to be deposited in a reserve fund.

18.3   Consideration of draft budget by association

The association may at a general meeting—

(a)   approve the draft budget subject to such variations as it may specify; or

(b)   reject the budget and direct the manager to prepare a revised draft budget for consideration by the association at a general meeting to be called by the manager and to take place not later than two months after the date of the meeting at which the budget is rejected.

18.4   Rejected budget—payment of service charge

Where the budget is rejected the service charge exigible under the budget last approved is, until a new budget is approved, to continue to be exigible and is to be due for payment on the anniversary (or anniversaries) of the date (or dates) on which it was originally due for payment.

18.5   Revised draft budget

At a general meeting at which a revised draft budget is considered, the association may approve or reject the budget as mentioned in rule 18.3(a) and (b).

Rule 19—Service charge

19.1   Amount of service charge

Except where rule 19.2 applies, the amount of any service charge imposed under this scheme is the same as respects each unit.

19.2   Service charge exemption

The association may at a general meeting decide as respects a particular owner and in relation to a particular payment that no service charge (or a service charge of a reduced amount) is payable.

19.3   Manager to collect service charge

When the draft budget has been approved in accordance with this scheme, the manager—

(a)   must send to each owner a notice requiring payment, on the date (or dates) specified in the budget, of the amount of the service charge so specified; and

(b)   may send to each owner at any time a notice—

(i)   requiring payment, on the date (or dates) stated in the notice, of an additional amount of service charge determined under rule 20.1; and

(ii)   explaining why the additional amount is payable, and each owner is liable for that amount accordingly.

19.4   Redistribution of share of costs

Where an owner is liable for a service charge but the service charge cannot be recovered (for example because the estate of that owner has been sequestrated, or that owner cannot, by reasonable inquiry, be identified or found) then that service charge is to be shared equally among the other owners or, if they so decide, is to be met out of any reserve fund; but that owner remains liable for the service charge.

19.5   Interest payable on overdue service charge

Where any service charge (or part of it) remains outstanding not less than twenty eight days after it became due for payment, the manager may send a notice to the owner concerned requiring that person to pay interest on the sum outstanding at such reasonable rate and from such date as the manager may specify in the notice.

19.6   Interpretation of rule 19

In rule 19 references to 'owner' are references to an owner of a unit.

Rule 20—Additional service charge

20.1   Additional service charge
The manager may from time to time determine that an additional service charge, limited as is mentioned in rule 20.2, is payable by the members to enable the association to meet any expenses that are due (or soon to become due) and which could not be met otherwise than out of the reserve fund.

20.2   Limit on amount of additional service charge
In any financial year the total amount of any additional service charge determined under rule 20.1 is not to exceed twenty-five per cent of the total service charge for that year as set out in the budget approved by the association; but in calculating that percentage no account is to be taken of any additional service charge payable in respect of the cost of emergency work (as defined in rule 14.3).

20.3   Supplementary budget
If in any financial year the manager considers that any additional service charge exceeding the percentage mentioned in rule 20.2 should be payable, the manager must prepare and submit to the association at a general meeting a draft supplementary budget setting out the amount of the additional service charge and the date (or dates) on which the charge will be due for payment; and rules 18.3, 18.4 and 19.3(a) apply as respects that draft supplementary budget as they apply as respects a draft budget and revised draft budget.

Rule 21—Funds

21.1   Association funds
Any association funds must be—
    (a)   held in the name of the association; and
    (b)   subject to rule 21.2, deposited by the manager in a bank or building society account.

21.2   Special treatment of certain funds
The manager must ensure that any association funds which are likely to be held for some time are—
    (a)   deposited in an account which is interest bearing; or
    (b)   invested in such other way as the association may at a general meeting decide.

21.3   Reserve fund
The manager must ensure that any association funds forming a reserve fund are kept separately from other association funds.

Rule 22—Sending

22.1   Sending
Where a rule requires that a thing be sent—
    (a)   to a person it shall suffice, for the purposes of that rule, that the thing be sent to an agent of the person;
    (b)   to a member and that member cannot by reasonable inquiry be identified or found, it shall suffice, for the purposes of that rule, that the thing be sent to the member's unit addressed to 'The Owner' (or using some other such expression, as for example 'The Proprietor').

22.2   Method of sending
Any reference to a thing being sent shall be construed as a reference to its being—
    (a)   posted;
    (b)   delivered; or
    (c)   transmitted by electronic means.

22.3 Date of sending

A thing posted shall be taken to be sent on the day of posting; and a thing transmitted by electronic means, to be sent on the day of transmission.

SCHEDULE 2

Article 9(2)

FORM OF NOTICE OF PROPOSAL TO REGISTER DEED OF VARIATION

'NOTICE OF PROPOSAL TO REGISTER DEED OF VARIATION'

Owners' Association:
(see note for completion 1)

Description of unit(s) in relation to which a rule is to be varied or discharged:
(see note for completion 2)

Terms of rule(s):
(see note for completion 3)

Effect of registration of deed on rule(s):
(see note for completion 4)

An application to the Lands Tribunal for Scotland for preservation of the scheme must be made not later than [specify the date on which the period mentioned in article 9(3) of the Title Conditions (Scotland) Act 2003 (Development Management Scheme) Order 2009 expires].

Signature of proposer:

Date:

NOTE

This notice is given under Article 9 of the Title Conditions (Scotland) Act 2003 (Development Management Scheme) Order 2009. The sender is the owners' association for the development and wishes [to free a property of a rule of the scheme] *or* [to vary a rule of the scheme].

A deed of variation has already been granted. A copy of the deed in question is attached. If the deed is duly registered the rule will be [discharged] *or* [varied] in relation to the unit.

If you want to preserve the scheme unvaried, you can apply to the Lands Tribunal for Scotland in that regard. The address of the Lands Tribunal is [*insert address*] and their telephone number is [*insert telephone number*]. For further guidance you may wish to consult a solicitor or other adviser.

An application to the Lands Tribunal must be made by the date stated in the notice. If no application is made by then the scheme may be varied on registration of the deed of variation.'

NOTES FOR COMPLETION OF THE NOTICE
(These notes have no legal effect)

1   Give the name and address of the owners' association (see rule 2.4).

2   Describe the unit in a way that is sufficient to identify it. Where the unit has a postal address the description should include that address. Where the title has been registered in the Land Register the description should refer to the title number of the property or of the larger subjects of which the unit forms part. Otherwise it should normally refer to and identify a deed recorded in a specified division of the Register of Sasines.

3   Identify the deed of application by reference to the appropriate Register, and set out the rule(s) in full.

4   If a rule of the scheme is wholly to be discharged say so; otherwise describe the extent of variation or discharge.

5   Intimation is by sending (or delivering) the notice. Since evidence of sending may be required at the time of registration in the Land Register, it is recommended that the notice be sent by recorded delivery or registered post.

6   There is to be endorsed on the deed before registration the certificate required by Article 9(4) of the Title Conditions (Scotland) Act 2003 (Development Management Scheme) Order 2008.

APPLICATIONS BY CREDITORS (PRE-ACTION REQUIREMENTS) (SCOTLAND) ORDER 2010
(SSI 2010/317)

1   Citation, commencement and interpretation

(1)   This Order may be cited as the Applications by Creditors (Pre-Action Requirements) (Scotland) Order 2010 and comes into force on the day after the day on which it is made.

(2)   In this Order—

'the 1894 Act' means the Heritable Securities (Scotland) Act 1894; and

'the 1970 Act' means the Conveyancing and Feudal Reform (Scotland) Act 1970.

2   Requirement to provide information about the default

(1)   In section 5B(2)(b) of the 1894 Act and section 24A(2)(b) of the 1970 Act the requirement that information about the amount due include information about charges in respect of redemption is removed.

(2)   In providing the debtor with clear information for the purposes of section 5B(2) of the 1894 Act and section 24A(2) of the 1970 Act—

(a)   information about the terms of the security must include a description of the nature and level of any charges that may be incurred by virtue of the contract to which the security relates if the default is not remedied; and

(b)   information about the amount due to the creditor under the security, including any arrears and any charges in respect of late payment must be broken down so as to show—

(i)   the total amount of the arrears; and

(ii)   the total outstanding amount due including any charges already incurred.

(3)   For the purposes of those sections 'charges' do not include any expenses for which the debtor is personally liable to the creditor by virtue of paragraph 12 of Schedule 3 to the 1970 Act, as read with section 11 of that Act.

(4)   The information required to be provided to the debtor by virtue of those sections must be provided as soon as is reasonably practicable upon the debtor entering into default.

3   Requirement to make reasonable efforts to agree proposals

(1)   In complying with the pre-action requirement contained in section 5B(3) of the 1894 Act and section 24A(3) of the 1970 Act the creditor must—

(a)   make reasonable attempts to contact the debtor to discuss the default;

(b)   provide the debtor with details of any proposal made by the creditor, set out in such a way as to allow the debtor to consider the proposal;

(c)   allow the debtor reasonable time to consider any proposal made by the creditor;

(d)   notify the debtor within a reasonable time of any decision taken by the creditor to accept or reject a proposal made by the debtor; and

(e)   consider the affordability of any proposal for the debtor taking into account, where known to the creditor, the debtor's personal and financial circumstances.

(2)   Where a proposal is made by the debtor which the creditor rejects the creditor must provide reasons for rejecting the proposal in writing within 10 working days of the notification referred to in paragraph (1)(d).

(3)   Where the debtor fails to comply with any condition of an agreement reached with the creditor in respect of any proposal and the creditor decides to make an application under section 5(1) of the 1894 Act or section 24(1B) of the 1970 Act, and the debtor has not previously failed to comply with any condition of the agreement, the following provisions of this paragraph apply—

(a)   the creditor must give the debtor notice in writing of the decision to make an application and the ground of the proposed application;

(b)   the creditor must not make an application before the expiry of 15 working days beginning with the date on which the debtor is deemed to receive the notice; and

(c)   the creditor must not make an application if the failure by the debtor to comply with a condition of the agreement, constituting the ground of the proposed application, is remedied during that period.

(4)   For the purposes of this article, the debtor is deemed to receive the notice given under paragraph (3)(a)—

(a)   if sent by post, at the time at which the letter would be delivered in the ordinary course of post;

(b)   if sent by electronic communication, on the day after the day on which the electronic communication containing it was sent; and

(c)   if otherwise given to the debtor, at the time of delivery.

(5)   In this article—

(a)   'working day' means a day that is not a Saturday or Sunday, nor any day that is a bank holiday under the Banking and Financial Dealings Act 1971 in any part of the United Kingdom; and

(b)   'electronic communication' has the meaning given by section 15(1) of the Electronic Communications Act 2000; such communications referred to in paragraph (4) must be sent to an address notified to the creditor by the debtor for the purpose of receiving communications relating to the security, and must be—

(i)   capable of being accessed by the recipient;

(ii)   legible in all other material respects; and

(iii)   sufficiently permanent to be used for subsequent reference.

4   Steps which are likely to result in payment within a reasonable time

(1)   Steps taken by the debtor which are steps within the meaning of section 5B(4)(a) of the 1894 Act and section 24A(4)(a) of the 1970 Act include providing documentary evidence to the creditor—

(a)   of submission of a claim to an insurer under a payment protection policy currently held by the debtor in respect of the security or the contract to which the security relates, where the evidence demonstrates a reasonable expectation of eligibility for payment from the insurer, unless paragraph (3) applies;

(b)   of submission of an application by the debtor to a support scheme run by Scottish Ministers or the United Kingdom Government, where the evidence demonstrates a reasonable expectation of being eligible for support in respect of the security or the contract to which the security relates, unless the creditor does not participate in, does not agree with any term of, or does not agree to the sale of the property in accordance with such a scheme or unless paragraph (3) applies; and

(c) demonstrating that the debtor or a person acting as agent for the debtor is actively marketing the property for sale at an appropriate price in accordance with professional advice, unless paragraph (4) applies.

(2) Documentary evidence for the purposes of paragraph (1)(c) must include the documents prescribed for the purposes of sections 98, 99(1) and 101(2) of the Housing (Scotland) Act 2006, where section 98 requires the person responsible for marketing the property to possess those documents.

(3) This paragraph applies where either the step in paragraph (1)(a) or (1)(b) is taken and—

(a) the debtor's claim or application has not been determined within a reasonable time or is refused; or

(b) the debtor is unable to pay any amount due under the security which is not covered by the insurance policy or support scheme.

(4) This paragraph applies where the step in paragraph (1)(c) is taken and—

(a) the debtor rejects a reasonable offer to purchase the property;

(b) the property has not sold within a reasonable time of that step being taken; or

(c) the debtor refuses to provide the creditor with details of any agent acting for him in relation to the marketing or sale of the property or to authorise any such agent to communicate with the creditor, resulting in the creditor being unable to readily ascertain if the circumstances in sub-paragraphs (a) or (b) have occurred.

5   Requirement to provide information about sources of advice and assistance
For the purposes of the pre-action requirement contained in section 5B(5) of the 1894 Act and section 24A(5) of the 1970 Act, sources of advice and assistance include—

(a) where the security is regulated, any relevant information sheet published by the appropriate regulatory body;

(b) a citizens advice bureau or other advice organisation; and

(c) the housing department of the local authority in whose area the property which is subject to the security is situated.

LAND REGISTER RULES ETC (SCOTLAND) REGULATIONS 2014
(SSI 2014/150)

PART 1
INTRODUCTORY

1   Citation, commencement and interpretation
(1) These Regulations may be cited as the Land Register Rules etc (Scotland) Regulations 2014 and come into force on 8th December 2014.

(2) In these Regulations—
'the Act' means the Land Registration etc (Scotland) Act 2012; and
'plot of land comprising seabed' means a plot of land entirely covered by water that lies within the territorial sea of the United Kingdom adjacent to Scotland.

PART 2
ADVANCE NOTICES

2   Forms to apply for, or to discharge, an advance notice
An application for—
(a) an advance notice under section 57(1) of the Act must be made—

(i) in respect of the whole of a registered plot, using the Form set out in Part 1 of Schedule 1;

(ii) in respect of part of a registered plot, using the Form set out in Part 2 of Schedule 1;

(b) discharge of an advance notice under section 63(1) of the Act must be made using the Form set out in Part 3 of Schedule 1.

3 Procedure for application for an advance notice

(1) [Subject to paragraph (3) an application] for an advance notice relating to [. . .] a registered plot or discharge of an advance notice must be sent to the Keeper electronically using a computer system for advance notices under the management and control of the Keeper, unless—

(a) the computer system notifies the applicant who attempts to use it that it is unavailable for a period of 48 hours or longer;

(b) the applicant—

(i) has no computer facilities with access to the internet;

[. . .] [; or

(c) the Keeper is otherwise satisfied that exceptional circumstances make it impractical to do so.]

[(1A) In particular, paragraph (1)(c) is met—

(a) if the applicant is a natural person who granted the deed to which the advance notice relates; and

(b) the application is not made by a person who, in connection with the grant, acts as a solicitor or other legal adviser to the granter.]

(2) Only a person authorised by the Keeper may use that computer system.

[(3) Except in respect of advance notices relating to the whole of a registered plot, paragraph (1) does not apply unless the Keeper has notified a date in accordance with paragraph (4).

(4) Such a notification by the Keeper must state the date on which it comes into effect, which date may not be earlier than 6 months after the date of its publication on the Keeper's website.

(5) Before making such notification, the Keeper must consult the Scottish Ministers.]

4 Description of an unregistered plot or unregistered lease in an advance notice

(1) An advance notice by virtue of section 56(1)(e) of the Act must contain a description of the subjects of the lease or plot of land sufficient to enable the Keeper to identify those subjects or that plot.

(2) The description mentioned in paragraph (1) must identify the subjects of the lease or plot of land by reference to the—

(a) description in a deed recorded in the Register of Sasines [if such a deed exists]; and

(b) postal address (if any).

(3) Where the subjects of the lease or plot of land [have not been recorded in or] form part only of the subjects described in a deed recorded in the Register of Sasines, the description mentioned in paragraph (2) must be accompanied by a plan of that part which satisfies the Keeper that the Keeper can delineate its boundaries on the cadastral map.

5 Notification of acceptance of advance notice

(1) The Keeper must notify the applicant or applicant's agent that the advance notice has been entered in the application record.

(2) A notification given under paragraph (1) must be made by email to the email address contained in the application, except in cases where an application has been made using a paper form under regulation 3(1)(b) or (3)(b).

(3)   The notification given under paragraph (1) must contain the—
(a)   granter's name and designation;
(b)   grantee's name and designation;
(c)   application number;
(d)   advance notice number;
(e)   type of intended deed;
(f)   particulars of the—
   (i)   plot of land; or
   (ii)   subjects of lease;
(g)   where section 57(4)(a)(ii) of the Act applies, a PDF(2) file of the delineation on the cadastral map; and
(h)   date when the advance notice is entered on the application record.

6   Removal of delineation from the cadastral map where intended deed not registered

In respect of an advance notice for a deed which is not registered during the protected period, the period prescribed under section 62(2) of the Act, after which the Keeper must remove the delineation on the cadastral map, is 35 days beginning on the day after the date when the notice is entered in the application record.

PART 3
REGISTRATION

[7   **Procedure and form to apply for registration in the Land Register [– *deeds or voluntary registration*]**
(1)   From a date notified by the Keeper in accordance with paragraph (5), an application for registration of—
(a)   a kind of deed under section 21 of the Act [(*other than by submission of a copy of the deed*)]; or
(b)   an unregistered plot under section 27 of the Act, must be sent to the Keeper in accordance with paragraphs (2) and (3).
(2)   The application must be sent in electronic form using a computer system under section 99 of the Act unless—
(a)   the computer system notifies the applicant who attempts to use it that it is unavailable for a period of 48 hours or longer;
(b)   the applicant has no computer facilities with access to the internet; or
(c)   the Keeper is otherwise satisfied that exceptional circumstances make it impractical to do so.
(3)   In particular, paragraph (2)(c) is met—
(a)   if the applicant is a natural person who granted the deed, or to whom the deed is granted; and
(b)   the application is not made by a person who, in connection with the grant, acts as a solicitor or other legal adviser to the person.
(4)   Where an application under paragraph (1)(a) must be sent in electronic form, the deed must be an electronic document within the meaning given by the Requirements of Writing (Scotland) Act 1995.
(5)   Such a notification by the Keeper must state the date on which it comes into effect, which date may not be earlier than 6 months after the date of its publication on the Keeper's website.
(6)   Before making such a notification, the Keeper must consult the Scottish Ministers.]

[7A   *Procedure and form to apply for registration in the Land Register – copy deeds*
(1)   *An application for registration by submission by electronic means of a copy of a deed which is a traditional document must be sent to the Keeper in accordance with paragraphs (2) and (3).*

(2)   *The application must be sent using a computer system under section 99 of the Act unless—*

(a)   *the computer system notifies the applicant who attempts to use it that it is unavailable for a period of 48 hours or longer,*

(b)   *the applicant has no computer facilities with access to the internet, or*

(c)   *the Keeper is otherwise satisfied that exceptional circumstances make it impractical to do so.*

(3)   *In particular, paragraph (2)(c) is met—*

(a)   *if the applicant is a natural person who granted the deed, or to whom the deed is granted, and*

(b)   *the application is not made by a person who, in connection with the grant, acts as a solicitor or other legal adviser to the person.*

(4)   *In this regulation 'traditional document' bears the meaning it has in the Requirements of Writing (Scotland) Act 1995.]*

8   Application for registration of plot of land comprising seabed

In respect of an application for registration of a deed in relation to a plot of land comprising seabed, the deed must contain—

(a)   a description of the plot of land based on OSGB36 coordinates; and

(b)   a plan, in a form that the Keeper considers reasonably identifies the location of the plot of land in relation to the coast of Scotland.

9   Affidavits to accompany applications for registration

An affidavit which—

(a)   accompanies an application for registration;

(b)   accompanies an application to vary warranty; or

(c)   provides evidence in respect of rectification of the register,

must be made before a notary public.

10   Application record

(1)   Where the Keeper enters an application in the application record, the Keeper must allocate an application number to that application.

(2)   An application number is an unique identifier consisting of numerals or of letters and numerals.

(3)   Where an application for registration requires the creation of a—

(a)   cadastral unit;

(b)   lease title sheet; or

(c)   title sheet for a flat,

the Keeper must allocate a provisional title number to that application.

(4)   Where additional cadastral units require to be created in respect of an application, the Keeper may allocate additional application numbers and provisional title numbers until registration is completed under section 30 or 31 of the Act.

(5)   Where registration is completed under section 30 or 31 of the Act, the provisional title number will become the title number assigned under section 4(1) of the Act.

11   Acknowledgement of application for registration

(1)   After an application for registration is entered in the application record, the Keeper must acknowledge receipt of that application if an email address for acknowledgment is contained in the application.

(2)   An acknowledgment given under paragraph (1) must contain the—

(a)   type of deed;

(b)   names of the parties;

(c)   date of application;

(d)   application number allocated under regulation 10(1);

(e)   title number or provisional title number allocated under regulation 10(3); and

(f)   particulars of the plot of land or the subjects of lease.

12   Title sheets
(1)   In addition to the information required to be entered in the property section by virtue of section 6 of the Act, the property section must contain—
   (a)   the date of—
      (i)   registration of the plot of land; and
      (ii)   the last entry in the title sheet;
   (b)   the terms of any caveat;
   (c)   in respect of a title sheet created for registration of—
      (i)   a deed relating to—
         (aa)   an unregistered plot; or
         (bb)   part of a registered plot; or
      (ii)   an unregistered plot,
particulars of any deed in which servitude rights are constituted;
   (d)   a statement where minerals are excepted;
   (e)   for a plot of land comprising seabed, the OSGB36 coordinates representing the boundaries of that plot; and
   (f)   in respect of a title sheet created for registration of—
      (i)   a deed relating to—
         (aa)   an unregistered plot; or
         (bb)   part of a registered plot; or
      (ii)   an unregistered plot,
the area measurement of the cadastral unit where it is greater than 0.5 hectare.
(2)   In addition to the information required to be entered in the property section by virtue of section 7 of the Act, the proprietorship section must contain the—
   (a)   consideration; and
   (b)   date of entry.

13   Amendments etc of application
Where the Keeper has consented under section 34(1)(b) of the Act to substitution or amendment of an application, the substituted or amended application must be received by the Keeper before the expiry of the period of 42 days beginning on the day after the date of consent.

[13A   Amendments of applications relating to an unregistered plot
Where—
   (a)   an application for registration of a deed which is an electronic document which relates to an unregistered plot is received by the Keeper; and
   (b)   within a period of 14 days from receipt of the application the Keeper receives prior deeds necessary to allow the Keeper to comply, in respect of the application, with the Keeper's duties under Part 1 of the Act,
the Keeper must consent to amendment of the application in order to include those deeds.]

14   Combination of cadastral units
Where—
   (a)   the Keeper combines cadastral units under section 13(2)(a) of the Act; and
   (b)   each registered plot of land has a different date of registration,
the earliest date of registration entered in the title sheet of one of those registered plots will be the date of registration of the resultant plot of land.

15   Form to place a caveat on a title sheet
An application to—
   (a)   place on a title sheet a caveat granted under section 67(3) of the Act;
   (b)   renew a caveat granted under section 69(2) of the Act;
   (c)   restrict a caveat granted under section 70(2) of the Act;

    (d)   recall a caveat granted under section 71(2) of the Act; or

    (e)   discharge a caveat under section 72 of the Act,

must be made using the Form set out in Part 5 of Schedule 1.

16   Form to vary warranty

An application to vary warranty under section 76(2) of the Act must be made using the Form set out in Part 6 of Schedule 1.

17   Corrections

    (1)   Where the Keeper becomes aware of a typographical error in a title sheet, the Keeper may correct the error.

    (2)   In paragraph (1), 'typographical error' means an error which is not an inaccuracy (within the meaning of section 65 of the Act).

PART 4

PRESCRIPTIVE CLAIMANTS

18   Notification by prescriptive claimants

    (1)   An applicant must notify the person mentioned in section 43(4) of the Act by sending the notification—

    (a)   at least 60 days prior to submitting to the Keeper the application for registration of a disposition mentioned in section 43(1) of the Act; and

    (b)   by a postal service which provides for the delivery of the notification to be recorded.

    (2)   The notification made under section 43(4) of the Act must be in the form set out in Schedule 2.

Regulations 2, 7, 15 and 16   SCHEDULE 1

APPLICATION FORMS TO BE USED IN CONNECTION WITH LAND REGISTRATION

List of forms

Form	Purpose	Relevant provisions of the Rules
PART 1	Application for an Advance Notice relating to Whole of a Registered Plot	Regulation 2(a)(i)
PART 2	Application for an Advance Notice relating to Part of Registered Plot	Regulation 2(a)(ii)
PART 3	Application to Discharge an Advance Notice	Regulation 2(b)
[. . .]		
PART 5	Application relating to a Caveat	Regulation 15
PART 6	Application to Vary Warranty	Regulation 16

PART 1   Regulation 2(a)(i)

LAND REGISTRATION ETC (SCOTLAND) ACT 2012

Application for an Advance Notice relating to Whole of a Registered Plot

In accordance with section 56(1) of the Land Registration etc (Scotland) Act 2012 an advance notice is a notice stating that a person ('the Granter') intends to grant a deed ('Intended Deed Type') to another person (the 'Grantee').

Agent Details
Agent's reference
Agent's telephone number
Agent's email address
Agent's name and address

Payment Details
FAS Number
Payment method

Intended Deed Type

Subjects
Title numbers(s) of registered plot of land or lease affected by this advance notice
Property name
Property number
Street name
Town
Postcode
Description of plot of land with no postal address

Granter Details
Individual
Prefix
Forename
Surname
Property name
Property number
Street name
Town
Postcode
Country
Non-natural person
Prefix
Name
Allocated number (if any, eg company number)
Property name
Property number
Street name
Town
Postcode
Country

Grantee Details
Individual
Prefix
Forename
Surname
Property name

Property number
Street name
Town
Postcode
Country
Non-natural person
Prefix
Name
Allocated number (if any, e.g. company number)
Property name
Property number
Street name
Town
Postcode
Country

Applicant Statement and Declaration

I/We apply for an advance notice in terms of section 57 of the Land Registration etc (Scotland) Act 2012 in respect of a registrable deed which I/we intend to grant. By making such application I/we confirm that (i) I/we may validly grant such a deed (or) (ii) I/we have the consent of a person who may validly do so, in accordance with section 57(2)(a) of (b) respectively, of the Land Registration etc (Scotland) Act 2012.

I/We certify that the information supplied on this Form is complete and correct to the best of my/our knowledge and belief.

Signature(s)

Date

PART 2   Regulation 2(a)(ii)
LAND REGISTRATION ETC (SCOTLAND) ACT 2012

Application for an Advance Notice relating to Part of the Registered Plot

In accordance with section 56(1) of the Land Registration etc (Scotland) Act 2012 an advance notice is a notice stating that a person ('the Granter') intends to grant a deed ('Intended Deed Type') to another person (the 'Grantee').

Agent Details
Agent's reference
Agent's telephone number
Agent's email address
Agent's name and address

Payment Details
FAS Number
Payment method

Intended Deed Type
Subjects
Title numbers(s) of registered plot of land or lease affected by this advance notice
Are the subjects a flatted building capable of being represented as a single cadas-

tral unit in accordance with section 56(2) of the Land Registration etc (Scotland) Act 2012?

Property name

Property number

Street name

Town

Postcode

Description of plot of land with no postal address

Related Plan

Where application is accepted by the Keeper on paper:

Submit a paper plan

Where application is accepted electronically by the Keeper:

Development Plan Approval Number and Development Plan Approval Plot Number

or

Provide co-ordinates

or

Upload shape file

Granter Details

Individual

Prefix

Forename

Surname

Property name

Property number

Street name

Town

Postcode

Country

Non-natural person

Prefix

Name

Allocated number (if any, eg company number)

Property name

Property number

Street name

Town

Postcode

Country

Grantee Details

Individual

Prefix

Forename

Surname

Property name
Property number
Street name
Town
Postcode
Country
Non-natural person
Prefix
Name
Allocated number (if any, eg company number)
Property name
Property number
Street name
Town
Postcode
Country

Applicant Statement and Declaration

I/We apply for an advance notice in terms of section 57 of the Land Registration etc (Scotland) Act 2012 in respect of a registrable deed which I/we intend to grant. By making such application I/we confirm that (i) I/we may validly grant such a deed (or) (ii) I/we have the consent of a person who may validly do so, in accordance with section 57(2)(a) of (b) respectively, of the Land Registration etc (Scotland) Act 2012.

I/We certify that the information supplied on this Form is complete and correct to the best of my/our knowledge and belief.

Signature(s)

Date

PART 3   Regulation 2(b)
LAND REGISTRATION ETC (SCOTLAND) ACT 2012

Application to Discharge an Advance Notice

Agent Details
Agent's reference
Agent's telephone number
Agent's email address
Agent's name and address

Payment Details
FAS Number
Payment method
Advance Notice Number to be discharged

Intended Deed Type

Subjects
Title numbers(s) of registered plot of land or lease affected by this advance notice

Property name
Property number
Street name
Town
Postcode
Description of plot of land with no postal address

Granter Details

Individual
Prefix
Forename
Surname
Property name
Property number
Street name
Town
Postcode
Country

Non-natural person
Prefix
Name
Allocated number (if any, e.g. company number)
Property name
Property number
Street name
Town
Postcode
Country

Grantee Details

Individual
Prefix
Forename
Surname
Property name
Property number
Street name
Town
Postcode
Country

Non-natural person
Prefix
Name
Allocated number (if any, eg company number)
Property name
Property number
Street name

Town
Postcode
Country

Applicant Statement and Declaration

I/We hereby certify that the person to whom the intended deed would be granted consents to this application to discharge the advance notice relating to that deed in accordance with section 63(3)(a) of the Land Registration etc (Scotland) Act 2012.

I/We certify that the information supplied on this Form is complete and correct to the best of my/our knowledge and belief.

Signature(s)

Date

PART 5　　　　　　　　　　Regulation 15
LAND REGISTRATION ETC (SCOTLAND) ACT 2012

Application relating to a caveat

Agent Details
Agent's reference
Agent's telephone number
Agent's email address
Agent's name and address

Payment Details
FAS number
Payment method

Subjects affected by caveat
Title number(s)
Property name
Property number
Street name
Town
Postcode
Description of plot of land with no postal address

Application type

- Noting of a caveat on a title sheet ☐
- Renewal of a caveat ☐
- Restriction of a caveat ☐
- Recall of a caveat ☐
- Discharge of a caveat ☐

Existing caveat application number (if affected by the application)

Applicant Details

Individual
Prefix
Forename
Surname
Property name
Property number
Street name
Town
Postcode
Country
Non-natural person
Prefix
Name
Allocated number (if any, eg company number)
Property name
Property number
Street name
Town
Postcode
Country

Registered Proprietor Details

Name

Designation

Signature

Date

PART 6   Regulation 16
LAND REGISTRATION ETC (SCOTLAND) ACT 2012

Application to vary warranty

Agent Details

Agent's reference
Agent's telephone number
Agent's email address
Agent's name and address

Payment Details

FAS Number
Payment method

Subjects

Title number(s)
Property name
Property number

Street name

Town

Postcode

Description of plot of land with no postal address

Applicant Details

Individual

Prefix

Forename

Surname

Property name

Property number

Street name

Town

Postcode

Country

Non-natural person

Prefix

Name

Allocated number (if any, eg company number)

Property name

Property number

Street name

Town

Postcode

Variation of Warranty

In what respect is a variation of warranty sought?

Explain why it is appropriate for the Keeper to vary the warranty currently provided for.

To support this application, I/we enclose the documents/evidence listed below

Signature

Date

Regulation 18(2)   SCHEDULE 2
               FORM OF NOTIFICATION BY PRESCRIPTIVE CLAIMANTS

Name and address of prescriptive claimant
(See note 1 for completion)

Name and address of person notified
(See note 2 for completion)

Description of the land over which a prescriptive claim is sought
(See note 3 for completion)

Applicable paragraph of section 43(4) of the Act
(See note 4 for completion)

Evidence of links in title (required only where person notified under section 43(4)(b) of the Act)
(See note 5 for completion)

Service
(See note 6 for completion)

I swear or affirm that the information contained in this notice is, to the best of my knowledge and belief, true.

Signature of person sending notice

Date

ELECTRONIC DOCUMENTS (SCOTLAND) REGULATIONS 2014
(SSI 2014/83)

1 Citation, commencement and interpretation

(1) These Regulations may be cited as the Electronic Documents (Scotland) Regulations 2014 and come into force on 11th May 2014.

(2) In these Regulations—

'the 1995 Act' means the Requirements of Writing (Scotland) Act 1995; [. . .]

['advanced electronic signature' means an advanced electronic signature within the meaning given in Article 3(11) of Regulation (EU) No 910/2014 of the European Parliament and of the Council on electronic identification and trust services for electronic transactions in the internal market;]

[. . .]

['digital registration document'] means a document created as an electronic communication within the ['digital registration' system];

'digital certificate' means an electronic document in a standardised format which proves ownership of a 'public key', includes information about its owner's identity and is digitally signed by the organisation that has verified the certificate's contents are correct and issued the certificate;]

['digital registration system' means a computer system managed and controlled by the Keeper in accordance with section 99(1) of the Land Registration etc (Scotland) Act 2012;]

'electronic document' has the meaning given in section 9A of the 1995 Act.

['electronic signature creation data' has the meaning given in Article 3(13) of Regulation (EU) No 910/2014 of the European Parliament and of the Council on electronic identification and trust services for electronic transactions in the internal market;]

['the Keeper' means the Keeper of the Registers of Scotland;

'public key' is one of a pair of mathematical keys that are used in the authentication of electronic documents, which is intrinsically linked with the private key (although it is computationally infeasible to determine one key from knowledge of the other key) and is made public and forms part of the digital certificate;

'private key' is one of a pair of mathematical keys that are used in the authentication of electronic documents, which is intrinsically linked with the public key (although it is computationally infeasible to determine one key from knowledge of the other key) and is kept private to be used, in combination with data from an electronic document, to create a digital signature which is uniquely linked to both the signer of the document and the document itself;

[. . .].]

['qualified electronic signature' means a qualified electronic signature as defined in Article 3(12) of Regulation (EU) No 910/2014 of the European Parliament and of the Council on electronic identification and trust services for electronic transactions in the internal market.]

2   Requirements of formally valid electronic document

For an electronic document required by section 1(2) of the 1995 Act to be valid the electronic signature of a granter incorporated into or logically associated with that document must be an advanced electronic signature.

3   Requirements of self-proving electronic document

For an electronic document to be presumed authenticated by a granter under section 9C of the 1995 Act the electronic signature incorporated into or logically associated with that document [must be a qualified electronic signature].

4   Annexations to electronic documents

[(1)   Subject to paragraphs (2) and (3) and except where an enactment expressly otherwise provides, any annexation to an electronic document is to be regarded as incorporated in the document if it is—

    (a)   referred to in the document, and

    (b)   identified on its face as being the annexation referred to in the document, without the annexation having to be authenticated.

(2)   Where writing is required under section 1(2) of the 1995 Act for an electronic document, an annexation to it is to be regarded as incorporated in the document if and only if it is—

    (a)   referred to in the document,

    (b)   identified on its face as being the annexation referred to in the document, and

    (c)   annexed to the document before an electronic signature under regulation 2 or 3 is incorporated into or logically associated with the document and the annexation.

(3)   Where writing is not required under section 1(2) of the 1995 Act for an electronic document which relates to land and an annexation to it describes or shows all or any part of the land to which the document relates, the annexation is to be regarded as incorporated in the document if and only if it—

    (a)   is referred to in the document,

    (b)   is identified on its face as being the annexation referred to in the document, and

    (c)   meets one of the conditions in paragraph (4)(a) or (b).

(4)   Those conditions are that—

    (a)   the annexation is annexed to the document before an advanced electronic signature or a qualified electronic signature is incorporated into or logically associated with the document and the annexation, or

    (b)   the annexation is authenticated with an electronic signature which is neither an advanced electronic signature nor a qualified electronic signature, on—

        (i)   each page, where it is a plan, drawing, photograph or other representation, or

        (ii)   the last page, where it is an inventory, appendix, schedule or other writing.

(5)   In respect of any annexation referred to in paragraph (4)(b)—

    (a)   if it bears to have been authenticated by a granter of the document it is presumed to have been authenticated by the person who authenticated the document as that granter,

    (b)   it is competent to sign it at any time before the document is founded on in legal proceedings,

(c)   where there is more than one granter, the requirement under paragraph (4)(b)(ii) of signing on the last page is complied with (provided that at least one granter signs at the end of the last page) if any other granter signs on an additional page.]

[5   Authentication of electronic documents: special cases
[(1)   Any reference in the 1995 Act or these Regulations to authentication by a granter of an electronic document, in a case where the granter is a person to whom any of paragraphs (2) to (7) applies, is to be construed as a reference to authentication by a person in accordance with that paragraph, unless the context otherwise requires.]
(2)   Where the granter is a partnership, an electronic signature on behalf of the partnership must be applied by—
(a)   a partner; or
(b)   a person authorised to sign by the partnership.
(3)   Where the granter is a limited liability partnership, an electronic signature on behalf of the limited liability partnership must be applied by a member of the limited liability partnership.
(4)   Where the granter is a company, an electronic signature on behalf of the company must be applied by—
(a)   a director of the company;
(b)   a secretary of the company; or
(c)   a person authorised to sign by the company.
(5)   Where the granter is a local authority, an electronic signature on behalf of the local authority must be applied by a proper officer of the authority.
(6)   Where the granter is a body corporate other than a company or a local authority, the electronic signature on behalf of the body corporate must be applied by—
(a)   a member of the body's governing board;
(b)   a member of the body;
(c)   a secretary of the body; or
(d)   a person authorised to sign by the body.
(7)   Where the granter is a Minister or office holder, the electronic signature by or on behalf of the Minister or office holder must be applied by—
(a)   the Minister or office holder;
(b)   where permitted by an enactment that a document may be signed by an officer of the Minister or by any other Minister, the officer or other Minister;
(c)   where permitted by an enactment that a document may be signed by an officer of the office holder, the officer; or
(d)   a person authorised to sign by the Minister or office holder.]

[6   Registration of electronic documents in the Land Register [and Register of Sasines]
[(1)]   A [digital registration document] to be registered in the Land Register of Scotland must be—
(a)   in the form of a PDF created in the [digital registration system]; and
(b)   authenticated by [. . .]—
(i)   [the type of electronic signature] created by electronic signature creation data associated with a digital certificate supplied by the Keeper in accordance with paragraph (c); or
[(ii)   a qualified electronic signature;]
(c)   [in the case of an electronic signature under paragraph (b)(i),] certified by a digital certificate which must—
(i)   comply with the International Telecommunication Union Telecommunication Standardization Sector (ITU-T) cryptography standard X509 ('X509');

(ii)   be bound to the holder in an identification process which meets a minimum of [having regard to] the Cabinet Office Good Practice Guide No. 45, Identity proofing and verification of an individual;

(iii)   use a public key and private key pair which are at least 1024 bits;

(iv)   employ a hashing algorithm no less satisfactory than [Secure Hash Algorithm-2 (SHA-2(2))];

(v)   not be subject to any limitation preventing use for authentication of conveyancing deeds and documents [; land and buildings transaction tax land transaction returns] or certification of Stamp Duty Land Tax land transaction returns;

(vi)   be certified under a certificate in respect of which revocation is managed by a Certificate Revocation List compliant with X509;

(vii)   be issued under policy, contractual and reliance documentation which contains no exclusion or limitation of liability clauses inappropriate to the reliance placed on conveyancing deeds, land registration applications and tax returns; and

(viii)   not be created under policy, contractual or reliance documentation including choice of law or prorogation of jurisdiction clauses serving to refer Scots land law and property registration issues to the courts or legal system of a jurisdiction other than Scotland; or to refer [land and buildings transaction tax or] Stamp Duty Land Tax issues to the courts or legal system of a jurisdiction outwith the United Kingdom.]

[(2)   A digital registration document to be recorded in the Register of Sasines against burdened or benefitted property (or both) which is capable of being, and is also to be, dual registered in the Land Register of Scotland under section 4(5) or 75(1) of the Title Conditions (Scotland) Act 2003—

(a)   must comply with the requirements of paragraph (1)(a) to (c); and

(b)   may be registered using the digital registration system.]

[7   Registration of [electronic] standard securities for preservation and execution

(1)   An extract of an electronic standard security that has been created as [a digital registration document] may be registered for preservation and execution in the Books of Council and Session.

(2)   An extract registered in accordance with paragraph (1) is to be treated for the purposes of executing any diligence as if—

(a)   the standard security were created by a document to which section 9C(1) of the 1995 Act applies; and

(b)   the extract were that electronic standard security.]

[8   *Registration of other electronic documents for preservation and execution*

(1)   An electronic document may be registered for preservation or execution (or both) in the register of deeds and probative writs in the Books of Council and Session if it is—

(a)   in the form of a PDF, and

(b)   authenticated by a qualified electronic signature.

(2)   This regulation does not apply to an extract of an electronic standard security.]

EUROPEAN CONVENTION ON HUMAN RIGHTS

Article 6
Right to a fair trial

1.   In the determination of his civil rights and obligations or of any criminal charge against him, everyone is entitled to a fair and public hearing within a reasonable time by an independent and impartial tribunal established by law. Judgment shall be pronounced publicly but the press and public may be excluded from all or part of the trial in the interests of morals, public order or national security in a democratic society, where the interests of juveniles or the protection of the private life of the parties so require, or to the extent strictly necessary in the opinion of the court in special circumstances where publicity would prejudice the interests of justice.

2.   Everyone charged with a criminal offence shall be presumed innocent until proved guilty according to law.

3.   Everyone charged with a criminal offence has the following minimum rights:

(a)   to be informed promptly, in a language which he understands and in detail, of the nature and cause of the accusation against him;

(b)   to have adequate time and facilities for the preparation of his defence;

(c)   to defend himself in person or through legal assistance of his own choosing or, if he has not sufficient means to pay for legal assistance, to be given it free when the interests of justice so require;

(d)   to examine or have examined witnesses against him and to obtain the attendance and examination of witnesses on his behalf under the same conditions as witnesses against him;

(e)   to have the free assistance of an interpreter if he cannot understand or speak the language used in court.

Article 8
Right to respect for private and family life

1.   Everyone has the right to respect for his private and family life, his home and his correspondence.

2.   There shall be no interference by a public authority with the exercise of this right except such as is in accordance with the law and is necessary in a democratic society in the interests of national security, public safety or the economic wellbeing of the country, for the prevention of disorder or crime, for the protection of health or morals, or for the protection of the rights and freedoms of others.

PROTOCOL 1

Article 1
Protection of property

Every natural or legal person is entitled to the peaceful enjoyment of his possessions. No one shall be deprived of his possessions except in the public interest and subject to the conditions provided for by law and by the general principles of international law.

The preceding provisions shall not, however, in any way impair the right of a State to enforce such laws as it deems necessary to control the use of property in accordance with the general interest or to secure the payment of taxes or other contributions or penalties.

PART II
TRUSTS AND SUCCESSION

ACT OF SEDERUNT OF 28 FEBRUARY 1662

ACT ANENT EXECUTORS-CREDITORS

THE whilk day, the Lords of Councill and Session considering the great confusion that arises amongst creditors of defunct persons, and prejudice sustained by many of them, in prosecution of their respective diligence against the executors of defunct persons, and otherways, by obtaining the saids creditors to be themselves decerned executors-creditors to the defunct, to the prejudice of other creditors, who either dwelling at ane far distance, or being out of the countrie, or otherways not knowing of the death of their debitors, are postponed, and others useing sudden diligence are preferred: in respect whereof, and for ane remedie in time to come, the saids Lords declares and ordaines, that all creditors of defunct persons useing legall diligence at any time within half an yeir of the defunct's death, by citation of the executors and intrometters with the defunct's goods, or by obtaining themselves decerned and conçrmed executors-creditors, or by citeing of any other executors-creditors conçrmed, the saids creditors, useing any such diligence before the expireing of half ane yeir, as said is, shall com *in pari passu* with any other creditors, who have used more timely diligence, by obtaining themselves decerned and confirmed executors-creditors, or otherways. It is always declared, That the creditors useing posterior diligence, shall bear ane proportionall pairt of the charges waired out by the executor-creditor first decerned and confirmed, before he have any benefite of the inventarie confirmed: and that it shall be lawfull to the said creditor to obtain himselff joyned to the said office of executrie; and ordains thir presents to be insert in the bookes of sederunt, and to be proclaimed at the mercatcroce of Edinburgh.

TRUSTS (SCOTLAND) ACT 1921
(1921, 11 & 12 GEO 5, C 58)

1 Citation
This Act may be cited as the Trusts (Scotland) Act 1921.

2 Definitions
In the construction of this Act unless the context otherwise requires—
'Trust' shall mean and include—
  (a) any trust constituted by any deed or other writing, or by private or local Act of Parliament, or by Royal Charter, or by resolution of any corporation or public or ecclesiastical body, and
  (b) the appointment of any [. . .] judicial factor by deed, decree, or otherwise;
'Trust deed' shall mean and include—
  (a) any deed or other writing, private or local Act of Parliament, Royal Charter, or resolution of any corporation or ecclesiastical body, constituting any trust, and
  (b) any decree, deed, or other writing appointing a [. . .] judicial factor;

'Trustee' shall mean and include any trustee under any trust whether nominated, appointed, judicially or otherwise, or assumed, whether sole or joint, and whether entitled or not to receive any benefit under the trust or any remuneration as trustee for his services, and shall include any trustee *ex officio*, executor nominate [. . .] and judicial factor;

[. . .]

'Judicial factor' shall mean any person holding a judicial appointment as a factor [. . .] on another person's estate;]

'Local authority' and 'rate' shall have respectively the meanings assigned to these expressions by the Local Authorities Loans (Scotland) Act 1891;

'The court' shall mean the Court of Session.

3 What trusts shall be held to include

All trusts shall be held to include the following powers and provisions unless the contrary be expressed (that is to say):—

(a) Power to any trustee to resign the office of trustee;

(b) Power to the trustee, if there be only one, or to the trustees, if there be more than one, or to a quorum of the trustees, if there be more than two, to assume new trustees;

(c) A provision that a majority of the trustees accepting and surviving shall be a quorum;

(d) A provision that each trustee shall be liable only for his own acts and intromissions and shall not be liable for the acts and intromissions of co-trustees and shall not be liable for omissions:

Provided that—

(1) A sole trustee shall not be entitled to resign his office by virtue of this Act unless either (1) he has assumed new trustees and they have declared their acceptance of office, or (2) the court shall have appointed new trustees or a judicial factor as hereinafter in this Act provided; and

(2) A trustee who has accepted any legacy or bequest or annuity expressly given on condition of the recipient thereof accepting the office of trustee under the trust shall not be entitled to resign the office of trustee by virtue of this Act, unless otherwise expressly declared in the trust deed, nor shall any trustee appointed to the office of trustee on the footing of receiving remuneration for his services be entitled so to resign that office in the absence of an express power to resign; but it shall be competent to the court, on the petition of any trustee to whom the foregoing provisions of this proviso apply, to grant authority to such trustee to resign the office of trustee on such conditions (if any) with respect to repayment or otherwise of his legacy as the court may think just; and

(3) A judicial factor shall not, by virtue of this Act, have the power of assumption, nor shall he have the power by virtue of this Act to resign his office without judicial authority.

Nothing in this section shall affect any liability incurred by any trustee prior to the date of any resignation or assumption under the provisions of this Act or of any Act repealed by this Act.

4 General powers of trustees

(1) In all trusts the trustees shall have power to do the following acts, where such acts are not at variance with the terms or purposes of the trust, and such acts when done shall be as effectual as if such powers had been contained in the trust deed, *viz:*—

(a) To sell the trust estate or any part thereof, heritable as well as moveable.

[. . .]

(c) To grant leases of any duration (including mineral leases) of the heritable estate or any part thereof and to remove tenants.

(d) To borrow money on the security of the trust estate or any part thereof, heritable as well as moveable.

(e) To excamb any part of the trust estate which is heritable.

[(ea) To make any kind of investment of the trust estate (including an investment in heritable property).

(eb) To acquire heritable property for any other reason.]

(f) To appoint factors and law agents and to pay them suitable remuneration.

(g) To discharge trustees who have resigned and the representatives of trustees who have died.

(h) To uplift, discharge, or assign debts due to the trust estate.

(i) To compromise or to submit and refer all claims connected with the trust estate.

(j) To refrain from doing diligence for the recovery of any debt due to the truster which the trustees may reasonably deem irrecoverable.

(k) To grant all deeds necessary for carrying into effect the powers vested in the trustees.

(l) To pay debts due by the truster or by the trust estate without requiring the creditors to constitute such debts where the trustees are satisfied that the debts are proper debts of the trust.

(m) To make abatement or reduction, either temporary or permanent, of the rent, lordship, royalty, or other consideration stipulated in any lease of land, houses, tenements, minerals, metals, or other subjects, and to accept renunciations of leases of any such subjects.

(n) To apply the whole or any part of trust funds which the trustees are empowered or directed by the trust deed to invest in the purchase of heritable property in the payment or redemption of any debt or burden affecting heritable property which may be destined to the same series of heirs and subject to the same conditions as are by the trust deed made applicable to heritable property directed to be purchased.

[(o) To concur, in respect of any securities of a company (being securities comprised in the trust estate), in any scheme or arrangement—

(i) for the reconstruction of the company,

(ii) for the sale of all or any part of the property and undertaking of the company to another company,

(iii) for the acquisition of the securities of the company, or of control thereof, by another company,

(iv) for the amalgamation of the company with another company, or

(v) for the release, modification, or variation of any rights, privileges or liabilities attached to the securities or any of them,

in like manner as if the trustees were entitled to such securities beneficially; to accept any securities of any denomination or description of the reconstructed or purchasing or new company in lieu of, or in exchange for, all or any of the first mentioned securities; and to retain any securities so accepted as aforesaid for any period for which the trustees could have properly retained the original securities,

(p) To exercise, to such extent as the trustees think fit, any conditional or preferential right to subscribe for any securities in a company (being a right offered to them in respect of any holding in the company), to apply capital money of the trust estate in payment of the consideration, and to retain any such securities for which they have subscribed for any period for which they have power to retain the holding in respect of which the right to subscribe for the securities was offered (but subject to any conditions subject to which they have that power); to renounce, to such extent as they think fit, any such right; or to assign, to such extent as they think fit and for the best consideration that can reasonably be obtained, the benefit of such right or the title thereto to any person, including any beneficiary under the trust.]

[(1A) The power to act under subsection (1)(ea) or (eb) above is subject to any restriction or exclusion imposed by or under any enactment.

(1B)   The power to act under subsection (1)(ea) or (eb) above is not conferred on any trustees who are—

    (a)   the trustees of a pension scheme,

    (b)   the trustees of an authorised unit trust, or

    (c)   trustees under any other trust who are entitled by or under any other enactment to make investments of the trust estate.

(1C)   No term relating to the powers of a trustee contained in a trust deed executed before 3rd August 1961 is to be treated as restricting or excluding the power to act under subsection (1)(ea) above.

(1D)   No term restricting the powers of investment of a trustee to those conferred by the Trustee Investments Act 1961 (c 62) contained in a trust deed executed on or after 3rd August 1961 is to be treated as restricting or excluding the power to act under subsection (1)(ea) above.

(1E)   The reference in subsection (1D) above to a trustee does not include a reference to a trustee under a trust constituted by a private or local Act of Parliament or a private Act of the Scottish Parliament; and 'trust deed' shall be construed accordingly.

(1F)   In this section—

    'authorised unit trust' means a unit trust scheme in the case of which an order under section 243 of the Financial Services and Markets Act 2000 (c 8) is in force,

    'enactment' has the same meaning as in the Scotland Act 1998 (c 46),

    'pension scheme' means an occupational pension scheme (within the meaning of the Pension Schemes Act 1993 (c 48)) established under a trust and subject to the law of Scotland.]

(2)   This section shall apply to acts done before as well as after the passing of this Act, but shall not apply so as to affect any question relating to an act enumerated in head (a), (b), (c), (d), or (e) of this section which may, at the passing of this Act, be the subject of a depending action.

[4A   Exercise of power of investment: duties of trustee

(1)   Before exercising the power of investment under section 4(1)(ea) of this Act, a trustee shall have regard to—

    (a)   the suitability to the trust of the proposed investment, and

    (b)   the need for diversification of investments [of the trust, in so far as is appropriate to the circumstances of the trust].

(2)   Before exercising that power of investment, a trustee shall (except where subsection (4) applies) obtain and consider proper advice about the way in which the power should be exercised.

(3)   When reviewing the investments of the trust, a trustee shall (except where subsection (4) applies) obtain and consider proper advice about whether the investments should be varied.

(4)   If a trustee reasonably concludes that in all the circumstances it is unnecessary or inappropriate to obtain such advice, the trustee need not obtain it.

(5)   In this section, 'proper advice' means the advice of a person who is reasonably believed by the trustee to be qualified by the person's ability and practical experience of financial and other matters relating to the proposed investment.

4B   Exercise of power of investment: power to appoint nominees

(1)   The trustees of a trust may, for the purpose of exercising the power of investment under section 4(1)(ea) of this Act—

    (a)   appoint a person to act as their nominee in relation to such of the trust estate, heritable as well as moveable, as they may determine, and

    (b)   take such steps as are necessary to secure the transfer of title to that property to their nominee.

(2)   A person may not be appointed as a nominee unless the trustees reasonably believe—

   (a) that the appointment is appropriate in the circumstances of the trust, and
   (b) that the proposed nominee has the skills, knowledge and expertise that it is reasonable to expect of a person acting as a nominee.

(3) The power to appoint a nominee is subject to any restriction or exclusion imposed by or under—
   (a) the trust deed, or
   (b) any enactment (within the meaning of the Scotland Act 1998 (c 46)).

(4) An appointment as a nominee shall—
   (a) be made in writing,
   (b) be subject to the trustees' retaining power to—
      (i) direct the nominee, and
      (ii) revoke the nominee's appointment, and
   (c) subject to subsection (4), otherwise be on such terms as to suitable remuneration and other matters as the trustees may determine.

(5) The trustees may not appoint a nominee on any of the following terms unless it is reasonably necessary for them to do so—
   (a) a term permitting the nominee to appoint a substitute,
   (b) a term restricting the liability of the nominee, or of any substitute, to the trustees or to any beneficiary,
   (c) a term permitting the nominee, or any substitute, to act in circumstances capable of giving rise to a conflict of interest.

(6) While a nominee continues to act for the trust, the trustees shall—
   (a) keep under review the arrangements under which the nominee acts and how those arrangements are being put into effect,
   (b) if circumstances make it appropriate to do so, consider whether there is a need to exercise their power—
      (i) to direct the nominee, or
      (ii) to revoke the nominee's appointment, and
   (c) exercise either or both of those powers if they consider that there is a need to do so.

4C Declaration of power to delegate investment management functions
(1) It is declared that the trustees of a trust have and have always had the power, subject to any restriction or exclusion imposed by or under the trust deed or any enactment, to authorise an agent to exercise any of their investment management functions at the agent's discretion or in such other manner as the trustees may direct.

(2) In this section—
'enactment' has the same meaning as in the Scotland Act 1998 (c 46), and
'investment management functions' means functions relating to the management of investments of the trust estate, heritable as well as moveable.]

5 Powers which may be granted to trustees by the court
It shall be competent to the court, on the petition of the trustees under any trust, to grant authority to the trustees to do any of the acts mentioned in the section of this Act relating to general powers of trustees, notwithstanding that such act is at variance with the terms or purposes of the trust, on being satisfied that such act is in all the circumstances expedient for the execution of the trust.

  In this section the expression 'trust' shall not include any trust constituted by private or local Act of Parliament, and the expression 'trustees' shall be construed accordingly.

6 Method of sale by trustees
All powers of sale conferred on trustees by the trust deed or by virtue of this Act may be exercised either by public roup or private bargain unless otherwise directed in the trust deed or in the authority given by the court, and when the

estate is heritable it shall be lawful in the exercise of such powers to [. . .] reserve the mines and minerals.

7   Deeds granted by trustees

Any deed bearing to be granted by the trustees under any trust, and in fact executed by a quorum of such trustees in favour of any person other than a beneficiary or a co-trustee under the trust where such person has dealt onerously and in good faith shall not be void or challengeable on the ground that any trustee or trustees under the trust was or were not consulted in the matter, or was or were not present, at any meeting of trustees where the same was considered, or did not consent to or concur in the granting of the deed, or on the ground of any other omission or irregularity of procedure on the part of the trustees or any of them in relation to the granting of the deed.

Nothing in this section shall affect any question of liability or otherwise between any trustee under any trust on the one hand and any co-trustee or beneficiary under such trust on the other hand. This section shall apply to deeds granted before as well as after the passing of this Act, but shall not apply so as to affect any question which may, at the passing of this Act, be the subject of a depending action.

In this section the expression 'quorum' means a quorum of the trustees under any trust entitled to act in terms of the trust deed or in virtue of this Act, or of any Act repealed by this Act, as the case may be.

8   Conveyances to non-existing or unidentifiable persons

(1)   Where in any deed, whether *inter vivos* or *mortis causa*, heritable or moveable property is conveyed to any person in liferent, and in fee to persons who, when such conveyance comes into operation, are unborn or incapable of ascertainment, the person to whom the property is conveyed in liferent shall not be deemed to be beneficially entitled to the property in fee by reason only that the liferent is not expressed in the deed to be a liferent allenarly; and all such conveyances as aforesaid shall, unless a contrary intention appears in the deed, take effect in the same manner and in all respects as if the liferent were declared to be a liferent allenarly; provided always that this subsection shall not apply to any conveyance which has come into operation before the passing of this Act.

For the purposes of this subsection, the date at which any conveyance in liferent and fee as aforesaid comes into operation shall be deemed to be the date at which the person to whom the liferent is conveyed first becomes entitled to receive the rents or income of the property.

(2)   Where under any conveyance, whether coming into operation before or after the passing of this Act, any property is conveyed to one person in liferent and in fee to persons who, when such conveyance comes into operation, are unborn or incapable of ascertainment, it shall be competent to the court, on the application of the liferenter, whether or not he would, according to the existing law, be deemed to be fiduciary fiar, or of any person to whom the fee or any part thereof bears to be presumptively destined, or who may have an interest under such conveyance notwithstanding that such interest is prospective or contingent, or of the accountant of court:—

(a)   To grant authority to the fiduciary fiar to exercise all or such of the powers, or to do all or such of the acts, competent to a trustee at common law or under this Act, as to the court may seem fit:

(b)   To appoint a trustee or trustees (of whom the liferenter or fiduciary fiar may be one) with all the powers of trustees at common law and under this Act, or a judicial factor, to hold the said property in trust in place of the liferenter or fiduciary fiar; and to authorise and ordain the fiduciary fiar to execute and deliver all such deeds as may be necessary for the completion of title to the said property by such trustee or trustees or judicial factor; or otherwise, to grant warrant to such trustee or trustees or judicial factor to complete a title to the said property in the same manner and to the same effect as under a warrant in favour of a trustee or trustees granted in terms of the section of this Act relating to the appointment of new trustees by the court, or a warrant in favour of a judicial factor granted in terms of section 24 of the Titles to Land Consolidation (Scotland) Act 1868 or section 44 of the Conveyancing (Scotland) Act 1874, as the case may be. The expense of completing the title as aforesaid shall, unless the court otherwise directs, be a charge against the capital of the estate.

(3)   For the purposes of this section, all references to a trust deed in this Act contained shall be read and construed as a reference to the conveyance of the property in liferent and fee as aforesaid.

9   Liferents of personal estate beyond certain limits prohibited

It shall be competent to constitute or reserve by means of a trust or otherwise a liferent interest in moveable and personal estate in Scotland in favour only of a person in life at the date of the deed constituting or reserving such liferent, and, where any moveable or personal estate in Scotland shall, by virtue of any deed dated after the 31st day of July 1868 (the date of any testamentary or *mortis causa* deed being taken to be the date of the death of the granter, and the date of any contract of marriage being taken to be the date of the dissolution of the marriage) be held in liferent by or for behoof of a person of full age born after the date of such deed, such moveable or personal estate shall belong absolutely to such person, and, where such estate stands invested in the name of any trustees, such trustees shall be bound to deliver, make over, or convey such estate to such person:

Provided always that, where more persons than one are interested in the moveable or personal estate held by trustees as hereinbefore mentioned, all the expenses connected with the transference of a portion of such estate to any of the beneficiaries in terms of this section shall be borne by the beneficiary in whose favour the transference is made.

[. . .]

15   Trustees not to hold certificates or bonds payable to bearer

(1)   A trustee, unless authorised by the terms of his trust, shall not apply for purchase, acquire, or hold beyond a reasonable time for realisation or conversion into registered or inscribed stock any certificate to bearer or debenture or other bond or document payable to bearer.

(2)   Nothing in this section shall impose on the Bank of England or the Bank of Ireland or on any person authorised by or under any Act of Parliament to issue any such certificate, bond, or document any obligation to inquire whether a person applying for such a certificate, bond, or document is or is not a trustee, or subject them to any liability in the event of their granting any such certificate, bond or document to a trustee, nor invalidate any such certificate, bond or document if granted.

16   The court may authorise the advance of part of the capital of a trust fund

The court may, from time to time under such conditions as they see fit, authorise trustees to advance any part of the capital of a fund destined either absolutely or contingently to beneficiaries who at the date of the application to the court are not of full age, if it shall appear that the income of the fund is insufficient or not applicable to, and that such advance is necessary for, the maintenance or education of such beneficiaries or any of them, and that it is not expressly prohibited by the trust deed, and that the rights of such beneficiaries, if contingent, are contingent only on their survivance.

17   Trustees may apply to court for superintendence order as to investment and distribution of estate

It shall be competent for the trustees under any trust deed or one or more of them to apply to the court for an order of the accountant of court to superintend their administration of the trust insofar as it relates to the investment of the trust funds and the distribution thereof among the creditors interested and the beneficiaries under the trust, and the court may grant such order accordingly, and if such order be granted the accountant of court shall annually examine and audit the accounts of such trustees, and at any time, if he thinks fit, he may report to the court upon any question that may arise in the administration of the trust with regard to any of the foresaid matters and obtain the directions of the court thereupon.

18 Discharge of trustees resigning and heirs of trustees dying during the subsistence of the trust

When a trustee who resigns or the representatives of a trustee who has died or resigned cannot obtain a discharge of his acts and intromissions from the remaining trustees, and when the beneficiaries of the trust refuse or are unable from absence, incapacity or otherwise to grant a discharge, the court may on petition to that effect at the instance of such trustee or representative and after such intimation and inquiry as may be thought necessary, grant such discharge.

19 Form of resignation of trustees

(1) Subject to the provisions of subsection (2) of this section, any trustee entitled to resign his office may do so by minute of the trust entered in the sederunt book of the trust and signed in such sederunt book by such trustee and by the other trustee or trustees acting at the time, or he may do so by signing a minute of resignation in the form of Schedule A to this Act annexed or to the like effect, and may register the same in the books of council and session, and in such case he shall be bound to intimate the same to his co-trustee or trustees, and the resignation shall be held to take effect from and after the date of the receipt of such intimation, or the last date thereof if more than one, and in case after inquiry the residence of any trustee to whom intimation should be given under this provision cannot be found, such intimation shall be sent by post in a registered letter addressed to the Keeper of the Register of Edictal Citations.

(2) A sole trustee desiring to resign his office may apply to the court stating such desire and praying for the appointment of new trustees or of a judicial factor to administer the trust, and the court, after intimation to the beneficiaries under the trust, or such of them as the court may direct, may thereafter appoint either a judicial factor or new trustees, and if the court appoint new trustees the court may grant warrant to complete title as provided in the section of this Act relating to appointment of new trustees by the court.

20 Effect of resignation

Where a trustee entitled to resign his office shall have resigned in either of the modes provided by the immediately preceding section or otherwise, and his resignation shall have been duly completed, such trustee shall be thereby divested of the whole property and estate of the trust, which shall accrue to or devolve upon the continuing trustees or trustee without the necessity of any conveyance or other transfer by the resigning trustee, but without prejudice to the right of the continuing trustee or trustees to require the resigning trustee to execute and deliver to the continuing trustees or trustee at the expense of the trust a conveyance or transfer (or conveyances or transfers) of the property or estate belonging to the trust, or any part thereof if the continuing trustees or trustee shall consider this expedient, and the resigning trustee when so required shall be bound at the expense of the trust to execute and deliver such conveyance or conveyances, transfer or transfers accordingly.

21 Appointment of new or additional trustees by deed of assumption

When trustees have the power of assuming new trustees, such new trustees may be assumed by deed of assumption executed by the trustee or trustees acting under the trust deed or by a quorum of such trustees, if more than two, in the form of Schedule B to this Act annexed or to the like effect, and a deed of assumption so executed, in addition to a general conveyance of the trust estate, may contain a special conveyance of heritable property belonging to the trust estate, and in such case shall be effectual as a conveyance of such heritable property in favour of the existing trustees and the trustees so to be assumed, and such deed of assumption shall also be effectual as an assignation in favour of such existing and assumed trustees of the whole personal property belonging to the trust estate, and in the event of any trustee acting under any trust deed being insane or incapable of acting by reason of physical or mental disability or by continuous absence from the United Kingdom for a period of six months or upwards, such deed of assumption may be executed by the remaining trustee or trustees acting under such trust deed: Provided that, when the signatures of a quorum of trustees cannot be obtained, it shall be necessary to obtain the consent of the court to such deed of assumption on application either by the acting trustee or trustees or by any one or more of the beneficiaries under the trust deed.

22   Appointment of new trustees by the court
When trustees cannot be assumed under any trust deed, or when any person who is the sole trustee appointed in or acting under any trust deed is or has become insane or is or has become incapable of acting by reason of physical or mental disability, or by being absent continuously from the United Kingdom for a period of at least six months, or by having disappeared for a like period, the [Court of Session or an appropriate sheriff court] may, upon the application of any party having interest in the trust estate, after such intimation and inquiry as may be thought necessary, appoint a trustee or trustees under such trust deed with all the powers incident to that office, and, on such appointment being made in the case of any person becoming insane or incapable of acting as aforesaid, such person shall cease to be a trustee under such trust deed, and the court [to which application is made] may, on such application, grant a warrant to complete a title to any heritable property forming part of the trust estate in favour of the trustee or trustees so appointed, which warrant shall specify and describe the heritable property to which it is applicable, or refer in terms of law to a recorded deed containing a description thereof, and shall also specify the moveable or personal property, or bear reference to an inventory appended to the petition to the court in which such moveable or personal property is specified, and such warrant shall be effectual as a conveyance of such heritable property in favour of the trustee or trustees so appointed in like manner and to the same effect as a warrant in favour of a judicial factor granted under the authority of section 24 of the Titles to Land Consolidation (Scotland) Act 1868, or section 44 of the Conveyancing (Scotland) Act 1874, and shall also be effectual as an assignation of such moveable or personal property in favour of the trustee or trustees so appointed.

23   Court may remove trustees in certain cases
In the event of any trustee being or becoming insane or incapable of acting by reason of physical or mental disability or being absent from the United Kingdom continuously for a period of at least six months, or having disappeared for a like period, such trustee, in the case of insanity or incapacity of acting by reason of physical or mental disability, shall, and in the case of continuous absence from the United Kingdom or disappearance for a period of six months or upwards, may, on application in manner in this section provided by any co-trustee or any beneficiary or other person interested in the trust estate, be removed from office upon such evidence as shall satisfy the court to which the application is made of the insanity, incapacity or continuous absence or disappearance of such trustee. Such application [may be made either to the Court of Session or to an appropriate sheriff court.]

24   Completion of title by the beneficiary of a lapsed trust
Any person who shall be entitled to the possession for his own absolute use of any heritable property or moveable or personal property the title to which has been taken in the name of any trustee who has died or become incapable of acting without having executed a conveyance of such property, or any other person deriving right whether immediately or otherwise from the person entitled as aforesaid, may apply by petition to the [Court of Session or an appropriate sheriff court] for authority to complete a title to such property in his own name, and such petition shall specify and describe the heritable property, or refer to a description thereof in terms of law, and refer to an inventory to which the moveable or personal property is specified to which such title is to be completed and after such intimation and inquiry as may be thought necessary it shall be lawful for the court [to which application is made] to grant a warrant for completing such title as aforesaid, which warrant shall specify and describe the heritable property to which it is applicable, or refer in terms of law to a description thereof, and shall also specify the moveable or personal property or shall bear reference to an inventory appended to the petition in which such moveable or personal property is specified, and such warrant shall be effectual as a conveyance of such heritable property in favour of the petitioner in like manner and to the same effect as a warrant in favour of a judicial factor granted under the authority of section 24 of the Titles to Land Consolidation (Scotland) Act 1868, or section 44 of the Conveyancing (Scotland) Act 1874, and shall also be effectual as an assignation of such moveable or personal property in favour of the petitioner.

[24A   Interpretation of sections 22–24
In sections 22 to 24 of this Act the expression 'appropriate sheriff court' means—
  (a)   in the case of a trust other than a marriage contract—
      (i)   where the truster, or any of the trusters, was at the date of the coming into operation of the trust domiciled in a sheriffdom, a sheriff court of that sheriffdom; or
      (ii)   where sub-paragraph (i) of this paragraph does not apply, or where the applicant does not possess sufficient information to enable him to determine which sheriff court, if any, would by virtue of that sub-paragraph be an appropriate sheriff court, the sheriff court at Edinburgh;
  (b)   in the case of a marriage contract—
      (i)   where either spouse is, or was when he died, domiciled in a sheriffdom, a sheriff court of that sheriffdom; or
      (ii)   where sub-paragraph (i) of this paragraph does not apply, or where the applicant does not possess sufficient information to enable him to determine which sheriff court, if any, would by virtue of that sub-paragraph be an appropriate sheriff court, the sheriff court at Edinburgh.]

25   Completion of title of judicial factors
Application for authority to complete the title of a judicial factor to any trust property or estate may be contained in the petition for the appointment of such factor, and such application may include moveable or personal property.

26   Powers of court under this Act to be exercised by Lord Ordinary
Applications to the court under the authority of this Act shall be by petition addressed to the court, and shall be brought in the first instance before one of the Lords Ordinary officiating in the Outer House, who may direct such intimation and service thereof and such investigation or inquiry as he may think fit, and the power of the Lord Ordinary before whom the petition is enrolled may be exercised by the Lord Ordinary on the Bills during vacation, and all such petitions shall, as respects procedure, disposal and review, be subject to the same rules and regulations as are enacted with respect to petitions coming before the Junior Lord Ordinary in virtue of the Court of Session Act 1857: Provided that, when in the

exercise of the powers pertaining to the court of appointing trustees and regulating trusts, it shall be necessary to settle a scheme for the administration of any charitable or other permanent endowment, the Lord Ordinary shall, after preparing such scheme, report to one of the divisions of the court, by whom the same shall be finally adjusted and settled, and in all cases where it shall be necessary to settle any such scheme, intimation shall be made to His Majesty's Advocate, who shall be entitled to appear and intervene for the interests of the charity or any object of the trust or the public interest.

27   Court may pass Acts of Sederunt
The court shall be and is hereby empowered from time to time to make such regulations by Act or Acts of Sederunt as may be requisite for carrying into effect the purposes of this Act. [. . .]

28   Resignation of trustee who is also executor to infer resignation as executor
In all cases where a trust deed appoints the trustees to be also executors the resignation of any such trustee shall infer, unless where otherwise expressly declared, his resignation also as an executor under such trust deed.

29   Extent of liability of trustee
Where a trustee shall have improperly advanced trust money on a heritable security which would, at the time of the investment, have been a proper investment in all respects for a less sum than was actually advanced thereon, the security shall be deemed an authorised investment for such less sum, and the trustee shall only be liable to make good the sum advanced in excess thereof with interest.

[29A   Errors in distribution: circumstances in which trustee not personally liable
(1)   A trustee is not personally liable for any error in the distribution of any property, or the income of property, vested in the person as trustee if—
   (a)   the error was caused by the trustee not knowing (either or both)—
      (i)   of the existence, or non-existence, of a person,
      (ii)   of a person's relationship, or lack of relationship, to another person, and
   (b)   the distribution takes place—
      (i)   in good faith and after such enquiries as any reasonable and prudent trustee would have made in the circumstances of the case, or
      (ii)   in accordance with an order of the court.
(2)   Subsection (1) does not affect any right which a person entitled to the property or income concerned has to recover it from another person.
(3)   Subsection (2) is without prejudice to section 24 of the Succession (Scotland) Act 2016.
(4)   This section applies only in relation to a distribution which takes place on or after the day on which section 23 of the Succession (Scotland) Act 2016 comes into force.]

30   Trustee not to be chargeable with breach of trust for lending money on security of any property on certain conditions
(1)   Any trustee lending money on the security of any property shall not be chargeable with breach of trust by reason only of the proportion borne by the amount of the loan to the value of such property at the time when the loan was made, provided that it shall appear to the court that in making such loan the trustee was acting upon a report as to the value of the property made by a person whom the trustee reasonably believed to be an able practical valuator instructed and employed independently of any owner of the property, whether such valuator carried on business in the locality where the property is situated or elsewhere, and that the amount of the loan by itself or in combination with any other loan or loans upon the property ranking prior to or *pari passu* with the loan in question does not exceed two equal third parts of the value of the property as stated in such report,

and this section shall apply to a loan upon any property on which the trustees can lawfully lend.

(2)   This section shall apply to transfers of existing securities as well as to new securities, and in its application to a partial transfer of an existing security the expression 'the amount of the loan' shall include the amount of any other loan or loans upon the property ranking prior to or *pari passu* with the loan in question.

31   Power of court to make orders in case of breach of trust

Where a trustee shall have committed a breach of trust at the instigation or request or with the consent in writing of a beneficiary, the court may, if it shall think fit, make such order as to the court shall seem just for applying all or any part of the interest of the beneficiary in the trust estate by way of indemnity to the trustee or person claiming through him.

32   Court may relieve trustee from personal liability

(1)   If it appears to the court that a trustee is or may be personally liable for any breach of trust, whether the transaction alleged to be a breach of trust occurred before or after the passing of this Act, but has acted honestly and reasonably, and ought fairly to be excused for the breach of trust, then the court may relieve the trustee either wholly or partly from personal liability for the same.

(2)   In this section and in the two immediately preceding sections the expression 'the court' shall mean any court of competent jurisdiction in which a question relative to the actings, liability, or removal of a trustee comes to be tried.

33   Investment ceasing to be an authorised investment

A trustee shall not be liable for breach of trust by reason only of his continuing to hold an investment which has ceased to be an investment authorised by the trust deed or by or under this Act.

34   Expenses of applications under this Act

(1)   The court shall determine all questions of expenses in relation to any application made under this Act, and may direct that any such expenses shall be paid out of the trust estate where the court considers this reasonable.

(2)   In this section the expression 'the court' shall include any court to which an application may be made under this Act.

35   Application of Act

Save as in this Act expressly otherwise provided—

(1)   This Act shall apply to trusts which have come into operation before as well as to trusts coming into operation after the passing of this Act.

(2)   Nothing in this Act contained shall be held to extend the liability of trustees.

[. . .]

SCHEDULES

SCHEDULE A   Section 19

FORM OF MINUTE OF RESIGNATION

I, *AB*, do hereby resign the office of trustee under the trust disposition and settlement (*or other deed*) granted by *CD* dated the   day of   ,* (*If the trustee was assumed add,* and to which office of trustee I was assumed by deed of assumption granted by *EF* and *GH*, dated   day of   .*).

[Testing clause†]

* If recorded specify register and date of recording.

[† Note—[In the case of a traditional document, subscription of it by the granter] will be sufficient for the document to be formally valid, but witnessing of it may be necessary or desirable for other purposes (see the Requirements of Writing (Scotland) Act 1995) [, which also makes provision as regards the authentication of an electronic document].]

SCHEDULE B   Section 21
FORM OF DEED OF ASSUMPTION

I, *AB* (*or* we, *AB* and *CD*), the accepting and surviving (*or* remaining) trustee (*or* trustees, *or* a majority and quorum of the accepting and surviving trustees), acting under a trust disposition and settlement (*or other deed*) granted by *EF*, dated the   day of   (*if recorded, specify register and date of recording*), do hereby assume *GH* (*or GH* and *IK*) as a trustee (*or* trustees) under the said trust disposition and settlement (*or other deed*); and I (*or* we) dispone and convey to myself (*or* ourselves) and the said *GH* (*or GH* and *IK*) as trustees under the said trust disposition and settlement (*or other deed*), and the survivors or survivor, and the heir of the last survivor, the majority, while more than two are acting, being a quorum (*or otherwise in accordance with the terms of the trust deed*), all and sundry the whole trust, estate and effects, heritable and moveable, real and personal, of every description and wherever situated, at present belonging to me (*or* us) or under my (*or* our) control as trustee (*or* surviving trustees, *or otherwise as the case may be*), under the said trust disposition and settlement (*or other deed*), together with the whole vouchers, titles, and instructions thereof. (*Then may follow, if wished, special conveyances of heritable or personal property, with the usual clauses of a conveyance applicable to such property, and as the case may require.*)

[Testing clause†]

[† Note—[In the case of a traditional document, subscription of it by the granter or granters] will be sufficient for the document to be formally valid, but witnessing of it may be necessary or desirable for other purposes (see the Requirements of Writing (Scotland) Act 1995) [, which also makes provision as regards the authentication of an electronic document].]

[...]

TRUSTS (SCOTLAND) ACT 1961
(1961, 9 & 10 Eliz 2, c 57)

1   Jurisdiction of court in relation to variation of trust purposes

(1)   In relation to any trust taking effect, whether before or after the commencement of this Act, under any will, settlement or other disposition, the court may if it thinks fit, on the petition of the trustees or any of the beneficiaries, approve on behalf of—

(a)   any of the beneficiaries who [because of any legal disability] by reason of nonage or other incapacity is incapable of assenting, or

(b)   any person (whether ascertained or not) who may become one of the beneficiaries as being at a future date or on the happening of a future event a person of any specified description or a member of any specified class of persons, so however that this paragraph shall not include any person who is capable of assenting and would be of that description, or a member of that class, as the case may be, if the said date had fallen or the said event had happened at the date of the presentation of the petition to the court, or

(c)   any person unborn,

any arrangement (by whomsoever proposed, and whether or not there is any other person beneficially interested who is capable of assenting thereto) varying or revoking all or any of the trust purposes or enlarging the powers of the trustees of managing or administering the trust estate:

Provided that the court shall not approve an arrangement under this subsection on behalf of any person unless it is of the opinion that the carrying out thereof would not be prejudicial to that person.

(2) For the purposes of the foregoing subsection a person who is [of or over the age of 16 years] but has not attained the age of [18 years] shall be deemed to be incapable of assenting: but before approving an arrangement under that subsection on behalf of any such person the court shall take such account as it thinks appropriate of his attitude to the arrangement.

(3) [...]

(4) Where under any trust such as is mentioned in subsection (1) of this section a trust purpose entitles any of the beneficiaries (in this subsection referred to as 'the alimentary beneficiary') to an alimentary liferent of, or any alimentary income from the trust estate or any part thereof, the court may if it thinks fit, on the petition of the trustees or any of the beneficiaries, authorise any arrangement varying or revoking that trust purpose and making new provisions in lieu thereof, including, if the court thinks fit, new provision for the disposal of the fee or capital of the trust estate or, as the case may be, of such part thereof as was burdened with the liferent or the payment of the income:

Provided that the court shall not authorise an arrangement under this subsection unless—

(a) it considers that the carrying out of the arrangement would be reasonable, having regard to the income of the alimentary beneficiary from all sources, and to such other factors, if any, as the court considers material, and

(b) the arrangement is approved by the alimentary beneficiary, or, where the alimentary beneficiary is a person on whose behalf the court is empowered by subsection (1) of this section or that subsection as extended by subsection (2) of this section to approve the arrangement, the arrangement is so approved by the court under that subsection.

(5) Nothing in the foregoing provisions of this section shall be taken to limit or restrict any power possessed by the court apart from this section under any Act of Parliament or rule of law.

(6) In this section the expression 'beneficiary' in relation to a trust includes any person having, directly or indirectly, an interest, whether vested or contingent, under the trust.

2 Validity of certain transactions by trustees

(1) Where, after the commencement of this Act, the trustees under any trust enter into a transaction with any person (in this section referred to as 'the second party'), being a transaction under which the trustees purport to do in relation to the trust estate or any part thereof an act of any of the descriptions specified in paragraphs (a) to [(eb)] of subsection (1) of section 4 of the Act of 1921 (which empowers trustees to do certain acts where such acts are not at variance with the terms or purposes of the trust) the validity of the transaction and of any title acquired by the second party under the transaction shall not be challengeable by the second party or any other person on the ground that the act in question is at variance with the terms or purposes of the trust:

Provided that in relation to a transaction [other than a transaction such as is specified in paragraph (ea) of that subsection] entered into by trustees who are acting under the supervision of the accountant of court this section shall have effect only if the said accountant consents to the transaction.

[(2) Nothing in subsection (1) of this section shall affect any question of liability between any of the trustees on the one hand and any co-trustee or any of the beneficiaries on the other hand.

(3) Without prejudice to the operation of subsection (1) of this section, where in relation to the trust estate or any part thereof a judicial factor thinks it expedient to do any of the acts mentioned in that subsection but the act in question might be at variance with the terms or purposes of the trust, he may, subject to the following provisions of this section, apply to the accountant of court for his consent to the doing of the act.

(4)   Where an application is made under subsection (3) of this section to the accountant of court for his consent to the doing of an act to which that subsection applies, he may grant the application subject to such conditions (including conditions as to price) as he thinks fit if—

(a)   he considers that the doing of the act is in the best interests of the owner of the trust estate to which the judicial factor's appointment relates or of any person to whom the owner owes a duty of support; and

(b)   he is satisfied—

(i)   that the judicial factor is not expressly prohibited by the terms of his appointment from doing the act; and

(ii)   that there has been compliance with the provisions of subsection (5) of this section and of any rules made thereunder; and

(c)   no objection is made to the doing of the act under subsection (5) of this section.

(5)   A judicial factor proposing to make an application under subsection (3) of this section to the accountant of court shall notify such persons or such class or classes of persons as may be specified in rules of court in such manner as may be so specified of the proposed application, the act to which it relates, and of their right to object to him doing that act within such time and in such manner as the rules may specify; and the rules may make different provision in respect of different classes of judicial factors, and may make provision exempting a judicial factor or a class of judicial factors from giving notification under this subsection in such circumstances as the rules may specify.

(6)   Where a judicial factor does any act in accordance with the consent of the accountant of court granted under subsection (4) of this section and in compliance with the provisions of this section and of any rules made thereunder, it shall be treated as being not at variance with the terms or purposes of the trust.]

3–4   [*Amend Trusts (Scotland) Act 1921.*]

5   Accumulations of income

(1)   The following provisions of this section shall have effect in substitution for the provisions of the Accumulations Act 1800, and that Act is hereby repealed.

(2)   No person may by any will, settlement or other disposition dispose of any property in such manner that the income thereof shall be wholly or partially accumulated for any longer period than one of the following, that is to say—

(a)   the life of the grantor; or

(b)   a term of twenty-one years from the death of the grantor; or

(c)   the duration of the minority or respective minorities of any person or persons living or *in utero* at the death of the grantor; or

(d)   the duration of the minority or respective minorities of any person or persons who, under the terms of the will, settlement or other disposition directing the accumulation, would for the time being, if of full age, be entitled to the income directed to be accumulated.

(3)   In every case where any accumulation is directed otherwise than as aforesaid, the direction shall, save as hereinafter provided, be void, and the income directed to be accumulated shall, so long as the same is directed to be accumulated contrary to this section, go to and be received by the person or persons who would have been entitled thereto if such accumulation had not been directed.

(4)   For avoidance of doubt it is hereby declared that, in the case of a settlement or other disposition *inter vivos*, a direction to accumulate income during a period specified in paragraph (d) of subsection (2) of this section shall not be void, nor shall the accumulation of the income be contrary to this section, solely by reason of the fact that the period begins during the life of the grantor and ends after his death.

(5)   The restrictions imposed by this section apply to wills, settlements and other dispositions made on or after the twenty-eighth day of July, 1800, but, in the

case of wills, only where the testator was living and of testamentary capacity after the end of one year from that date.

(6)   In this section 'minority' in relation to any person means the period beginning with the birth of the person and ending with his attainment of the age of twenty-one years, and 'grantor' includes settlor and, in relation to a will, the testator.

6   Interpretation

(1)   In this Act, unless the context otherwise requires,—

'Act of 1921' means the Trusts (Scotland) Act 1921;

'the court' means the Court of Session; and

'trust' and 'trustee' have the same meanings respectively as in the Act of 1921.

(2)   Unless the context otherwise requires references in this Act to any other Act are references to that Act as amended, modified or extended by any Act including this Act.

7   Short title, citation, application and commencement

(1)   This Act may be cited as the Trusts (Scotland) Act 1961, and this Act and the Act of 1921 may be cited together as the Trusts (Scotland) Acts 1921 and 1961.

(2)   This Act shall apply to trusts which have come into operation before, as well as to trusts coming into operation after, the commencement of this Act.

(3)   This Act shall come into operation on the expiration of the period of one month beginning with the date of the passing thereof.

WILLS ACT 1963
(1963, c 44)

1   General rule as to formal validity

A will shall be treated as properly executed if its execution conformed to the internal law in force in the territory where it was executed, or in the territory where, at the time of its execution or of the testator's death, he was domiciled or had his habitual residence, or in a state of which, at either of those times, he was a national.

2   Additional rules

(1)   Without prejudice to the preceding section, the following shall be treated as properly executed—

(a)   a will executed on board a vessel or aircraft of any description, if the execution of the will conformed to the internal law in force in the territory with which, having regard to its registration (if any) and other relevant circumstances, the vessel or aircraft may be taken to have been most closely connected;

(b)   a will so far as it disposes of immovable property, if its execution conformed to the internal law in force in the territory where the property was situated;

(c)   a will so far as it revokes a will which under this Act would be treated as properly executed or revokes a provision which under this Act would be treated as comprised in a properly executed will, if the execution of the later will conformed to any law by reference to which the revoked will or provision would be so treated;

(d)   a will so far as it exercises a power of appointment, if the execution of the will conformed to the law governing the essential validity of the power.

(2)   A will so far as it exercises a power of appointment shall not be treated as improperly executed by reason only that its execution was not in accordance with any formal requirements contained in the instrument creating the power.

3   Certain requirements to be treated as formal

Where (whether in pursuance of this Act or not) a law in force outside the United Kingdom falls to be applied in relation to a will, any requirement of that law whereby special formalities are to be observed by testators answering a particular description, or witnesses to the execution of a will are to possess certain qualifications, shall be treated, notwithstanding any rule of that law to the contrary, as a formal requirement only.

4 Construction of wills
The construction of a will shall not be altered by reason of any change in the testator's domicile after the execution of the will.

[. . .]

6 Interpretation
(1) In this Act—
'internal law' in relation to any territory or state means the law which would apply in a case where no question of the law in force in any other territory or state arose;
'state' means a territory or group of territories having its own law of nationality;
'will' includes any testamentary instrument or act, and 'testator' shall be construed accordingly.
(2) Where under this Act the internal law in force in any territory or state is to be applied in the case of a will, but there are in force in that territory or state two or more systems of internal law relating to the formal validity of wills, the system to be applied shall be ascertained as follows—
(a) if there is in force throughout the territory or state a rule indicating which of those systems can properly be applied in the case in question, that rule shall be followed; or
(b) if there is no such rule, the system shall be that with which the testator was most closely connected at the relevant time, and for this purpose the relevant time is the time of the testator's death where the matter is to be determined by reference to circumstances prevailing at his death, and the time of execution of the will in any other case.
(3) In determining for the purposes of this Act whether or not the execution of a will conformed to a particular law, regard shall be had to the formal requirements of that law at the time of execution, but this shall not prevent account being taken of an alteration of law affecting wills executed at that time if the alteration enables the will to be treated as properly executed.

7 Short title, commencement, repeal and extent
(1) This Act may be cited as the Wills Act 1963.
(2) This Act shall come into operation on 1st January 1964.
(3) The Wills Act 1861 is hereby repealed.
(4) This Act shall not apply to a will of a testator who died before the time of the commencement of this Act and shall apply to a will of a testator who dies after that time whether the will was executed before or after that time, but so that the repeal of the Wills Act 1861 shall not invalidate a will executed before that time.
(5) It is hereby declared that this Act extends to Northern Ireland [. . .].

SUCCESSION (SCOTLAND) ACT 1964
(1964, c 41)

PART I
INTESTATE SUCCESSION

1   Assimilation of heritage to moveables for purpose of devolution on intestacy
   (1)   The whole of the intestate estate of any person dying after the commencement of this Act (so far as it is estate the succession to which falls to be regulated by the law of Scotland) shall devolve, without distinction as between heritable and moveable property, in accordance with—
   (a)   the provisions of this Part of this Act, and
   (b)   any enactment or rule of law in force immediately before the commencement of this Act which is not inconsistent with those provisions and which, apart from this section, would apply to that person's moveable intestate estate, if any;
and, subject to section 37 of this Act, any enactment or rule of law in force immediately before the commencement of this Act with respect to the succession to intestate estates shall, in so far as it is inconsistent with the provisions of this Part of this Act, cease to have effect.
   (2)   Nothing in this Part of this Act shall affect legal rights or the prior rights of a surviving spouse [or civil partner]; and accordingly any reference in this Part of this Act to an intestate estate shall be construed as a reference to so much of the net intestate estate as remains after the satisfaction of those rights, or the proportion thereof properly attributable to the intestate estate.

2   Rights of succession to intestate estate
   (1)   Subject to the following provisions of this Part of this Act—
   (a)   where an intestate is survived by children, they shall have right to the whole of the intestate estate;
   (b)   where an intestate is survived by either of, or both, his parents and is also survived by brothers or sisters, but is not survived by any prior relative, the surviving parent or parents shall have right to one half of the intestate estate and the surviving brothers and sisters to the other half thereof;
   (c)   where an intestate is survived by brothers or sisters, but is not survived by any prior relative, the surviving brothers and sisters shall have right to the whole of the intestate estate;
   (d)   where an intestate is survived by either of, or both, his parents, but is not survived by any prior relative, the surviving parent or parents shall have right to the whole of the intestate estate;
   (e)   where an intestate is survived by a husband [, wife or civil partner], but is not survived by any prior relative, the surviving spouse [or civil partner] shall have right to the whole of the intestate estate;
   (f)   where an intestate is survived by uncles or aunts (being brothers or sisters of either parent of the intestate), but is not survived by any prior relative, the surviving uncles and aunts shall have right to the whole of the intestate estate;
   (g)   where an intestate is survived by a grandparent or grandparents (being a parent or parents of either parent of the intestate), but is not survived by any prior relative, the surviving grandparent or grandparents shall have right to the whole of the intestate estate;
   (h)   where an intestate is survived by brothers or sisters of any of his grandparents (being a parent or parents of either parent of the intestate), but is not survived by any prior relative, those surviving brothers and sisters shall have right to the whole of the intestate estate;
   (i)   where an intestate is not survived by any prior relative, the ancestors of the intestate (being remoter than grandparents) generation by generation successively, without distinction between the paternal and maternal lines, shall have

right to the whole of the intestate estate; so however that, failing ancestors of any generation, the brothers and sisters of any of those ancestors shall have right thereto before ancestors of the next more remote generation.

(2)   References in the foregoing subsection to brothers or sisters include respectively brothers and sisters of the half blood as well as of the whole blood; and in the said subsection 'prior relative', in relation to any class of person mentioned in any paragraph of that subsection, means a person of any other class who, if he had survived the intestate, would have had right to the intestate estate or any of it by virtue of an earlier paragraph of that subsection or by virtue of any such paragraph and section 5 of this Act.

3   Succession of collaterals

Subject to section 5 of this Act, where brothers and sisters of an intestate or of an ancestor of an intestate (in this section referred to as 'collaterals') have right to the whole, or, in a case to which subsection (1)(b) of the last foregoing section applies, to a half, of the intestate estate, the collaterals of the whole blood shall be entitled to succeed thereto in preference to the collaterals of the half blood; but where the collaterals of the half blood have right as aforesaid they shall rank without distinction as between those related to the intestate, or, as the case may be, the ancestor, through their father and those so related through their mother.

[. . .]

5   Representation

(1)   Subject to section 6 of this Act, where a person who, if he had survived an intestate, would, by virtue of any of the foregoing provisions of this Part of this Act, have had right (otherwise than as a parent [, spouse or civil partner] of the intestate) to the whole or to any part of the intestate estate has [failed to survive] the intestate, but has left issue who survive the intestate, such issue shall have the like right to the whole or to that part of the intestate estate as the said person would have had if he had survived the intestate.

(2)   The right of any issue entitled to share in an intestate estate by virtue of the foregoing subsection to be appointed to the office of executor on the intestate estate shall be postponed to the right thereto of any person who succeeds to the whole or part of the intestate estate by virtue of the foregoing provisions of this Act apart from this section and who applies for appointment to that office.

6   Division of intestate estate among those having right thereto

If, by virtue of the foregoing provisions of this Part of this Act, there are two or more persons having right among them to the whole, or, in a case to which section 2(1)(b) of this Act relates, to a half, of an intestate estate, then the said estate, or, as the case may be, that half thereof, shall—

(a)   if all of those persons are in the same degree of relationship to the intestate, be divided among them equally, and

(b)   in any other case, be divided equally into a number of parts equal to the aggregate of—

(i)   those of the said persons who are nearest in degree of relationship to the intestate (in this section referred to as 'the nearest surviving relatives') and

(ii)   any other persons who were related to the intestate in that degree, but who have [failed to survive] him leaving issue who survive him;

and, of those parts, one shall be taken by each of the nearest surviving relatives, and one shall be taken *per stirpes* by the issue of each of the said [persons who have failed to survive the deceased].

7   Saving of right of Crown as *ultimus haeres*

Nothing in this Part of this Act shall be held to affect the right of the Crown as *ultimus haeres* to any estate to which no person is entitled by virtue of this Act to succeed.

PART II
LEGAL AND OTHER PRIOR RIGHTS IN ESTATES OF DECEASED PERSONS

8 Prior rights of surviving spouse, on intestacy, in dwelling house and furniture

(1) Where a person dies intestate leaving a spouse [or civil partner], and the intestate estate includes a relevant interest in a [dwelling house mentioned in subsection (4)(a) of this section], the surviving spouse [or civil partner] shall be entitled [subject to subsection (2B) of this section] to receive out of the intestate estate—

(a) where the value of the relevant interest does not exceed [[£473,000] or such larger amount as may from time to time be fixed by order of the Secretary of State:]

(i) if subsection (2) of this section does not apply, the relevant interest;

(ii) if the said subsection (2) applies, a sum equal to the value of the relevant interest;

(b) in any other case, the sum of [[£473,000] or such larger amount as may from time to time be fixed by order of the Secretary of State].

[. . .]

(2) This subsection shall apply for the purposes of paragraph (a) of the foregoing subsection if—

(a) the dwelling house forms part only of the subjects comprised in one tenancy or lease under which the intestate was the tenant; or

(b) the dwelling house forms the whole or part of subjects an interest in which is comprised in the intestate estate and which were used by the intestate for carrying on a trade, profession or occupation, and the value of the estate as a whole would be likely to be substantially diminished if the dwelling house were disposed of otherwise than with the assets of the trade, profession or occupation.

[(2A) Where the tenant of a croft dies intestate leaving a spouse or civil partner or, where he dies leaving no spouse or civil partner, leaving a cohabitant, and the intestate estate includes a relevant interest in a dwelling house mentioned in subsection (4)(b) of this section, the surviving spouse, civil partner or, as the case may be, cohabitant shall be entitled, subject to subsection (2B) of this section, to receive out of the intestate estate—

(a) where the value of the relevant interest does not exceed the amount for the time being fixed by order under subsection (1)(a) of this section, the tenancy of the croft;

(b) in any other case, the sum for the time being fixed by order under subsection (1)(b) of this section.

(2B) If the intestate estate comprises—

(a) a relevant interest in two or more dwelling houses mentioned in subsection (4)(a) of this section, subsection (1) of this section shall have effect only in relation to such one of them as the surviving spouse or civil partner may elect for the purposes of subsection (1) within 6 months after the date of death of the intestate;

(b) a relevant interest in two or more dwelling houses mentioned in subsection (4)(b) of this section, subsection (2A) of this section shall have effect only in relation to such one of them as the surviving spouse, civil partner or cohabitant may elect for the purposes of subsection (2A) within 6 months after that date;

(c) a relevant interest in both—

(i) one or more dwelling houses mentioned in subsection (4)(a) of this section; and

(ii) one or more dwelling houses mentioned in subsection (4)(b) of this section,

the surviving spouse or civil partner shall not be entitled to receive both the entitlement under subsection (1) of this section and that under subsection (2A) of this section and must elect within 6 months after that date whether to take the entitlement under the said subsection (1) or under the said subsection (2A).]

(3)   Where a person dies intestate leaving a spouse [or civil partner], and the intestate estate includes the furniture and plenishings of a dwelling house to which this section applies (whether or not the dwelling house is comprised in the intestate estate), the surviving spouse [or civil partner] shall be entitled to receive out of the intestate estate—

(a)   where the value of the furniture and plenishings does not exceed [[£29,000] or such larger amount as may from time to time be fixed by order of the Secretary of State] the whole thereof;

(b)   in any other case, such part of the furniture and plenishings, to a value not exceeding [[£29,000] or such larger amount as may from time to time be fixed by order of the Secretary of State] as may be chosen by the surviving spouse [or civil partner]:

Provided that, if the intestate estate comprises the furniture and plenishings of two or more such dwelling houses, this subsection shall have effect only in relation to the furniture and plenishings of such one of them as the surviving spouse [or civil partner] may elect for the purposes of this subsection within six months of the date of death of the intestate.

[(4)   The dwelling house is—

(a)   in a case mentioned in subsection (1) of this section, any dwelling house in which the surviving spouse or civil partner of the intestate was ordinarily resident at the date of death of the intestate and which did not, at that date, form part of a croft of which the intestate was tenant;

(b)   in a case mentioned in subsection (2A) of this section, any dwelling house in which the surviving spouse, civil partner or cohabitant was ordinarily resident at the date of death of the intestate and which, at that date, formed part of a croft of which the intestate was tenant.]

(5)   Where any question arises as to the value of any furniture or plenishings, or of any interest in a dwelling house, for the purposes of any provision of this section the question shall be determined by arbitration by a single arbiter appointed, in default of agreement, by the sheriff of the county in which the intestate was domiciled at the date of his death or, if that county is uncertain or the intestate was domiciled furth of Scotland, the sheriff of the Lothians and Peebles at Edinburgh.

(6)   In this section—

[(za) 'cohabitant' means a person—

(i)   who was living with the intestate as if married to him,

(ii)   who was living with the intestate as if in civil partnership with him, and had been so living for at least 2 years.]

(a)   'dwelling house' includes a part of a building occupied (at the date of death of the intestate) as a separate dwelling; and any reference to a dwelling house shall be construed as including any garden or portion of ground attached to, and usually occupied with, the dwelling house or otherwise required for the amenity or convenience of the dwelling house;

(b)   'furniture and plenishings' includes garden effects, domestic animals, plate, plated articles, linen, china, glass, books, pictures, prints, articles of household use and consumable stores; but does not include any article or animal used at the date of death of the intestate for business purposes, or money or securities for money, or any heirloom;

(c)   'heirloom', in relation to an intestate estate, means any article which has associations with the intestate's family of such nature and extent that it ought to pass to some member of that family other than the surviving spouse of the intestate;

(d)   'relevant interest', in relation to a dwelling house, means the interest therein of an owner, or the interest therein of a tenant, subject in either case to any heritable debt secured over the interest; and for the purposes of this definition 'tenant' means a tenant under a tenancy or lease (whether of the dwelling house alone or of the dwelling house together with other subjects) which is not a tenancy to which the Rent and Mortgage Interest Restrictions Acts 1920 to 1939 apply.

Note
The figures in s 8 have been increased over the years to take account of inflation. The earlier figures for the dwellinghouse right in s 8(1)(b) and the plenishings right in s 8(3)(b) were:

	dwelling house right (s 8(1)(b))	plenishings right (s 8(3) (b))
10 Sept 1964 to 22 May 1973	£15,000	£5,000
23 May 1973 to 31 July 1981	£30,000	£8,000
1 Aug 1981 to 30 April 1988	£50,000	£10,000
1 May 1988 to 25 Nov 1993	£60,000	£12,000
26 Nov 1993 to 31 March 1999	£110,000	£20,000
1 April 1999 to 31 May 2005	£130,000	£22,000
1 June 2005 to 31 January 2012	£300,000	£24,000

9   Prior right of surviving spouse to financial provision on intestacy
   (1)   Where a person dies intestate and is survived by a husband [, wife or civil partner, the survivor] shall be entitled to receive out of the intestate estate—
      (a)   if the intestate is survived by issue [. . .] the sum of [[£50,000] or such larger amount as may from time to time be fixed by order of the Secretary of State; or]
      (b)   if the intestate is not survived by issue [. . .] the sum of [[£89,000] or such larger amount as may from time to time be fixed by order of the Secretary of State,] together with, in either case, interest at the rate of [7] per cent per annum [or at such rate as may from time to time be fixed by order of the Secretary of State} on such sum from the date of the intestate's death until payment:
      Provided that where the surviving spouse [or civil partner] is entitled to receive a legacy out of the estate of the intestate (other than a legacy of any dwelling house to which the last foregoing section applies or of any furniture and plenishings of any such dwelling house), he or she shall, unless he or she renounces the legacy, be entitled under this subsection to receive only such sum, if any, as remains after deducting from the sum [fixed by virtue of paragraph (a) of this subsection or the sum fixed by virtue of paragraph (b) of this subsection], as the case may be, the amount or value of the legacy.
   (2)   Where the intestate estate is less than the amount which the surviving spouse [or civil partner] is entitled to receive by virtue of subsection (1) of this section the right conferred by the said subsection on the surviving spouse [or civil partner] shall be satisfied by the transfer to him or her of the whole of the intestate estate.
   (3)   The amount which the surviving spouse [or civil partner] is entitled to receive by virtue of subsection (1) of this section shall be borne by, and paid out of, the parts of the intestate estate consisting of heritable and moveable property respectively in proportion to the respective amounts of those parts.
   (4)   Where by virtue of subsection (2) of this section a surviving spouse [or civil partner] has right to the whole of the intestate estate, he or she shall have the right to be appointed executor.

(5)   The rights conferred by the Intestate Husband's Estate (Scotland) Acts 1911 to 1959 on a surviving spouse in his or her deceased spouse's estate shall not be exigible out of the estate of any person dying after the commencement of this Act.

(6)   For the purposes of this section—

(a)   the expression 'intestate estate' means so much of the net intestate estate as remains after the satisfaction of any claims under the last foregoing section; and

(b)   the expression 'legacy' includes any payment or benefit to which a surviving spouse [or civil partner] becomes entitled by virtue of any testamentary disposition; and the amount or value of any legacy shall be ascertained as at the date of the intestate's death.

Note

The figures in s 9 have been increased over the years to take account of inflation. The earlier figures in s 9(1)(a) and (b) were:

10 Sept 1964 to 22 May 1973	£2,500 and £5,000
23 May 1973 to 30 Dec 1977	£4,000 and £8,000
31 Dec 1977 to 31 July 1981	£8,000 and £16,000
1 Aug 1981 to 30 April 1988	£15,000 and £25,000
1 May 1988 to 25 Nov 1993	£21,000 and £35,000
26 Nov 1993 to 31 March 1999	£30,000 and £50,000
1 April 1999 to 31 May 2005	£35,000 and £58,000
1 June 2005 to 31 January 2012	£42,000 and £75,000

[9A   Provisions supplementary to ss 8 and 9

Any order of the Secretary of State, under section 8 or 9 of this Act, fixing an amount or rate—

(a)   shall be made by statutory instrument which shall be subject to annulment in pursuance of a resolution of either House of Parliament; and

(b)   shall have effect in relation to the estate of any person dying after the coming into force of the order.]

10   Abolition of terce and courtesy, and calculation of legal rights

(1)   The right of courtesy of a surviving husband in his deceased wife's estate and the right of terce of a surviving wife in her deceased husband's estate shall not be exigible out of the estate of a person dying after the commencement of this Act.

(2)   The amount of any claim to [legal rights] out of an estate shall be calculated by reference to so much of the net moveable estate as remains after the satisfaction of any claims thereon under the two last foregoing sections.

11   Representation in, and division of, legitim

(1)   Subject to the next following subsection, where a person (hereinafter in this section referred to as 'the deceased') dies [in circumstances where a child who has failed to survive the deceased] has left issue who survive the deceased, and the child would, if he had survived the deceased, have been entitled [. . .] to legitim out of the deceased's estate, such issue shall have the like right to legitim as the child would have had if he had survived the deceased [. . .].

(2)   If, by virtue of the foregoing subsection or otherwise, there are two or more persons having right among them to legitim, then the legitim shall—

(a)   if all of those persons are in the same degree of relationship to the deceased, be divided among them equally, and

(b)   in any other case, be divided equally into a number of parts equal to the aggregate of—

(i)   those of the said persons who are nearest in degree of relationship to the deceased (in this paragraph referred to as 'the nearest surviving relatives') and

(ii)   any other persons who were related to the deceased in that degree and who (if they had survived him) would have been entitled to legitim out of his estate, but who have [failed to survive] him leaving issue who survive him and are entitled to legitim out of his estate;

and, of those parts, one shall be taken by each of the nearest surviving relatives, and one shall be taken *per stirpes* by the issue of each of the said [persons who have failed to survive the deceased], being issue who are entitled as aforesaid [. . .].

(3)   Nothing in the last foregoing subsection shall be construed as altering any rule of law as to collation of advances; and where any person is entitled to claim legitim out of the estate of a deceased person by virtue of subsection (1) of this section he shall be under the like duty to collate any advances made by the deceased to him, and the proportion appropriate to him of any advances so made to any person through whom he derives such entitlement, as if he had been entitled to claim such legitim otherwise than by virtue of the said subsection (1).

(4)   For the avoidance of doubt it is hereby declared that where any person is entitled by virtue of subsection (1) of this section to legitim out of the estate of the deceased, and the deceased is not survived by any child, the proportion of the estate due to any surviving spouse in respect of *jus relicti* or *jus relictae* shall be ascertained as if the deceased had been survived by a child.

12   Legitim not to be discharged by ante-nuptial marriage contract

Nothing in any ante-nuptial contract of marriage executed after the commencement of this Act shall operate so as to exclude, on the occurrence of the death of either party to the marriage, the right of any child of the marriage (or of any issue of his coming in his place by virtue of the last foregoing section) to legitim out of the estate of that party unless such child or issue shall elect to accept in lieu of legitim the provision made in his favour under the contract.

13   Equitable compensation

Every testamentary disposition executed after the commencement of this Act by which provision is made in favour of the spouse or of any issue of the testator and which does not contain a declaration that the provision so made is in full and final satisfaction of the right to any share in the testator's estate to which the spouse or the issue, as the case may be, is entitled by virtue of *jus relicti*, *jus relictae* or legitim, shall (unless the disposition contains an express provision to the contrary) have effect as if it contained such a declaration [. . .].

PART III
ADMINISTRATION AND WINDING UP OF ESTATES

14   Assimilation for purposes of administration, etc, of heritage to moveables

(1)   Subject to subsection (3) of this section the enactments and rules of law in force immediately before the commencement of this Act with respect to the administration and winding up of the estate of a deceased person so far as consisting of moveable property shall have effect (as modified by the provisions of this Act) in relation to the whole of the estate without distinction between moveable property and heritable property; and accordingly on the death of any person (whether testate or intestate) every part of his estate (whether consisting of moveable property or heritable property) falling to be administered under the law of Scotland shall, by virtue of confirmation thereto, vest for the purposes of administration in the executor thereby confirmed and shall be administered and disposed of according to law by such executor.

(2)   Provision shall be made by the Court of Session by act of sederunt made

under the enactments mentioned in section 22 of this Act (as extended by that section) for the inclusion in the confirmation of an executor, by reference to an appended inventory or otherwise, of a description, in such form as may be so provided, of any heritable property forming part of the estate.

(3)   Nothing in this section shall be taken to alter any rule of law whereby any particular debt of a deceased person falls to be paid out of any particular part of his estate.

15   Provisions as to transfer of heritage

(1)   Section 5(2) of the Conveyancing (Scotland) Act 1924 (which provides that a confirmation which includes a heritable security shall be a valid title to the debt thereby secured) shall have effect as if any reference therein to a heritable security, or to a debt secured by a heritable security, included a reference to any interest in heritable property which has vested in an executor in pursuance of the last foregoing section by virtue of a confirmation

Provided that a confirmation [(other than an implied confirmation within the meaning of the said section 5(2))] shall not be deemed for the purposes of the said section 5(2) to include any such interest unless a description of the property, in accordance with any act of sederunt such as is mentioned in subsection (2) of the last foregoing section, is included or referred to in the confirmation.

(2)   Where in pursuance of the last foregoing section any heritable property has vested in an executor by virtue of a confirmation, and it is necessary for him in distributing the estate to transfer that property—

(a)   to any person in satisfaction of a claim to legal rights or the prior rights of a surviving spouse [or civil partner] out of the estate, or

(b)   to any person entitled to share in the estate by virtue of this Act, or

(c)   to any person entitled to take the said property under any testamentary disposition of the deceased,

the executor may effect such transfer by endorsing on the confirmation (or where a certificate of confirmation relating to the property has been issued in pursuance of any act of sederunt, on the certificate) a docket in favour of that person in the form set out in Schedule 1 to this Act, or in a form as nearly as may be to the like effect, and any such docket may be specified as a midcouple or link in title in any deduction of title; but this section shall not be construed as prejudicing the competence of any other mode of transfer.

16   Provisions relating to leases

(1)   This section applies to any interest, being the interest of a tenant under a lease, which is comprised in the estate of a deceased person and has accordingly vested in the deceased's executor by virtue of section 14 of this Act; and in the following provisions of this section 'interest' means an interest to which this section applies.

(2)   [Subject to subsection (4A)] where an interest—

(a)   is not the subject of a valid bequest by the deceased, or

(b)   is the subject of such a bequest, but the bequest is not accepted by the legatee, or

(c)   being an interest under an agricultural lease, is the subject of such a bequest, but the bequest is declared null and void in pursuance of section 16 of the Act of 1886 or [section 11 of the 1991 Act] [or becomes null and void under section 10 of the Act of 1955],

and there is among the conditions of the lease (whether expressly or by implication) a condition prohibiting assignation of the interest, the executor shall be entitled, [subject to subsection (2A) of this section, to transfer the interest].

[(2A)   Transfer by an executor pursuant to subsection (2) of this section—

[. . .]

(b)   of an interest under any [lease (other than the lease of a croft within the meaning of section 3(1) of the Crofters (Scotland) Act 1993)] and which is not a transfer to one of the persons entitled to succeed to the deceased's intestate estate or to claim legal rights or the prior rights of a surviving spouse or civil partner out of the estate, in satisfaction of that person's entitlement or claim, shall require the consent of the landlord.]

(3) [Subject to subsection (4C)] if in the case of any interest—

(a) at any time the executor is satisfied that the interest cannot be disposed of according to law and so informs the landlord, or

(b) [subject to subsection (3A)] the interest is not so disposed of within a period of one year or such longer period as may be fixed by agreement between the landlord and the executor or, failing agreement, by the [relevant court on the application of] the executor—

(i) in the case of an interest under an agricultural lease which is the subject of a petition to the Land Court under section 16 of the Act of 1886 or an application to that court under [section 11 of the 1991 Act] from the date of the determination or withdrawal of the petition or, as the case may be, the application,

[...]

(ii) in any other case, from the date of death of the deceased, either the landlord or the executor may, on giving notice in accordance with the next following subsection to the other, terminate the lease (in so far as it relates to the interest) notwithstanding any provision therein, or any enactment or rule of law, to the contrary effect.

[(3A) In the case of an interest in an agricultural lease which is a lease of a croft within the meaning of section 3(1) of the Crofters (Scotland) Act 1993 (c 44) the period for the purposes of subsection (3)(b) is 24 months.]

(4) The period of notice given under the last foregoing subsection shall be—

(a) in the case of an agricultural lease, such period as may be agreed, or, failing agreement, a period of not less than one year and not more than two years ending with such term of Whitsunday or Martinmas as may be specified in the notice; and

(b) in the case of any other lease, a period of six months:

Provided that paragraph (b) of this subsection shall be without prejudice to any enactment prescribing a shorter period of notice in relation to the lease in question.

[(4A) Where an interest, being an interest under a lease constituting a short limited duration tenancy [, a limited duration tenancy, a modern limited duration tenancy or a repairing tenancy]—

(a) is not the subject of a valid bequest by the deceased; or

(b) is the subject of such a bequest, but the bequest is not accepted by the legatee; or

(c) is the subject of such a bequest, but the bequest is declared null and void by virtue of section 21 of the 2003 Act,

and there is among the conditions of the lease (whether expressly or by implication) a condition prohibiting assignation of the interest, the executor shall be entitled, notwithstanding that condition, to transfer the interest to a person to whom subsection (4B) below applies; and the executor shall be entitled so to transfer the interest without the consent of the landlord.

(4B) This subsection applies to—

(a) any one of the persons entitled to succeed to the deceased's intestate estate, or to claim legal rights or the prior rights of a surviving spouse out of the estate, in or towards satisfaction of that person's entitlement or claim; or

(b) any other person.

(4C) In the case of any interest under a lease constituting a short limited duration tenancy [, a limited duration tenancy, a modern limited duration tenancy or a repairing tenancy]—

(a) if at any time the executor is satisfied that the interest cannot be disposed of according to law and so informs the landlord, the executor may terminate the tenancy (in so far as it relates to the interest); and

(b) if the interest is not so disposed of within the period referred to in subsection (4D) below, the lease shall (in so far as it relates to the interest) terminate at the expiry of the period, notwithstanding any provision in the lease, or any enactment or rule of law, to the contrary effect.

(4D)   The period is one year or such longer period as may be fixed by agreement or, failing agreement, by the Land Court on the application of the executor—

(a) in the case of an interest which is the subject of an application to that court by virtue of section 21 of the 2003 Act, from the date of the determination or withdrawal of the application; and

(b) in any other case, from the date of death of the deceased.

(4E)   The—

(a)   interest may be transferred under subsections (4A) and (4B) above; or

(b)   tenancy may be terminated under subsection (4C)(a) above,

only if the transfer, or as the case may be, termination is in the best interests of the deceased's estate.]

(5)   Subsection (3) of this section shall not prejudice any claim by any party to the lease for compensation or damages in respect of the termination of the lease (or any rights under it) in pursuance of that subsection; but any award of compensation or damages in respect of such termination at the instance of the executor shall be enforceable only against the estate of the deceased and not against the executor personally.

(6)   Where an interest is an interest under an agricultural lease, and—

(a) an application is made under section 3 of the Act of 1931 [or section 13 of the Act of 1955] to the Land Court for an order for removal, or

(b) a reference is made under [section 23(2) and (3) of the 1991 Act] [for the determination of] any question which has arisen under [section 22(2)(e)] of that Act in connection with a notice to quit,

the [order or determination shall not be] in favour of the landlord, unless [. . .] it is reasonable, having regard to the fact that the interest is vested in the executor in his capacity as executor, that it should be made.

(7)   Where an interest is not an interest under an agricultural lease, and the landlord brings an action of removing against the executor in respect of a breach of a condition of the lease, the court shall not grant decree in the action unless it is satisfied that the condition alleged to have been breached is one which it is reasonable to expect the executor to have observed, having regard to the fact that the interest is vested in him in his capacity as an executor.

(8)   Where an interest is an interest under an agricultural lease and is the subject of a valid bequest by the deceased, the fact that the interest is vested in the executor under the said section 14 shall not prevent the operation, in relation to the legatee, of paragraphs (a) to (h) of section 16 of the Act of 1886, or, as the case may be, [section 11(2) to (8) of the 1991 Act] [or, as the case may be, section 21(2) and (3) of the 2003 Act], [or, as the case may be, subsections (2) to (7) of section 10 of the Act of 1955].

[(8A)   For the purposes of subsection (3)(b) above the 'relevant court' is—

(a) in the case of an interest under a lease constituting a 1991 Act tenancy, the Land Court; and

(b) in any other case, the sheriff,

and an application to the sheriff in any such other case shall be by summary application.]

(9)   In this section—

'agricultural lease' means a lease of a holding within the meaning of the Small Landholders (Scotland) Acts 1886 to 1931 [, or a lease of a croft within the meaning of section 3(1) of the [Crofters (Scotland) Act 1993 (or of any part of a croft if it is a part consisting of a right mentioned in section 3(4)(a) of that Act)]; or a lease con-

stituting a 1991 Act tenancy, or lease constituting a short limited duration tenancy [, a limited duration tenancy, a modern limited duration tenancy or a repairing tenancy]];
'the Act of 1886' means the Crofters Holdings (Scotland) Act 1886;
'the Act of 1931' means the Small Landholders and Agricultural Holdings (Scotland) Act 1931;
['the 1991 Act' means the Agricultural Holdings (Scotland) Act 1991];
['the 2003 Act' means the Agricultural Holdings (Scotland) Act 2003 (asp 11);] ['the Act of 1955' means the Crofters (Scotland) Act 1955];
'lease' includes tenancy.
['1991 Act tenancy', 'short limited duration tenancy' [, 'limited duration tenancy', a modern limited duration tenancy or a repairing tenancy] shall be construed in accordance with the 2003 Act.]

[...]

18 Provisions as to entails and special destinations

(1) [...]

(2) On the death of a person entitled to any heritable property subject to a special destination in favour of some other person, being a destination which the deceased could not competently have, or in fact has not, evacuated by testamentary disposition or otherwise, the property shall, if the executor of the deceased is confirmed thereto, vest in the executor for the purpose of enabling it to be conveyed to the person next entitled thereto under the destination (if such conveyance is necessary) and for that purpose only.

(3) Section 14(2) of this Act shall apply in relation to property to which this section refers as it applies to property to which the said section 14(2) refers.

(4) Sections 15 and 17 of this Act shall apply to property which has vested in an executor by virtue of this section as they apply to property which has vested in an executor by virtue of section 14 of this Act, as if the person next entitled to the first mentioned property were a person entitled to share in the estate of the deceased.

[...]

20 Executor dative to have powers of a trustee

An executor dative appointed to administer the estate of a deceased person shall have in his administration of such estate the whole powers, privileges and immunities, and be subject to the same obligations, limitations and restrictions, which gratuitous trustees have, or are subject to, under any enactment or under common law, and the Trusts (Scotland) Acts 1921 and 1961 shall have effect as if any reference therein to a trustee included a reference to such an executor dative:

Provided that nothing in this section shall exempt an executor dative from finding caution for his intromissions or confer upon him any power to resign or to assume new trustees.

21 Evidence as to holograph wills in commissary proceedings

(1) Notwithstanding any rule of law or practice to the contrary, confirmation of an executor to property disposed of in a holograph testamentary disposition shall not be granted unless the court is satisfied by evidence consisting at least of an affidavit by each of two persons that the writing and signature of the disposition are in the handwriting of the testator.

[(2) This section shall not apply to a testamentary document executed after the commencement of the Requirements of Writing (Scotland) Act 1995.]

[21A Evidence as to testamentary documents in commissary proceedings

Confirmation of an executor to property disposed of in a testamentary document executed after the commencement of the Requirements of Writing (Scotland) Act 1995 shall not be granted unless the formal validity of the document is governed—

(a)   by Scots law and the document is presumed under section 3 [or 9D] of that Act to have been subscribed [or under section 9C or 9D (or by virtue of section 9E(1)) of that Act to have been authenticated] by the granter so disposing of that property; or

(b)   by a law other than Scots law and the court is satisfied that the document is formally valid according to the law governing such validity.]

22   Court of Session may regulate procedure in commissary proceedings

(1)   The powers exercisable by the Court of Session by act of sederunt under section 18 of the Confirmation of Executors (Scotland) Act 1858, section 16 of the Sheriff Courts and Legal Officers (Scotland) Act 1927 and section 34 of the Administration of Justice (Scotland) Act 1933 (which empower the court to regulate *inter alia* procedure in proceedings in the sheriff court and in proceedings for the confirmation of executors) shall include power to regulate the procedure to be followed, and to prescribe the form and content of any petition, writ or other document to be used, in connection with the confirmation of executors in cases where, by virtue of this Act, heritable property devolves upon the executor.

(2)   Without prejudice to the generality of the powers conferred on the court by the said sections and by this section, the power conferred by the said section 34 to modify, amend or repeal by act of sederunt enactments relating to certain matters shall include power so to modify, amend or repeal any enactment relating to the procedure to be followed in proceedings for the confirmation of executors in such cases as aforesaid.

[. . .]

PART IV
ADOPTED PERSONS

23   Adopted person to be treated for purposes of succession etc as child of adopter

(1)   For all purposes relating to—

(a)   the succession to a deceased person (whether testate or intestate), and

(b)   the disposal of property by virtue of any *inter vivos* deed,

an adopted person shall be treated as the child of the adopter and not as the child of any other person.

In this subsection and in the following provisions of this Part of this Act any reference to succession to a deceased person shall be construed as including a reference to the distribution of any property in consequence of the death of the deceased person and any claim to legal rights or the prior rights of a surviving spouse out of his estate.

(2)   In any deed whereby property is conveyed or under which a succession arises, being a deed executed after the making of an adoption order, unless the contrary intention appears, any reference (whether express or implied)—

(a)   to the child or children of the adopter shall be construed as, or as including, a reference to the adopted person;

(b)   to the child or children of the adopted person's natural parents or either of them shall be construed as not being, or as not including, a reference to the adopted person; and

(c)   to a person related to the adopted person in any particular degree shall be construed as a reference to the person who would be related to him in that degree if he were the child of the adopter and were not the child of any other person:

Provided that for the purposes of this subsection a deed containing a provision taking effect on the death of any person shall be deemed to have been executed on the date of death of that person.

(3)   Where the terms of any deed provide that any property or interest in property shall devolve along with a title, honour or dignity, nothing in this section [or

in the Children Act 1975 or in the Adoption (Scotland) Act 1978 [or in the Adoption and Children (Scotland) Act 2007 (asp 4)]] shall prevent that property or interest from so devolving.

(4)   Nothing in this section shall affect any deed executed, or the devolution of any property on, or in consequence of, the death of a person who dies, before the commencement of this Act.

(5)   In this Part of this Act the expression 'adoption order'—

[(a)]   [has the same meaning as in section 38 of the Adoption (Scotland) Act 1978 (whether the order took effect before or after the commencement of this Act) [; and

(b)   includes an adoption order within the meaning of section 28(1) of the Adoption and Children (Scotland) Act 2007 (asp 4).]

and 'adopted' means adopted in pursuance of an adoption order].

24   Provisions supplementary to s 23

(1)   For the purposes of the law regulating the succession to any property and for the purposes of the construction of any such deed as is mentioned in the last foregoing section, an adopted person shall be deemed to be related to any other person, being the child or the adopted child of the adopter or (in the case of a joint adoption) of either of the adopters,

(a)   where he or she was adopted by two spouses jointly and that other person is the child or adopted child of both of them, as a brother or sister of the whole blood;

(b)   in any other case, as a brother or sister of the half blood.

[(1A)   Where, in relation to any purpose specified in section 23(1) of this Act, any right is conferred or any obligation is imposed, whether by operation of law or under any deed coming into operation after the commencement of the Children Act 1975, by reference to the relative seniority of the members of a class of persons, then, [. . .],

(a)   any member of that class who is an adopted person shall rank as if he had been born on the date of his adoption, and

(b)   if two or more members of the class are adopted persons whose dates of adoption are the same, they shall rank as between themselves in accordance with their respective times of birth.]

[. . .]

(3) Where an adoption order is made in respect of a person who has been previously adopted, the previous adoption shall be disregarded for the purposes of the last foregoing section in relation to the devolution of any property on the death of any person dying after the date of the subsequent adoption order, and in relation to any deed executed after that date whereby property is conveyed or under which a succession arises.

(4)   [. . .]

PART VI
MISCELLANEOUS AND SUPPLEMENTARY

29   Right of tenant to bequeath interest under lease

(1)   A bequest by a tenant of his interest under a tenancy or lease to any one of the persons who, if the tenant had died intestate, would be, or would in any circumstances have been, entitled to succeed to his intestate estate by virtue of this Act shall not be treated as invalid by reason only that there is among the conditions of the tenancy or lease an implied condition prohibiting assignation.

(2)   This section shall not prejudice the operation of section 16 of the Crofters Holdings (Scotland) Act 1886 or [section 11 of the Agricultural Holdings (Scotland) Act 1991 or section 21 of the Agricultural Holdings (Scotland) Act 2003 (asp 11)] (which relate to bequests in the case of agricultural leases) [or of section 10 of the Crofters (Scotland) Act 1955 (which makes similar provision in relation to crofts).]

30   Effect of testamentary dispositions on special destinations
A testamentary disposition executed after the commencement of this Act shall not
have effect so as to evacuate a special destination (being a destination which could
competently be evacuated by the testamentary disposition) unless it contains a
specific reference to the destination and a declared intention on the part of the testator to evacuate it.

[. . .]

[32   Certain testamentary dispositions to be formally valid
   (1)   For the purpose of any question arising as to entitlement, by virtue of a testamentary disposition, to any relevant property or to any interest therein, the disposition shall be treated as valid in respect of the formalities of execution.
   (2)   Subsection (1) above is without prejudice to any right to challenge the validity
of the testamentary disposition on the ground of forgery or on any other ground of
essential invalidity.
   (3)   In this section 'relevant property' means property disposed of in the testamentary disposition in respect of which—
      (a)   confirmation has been granted; or
      (b)   probate, letters of administration or other grant of representation—
         (i)   has been issued, and has noted the domicile of the deceased to be, in
England and Wales or Northern Ireland; or
         (ii)   has been issued outwith the United Kingdom and had been sealed in
Scotland under section 2 of the Colonial Probates Act 1892.]

33   Construction of existing deeds
   (1)   Subject to subsection (2) of this section, any reference in any deed taking effect
after the commencement of this Act to jus relicti, jus relictae or legitim shall be construed as a reference to the right to jus relicti, jus relictae or legitim, as the case may
be, as modified by Part II of this Act; and any reference in any such deed to courtesy
or terce shall be of no effect.
   (2)   Any reference to legal rights in a marriage contract made before the commencement of this Act and taking effect in consequence of a decree of divorce granted
in an action commenced after the commencement of this Act shall be construed as
a reference to any right which the husband or the wife, as the case may be, might
obtain by virtue of the provisions of section 26 of this Act [or section 5 of the Divorce
(Scotland) Act 1976, or section 29 of the Matrimonial and Family Proceedings Act
1984, or section 8 of the Family Law (Scotland) Act 1985].

34   Modification of enactments and repeals
   (1)   Subject to the provisions of section 37 of this Act, the enactments mentioned
in Schedule 2 to this Act shall have effect subject to the modifications specified in that
Schedule, being modifications consequential on the provisions of this Act.
   (2) [. . .]

35   Transfer of certain jurisdiction to Sheriff of Chancery
   (1)   If at any time it appears to the Secretary of State expedient to do so he may by
order transfer to the Sheriff of Chancery the jurisdiction of any other sheriff in relation to the service of heirs.
   (2)   An order made under this section may contain such consequential provisions
as appears to the Secretary of State to be necessary, including provisions for the consequential repeal or consequential modification of any enactment relating to the matters dealt with in the order.
   (3)   Any order made under this section shall be made by statutory instrument.

36   Interpretation
   (1)   In this Act the following expressions shall, unless the context otherwise
requires, have the meanings hereby respectively assigned to them, that is to say—

'deed' includes any disposition, contract, instrument or writing, whether *inter vivos* or *mortis causa*;

'an intestate' means a person who has died leaving undisposed of by testamentary disposition the whole or any part of his estate, and 'intestate' shall be construed accordingly;

'intestate estate', in relation to an intestate, means (subject to sections 1(2) and 9(6) (a) of this Act) so much of his estate as is undisposed of by testamentary disposition;

'issue' means issue however remote;

'Land Court' means the Scottish Land Court;

'lease' and 'tenancy' include sub-lease and sub-tenancy, and tenant shall be construed accordingly;

'legal rights' means *jus relicti, jus relictae*, and legitim;

'net estate' and 'net intestate estate' mean respectively so much of an estate or an intestate estate as remains after provision for the satisfaction of estate duty and other liabilities of the estate having priority over legal rights, the prior rights of a surviving spouse and rights of succession, or, as the case may be, the proportion thereof properly attributable to the intestate estate;

'owner' in relation to any heritable property means the person entitled to receive the rents thereof (other than rents under a sub-lease or sub-tenancy);

'prior rights', in relation to a surviving spouse [or civil partner], means the rights conferred by sections 8 and 9 of this Act;

'testamentary disposition', in relation to a deceased, includes any deed taking effect on his death whereby any part of his estate is disposed of or under which a succession thereto arises.

(2)   Any reference in this Act to the estate of a deceased person shall, unless the context otherwise requires, be construed as a reference to the whole estate, whether heritable or moveable, or partly heritable and partly moveable, belonging to the deceased at the time of his death or over which the deceased had a power of appointment and, where the deceased immediately before his death held the interest of a tenant under a tenancy or lease which was not expressed to expire on his death, includes that interest:

Provided that—

(a)   where any heritable property belonging to a deceased person at the date of his death is subject to a special destination in favour of any person, the property shall not be treated for the purposes of this Act as part of the estate of the deceased unless the destination is one which could competently be, and has in fact been, evacuated by the deceased by testamentary disposition or otherwise; and in that case the property shall be treated for the purposes of this Act as if it were part of the deceased's estate on which he has tested; and

(b)   where any heritable property over which a deceased person had a power of appointment has not been disposed of in exercise of that power and is in those circumstances subject to a power of appointment by some other person, that property shall not be treated for the purposes of this Act as part of the estate of the deceased.

(3)   Without prejudice to the proviso to section 23(2) of this Act, references in this Act to the date of execution of a testamentary disposition shall be construed as references to the date on which the disposition was actually executed and not to the date of death of the testator.

(4)   References in this Act to any enactment shall, except where the context otherwise requires, be construed as references to that enactment as amended by or under any other enactment, including this Act.

[(5)   Section 1(1) (legal equality of children) of the Law Reform (Parent and Child) (Scotland) Act 1986 shall apply to this Act; and any reference (however expressed) in this Act to a relative shall be construed accordingly.]

37   Exclusion of certain matters from operation of Act

(1)   Save as otherwise expressly provided, nothing in this Act [or (as respects paragraph (a) of this subsection) in the Children Act 1975 or the Adoption (Scotland) Act 1978 or the Adoption and Children (Scotland) Act 2007 (asp 4)] shall—

(a)   apply to any title, coat of arms, honour or dignity transmissible on the death of the holder thereof or affect the succession thereto or the devolution thereof;

(b)   [...]

(c)   affect any right on the part of a surviving spouse to claim from the representatives of his or her deceased spouse payment of aliment out of the estate of that spouse;

(d)   affect the administration, winding up or distribution of or the making up of title to any part of the estate of any person who died before the commencement of this Act or the rights of succession to such an estate or any claim for legal rights or terce or courtesy or any rights arising under the Intestate Husband's Estate (Scotland) Acts 1911 to 1959 out of such an estate or the right to take any legal proceedings with respect to any such matters;

(e)   affect any claim for legal rights arising out of an action of divorce commenced before the commencement of this Act;

and in relation to the matters aforesaid the law in force immediately before the commencement of this Act shall continue to have effect as if this Act had not passed.

(2)   Nothing in this Act shall be construed as affecting the operation of any rule of law applicable immediately before the commencement of this Act to the choice of the system of law governing the administration, winding up or distribution of the estate, or any part of the estate, of any deceased person.

38   Citation, extent and commencement

(1)   This Act may be cited as the Succession (Scotland) Act 1964.

(2)   This Act shall extend to Scotland only.

(3)   This Act shall come into operation on the expiration of the period of three months beginning with the date on which it is passed.

SCHEDULES

Section 15

SCHEDULE 1
FORM OF DOCKET

I, AB, being by virtue of the within confirmation [or certificate of confirmation] the executor on the estate of the deceased CD so far as specified in the confirmation [or certificate or inventory attached hereto] hereby nominate EF [design] as the person entitled—

(a)   in [part] satisfaction of his claim to prior rights, as a surviving spouse, on the death of the deceased,

(b)   in [part] satisfaction of his claim to legal rights on the death of the deceased,

(c)   in [part] satisfaction of his share in the said estate,

(d)   in [part] implement of a trust disposition and settlement, [or will, or as the case may be] of the deceased dated   and registered in the Books of Council and Session   ,

to the following item of estate, that is to say, [short description] being number   of the items of the estate specified in the said confirmation [or certificate or inventory].

[Testing clause†

† Note—Subscription of the document by the granter of it will be sufficient for the document to be formally valid, but witnessing of it may be necessary or desirable for other purposes (see the Requirements of Writing (Scotland) Act 1995).]

SCHEDULE 2

Section 34

MODIFICATION OF ENACTMENTS

General modifications

1.   Subject to the specific modifications made by the following provisions of this Schedule, references in any enactment to the heir-at-law of a deceased person in relation to any heritable property [. . .] shall be construed as references to the persons who by virtue of this Act are entitled to succeed to such property on intestacy.

2.   Subject as aforesaid references in general terms in any enactment to the heirs of a deceased person shall include—

(a)   the persons entitled by virtue of this Act to succeed on intestacy to any part of the estate of the deceased; and

(b)   so far as is necessary for the purposes of Part III of this Act, the executor of the deceased.

3.   References in any enactment relating to the confirmation of executors or the administration of the moveable estates of deceased persons to the moveable or personal property or estate of a deceased person shall, except where the context otherwise requires, be construed as references to the whole estate of the deceased person.

4.   References in any enactment (other than in this Act) to courtesy or terce shall be of no effect.

LAW REFORM (MISCELLANEOUS PROVISIONS) (SCOTLAND) ACT 1966
(1966, c 19)

6   Amendment of s 5 of Trusts (Scotland) Act 1961

(1)   The periods for which accumulations of income under a settlement or other disposition are permitted by section 5 of the Trusts (Scotland) Act 1961 shall include—

(a)   a term of twenty-one years from the date of the making of the settlement or other disposition, and

(b)   the duration of the minority or respective minorities of any person or persons living or in utero at that date,

and a direction to accumulate income during a period specified in paragraph (a) or paragraph (b) of this subsection shall not be void, nor shall the accumulation of the income be contrary to the said section 5, solely by reason of the fact that the period begins during the life of the grantor and ends after his death.

(2)   The restrictions imposed by the said section 5 shall apply in relation to a power to accumulate income whether or not there is a duty to exercise that power, and they shall apply whether or not the power to accumulate extends to income produced by the investment of income previously accumulated.

(3)   This section shall apply only in relation to instruments taking effect after the passing of this Act, and in the case of an instrument made in the exercise of a special power of appointment shall apply only where the instrument creating the power takes effect after the passing of this Act.

LAW REFORM (MISCELLANEOUS PROVISIONS) (SCOTLAND) ACT 1968
(1968, c 70)

18   Restriction on duration of liferents

(1)   Where by any deed executed after the commencement of this Act there is created a liferent interest in any property and a person who was not living or *in utero* at the date of the coming into operation of the said deed becomes entitled to that interest, then—

  (a)   if that person is of full age at the date on which he becomes entitled to the liferent interest, as from that date, or

  (b)   if that person is not of full age at that date, as from the date on which, being still entitled to the liferent interest, he becomes of full age,

the said property shall, subject to subsection (2) of this section, belong absolutely to that person, and, if the property is vested in trustees, those trustees shall, subject as aforesaid, be bound to convey, deliver or make over the property to that person.

(2)   The fact that, by virtue of subsection (1) of this section, any property has come to belong absolutely to any person shall not affect—

  (a)   the rights in the property of any person holding a security over the property;

  (b)   any rights in the property created independently of the deed by which the liferent interest in question was created;

  [. . .]

(3)   The expenses of the conveyance, delivery or making over of any property to any person in pursuance of subsection (1) of this section shall be borne by that person.

(4)   Section 48 of the Entail Amendment Act 1848 and section 9 of the Trusts (Scotland) Act 1921 shall not have effect in relation to any deed executed after the commencement of this Act.

(5)   For the purposes of this section—

  (a)   the date of the coming into operation of any testamentary or other *mortis causa* deed shall, subject to paragraph (c) below, be taken to be the date of the death of the granter thereof;

  (b)   the date of the coming into operation of any marriage contract shall, subject as aforesaid, be taken to be the date of the dissolution of the marriage;

  (c)   the date of the execution, or of the coming into operation, of any deed made in the exercise of a special power of appointment shall be taken to be the date of the execution, or as the case may be of the coming into operation, of the deed creating that power.

PRESUMPTION OF DEATH (SCOTLAND) ACT 1977
(1977, c 27)

1   Action of declarator

(1)   Where a person who is missing is thought to have died or has not been known to be alive for a period of at least seven years, any person having an interest may raise an action of declarator of the death of that person (hereafter in this Act referred to as the 'missing person') in the Court of Session or the sheriff court in accordance with the provisions of this section.

(2)   An action such as is mentioned in subsection (1) above is, in this Act, referred to as an 'action of declarator'.

(3)   The Court of Session shall have jurisdiction to entertain an action of declarator if and only if—

  (a)   the missing person was domiciled in Scotland on the date on which he was last known to be alive or had been habitually resident there throughout the period of one year ending with that date; or

(b) the pursuer in the action—
    (i)   is the spouse [or civil partner] of the missing person, and
    (ii) is domiciled in Scotland at the date of raising the action or was habitu-
ally resident there throughout the period of one year ending with that date [; or
(c) in a case where the pursuer in the action is the civil partner of the missing
person, the following conditions are met—
    (i)   the two people concerned registered as civil partners of each other in
Scotland; and
    (ii) it appears to the court to be in the interests of justice to assume jurisdic-
tion in the case.]
(4)   The sheriff court shall have jurisdiction to entertain an action of declarator if
and only if—
  (a) the provisions of subsection (3)(a) above are satisfied and the missing person's last known place of residence in Scotland is in the sheriffdom; or
  (b) the provisions of subsection (3)(b) above are satisfied and the pursuer was
resident in the sheriffdom for a period of not less than forty days ending with the
date of raising the action.
[(4A)   Despite subsection (4), the sheriff court of the sheriffdom of Lothian and
Borders at Edinburgh also has jurisdiction to entertain an action of declarator if—
  (a) the pursuer in the action and the missing person are married to each other
and are of the same sex,
  (b) they married each other in Scotland, and
  (c) it appears to the court to be in the interests of justice to assume jurisdiction
in the case.]
(5)   Any person having an interest may, in an action of declarator, lodge a minute
seeking the making by the court under section 2 of this Act of any determination or
appointment not sought by the pursuer.
(6)   At any stage of the proceedings the sheriff may, of his own accord or on the
application of any party to the action, and shall, if so directed by the Court of Session
(which direction may be given on the application of any party to the action), remit to
the Court of Session an action of declarator raised in the sheriff court where he or, as
the case may be, the Court of Session considers such remit desirable because of the
importance or complexity of the matters at issue.

2   Decree in action of declarator and determination of incidental questions in other proceedings

(1)   In an action of declarator, the court, having heard proof and being satisfied on
a balance of probabilities that the missing person—
  (a) has died, shall grant decree accordingly and shall include in the decree a
finding as to the date and time of death:
Provided that where it is uncertain when, within any period of time, the missing
person died, the court shall find that he died at the end of that period;
  (b) has not been known to be alive for a period of at least seven years, shall find
that the missing person died at the end of the day occurring seven years after the
date on which he was last known to be alive and shall grant decree accordingly.
(2)   The court, in granting decree under subsection (1) above, shall have power
to—
  (a) determine the domicile of the missing person at the date of his death;
  (b) determine any question relating to any interest in property which arises as
a consequence of the death of the missing person;
  (c) appoint a judicial factor on the estate of the missing person notwithstanding
(in relation to such an appointment by the sheriff) what the value of the estate may
be.
(3)   Where, for the purpose of deciding any issue before it, a court or statutory

tribunal has to determine any incidental question as to the death of a person, the court or tribunal may, if it thinks fit, determine that question (but for the purpose only of deciding that issue); and in the determination of that question the court or tribunal shall apply the criteria set out in subsection (1) above.

3 Effect of decree

(1)   Subject to the provisions of this section and sections 4 and 5 of this Act, where no appeal is made against decree in an action of declarator within the time allowed for appeal, or where an appeal against such a decree has been made and refused or withdrawn, the decree shall be conclusive of the matters contained in the decree and shall, without any special form of words, be effective against any person and for all purposes including the dissolution of a marriage [or of a civil partnership] to which the missing person is a party and the acquisition of rights to or in property belonging to any person.

(2)   A decree under section 2(1)(b) of this Act or a determination as mentioned in section 2(3) of this Act shall not determine a substantive question which is properly referable to a foreign law otherwise than in accordance with that law.

(3)   Where a marriage [or civil partnership] to which the missing person is a party has been dissolved by virtue of decree in an action of declarator, [its dissolution] shall not be invalidated by the circumstance that the missing person was in fact alive at the date specified in the decree as the date of death.

(4)   Where the missing person or any other person has committed any crime or offence, the responsibility of that person therefor shall not be affected by the circumstance that decree in an action of declarator has been granted if the missing person was in fact alive at the date specified in the decree as the date of death.

4 Recall or variation of decree

(1)   Decree in an action of declarator may, on application made at any time by any person having an interest, be varied or recalled by an order of the court which granted the decree or, in a case to which subsection (4) below applies, by an order of the Court of Session.

An order of the court pronounced under this subsection is hereafter in this Act referred to as a 'variation order'.

(2)   By a variation order the court may make any determination or appointment referred to in section 2 of this Act.

(3)   Any person having an interest may, in an application for a variation order, [make an application to the court] seeking the making by the court of any determination or appointment referred to in section 2 of this Act, which has not been sought by the person making the application for the variation order.

(4)   At any stage of the proceedings the sheriff may, of his own accord or on the application of any party to the proceedings, and shall, if so directed by the Court of Session (which direction may be given on the application of any party to the proceedings), remit to the Court of Session an application made in the sheriff court for a variation order where he or, as the case may be, the Court of Session considers such remit desirable because of the importance or complexity of the matters at issue.

(5)   Nothing in this section shall operate so as to revive a marriage of the missing person dissolved by virtue of decree in an action of declarator.

5 Effect on property rights of recall or variation of decree

(1)   Subject to the following provisions of this section, a variation order shall have no effect on rights to or in any property acquired as a result of a decree under section 2 of this Act.

(2)   Notwithstanding the generality of subsection (1) above, where a decree under section 2 of this Act has been varied or recalled by a variation order, the court shall make such further order, if any, in relation to any rights to or in any

property acquired as a result of that decree as it considers fair and reasonable in all the circumstances of the case; but no such further order shall affect any income accruing between the date of that decree and the date of the variation order.

(3)   In considering what order shall be made under subsection (2) above, the court shall, so far as practicable in the circumstances, have regard to the following considerations, namely:—

(a)   that, in the case of any property which is being or has been administered under a trust, any person who on account of the variation order would, apart from subsection (1) above, have been entitled to rights to or in any such property, or any person deriving right from him, shall be entitled to have made over to him by the trustee in full satisfaction of these rights only—

(i)   the said rights to or in any such property or other property for the time being representing it which is still in the hands of the trustee at the date of the variation order, and

(ii)   the value, as at the date of distribution, of the said rights to or in any such property which has been distributed;

(b)   that any capital sum paid by an insurer as a result of the said decree (other than a capital sum which has been distributed by way of an annuity or other periodical payment) or any part of such sum should be repaid to the insurer if the facts in respect of which the variation order was pronounced justify such repayment.

(4)   The court shall not make an order under subsection (2) above unless application for the variation order has been made to the court within the period of five years beginning with the date of the decree under section 2 of this Act.

(5)   Where any person who has acquired rights to or in any property as a result of a decree under section 2 of this Act, or any person deriving right from him, enters into a transaction with another person whereby that other person acquires in good faith and for value any right to or in that property or any part of it, the transaction and any title acquired under it by that other person shall not be challengeable on the ground that an order under subsection (2) above has been made in relation to that property.

(6)   A trustee shall be liable to any person having entitlement by virtue of an order under subsection (2) above for any loss suffered by that person on account of any breach of trust by the trustee in the administration or distribution of the whole or any part of the property, except in so far as the liability of the trustee may be restricted under any enactment or by any provision in any deed regulating the administration of the trust.

(7)   Nothing in this section shall apply to estate duty or capital transfer tax which falls to be repaid as a result of a variation order having been pronounced.

6   Insurance against claims

(1)   Where decree has been granted under section 2 of this Act then, unless the court otherwise directs, the trustee, if any, shall as soon as may be effect a policy of insurance in respect of any claim which may arise by virtue of an order under section 5(2) of this Act.

(2)   Any premium payable by the trustee in respect of a policy of insurance effected under subsection (1) above shall be a proper charge on the estate being administered by the trustee.

(3)   Where decree has been granted under section 2 of this Act, an insurer may, before making payment of any capital sum (other than in respect of an annuity or other periodical payment) to any person as a result of that decree, require that person to effect in his own name for the benefit of that insurer a policy of insurance to satisfy any claim which that insurer may establish in the event of a variation order being pronounced.

7   Value of certain rights may be declared irrecoverable

Where decree has been granted under section 2 of this Act, the court may—

(a) on the application of—

    (i) any person whom the missing person would, at the time of the making of the said application (apart from the said decree), have had a duty (other than a contractual duty) to aliment, or

    (ii) the trustee, and

(b) subject to such conditions, if any, as it thinks fit,

then or at any time thereafter, make an order directing that the value of any rights to or in any property acquired as a result of the said decree shall not be recoverable by virtue of an order under section 5(2) of this Act.

8 Repayment of estate duty

Where estate duty or capital transfer tax falls to be repaid as a result of a variation order having been pronounced—

(a) the court which pronounced the variation order may order the duty or tax to be repaid to the person entitled to receive repayment;

(b) nothing in this Act shall affect the obligation of any person to whom the duty or tax is repaid to account for the amount of the duty or tax to any other person.

9 Disclosure of information

(1) Any person (including the Secretary of State for Social Services) who possesses information relating to the survival or death of the missing person, and who is aware that an action of declarator has been raised or an application for a variation order has been made, shall have a duty to disclose that information—

(a) by means of written communication to the Principal Clerk of Session or, as the case may require, the appropriate sheriff clerk; or

(b) in such other manner as may be prescribed by act of sederunt.

(2) Nothing in this section shall impose any duty to disclose information where the person possessing the information would, if cited as a witness or haver, have been entitled to refuse to disclose such information under any rule of law or practice relating to the privilege of witnesses and havers, confidentiality of communications and withholding or non-disclosure of information on the grounds of public interest.

(3) A statement purporting to be an instrument made or issued by or on behalf of any Minister of the Crown and disclosing to the court facts relating to an action of declarator which has been raised or an application for a variation order which has been made in that court shall be sufficient evidence of those facts.

10 Decree of court furth of Scotland to be sufficient evidence

Where a court in any country furth of Scotland in which a person was domiciled or habitually resident on the date on which he was last known to be alive issues a decree or judgment declaring that that person has died or is presumed to have died, or has died or is presumed to have died on a specified date or within a specified period, that decree or judgment shall, in any proceedings in Scotland, be sufficient evidence of the facts so declared.

11 Appointment or confirmation of executor

(1) Where, in proceedings for the appointment or confirmation of an executor of any person, a document to which subsection (2) below refers is produced, an oath or affirmation that to the best of the deponent's knowledge and belief that person is dead shall, for the purposes of those proceedings, be equivalent to an oath or affirmation that that person has died or died at any place or on any date appearing in such document as the place or date at or on which he died or was presumed to have died or was lost or missing.

(2) This subsection refers to the following documents, that is to say—

(a) a duly certified copy of a decree or judgment such as is referred to in section 10 of this Act;

(b) a certificate or intimation issued by or on behalf of a competent authority within the United Kingdom that the person—

    (i)   has died.

    (ii) is presumed to have died, or

    (iii) is lost or missing in circumstances affording reasonable ground for the belief that he has died as a result of an incident in or in connection with a ship, aircraft, hovercraft or off-shore installation.

(3)   Notwithstanding any provision in or under any enactment, it shall not be necessary, in any petition for appointment as executor of any person in regard to whom a duly certified copy of such a decree or judgment as aforesaid or such a certificate or intimation as aforesaid is produced with the petition, to aver that the person died at any specified place or on any specified date, but it shall be sufficient to aver that the duly certified copy of the decree or judgment or (as the case may be) the certificate or intimation is produced and that to the best of the petitioner's knowledge and belief the person is dead.

12   Particulars of decree or variation order to be intimated to Registrar General

(1)   Where a decree under section 2 of this Act or a variation order has been granted by any court, the clerk of court shall, where no appeal has been made against such decree or order, on the expiration of the time within which such an appeal may be made, or where an appeal has been made against such a decree or order, on the conclusion of any appellate proceedings, notify the prescribed particulars in connection with such decree or order to the Registrar General of Births, Deaths and Marriages for Scotland, who shall thereupon cause to be made such entry, if any, as appears to him to be appropriate, in a register kept for that purpose.

(2)   In this section, 'prescribed' means prescribed by regulations made under section 54 of the Registration of Births, Deaths and Marriages (Scotland) Act 1965.

13   Defence to charge of bigamy

It shall be a defence against a charge of [committing an offence under section 24(A1) of the Marriage (Scotland) Act 1977 or section 100(1) of the Civil Partnership Act 2004] for the accused to prove that at no time within the period of seven years immediately preceding the date of the purported marriage [or civil partnership] forming the substance of the charge had he any reason to believe that his spouse [or civil partner] was alive.

14   Report of proceedings

For the avoidance of doubt, it is hereby declared that section 1(1)(b) of the Judicial Proceedings (Regulation of Reports) Act 1926 does not apply to an action of declarator.

15   Rules of procedure

(1)   Without prejudice to the generality of the powers conferred on the Court of Session by section 16 of the Administration of Justice (Scotland) Act 1933 and section 32 of the Sheriff Courts (Scotland) Act 1971 to regulate procedure by act of sederant, the said powers shall include power to make rules of procedure for the purpose of giving effect to the provisions of this Act.

(2)   Such rules of procedure shall include provisions—

    (a) specifying the persons (including the Lord Advocate) upon or to whom service or intimation of the summons or initial writ in an action of declarator or of an application for a variation order is to be made; and

    (b) relating to the advertisement of the raising of the said action or the making of the said application.

16   Entailed estates

(1)   The following provisions of this section shall apply where decree has been granted under section 2 of this Act declaring the death of the missing person who is the heir in possession of an entailed estate.

(2)   In the circumstances set out in subsection (1) above, the next heir may apply to the court for authority to disentail the estate and the court may make it a con-

dition of granting such authority that the next heir gives security of such amount and in such manner as the court may direct to meet any contingent interest of the heir if he shall reappear and, within the period of five years beginning with the date of the said decree, application for the relative variation order shall be made.

(3)   Where, in the circumstances set out in subsection (1) above—

(a)   the estate has not been disentailed,

(b)   the absent heir reappears,

(c)   application for the relative variation order is made within the period of five years beginning with the date of the said decree, and

(d)   the relative variation order is pronounced,

then, notwithstanding section 5 of this Act, the absent heir who reappears shall be entitled to resume possession of the estate but shall not be entitled to recover the fruits or income of the estate from any following heir in respect of the period of that heir's possession.

(4)   In this section, 'the court' means the Court of Session.

17   Interpretation

In this Act, unless the context otherwise requires,

'action of declarator' has the meaning assigned to it by section 1 of this Act;

'any person having an interest' includes the Lord Advocate for the public interest;

'the court' means the Court of Session or the sheriff;

'insurer' includes a society registered under the Acts relating to friendly and industrial and provident societies and any person or body which provides for the payment of benefits on the death of another person;

'missing person' has the meaning assigned to it by section 1(1) of this Act;

'statutory tribunal' means a tribunal established by or under any enactment;

'trust' means—

(a)   any trust or executry for the administration of property which comes into operation as a result of a decree under section 2 of this Act, or

(b)   any trust under which property devolves upon or is transmitted to any person by reason of the death of the missing person;

and 'trustee' means the trustee, executor, judicial factor or other person administering any such property;

'variation order' has the meaning assigned to it by section 4(1) of this Act.

18, 19   [*Amendments and repeals*]

20   Short title, commencement and extent

(1)   This Act may be cited as the Presumption of Death (Scotland) Act 1977.

(2)   This Act, except this section, shall come into force on such date as the Lord Advocate may by order made by statutory instrument appoint.

(3)   This Act shall extend to Scotland only.

FORFEITURE ACT 1982
(1982 c 34)

1 The 'forfeiture rule'

(1)   In this Act, the 'forfeiture rule' means the rule of public policy which in certain circumstances precludes a person who has unlawfully killed another from acquiring a benefit in consequence of the killing.

(2)   References in this Act to a person who has unlawfully killed another include a reference to a person who has unlawfully aided, abetted, counselled or procured the death of that other and references in this Act to unlawful killing shall be interpreted accordingly.

2   Power to modify the rule

(1)   Where a court determines that the forfeiture rule has precluded a person (in this section referred to as 'the offender') who has unlawfully killed another from acquiring any interest in property mentioned in subsection (4) below, the court may make an order under this section modifying [or excluding] the effect of that rule.

(2)   The court shall not make an order under this section modifying [or excluding] the effect of the forfeiture rule in any case unless it is satisfied that, having regard to the conduct of the offender and of the deceased and to such other circumstances as appear to the court to be material, the justice of the case requires the effect of the rule to be so modified [or excluded] in that case.

(3)   In any case where a person stands convicted of an offence of which unlawful killing is an element, the court shall not make an order under this section modifying [or excluding] the effect of the forfeiture rule in that case unless proceedings for the purpose are brought before the expiry of the [relevant period].

[(3A)   In subsection (3) above, the 'relevant period' is the period of 6 months beginning with—

(a)   the end of the period allowed for bringing an appeal against the conviction, or

(b)   if such an appeal is brought, the conclusion of proceedings on the appeal.]

(4)   The interests in property referred to in subsection (1) above are—

(a)   any beneficial interest in property which (apart from the forfeiture rule) the offender would have acquired—

(i)   under the deceased's will (including, as respects Scotland, any writing having testamentary effect) or the law relating to intestacy or by way of ius relicti, ius relictae or legitim;

(ii)   on the nomination of the deceased in accordance with the provisions of any enactment;

(iii)   as a donatio mortis causa made by the deceased; or

(iv)   under a special destination (whether relating to heritable or moveable property); or

(b)   any beneficial interest in property which (apart from the forfeiture rule) the offender would have acquired in consequence of the death of the deceased, being property which, before the death, was held on trust for any person.

(5)   An order under this section may modify [or exclude] the effect of the forfeiture rule in respect of any interest in property to which the determination referred to in subsection (1) above relates and may do so in either or both of the following ways, that is—

(a)   where there is more than one such interest, by excluding the application of the rule in respect of any [or all] of those interests; and

(b)   in the case of any such interest in property, by excluding the application of the rule in respect of [all or any] part of the property.

(6)   On the making of an order under this section [modifying the effect of the forfeiture rule], the forfeiture rule shall have effect for all purposes (including

purposes relating to anything done before the order is made) subject to the modifications made by the order.

(7)   The court shall not make an order under this section modifying the effect of the forfeiture rule in respect of any interest in property which, in consequence of the rule, has been acquired before the coming into force of this section by a person other than the offender or a person claiming through him.

(8)   In this section—
'property' includes any chose in action or incorporeal moveable property; and 'will' includes codicil.

3   Application for financial provision not affected by the rule

(1)   The forfeiture rule shall not be taken to preclude any person from making any application under a provision mentioned in subsection (2) below or the making of any order on the application.

(2)   The provisions referred to in subsection (1) above are—
    (a)   any provision of the Inheritance (Provision for Family and Dependants) Act 1975;
    [(b)   sections 31(6) and 36(1) of the Matrimonial Causes Act 1973 (variation by court in England and Wales of periodical payments order and maintenance agreements in respect of marriages),
    (c)   paragraphs 60(2) and 73(2) of Schedule 5 to the Civil Partnership Act 2004 (variation by court in England and Wales of periodical payments orders and maintenance agreements in respect of civil partnerships), and
    (d)   section 13(4) of the Family Law (Scotland) Act 1985 (variation etc of periodical allowances in respect of marriages and civil partnerships)].

4   [Upper Tribunal] to decide whether rule applies to social security benefits

(1)   Where a question arises as to whether, if a person were otherwise entitled to or eligible for any benefit or advantage under a relevant enactment, he would be precluded by virtue of the forfeiture rule from receiving the whole or part of the benefit or advantage, that question shall (notwithstanding anything in any relevant enactment) be determined by [the Upper Tribunal].

[(1A)   Where [the Upper Tribunal] determines that the forfeiture rule has precluded a person (in this section referred to as 'the offender') who has unlawfully killed another from receiving the whole or part of any such benefit or advantage, [the Upper Tribunal] may make a decision under this subsection modifying the effect of that rule and may do so whether the unlawful killing occurred before or after the coming into force of this subsection.

(1B)   [The Upper Tribunal] shall not make a decision under subsection (1A) above modifying the effect of the forfeiture rule in any case unless [it] is satisfied that, having regard to the conduct of the offender and of the deceased and to such other circumstances as appear to [the Upper Tribunal] to be material, the justice of the case requires the effect of the rule to be so modified in that case.

(1C)   Subject to subsection (1D) below, a decision under subsection (1A) above may modify the effect of the forfeiture rule in either or both of the following ways—
    (a)   so that it applies only in respect of a specified proportion of the benefit or advantage;
    (b)   so that it applies in respect of the benefit or advantage only for a specified period of time.

(1D)   Such a decision may not modify the effect of the forfeiture rule so as to allow any person to receive the whole or any part of a benefit or advantage in respect of any period before the commencement of this subsection.

(1E)   If [the Upper Tribunal] thinks it expedient to do so, [the Upper Tribunal may direct that its] decision shall apply to any future claim for a benefit or advantage under a relevant enactment, on which a question such as is mentioned in subsection (1) above arises by reason of the same unlawful killing.

(1F)   It is immaterial for the purposes of subsection (1E) above whether the claim is in respect of the same or a different benefit or advantage.

(1G)   For the purpose of obtaining a decision whether the forfeiture rule should be modified the Secretary of State may refer to [the Upper Tribunal] for review any determination of a question such as is mentioned in subsection (1) above that was made before the commencement of subsections (1A) to (1F) above (whether by [the Upper Tribunal] or not) and shall do so if the offender requests him to refer such a determination.

(1H)   Subsections (1A) to (1F) above shall have effect on a reference under subsection (1G) above as if in subsection (1A) the words 'it has been determined' were substituted for the words '[the Upper Tribunal] determines'.]

(2)   [Tribunal procedure rules may make provision] for carrying this section into effect; and (without prejudice to the generality of that) [the rules] may, in relation to the question mentioned in subsection (1) above or any determination under that subsection [or any decision under subsection (1A) above]—

(a)   apply any provision of any relevant enactment, with or without modifications, or exclude or contain provision corresponding to any such provision [. . .].

[. . .]

(5)   In this section—

[. . .]

'relevant enactment' means any provision of the following and any instrument made by virtue of such a provision:

the Personal Injuries (Emergency Provisions) Act 1939,

[the Pension Schemes Act 1993]

the Pensions (Navy, Army, Air Force and Mercantile Marine) Act 1939,

the Polish Resettlement Act 1947,

[. . .], [the Social Security Acts 1975 to 1991],

[the Social Security Contributions and Benefits Act 1992,]

[section 1 of the Armed Forces (Pensions and Compensation) Act 2004,]

and any other enactment relating to pensions or social security prescribed by regulations under this section.

5   Exclusion of murderers

Nothing in this Act or in any order made under section 2 or referred to in section 3(1) of this Act [or in any decision made under section 4(1A) of this Act] shall affect the application of the forfeiture rule in the case of a person who stands convicted of murder.

6   [*Applies to Northern Ireland only.*]

7   Short title, etc

(1)   This Act may be cited as the Forfeiture Act 1982.

(2)   Section 4 of this Act shall come into force on such day as the Secretary of State may appoint by order made by statutory instrument; and sections 1 to 3 and 5 of this Act shall come into force on the expiry of the period of three months beginning with the day on which it is passed.

(3)   This Act, except section 6, does not extend to Northern Ireland.

(4)   Subject to section 2(7) of this Act, an order under section 2 of this Act or an order referred to in section 3(1) of this Act and made in respect of a person who has unlawfully killed another may be made whether the unlawful killing occurred before or after the coming into force of those sections.

LAW REFORM (MISCELLANEOUS PROVISIONS) (SCOTLAND) ACT 1990
(1990, c 40)

Reorganisation of public trusts

9   Reorganisation of public trusts by the court

(1)   Where, in the case of any public trust, the court is satisfied—

(a)   that the purposes of the trust, whether in whole or in part—

(i)   have been fulfilled as far as it is possible to do so; or

(ii)   can no longer be given effect to, whether in accordance with the directions or spirit of the trust deed or other document constituting the trust or otherwise;

(b)   that the purposes of the trust provide a use for only part of the property available under the trust;

(c)   that the purposes of the trust were expressed by reference to—

(i)   an area which has, since the trust was constituted, ceased to have effect for the purpose described expressly or by implication in the trust deed or other document constituting the trust; or

(ii)   a class of persons or area which has ceased to be suitable or appropriate, having regard to the spirit of the trust deed or other document constituting the trust, or as regards which it has ceased to be practicable to administer the property available under the trust; or

(d)   that the purposes of the trust, whether in whole or in part, have, since the trust was constituted—

(i)   been adequately provided for by other means; or

(ii)   ceased to be such as would enable the trust to [be entered in the Scottish Charity Register]; or

(iii)   ceased in any other way to provide a suitable and effective method of using the property available under the trust, having regard to the spirit of the trust deed or other document constituting the trust,

the court, on the application of the trustees, may, subject to subsection (2) below, approve a scheme for the variation or reorganisation of the trust purposes.

(2)   The court shall not approve a scheme as mentioned in subsection (1) above unless it is satisfied that the trust purposes proposed in the scheme will enable the resources of the trust to be applied to better effect consistently with the spirit of the trust deed or other document constituting the trust, having regard to changes in social and economic conditions since the time when the trust was constituted.

(3)   Where any of paragraphs (a) to (d) of subsection (1) above applies to a public trust, an application may be made under this section for the approval of a scheme—

(a)   for the transfer of the assets of the trust to another public trust, whether involving a change to the trust purposes of such other trust or not; or

(b)   for the amalgamation of the trust with one or more public trusts,

and the court, if it is satisfied that the conditions specified in subsection (2) above are met, may approve such a scheme.

(4)   Subject to subsection (5) below, an application for approval of a scheme under this section shall be made to the Court of Session.

(5)   From such day as the Lord Advocate may, by order, appoint, an application for approval of a scheme under this section may be made by a public trust having an annual income not exceeding such amount as the Secretary of State may, by order, prescribe—

(a)   to the sheriff for the place with which the trust has its closest and most real connection;

(b)   where there is no such place as is mentioned in paragraph (a) above, to the sheriff for the place where any of the trustees resides;

    (c)   where neither paragraph (a) nor (b) above applies, to the sheriff of Lothian and Borders at Edinburgh.

    (6)   Every application under this section shall be intimated to the Lord Advocate who shall be entitled to enter appearance as a party in any proceedings on such application, and he may lead such proof and enter such pleas as he thinks fit; and no expenses shall be claimable by or against the Lord Advocate in any proceedings in which he has entered appearance under this subsection.

    (7)   This section shall be without prejudice to the power of the Court of Session to approve a cy pres scheme in relation to any public trust.

10 Small trusts

    (1)   Where a majority of the trustees of any public trust having an annual income not exceeding £5,000 are of the opinion—

    (a)   that the purposes of the trust, whether in whole or in part—

        (i)   have been fulfilled as far as it is possible to do so; or

        (ii)   can no longer be given effect to, whether in accordance with the directions or spirit of the trust deed or other document constituting the trust or otherwise;

    (b)   that the purposes of the trust provide a use for only part of the property available under the trust;

    (c)   that the purposes of the trust were expressed by reference to—

        (i)   an area which has, since the trust was constituted, ceased to have effect for the purpose described expressly or by implication in the trust deed or other document constituting the trust; or

        (ii)   a class of persons or area which has ceased to be suitable or appropriate, having regard to the spirit of the trust deed or other document constituting the trust, or as regards which it has ceased to be practicable to administer the property available under the trust; or

    (d)   that the purposes of the trust, whether in whole or in part, have, since the trust was constituted—

        (i)   been adequately provided for by other means; or

        (ii)   ceased to be such as would enable the trust to [be entered in the Scottish Charity Register]; or

        (iii)   ceased in any other way to provide a suitable and effective method of using the property available under the trust, having regard to the spirit of the trust deed or other document constituting the trust,

subsection (2) below shall apply in respect of the trust.

    (2)   Where this subsection applies in respect of a trust, the trustees may determine that, to enable the resources of the trust to be applied to better effect consistently with the spirit of the trust deed or other document constituting the trust—

    (a)   a modification of the trust's purposes should be made;

    (b)   the whole assets of the trust should be transferred to another public trust; or

    (c)   that the trust should be amalgamated with one or more public trusts.

    (3)   Where the trustees of a trust determine as mentioned in subsection (2)(a) above, they may, subject to subsections (4) to (6) below, pass a resolution that the trust deed be modified by replacing the trust purposes by other purposes specified in the resolution.

    (4)   The trustees shall ensure that, so far as is practicable in the circumstances, the purposes so specified are not so far dissimilar in character to those of the purposes set out in the original trust deed or other document constituting the trust that such modification of the trust deed would constitute an unreasonable departure from the spirit of such trust deed or other document.

    (5)   Before passing a resolution under subsection (3) above the trustees shall have regard—

(a)   where the trust purposes relate to a particular locality, to the circumstances of the locality; and

(b)   to the extent to which it may be desirable to achieve economy by amalgamating two or more trusts.

[. . .]

(7)   Subject to subsection (14) below, a modification of trust purposes under this section shall not have effect before the expiry of a period of two months commencing with the date on which any advertisement in pursuance of regulations made under subsection (13) below is first published.

(8)   Where the trustees determine as mentioned in subsection (2)(b) above they may pass a resolution that the trust be wound up and that the assets of the trust be transferred to another trust or trusts the purposes of which are not so dissimilar in character to those of the trust to be wound up as to constitute an unreasonable departure from the spirit of the trust deed or other document constituting the trust to be wound up.

(9)   Before passing a resolution under subsection (8) above, the trustees shall—

(a)   where the trust purposes relate to a particular locality, have regard to the circumstances of the locality; and

[. . .]

(c)   ascertain that the trustees of the trust to which it is proposed to transfer the assets will consent to the transfer of the assets.

(10)   Where the trustees determine as mentioned in subsection (2)(c) above, they may pass a resolution that the trust be amalgamated with one or more other trusts so that the purposes of the trust constituted by such amalgamation will not be so dissimilar in character to those of the trust to which the resolution relates as to constitute an unreasonable departure from the spirit of the trust deed or other document constituting the last mentioned trust.

(11)   Before passing a resolution under subsection (10) above, the trustees shall—

(a)   where the trust purposes relate to a particular locality, have regard to the circumstances of the locality; and

[. . .]

(c)   ascertain that the trustees of any other trust with which it is proposed that the trust will be amalgamated will agree to such amalgamation.

(12)   Subject to subsection (14) below, a transfer of trust assets or an amalgamation of two or more trusts under this section shall not be effected before the expiry of a period of two months commencing with the date on which any advertisement in pursuance of regulations made under subsection (13) below is first published.

(13)   The Secretary of State may, by regulations, prescribe the procedure to be followed by trustees following upon a resolution passed under subsection (3), (8) or (10) above, and such regulations may, without prejudice to the generality, include provision as to advertisement of the proposed modification or winding up, the making of objections by persons with an interest in the purposes of the trust, notification to the Lord Advocate of the terms of the resolution and the time within which anything requires to be done.

(14)   If it appears to the Lord Advocate, whether in consideration of any objections made in pursuance of regulations made under subsection (13) above or otherwise—

(a)   that the trust deed should not be modified as mentioned in subsection (3) above;

(b)   that the trust should not be wound up as mentioned in subsection (8) above; or

(c)   that the trust should not be amalgamated as mentioned in subsection (10) above, he may direct the trust not to proceed with the modification or, as the case may be winding up and transfer of funds or amalgamation.

(15)   The Secretary of State may, by order, amend subsection (1) above by substituting a different figure for the figure, for the time being, mentioned in that subsection.

(16)   This section shall apply to any trust to which section 223 of the Local Government (Scotland) Act 1973 (property held on trust by local authorities) applies.

11   Expenditure of capital

(1)   This section applies to any public trust which has an annual income not exceeding £1,000 where the trust deed or other document constituting the trust prohibits the expenditure of any of the trust capital.

(2)   In the case of any trust to which this section applies where the trustees—

(a)   have resolved unanimously that, having regard to the purposes of the trust, the income of the trust is too small to enable the purposes of the trust to be achieved; and

(b)   are satisfied that either there is no reasonable prospect of effecting a transfer of the trust's assets under section 10 of this Act or that the expenditure of capital is more likely to achieve the purposes of the trust,

they may, subject to subsection (3) below, proceed with the expenditure of capital.

(3)   Not less than two months before proceeding to expend capital, the trustees shall advertise their intention to do so in accordance with regulations made by the Secretary of State and shall notify the Lord Advocate of such intention.

(4)   If it appears to the Lord Advocate that there are insufficient grounds for the expenditure of capital he may apply to the court for an order prohibiting such expenditure, and if the court is satisfied that there are such insufficient grounds it may grant the order.

(5)   The Secretary of State may, by order, amend subsection (1) above by substituting a different figure for the figure, for the time being, mentioned in that subsection.

CIVIL PARTNERSHIP ACT 2004
(2004, c 33)

131   Succession: legal rights arising by virtue of civil partnership

(1)   Where a person dies survived by a civil partner then, unless the circumstance is as mentioned in subsection (2), the civil partner has right to half of the moveable net estate belonging to the deceased at the time of death.

(2)   That circumstance is that the person is also survived by issue, in which case the civil partner has right to a third of that moveable net estate and those issue have right to another third of it.

(3)   In this section—

'issue' means issue however remote, and

'net estate' has the meaning given by section 36(1) (interpretation) of the Succession (Scotland) Act 1964 (c 41).

(4)   Every testamentary disposition executed after the commencement of this section by which provision is made in favour of the civil partner of the testator and which does not contain a declaration to the effect that the provision so made is in full and final satisfaction of the right to any share in the testator's estate to which the civil partner is entitled by virtue of subsection (1) or (2), has effect (unless the disposition contains an express provision to the contrary) as if it contained such a declaration.

(5)   In section 36(1) of the Succession (Scotland) Act 1964 (c 41), in the definition of 'legal rights', for 'and legitim' substitute 'legitim and rights under section 131 of the Civil Partnership Act 2004'.

CHARITIES AND TRUSTEE INVESTMENT (SCOTLAND) ACT 2005
(2005, asp 10)

PART 1
CHARITIES

CHAPTER 1
OFFICE OF THE SCOTTISH CHARITY REGULATOR

1   Office of the Scottish Charity Regulator
(1)   There is to be an office to be known as the Office of the Scottish Charity Regulator.
(2)   There is established a body corporate, to be known as the Scottish Charity Regulator, which is to be the holder of that office.
(3)   That office-holder is referred to in this Act as 'OSCR'.
(4)   OSCR has the functions conferred on it by or under this Act and any other enactment.
(5)   OSCR's general functions are—
　　(a)   to determine whether bodies are charities,
　　(b)   to keep a public register of charities,
　　(c)   to encourage, facilitate and monitor compliance by charities with the provisions of this Act,
　　(d)   to identify and investigate apparent misconduct in the administration of charities and to take remedial or protective action in relation to such misconduct, and
　　(e)   to give information or advice, or to make proposals, to the Scottish Ministers on matters relating to OSCR's functions.
(6)   OSCR may do anything (whether in Scotland or elsewhere) which is calculated to facilitate, or is conducive or incidental to, the performance of its functions.
(7)   Subsection (6) does not enable OSCR to do anything in contravention of any express prohibition, restriction or limitation on its powers which is contained in any enactment (including this Act).
(8)   OSCR must perform its functions in a manner that encourages equal opportunities and in particular the observance of the equal opportunity requirements.
(9)   In performing its functions OSCR must, so far as relevant, have regard to—
　　(a)   the principles under which regulatory activities should be proportionate, accountable, consistent, transparent and targeted only at cases in which action is needed, and
　　(b)   any other principle appearing to OSCR to represent best regulatory practice.
(10)   Schedule 1 makes further provision about the Scottish Charity Regulator.

2   Annual reports
(1)   As soon as practicable after the end of each financial year, OSCR must—
　　(a)   prepare and publish a general report on the exercise of its functions during that year,
　　(b)   send a copy of the report to the Scottish Ministers, and
　　(c)   lay a copy of the report before the Scottish Parliament.
(2)   A general report may include, in particular, any general recommendations which OSCR may have arising from the exercise of its functions during that year and any previous financial year.
(3)   It is for OSCR to determine the form and content of a general report and by what means it is to be published.

CHAPTER 2
SCOTTISH CHARITY REGISTER

The Register

3 Scottish Charity Register

(1) OSCR must keep a register of charities to be known as the 'Scottish Charity Register' (and referred to in this Act as 'the Register').

(2) The Register is to be kept in such manner as OSCR thinks fit.

(3) The Register must contain a separate entry for each charity entered in it setting out—

(a) the name of the charity,

(b) the principal office of the charity or, where it does not have such an office, the name and address of one of its charity trustees,

(c) the purposes of the charity,

(d) where the charity is a designated religious charity or a designated national collector, that fact,

(e) where—

(i) a direction is given under section 11(3), 12(2) or (3), 16(6), 28(3), 30(1) or 31(5) to (9), or

(ii) a notice is given under section 31(4),

in relation to the charity, the fact that the direction or notice has been given and the date on which it was given,

(f) any other information in relation to the charity which the Scottish Ministers by regulations require to be set out in the Register, and

(g) any other information in relation to the charity which OSCR considers appropriate.

(4) OSCR must, despite subsection (3)(b), exclude the information specified in that provision from a charity's entry in the Register if, on the application of the charity (whether together with its application for entry in the Register or separately), OSCR is satisfied that including that information is likely to jeopardise the safety or security of any person or premises.

(5) OSCR must, if it is satisfied that a direction or notice of a type described in subsection (3)(e) has been complied with or no longer has effect, remove reference to the direction or notice from the charity's entry.

(6) OSCR must—

(a) from time to time, review each entry in the Register, and

(b) if it considers any information set out in a charity's entry to be inaccurate—

(i) amend the entry accordingly, and

(ii) notify the charity of the amendment made.

Applications

4 Application for entry in Register

An application for entry in the Register must—

(a) state the name of the body making the application (the 'applicant'),

(b) state the principal office of the applicant or, where it does not have such an office, the name and address of one of the persons who, if the applicant is entered in the Register, will be its charity trustees,

(c) be accompanied by—

(i) a statement of the applicant's purposes,

(ii) a copy of the applicant's constitution, and

(iii) the applicant's most recent statement of account (if any), and

(d) contain such other information, and be accompanied by such other documents, as may be—

     (i)   required by regulations under section 6(1), or
    (ii)   otherwise requested by OSCR.

5 Determination of applications

(1)   OSCR may enter an applicant in the Register only if it considers that the applicant meets the charity test.

(2)   OSCR must refuse to enter an applicant if—

   (a)   it considers that the applicant's name falls within section 10, or

   (b)   the application must, by virtue of regulations under section 6(1), be refused,

but must not otherwise refuse to enter an applicant which it considers meets the charity test.

6 Applications: further procedure

(1)   The Scottish Ministers may by regulations make such further provision in relation to the procedure for applying and determining applications for entry in the Register (including applications under section 54(1), 56(1) and 59(1)) as they think fit.

(2)   Such regulations may in particular make provision about—

   (a)   information and documents which must be specified in or accompany an application,

   (b)   the form and manner in which applications must be made,

   (c)   the period within which OSCR must make a decision on an application, and

   (d)   circumstances in which OSCR must refuse to enter a body in the Register.

The charity test

7 The charity test

(1)   A body meets the charity test if—

   (a)   its purposes consist only of one or more of the charitable purposes, and

   (b)   it provides (or, in the case of an applicant, provides or intends to provide) public benefit in Scotland or elsewhere.

(2)   The charitable purposes are—

   (a)   the prevention or relief of poverty,

   (b)   the advancement of education,

   (c)   the advancement of religion,

   (d)   the advancement of health,

   (e)   the saving of lives,

   (f)   the advancement of citizenship or community development,

   (g)   the advancement of the arts, heritage, culture or science,

   (h)   the advancement of public participation in sport,

   (i)   the provision of recreational facilities, or the organisation of recreational activities, with the object of improving the conditions of life for the persons for whom the facilities or activities are primarily intended,

   (j)   the advancement of human rights, conflict resolution or reconciliation,

   (k)   the promotion of religious or racial harmony,

   (l)   the promotion of equality and diversity,

   (m)   the advancement of environmental protection or improvement,

   (n)   the relief of those in need by reason of age, ill-health, disability, financial hardship or other disadvantage,

   (o)   the advancement of animal welfare,

   (p)   any other purpose that may reasonably be regarded as analogous to any of the preceding purposes.

(3) In subsection (2)—

(a) in paragraph (d), 'the advancement of health' includes the prevention or relief of sickness, disease or human suffering,

(b) paragraph (f) includes—

(i) rural or urban regeneration, and

(ii) the promotion of civic responsibility, volunteering, the voluntary sector or the effectiveness or efficiency of charities,

(c) in paragraph (h), 'sport' means sport which involves physical skill and exertion,

(d) paragraph (i) applies only in relation to recreational facilities or activities which are—

(i) primarily intended for persons who have need of them by reason of their age, ill-health, disability, financial hardship or other disadvantage, or

(ii) available to members of the public at large or to male or female members of the public at large,

(e) paragraph (n) includes relief given by the provision of accommodation or care, and

(f) for the purposes of paragraph (p), the advancement of any philosophical belief (whether or not involving belief in a god) is analogous to the purpose set out in paragraph (c).

(4) A body which falls within paragraphs (a) and (b) of subsection (1) does not, despite that subsection, meet the charity test if—

(a) its constitution allows it to distribute or otherwise apply any of its property (on being wound up or at any other time) for a purpose which is not a charitable purpose,

(b) its constitution expressly permits the Scottish Ministers or a Minister of the Crown to direct or otherwise control its activities, or

(c) it is, or one of its purposes is to advance, a political party.

(5) The Scottish Ministers may by order disapply either or both of paragraphs (a) and (b) of subsection (4) in relation to any body or type of body specified in the order.

8 Public benefit

(1) No particular purpose is, for the purposes of establishing whether the charity test has been met, to be presumed to be for the public benefit.

(2) In determining whether a body provides or intends to provide public benefit, regard must be had to—

(a) how any—

(i) benefit gained or likely to be gained by members of the body or any other persons (other than as members of the public), and

(ii) disbenefit incurred or likely to be incurred by the public,

in consequence of the body exercising its functions compares with the benefit gained or likely to be gained by the public in that consequence, and

(b) where benefit is, or is likely to be, provided to a section of the public only, whether any condition on obtaining that benefit (including any charge or fee) is unduly restrictive.

9 Guidance on charity test

OSCR must, after consulting representatives of the charitable sector and such other persons as it thinks fit, issue guidance on how it determines whether a body meets the charity test.

Charity names

10   Objectionable names

(1)   A body's name falls within this section if it is—

(a)   the same as, or too like, the name of a charity,

(b)   likely to mislead the public as to the true nature of the purposes of the body or of the activities which it carries on, or intends to carry on, in pursuit of those purposes,

(c)   likely to give the impression that the body is connected in some way to the Scottish Administration, Her Majesty's Government in the United Kingdom or any local authority, or with any other person, when it is not so connected, or

(d)   offensive.

(2)   The reference in subsection (1)(b) to a body's purposes are—

(a)   in the case of an applicant, the purposes set out in the statement accompanying its application,

(b)   in the case of a charity, the purposes set out in its entry in the Register, and

(c)   in the case of an SCIO proposed in an application under section 54(1), 56(1) or 59(1), the purposes set out in the SCIO's proposed constitution accompanying the application.

11   Change of name

(1)   A charity may change its name only with OSCR's consent.

(2)   A charity which proposes to change its name must, not less than 42 days before doing so, give notice to OSCR specifying its proposed new name.

(3)   Unless OSCR, within 28 days of the date on which a notice is given under subsection (2), directs the charity not to change its name, OSCR is to be taken as having given its consent.

(4)   OSCR may refuse to consent to a charity changing its name only where it considers that the proposed new name falls within section 10.

12   Power of OSCR to require charity to change name

(1)   A charity may, if it considers that the name of another charity is too like its name, request OSCR to review the names.

(2)   OSCR must, if satisfied following such a review that the names of two charities are too alike, direct either one or both of the charities to change its name.

(3)   OSCR must, where at any other time it considers that a charity's name falls within section 10, direct the charity to change its name.

(4)   Section 11 applies in relation to a change of name in compliance with a direction under this section (and the charity directed must give notice of its proposed new name under subsection (2) of that section within such period as may be specified in the direction).

(5)   OSCR must remove from the Register any charity which fails to comply with a direction under this section.

References to charitable status

13   References to charitable status

(1)   A body entered in the Register may refer to itself as a 'charity', a 'charitable body', a 'registered charity' or a 'charity registered in Scotland'.

(2)   If such a body is established under the law of Scotland, or is managed or controlled wholly or mainly in or from Scotland, it may also refer to itself as a 'Scottish charity' or a 'registered Scottish charity'.

(3)   A body which refers to itself in any of the ways described in subsection (1) is to be treated as representing itself as a body entered in the Register.

(4)   A body which refers to itself in any of the ways described in subsection (2) is to be treated as representing itself—

(a)   as a body entered in the Register, and

(b)   as being established under the law of Scotland or managed or controlled wholly or mainly in or from Scotland.

14   Exception for certain bodies not in Register

A body which is not entered in the Register may, despite section 13, refer to itself as a 'charity' without being treated as representing itself as a charity if, and only if—

(a)   it is—

(i)   established under the law of a country or territory other than Scotland,

(ii)   entitled to refer to itself as a 'charity' (by any means or in any language) in that country or territory, and

(iii)   managed or controlled wholly or mainly outwith Scotland,

(b)   it does not—

(i)   occupy any land or premises in Scotland, or

(ii)   carry out activities in any office, shop or similar premises in Scotland, and

(c)   in making that reference, it also refers to being established under the law of a country or territory other than Scotland.

15   References in documents

(1)   The Scottish Ministers may by regulations require each body entered in the Register to state, in legible characters—

(a)   that it is a charity,

(b)   such other information as may be specified in the regulations,

on such documents issued or signed on behalf of the charity as may be so specified.

(2)   Such regulations may—

(a)   exempt charities, or charities of a particular type, from any of the requirements imposed by the regulations,

(b)   provide that any statement required by them may, in the case of documents which are otherwise wholly or mainly in a language other than English, be made in that other language.

[(3) For the purposes of this section, a reference to a document issued or signed on behalf of the charity includes a reference to a web page on a website operated by or on behalf of the charity.]

Changes

16   Changes which require OSCR's consent

(1)   A charity may take any action set out in subsection (2) only with OSCR's consent and in accordance with any conditions attached to any such consent.

(2)   Those actions are—

(a)   amending its constitution so far as it relates to its purposes,

(b)   amalgamating with another body,

(c)   winding itself up or dissolving itself,

(d)   applying to the court in relation to any action set out in paragraphs (a) to (c).

(3)   Subsection (1) does not apply in relation to any action—

(a)   in pursuance of an approved reorganisation scheme, or

(b)   for which OSCR's consent is required by virtue of any other enactment.

(4)   Where a charity proposes to take any action set out in subsection (2) it must, not less than 42 days before the date on which the action is to be taken, give notice to OSCR of the proposal specifying that date.

(5)   In the case of an action set out in subsection (2)(a), the charity must not proceed unless and until OSCR has given its consent.

(6)   In any other case, unless OSCR, within 28 days of the date on which notice is given under subsection (4)—

(a)   refuses its consent, or

(b)   directs the charity not to take the action for a period of not more than 6 months specified in the direction,

OSCR is to be taken as having consented to it.

(7)   A direction under subsection (6)(b)—

(a)   may be revoked at any time,

(b)   may be varied, but not so as to have effect for a period of more than 6 months from the date on which it is given.

(8)   Where OSCR gives such a direction it must, after making such inquiries as it thinks fit—

(a)   give its consent, whether or not subject to conditions, or

(b)   refuse its consent.

17   Notification of other changes

(1)   A charity must give OSCR notice of—

(a)   any change in—

(i)   the principal office of the charity, or

(ii)   where it does not have such an office, the name or address of the charity trustee specified in the Register (or which would, but for section 3(4), be so specified),

(b)   any change in any other details set out in its entry in the Register,

(c)   any change to its constitution,

(d)   any action set out in section 16(2)(b) to (d) which the charity has taken,

(e)   any administration order or an order for winding up made by the court in respect of the charity,

(f)   the appointment of a receiver in respect of any of the charity's property, setting out the date on which the change, action, order or appointment took effect.

(2)   Subsection (1) does not apply in relation to any action which requires OSCR's consent under section 16.

(3)   A notice under any of paragraphs (a) to (d) of subsection (1) must be given within 3 months of the date of the change or action to which it relates.

(4)   A notice under paragraph (e) or (f) of subsection (1) must be given within 1 month of the date of the order or appointment to which it relates.

CHAPTER 3
CO-OPERATION AND INFORMATION

. . .

Information about charities

21   Public access to Register

(1)   OSCR must make the Register available for public inspection—

(a)   at all reasonable times at its principal office,

(b)   at such other places as it thinks fit, and

(c)   otherwise as it thinks fit.

(2)   It is for OSCR to determine the form and manner in which the Register is made available; but in doing so OSCR must ensure that the information in the Register is made reasonably obtainable.

(3)   OSCR must publicise the arrangements which it makes in pursuance of subsection (1).

(4)   OSCR may charge such fee (not exceeding the cost of supply) as it thinks fit for providing information under any arrangements it makes under subsection (1)(b) and (c).

22   Power of OSCR to obtain information from charities

(1)   OSCR may by notice require any charity to provide to it—
  (a)   any document, or a copy of or extract from any document,
  (b)   documents of any type, or copies of or extracts from such documents,
  (c)   other information or explanation,
which OSCR requires in relation to the charity's entry in the Register.

(2)   The notice must specify—
  (a)   the documents, type of documents, copies, extracts, information or explanation which the charity is to provide to OSCR, and
  (b)   the date (which must be at least 14 days after the date on which the notice is given) by which the charity must do so.

(3)   Subsection (1) does not authorise OSCR to require the disclosure of anything which a charity would be entitled to refuse to disclose on grounds of confidentiality in proceedings in the Court of Session.

23   Entitlement to information about charities

(1)   A person who requests a charity to provide a copy of its—
  (a)   constitution,
  (b)   latest statement of account prepared under section 44,
is, if the request is reasonable, entitled to be given that copy constitution or copy statement of account (if any) by the charity in such form as the person may reasonably request.

(2)   A charity may charge such fee as it thinks fit for complying with such a request; but such a fee must not exceed the cost of supplying the document requested or, if less, any maximum fee which the Scottish Ministers may by order prescribe.

(3)   The Scottish Ministers may by order exempt from the duty set out in subsection (1) any charities which meet such criteria as may be specified in the order.

CHAPTER 4
SUPERVISION OF CHARITIES ETC

Inquiries

28   Inquiries about charities etc

(1)   OSCR may at any time make inquiries, either generally or for particular purposes, with regard to—
  (a)   a charity,
  (b)   a body controlled by a charity (or by two or more charities, when taken together),
  (c)   a body which is not entered in the Register which appears to OSCR to represent itself as a charity (or which would, but for section 14, so appear),
  (d)   a person not falling within paragraph (a) to (c) who appears to OSCR to act, or to represent itself as acting, for or on behalf of—
      (i)   a charity, or
      (ii)   a body falling within paragraph (b) or (c),
  (e)   a person who appears to OSCR to represent a body which is not entered in the Register as a charity,
  (f)   any particular type of charity, of body falling within paragraph (b) or (c), or of person falling within paragraph (d) or (e).

(2)   OSCR may make inquiries under subsection (1) of its own accord or on the representation of any person.

(3)   OSCR may direct any charity, body or person with regard to which it is making inquiries under subsection (1) not to undertake activities specified in the direction for such period of not more than 6 months as is specified in the direction.

(4)   A direction under subsection (3) given to a person falling within paragraph (d) or (e) of subsection (1) may be given only in relation to activities which that person undertakes for or on behalf of the charity or body to which the inquiries relate.

(5)   A direction under subsection (3)—

(a)   may be revoked at any time,

(b)   may be varied, but not so as to have effect for a period of more than 6 months from the date on which it is given.

(6)   A person who, without reasonable excuse, refuses or fails to comply with a direction under subsection (3) is guilty of an offence.

(7)   A person guilty of an offence under subsection (6) is liable on summary conviction to a fine not exceeding level 4 on the standard scale or imprisonment for a period not exceeding 3 months, or to both.

29   Power of OSCR to obtain information for inquiries

(1)   OSCR may by notice require any person to provide to it—

(a)   any document, or a copy of or extract from any document,

(b)   documents of any type, or copies of or extracts from such documents,

(c)   any information or explanation,

which OSCR considers necessary for the purposes of inquiries under section 28.

(2)   The notice must specify—

(a)   the documents, type of documents, copies, extracts, information or explanation which the person is to provide to OSCR,

(b)   the date (which must be at least 14 days after the date on which the notice is given) by which the person must do so, and

(c)   the effect of subsection (6).

(3)   Subsection (1) does not authorise OSCR to require the disclosure of anything which a person would be entitled to refuse to disclose on grounds of confidentiality in proceedings in the Court of Session.

(4)   OSCR must not disclose any document, information or explanation provided in response to a requirement under subsection (1) except for the purposes of the inquiries in connection with which the requirement was made.

(5)   OSCR may pay to any person a sum in respect of expenses reasonably incurred by the person in complying with a requirement under subsection (1).

(6)   A person who, without reasonable excuse, refuses or fails to comply with a requirement under subsection (1) is guilty of an offence and liable on summary conviction to a fine not exceeding level 4 on the standard scale or imprisonment for a period not exceeding 3 months, or to both.

30   Removal from Register of charity which no longer meets charity test

(1)   Where it appears to OSCR, as a result of inquiries under section 28, that a charity no longer meets the charity test it must—

(a)   direct the charity to take, within such period as may be specified in the direction, such steps as OSCR considers necessary for the purposes of meeting the charity test, or

(b)   remove the charity from the Register.

(2)   Steps specified in a direction under subsection (1)(a) may include applying to OSCR for approval under section 39 of a reorganisation scheme in relation to the charity's constitution.

[(2A)   The power of OSCR to give a direction under subsection (1)(a) includes the power to—

    (a) vary the direction, but only by—
        (i) extending the time period specified in the direction, or
        (ii) removing steps which the charity is required to take, or
    (b) revoke such a direction.]
(3) OSCR must, if a charity fails to comply with a direction under subsection (1)(a), remove the charity from the Register.

31 Powers of OSCR following inquiries

(1) Subsections (4), (6) and (7) apply where it appears to OSCR, as a result of inquiries under section 28—
    (a) that there has been misconduct in the administration of—
        (i) a charity, or
        (ii) a body controlled by a charity, or
    (b) that it is necessary or desirable to act for the purpose of protecting the property of a charity or securing a proper application of such property for its purposes.
(2) Subsections (5) to (7) apply where it appears to OSCR, as a result of inquiries under section 28—
    (a) that a body which is not a charity is being or has been represented as a charity, or
    (b) that a charity which is not entitled to refer to itself in either of the ways described in section 13(2) is being or has been represented as being established under the law of Scotland or managed or controlled wholly or mainly in or from Scotland.
(3) Subsections (8) and (9) apply where it appears to OSCR, as a result of inquiries under section 28, that there is or has been misconduct by a person falling within section 28(1)(d) in any activity which the person undertakes for or on behalf of the charity or body referred to in that provision.
(4) OSCR may, by notice, suspend any person concerned in the management or control of the charity or body who appears to it to—
    (a) have been responsible for or privy to the misconduct,
    (b) have contributed to, or facilitated, the misconduct, or
    (c) be unable or unfit to perform that person's functions in relation to the property of the charity or body.
(5) OSCR may direct—
    (a) the body representing itself as a charity,
    (b) the person representing the body as a charity,
    (c) the charity representing itself as being established under the law of Scotland or managed or controlled wholly or mainly in or from Scotland, or, as the case may be
    (d) the person representing the charity as being established under the law of Scotland or managed or controlled wholly or mainly in or from Scotland,
to stop doing so.
(6) OSCR may give a direction restricting the transactions which may be entered into, or the nature or amount of the payments which may be made, in the administration of the charity or body without OSCR's consent.
(7) OSCR may direct any relevant financial institution or other person holding property on behalf of the charity or body or of any person concerned in its management or control not to part with the property without OSCR's consent.
(8) OSCR may direct the person—
    (a) to cease acting, or representing itself as acting, for or on behalf of the charity or body in any activity specified in the direction,
    (b) to pay to the charity or body, within such period as the direction may specify, any sums which it has collected for the charity or body and which are held by it or by any relevant financial institution or other person on its behalf,

after deducting any sums payable to the person or any other person under an agreement with the charity or body.

(9)　OSCR may direct any relevant financial institution or other person holding property which OSCR considers to be, or to represent, sums collected for the charity or body not to part with the property without OSCR's consent.

(10)　OSCR's power to suspend a person by giving notice under subsection (4) (a) or (b) does not apply if OSCR considers that the person has acted honestly and reasonably in relation to the misconduct concerned and ought fairly to be excused.

32　Suspensions and directions: procedure

(1)　A suspension under subsection (4) and a direction under any of subsections (5) to (9) of section 31—

(a)　has effect for such period of not more than 6 months as is specified in the suspension or direction,

(b)　may be revoked at any time,

(c)　may be varied, but not so as to have effect for a period of more than 6 months from the date on which the suspension or direction first has effect.

(2)　Where such a suspension has been made or direction has been given, a further suspension or direction may be made or given under section 31 but the further suspension or direction ceases to have effect on the same date as the original suspension or direction (unless stated to cease to have effect earlier).

(3)　A copy of the notice given under section 72 in respect of a—

(a)　suspension under subsection (4) of section 31, or

(b)　direction under subsection (5)(b) or (d) or (8) of that section, must be given to the charity or body in question.

(4)　A copy of the notice given under section 72 in respect of a direction under subsection (7) or (9) of that section must be given to the person directed.

(5)　A person who, without reasonable excuse—

(a)　contravenes a suspension under subsection (4) of section 31, or

(b)　refuses or fails to comply with a direction under any of subsections (5) to (9) of that section,

is guilty of an offence and liable on summary conviction to a fine not exceeding level 5 on the standard scale or imprisonment for a period not exceeding 6 months, or to both.

33　Reports on inquiries

(1)　OSCR must prepare a report of the subject matter of inquiries made under section 28 if—

(a)　as a result of the inquiries it—

(i)　gives a direction, or removes a charity from the Register, under section 30,

(ii)　suspends a person under subsection (4) of section 31, or

(iii)　gives a direction under any of subsections (5) to (9) of that section, or

(b)　in any other case, it is requested to do so by the person in respect of whom the inquiries were made and it has not previously prepared a report of the subject matter of those inquiries under this subsection or subsection (2).

(2)　OSCR may prepare a report of the subject matter of any other inquiries under section 28.

(3)　A report prepared under this section may relate to two or more inquiries.

(4)　Apart from identifying the person in respect of whom inquiries were made, a report under this section must not—

(a)　mention the name of any person, or

(b)　contain any particulars which, in OSCR's opinion—

(i)　are likely to identify any person, and

(ii)　can be omitted without impairing the effectiveness of the report,

unless OSCR considers it is necessary to do so.

(5)   OSCR must—
   (a)   send a copy of a report prepared under subsection (1) to the person in respect of whom the inquiries were made, and
   (b)   publish a report prepared under this section or such other statement of the result of inquiries made under section 28 as OSCR thinks fit in such manner as OSCR thinks fit.

Powers of Court of Session

34   Powers of Court of Session
(1)   Where, on an application by OSCR, it appears to the Court of Session—
   (a)   that there is or has been misconduct in the administration of—
      (i)   a charity, or
      (ii)   a body controlled by a charity (or by two or more charities, when taken together), or
   (b)   that it is necessary or desirable to act for the purpose of protecting the property of a charity or securing a proper application of such property for its purposes, the court may exercise any of the powers set out in subsection (5)(a) and (c) to (g).
(2)   Where, on an application by OSCR, it appears to the Court of Session that a body which is not a charity is or has been representing itself as a charity, the court may exercise any of the powers set out in subsection (5)(b) to (g).
(3)   Where, on an application by OSCR, it appears to the Court of Session that a person is or has been representing a body which is not a charity as a charity, the court may exercise any of the powers set out in subsection (5)(f) to (h).
(4)   Where, on an application by OSCR, it appears to the Court of Session that a charity which is not entitled to refer to itself in either of the ways described in section 13(2) is being or has been represented as being established under the law of Scotland or managed or controlled wholly or mainly in or from Scotland, the court may exercise any of the powers set out in subsections (5)(f), (g) and (i).
(5)   Those powers are power to—
   (a)   interdict (whether temporarily or permanently) the charity or body from such action as the court thinks fit,
   (b)   interdict (whether temporarily or permanently) the body from representing itself as a charity or from such other action as the court thinks fit,
   (c)   appoint a judicial factor (whether temporarily or permanently) to manage the affairs of the charity or body,
   (d)   where the charity or body is a trust, appoint a trustee,
   (e)   suspend or remove any person concerned in the management or control of the charity or body,
   [(ea)   make an order declaring that any person who was concerned in the management or control of a charity or body is to be treated, for the purpose of section 69(2)(c) (disqualification from being charity trustee) as having been removed from being concerned in the management or control of the charity or body, notwithstanding that—
      (i)   the person is no longer concerned in the management or control of the charity or body,
      (ii)   the body is no longer a charity,
      (iii)   the body is no longer controlled by a charity (or charities), or
      (iv)   the charity or body has ceased to exist,]
   (f)   order any relevant financial institution or other person holding property on behalf of the charity or body or of any person concerned in its management or control not to part with the property without the court's consent,
   (g)   make an order restricting the transactions which may be entered into, or

the nature or amount of the payments which may be made, in the administration of the charity or body without the court's consent,

(h) interdict (whether temporarily or permanently) the person from representing the body as a charity or from such other action as the court thinks fit,

(i) interdict (whether temporarily or permanently) the charity or, as the case may be, the person from representing the charity as being established under the law of Scotland or managed or controlled wholly or mainly in or from Scotland or from such other action as the court thinks fit.

(6) Where the court appoints a trustee in pursuance of subsection (5)(d), section 22 of the Trusts (Scotland) Act 1921 (c 58) applies as if the trustee had been appointed under that section.

(7) The power in subsection (5)(g) applies despite anything in the constitution of the charity or body.

(8) Subsection (9) applies where, on an application by OSCR, it appears to the Court of Session that there is or has been misconduct by a person falling within section 28(1)(d) in any activity which the person undertakes for or on behalf of the charity or body referred to in that provision.

(9) The court may—

(a) interdict (whether temporarily or permanently) the person from acting, or representing itself as acting, on behalf of the charity or body,

(b) order the person to pay to the charity or body any sums which it has collected for the charity or body and which are held by it, any relevant financial institution or other person holding money on its behalf, after deducting any sums payable to the person or any other person under an agreement with the charity or body,

(c) order any relevant financial institution or other person holding property which the court considers to be, or to represent, sums collected for the charity or body not to part with the property without the court's consent.

(10) The court may—

(a) recall the suspension of a person in pursuance of subsection (5)(e),

(b) vary or recall an order in pursuance of subsection (5)(f) or (g) or under subsection (9)(b) or (c).

35 Transfer schemes

(1) The Court of Session may, on an application by OSCR, approve a scheme prepared by OSCR in accordance with regulations made by the Scottish Ministers for the transfer to a charity specified in the scheme of any assets of—

(a) another charity,

(b) a body which is controlled by a charity (or by two or more charities, when taken together),

(c) a body which is not a charity but which is or has been representing itself as a charity.

(2) The court may approve a scheme in relation to a charity only if it is satisfied—

(a) that there is or has been misconduct in the administration of the charity,

(b) that it is necessary or desirable to act for the purpose of protecting the property of the charity or securing a proper application of such property for its purposes, and

(c) that the charity's purposes would be better achieved by transferring its assets to another charity.

(3) The court may approve a scheme in relation to a body falling with paragraph (b) of subsection (1) only if it is satisfied—

(a) that there is or has been misconduct in the administration of the body or any of the charities which control it,

(b) that it is necessary or desirable to act for the purpose of protecting the property of the body or any such charity, and

(c)   that the transfer provided for by the scheme is reasonable.

(4)   The court may approve a scheme in relation to a body falling within paragraph (c) of subsection (1) only if it is satisfied—

(a)   that the body falls within that paragraph, and

(b)   that the transfer provided for by the scheme is reasonable.

(5)   The court may approve a scheme under this section subject to modifications.

(6)   A charity receiving property in pursuance of a scheme approved under this section may apply that property for its purposes as it thinks fit.

Supplemental

38   Delegation of functions

[. . .]

(2)   OSCR may authorise any Scottish public authority with mixed functions or no reserved functions to exercise any of [OSCR's functions under sections 28 to 35 (other than section 30) and section 70A] in so far as they are exercisable in relation to—

(a)   such charities or bodies, or types of charity or body, as OSCR may specify in the authorisation, and

(b)   persons acting for or on behalf of those charities or bodies.

(3)   Such an authorisation may be made only if the authorised person has other regulatory functions conferred on it by an enactment in relation to the charities or types of charity in respect of which the authorisation is made.

(4)   OSCR must send a copy of such an authorisation to each charity to which it relates.

(5)   OSCR must, before making such an authorisation, consult such persons (including the person it proposes to authorise) as it thinks fit.

(6)   OSCR may, at any time, withdraw an authorisation under subsection (2) (and subsections (4) and (5) apply in relation to such a withdrawal as they apply in relation to an authorisation).

[. . .]

(8)   It is not competent for OSCR to exercise any of its functions which are, by virtue of subsection [. . .] (2), delegated to another public body or office-holder (unless it considers it necessary or expedient to do so in relation to its functions under section 30).

(9)   Sections 24 to 26 apply in relation to a public body or office-holder to whom OSCR's functions are delegated by virtue of subsection [. . .] (2) as they apply to OSCR, but subject to the following modifications—

(a)   references in those sections to OSCR and to OSCR's functions are to be read as references to the public body or office-holder and to the functions delegated to it, and

(b)   the reference in section 25(1)(d) to section 46 is to be read as a reference to subsection (10).

(10)   Where any of OSCR's functions are delegated to another public body or office-holder by virtue of subsection [. . .] (2), a person to whom section 46 applies—

(a)   must report to the body or office-holder on any matter which the person would, but for that delegation, be required by section 46(2) to report on to OSCR,

(b)   may report to the body or office-holder on any matter which the person would, but for that delegation, be authorised by subsection 46(3) to report on to OSCR.

(11)   A duty or power which arises under subsection (10) is not affected if the person in relation to whom it arises subsequently stops acting in the capacity mentioned in section 46(1).

[. . .]

CHAPTER 5
REORGANISATION OF CHARITIES

39   Reorganisation of charities: applications by charity
(1)   OSCR may, on the application of a charity, approve a reorganisation scheme proposed by the charity if it considers—
(a)   that any of the reorganisation conditions is satisfied in relation to the charity, and
(b)   that the proposed reorganisation scheme will—
(i)   where the condition satisfied is that set out in paragraph (a) or (b) of section 42(2), enable the resources of the charity to be applied to better effect for charitable purposes consistently with the spirit of its constitution, having regard to changes in social and economic conditions since it was constituted, or
(ii)   where the condition satisfied is that set out in paragraph (c) [or (d)] of that section, enable the charity to be administered more effectively.
[(1A)   But OSCR must not approve a reorganisation scheme where—
(a)   the reorganisation condition satisfied is that set out in section 42(2)(d), and
(b)   the proposed provision would enable the charity to make amendments to its constitution which would not be consistent with the spirit of the constitution.]
(2)   The Scottish Ministers may by regulations make such provision as they think fit in relation to the procedure for applying for and determining applications under this section.
(3)   Such regulations may in particular make provision about—
(a)   the form and manner in which applications must be made,
(b)   the period within which OSCR must make a decision on an application,
(c)   publication of proposed reorganisation schemes,
and may make different provision in relation to different types of charity.

40   Reorganisation of charities: applications by OSCR
(1)   Where OSCR considers—
(a)   that any of the reorganisation conditions is satisfied in relation to a charity, and
(b)   that a reorganisation scheme proposed by it or by the charity trustees of the charity will—
(i)   where the condition satisfied is that set out in paragraph (a) or (b) of section 42(2), enable the resources of the charity to be applied to better effect for charitable purposes consistently with the spirit of its constitution, having regard to changes in social and economic conditions since it was constituted, or
(ii)   where the condition satisfied is that set out in paragraph (c) [or (d)] of that section, enable the charity to be administered more effectively,
OSCR may, of its own accord or on the application of the charity trustees of the charity, apply to the Court of Session for approval of the scheme.
(2)   The Court of Session may, on an application under subsection (1), approve the proposed reorganisation scheme if it considers that the matters set out in paragraphs (a) and (b) of that subsection are satisfied in relation to the charity to which the application relates.
[(2A)   But the Court of Session must not approve a reorganisation scheme where—
(a)   the reorganisation condition satisfied is that set out in section 42(2)(d), and
(b)   the proposed provision would enable the charity to make amendments to its constitution which would not be consistent with the spirit of the constitution.]
(3)   The charity trustees of a charity may enter appearance as a party in proceedings on an application under subsection (1) in relation to the charity.

(4)   OSCR must, not less than 28 days before making an application under subsection (1), notify the charity in question of its intention to do so.

41   Approved schemes
A charity may, despite any provision of its constitution having contrary effect, proceed with any variation, transfer or amalgamation for which an approved reorganisation scheme makes provision.

42   Reorganisation: supplementary
(1)   This section applies for the interpretation of Chapter 5.
(2)   The 'reorganisation conditions' are—
   (a)   that some or all of the purposes of the charity—
      (i)   have been fulfilled as far as possible or adequately provided for by other means,
      (ii)   can no longer be given effect to (whether or not in accordance with the directions or spirit of its constitution),
      (iii)   have ceased to be charitable purposes, or
      (iv)   have ceased in any other way to provide a suitable and effective method of using its property, having regard to the spirit of its constitution,
   (b)   that the purposes of the charity provide a use for only part of its property,
   (c)   that a provision of the charity's constitution (other than a provision setting out the charity's purposes) can no longer be given effect to or is otherwise no longer desirable [, and
   (d)   that it is desirable to introduce a provision (other than a provision setting out a new purpose) to a charity's constitution.]
(3)   A 'reorganisation scheme' is a scheme for—
   (a)   variation of the constitution of the charity (whether or not in relation to its purposes),
   (b)   transfer of the property of the charity (after satisfaction of any liabilities) to another charity (whether or not involving a change to the purposes of the other charity), or
   (c)   amalgamation of the charity with another charity.
(4)   Nothing in section 40 affects the power of the Court of Session to approve a cy pre`s scheme in relation to a charity.
(5)   Sections 39 and 40 do not apply to any charity constituted under a Royal charter or warrant or under any enactment.
(6)   But, despite subsection (5), those sections do apply to an endowment if its governing body is a charity.
(7)   In subsection (6), 'endowment' and 'governing body' have the same meaning as in Part 6 (reorganisation of endowments) of the Education (Scotland) Act 1980 (c 44)

43   [*Amends Education (Scotland) Act 1980.*]

[CHAPTER 5A
REORGANISATION OF RESTRICTED FUNDS

[43A   Reorganisation of restricted funds: applications by charity
(1)   OSCR may, on the application of a charity, approve a restricted funds reorganisation scheme proposed by the charity if—
   (a)   it considers—
      (i)   that any of the conditions specified in subsection (2) is satisfied in relation to the restricted funds, and

(ii)   that the proposed reorganisation will enable the resources of the restricted funds to be applied to better effect for charitable purposes consistently with the charity's constitution, and

(b)   it is satisfied that the charity is unable to ascertain the wishes of the donor.

(2)   The conditions are—

(a)   that some or all of the purposes of the restricted funds—

(i)   have been fulfilled as far as possible or adequately provided for by other means,

(ii)   can no longer be given effect to (whether or not in accordance with the directions or spirit of the restricted funds' purposes),

(iii)   have ceased to be charitable purposes,

(iv)   have ceased in any other way to provide a suitable and effective method of using the funds, having regard to the spirit of the restricted funds' purposes,

(b)   that the purposes of the restricted funds provide a use for only part of its property.

(3)   The Scottish Ministers may by regulations make such provision as they think fit in relation to making and determining applications under this section.

(4)   Such regulations may in particular make provision about—

(a)   the form and manner in which applications must be made,

(b)   the period within which OSCR must make a decision on an application,

(c)   publication of proposed restricted funds reorganisation schemes,

(d)   the action a charity may take in order to satisfy OSCR of the matters described in subsection (1)(b),

and may make different provision in relation to different types of charity.]

[43B   Reorganisations of restricted funds: applications by OSCR

(1)   Where OSCR—

(a)   considers—

(i)   that any of the conditions specified in section 43A(2) is satisfied in relation to a charity, and

(ii)   that a restricted funds reorganisation scheme proposed by it or by the charity trustees of the charity will enable the resources of the restricted funds to be applied to better effect for charitable purposes consistently with the charity's constitution, and

(b)   is satisfied that it is not possible to ascertain the wishes of the donor,

OSCR may, of its own accord or on the application of the charity trustees of the charity, apply to the Court of Session for approval of the scheme.

(2)   The Court of Session may, on an application under subsection (1), approve the proposed restricted funds reorganisation scheme if it considers that the matters set out in paragraphs (a) and (b) of that subsection are satisfied in relation to the restricted funds to which the application relates.

(3)   The charity trustees of a charity may enter appearance as a party in proceedings on an application under subsection (1) in relation to the charity.

(4)   OSCR must, not less than 28 days before making an application under subsection (1), notify the charity in question of its intention to do so.

(5)   The Scottish Ministers may by regulations make such provision as they think fit in relation to action which may be taken to satisfy OSCR of the matter described in subsection (1)(b).

(6)   Nothing in this section affects the power of the Court of Session to approve a cy pre`s scheme in relation to a charity.]

[43C   Approved restricted funds reorganisation schemes

A charity may, despite any condition relating to restricted funds having contrary effect, use the restricted funds in such manner as permitted by an approved restricted funds reorganisation scheme.]

[43D Restricted funds reorganisations: supplementary
In this chapter—
'donor' means such person or body who may vary the purpose of, or any conditions imposed in relation to, restricted funds as may be specified by regulations made by the Scottish Ministers as they think fit,
'restricted funds' means property (including money) given to a charity for a specific purpose and in respect of which conditions have been imposed as to its use,
a 'restricted funds reorganisation scheme' is a scheme for—
(a) the variation of the purpose for which restricted funds may be used,
(b) the variation or removal of any condition imposed on the charity in relation to the use of restricted funds.]]

CHAPTER 6
CHARITY ACCOUNTS

Duty to keep accounts etc

44 Accounts
(1) A charity must—
(a) keep proper accounting records,
(b) prepare for each financial year of the charity a statement of account, including a report on its activities in the financial year,
(c) have the statement of account independently examined or audited, and
(d) after such examination or audit, send a copy of the statement of account to OSCR,
in accordance with regulations under subsection (4).
(2) Accounting records kept in pursuance of subsection (1)(a) must be preserved by the charity for 6 years from the end of the financial year in which they are made.
(3) Subsection (2) is without prejudice to any other enactment or rule of law.
(4) The Scottish Ministers may by regulations make provision about the matters referred to in subsection (1) including—
(a) the meaning of 'financial year',
(b) the information to be contained in the accounting records and statement of account,
(c) the manner in which that information is to be presented,
(d) the keeping and preservation of the accounting records,
(e) the methods and principles according to which, and the time by which, the statement of account is to be prepared,
(f) the time by which the copy statement of account is to be sent to OSCR,
(g) examination or audit of the statement of account,
(h) such other matters in relation to the accounts of a charity as the Scottish Ministers think necessary or expedient.
(5) Regulations under subsection (4) may make different provision in relation to different types of charity, including provision exempting charities of a particular type from some or all of the requirements of this section.

45 Failure to provide statement of account
(1) This section applies where a charity fails, within such period as is specified in regulations under section 44(4), to send a copy of a statement of account to OSCR in pursuance of subsection (1)(d) of that section.
(2) OSCR may, after notifying the charity of its intention to do so, appoint a suitably qualified person (an 'appointed person') to prepare such a statement of account.

(3)   An appointed person is entitled—
(a)   on giving reasonable notice, to enter premises occupied by the charity at all reasonable times,
(b)   to have access to, and take possession of, any document appearing to the appointed person to relate to the financial affairs of the charity, and
(c)   to require any charity trustee, or agent or employee, of the charity to give the person such assistance, information or explanation as the appointed person may reasonably require.
(4)   The charity trustees of the charity are personally liable jointly and severally for—
(a)   any costs incurred by OSCR in relation to the appointment of the appointed person, and
(b)   the expenses of the appointed person in performing that person's functions under this section.
(5)   The appointed person must—
(a)   send to OSCR the statement of account prepared in pursuance of subsection (2),
(b)   submit to OSCR a report on the affairs and accounting records of the charity, and
(c)   send a copy of the statement of account and report to each person appearing to the appointed person to be a charity trustee of the charity.
(6)   A person who, without reasonable excuse, refuses or fails to comply with a requirement of an appointed person under subsection (3) is guilty of an offence and liable on summary conviction to a fine not exceeding level 3 on the standard scale.

CHAPTER 7
SCOTTISH CHARITABLE INCORPORATED ORGANISATIONS

Nature and constitution

49   Scottish charitable incorporated organisations
(1)   A charity may be constituted as a Scottish charitable incorporated organisation (a 'SCIO').
(2)   A SCIO is a body corporate having—
(a)   a constitution,
(b)   a principal office in Scotland,
(c)   2 or more members.
(3)   Its membership may, but need not, consist of or include some or all of its charity trustees.
(4)   The members are not liable to contribute to the assets of the SCIO if it is wound up.

50   Constitution and powers
(1)   A SCIO's constitution must state its name and its purposes.
(2)   A SCIO's constitution must make provision—
(a)   about who is eligible for membership, and how a person becomes a member, and
(b)   for the appointment of 3 or more persons ('charity trustees') who are to be charged with the general control of the SCIO's administration, and about any conditions of eligibility for becoming a charity trustee.
(3)   A SCIO's constitution must also provide for such other matters, and comply with such requirements, as are specified in regulations made by the Scottish Ministers.
(4)   A SCIO must use and apply its property in furtherance of its purposes and in accordance with its constitution.
(5)   Subject to anything in its constitution, a SCIO has power to do anything

which is calculated to further its purposes or is conducive or incidental to doing so.

(6)   For the purposes of managing the affairs of a SCIO, its charity trustees may exercise all the SCIO's powers.

51   General duty of members of SCIO

Subsections (1)(a), (3) and (4) of section 66 apply to the members of a SCIO who are not charity trustees as they apply to its charity trustees.

52   Name and status

(1)   The name of a SCIO must appear in legible characters on—
  (a)   such documents issued by or on behalf of the SCIO,
  (b)   such documents signed by or on behalf of the SCIO,
as may be specified in regulations made by the Scottish Ministers.

(2)   Subsection (3) applies where the name of a SCIO does not include—
  (a)   'Scottish charitable incorporated organisation', or
  (b)   'SCIO' (with or without a full stop after each letter),
whether or not capital letters are used.

(3)   Where this subsection applies, the fact that a SCIO is a SCIO must be stated in legible characters in all the documents referred to in subsection (1).

(4)   Section 15 does not apply in relation to a SCIO.

[(5)   For the purposes of this section, a reference to a document—
  (a)   issued by or on behalf of the SCIO, or
  (b)   signed by or on behalf of the SCIO,
includes a reference to a web page on a website operated by or on behalf of the SCIO.]

53   Offences etc

(1)   A charity trustee of a SCIO or a person on the SCIO's behalf who—
  (a)   issues, or authorises the issue of, any document referred to in subsection (1)
  (a) of section 52, or
  (b)   signs, or authorises the signature on behalf of the SCIO of, any document referred to in subsection (1)(b) of that section,
which does not comply with subsections (1) and (3) of that section is guilty of an offence and liable on summary conviction to a fine not exceeding level 3 on the standard scale.

(2)   OSCR may direct—
  (a)   any body which is not a SCIO and which is representing itself as being a SCIO,
  (b)   any person who is representing that any such body is a SCIO, to stop doing so by such date as OSCR may direct.

(3)   The Court of Session may, on an application by OSCR, interdict—
  (a)   any body which is not a SCIO from representing itself as a SCIO,
  (b)   a person who is representing that such a body is a SCIO from doing so.

(4)   OSCR may not apply for such an interdict against a body or person unless the body or person has failed to comply with a direction under subsection (2).

Creation of SCIO and entry in Register

54   Application for creation of SCIO

(1)   Any 2 or more individuals may apply to OSCR for a SCIO to be constituted and for its entry in the Register.

(2)   The application must—
  (a)   state the name of the SCIO,
  (b)   state the proposed principal office of the SCIO,
  (c)   be accompanied by a copy of the SCIO's proposed constitution,

(d) contain such other information, and be accompanied by such other documents, as may be—
    (i) required by regulations under section 6(1), or
    (ii) otherwise required by OSCR.

(3) OSCR may grant the application only if it considers that the SCIO, if constituted, would meet the charity test.

(4) OSCR must refuse the application if—
    (a) it considers that the SCIO's proposed name falls within section 10,
    (b) the SCIO's proposed constitution does not comply with one or more of the requirements of section 50 and any regulations made under that section, or
    (c) the application must, by virtue of regulations under section 6(1), be refused,
but must not otherwise refuse an application if it considers that the SCIO, if constituted, would meet the charity test.

(5) Sections 4 and 5 do not apply in relation to an application under subsection (1).

55 Entry in Register

(1) If OSCR grants an application under section 54(1) it must enter the SCIO to which the application relates in the Register.

(2) On the entry in the Register being made in accordance with subsection (5), subsections (3) and (4) apply.

(3) The SCIO becomes by virtue of this subsection a body corporate—
    (a) whose constitution is that proposed in the application,
    (b) whose name is that specified in the constitution, and
    (c) whose first members are the individuals who made the application.

(4) All property for the time being vested in those individuals (or any of them) on trust for the charitable purposes of the SCIO (when constituted) vests by virtue of this subsection in the SCIO.

(5) The entry for the SCIO in the Register must (in addition to the matters required by section 3(3)) include—
    (a) the date when the entry was made, and
    (b) a note stating that the charity is constituted as a SCIO.

(6) OSCR must send a copy of the entry in the Register to the SCIO at its principal office.

(7) If a SCIO ceases to be a charity, it ceases to be a SCIO.

CHAPTER 9
CHARITY TRUSTEES

General duties

66 Charity trustees: general duties

(1) A charity trustee must, in exercising functions in that capacity, act in the interests of the charity and must, in particular—
    (a) seek, in good faith, to ensure that the charity acts in a manner which is consistent with its purposes,
    (b) act with the care and diligence that it is reasonable to expect of a person who is managing the affairs of another person, and
    (c) in circumstances capable of giving rise to a conflict of interest between the charity and any person responsible for the appointment of the charity trustee—
        (i) put the interests of the charity before those of the other person, or
        (ii) where any other duty prevents the charity trustee from doing so, disclose the conflicting interest to the charity and refrain from participating in

any deliberation or decision of the other charity trustees with respect to the matter in question.

(2) The charity trustees of a charity must ensure that the charity complies with any direction, requirement, notice or duty imposed on it by virtue of this Act.

(3) Subsections (1) and (2) are without prejudice to any other duty imposed by enactment or otherwise on a charity trustee in relation to the exercise of functions in that capacity.

(4) Any breach of the duty under subsection (1) or (2) is to be treated as being misconduct in the administration of the charity.

(5) All charity trustees must take such steps as are reasonably practicable for the purposes of ensuring—

(a) that any breach of a duty under subsection (1) or (2) is corrected by the trustee concerned and not repeated, and

(b) that any trustee who has been in serious or persistent breach of either or both of those duties is removed as a trustee.

Remuneration

67 Remuneration for services

(1) A charity trustee may not be remunerated for services provided to the charity (including services provided in the capacity as a charity trustee or under a contract of employment) unless subsection (2) entitles the trustee to be so remunerated.

(2) Where a charity trustee of a charity—

(a) provides services to or on behalf of the charity, or

(b) might benefit from any remuneration for the provision of such services by a person with whom the trustee is connected,

the person providing the services (the 'service provider') is entitled to be remunerated from the charity's funds for doing so only if the conditions set out in subsection (3) are met.

(3) Those conditions are—

(a) that the maximum amount of the remuneration—

(i) is set out in a written agreement between the service provider and the charity (or, as the case may be, its charity trustees) under which the service provider is to provide the services in question, and

(ii) is reasonable in the circumstances,

(b) that, before entering into the agreement, the charity trustees were satisfied that it would be in the interests of the charity for those services to be provided by the service provider for that maximum amount,

(c) that, immediately after entering into the agreement, less than half of the total number of charity trustees of the charity fall within subsection (4), and

(d) that the charity's constitution does not contain any provision which expressly prohibits the service provider from receiving the remuneration.

(4) A charity trustee falls within this subsection if the trustee is—

(a) party (in the capacity of a service provider) to a written agreement of the type described in subsection (3)(a)(i) under which any obligation is still to be fully discharged,

(b) entitled to receive remuneration from the charity's funds otherwise than by virtue of such an agreement, or

(c) connected with any other charity trustee who falls within sub-paragraph (a) or (b).

(5) Nothing in subsections (1) or (2) prevents a charity trustee or other service provider from receiving any remuneration from a charity's funds which that service provider is entitled to receive by virtue of—

(a) any authorising provision of the charity's constitution which was in force on 15 November 2004,

(b) an order made by the Court of Session, or

(c) [this Act or any other] enactment.

(6) For the purposes of subsection (5)(a), an 'authorising provision' is a provision which refers specifically to the payment of remuneration—

(a) to the service provider concerned,

(b) where that service provider is a charity trustee, to a charity trustee, or

(c) where that service provider is connected to a charity trustee, to any person so connected.

(7) Where a charity trustee or other service provider is remunerated in contravention of this section, the charity may recover the amount of remuneration; and proceedings for its recovery must be taken if OSCR so directs.

68 Remuneration: supplementary

(1) In section 67—

'benefit' means any direct or indirect benefit,

'maximum amount', in relation to remuneration, means the maximum amount of the remuneration whether specified in or ascertainable under the terms of the agreement in question,

'remuneration' includes any benefit in kind (and 'remunerated' is to be construed accordingly),

'services' includes goods that are supplied in connection with the provision of services.

(2) For the purposes of that section, the following persons are 'connected' with a charity trustee—

(a) any person—

(i)   to whom the trustee is married,

(ii) who is the civil partner of the trustee, or

(iii) with whom the trustee is living as husband and wife or, where the trustee and the other person are of the same sex, in an equivalent relationship,

(b) any child, parent, grandchild, grandparent, brother or sister of the trustee (and any spouse of any such person),

(c) any institution which is controlled (whether directly or through one or more nominees) by—

(i)   the charity trustee,

(ii) any person with whom the charity trustee is connected by virtue of paragraph (a), (b), (d) or (e), or

(iii) two or more persons falling within sub-paragraph (i) or (ii), when taken together,

(d) a body corporate in which—

(i)   the charity trustee has a substantial interest,

(ii) any person with whom the charity trustee is connected by virtue of paragraph (a), (b), (c) or (e) has a substantial interest, or

(iii) two or more persons falling within sub-paragraph (i) or (ii), when taken together, have a substantial interest,

(e) a Scottish partnership in which one or more of the partners is—

(i)   the charity trustee, or

(ii) a person with whom the charity trustee is, by virtue of paragraph (a) or (b), connected.

(3) For the purposes of subsection (2) a person who is—

(a) another person's stepchild, or

(b) brought up or treated by another person as if the person were a child of the other person,

is to be treated as that other person's child.

(4) Section 105 sets out when a person is to be treated as being in control of an institution or as having a substantial interest in a body corporate.

[68A   Charity trustees' indemnity insurance

(1)   The charity trustees of a charity may arrange for the purchase, from the charity's funds, of insurance designed to indemnify the charity trustees against personal liability in respect of any negligence, default or breach of duty committed by them in their capacity as—

(a)   charity trustees, or

(b)   directors or officers of any body corporate carrying on any activities on behalf of the charity.

(2)   The terms of such insurance must, however, be framed to exclude the provision of any indemnity for a charity trustee in respect of any liability incurred by the charity trustee—

(a)   to pay—

(i)   a fine imposed in criminal proceedings,

(ii)   a sum payable to a regulatory authority by way of a penalty in respect of non-compliance with any requirement of a regulatory nature,

(b)   in respect of representation in any criminal proceedings in which the charity trustee is convicted of an offence arising out of any fraud or dishonesty, or wilful or reckless misconduct, by the charity trustee,

(c)   to the charity that arises out of any conduct which the charity trustee knew (or must reasonably be assumed to have known) was not in the interests of the charity or in the case of which the charity trustee did not care whether it was in the interests of the charity or not.

(3)   For the purposes of subsection (2)(b) the reference to conviction does not include a conviction—

(a)   quashed by an order under section 118(1)(b) or 183(1)(c) of the Criminal Procedure (Scotland) Act 1995 (c 46),

(b)   quashed by an order under section 118(1)(c) of that Act and which order has the effect of an acquittal by virtue of section 119(9) of that Act or otherwise,

(c)   in relation to which the verdict is set aside by an order under section 183(1) (d) of that Act and which order has the effect of an acquittal by virtue of section 185(9) of that Act or otherwise.

(4)   This section—

(a)   does not authorise the purchase of any insurance whose purchase is expressly prohibited by the charity's constitution,

(b)   has effect despite any provision prohibiting the charity trustees receiving any personal benefit from the charity's funds.]

Disqualification

69   Disqualification from being charity trustee

(1)   The persons specified in subsection (2) are disqualified from being charity trustees.

(2)   Those persons are any person who—

(a)   has been convicted of—

(i)   an offence involving dishonesty,

(ii)   an offence under this Act,

(b)   is an undischarged bankrupt,

(c)   has been removed, under section 7 of the Law Reform (Miscellaneous Provisions) (Scotland) Act 1990 (c 40) or section 34 of this Act, from being concerned in the management or control of any body,

(d)   has been removed from the office of charity trustee or trustee for a charity by an order made—

(i)   [by the Charity Commission for England and Wales under [section 79(2)(a) of the Charities Act 2011 or] section 18(2)(i) of the Charities Act 1993 or] by the Charity Commissioners for England and Wales [, whether under section [18(2)(i) of the 1993 Act]], section 20(1A)(i) of the Charities Act 1960 (c 58) or section 20(1) of that Act (as in force before the commencement of section 8 of the Charities Act 1992 (c 41)), or

    (ii)   by Her Majesty's High Court of Justice in England,

on the grounds of any misconduct in the administration of the charity for which the person was responsible or to which the person was privy, or which the person's conduct contributed to or facilitated,

    (e)   is subject to a disqualification order or disqualification undertaking under the Company Directors Disqualification Act 1986 (c 46) or the Company Directors Disqualification (Northern Ireland) Order 2002 (SI 2002/3150).

(3)   A person referred to in subsection (2)(a) is not disqualified under subsection (1) if the conviction is spent by virtue of the Rehabilitation of Offenders Act 1974 (c 53).

(4)   OSCR may, on the application of a person disqualified under subsection (1), waive the disqualification either generally or in relation to a particular charity or type of charity.

(5)   OSCR must notify a waiver under subsection (4) to the person concerned.

(6)   OSCR must not grant a waiver under subsection (4) if to do so would prejudice the operation of the Company Directors Disqualification Act 1986 (c 46) or the Company Directors Disqualification (Northern Ireland) Order 2002 (SI 2002/3150).

70   Disqualification: supplementary

(1)   A person who acts as a charity trustee while disqualified by virtue of section 69 is guilty of an offence and liable—

    (a)   on summary conviction, to imprisonment for a period not exceeding 6 months or a fine not exceeding level 5 on the standard scale or both,

    (b)   on conviction on indictment, to imprisonment for a period not exceeding 2 years or a fine or both.

(2)   Any acts done as a charity trustee by a person disqualified by virtue of section 69 from being a charity trustee are not invalid by reason only of the disqualification.

(3)   In section 69(2)(b), 'undischarged bankrupt' means a person—

    (a)   whose estate has been sequestrated, who has been adjudged bankrupt or who has granted a trust deed for or entered into an arrangement with creditors, and

    (b)   who has not been discharged under or by virtue of—

        (i)   section [137, 138 or 140 of the Bankruptcy (Scotland) Act 2016],

        [...]

        (iii)   section 279 or 280 of the Insolvency Act 1986 (c 45), or

        (iv)   any other enactment or rule of law subsisting at the time of the person's discharge.

[Appointment

[70A   Appointment of charity trustees

(1)   Subsection (2) applies where—

    (a)   a charity has an insufficient number of charity trustees to be able to appoint a charity trustee under its constitution, and

    (b)   the constitution does not provide a mechanism for appointing a charity trustee in such circumstances.

(2)   OSCR may, upon the request of—

    (a)   the majority of the charity trustees of a charity,

    (b)   if there are only two charity trustees, either of them, appoint a person as an acting charity trustee for the charity.

(3)   OSCR may appoint more than one acting charity trustee under subsection (2), but only as many as is necessary for the charity to be able to appoint charity trustees under its constitution.

(4)   A person appointed as an acting charity trustee under subsection (2)—

(a) is appointed for the period of 12 months (or such shorter period as OSCR thinks fit) starting with the date of appointment, and

(b) has the same functions as a charity trustee appointed under the charity's constitution.

(5)   Despite subsection (4)(a), if—

(a) at the end of the period mentioned in that subsection, the charity is still not (but for the acting charity trustee) able to appoint a charity trustee under its constitution, and

(b) OSCR, the majority of the charity trustees (or if only two trustees, either of them) and the acting charity trustee agree to an extension,

an acting charity trustee's period of appointment may be extended by one period of up to three months starting with the expiry of the original period of appointment.

(6)   Nothing in subsections (1) to (5) prevents a person appointed as an acting charity trustee by OSCR under subsection (2) from being appointed as a charity trustee by the charity under its constitution.

(7)   But the acting charity trustee may not vote on whether to make such an appointment.

(8)   Where an acting charity trustee is appointed as a charity trustee under the charity's constitution, the person's appointment as an acting charity trustee comes to an end on the date of that subsequent appointment.]]

PART 4
GENERAL AND SUPPLEMENTARY

. . .

99   Population of Register etc

(1)   OSCR must enter in the Register each body which was, immediately prior to the commencement of paragraph 7(a)(ii) of Schedule 4 to this Act, entitled by virtue of section 1(7) of the Law Reform (Miscellaneous Provisions) (Scotland) Act 1990 (c 40) to describe itself as a 'Scottish charity'.

(2)   Subsection (1) does not affect OSCR's power to remove a charity from the Register under section 30.

(3)   The Scottish Ministers may by order—

(a) disapply section 3(3) in so far as it would otherwise apply to any body entered in the Register under subsection (1) for such period ending no later than 18 months after the commencement of this section as may be specified in the order,

(b) provide—

(i)   that any unregistered charitable body (or any such body of a particular type) may, despite any contrary provision in this Act, refer to itself as a 'charity' for such period ending no later than 12 months after the commencement of this section as may be so specified, and

(ii)   that any provision of this Act or of any other enactment is to apply (with such modifications, if any, as may be so specified) to any such body as if it were entered in the Register for so long as it refers to itself as a 'charity'.

(4)   In subsection (3), 'unregistered charitable body' means a body which—

(a) is established under the law of a country or territory other than Scotland,

(b) is entitled to refer to itself as a 'charity' (by any means or in any language) in that country or territory, and

(c) does not require to be entered in the Register under subsection (1).

106   General interpretation

In this Act, unless the context otherwise requires—

'applicant' has the meaning given in section 4(a),

'benevolent body' has the meaning given in section 79,

'charitable purposes' means the purposes set out in section 7(2),

'charity' means a body entered in the Register,

'charity test' is to be construed in accordance with section 7,

'charity trustees' means the persons having the general control and management of the administration of a charity,

['company' means a company registered under the Companies Act 2006 in England and Wales or Scotland,]

'constitution'—

[(a) in relation to a charity or other body which is a company, means its articles of association,]

(b) in relation to a charity or other body which is a body of trustees, means the trust deed,

(c) in relation to a SCIO, has the meaning given in section 50,

(d) in relation to a charity or other body established by enactment, means the enactment which establishes it and states its purposes,

(e) in relation to charity or other body established by a Royal charter or warrant, means the Royal charter or warrant, and

(f) in the case of any other charity or body, means the instrument which establishes it and states its purposes,

'designated national collector' means a charity designated as such under section 87(4),

'designated religious charity' means a charity designated as such under section 65(1),

'equal opportunities' and 'equal opportunity requirements' have the meaning given in Section L2 of Part 2 of Schedule 5 to the Scotland Act 1998 (c 46),

'local authority' means a council constituted under section 2 of the Local Government etc. (Scotland) Act 1994 (c 39),

'misconduct' includes mismanagement,

'OSCR' means the holder of the Office of the Scottish Charity Regulator,

'the Panel' mean a Scottish Charity Appeals Panel constituted in accordance with section 75(1) of this Act,

'the Register' means the Scottish Charity Register,

'relevant financial institution' means—

(a) a person who has permission under [Part 4A] of the Financial Services and Markets Act 2000 (c 8) to accept deposits,

(b) an EEA firm of the kind mentioned in paragraph 5(b) of Schedule 3 to that Act which has permission under paragraph 15 of that Schedule (as a result of qualifying for authorisation under paragraph 12(1) of that Schedule) to accept deposits,

and this definition must be read with section 22 of and Schedule 2 to that Act and any relevant order under that section,

'reorganisation scheme' has the meaning given in section 42(3) and references to 'approved reorganisation schemes' are references to schemes approved under section 39 or 40,

['restricted funds reorganisation scheme' has the meaning given in section 43D and references to 'approved restricted funds reorganisation schemes' are references to schemes approved under section 43A or 43B,]

'SCIO' has the meaning given in section 49.

FAMILY LAW (SCOTLAND) ACT 2006
(2006 asp 2)

29 Application to court by survivor for provision on intestacy

(1)   This section applies where—
   (a)   a cohabitant (the 'deceased') dies intestate; and
   (b)   immediately before the death the deceased was—
      (i)   domiciled in Scotland; and
      (ii)   cohabiting with another cohabitant (the 'survivor').

(2)   Subject to subsection (4), on the application of the survivor, the court may—
   (a)   after having regard to the matters mentioned in subsection (3), make an order—
      (i)   for payment to the survivor out of the deceased's net intestate estate of a capital sum of such amount as may be specified in the order;
      (ii)   for transfer to the survivor of such property (whether heritable or moveable) from that estate as may be so specified;
   (b)   make such interim order as it thinks fit.

(3)   Those matters are—
   (a)   the size and nature of the deceased's net intestate estate;
   (b)   any benefit received, or to be received, by the survivor—
      (i)   on, or in consequence of, the deceased's death; and
      (ii)   from somewhere other than the deceased's net intestate estate;
   (c)   the nature and extent of any other rights against, or claims on, the deceased's net intestate estate; and
   (d)   any other matter the court considers appropriate.

(4)   An order or interim order under subsection (2) shall not have the effect of awarding to the survivor an amount which would exceed the amount to which the survivor would have been entitled had the survivor been the spouse or civil partner of the deceased.

(5)   An application under this section may be made to—
   (a)   the Court of Session;
   (b)   a sheriff in the sheriffdom in which the deceased was habitually resident at the date of death;
   (c)   if at the date of death it is uncertain in which sheriffdom the deceased was habitually resident, the sheriff at Edinburgh.

(6)   [Subject to section 29A] any application under this section shall be made before the expiry of the period of 6 months beginning with the day on which the deceased died.

(7)   In making an order under paragraph (a)(i) of subsection (2), the court may specify that the capital sum shall be payable—
   (a)   on such date as may be specified;
   (b)   in instalments.

(8)   In making an order under paragraph (a)(ii) of subsection (2), the court may specify that the transfer shall be effective on such date as may be specified.

(9)   If the court makes an order in accordance with subsection (7), it may, on an application by any party having an interest, vary the date or method of payment of the capital sum.

(10)   In this section—
'intestate' shall be construed in accordance with section 36(1) of the Succession (Scotland) Act 1964;
'legal rights' has the meaning given by section 36(1) of the Succession (Scotland) Act 1964;
'net intestate estate' means so much of the intestate estate as remains after provision for the satisfaction of—
   (a)   inheritance tax;

(b) other liabilities of the estate having priority over legal rights and the prior rights of a surviving spouse or surviving civil partner; and

(c) the legal rights, and the prior rights, of any surviving spouse or surviving civil partner; and

'prior rights' has the meaning given by section 36(1) of the Succession (Scotland) Act 1964.

SUCCESSION (SCOTLAND) ACT 2016
(asp 7)

Testamentary documents and special destinations

1   Effect of divorce, dissolution or annulment on will

(1) This section applies where—

(a) a person ('the testator') by a will—

(i)   confers a benefit or power of appointment on a person, or

(ii) appoints a person as a trustee or executor,

(b) that person ('P') is, or becomes, the testator's spouse or civil partner,

(c) the marriage or civil partnership is terminated, and

(d) the testator then dies.

(2) P is to be treated as having died before the testator for the purposes of the will except for the purposes of any appointment of P or another person as a guardian.

(3) Subsection (2) does not apply if the will expressly provides that P is to—

(a) have the benefit or power of appointment, or

(b) be so appointed as a trustee or executor, even if the marriage or civil partnership is terminated.

(4) For the purposes of this section, a marriage is terminated in the event of divorce or annulment and a civil partnership is terminated in the event of dissolution or annulment.

(5) In this section, references to 'divorce', 'dissolution' and 'annulment' are to divorce, dissolution or annulment—

(a) obtained from a court of civil jurisdiction in the United Kingdom, the Channel Islands or the Isle of Man, or

(b) if not so obtained, the validity of which is recognised in Scotland.

2   Effect of divorce, dissolution or annulment on special destination

(1) This section applies where—

(a) property is held in the name of—

(i)   a person ('A') and A's spouse or civil partner ('B') and the survivor of them,

(ii) A, B and another person or other persons and the survivor or survivors of them,

(iii) A with a special destination, on A's death, in favour of B,

(b) A and B's marriage or civil partnership is terminated, and

(c) A then dies.

(2) In relation to the succession to the property mentioned in subsection (1)(a) on A's death, B is to be treated as having died before A.

(3) Subsection (2) does not apply if the document under which the property is held expressly provides that succession to the property is to be unaffected by A and B's marriage or civil partnership being terminated.

(4) If a person has in good faith and for value (whether by purchase or otherwise) acquired title to the property, that title is not to be challengeable on the ground that, by virtue of subsection (2), the property falls to A's estate.

(5) For the purposes of this section, a marriage is terminated in the event of

divorce or annulment and a civil partnership is terminated in the event of dissolution or annulment.

(6)   In this section, references to 'divorce', 'dissolution' and 'annulment' are to divorce, dissolution or annulment—

(a)   obtained from a court of civil jurisdiction in the United Kingdom, the Channel Islands or the Isle of Man, or

(b)   if not so obtained, the validity of which is recognised in Scotland.

3   Rectification of will

(1)   This section applies where—

(a)   a person ('the testator') dies domiciled in Scotland, leaving a will,

(b)   the will was drafted not by the testator but on the testator's instructions,

(c)   after the date of death, a person applies to the court for rectification of the will, and

(d)   the court is satisfied that the will fails to express accurately what was instructed.

(2)   The court may order that the will be rectified in such manner as it may specify so as to give effect to the testator's instructions.

(3)   For the purposes of subsections (1)(d) and (2), the court may have regard to evidence extrinsic to the will.

(4)   A will rectified by virtue of this section has effect as if so rectified when executed (but see sections 4(7) and 24).

(5)   In this section, 'the court' means—

(a)   the Court of Session, or

(b)   a relevant sheriff.

(6)   In subsection (5)(b), 'a relevant sheriff' means—

(a)   a sheriff—

(i)   of the sheriffdom in which the testator was habitually resident at the date of death, or

(ii)   if subsection (7) applies, of the sheriffdom of Lothian and Borders sitting at Edinburgh, or

(b)   a sheriff of the sheriffdom in which the testator's executor obtains confirmation.

(7)   This subsection applies if at the date of death—

(a)   the testator was not habitually resident in a particular part of Scotland, or

(b)   the particular part of Scotland in which the testator was habitually resident is not known or is uncertain.

4   Rectification of will: supplementary

(1)   Subject to subsection (2), an application under section 3(1)(c) must be made within the period of 6 months commencing—

(a)   in a case where confirmation is obtained in respect of the testator's estate, on the date of its being obtained, or

(b)   in any other case, on the date of the testator's death.

(2)   The court may, on cause shown, consider an application which is made outwith that period of 6 months.

(3)   An order made by virtue of section 3(2) may be registered in—

(a)   the Books of Council and Session, or

(b)   the sheriff court books,

if the will to which the order relates is registered (either before or when the order is registered) in the books in question.

(4)   Subsections (5) and (6) apply if the court is satisfied, on an application, that—

(a)   execution by a person of a particular document is reasonably necessary to give effect to the rectified will, and

(b)   the person—

(i)   is refusing to execute the document, or

(ii)   is unable, or otherwise failing, to execute the document.

(5) The court may make an order—
    (a) dispensing with the execution of the document by the person, and
    (b) directing a clerk of session, or as the case may be the sheriff clerk, to execute the document.

(6) A document executed by a clerk of session or the sheriff clerk in accordance with an order under subsection (5) has the same force and effect as if it had been executed by the person.

(7) A trustee or executor is not personally liable for distributing property in good faith in accordance with a will which, by virtue of section 3, is rectified after the distribution.

(8) In this section, 'the court' has the same meaning as in section 3.

5 Revocation of will not to revive earlier revoked will

(1) This section applies where—
    (a) a will, or part of a will, is expressly or impliedly revoked by a subsequent will, and
    (b) the subsequent will, or part of it, is revoked.

(2) The revocation of the subsequent will, or part of it, does not revive the earlier will or (as the case may be) the revoked part of the earlier will.

6 Death before legacy vests: entitlement of issue

(1) This section applies where—
    (a) a person ('the testator') by a will bequeaths a legacy to—
        (i) a direct descendant of the testator, or
        (ii) more than one person where both or (as the case may be) all of those persons are direct descendants of the testator, and
    (b) the person to whom the legacy is bequeathed or, if it is bequeathed to more than one person, a person to whom it is bequeathed—
        (i) is alive when the will is executed, but
        (ii) fails to survive the date of vesting of the legacy.

(2) Any issue of the deceased legatee alive when the legacy would, but for the legatee's death, have vested in the legatee is entitled to receive the legacy unless it is clear from the terms of the will that the testator intended otherwise.

(3) Without prejudice to the generality of subsection (2), it is to be regarded as clear from the terms of the will that the testator intended otherwise if the will provides expressly that the legacy is bequeathed—
    (a) to the deceased legatee and another person (or other persons) and to the survivor (or survivors) of them, or
    (b) to the deceased legatee, whom failing to another person (or other persons).

(4) Where the legacy is bequeathed to more than one direct descendant, the share of it which the deceased legatee's issue is entitled to receive is the share which the deceased legatee would have received if alive.

(5) Any distribution made by virtue of this section between or among two or more of the deceased legatee's issue is to be made in the same way as if it were a distribution between or among them of the whole or part of an intestate estate.

(6) In this section—
'intestate estate' means an estate, or any part of an estate, which is not disposed of by will,
'issue' means issue however remote.

7 Liferent: vesting of fee other than on death

(1) This section applies where a liferent terminates other than on the death of the liferenter.

(2) If the fee has not vested in the fiar by the date of termination of the liferent, the fee vests in the fiar on that date unless—
    (a) the document creating the liferent expressly provides otherwise, or
    (b) there is an obligation requiring otherwise.

8 Destinations in wills and certain trusts: conditional institution

(1)   This section applies where—

(a) a destination of property in favour of a person ('A') whom failing another person ('B') is contained in a will or in a trust taking effect during the lifetime of the truster, and

(b) the property vests in A.

(2)   B loses all rights to the property under the destination unless—

(a) the will or trust expressly provides otherwise, or

(b) it is clear from the terms of the will or trust that the testator or truster intended otherwise.

Survivorship

9 Uncertainty of survivorship treated as failure to survive

(1)   Where two persons die simultaneously or in circumstances in which it is uncertain who survived whom, each is to be treated as having failed to survive the other for all purposes affecting title or succession to property.

(2)   Where a person mentioned in subsection (1) ('the testator') by a will confers a benefit on a person on the condition that the other person mentioned in subsection (1) dies before the testator, the condition that the person dies before the testator (however it is expressed) is to be read as a condition that the person fails to survive the testator.

(3)   This section is subject to section 10.

10 Equal division of property if order of beneficiaries' deaths uncertain

(1)   This section applies, instead of section 9, for the purposes of determining rights of succession or title to property where—

(a) property is to pass, or be transferred, to—

(i) the estate of whichever member of a group of persons dies first (or the estates of whichever members die first),

(ii) whichever member of a group of persons survives the other members (or whichever members survive the other members), or

(iii) the members of a group of persons equally or the survivor (or survivors) of them,

(b) two (or more) of the members of the group die simultaneously or in circumstances in which the order of death is uncertain,

(c) had the deaths not been simultaneous or (as the case may be) had the order of death been certain, the property would have passed, or been transferred, to one (or more) of the persons mentioned in paragraph (b), and

(d) apart from this section, no provision has been made to deal with that situation.

(2)   The property is to be divided equally between (or among) the estates of the persons mentioned in subsection (1)(b).

(3)   For the purposes of this section, a 'group of persons' may consist of two persons or more than two persons.

(4)   This section does not apply if the property is to pass under a will and the persons mentioned in subsection (1)(b) and the testator die simultaneously or in circumstances in which the order of death is uncertain.

11 Testamentary requirement of survival for a particular period

Where—

(a) a provision in a will requires that a person survives the testator for a specified period in order to receive a benefit under the will, and

(b) the person survives the testator but dies in circumstances in which it is uncertain whether the person survived for the specified period,

the person is to be treated as having failed to survive the testator for the specified period.

Forfeiture

12   Person forfeiting to be treated as having failed to survive victim

(1)   This section applies where, under the forfeiture rule, a person ('the offender') has forfeited—

(a)   rights of succession to the estate of the deceased,

(b)   a beneficial interest in trust property which (but for the forfeiture) the offender would have acquired in consequence of the deceased's death,

(c)   title to property which (but for the forfeiture) the offender would have acquired in consequence of the deceased's death by virtue of a special destination.

(2)   In subsection (1)(b), 'trust property' means property which, before the deceased's death, was held in trust for any person.

(3)   The offender is to be treated as having died before the deceased—

(a)   for the purposes of the rights of succession to the deceased's estate,

(b)   in relation to the beneficial interest mentioned in subsection (1)(b),

(c)   in relation to the title to property mentioned in subsection (1)(c), (as the case may be).

(4)   For the avoidance of doubt, references in this section to rights of succession to the estate of the deceased include references to—

(a)   a claim to jus relicti, jus relictae or legitim out of that estate,

(b)   an entitlement from that estate conferred by section 8 or 9 of the Succession (Scotland) Act 1964.

(5)   In this section, 'the deceased' means the person as a result of whose death the forfeiture arose.

13   Protection for persons acquiring in good faith and for value

(1)   This section applies where a person acquires title to property in good faith and for value (whether by purchase or otherwise).

(2)   The title is not challengeable on the ground that it was acquired (directly or indirectly) from a person who in relation to the property has incurred forfeiture under the forfeiture rule.

14   Power of sheriff to order sheriff clerk to execute document

(1)   This section applies where a relevant sheriff is satisfied, on an application, that—

(a)   execution by a person of a particular document is reasonably necessary to give effect to a forfeiture under the forfeiture rule, and

(b)   the person—

(i)   is refusing to execute the document, or

(ii)   is unable, or otherwise failing, to execute the document.

(2)   The sheriff may make an order—

(a)   dispensing with the execution of the document by the person, and

(b)   directing the sheriff clerk to execute the document.

(3)   A document executed by the sheriff clerk in accordance with an order under subsection (2) has the same force and effect as if it had been executed by the person.

(4)   In subsection (1), 'a relevant sheriff' means—

(a)   if the deceased died domiciled in Scotland, a sheriff—

(i)   of the sheriffdom in which the deceased was habitually resident at the date of death, or

(ii)   if subsection (5) applies, of the sheriffdom of Lothian and Borders sitting at Edinburgh,

(b)   if the deceased died domiciled other than in Scotland but at the date of death owned immoveable property situated in Scotland, a sheriff of the sheriffdom in which the immoveable property is situated,

(c) in any case, a sheriff of the sheriffdom in which the deceased's executor obtains confirmation.

(5) This subsection applies if at the date of death—

(a) the deceased was not habitually resident in a particular part of Scotland, or

(b) the particular part of Scotland in which the deceased was habitually resident is not known or is uncertain.

(6) In this section, 'the deceased' means the person as a result of whose death the forfeiture arose.

[Sections 15 and 16 amend the Forfeiture Act 1982]

17 Repeal of the Parricide Act

(1) The Parricide Act 1594 is repealed.

(2) For the avoidance of doubt, the forfeiture rule applies in relation to cases where a person has unlawfully killed the person's parent or grandparent as it applies in relation to other cases of unlawful killing.

. . .

24 Protection of persons acquiring title

(1) This section applies where a person, in good faith and for value (whether by purchase or otherwise)—

(a) acquires property which has vested, by virtue of confirmation, in an executor, and

(b) acquires title to that property directly or indirectly—

(i) from the executor, or

(ii) from a person ('A') who derived title directly from the executor.

(2) It is not a ground of challenge to the title—

(a) that the confirmation is reducible or has been reduced,

(b) that the property was distributed in accordance with a will which, by virtue of section 3, has been rectified after distribution, or

(c) where the title was acquired from A, that it should not have been transferred to A.

Other reforms

25 Gifts made in contemplation of death

(1) The customary mode of making a conditional gift in contemplation of death known as making a donation mortis causa is abolished.

(2) Subsection (1) does not prevent the making of a conditional gift other than in that customary mode.

26 Abolition of right to claim in respect of expense of mournings

Any right at common law to claim an allowance in respect of the expense of mournings from the estate of a deceased person is abolished.

. . .

General

28 Interpretation

(1) In this Act (unless the context otherwise requires)—

a reference to the 'estate' of a deceased person is a reference to the whole estate belonging to the person at the time of death but does not include property passing on the person's death to another person by virtue of a special destination,

'property' includes any interest in property.

(2) In this Act, the 'forfeiture rule' has the same meaning as in the Forfeiture Act 1982.

(3) In this Act, a 'will' means any document of a testamentary nature and includes ı reference to—

(a) a testamentary trust disposition and settlement,

(b) a codicil.

29 Consequential provision

(1) The rule of law known as the conditio si institutus sine liberis decesserit ceases to have effect.

(2) The schedule (which modifies provisions for the purposes of or in consequence of this Act) has effect.

30 Ancillary provision

(1) The Scottish Ministers may by regulations make such supplementary, incidental, consequential, transitional, transitory or saving provision as they consider appropriate for the purposes of, or in connection with, or for the purposes of giving full effect to, any provision of this Act.

(2) Regulations under this section may—

(a) modify this Act or any other enactment,

(b) make different provision for different purposes.

(3) Regulations under this section—

(a) are subject to the affirmative procedure if they contain provision which adds to, or replaces or omits any part of, the text of this or any other Act,

(b) otherwise, are subject to the negative procedure.

31 Commencement

(1) Sections 18 to 22, 30 and 32, and this section, come into force on the day after Royal Assent.

(2) The other provisions of this Act come into force on such day as the Scottish Ministers may by regulations appoint.

(3) Regulations under subsection (2) may—

(a) make different provision for different purposes,

(b) include transitional, transitory or saving provision.

32 Short title

The short title of this Act is the Succession (Scotland) Act 2016.

SUCCESSION (SCOTLAND) ACT 2016 (COMMENCEMENT, TRANSITIONAL AND SAVING PROVISIONS) REGULATIONS 2016 (SSI 2016/210)

Saving and transitional provisions

3.—(1) Section 5 of the 2016 Act applies only where the subsequent will, or part of it, referred to in section 5(1)(b) is revoked on or after 1st November 2016.

(2) Sections 6, 8 and 29(1) of the 2016 Act apply only if the will or trust was executed on or after 1st November 2016.

(3) The coming into force of section 25 does not affect a donation that was made before 1st November 2016.

(4) Despite the repeal of section 17 of the 1964 Act by paragraph 1(5)(a) of the schedule of the 2016 Act, it continues to apply to an acquisition which has taken place before 1st November 2016.

(5) Despite the repeal of—

(a) section 24(2) of the 1964 Act by paragraph 1(5)(b) of the schedule of the 2016 Act; and

(b) section 7 of the Law Reform (Miscellaneous Provisions) (Scotland) Act 1968(1) by paragraph 2 of the schedule of the 2016 Act,

they continue to apply to a distribution of property which has taken place before 1st November 2016.

INDEX OF STATUTES